TEXAS
REAL ESTATE

SEVENTH
EDITION

Charles J. Jacobus,
D.R.E.I., C.R.E.I.

Prentice Hall
Upper Saddle River, New Jersey 07458

Jan 10 2000
#39

Library of Congress Cataloging-in-Publication Data

Jacobus, Charles J.
    Texas Real Estate / Charles J. Jacobus. — 7th ed.
        p.   cm.
    Includes index.
    ISBN 0–13–080984–5
        1. Real estate business—Law and legislation—Texas.   2. Vendors
and purchasers—Texas.   3. Real property—Texas.   4. Real estate
business—Texas.   I. Title.
KFT1482.R4J32   1999
346.76404'37—dc21   98–7192
                                                                                        CIP

Acquisitions Editor: *Elizabeth Sugg*
Managing Editor: *Mary Carnis*
Production: *Holcomb Hathaway, Inc.*
Production Liaison: *Glenn Johnston*
Director of Manufacturing and Production: *Bruce Johnson*
Manufacturing Buyer: *Marc Bove*
Marketing Manager: *Danny Hoyt*
Cover Design: *Marianne Frasco*
Editorial Assistant: *Maria Kirk*
Marketing Assistant: *Christopher Eastman*

© 1999, 1995, 1991, 1987, 1983, 1980, 1978 by Prentice-Hall, Inc.
Simon & Schuster / A Viacom Company
Upper Saddle River, New Jersey 07458

Printed in the United States of America

10 9 8 7 6 5 4 3 2

ISBN 0-13-080984-5

Prentice-Hall International (UK) Limited, *London*
Prentice-Hall of Australia Pty. Limited, *Sydney*
Prentice-Hall Canada Inc., *Toronto*
Prentice-Hall Hispanoamericana, S.A., *Mexico*
Prentice-Hall of India Private Limited, *New Delhi*
Prentice-Hall of Japan, Inc., *Tokyo*
Simon & Schuster Asia Pte. Ltd., *Singapore*
Editora Prentice-Hall do Brasil, Ltda., *Rio de Janeiro*

Brief Contents

Contents

CHAPTER 4

FORMS OF OWNERSHIP   54

CHAPTER 5

TRANSFERRING TITLE   70

CHAPTER 6

RECORDATION, ABSTRACTS, AND TITLE INSURANCE 86

CHAPTER 7

CONTRACT LAW 100

CHAPTER 8

REAL ESTATE SALES CONTRACTS 116

CHAPTER 14

TAXES AND ASSESSMENTS 234

CHAPTER 15

TITLE CLOSING AND ESCROW 248

CHAPTER 16

REAL ESTATE LEASES 268

CHAPTER 17

REAL ESTATE APPRAISAL   278

CHAPTER 18

LICENSING LAWS AND PROFESSIONAL AFFILIATION   306

Preface

Is your goal a full-time or part-time career in real estate? Do you own or plan to own your own home or an investment property? Are you a student of real estate desiring to broaden your knowledge of this subject? If you answered "Yes" to one or more of these questions, the content of this book will be of immense help to you. After all, in the United States and in Texas, real estate is part of the great American dream. It touches all of our lives. We share stories about it, invest in it, live in it and on it, sell it, and hire people to advise us about it. The subject of real estate is always fun and interesting, but often complex.

Texas is on the forefront of real estate education, law, and practice. Our state currently has one of the highest educational requirements for real estate licensees. The Texas Real Estate Center in College Station, Texas, is the premier real estate research facility in the country. The State Bar of Texas is widely acknowledged as the leading bar association in the country for research and education. Texas offers many resources for students and practitioners, and this Seventh Edition of *Texas Real Estate* is a primary beneficiary of (and, we hope, an example of) Texas's efforts to pursue excellence in real estate education.

The subject of real estate has never been as simple as some have tried to make it. Authoritative national textbooks, while functional and complete, can't include many familiar local trends and practices of the business, and do include topics that are not applicable to Texas. This text was written and organized to be authoritative and specifically adapted to the Texas real estate practitioner and student.

In this book you will learn about Texas real estate brokerage, appraisal, financing, contracts, closing, and investment. Additionally, you will learn about land descriptions, rights and interests, fair housing, taxes, leases, condominiums, zoning, licensing, and the use of computers in real estate. You will find particularly valuable the attention given to such timely topics as a real estate agent's liability and professional obligation to buyers and sellers, buyer brokerage, errors and omission insurance, foreclosure, and timesharing. Included throughout the book are numerous examples from the actual practice of real estate in Texas.

This edition has been updated to reflect the 1995 and 1997 legislature changes. Although the legislature has eliminated the need to cover the subjects of contracts and agency, these topics are covered here. I believe that these subjects are basic to the principles of real estate and, in fact, I have expanded the discussion of agency in this edition. The new discussion includes information on changing liabilities, new disclosure requirements, and the growth of buyer brokerage.

This book is written in a clear and easily readable style to help you understand and apply the important information contained in these chapters. The book's explanations combine "how" things are done with "why" they are done. Figures and tables will help you to visualize real estate rights and interests, financing techniques, appraisal methods, closing statements, and map reading. Simplified, plain English examples of real estate documents are used so their key elements can be easily identified and not lost in a haze of legal language.

I have attempted to cover most substantive Texas topics in such depth that this book can be used for future reference as well as for an introduction to Texas real estate. For your convenience, the Texas Real Estate Licensing Act has been included. The official regulations are detailed and voluminous. They are readily available in a convenient booklet format, from the Texas Real Estate Commission, P.O. Box 12188, Capital Station, Austin, Texas 78711. As a first assignment, you should write for the booklet and get to know it well.

Special Features of this Book

- Beginning with Chapter 2, each chapter offers a list of key terms and their definitions. Key terms are also boldfaced at first use within the chapter.
- Chapters also begin with a chapter Overview that previews the chapter's main topics.
- This edition introduces a new feature. Within chapters you'll encounter "Putting It to Work," brief capsules of practical information that help you understand how the discussion relates to the everyday practice of real estate in Texas.
- Each chapter ends with Multiple Choice questions. These questions will help you review the material and will alert you to areas that may need more study if you are preparing for your Texas real estate licensing examination. The questions are much like the ones you will encounter on your real estate exam and should provide valuable practice for that exam. The answers to these chapter-end questions are found in the Answer Key in the back of the book so that you can check your responses.
- For those of you preparing for your licensing exam, the book now offers two Practice Examinations. These tests contain 90 questions each, as on the NAI exam, in the multiple choice format used by the NAI testing service. Although answers for the Practice Exams are also found in the Answer Key, take the exam in its completion, timing yourself as will be the case when you take the real exam. Then use the Answer Key to identify the areas in which you need to review.
- To aid your review and help you locate topics, this book offers a comprehensive, combined Glossary/Index. This feature allows you to look up a term and find not only the definition, but also page references alerting you to where the topic is discussed throughout the book.
- Finally, this book also includes a useful, clear, and concise math review. Many of you probably worry that you will be unprepared for the math you'll encounter in this book and in your profession. This appendix will help you identify the basic skills you'll use and help you review and develop those skills.
- All of these features and the book's readable style make it perfect for distance learning courses. If you are taking the course via computer link, telecourse, mail, or any other distance learning method, you'll find the book easy to use.

This Edition's New Look

Many of you who have used this book in previous editions will notice that it has a new look. The book's new "trim size" has helped to make it shorter and, we hope, easier to read and review. For reader convenience and to make the book more affordable for you, the book is now a paperback. The type is still large and readable and the headings are bigger and bolder so you can find them more easily. We've retained the wide margins for your note-taking. All in all, the book looks friendlier and more readable, and that was our goal.

Study Aids

Two new and important study aids are available for use with this text.

Audiotapes: This two-tape set will help you make the most of your study time in the car or at home. The set contains a thorough review of the most important points of each book chapter.

Interactive Software Tutorial: More than 500 questions allow you to review each chapter in detail. Also generates practice tests for you to take at your convenience on your own computer (if you wish, set the program's timer to allow only the same amount of time allowed for the actual test).

Instructor's Manual

The complete Instructor's Manual available with adoption of this text includes chapter outlines and lots of extra review/test questions (40–50 per chapter) for each chapter.

Acknowledgments

Special thanks to the following individuals for their help in preparing this and previous editions of the book: Paddy Amyett, Katy Peeples, Minor Peeples, Dorothy A. Lewis, Carl K. Sheffield, Mark Moseley, Richard Chumbley, Jim Howze, Rita Vitale, Ralph Tamper, Ken Combs, Drue Combs, Dorothy Turner, Kay Wilson, Bill Proctor, and John P. Wiedemer. I appreciate their assistance and support.

TEXAS
REAL ESTATE

SEVENTH
EDITION

CHAPTER 1

REAL ESTATE is a unique subject, and because it is unique, real estate has spawned complex legal theories and very unusual fact situations. No two situations are ever exactly alike, and the subject never ceases to be intellectually stimulating. Everyone has a favorite story about real estate, and it has remained a fascinating topic for centuries. This fascination is what makes the real estate business such a fun, interesting business.

As a new real estate student, one must be prepared to learn a lot of new concepts and be willing to commit the time and effort to that end. There are some who say that the only way to learn real estate is by experience. Many years ago this was the traditional concept. Real estate was then considered to be a "marketing" or "salesmanship" business, and experience was the best teacher. Recent years, however, have seen the development of extensive academic applications in real estate education. Real estate has come to the academic forefront; undergraduate degrees in real estate are becoming more common, as are graduate level degree programs. There is also a resulting emphasis on the professionalism and duty of these new real estate professionals. Unlike many other academic subjects, however, real estate continues to emphasize the "people-oriented" aspects of the business. Experience and hard work have a very high correlation with success in the real estate business.

With these combinations in mind, this book has been written to provide an understanding of the basic principles and business fundamentals of real estate. Emphasis is placed on an easily readable presentation that combines explanations of the basic principles of the subject with "why" things are done and "how" these principles apply to everyday activities.

Introduction to Real Estate

HOW TO READ THIS BOOK

At the beginning of each chapter (2 through 23) there is a list of the new "Key Terms" that you will learn, along with brief definitions. Read these before starting your work in each chapter. In the body of each chapter these terms, as well as other terms important to real estate, are set in **boldface type** and given an in-depth discussion. At the end of each chapter are questions designed to help you test yourself on your comprehension of the material in the chapter you've just read. The answers are given in Appendix D in the back of the book.

A combined index-glossary is also in the back of this book. This approach was taken to help reinforce your familiarity with the language of real estate. When you use this index-glossary, you will receive a short definition followed by a page reference for more detailed discussion.

Another special feature of this book is the wide margin on each page. Besides its eye appeal, it provides a handy place for your study notes.

TRANSACTION OVERVIEW

Figure 1.1 provides a visual summary of the real estate transaction cycle. It is included here to give you an overview of the different steps involved in the sale of real property and to show how the steps are related to each other. The chapter in which each step is discussed is also shown. Whether your point of view is that of a real estate agent, owner, buyer, or seller, you will find the chapters that follow to be informative and valuable.

CHAPTER ORGANIZATION

Great care has been taken in organizing this text so as to carefully build your knowledge of real estate. For example, land description methods and rights and interests in land are necessary to sales contracts, abstracts, deeds, mortgages, and listings and therefore are discussed early in the text.

In Chapter 2 you will find such topics as metes and bounds and tract maps. You will also find a discussion of what is real estate and what is not, and how land is physically and economically different from other commodities. Having described real estate, the next logical step is to look at the various rights and interests that exist in a given

FIGURE 1.1
An overview of a real estate transaction.

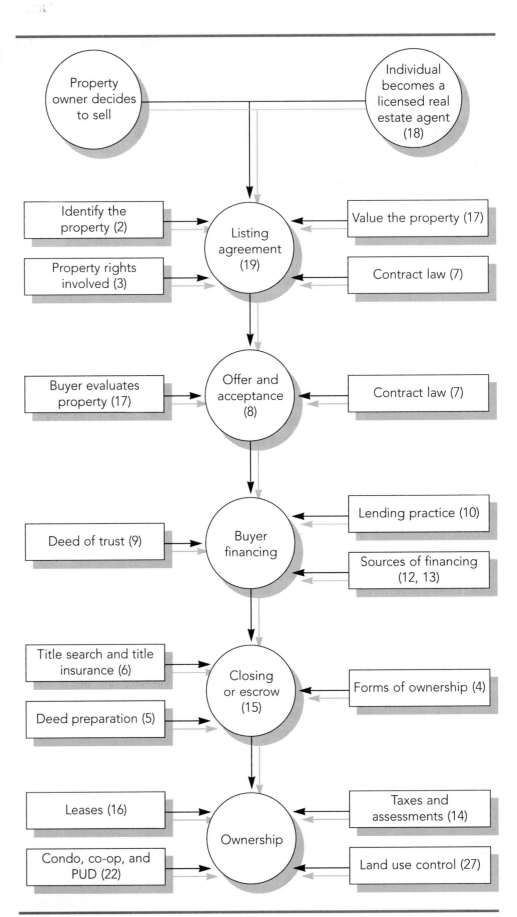

parcel of land. In Chapter 3 you will see that there is much more to ownership of land than meets the eye! In Chapter 4 we look at how a given right or interest in land can be held by an individual, by two or more persons, or by a business entity. Included in this chapter are discussions of joint tenancy, tenancy in common, and community property.

Chapters 5 and 6 deal with the process by which the ownership of real estate is transferred from one person to another. In particular, Chapter 5 discusses deeds and wills, and Chapter 6 deals with how a person gives evidence to the world that he possesses a given right or interest in land. Abstracts and title insurance are among the topics included.

In Chapters 7 and 8 we turn to contract law and its application to offers and acceptances. Because so much of what takes place in real estate is in the form of contracts, you will want to have a solid understanding of what makes a contract legally binding and what doesn't.

Chapters 9 through 13 are devoted to real estate finance. In Chapter 9 mortgages and the laws regarding their use are explained. Amortized loans, points, FHA and VA programs, loan application, and mortgage insurance are discussed in Chapter 10. Consumer loan issues are discussed in Chapter 11. Mortgage lenders, the secondary mortgage market, due-on-sale clauses, adjustable rate mortgages, and financing alternatives are covered in Chapters 12 and 13.

In Chapter 14 we see how property taxes and assessments are calculated; and Chapter 15 explains title closing and escrow. Chapter 16 deals with leasing real estate and includes a sample lease document with discussion. Chapter 17 explores the language, principles, and techniques of real estate appraisal.

In Chapters 18 through 20 we examine the relationship between real estate agents, buyers, and sellers. Chapter 18 deals with real estate license law requirements, how a salesperson goes about choosing a broker to affiliate with, and professional ethics. Chapter 19 discusses an agent's employment, commission issues, and ethics. Chapter 20 explains the concepts of agency and intermediary status. Chapter 21 introduces the reader to fair housing, equal credit opportunity, and the Americans with Disabilities Act (ADA).

The remaining chapters of this book deal with a number of individual and specialized real estate topics. Chapter 22 explores the condominium, cooperative, and planned unit development and timeshare forms of real estate ownership. Included is a look at how they are created and the various rights and interests in land that are created by them.

Zoning, land planning, and deed restrictions are covered in Chapter 23. These are important topics because any limitations on a landowner's right to develop and use land can have a substantial effect on the value of the property. The final chapter, Chapter 24, is an introduction to the opportunities available to you as a real estate investor. Topics include tax shelter, equity build-up, what to buy, and when to buy.

Following the final chapter are several appendices that you will find useful. Appendices include the Texas Real Estate License Act and the Texas Canons of Professional Conduct. In addition, you will find a short real estate math review section, and the answers to the problems found at the end of Chapters 2 through 24.

CAREER OPPORTUNITIES

The contents and organization of this book are designed for people who are interested in real estate because they now own or plan to own real estate and for people who are interested in real estate as a career. It is to those who are considering real estate as a profession that the balance of this chapter is devoted.

Most people who are considering a career in real estate think of becoming a real estate agent who specializes in selling homes. This is quite natural because home selling is the most visible segment of the real estate industry. It is the area of the business most people enter and the one in which most practicing real estate licensees make their living. Residential sales experience is a good way to find out whether real estate sales appeals to you and whether residential property is the type of property in which you wish to specialize.

Residential Brokerage

Residential brokerage requires a broad knowledge of the community and its neighborhoods, finance, real estate law, economics, and the money market. Working hours will often include nights and weekends as these times are usually most convenient to buyers and sellers. A residential agent must also possess an automobile that is suitable for taking clients to see property.

A person who is adept at interpersonal relations, who can identify clients' buying motives and find the property to fit, will probably be quite successful in this business.

Putting It To Work

In only a few real estate offices are new residential salespersons given a minimum guaranteed salary or a draw against future commissions. Therefore, a newcomer should have enough capital to survive until the first commissions are earned—and that can take four to six months. Additionally, the salesperson must be capable of developing and handling a personal budget that will withstand the feast and famine cycles that can occur in real estate selling.

Commercial Brokerage

Commercial brokers specialize in income-producing properties such as apartment and office buildings, retail stores, and warehouses. In this specialty, the salesperson is primarily selling monetary benefits. These benefits are the income, appreciation, mortgage reduction, and tax shelter that a property can reasonably be expected to produce.

To be successful in commercial brokerage, one must be very competent in mathematics, know how to finance transactions, and be aware of current tax laws. One must also have a sense of what makes a good investment, what makes an investment salable, and what the growth possibilities are in the neighborhood where a property is located.

Commission income from commercial brokerage is likely to be less frequent but in larger amounts compared to residential brokerage. The time required to break into the business is longer, but once in the business, agent turnover is low. The working hours of a commercial broker are much closer to regular business hours than for those in residential selling.

Industrial Brokerage

Industrial brokers specialize in finding suitable land and buildings for industrial concerns. This includes leasing and developing industrial property as well as listing and selling it. An industrial broker must be familiar with industry requirements such as proximity to raw materials, water and power, labor supplies, and transportation. He must also know about local building, zoning, and tax laws as they pertain to possible sites, and about the schools, housing, and cultural and recreational facilities that would be used by future employees of the plant.

Commissions are irregular, but are usually substantial. Working hours are regular business hours, and sales efforts are primarily aimed at locating facts and figures and presenting them to clients in an orderly fashion. Industrial clients are usually sophisticated business people. Gaining entry to an industrial brokerage and acquiring a client list can be slow.

FARM BROKERAGE

With the rapid disappearance of the family farm, the farm broker's role is changing. Today a farm broker must be equally capable of handling the 160-acre spread of Farmer Jones and the 10,000-acre operation owned by an agribusiness corporation. College training in agriculture is an advantage and on-the-job training is a must. Knowledge of soil types, seeds, fertilizers, production methods, new machinery, government subsidies, and tax laws is vital to success. Farm brokerage offers as many opportunities to earn commissions and fees from leasing and property management as from listing and selling property.

PROPERTY MANAGEMENT

For an investment property, the property manager's job is to supervise every aspect of a property's operation so as to produce the highest possible financial return over the longest period of time. The manager's tasks include renting, tenant relations, building repair and maintenance, accounting, advertising, and supervision of personnel and tradespeople.

The expanded development of condominiums has resulted in a growing demand for property managers to maintain them. In addition, large businesses that own property for their own use hire property managers.

PUTTING IT TO WORK

Property managers are usually paid a salary and, if the property is a rental, a bonus for keeping the building fully occupied. To be successful, a property manager should be at ease with tenants, a public relations expert, handy with tools, a good bookkeeper, and knowledgeable about laws applicable to rental units.

APARTMENT LOCATORS

In recent years, the service of helping tenants find rental units and helping landlords find tenants has become increasingly popular. This is normally a free service to the public. Locators are paid commissions by management companies and owners of apartment projects for finding qualified tenants. A locating agent must have an in-depth knowledge of the apartment complexes in the community and their requirements for tenants. The locating business has expanded in the last few years to include the leasing of condominiums, townhouses, and single-family homes.

An offshoot of apartment locators are roommate locators. These are especially popular in cities with substantial numbers of single persons. Roommate locators are central places where people looking for other people who are willing to share living space can meet. The locator service maintains files on people with space to share (such as the second bedroom in a two-bedroom apartment) and those looking for space. The files will contain information on location, rent, male or female, smoking or nonsmoking, etc.

PUTTING IT TO WORK

Most roommate and tenant locator services have been started by individual entrepreneurs and are not affiliated with real estate offices. In Texas, a real estate license is required to operate as an apartment locator or a roommate locator.

REAL ESTATE APPRAISING

The job of the real estate appraiser is to gather and evaluate all available facts affecting a property's value. Appraisal is a real estate career opportunity that demands a special set of skills. The job requires practical experience, technical education, and good judgment. If you have an analytical mind and like to collect and interpret data, you might consider becoming a real estate appraiser. The job combines office work and field work, and the income of an expert appraiser can match that of a top real estate salesperson. One can be an independent appraiser, or there are numerous opportunities to work as a salaried appraiser for local tax authorities or lending institutions. The appraisal process is now becoming more complex, however. Most lenders and taxing authorities require that their appraisers have some advanced credential designation to ensure an adequate level of competence.

GOVERNMENT SERVICE

Approximately one-third of the land in the United States is government owned. This includes vacant and forested lands, office buildings, museums, parks, zoos, schools, hospitals, public housing, libraries, fire and police stations, roads and highways, subways, airports, and courthouses. All of these are real estate and all of these require government employees who can negotiate purchases and sales, appraise, finance, manage, plan, and develop. Cities, counties, and state governments all have extensive real estate holdings. At the federal level, the Forest Service, Park Service, Department of Agriculture, Army Corps of Engineers, Bureau of Land Management, and General Services Administration are all major landholders. In addition to outright real estate ownership, government agencies such as the Federal Housing Administration, Department of Veterans Affairs, and Federal Home Loan Bank employ thousands of real estate specialists to keep their real estate lending programs operating.

LAND DEVELOPMENT

Most new houses in the United States are built by developers who in turn sell them to homeowners and investors. Some houses are built by small-scale developers who produce only a few a year. Others are part of 400-house subdivisions and 40-story condominiums that are developed and constructed by large corporations that have their own planning, appraising, financing, construction, and marketing personnel. There is equal opportunity for success in development whether you build 4 houses a year or work for a firm that builds 400 a year.

URBAN PLANNING

Urban planners work with local governments and civic groups for the purpose of anticipating future growth and land use changes. The urban planner makes recommendations for new streets, highways, sewer and water lines, schools, parks, and libraries. The current emphasis on environmental protection and controlled growth has made urban planning one of real estate's most rapidly expanding specialties. An urban planning job is usually a salaried position and does not emphasize sales ability.

MORTGAGE FINANCING

Specialists in mortgage financing have a dual role: (1) to find economically sound properties for lenders and (2) to locate money for borrowers. A mortgage specialist can work independently, receiving a fee from the borrower for locating a lender, or as a salaried employee of a lending institution. The commission paid to a mortgage specialist on a multi-million dollar loan can be quite substantial.

SECURITIES AND SYNDICATIONS

Limited partnerships and other forms of real estate syndications that combine the investment capital of a number of investors to buy large properties number in the thousands. The investment opportunities and professional management offered by syndications are eagerly sought after by people with money to invest in real estate. As a result, there are job opportunities in creating, promoting, and managing real estate syndications.

CONSULTING

Real estate consulting involves giving others advice about real estate for a fee. A consultant must have a very broad knowledge of real estate—including financing, appraising, brokerage, management, development, construction, investing, leasing, zoning, taxes, title, economics, and law. To remain in business as a consultant, one must develop a good track record of successful suggestions and advice.

RESEARCH AND EDUCATION

A person interested in real estate research can concentrate on such matters as improved construction materials and management methods or on finding answers to economic questions such as "What is the demand for homes going to be next year in this community (state, country)?"

Opportunities abound in real estate education. Nearly all states require the completion of specified real estate courses before a real estate license can be issued. All states require continuing education for license renewal. As a result, people with experience in the industry and an ability to effectively teach the subject are much sought after as instructors.

Real estate teachers organizations, such as the Texas Real Estate Teachers Association (TRETA) with their CREI designation and the Real Estate Educators Association (REEA) with their DREI designation are now also making a significant impact on improving the quality of real estate education.

FULL-TIME INVESTOR

One of the advantages of the free-enterprise system is that you can choose to become a full-time investor solely for yourself. A substantial number of people have quit their jobs to work full time with their investment properties and have done quite well at it. A popular and successful route for many has been to purchase, inexpensively and with a low down payment, a small apartment building that has not been well maintained but is in a good neighborhood. The property is then thoroughly reconditioned and rents are raised. This process increases the value of the property. The increase is parlayed into a larger building—often through a tax-deferred exchange—and the process is repeated. Alternatively, the investor can increase the mortgage loan on the building and take the cash he receives as a "salary" for himself or use it as a down payment on another not-too-well maintained apartment building in a good neighborhood.

Other individual investors have done well financially by searching newspaper ads and regularly visiting real estate brokerage offices looking for underpriced properties that can be sold at a mark-up. A variation of this is to write to out-of-town property owners in a given neighborhood to see if any wish to sell at a bargain price. Another approach is to become a small-scale developer and contractor. (No license is needed if you work with your own property.) Through your own personal efforts you create value in your projects and then hold them as investments. One should be cautioned, however, that there are very few legitimate "get rich quick" schemes in the real estate business.

LICENSE REQUIREMENTS

As stated previously, property owners who deal only with their own property are not required to hold a real estate license. However, any person who **for another,** and for compensation or the promise of compensation lists or offers to list, sells or offers to sell, buys or offers to buy, negotiates or offers to negotiate, either directly or indirectly, for the purpose of bringing about a sale, purchase, or option to purchase, exchange, auction, lease, or rental of real estate, or any interest in real estate, is required to hold a valid real estate license. Texas also requires people offering their services as real estate appraisers and property managers to hold real estate licenses.

If your real estate plans are such that you may need a license, you should turn to Chapter 18 and read the material on real estate licensing.

KEY TERMS

Base line: an east-west or geographer's line selected as a basic reference in the rectangular survey system

Fixture: an object that has been attached to land so as to become real estate

Improvements: any form of land development, such as buildings, roads, fences, pipelines, etc.

Meridian: imaginary lines running north and south, used as references in mapping land

Metes and bounds: a detailed method of land description that identifies a parcel by specifying its shape and boundaries

Monument: an iron pipe, stone, tree, or other fixed point used in making a survey

Personal property: a right or interest in things of a temporary or movable nature; anything not classed as real property

Real estate: land and improvements in a physical sense as well as the rights to own or use them

Recorded plat: a subdivision map filed in the county recorder's office that shows the location and boundaries of individual parcels of land

Riparian right: the right of a landowner whose land borders a river or stream to use and enjoy that water

Nature and Description of Real Estate

IN THIS CHAPTER *In this chapter you will be introduced to the terminology used to define and describe real estate. Real estate is defined, and rights in land are also described. Other topics include fixtures, appurtenances, water rights, and land descriptions. The metes and bounds description of land and the rectangular survey system of describing land are also covered as are other land descriptive survey systems. The chapter is concluded with coverage of the physical and economic characteristics of land. Key terms, such as scarcity, homogeneity, immobility, fixity, and situs are also defined. These and the other terms defined within this second chapter should be studied thoroughly and be remembered to enhance your understanding of material in subsequent chapters.*

What is real estate? **Real estate** *or* **real property** *is land and the improvements made to land and the rights to use them. Let's begin in this chapter by looking more closely at what is meant by land and improvements. Then in the next chapter we shall focus our attention on the various rights one may possess in land and improvements.*

LAND

Often we think of land as only the surface of the earth. But it is substantially more than that. As Figure 2.1 illustrates, land starts at the center of the earth, passes through the earth's surface, and continues on into space. An understanding of this concept is important because, given a particular parcel of land, it is possible for one person to own the rights to use its surface **(surface rights),** another to own the rights to drill or dig below its surface **(subsurface rights),** and still another to own the rights to use the air space above it **(air rights).**

Realty refers to land and buildings and other improvements from a physical standpoint; **real property** refers to the right to own land and improvements; and **real estate** refers to land and improvements and the rights to own or use them. As a practical matter, however, these three terms are used interchangeably in everyday usage.

IMPROVEMENTS

Anything affixed to land with the intent of being permanent is considered to be part of the land and therefore real estate. Thus houses, schools, factories, barns, fences, roads, pipelines, and landscaping are real estate. As a group, these are referred to as **improvements** because they improve or develop land.

FIGURE 2.1
Land includes the
surface of the earth
and the sky above
and everything to the
center of the earth.

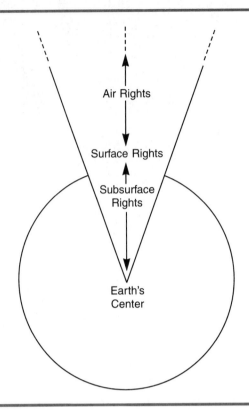

Being able to identify what is real estate and what is not is important. For example, in conveying ownership to a house, only the lot is described in the deed. It is not necessary to describe the dwelling unit itself, or the landscaping, driveways, sidewalks, wiring, or plumbing. Items that are not a part of the land, such as tables, chairs, beds, desks, automobiles, farm machinery, and the like, are classified as **personal property,** or **personalty,** if the right to use them is to be transferred to the buyer, the seller should sign a separate **bill of sale,** in addition to the deed.

FIXTURES

When an object that was once personal property is attached to land (or a building thereon) so as to become real estate, it is called a **fixture.** As a rule, a fixture is the property of the landowner and when the land is conveyed to a new owner, it is automatically included with the land.

Tests of a Fixture

Whether or not an object becomes real estate depends on whether the object was affixed or installed with the apparent intent of permanently improving the land. In Texas, the determination of what constitutes a fixture has primarily revolved around three criteria:

1. Method of annexation to the real estate
2. Fitness or adaptation to a particular use of the premises
3. The intention of the parties

Annexation

The first test, **method of annexation,** refers to how the object is attached to the land. Ordinarily, when an object that was once personal property is attached to land by virtue of its being imbedded in the land or affixed to the land by means of cement, nails, bolts, etc., it becomes a fixture. To illustrate, when asphalt and concrete for driveways and sidewalks are still on the delivery truck, they are movable and therefore personal property. But once they are poured into place, the asphalt and concrete become part of the land. Similarly, lumber, wiring, pipes, doors, toilets, sinks, water heaters, furnaces, and other construction materials change from personal property to real estate when they become part of a building. Items brought into the house that do not become permanently affixed to the land remain personal property; for example, furniture, clothing, cooking utensils, radios, and television sets.

Adaptation

Historically, the **manner of attachment** was the only method of classifying an object as personal property or real estate, but as time progressed, this test alone was no longer adequate. For example, how would you classify custom-made drapes made for an unusual window? For the answer, we must apply a second test: **How is the article adapted** to the building? If the drapes were custom cut for the windows in the building, they are automatically included in the purchase or rental of the building. Drapes of a standard size that may be suitable for use in other buildings are personal property and are not automatically included with the building. Note the difference: In the first case, the drapes are specifically adapted to the building; in the second case, they are not.

Intention

Of the three tests, pre-eminence is given to the question of intention of the parties. **Intention** is inferred from the nature of the article, the relationship and situation of the parties involved, the policy of the law, the mode of annexation, and the purpose or use for which the annexation is made. So intention, in its broadest sense, includes the other two criteria.

Prior Liens Against Fixtures

In addition to the misunderstandings that often arise between buyer and seller in determining the intention of the parties regarding fixtures, there are also priorities given in the law that create a priority interest in fixtures if that interest is timely and properly recorded. If the interest is of record, the buyer may find that an important fixture may have prior claims by a supplier or vendor that gives the purchase an inferior priority in the event of nonpayment or subsequent default by the seller. For instance, if a homeowner purchased a central air conditioning unit, the air conditioning contractor or vendor would probably record and properly file a chattel mortgage to reflect their interest in the air conditioning system until it is fully paid for.

PUTTING IT TO WORK

The air conditioning system once affixed to the real estate is a part of that real estate. However, Texas statute gives that air conditioning contractor, as a materialman and supplier, the right to remove that air conditioner in the event that it is not paid for. Therefore, even a subsequent purchaser may discover that the air conditioning unit can be removed after they take possession of the premises.

Trade Fixtures

Normally, when a tenant makes permanent additions to the property they are renting, the additions belong to the landlord when the lease or rental agreement expires. However, this can work a particular hardship on tenants operating a trade or business. For example, a supermarket moves into a rented building, then buys and bolts to the floor various **trade fixtures** such as display shelves, meat and dairy coolers, frozen food counters, and checkout stands. When the supermarket later moves out, do these items, by virtue of their attachment, become the property of the building owner? Modern courts hold that tenant-owned trade fixtures do not become the property of the landlord. However, for the tenant to keep the trade fixtures, they must be removed in a timely manner before the expiration of the lease and without seriously damaging the building.

Plants, Trees, and Crops

Trees, cultivated perennial plants, and uncultivated vegetation of any sort are classed as **fructus naturales** and are considered part of the land. Annual cultivated crops are called **fructus industriales** or **emblements** and most courts of law regard them as personal property even though they are attached to the soil.

APPURTENANCES

The conveyance of land carries with it any appurtenances to the land. An **appurtenance** is a right or privilege or improvement that belongs to and passes with land but is not necessarily a part of the land. Examples of appurtenances are easements and rights-of-way (discussed in Chapter 3), condominium parking stalls, and shares of stock in a mutual water company that services the land.

WATER RIGHTS

The ownership of land that borders on a river or stream carries with it the right to use that water in common with the other landowners whose land borders on the same watercourse. This is known as a **riparian right.** The landowner does not have absolute ownership of the water that flows through or past their land, but they may use it in a reasonable manner. Where land borders on a lake or sea, it is said to carry **littoral rights** rather than riparian rights. Littoral rights allow a landowner to use and enjoy the water touching their land provided they do not alter the water's position by artificial means.

Ownership of land normally includes the right to drill for and remove water found below the surface. Where water is not confined to a defined underground waterway, it is known as **percolating water.** When speaking of underground water, the term **water table** refers to the upper limit of percolating water below the earth's surface. It is also called the **groundwater level.** This may be only a few feet below the surface or hundreds of feet down.

Texas Natural Resources and Conservation Commission

The laws of the State of Texas with respect to water rights are contained in the State's Water Code. The agency of the state given primary responsibility for implementing the provisions of the Constitution and laws of the State of Texas is the Texas Natural

Resources and Conservation Commission. This agency is responsible for carrying out legislative, executive, and judicial functions provided under the Texas Water Code, delegated to it by the Constitution and other laws of the State of Texas. The legislative functions of the Natural Resources and Conservation Commission are vested in the Texas Water Development Board.

The commission is composed of three members who are appointed by the Governor with the advice and consent of the Senate. Each must be from a different section of the state. They hold staggered terms for six years, and no person may serve more than two six-year terms. This agency has the function of holding hearings to authorize the issuing of permits and judicial review. Any person affected by a ruling, order, decision, or other act of the department may file a petition to review, set aside, modify, or suspend the act of the department.

Water Development Board

The Texas Water Development Board is composed of six members who are appointed by the Governor with the advice and consent of the state Senate. The board establishes and approves all general policies of the Natural Resource Conservation Commission.

Ownership of Waterways

The Texas Water Code specifies that the water of the ordinary flow, underflow, and tides of every flowing river, natural stream, and lake, and of every bay or arm of the Gulf of Mexico, and the storm water, flood water, and rain water, of every river, natural stream, canyon, ravine, depression, and watershed in the State is the property of the State.

Water imported from any source outside the boundaries of the State for use in the State that is transported through the beds and banks of any applicable stream within the State or by utilizing any facilities owned or operated by the State, is the property of the State. The State may authorize the use of state water which may be acquired by appropriation in the manner provided for by statute. Once the permit has been obtained from the Natural Resources and Conservation Commission, the right to use the state water under that permit is limited not only to the amount specifically appropriated, but also to the amount that can be beneficially used for the purposes specified in the appropriation. All water not used within the specified limits is not considered as having been appropriated. If one doesn't use their appropriation, it may be limited or prohibited in future years.

Texas also reserves, under the Open Beaches Act, the free and unrestricted right of ingress or egress to and from the state-owned beaches on the shore of the Gulf of Mexico. This area extends from the line of mean low tide to the line of vegetation bordering on the Gulf of Mexico.

Conflicting Claims

If the appropriation has been given to two conflicting claimants, the first in time is first in right. The only exception to the doctrine of appropriation by the Department of Water Resources is that any city or town can make further appropriations of the water for domestic or municipal use without paying for the water. When a person uses water under the terms of a certified filing or permit for a period of three years, she acquires title to her appropriation against any other claimant of the water. Conversely, if any lawful appropriation or use of state water is willfully abandoned during the three years, the right to use the water is forfeited and the water is again subject to appropriation. All persons having an appropriation by the State must file by March 1 of each and every year a written report to the Department on forms prescribed by the Department or be subject to a statutory penalty.

State Rights

The Code basically vests water rights in the State. It does not recognize any riparian rights in the owner of any land to which the title passed out of the State of Texas after July 1, 1895. Current owners who can trace their riparian rights to a date prior to that date may still claim them.

State Water Agencies

There are other state agencies that are concerned with specific requirements for water use and water development. They include Water Control and Improvement Districts, Underground Water Conservation Districts, Fresh Water Supply Districts, Municipal Utility Districts, Water Improvement Districts, Drainage Districts, Levee Improvement Districts, and Navigation Districts. There have recently been established Subsidence Districts that affect control and permit procedures for development along the Texas coastal areas. There is a very good chance that if any development is to take place, one or several of the preceding districts or agencies will significantly affect the proposed project.

LAND DESCRIPTIONS

There are six commonly used methods of describing the location of land: (1) informal reference, (2) metes and bounds, (3) rectangular survey system, (4) recorded plat, (5) assessor parcel number, and (6) reference to documents other than maps. We shall look at each in detail.

Informal References

Street numbers and place names are informal references: the house located at 7216 Maple Street; the apartment identified as Apartment 101, 875 First Street; the office identified as Suite 222, 3570 Oakview Boulevard; or the ranch known as the Rocking K Ranch—in each case followed by the city (or county) and state where it is located. The advantage of an informal reference is that it is easily understood. The disadvantage from a real estate standpoint is that it is not a precise method of land description: A street number or place name does not provide the boundaries of the land at that location, and these numbers and names change over the years. Consequently, in real estate the use of informal references is limited to situations in which convenience is more important than precision. Thus, in a rental contract, Apartment 101, 875 First Street, City and State, is sufficient for a tenant to find the apartment unit. The apartment need not be described by one of the following more formal land descriptions.

Metes and Bounds

A **metes and bounds** land description is one that identifies a parcel by specifying its shape and boundaries. Early land descriptions in America depended on convenient natural or man-made objects. A stream might serve to mark one side of a parcel, an old

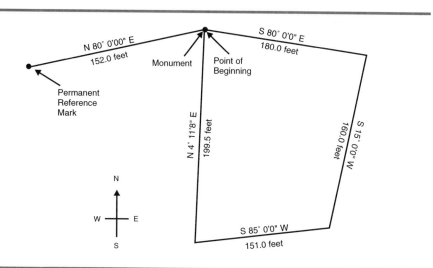

FIGURE 2.2
Describing land by
metes and bounds.

oak tree to mark a corner, a road another side, a pile of rocks a second corner, a fence another side, and so forth. This method was handy, but it had two major drawbacks: there might not be a convenient corner or boundary marker where one was needed, and over time, oak trees died, stone heaps were moved, streams and rivers changed course, stumps rotted, fences were removed, and unused roads became overgrown with vegetation.

Possible drawbacks of the metes and bounds method of land description are resolved by setting a permanent man-made **monument** at one corner of the parcel, and then describing the parcel in terms of distance and direction from that point. From the monument, the surveyor runs the parcel's outside lines by compass and distance so as to take in the land area being described. Distances are measured in feet, usually to the nearest tenth or one-hundredth of a foot. Direction is shown in degrees, minutes, and seconds. There are 360 degrees (°) in a circle, 60 minutes (') in each degree, and 60 seconds (") in each minute. The abbreviation 29°14'52" would be read as 29 degrees, 14 minutes, and 52 seconds. Figure 2.2 illustrates a modern metes and bounds land description.

At the corner where the survey begins, a monument in the form of an iron pipe or bar one to two inches in diameter is driven into the ground. Alternatively, concrete or stone monuments are sometimes used. To guard against the possibility that the monument might later be destroyed or removed, it is referenced by means of a **connection line** to a nearby **permanent reference mark** established by a government survey agency. The corner where the parcel survey begins is called the **point of beginning** or **point of commencement.** From this point in Figure 2.2, we travel clockwise along the parcel's perimeter, reaching the next corner by going in the direction 80 degrees east of south for a distance of 180 feet. We then travel in a direction 15 degrees west of south for 160 feet, thence 85 degrees west of south for 151 feet, and thence 4 degrees, 11 minutes, and 8 seconds east of north for 199.5 feet back to the point of beginning. In mapping shorthand, this parcel would be described by first identifying the monument, then the county and state within which it lies, and "thence S80°0'0", 180.0'; thence S15°0'0"W, 160.0'; thence S85°0'0"W, 151.0'; thence N4°11'18"E, 199.5' back to the p.o.b." It is customary, but not required, to describe a parcel as if traveling clockwise around it.

Compass Directions

The compass illustrated in Figure 2.3A shows how the direction of travel along each side of the parcel in Figure 2.2 is determined. Note that the same line can be labeled

FIGURE 2.3
Metes and bounds
mapping.

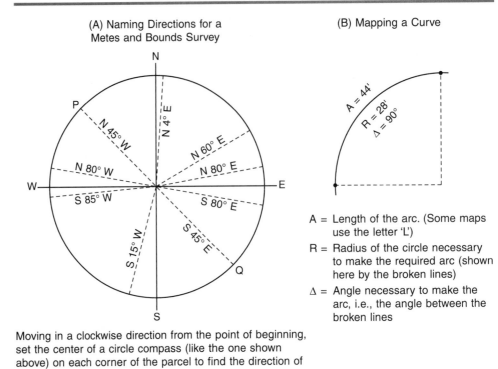

(A) Naming Directions for a
Metes and Bounds Survey

(B) Mapping a Curve

A = Length of the arc. (Some maps
use the letter 'L')

R = Radius of the circle necessary
to make the required arc (shown
here by the broken lines)

Δ = Angle necessary to make the
arc, i.e., the angle between the
broken lines

Moving in a clockwise direction from the point of beginning,
set the center of a circle compass (like the one shown
above) on each corner of the parcel to find the direction of
travel to the next corner.

two ways depending on which direction you are traveling. To illustrate, look at the line from *P* to *Q*. If you are traveling toward *P* on the line, you are going N45°W. But, if you are traveling toward point *Q* on the line, you are going S45°E.

Curved boundary lines are produced by using arcs of a circle. The length of the arc is labeled *L* or *A;* the radius of the circle producing the arc is labeled *R*. The symbol Δ (delta) indicates the angle used to produce the arc (see Figure 2.3 B).

Bench marks are commonly used as permanent reference markers. A bench mark is a fixed marker of known location and elevation. It may be as simple as an iron post or as elaborate as an engraved 3 ³/₄" brass disc set into concrete. The mark is usually set in place by a government survey team from the U.S. Geological Survey (USGS) or the U.S. Coast and Geodetic Survey (USCGS). Bench marks are referenced to each other by distance and direction. The advantages of this type of reference point, compared to trees, rocks, and the like, are permanence and accuracy to within a fraction of an inch. Additionally, even though it is possible to destroy a reference point or monument, it can be replaced in its exact former position because the location of each is related to other reference points.

It is also possible to describe a parcel using metes and bounds when there is no physical monument set in the ground. This is done by identifying a corner of a parcel of land by using the rectangular survey system or a recorded plat map, and then using that corner as a reference point to begin a metes and bounds description. As long as the starting place for a metes and bounds description can be accurately located by future surveyors, it will serve the purpose.

Rectangular Survey System

The **rectangular survey system** was authorized by Congress in May 1785 in order to systematically divide the land north and west of the Ohio River into six-mile

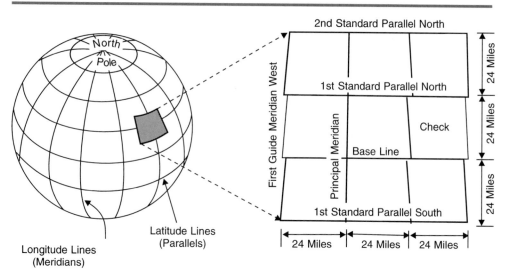

squares, now called congressional townships. It was also designed to provide a faster and simpler method than metes and bounds for describing land in newly annexed territories and states. Rather than using physical monuments, the rectangular survey system, also known as the **government survey** or **U.S. public lands survey,** is based on the system of mapping lines first imagined by ancient geographers and navigators. These are the east-west **latitude** lines and the north-south **longitude** lines that encircle the earth.

Certain longitude lines were selected to act as principal **meridians.** For each of these an intercepting latitude line was selected as a **base line.** Every 24 miles north and south of a base line, **correction lines** or **standard parallels** were established. Every 24 miles east and west of a principal meridian, guide **meridians** were established to run from one standard parallel to the next. These are needed because the earth is a sphere, not a flat surface. As one travels north in the United States, longitude (meridian) lines come closer together; that is, they converge toward the pole. Figure 2.4 shows how guide meridians and correction lines adjust for this problem. Each 24 by 24 mile area created by the guide meridians and correction lines is called a **check.**

There are 36 principal meridians and their intersecting base lines in the U.S. public land survey system. Figure 2.5 shows the states in which this system is used and the land area for which each principal meridian and base line act as a reference. For example, the Sixth Principal Meridian is the reference point for land surveys in Kansas, Nebraska, and portions of Colorado, Wyoming, and South Dakota. In addition to the U.S. public land survey system, a portion of western Kentucky was surveyed into townships by a special state survey. Also, the state of Ohio contains eight public land surveys that are rectangular in design, but which use state boundaries and major rivers rather than latitude and longitude as reference lines.

Range

Figure 2.6 shows how land is referenced to a principal meridian and base line. Every six miles east and west of each principal meridian, parallel survey lines are drawn. The resulting six-mile-wide columns are called **ranges** and are numbered consecutively east and west of the principal meridian. For example, the first range west is called Range 1 West and abbreviated R1W. The next range west is R2W, and so forth. The fourth range east is R4E.

FIGURE 2.5
The public lands
survey of the
United States.

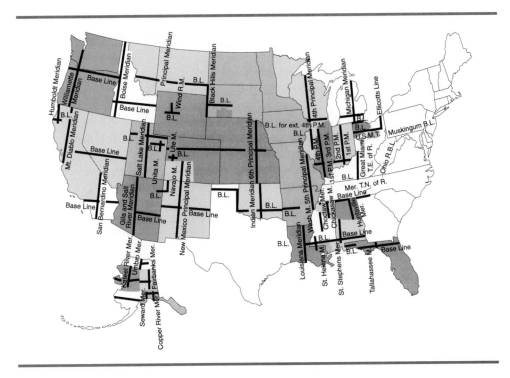

Township

Every six miles north and south of a base line, township lines are drawn. They intersect with the range lines and produce six-by-six-mile mapped squares called **townships** (not to be confused with the word *township* as applied to political subdivisions). Each tier or row of townships thus created is numbered with respect to the base line. Townships lying in the first tier north of a base line all carry the designation Township 1 North, abbreviated T1N. Townships lying in the first tier south of the base line are

FIGURE 2.6
Identifying townships
and sections.

Identifying Townships   Township Divided into Sections

all designated T1S, and in the second tier south, T2S. By adding a range reference, an individual township can be identified. Thus, T2S, R2W would identify the township lying in the second tier south of the base line and the second range west of the principal meridian. T14N, R52W would be a township 14 tiers north of the base line and 52 ranges west of the principal meridian.

Section

Each 36-square-mile township is divided into 36 one-square-mile units called **sections.** When one flies over farming areas, particularly in the Midwest, the checkerboard pattern of farms and roads that follow section boundaries can be seen. Sections are numbered 1 through 36, starting in the upper-right corner of the township. With this numbering system, any two sections with consecutive numbers share a common boundary. The section numbering system is illustrated in the right half of Figure 2.6 where the shaded section is described as Section 32, T2N, R3E, 6th Principal Meridian.

Acre

Each square-mile **section** contains 640 acres, and each **acre** contains 43,560 square feet. Any parcel of land smaller than a full 640-acre section is identified by its position in the section. This is done by dividing the section into quarters and halves as shown in Figure 2.7. For example, the shaded parcel shown at A is described by dividing the section into quarters and then dividing the southwest quarter into quarters. Parcel A is described as the NW $^1/_4$ of the SW $^1/_4$ of Section 32, T2N, R3E, 6th P.M. Additionally, it is customary to name the county and state in which the land lies. How much land does the NW $^1/_4$ of the SW $^1/_4$ of a section contain? A section contains 640 acres; therefore, a quarter-section contains 160 acres. Dividing a quarter-section again into quarters results in four 40-acre parcels. Thus, the northwest quarter of the southwest quarter contains 40 acres.

The rectangular survey system is not limited to parcels of 40 or more acres. To demonstrate this point, the SE $^1/_4$ of section 32 is exploded in the right half of Figure 2.7. Parcel B is described as the SE $^1/_4$ of the SE $^1/_4$ of the SE $^1/_4$ of the SE $^1/_4$ of section 32 and contains 2$^1/_2$ acres. Parcel C is described as the west 15 acres of the NW

FIGURE 2.7
Subdividing a section.

$^1/_4$ of the SE $^1/_4$ of section 32. Parcel D would be described in metes and bounds using the northeast corner of the SE $^1/_4$ of section 32 as the starting point.

Not all sections contain exactly 640 acres. Some are smaller because the earth's longitude lines converge toward the North Pole. Also, a section may be larger or smaller than 640 acres due to historical accommodations or survey errors dating back a hundred years or more. For the same reasons, not all townships contain exactly 36 square miles.

In terms of surface area, more land in the United States is described by the rectangular survey system than by any other survey method. But in terms of number of properties, the recorded plat is the most important survey method.

As shown on the map in Figure 2.5, Texas has not seen fit to adopt it. Note, however, that it has had limited use in portions of west Texas.

Recorded Plat

When a tract of land is ready for subdividing into lots for homes and businesses, reference by **recorded plat** provides the simplest and most convenient method of land description. A **plat** is a map that shows the location and boundaries of individual properties. Also known as the lot-block-tract system, **recorded map,** or **recorded survey**, this method of land description is based on the filing of a surveyor's plat in the public recorder's office of the county where the land is located. Figure 2.8 illustrates a plat. Notice that a metes and bounds survey has been made and a map prepared to show in detail the boundaries of each parcel of land. Each parcel is then assigned a lot number. Each block in the tract is given a block number, and the tract itself is given a name or

FIGURE 2.8
Land description by recorded plat.

number. A plat showing all the blocks in the tract is delivered to the county recorder's office, where it is placed in **map books** or **survey books,** along with plats of other subdivisions in the county.

Each plat is given a book and page reference number, and all map books are available for public inspection. From that point on, it is no longer necessary to give a lengthy metes and bounds description to describe a parcel. Instead, one need only provide the lot and block number, tract name, map book reference, county, and state. To find the location and dimensions of a recorded lot in Texas, one simply looks at the map book at the county clerk's office.

Note that the plat in Figure 2.8 combines both of the land descriptions just discussed. The boundaries of the numbered lots are in metes and bounds. These, in turn, are referenced to a section corner in the rectangular survey system.

Assessor Parcel Number

In many Texas counties the appraisal district assigns an **assessor parcel number** to each parcel of land in the county. The primary purpose is to aid in the assessment of property for tax collection purposes. However, these parcel numbers are public information and real estate brokers, appraisers, and investors can and do use them extensively to assist in identifying real properties.

The method used in Texas is to divide the county into map books. Each book is given a number and covers a given portion of the county. Depending on the size of the county and the number of separate parcels of land in the county, the number of map books necessary to cover a county can range from less than a dozen to several hundred. On each page of the map book are parcel maps, each with its own number. For subdivided lots, these maps are based on the plats submitted by the subdivider to the county clerk's office when the subdivision was made. For unsubdivided land, the appraisal district prepares its own maps.

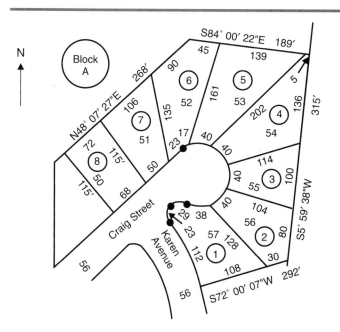

FIGURE 2.9
Assessor's map.

Assessor's Map
Book 34
Page 18

Assessor Parcel Numbers
shown in circles

Lots 50 through 57 of
Tract 2118, filed in
Recorded Maps, Book 63,
page 39.

The tax assessor assigns every parcel of land in the county its own parcel number. For example, the westernmost parcel (Lot 50) in the map would carry the number 34-18-8, meaning Book 34, Page 18, Parcel 8.

Each parcel of land on the map is assigned a parcel number by the appraisal district. The assessor parcel number may or may not be the same as the lot number assigned by the subdivider. To reduce confusion, the parcel number is either circled or underlined. Figure 2.9 illustrates a page out of an appraisal district's map book.

The appraisal district's maps are open to viewing by the public at the appraisal district's office. In many counties, private firms reproduce the maps and rolls and make them available to real estate brokers, appraisers, lenders, etc., for a fee.

PUTTING IT TO WORK

Before leaving the topic of the appraisal district's maps, a word of caution is in order. These maps should not be relied upon as the final authority for the legal description of a parcel. That can come only from a title search that will include looking at the current deed to the property and the recorded copy of the subdivider's plat. Note also that the assessor parcel number is never used as a legal description in a deed.

Reference to Documents Other than Maps

Land can also be described by referring to another publicly recorded document, such as a deed or a mortgage, that contains a full legal description of the parcel in question. For example, suppose that several years ago Baker received a deed from Adams that contained a long and complicated metes and bounds description. Baker recorded the deed in the public records office, where a photocopy was placed in Book 1089, Page 456. If Baker later wants to deed the same land to Cooper, Baker can describe the parcel in his deed to Cooper by saying, "all the land described in the deed from Adams to Baker recorded in Book 1089, Page 456, county of ABC, state of XYZ, at the public recorder's office for said county and state." Since these books are open to the public, Cooper (or anyone else) could go to Book 1089, Page 456 and find a detailed description of the parcel's boundaries.

PUTTING IT TO WORK

The key test of a land description is: "Can another person, reading what I have written or drawn, understand my description and go out and locate the boundaries of the parcel?"

VERTICAL LAND DESCRIPTION

In addition to surface land descriptions, land may also be described in terms of vertical measurements. This type of measurement is necessary when air rights or subsurface rights need to be described.

A point, line, or surface from which a distance, vertical height, or depth is measured is called a **datum.** The most commonly used datum plane in the United States is mean sea level, although a number of cities have established other data surfaces for use in local surveys. Starting from a datum, **bench marks** are set at calculated inter-

FIGURE **2.10**
Air lot and contour
lines.

(A) An air lot over Lot 26 of Block 17
and lying between an elevation of
575 ft. and 625 ft. above sea level.

(B) Contour map (*above*) showing a
profile (*below*) through X-X'.

vals by government survey teams; thus, a surveyor need not travel to the original
datum to determine an elevation. These same bench marks are used as reference points
for metes and bounds surveys.

In selling or leasing subsurface drilling or mineral rights, the chosen datum is
often the surface of the parcel. For example, an oil lease may permit the extraction of
oil and gas from a depth greater than 500 feet beneath the surface of a parcel of land.
(Subsurface rights are discussed more in the next chapter.)

An **air lot** (a space over a given parcel of land) is described by identifying both
the parcel of land beneath the air lot and the elevation of the air lot above the parcel
(see Figure 2.10A). Multi-story condominiums use this system of land description.

Contour maps (topographic maps) indicate elevations. On these maps, **contour
lines** connect all points having the same elevation. The purpose is to show hills and
valleys, slopes, and water runoff. If the land is to be developed, the map shows where
soil will have to be moved to provide level building lots. Figure 2.10B illustrates how
vertical distances are shown using contour lines.

PHYSICAL CHARACTERISTICS OF LAND

The physical characteristics of land are immobility, indestructibility, and nonhomogeneity. This combination of characteristics makes land different from other commodities and directly and indirectly influences our use of it.

Immobility

A parcel of land cannot be moved. It is true that soil, sand, gravel, and minerals can be
moved by the action of nature (erosion) or humans (digging); however, the parcel itself
still retains its same geographical position on the globe. Because land is **immobile,** a
person must go to the land; it cannot be brought to him. When land is sold, the seller
cannot physically deliver his land to the buyer. Instead, the seller gives the buyer a
document called a deed that transfers to the buyer the right to go onto that land and
use it. Because land is immobile, real estate offices nearly always limit their sales
activities to nearby properties. Even so, a great deal of a salesperson's effort consists

of traveling to show properties to clients. Immobility also creates a need for property-management firms, because unless an owner of rental property lives on the property or nearby, neither land nor buildings can be efficiently managed.

Indestructibility

Land is **indestructible,** that is, durable. For example, today one can travel to the Middle East and walk on the same land that was walked on in Biblical days, and most of the land that we use in the United States today is the same land used by the American Indians a thousand years ago.

The characteristic of physical durability encourages many people to buy land as an investment because they feel that paper money, stocks and bonds, and other commodities may come and go, but land will always be here. Although this is true in a physical sense, whether a given parcel has and will have economic value depends on one's ability to protect his ownership and on subsequent demand for that land by other people. In other words, physical durability must not be confused with economic durability.

Nonhomogeneity

The fact that no two parcels of land are exactly alike because no two parcels can occupy the same position on the globe is known as **nonhomogeneity** (heterogeneity). Courts of law recognize this characteristic of land and consequently treat land as a **nonfungible** commodity; that is, nonsubstitutable. Thus, in a contract involving the sale or rental of land (and any improvements to that land), the courts can be called upon to enforce specific performance of the contract. For example, in a contract to sell a home, if the buyer carries out his obligations and the seller fails to convey ownership to the buyer, a court of law will force the seller to convey ownership of *that* specific home to the buyer. The court will not require the buyer to accept a substitute home. This is different from a homogeneous or **fungible** commodity that is freely substitutable in carrying out a contract. For example, one bushel of No. 1 grade winter wheat can be freely replaced by another bushel of the same grade, and one share of United States Steel common stock can be substituted for another as all are identical.

Although land is nonhomogeneous, there can still be a high degree of physical and economic similarity. For example, in a city block containing 20 house lots of identical size and shape, there will be a high degree of similarity even though the lots are still nonhomogeneous. Finding similar properties is, in fact, the basis for the market-comparison approach to appraising real estate.

ECONOMIC CHARACTERISTICS OF LAND

The dividing line between the physical and economic characteristics of land is sometimes difficult to define because the physical aspects of land greatly influence our economic behavior toward land. However, four economic characteristics are generally recognized: scarcity, modification, permanence of investment (fixity), and area preference (situs).

Scarcity

The shortage of land in a given geographical area where there is great demand for land is referred to as **scarcity.** It is a man-made characteristic. For example, land is scarce in Dallas and Houston, because a relatively large number of people want to use a relatively small area of land. Yet outside of Texas cities there is plenty of uncrowded land available for purchase at very reasonable prices.

Land scarcity is also influenced by our ability to use land more efficiently. To illustrate, in agricultural areas production per acre of land has more than doubled for many crops since 1940. This is not due to any change in the land, but is the result of improved fertilizers and irrigation systems, better seeds, and modern crop management. Likewise, in urban areas, an acre of land that once provided space for five houses can be converted to high-rise apartments to provide homes for 100 or more families.

Thus, although there is a limited physical amount of land on the earth's surface, scarcity is chiefly a function of demand for land in a given geographical area and the ability of man to make land more productive. The persistent notion that all land is scarce has led to periodic land sale booms in undeveloped areas, which can be followed by a collapse in land prices when it becomes apparent that that particular land is not economically scarce.

Modification

Land use and value are greatly influenced by **modification,** that is, improvements made by individuals to surrounding parcels of land. For example, the construction of an airport will increase the usefulness and value of land parallel to runways, but will have a negative effect on the use and value of land at the ends of runways because of noise from landings and takeoffs. Similarly, land subject to flooding will become more useful and valuable if government-sponsored flood control dams are built upriver.

PUTTING IT TO WORK

One of the most widely publicized cases of land modification occurred near Orlando, Florida when Disney World was constructed. Nearby land previously used for agricultural purposes suddenly became useful as motel, gas station, restaurant, house, and apartment sites and increased rapidly in value.

Fixity

The fact that land and buildings and other improvements to land require long periods of time to pay for themselves is referred to as **fixity** or **investment permanence.** For example, it may take 20 or 30 years for the income generated by an apartment or office building to repay the cost of the land and building plus interest on the money borrowed to make the purchase. Consequently, real estate investment and land use decisions must consider not only how the land will be used next month or next year, but also the usefulness of the improvements 20 years from now. There is no economic logic in spending money to purchase land and improvements that will require 20 to 30 years to pay for themselves, if their usefulness is expected to last only 5 years.

Fixity also reflects the fact that land cannot be moved from its present location to another location where it will be more valuable. With very few exceptions, improvements to land are also fixed. Even with a house, the cost of moving it plus building a foundation at the new site can easily exceed the value of the house after the move. Thus, when an investment is made in real estate, it is regarded as a **fixed** or **sunk cost.**

Situs

Situs, or **location preference,** refers to location from an economic rather than a geographic standpoint. It has often been said that the single most important word in real estate is "location." What this means is the preference of people for a given area. For a residential area, these preferences are the result of *natural* factors, such as weather, air quality, scenic views, and closeness to natural recreation areas, and man-made factors, such as job opportunities, transportation facilities, shopping, and schools. For an industrial area, situs depends on such things as an available labor market, adequate supplies of water and electricity, nearby rail lines, and highway access. In farming areas, situs includes soil and weather conditions, water and labor availability, and transportation facilities.

Situs is the reason that house lots on street corners sell for more than identical-sized lots not on corners. This reflects a preference for open space. The same is true in apartments; corner units usually rent for more than similar-sized noncorner units. In a high-rise apartment building, units on the top floors, if they offer a view, command higher prices than identical units on lower floors. On a street lined with stores, the side of the street that is shaded in the afternoon will attract more shoppers than the unshaded side. Consequently, buildings on the shaded side will generate more sales and, as a result, will be worth more.

It is important to realize that since situs is a function of people's preferences and preferences can change with time, situs can also change. For example, the freeway and expressway construction boom that started up in the 1950s and accelerated during the 1960s, increased the preference for suburban areas. This resulted in declining property values in inner city areas and increasing land values in the suburbs. Today, people are starting to show a preference for living closer to the centers of cities, due to transportation convenience and proximity to work.

REVIEW QUESTIONS

Answers to these questions are found in the Answer Key section at the back of the book.

1. In determining whether an article of personal property has become a fixture, which of the following tests would NOT be applied?
   A. The manner of attachment.
   B. The cost of the article.
   C. The adaptation of the article to the land.
   D. The existence of an agreement between the parties.

2. The term "real estate" includes
   A. the right to use land.
   B. anything affixed to land with the intent of being permanent.
   C. rights to the air above the land.
   D. rights to subsurface minerals.
   E. All of the above.

3. Determining what is a fixture and what is not is important when
   A. property taxes are calculated.
   B. real estate is mortgaged.
   C. a tenant attaches an object to a rented building.
   D. hazard insurance is purchased.
   E. All of the above.

4. In remodeling their home, the Wades put the items described below in the home. Once in place all would be fixtures EXCEPT:
   A. an oriental throw rug in the front entry hall.
   B. the built-in kitchen range.
   C. the built-in dishwasher.
   D. custom fitted wall-to-wall carpet installed over plywood sub-flooring.

5. Which of the following are NOT classified as real property?
   A. Fixtures.
   B. Emblements.
   C. A shrub planted in the ground.
   D. Air rights.

6. The right of an owner to use water from a stream for his own use is called
   A. an emblement right.
   B. a riparian right.
   C. a littoral right.
   D. a percolated right.

7. Which of the following land description methods identifies a parcel of land by specifying its shape and boundaries?
   A. Metes and bounds.
   B. Government survey.
   C. Recorded plat.
   D. Assessor's parcel number.
   E. All of the above.

8. Which of the following have been utilized as monuments to designate the corner of a parcel of land in the metes and bounds description of the land?
   A. An iron pipe driven in the ground.
   B. A tree.
   C. A fence corner.
   D. All of the above.
   E. None of the above.

9. The term "point of beginning" refers to
   A. a permanent reference marker.
   B. the first corner of the parcel to be surveyed.
   C. a benchmark.
   D. the intersection of a principal meridian with its base line.

10. 1/60th of 1/60th of 1/360th of a circle is known as a
    A. degree.
    B. minute.
    C. second.
    D. None of the above.

11. The major drawbacks of the early land descriptions were
    A. the possible lack of convenient monuments or boundaries.
    B. the possibility that monuments or boundaries could be moved or might disappear.
    C. Both A and B.
    D. Neither A nor B.

12. As measured from the north, an angular bearing of 135 degrees would be equivalent to which of the following in a surveyor's description of the same angle?
    A. S 45 degrees W
    B. N 45 degrees W
    C. N 45 degrees E
    D. S 45 degrees E

13. Goodwin, a surveyor, was called upon to make a metes and bounds survey of an irregularly shaped parcel of land. Which of the following statements would be correct?
    A. Goodwin could travel in either a clockwise or counterclockwise direction in making the survey.
    B. Goodwin must always travel in a clockwise direction in making the survey.
    C. The angular bearings of all boundary lines would be measured from the north.
    D. The corner where the survey was begun would be identified as the point of beginning.
    E. Both A and D.

14. A township is
    A. six miles square.
    B. one mile square.
    C. six square miles.
    D. one square mile.

15. Forty-three thousand, five hundred and sixty is the number of square feet in
    A. an acre.
    B. a section.
    C. a township.
    D. a tier.

16. The NW 1/4 of the NW 1/4 of the NW 1/4 of a section contains
    A. 80 acres.
    B. 10 acres.
    C. 20 acres.
    D. 40 acres.

17. An assessor's parcel number
    A. is the final authority for the legal description of a parcel of land.
    B. is often used as a legal description in a deed.
    C. Both A and B.
    D. Neither A nor B.

KEY TERMS

Chattel: an article of personal property

Easement: the right or privilege one party has to use land belonging to another for a special purpose not inconsistent with the owner's use of the land

Eminent domain: the right of government to take privately held land for public use provided fair compensation is paid

Encroachment: the unauthorized intrusion of a building or other improvement onto another person's land

Encumbrance: any impediment to a clear title, such as a lien, lease, or easement

Fee simple: the largest, most complete bundle of rights one can hold in land; land ownership

Homestead protection: state laws that protect against the forced sale of a person's home

Lien: a hold or claim that one person has on the property of another to secure payment of a debt or other obligation

Title: the right to or ownership of something; also the evidence of ownership, such as a deed or bill of sale

Rights and Interests in Land

IN THIS CHAPTER *This chapter provides the student with general and legal information concerning rights and interests in land. It begins with a brief discussion of government rights in land, individual rights, easements, encroachments, deed restrictions, and types of liens. Other topics covered in this chapter include various types of estates, homestead rights, chattels, and subsurface rights.*

FEUDAL AND ALLODIAL SYSTEMS

Early humans were nomadic and had no concept of real estate. Roaming bands followed game and the seasons and did not claim the exclusive right to use a given area. When humans began to cultivate crops and domesticate animals, the concept of an exclusive right to the use of land became important. This right was claimed for the tribe as a whole, and each family in the tribe was given the right to the exclusive use of a portion of the tribe's land. In turn, each family was obligated to aid in defending the tribe's claim against other tribes.

Feudal System

As time passed, individual tribes allied with each other for mutual protection; eventually these alliances resulted in political states. In the process, land ownership went to the head of the state, usually a king. The king, in turn, gave the right (called a feud) to use large tracts of land to select individuals, called lords. The lords did not receive ownership. They were tenants of the king, and were required to serve and pay duties to the king and to help fight the king's wars. It was customary for the lords to remain tenants for life, subject, of course, to the defeat of their king by another king. This system, wherein all land ownership rested in the name of the king, became known as the **feudal system.**

The lords gave their subjects the right to use small tracts of land. For this, the subjects owed their lord a share of their crops and their allegiance in time of war. The subjects (vassals) were, in effect, tenants of the lord and subtenants of the king. Like the lord, the vassal could not sell his rights nor pass them to his heirs.

Allodial System

The first major change in the feudal system occurred in 1285 when King Edward I of England gave his lords the right to pass their tenancy rights to their heirs. Subsequently, tenant vassals were permitted to convey their tenancy rights to others. By the year

1650, the feudal system had come to an end in England; in France it ended with the French Revolution in 1789. In its place arose the **allodial system** of land ownership under which individuals were given the right to own land. Initially, lords became owners and the peasants remained tenants of the lord. As time passed, the peasants became landowners either by purchase or by a gift from the lord.

When the first European explorers reached North American shores, they claimed the land in the name of the king or queen whom they represented. When the first settlers later came to America from England, they claimed the land in the name of their mother country. However, since the feudal system had been abolished in the meantime, the king of England granted the settlers private ownership of the land upon which they settled, while retaining the claim of ownership to the unsettled lands.

Claims by the king of England to land in the 13 colonies were ended with the American Revolution. Subsequently, the U.S. government acquired the ownership right to additional lands by treaty, wars, and purchase, resulting in the borders of the United States as we know them today. The United States adopted the allodial system of ownership and not only permits, but encourages, its citizens to own land within its borders.

GOVERNMENT RIGHTS IN LAND

Under the feudal system, the king was responsible for organizing defense against invaders, making decisions on land use, providing services such as roads and bridges, and the general administration of the land and his subjects. An important aspect of the transition from feudal to allodial ownership was that the need for these services did not end. Consequently, even though ownership could now be held by private citizens, it became necessary for the government to retain the rights of taxation, eminent domain, police power, and escheat. Let us look at each of these more closely.

Property Taxes

Under the feudal system, governments financed themselves by requiring lords and vassals to share a portion of the benefits they received from the use of the king's lands. With the change to private ownership, the need to finance governments did not end. Thus, the government retained the right to collect **property taxes** from landowners. Before the advent of income taxes, taxes levied against land were the main source of government revenues. Taxing land was a logical method of raising revenue for two reasons: (1) until the Industrial Revolution, which started in the mid-eighteenth century, land and agriculture were the primary sources of income; the more land one owned, the wealthier one was considered to be and therefore the better able to pay taxes to support the government; and (2) land is impossible to hide, making it easily identifiable for taxation. This is not true of other valuables such as gold or money.

The real property tax has endured over the centuries, and today it is still a major source of government revenue. The major change in real estate taxation is that ini-

PUTTING IT TO WORK

To encourage property owners to pay their taxes in full and on time, the right of taxation also enables the government to seize ownership of real estate upon which taxes are delinquent and to sell the property to recover the unpaid taxes.

tially it was used to support all levels of government, including defense. Today, defense is supported by the income tax, and real estate taxes are sources of city, county, and, in some places, state revenues. At state and local government levels, the real property tax provides money for such things as schools, fire and police protection, parks, and libraries.

Eminent Domain

The right of government to take ownership of privately held real estate regardless of the owner's wishes is called **eminent domain.** Land for schools, freeways, streets, parks, urban renewal, public housing, public parking, and other social and public purposes is obtained this way. Quasi-public organizations, such as utility companies and railroads, are also permitted by state law to obtain land needed for utility lines, pipes, and tracks. The legal proceeding involved in eminent domain is a **condemnation proceeding,** and the property owner must be paid the fair market value of the property taken from him. The actual condemnation is usually preceded by negotiations between the property owner and an agent of the public body wanting to acquire ownership. If the agent and the property owner can arrive at a mutually acceptable price, the property is purchased outright. If an agreement cannot be reached, a formal proceeding in eminent domain is filed against the property owner in a court of law. The court hears expert opinions from appraisers brought by both parties, and then sets the price the property owner must accept in return for the loss of ownership.

When only a portion of a parcel of land is being taken, **severance damages** may be awarded in addition to payment for land actually being taken. For example, if a new highway requires a 40-acre strip of land through the middle of a 160-acre farm, the farm owner will not only be paid for the 40 acres; she will also receive severance damages to compensate for the fact that her farm will be more difficult to work because it is no longer in one piece.

An **inverse condemnation** is a proceeding brought about by a property owner demanding that his land be purchased from him. In a number of cities, homeowners at the end of airport runways have forced airport authorities to buy their homes because of the deafening noise of jet aircraft during takeoffs. Damage awards may also be made when land itself is not taken but its usefulness is reduced because of a nearby condemnation. These are **consequential damages** and might be awarded, for instance, when land is taken for a sewage treatment plant, and privately owned land downwind from the plant suffers a loss in value owing to the prevalence of foul odors.

Police Power

The right of government to enact laws and enforce them for the order, safety, health, morals, and general welfare of the public is called **police power.** Examples of police power applied to real estate are zoning laws; planning laws; building, health, and fire codes; and rent control. A key difference between police power and eminent domain is that although police power restricts how real estate may be used, there is no legally recognized "taking" of property. Consequently, there is no payment to an owner who suffers a loss of value through the exercise of police power. A government may not utilize police power in an offhand or capricious manner; any law that restricts how an owner may use his real estate must be deemed in the public interest and must be applied evenhandedly to be valid. The breaking of a law based upon police power results in either a civil or criminal penalty rather than in the seizure of real estate, as in the case of unpaid property taxes. Of the various rights government holds in land, police power has the most impact on land value.

Escheat

When a person dies and leaves no heirs and no instructions as to how to dispose of her real and personal property, or when property is abandoned, the ownership of that property reverts to the state. This reversion to the state is called **escheat** from the Anglo-French word meaning *to fall back.* Escheat solves the problem of property becoming ownerless.

PROTECTING OWNERSHIP

It cannot be overemphasized that in order to have real estate there must be a system or means of protecting rightful claims to the use of land and the improvements thereon. In the United States, the federal government is given the task of organizing a defense system to prevent confiscation of those rights by a foreign power. The federal government, in combination with state and local governments, also establishes laws and courts within the country to protect the ownership rights of one citizen in relation to another citizen. Whereas the armed forces protect against a foreign takeover from outside, written deeds, public records, contracts, and other documents have replaced the need for brute force to prove and protect ownership of real estate within the country.

FEE SIMPLE

The concept of real estate ownership can be more easily understood when viewed as a collection or bundle of rights. Under the allodial system, the rights of taxation, eminent domain, police power, and escheat are retained by the government. The remaining bundle of rights, called **fee simple,** is available for private ownership. The fee simple bundle of rights can be held by a person and his heirs forever or until his government can no longer protect those rights. Figure 3.1 illustrates the fee simple bundle of rights concept.

The term **estate** refers to one's legal interest or rights in land. A fee simple is the largest estate one can hold in land. Most real estate sales are for the fee simple estate. When a person says she "owns" or has "title" to real estate, it is usually the fee simple estate that is being discussed. The word **title** refers to the ownership of something. All other lesser estates in land, such as life estates and leaseholds, are created from the fee estate.

Real estate is concerned with the "sticks" in the bundle—how many there are, how useful they are, and who possesses the sticks not in the bundle. With that in mind, let us describe what happens when sticks are removed from the bundle.

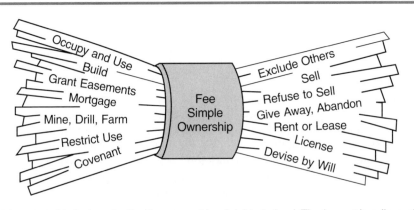

Real estate ownership is, in actuality, the ownership of rights to land. The largest bundle available for private ownership is called "fee simple."

ENCUMBRANCES

Whenever a stick is removed from the fee simple bundle, it creates an impediment to the free and clear ownership and use of that property. These impediments to title are called encumbrances. An **encumbrance** is defined as any claim, right, lien, estate, or liability that limits the fee simple title to property. An encumbrance is, in effect, a stick that has been removed from the bundle. Commonly found encumbrances are easements, encroachments, deed restrictions, liens, leases, and air and subsurface rights. In addition, qualified fee estates are encumbered estates, as are life estates.

The party holding a stick from someone else's fee simple bundle is said to hold a claim to or a right or interest in that land. In other words, what is one person's encumbrance is another person's right or interest or claim. For example, a lease is an encumbrance from the standpoint of the fee simple owner. But from the tenant's standpoint, it is an interest in land that gives the tenant the right to the exclusive use of land and buildings. A mortgage is an encumbrance from the fee owner's viewpoint, but a right to foreclose from the lender's viewpoint. A property that is encumbered with a lease and a mortgage is called "a fee simple subject to a lease and a mortgage." Figure 3.2 illustrates how a fee simple bundle shrinks as rights are removed from it. Meanwhile, let us turn our attention to a discussion of individual sticks found in the fee simple bundle.

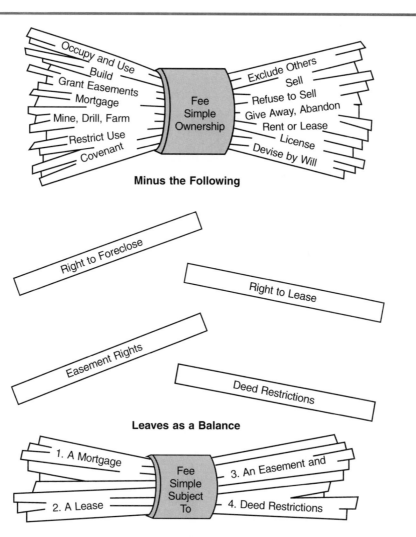

FIGURE 3.2
Removing sticks from the fee simple bundle.

Notice that the fee simple bundle shrinks as an owner voluntarily removes rights from it.

FIGURE 3.3
Commonly found
easements.

Easements

An **easement** is a right or privilege one party has to the use of the land of another for a special purpose consistent with the general use of the land. The landowner is not dispossessed from his land, but rather coexists side by side with the holder of the easement. Examples of easements are those given to telephone and electric companies to erect poles and to run lines over private property, easements given to people to drive or walk across someone else's land, and easements given to gas and water companies to run pipelines to serve their customers. Figure 3.3 illustrates several examples of easements.

The usual procedure in creating an easement is for the landowner to use a written document to specifically grant an easement to someone else or to reserve an easement to himself in the deed when he sells the property. A land developer may reserve easements for utility lines and then grant them to the utility companies that will service the lots.

It is also possible for an easement to arise without a written document. For example, a parcel of land fronts on a road and the owner sells the back half of the parcel. If the only access to the back half is by crossing over the front half, even if the seller did not expressly grant an easement, the law may protect the buyer's right to travel over the front half to get to his land. This may create an **easement by implication.** Another method of acquiring an easement without a written document is by constant use, or **easement by prescription:** If a person acts as though she owns an easement long enough, she will have a legally recognized easement. Persons using a private road without permission for a long enough period of time can acquire a legally recognized easement by this method.

Easement Appurtenant

In Figure 3.3, the driveway from the road to the back lot is called an **easement appurtenant.** This driveway is automatically included with the back lot whenever the back lot is sold or otherwise conveyed. This is so because this easement is physically and legally connected (appurtenant) to the back lot, which is the dominant estate. Please note that just as the back lot benefits from this easement, the front lot is burdened by it. Whenever the front lot is sold or otherwise conveyed, the new owners must continue to respect the easement to the back lot. The owner of the front lot owns all the front lot, but cannot put a fence across the easement, or plant trees on it or grow a garden on it or otherwise hamper access to the back lot. The front lot, being burdened by the easement, is called the **servient estate,** and the back lot, which benefits from the easement, is called the **dominant estate.**

Easement in Gross

An **easement in gross** is given to a person or business, and a subsequent sale of the land does not usually affect ownership of the easement. It benefits the user only and is an encumbrance to the fee estate (no benefit to the contiguous land owner). Therefore, there is neither a dominant or a servient estate. Telephone, electricity, and gas line easements are examples of easements in gross. The holder of a commercial easement usually has the right to sell, assign, or devise it. However, easements in gross for personal use are not transferable and terminate with the death of the person holding the easement. An example of a personal easement in gross would be a landowner giving a friend an easement to travel over his land to reach a choice fishing area.

Party Wall Easement

Party wall easements exist when a single wall straddles the lot line that separates two parcels of land. The wall may be either a fence or the wall of a building. In either case, each lot owner owns that portion of the wall on his land, plus an easement in the other half of the wall for physical support. Party walls are common where stores and office buildings are built right up to the lot line. Such a wall can present an interesting problem when the owner of one lot wants to demolish his building. Because the wall provides support for the building next door, it is usually her responsibility to either leave the wall or provide special supports for the adjacent building during demolition and until another building is constructed on the lot.

Easement Termination

Easements may be terminated when the purpose for the easement no longer exists (e.g., a public road is built adjacent to the back half of the lot mentioned earlier), or when the dominant and servient estates are combined with the intent of extinguishing the easement, or by release from the owner of the dominant estate to the servient estate, or by lack of use.

Encroachments

The unauthorized intrusion of a building or other improvement onto another person's land is called an **encroachment.** A tree that overhangs into a neighbor's yard or a building or eave of a roof that crosses a property line are examples of encroachments. The owner of the property being encroached upon has the right to force the removal of the encroachment. Failure to do so may eventually injure his title and make his land more difficult to sell. Ultimately, inaction may result in the encroaching neighbor claiming a legal right to continue his use. Figure 3.4 illustrates several commonly found encroachments.

FIGURE 3.4
Commonly found
encroachments.

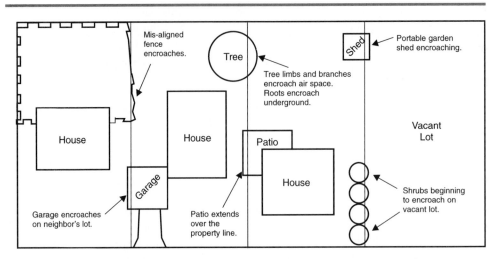

Most commonly found encroachments are not intentional but are due to poor or nonexistent planning. For example, a weekend garden shed, fence, or patio project is built without surveying to find the lot line, or a tree or bush grows so large it encroaches upon a neighbor's land.

Deed Restrictions

Private agreements that govern the use of land are known as **deed restrictions** or **deed covenants.** For example, a land subdivider can require that persons who purchase lots from her build only single-family homes containing 1,200 square feet or more. The purpose would be to protect those who have already built houses from an erosion in property value due to the construction of nearby buildings not compatible with the neighborhood. Where scenic views are important, deed restrictions may limit the height of buildings and trees to 15 feet. A buyer would still obtain fee simple ownership, but at the same time would voluntarily give up some of his rights to do as he pleases. As a buyer, he is said to receive a fee simple title subject to deed restrictions.

PUTTING IT TO WORK

The right to enforce the deed restrictions is usually given by the developer to the subdivision's homeowner association. Violation of a deed restriction can result in a civil court action brought by other property owners who are bound by the same deed restriction.

Liens

A hold or claim that one person has on the property of another to secure payment of a debt or other obligation is called a **lien.** Common examples are property tax liens, mechanic's liens, judgment liens, and mortgage liens. From the standpoint of the property owner, a lien is an encumbrance on his title. Note that a lien does not transfer title to property. The debtor retains title until the lien is foreclosed. When there is more than one lien against a property, the lien that was recorded first usually has the highest priority in the event of foreclosure.

Property Tax Lien

Property tax liens are superior to other liens. A **property tax lien** results from the right of government to collect taxes from property owners. At the beginning of each tax year, a tax lien is placed on taxable property and remains until the property taxes are paid. If they are not paid, the lien gives the government the right to force the sale of the property in order to collect the unpaid taxes.

Mechanic's Lien

Mechanic's lien laws give anyone who has furnished labor or materials for the improvement of land the right to place a lien against that land if payment has not been received. A sale of the property can then be forced to recover the money owed. To be entitled to a mechanic's lien, the work or materials must have been provided pursuant to an agreement with the property owner or his representative.

The legal theory behind mechanic's lien rights is that the labor and materials supplied enhance the value of the property. Therefore, the property should be security for payment. If the property owner does not pay voluntarily, the lien can be enforced with a court-supervised foreclosure sale. To be valid, a mechanic's lien must be recorded in the county clerk's office within the time limits set by state law.

Judgment Lien

Judgment liens arise from lawsuits for which money damages are awarded. The law permits a hold to be placed against the real and personal property of the debtor until the judgment is paid. Usually the lien created by the judgment covers only property in the county where the judgment was awarded. However, the creditor can extend the lien to property in other counties by filing an **abstract of judgment** in each of those counties. If the debtor does not repay the lien voluntarily, and the property is not the debtor's homestead (or is in excess of allowable homestead limits), the creditor can ask the court to issue a **writ of execution** that directs the county sheriff to seize and sell a sufficient amount of the debtor's property to pay the debt and expenses of the sale. If a writ of execution is not issued, the creditor must renew the abstract of judgment every ten years or it will expire and be of no further effect.

PUTTING IT TO WORK

If a landowner hires a contractor to build a house or add a room to his existing house, and then fails to pay the contractor, the contractor may file a mechanic's lien against the land and its improvements. Furthermore, if the landowner pays the contractor, but the contractor does not pay his subcontractors, the subcontractors are entitled to file a mechanic's lien against the property. In this situation, the owner may have to pay twice. The Texas legislature has also extended the lien rights to architects, engineers, and surveyors, provided that certain requirements are met.

Mortgage Lien

A **mortgage lien** is a pledge of property by its owner to secure the repayment of a debt. In contrast to a property tax lien which is imposed by law, a mortgage lien is a voluntary lien created by the property owner. In contrast to a judgment lien, which applies to all the debtor's property, a mortgage lien covers only the specific property that its owner elects to pledge. If the debt secured by the mortgage lien is not repaid, the creditor can foreclose and sell the pledged property. If this is insufficient to repay the debt, some states allow the creditor to petition the court for a judgment lien for the balance due. (Mortgage law is covered in more detail in Chapter 9.)

Voluntary and Involuntary Liens

A **voluntary lien** is a lien created by the property owner. A mortgage lien is an example of a voluntary lien; the owner voluntarily creates a lien against his or her own property in order to borrow money. An **involuntary lien** is one that is created by operation of law, against the wishes of the owner. Examples are property tax liens and judgment liens.

Specific and General Liens

A **specific lien** is a lien on a specific property. A property tax lien is a specific lien because it is a lien against a specific property and no other. Thus, if a person owns five parcels of land scattered throughout a given county and fails to pay the taxes on one of those parcels, the county can force the sale of just that one parcel; the others cannot be touched. Mortgages and mechanic's liens are also specific liens in that they apply to only the property receiving the materials or labor. In contrast, a **general lien** is a lien on all the property of a person in a given jurisdiction. For example, a judgment lien is a lien on all the debtor's property in the county or counties in which the judgment has been filed. Federal tax liens are also general liens.

QUALIFIED FEE ESTATES

A **qualified fee estate** is a fee estate that is subject to certain limitations imposed by the person creating the estate. Qualified fee estates fall into three categories: determinable, condition subsequent, and condition precedent. They will be discussed only briefly as they are rather uncommon.

A **fee on conditional limitation,** also called a **fee simple determinable estate,** results when the estate created is limited by the happening of a certain event. For example, Mr. Smith donates a parcel of land to a church so long as the land is used for religious purposes. The key words are "so long as." So long as the land is used for religious purposes the church has all the rights of fee simple ownership. But, if some other use is made of the land, it reverts to the grantor (Mr. Smith) or someone else named by Mr. Smith (called a **remainderman**). Note that the termination of the estate is automatic if the land is used contrary to the limitation stated in the deed.

A **fee simple subject to condition subsequent** is similar to a determinable fee except that it gives the grantor the right to terminate the estate rather than wait for it to terminate automatically. Continuing the above example, Mr. Smith would have the right to reenter the property and take it back if it was no longer being used for religious purposes.

With a **fee simple upon condition precedent,** the title will not take effect until a condition is performed. For example, Mr. Smith could deed his land to a church with the condition that the deed will not take effect until a religious sanctuary is built.

Occasionally, qualified fees have been used by land developers in lieu of deed restrictions or zoning. For example, the buyer has fee title so long as she uses the land for a single-family residence. In another example, a land developer might use a condition precedent to encourage lot purchasers to build promptly. This would enhance the value of her unsold lots. From the standpoint of the property owner, a qualification is an encumbrance to her title.

LIFE ESTATES

A **life estate** conveys an estate for the duration of someone's life. The duration of the estate can be tied to the land of the **life tenant** (the person holding the life estate) or to a third party. In addition, someone must be named to acquire the estate upon its termination. The following example will illustrate the life estate concept. Suppose you have an aunt who needs financial assistance and you have decided to grant her, for the rest of her life, a house to live in. When you create the life estate, she becomes the life tenant. Additionally, you must decide who gets the house upon her death. If you want it back, you would want a **reversionary interest** for yourself. This way the house reverts to you, or if you predecease her, to your heirs. If you want the house to go to someone else, your son or daughter for example, you could name him or her as the **remainderman.** Alternatively, you could name a friend, relative, or charity as the remainderman. While your aunt is alive, the remainderman is said to hold a **remainder interest** in the house. When she dies, that interest changes to a fee simple estate.

A life estate does not have to be based on the life span of the life tenant. It can be based upon the life span of a third party in which case it is called a life estate **pur autre vie** (i.e., for the life of another). Continuing the above example, suppose that you know your rich uncle is naming your aunt to receive a substantial portion of his wealth upon his death. If this would adequately take care of her future financial needs, you could grant your aunt a life estate until your uncle dies. Sometimes a life estate is used to avoid the time and expense of probating a will and to reduce estate taxes. For example, an aging father could deed his real estate to his children but retain a life estate for himself.

Prohibition of Waste

Since a life estate arrangement is temporary, the life tenant must not commit **waste** by destroying or harming the property. Furthermore, the life tenant is required to keep the property in reasonable repair and to pay any property taxes, assessments, and interest on debt secured by the property. During the tenancy, the life tenant is entitled to the use and/or income generated by the property, and may sell, lease, rent, or mortgage his or her interest. Note, however, that it is impossible for the life tenant to sell, lease, or mortgage any greater interest than the life tenant holds.

STATUTORY ESTATES

Statutory estates are created by state law. They include **dower,** which gives a wife rights in her husband's real property; **curtesy,** which gives a husband rights in his wife's real property; and **community property,** which gives each spouse a one-half interest in marital property. Additionally there are **homesteads,** which are designed to protect the family's home from certain debts and, upon the death of one spouse, provide the other with a home for life. In Texas there is homestead protection and community property, but no dower or curtesy.

Dower

Historically, **dower** came from old English common law, in which the marriage ceremony was viewed as merging the wife's legal existence into that of her husband's. From this viewpoint, property bought during marriage belongs to the husband, with both husband and wife sharing the use of it. As a counterbalance, the dower right recognizes the wife's efforts in marriage and grants her legal ownership to one-third (in some states one-half) of the family's real property for the rest of her life. This prevents the husband from conveying ownership of the family's real estate without the wife's permission and protects her even if she is left out of her husband's will.

Because the wife's dower right does not ripen into actual ownership until her husband's death, her right is described as being **inchoate** until then. Once she obtains her life estate, she can sell, give, rent, or mortgage it, as described previously. Recognizing the impractical nature of an undivided life estate and the need for equal rights between husband and wife, some states award the wife an undivided fee simple estate rather than a life estate.

In real estate sales, the effect of dower laws is that when a husband and wife sell their property, the wife must relinquish her dower rights. This is usually accomplished by the wife signing the deed with her husband or by signing a separate quit claim deed. If she does not relinquish her dower rights, the buyer (or even a future buyer) may find that, upon the husband's death, the wife may return to legally claim an undivided ownership in the property. This is an important reason why, if you are buying real estate, you should have the property's ownership researched by a competent abstractor and have the title you receive insured by a title insurance company. Because the wife's dower right is inchoate while her husband is alive, she cannot sell it or otherwise part with it except when they mutually sell family real estate.

Curtesy

Roughly the opposite of dower, **curtesy** gives the husband benefits in his deceased wife's property as long as he lives. However, unlike dower, the wife can defeat those rights in her will. Furthermore, state law may require the couple to have had a child in order for the husband to qualify for curtesy. In some states, husbands are given dower rights rather than curtesy.

Community Property

Nine states (Arizona, California, Idaho, Louisiana, Nevada, New Mexico, Texas, Washington, and Wisconsin) subscribe to the legal theory that during marriage each spouse has an equal interest in all property acquired by their joint efforts during the marriage. This jointly produced property is called **community property.** Upon the death of one spouse, one-half of the community property passes to his or her heirs. The other one-half is retained by the surviving spouse. When community property is sold or mortgaged, both spouses should sign the document. Community property rights arise upon marriage (either formal or common law) and terminate upon divorce or death. Community property is discussed at greater length in Chapter 4.

Homestead Protection

Forty-two of the fifty states have passed **homestead laws,** usually with two purposes in mind: (1) to provide some legal protection for the homestead claimants from debts and judgments against them that might result in the forced sale and loss of the home, and (2) to provide a home for a widow, and sometimes a widower, for life. Homestead laws also restrict one spouse from acting without the other when conveying the homestead or using it as collateral for a loan. Dower, curtesy, and community property rights are automatic in those states that have them. In some states the homestead right may require that a written declaration be recorded in the public records. This is not required in Texas, however. Additionally, the "homestead" exemption from forced sale should not be confused with the "homestead exemption," which Texas grants to homeowners in order to reduce their property taxes.

Texas Homestead Rights

In Texas, the homestead right is constitutional and, as a constitutional right, cannot be waived through any contractual agreement or change in state law. Basically, homestead rights are expressed as exemptions from forced sale. All rights vested under the homestead laws are rights secure in the homestead claimant. The independence and security of a home may be enjoyed without the danger of its loss or harassment by reason of the improvidence or misfortune of a head, *or any member,* of the family. That is, the homestead claimant cannot be deprived of the homestead by creditors in the normal course of business. Therefore, a homeowner could own a very expensive house, which falls within the homestead exemption limits, and *no creditor,* regardless of the amount of the debt, could force the homeowner to sell her home to satisfy the debt, except under certain constitutionally specified circumstances.

Article 16, Section 50 of the Texas Constitution, specifically states that the homestead of a family, or a single adult person, is protected from forced sale for payment of all debts, with the following exceptions: (1) purchase money mortgages, which secure the payment of the purchase price of the house, (2) taxes, (3) mechanics' and materialmen's liens levied because of construction improvements to the homestead, *if* the improvements were contracted for in writing and signed by the husband and wife before any work was performed in constructing said improvements, (4) federal tax liens of both spouses, (5) refinancing of liens against the homestead, (6) an owelty of partition imposed against the whole for the acquisition of a partial interest, (7) a home equity lien, and (8) a reverse mortgage. There is also some authority that a homestead can be foreclosed upon for nonpayment of subdivision maintenance fund liens.

The homestead may not be conveyed without the consent of the spouse if the homestead claimant is married.

Protection is Automatic

There is no official document one must sign to create homestead rights. The fact that the realty is in the possession of the owner and that the owner resides upon it as his principal residence makes it the homestead of the family in law and in fact. Additionally, even if the homestead is not occupied by the owner, the intent of making it the owner's homestead, accompanied by circumstances manifesting said intention, is enough to vest the homestead character of the property and make the exemption rights applicable to it. There must be a declaration of homestead, however, in order to get the benefit of certain tax exemptions provided for under state and county taxing authorities. However, this declaration is not required to create homestead rights. Note that in both situations only one property (the principal residence) can be claimed as a homestead.

Once the homestead rights have vested in a certain parcel of real property, it maintains its homestead character during the entire life of the occupant and loses its homestead character only by (1) death, (2) abandonment, or (3) alienation (subsequent sale).

While death and alienation are self-explanatory, abandonment is a fact question. Abandonment of a homestead property cannot be accomplished by mere intention. There must be a discontinuance of use of the property coupled with an intention not to use it again as a home before it will constitute abandonment.

Homestead Limitations

There are limits established as to the homestead, however, depending on the type of homestead exemption one wishes to claim. The Constitution of Texas states that a **rural homestead** for married claimants consists of not more than 200 acres of land, which may be in one or more parcels, with the improvements thereon. If more than 200 acres is owned, the owner may designate which 200 acres constitutes the homestead, so long as the designated 200 acres do contain the owner's home. A state statute limits the **homestead** of a single person to only 100 acres.

An **urban homestead** is a homestead in a city, town, or village and can consist of a lot or lots amounting to not more than one acre of land, together with any improvement on the land. The urban homestead can consist of both a business and residential homestead, provided that the amount of both homestead claims does not exceed one acre. The value of the improvements has no bearing whatsoever in the homestead designation. The temporary renting of a homestead does not change the character of the homestead when no other homestead has been acquired; and, even if another house had been acquired, there must have been sufficient abandonment of the previous homestead before the homestead rights vest in the newly acquired home.

Homestead rights are constitutional and can only be changed by constitutional amendment, ratified by the voters of the State of Texas.

Home Equity Liens

Texas recently (1997) passed a constitutional amendment to allow home equity loans in Texas. This proposal is very restrictive, allowing for only *one* such loan at a time, with no personal liability, without prepayment penalty, that cannot be called (accelerated) because of the home's decrease in market value. The amendment allows the homeowner a *3-day* right to rescind, and allows many other protections for consumers. Because there are so many restrictions, there is some question as to how popular these new loans will be with some lenders. For the first time in Texas, however, they are legal, and will be discussed in greater detail in a later chapter.

FREEHOLD ESTATES

In a carryover from the old English court system, estates in land are classified as either **freehold estates** or **leasehold estates.** The main difference is that freehold estate cases are tried under real property laws whereas leasehold (also called non-freehold or less-than-freehold) estates are tried under personal property laws.

The two distinguishing features of a freehold estate are the following: (1) there must be actual ownership of the land, and (2) the estate must be of unpredictable duration. Fee estates, life estates, and estates created by statute are freehold estates.

LEASEHOLD ESTATES

The distinguishing features of a leasehold estate are (1) although there is possession of the land, there is no ownership, and (2) the estate is of definite duration.

As previously noted, the user of a property need not be its owner. Under a leasehold estate, the user is called the **lessee** or **tenant,** and the person from whom he leases is the **lessor** or **landlord.** As long as the tenant has a valid lease, abides by it, and pays the rent on time, the owner, even though he owns the property, cannot occupy it until the lease has expired. During the lease period, the freehold estate owner is said to hold a **reversionary interest.** This is his right to recover possession at the end of the lease period. Meanwhile, the lease is an encumbrance against the property.

There are four categories of leasehold estates: estate for years, periodic estate, estate at will, and tenancy at sufferance. Note that in this chapter, we will be examining leases primarily from the standpoint of estates in land. Leases as financing tools are discussed in Chapter 12, and lease contracts are covered in Chapter 16.

Estate for Years

Also called a tenancy for years, the **estate for years** is somewhat misleadingly named as it implies that a lease for a number of years has been created. Actually, the key criterion is that the lease has a specific starting time and a specific ending time. It can be for any length of time, ranging from less than a day to many years. An estate for years does not automatically renew itself. Neither the landlord nor the tenant must act to terminate it, as the lease agreement itself specifies a termination date.

Usually the lessor is the freehold estate owner. However, the lessor could be a lessee. To illustrate, a fee owner leases property to a lessee, who, in turn, leases the right to still another person. By doing this, the first lessee has become a **sublessor** and is said to hold a **sublease.** The person who then leases is a **sublessee.** It is important to realize that in no case can a sublessee acquire from the lessee any more rights than the lessee has under the lease. Thus, if a lessee has a five-year lease with three years remaining, only the remaining three years or a portion of that can be subleased to the sublessee.

Periodic Estate

Also called an estate from year-to-year or a periodic tenancy, a **periodic estate** has an original lease period with fixed length; when it runs out, unless the tenant or his landlord acts to terminate it, renewal is automatic for another like period of time. A month-to-month apartment rental is an example of this arrangement. To avoid last minute confusion, rental agreements usually require that advance notice be given if either the landlord or the tenant wishes to terminate the tenancy.

Estate at Will

Also called a tenancy at will, an **estate at will** is a landlord-tenant relationship with all the normal rights and duties of a lessor-lessee relationship, except that the estate may be terminated by either the lessor or the lessee at anytime. However, most states recognize the inconvenience a literal interpretation of "anytime" can cause and require that reasonable advance notice be given.

Tenancy at Sufferance

A **tenancy at sufferance** occurs when a tenant stays beyond legal tenancy without the consent of the landlord. In other words, the tenant wrongfully holds the property against the owner's wishes. In a tenancy at sufferance, the tenant is commonly called a **holdover tenant,** although once he stays beyond his legal tenancy he is not actually a tenant in the normal landlord-tenant sense. The landlord is entitled to evict him and recover possession of the property, provided the landlord does so in a timely manner. A tenant at sufferance differs from a trespasser only in that his original entry was rightful. If, during the holdover period, the tenant pays and the landlord accepts rent, the tenancy at sufferance changes to a periodic estate.

SUBSURFACE RIGHTS

In Texas, oil and mineral rights are subsurface estates in real estate and occupy a unique position. Once the subsurface rights have been leased or conveyed, there is an immediate conflict of rights as to surface control. The subsurface mineral owner has the dominant estate in Texas; that is, an owner of mineral rights has the right, unless otherwise specified, to reasonably enter upon any property to extract the minerals to which he holds a fee or leasehold estate. A mineral owner or lessee may waive these rights by relinquishing surface control of the property so that the surface estate owner can develop his property without worry of interference from the subsurface interest below.

Any rights to the subsurface oil, gas, or minerals are always subject to prior notices of record, local land use legislation and regulation, and any other prior existing interests that may affect the surface estate as well as the subsurface estate. Therefore, one could assume that any oil, gas, or mineral rights acquired after the property has been deed restricted would be subject to those deed restrictions, and owners of any oil, gas, and mineral rights within a municipality that has an ordinance against drilling would probably not be allowed to drill without a special permit from the city's governing body.

Although the oil or minerals in the ground are considered real property, once they are extracted from the ground they become personalty. Texas courts have held that once oil and minerals are extracted from the ground and then later injected into the ground for storage purposes, the oil and minerals still maintain their character as personal property and do not revert to real estate.

PUTTING IT TO WORK

It is important for a developer in Texas to recognize that even though he has built on a parcel of land, the mineral estate owner has the right to extract his mineral interests, regardless of the nuisance or inconvenience to the subsequent property owner. This may create a serious problem in subdivision property or fully developed property where the mineral rights have not been waived, or surface control has not been relinquished by the mineral estate owner.

LICENSE

A **license** is not a right or an estate in land, but a personal privilege given to someone to use land. It is nonassignable and can be canceled by the person who issues it. A license to park is typically what an automobile parking lot operator provides for persons parking in her lot. The contract creating the license is usually written on the stub that the lot attendant gives the driver, or it is posted on a sign on the lot. Tickets to theaters and sporting events also fall into this category. Because it is merely a personal privilege, a license is not an encumbrance against land.

CHATTELS

A chattel is an article of personal property. Chattels are divided into two categories: chattels personal and chattels real. Examples of **chattels personal** are automobiles, clothes, food, and furniture. **Chattels real** are interests in real estate that remain personal property; for example, a contract for the purchase of real estate or a lease. In the United States, chattels are governed by personal property laws. Freehold estates are governed by real property laws.

PICTORIAL SUMMARY

Let's conclude this chapter by combining what has been discussed in Chapter 2 regarding the physical nature of land with what has been covered in this chapter regarding estates and rights in land. The results, diagrammed in Figure 3.6, show why real estate is both complicated and exciting. A single parcel of land can be divided into subsurface, surface, and air-space components, and each of these carries its own fee simple bundle of rights, which can be divided into the various estates and rights discussed in this chapter.

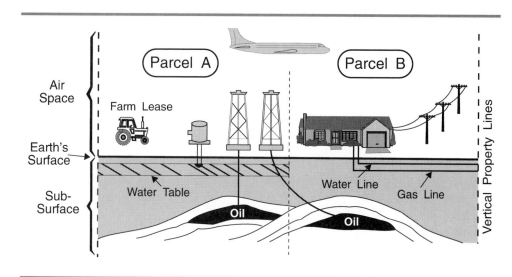

FIGURE 3.6
Cross section of estates and rights in land.

To more clearly convey this idea, let us turn our attention to Figure 3.6. In Parcel A, the fee landowner has leased the bulk of her surface and air rights, plus the right to draw water from her wells, to a farmer for the production of crops and livestock. This leaves the fee owner with the right to lease or sell subterranean rights for mineral, oil, and gas extraction. With a single parcel of land, the fee owner has created two estates, one for farming and another for oil and gas production. With the minor exception of the placement of the well platforms, pumps, and pipes, neither use interferes with the other and both bring income to the landowner. The farmer, in turn, can personally utilize the leasehold estate he possesses or he can sublease it to another farmer. The oil company, if it has leased its rights, can sublease them; if it has purchased them, it can sell or lease them. A variation would be for an oil company to buy the land in fee, conduct its drilling operations, and lease the remainder to a farmer. In the public interest, the government has claimed the right to allow aircraft to fly over the land. Although technically a landowner owns from the center of the earth out to the heavens, the right given aircraft to fly overhead creates a practical limit on that ownership.

OVERVIEW OF RIGHTS AND INTERESTS IN THE LAND

Figure 3.5 provides an overview of the various rights and interests in land that are discussed in this chapter and the previous chapter. This chart is designed to give you an overall perspective of what the term *real estate* includes.

Figure 3.6
Rights and interests in land.

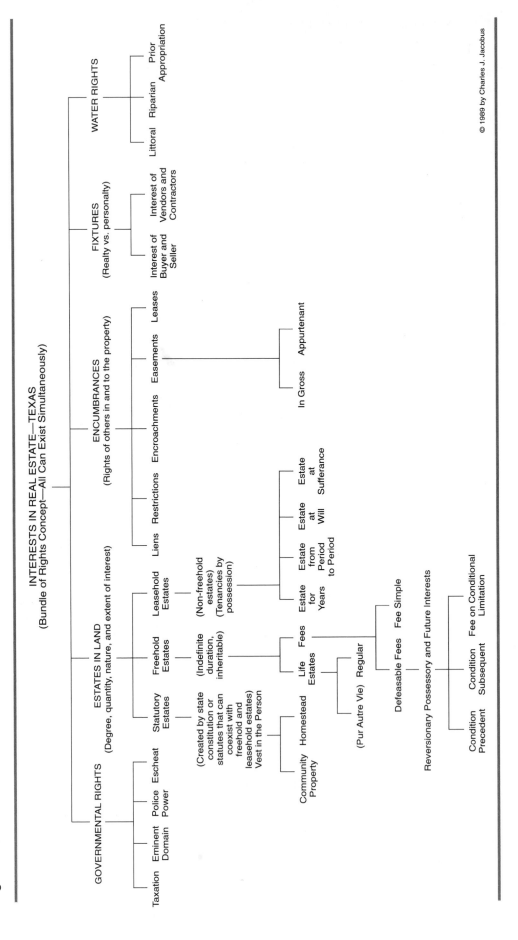

© 1989 by Charles J. Jacobus

Answers to these questions are found in the Answer Key section at the back of the book.

1. The system under which individuals are given the right to own land is known as the
   A. feudal system.
   B. allodial system.
   C. chattel system.
   D. fee system.

2. By which of the following processes may a government acquire ownership of privately held land?
   A. Condemnation.
   B. Taxation.
   C. Police power.
   D. Escheat.
   E. Both A and D.

3. The right of the government to place reasonable restrictions on the use of privately held land is known as
   A. a restrictive covenant.
   B. police power.
   C. escheat.
   D. estate.

4. Which of the following is NOT an example of a government's exercise of its police power?
   A. Rent controls.
   B. Building codes.
   C. Zoning laws.
   D. Restrictive covenants.

5. Property owned by a person who dies intestate and without heirs will escheat to the
   A. city.
   B. county.
   C. state.
   D. federal government.

6. A property owner who holds fee simple title to land will have all of the following "sticks" in his bundle of rights EXCEPT the right to:
   A. occupy and use it.
   B. restrict the use of the land.
   C. devise it by will.
   D. violate building, health, and safety codes.

7. The term "estate" refers to
   A. the quantity of land as shown on a plat of the property.
   B. one's legal rights in the land.
   C. both A and B.
   D. neither A nor B.

8. All of the following constitute an encumbrance on the fee simple title to real property EXCEPT
   A. a will conveying the property to the owner's heirs upon death of the owner.
   B. a restrictive covenant in the deed to the property.
   C. a mortgage.
   D. a lease.

9. Which of the following easements could be created without a written document?
   A. An easement by necessity.
   B. An easement by prescription.
   C. both A and B.
   D. neither A nor B.

10. An easement is
    A. an appurtenance to the holder of the dominant tenement.
    B. an encumbrance to the holder of the servient tenement.
    C. Both A and B.
    D. Neither A nor B.

11. Morris sold the back half of her lot to Katz and gave Katz a permanent easement across her land in order for Katz to have access to the road. Which of the following statements is true?
    A. The easement is an easement in gross.
    B. The easement is an easement appurtenant.
    C. The servient estate is held by Katz.
    D. The dominant estate is held by Morris.

12. An easement appurtenant may NOT be terminated
    A. by combination of the dominant and servient tenements.
    B. when the purpose for the easement no longer exists.
    C. by lack of use.
    D. unilaterally by the holder of the servient tenement.

13. All of the following may constitute a lien on real property EXCEPT:
    A. a mortgage.
    B. unpaid real property taxes.
    C. a restrictive covenant in a deed.
    D. a judgment against the owner.

14. Which of the following are examples of specific liens?

    A. Mechanic's liens.

    B. Judgment liens.

    C. Ad valorem tax liens.

    D. Federal income tax liens.

    E. Both A and C.

15. Which of the following is NOT classified as a freehold estate?

    A. An estate created by statute.

    B. A life estate.

    C. A fee simple estate.

    D. A leasehold estate.

16. Real estate held as a leasehold

    A. is used by the owner rather than by the tenant.

    B. reverts to the tenant upon termination of the lease.

    C. both A and B.

    D. neither A nor B.

17. Unless the landlord or tenant acts to terminate it, an estate from period-to-period

    A. automatically renews itself.

    B. continues for an indefinite time.

    C. both A and B.

    D. neither A nor B.

18. The lessor holds a reversion in which of the following situations?

    A. Estate for years.

    B. Periodic estate.

    C. Estate at will.

    D. Tenancy at sufferance.

    E. All of the above.

19. A tenant at sufferance is

    A. a legal tenant.

    B. a trespasser.

    C. a licensee.

    D. a guest.

20. A chattel is

    A. an item of personal property.

    B. an item of real property such as a building.

    C. a freehold estate in land.

    D. a term that refers to land used for cattle ranching.

KEY TERMS

Association: a not-for-profit organization that can own property and transact business in its own name

Community property: spouses are treated as equal partners with each owning a one-half interest

Estate in severalty: owned by one person; sole ownership

Financial liability: the amount of money one can lose; one's risk exposure

Joint tenancy: a form of property co-ownership that features the right of survivorship

Joint venture: an association of two or more persons or firms in order to carry out a single business project

Limited liability company: a company consisting of members or managers that is governed by its by-laws

Partnership: two or more persons engaged in business for a profit

Right of survivorship: a feature of joint tenancy whereby the surviving joint tenants automatically acquire all the rights, title, and interest of the deceased joint tenant

Tenants in common: shared ownership of a single property among two or more persons; interests need not be equal and no right of survivorship exists

Undivided interest: ownership by two or more persons that gives each the right to use the entire property

Forms of Ownership

IN THIS CHAPTER *This chapter will look at how a given right or interest in land is held by one or more individuals. It covers such topics as sole ownership, tenants in common, joint tenancy, tenancy by the entirety, and community property. In Chapter 2 we looked at land from a physical standpoint: the size and shape of a parcel, where it is located, and what was affixed to it. In Chapter 3 we explored various legal rights and interests that can be held in land. In this chapter, we shall look at how a given right or interest in land can be held by one or more individuals.*

SOLE OWNERSHIP

When title to property is held by one person, it is called an estate in **severalty** or **sole ownership.** Although the word "severalty" seems to imply that several persons own a single property, the correct meaning can be easily remembered by thinking of "severed" (separated) ownership. Sole ownership is available to single and married persons. However, in the case of married persons, most states require one spouse to waive community property, dower, or curtesy rights in writing. Businesses usually hold title to property in severalty. It is from the estate in severalty that all other tenancies are carved.

The major advantage of sole ownership for an individual is flexibility. As a sole owner you can make all the decisions regarding a property without having to get the agreement of co-owners. You can decide what property or properties to buy, when to buy, and how much to offer. You can decide whether to pay all cash or to seek a loan by using the property as collateral. Once bought, you control (within the bounds of the law) how the property will be used, how much will be charged if it is rented, and how it will be managed. If you decide to sell, you alone decide when to offer the property for sale and at what price and terms.

But freedom and responsibility go together. For example, if you purchase a rental property you must determine the prevailing rents, find tenants, prepare contracts, collect the rent, and keep the property in repair; or you must hire and pay someone else to manage the property. Another deterrent to sole ownership is the high entry cost. This form of real estate ownership is not possible for someone with only a few hundred dollars to invest.

TENANTS IN COMMON

When two or more persons wish to share the ownership of a single property, they may do so as **tenants in common.** As tenants in common, each owns an **undivided interest** in the whole property. This means that each owner has a right to possession of the entire property. None can exclude the others nor claim any specific portion. In a tenancy in common, these interests need not be the same size, and each owner can independently sell, mortgage, give away, or devise his individual interest. This independence is possible because each tenant in common has a separate legal title to his undivided interest.

Suppose that you invest $20,000 along with two of your friends, who invest $30,000 and $50,000, respectively; together you buy 100 acres of land as tenants in common. Presuming that everyone's ownership interest is proportional to his or her cash investment, you will hold a 20% interest in the entire 100 acres and your two friends will hold 30% and 50%. You cannot pick out 20 acres and exclude the other co-owners from them, nor can you pick out 20 acres and say, "These are mine and I'm going to sell them"; nor can they do that to you. You do, however, have the legal right to sell or otherwise dispose of your 20% interest (or a portion of it) without the permission of your two friends. Your friends have the same right. If one of you sells, the purchaser becomes a new tenant in common with the remaining co-owners.

Wording of the Conveyance

As a rule, a tenancy in common is indicated by naming the co-owners in the conveyance and adding the words "as tenants in common." For example, a deed might read, "Samuel Smith, John Jones, and Robert Miller, as tenants in common." If nothing is said regarding the size of each co-owner's interest in the property, the law presumes that all interests are equal. Therefore, if the co-owners intend their interests to be unequal, the size of each co-owner's undivided interest must be stated as a percent or a fraction such as 60 and 40 or one-third and two-thirds.

PUTTING IT TO WORK

In Texas, if two or more persons are named as owners, and there is no specific indication as to how they are taking title, they are presumed to be tenants in common. Thus, if a deed is made out to "Donna Adams and Barbara Kelly," the law would consider them to be tenants in common, each holding an undivided one-half interest in the property. An important exception to this presumption is when the co-owners are married to each other. In this case, they may be automatically considered to be taking ownership as community property.

No Right of Survivorship

When a tenancy in common exists, if a co-owner dies her interest passes to the heirs or devisees, who then become tenants in common with the remaining co-owners. There is no **right of survivorship;** that is, the remaining co-owners do not acquire the deceased's interest unless they are named in the deceased's last will and testament to do so. When a creditor has a claim on a co-owner's interest and forces its sale to satisfy the debt, the new buyer becomes a tenant in common with the remaining co-owners. If one co-owner wants to sell (or give away) only a portion of his undivided interest, he may; the new owner becomes a tenant in common with the other co-owners.

Any income generated by the property belongs to the tenants in common in proportion to the size of their interests. Similarly, each co-owner is responsible for paying his proportionate share of property taxes, repairs, upkeep, and so on, plus interest and debt repayment, if any. If any co-owner fails to contribute his proportionate share, the other co-owners can pay on his behalf and then sue him for that amount. If co-owners find that they cannot agree as to how the property is to be run and cannot agree on a plan for dividing or selling it, it is possible to request a court-ordered partition. A **partition** divides the property into distinct portions so that each person can hold his or her proportionate interest in severalty. If this is physically impossible, such as when three co-owners each have a one-third interest in a house, the court will order the property sold and the proceeds divided among the co-owners.

The major advantage of tenancy in common is that it allows two or more persons to achieve goals that one person could not accomplish alone. However, prospective co-owners should give advance thought to what they will do (short of going to court) if (1) a co-owner fails to pay his share of ownership expenses, (2) differences arise regarding how the property is to be operated, (3) an agreement cannot be reached as to when to sell, for how much, and on what terms, and (4) what happens if a co-owner dies and those who inherit his interest have little in common with the surviving co-owners. The counsel of an attorney experienced in property ownership can be very helpful when considering the co-ownership of property.

JOINT TENANCY

Another form of multiple-person ownership is **joint tenancy.** The most distinguishing characteristic of joint tenancy is the right of survivorship. Upon the death of a joint tenant, his interest does not descend to his heirs or pass by his will. Rather, the entire ownership remains in the surviving joint tenant(s). In other words, there is just one less owner.

Four Unities

To create a joint tenancy, **four unities** must be present. They are the unities of time, title, interest, and possession.

Unity of time means that each joint tenant must acquire his or her ownership interest at the same moment. Once a joint tenancy is formed, it is not possible to add new joint tenants later unless an entirely new joint tenancy is formed among the existing co-owners and the new co-owner. To illustrate, suppose that *A, B,* and *C* own a parcel of land as joint tenants. If *A* sells his interest to *D,* then *B, C,* and *D* must sign documents to create a new joint tenancy among them. If this is not done, *D* automatically becomes a tenant in common with *B* and *C* who, between themselves, remain joint tenants. *D* will then own an undivided one-third interest in common with *B* and *C* who will own an undivided two-thirds interest as joint tenants.

Unity of title means that the joint tenants acquire their interests from the same source; i.e., the same deed or will. (Some states allow a property owner to create a valid joint tenancy by conveying to himself, or herself, and another without going through a third party.)

Unity of interest means that the joint tenants own one interest together and each joint tenant has exactly the same right in that interest. (This, by the way, is the foundation upon which the survivorship feature rests.) If the joint tenants list differing individual interests, they lack unity of interest and will be treated as tenants in common. Unity of interest also means that if one joint tenant holds a fee simple interest in the property, the others cannot hold anything but a fee simple interest.

Unity of possession means that the joint tenants must enjoy the same undivided possession of the whole property. All joint tenants have the use of the entire property, and no individual owns a particular portion of it. By way of contrast, unity of possession is the only unity essential to a tenancy in common.

PUTTING IT TO WORK

Texas requires that the joint tenancy be expressly agreed to in writing by the parties involved. Any automatic presumption of joint tenancy has been abolished by statute.

Right of Survivorship

The feature of joint tenancy ownership that is most widely recognized is its **right of survivorship.** Upon the death of a joint tenant, that interest in the property is extinguished. In a two-person joint tenancy, when one person dies, the other immediately becomes the sole owner. With more than two persons as joint tenants, when one dies the remaining joint tenants are automatically left as owners. Ultimately, the last survivor becomes the sole owner. The legal philosophy is that the joint tenants constitute a single owning unit. The death of one joint tenant does not destroy that unit—it only reduces the number of persons owning the unit. For the public record, a copy of the death certificate and an affidavit of death of the joint tenant is recorded in the county where the property is located. The property must also be released from any estate tax liens.

It is the right of survivorship that has made joint tenancy a popular form of ownership among married couples in other states. Married couples often want the surviving spouse to have sole ownership of the marital property. Any property held in joint tenancy goes to the surviving spouse without the delay of probate and usually with less legal expense. Community property (discussed later in this chapter) may not be held in joint tenancy.

"Poor Man's Will"

Because of the survivorship feature, joint tenancy has loosely been labeled a "poor man's will." However, it should not replace a properly drawn will as it affects only that property held in joint tenancy. Moreover, a will can be changed if the persons named therein are no longer in one's favor. But once a joint tenancy is formed, title is permanently conveyed and no further opportunity for change exists, unless the joint tenancy is terminated. A joint tenant cannot name someone in his will to receive the joint tenant interest because his interest ends upon his death. One should also be aware of the possibility that ownership in joint tenancy may result in additional estate taxes.

Another important aspect of joint tenancy ownership is that it can be used to defeat dower or curtesy rights. If a married man forms a joint tenancy with someone other than his wife (such as a business partner) and then dies, his wife has no dower rights in that joint tenancy. As a result, courts have begun to look with disfavor upon the right of survivorship. Louisiana, Ohio, and Oregon either do not recognize joint tenancy or have abolished it. Of the remaining, 47 states and the District of Columbia recognize joint tenancy ownership, but 14 (including Texas) have abolished the automatic presumption of survivorship (see Table 4.1). In those 14 states, if the right of survivorship is desired in a joint tenancy, it must be clearly stated in the conveyance. For example, a deed might read, "Karen Carson and Judith Johnson, as joint tenants with the right of survivorship and not as tenants in common." Even in those states not requiring it, this wording is often used to ensure that the right of survivorship is intended. In community property states, one spouse cannot take community funds and establish a valid joint tenancy with a third party.

There is a popular misconception that a debtor can protect himself from creditors' claims by taking title to property as a joint tenant. It is true that in a joint tenancy, the surviving joint tenant(s) acquire(s) the property free and clear of any liens against the deceased. However, this can happen only if the debtor dies before the creditor seizes the debtor's interest.

Only a human being can be a joint tenant. A corporation cannot be a joint tenant. This is because a corporation is an artificial legal being and can exist in perpetuity;

TABLE 4.1
Concurrent ownership by states.

State	L.L.P.*	L.L.C.**	Tenancy in common	Joint tenancy	Tenancy by the entirety	Community property
Alabama	X	X	X	X		
Alaska		X	X	X	X	
Arizona	X	X	X	X		X
Arkansas		X	X	X	X	
California		X	X	X		X
Colorado		X	X	X		
Connecticut		X	X	X		
Delaware	X	X	X	X	X	
District of Columbia	X	X	X	X	X	
Florida		X	X	X	X	
Georgia	X	X	X	X		
Hawaii		X	X	X	X	
Idaho	X	X	X	X		X
Illinois		X	X	X		
Indiana		X	X	X	X	
Iowa	X	X	X	X		
Kansas	X	X	X	X		
Kentucky		X	X	X	X	
Louisiana	X	X				X
Maine		X	X	X		
Maryland	X	X	X	X	X	
Massachusetts		X	X	X	X	
Michigan	X	X	X	X	X	
Minnesota	X	X	X	X		
Mississippi	X	X	X	X	X	
Missouri		X	X	X	X	
Montana		X	X	X		
Nebraska		X	X	X		
Nevada		X	X	X		X
New Hampshire		X	X	X		
New Jersey	X	X	X	X	X	
New Mexico		X	X	X		X
New York		X	X	X	X	
North Carolina	X	X	X	X	X	
North Dakota		X	X	X		
Ohio	X	X	X		X	
Oklahoma		X	X	X	X	
Oregon		X	X		X	
Pennsylvania		X	X	X	X	
Rhode Island		X	X	X	X	
South Carolina		X	X	X		
South Dakota		X	X	X		
Tennessee		X	X	X	X	
Texas	X	X	X	X		X
Utah	X	X	X	X	X	
Vermont		X	X	X	X	
Virginia	X	X	X	X	X	
Washington		X	X	X		X
West Virginia		X	X	X	X	
Wisconsin		X	X	X		X
Wyoming		X	X	X	X	

*Limited Liability Partnership

**Limited Liability Company

In Ohio and Oregon other means are available to achieve rights of survivorship between nonmarried persons. When two or more persons own property together in Louisiana, it is termed an "ownership in indivision" or a "joint ownership." Louisiana law is based on an old French civil law.

that is, never die. Joint tenancy ownership is not limited to the ownership of land; any estate in land and any chattel interest may be held in joint tenancy.

TENANCY BY THE ENTIRETY

Tenancy by the entirety (also called tenancy by the entireties) is a form of joint tenancy specifically for married persons. To the four unities of a joint tenancy is added a fifth: **unity of person.** The basis for this is the legal premise that a husband and wife are an indivisible legal unit. Two key characteristics of a tenancy by the entirety are the following: (1) the surviving spouse becomes the sole owner of the property upon the death of the other, and (2) neither spouse has a disposable interest in the property during the lifetime of the other. Thus, while both are alive and married to each other, both signatures are necessary to convey title to the property. With respect to the first characteristic, tenancy by the entirety is similar to joint tenancy because both feature the right of survivorship. They are quite different, however, with respect to the second characteristic. A joint tenancy can be terminated by one tenant's conveyance of his or her interest, but a tenancy by the entirety can be terminated only by joint action of husband and wife. Since Texas has community property laws, tenancy by the entireties is not recognized here.

States that recognize tenancy by the entirety are listed in Table 4.1. Some of these states automatically assume that a tenancy by the entirety is created when married persons buy real estate. However, it is best to use a phrase such as "John and Mary Smith, husband and wife as tenants by the entirety with the right of survivorship" on deeds and other conveyances. This avoids later questions as to whether their intention might have been to create a joint tenancy or a tenancy in common.

COMMUNITY PROPERTY

Due largely to its Spanish heritage, Texas has adopted community property laws that vest particular rights in property as a result of the marital community. Table 4.1 identifies the nine community property states. The laws of each community property state vary slightly, but the underlying concept is that the husband and wife contribute jointly and equally to their marriage and thus should share equally in any property purchased during marriage. Whereas English law is based on the merging of husband and wife's interest upon marriage, community property law treats husband and wife as equal partners, with each owning an undivided one-half interest.

Community Property, Separate Property

Community property rights do not come into effect until there is a marriage and, similarly, end with the dissolution of that marriage. The law in Texas presumes that all property acquired after marriage is **community property.**

Property that is not community property is referred to as **separate property.** The Texas Constitution constitutionally defines separate property as property acquired prior to marriage (even if the owner subsequently marries, the real estate remains separate property) and property acquired by gift, devise, or descent after marriage. In addition, spouses can agree in writing, before or during marriage, that property can be separate rather than community. Courts have held that property purchased after marriage with separate funds can also be construed as separate property. However, rents and revenues from separate property are construed to be community property, unless the spouses agree otherwise.

Community property cannot be generally conveyed without both spouses' signatures. There are statutes that will allow property under the sole management and control of one spouse to be sold without the signature of the other spouse. As a good business practice, however, the wise real estate agent should obtain the other spouse's signature on any pertinent documents for real estate believed to be community property.

The major advantage of the community property system is found in its philosophy: it treats the spouses as equal partners in property acquired through their mutual efforts during marriage. Even if the wife elects to be a full-time homemaker and all the money brought into the household is the result of her husband's job (or vice versa), the law treats them as equal co-owners in any property bought with that money. This is true even if only one spouse is named as the owner.

In the event of divorce, if the parting couple cannot amicably decide how to divide their community property, the courts will usually do so. If the courts do not, the ex-spouses will become tenants in common with each other. If it later becomes necessary, either can file suit for partition.

Community Property Right of Survivorship

The Texas Constitution was amended in 1987 to provide that husbands and wives could own community property with rights of survivorship. Don't confuse this with joint tenancy. In joint tenancy, you will recall, each spouse is liable for their proportionate share of ownership. In community property, both spouses are jointly and severally liable for all community debts. This 1987 constitutional amendment allows Texans to own community property, plus have the additional benefits of the right of survivorship, if they choose to do so. To create the right of survivorship, there must be a written agreement signed by both spouses that must be recorded in the county courthouse. Legal counsel should be consulted before utilizing this form of ownership.

PARTNERSHIP

A **partnership** exists when two or more persons, as partners, unite their property, labor, and skill as a business to share the profits created by it. The agreement between the partners may be oral or written. The partners may hold the partnership property either in their own names (as tenants in common or as joint tenants) or in the name of the partnership (which would hold title in severalty). For convenience, especially in a large partnership, the partners may designate two or three of their group to make contracts and sign documents on behalf of the entire partnership. There are four types of partnerships: general partnerships made up entirely of general partners, limited partnerships composed of general and limited partners, limited liability partnerships that limit the liability of a general partner from the misconduct of other general partners, and joint ventures.

General Partnership

The **general partnership** is an outgrowth of common law. However, to introduce clarity and uniformity into general partnership laws across the United States, 49 states and the District of Columbia have adopted the **Uniform Partnership Act** either in total or with local modifications. The only exception is Louisiana. Briefly, the highlights of the Act are that (1) title to partnership property may be held in the partnership's name, (2) each partner has an equal right of possession of partnership property—but only for partnership purposes, (3) upon the death of one partner their rights in the partnership property vest in the surviving partners—but the decedent's estate must be reimbursed for the value of their interest in the partnership, (4) a partner's right to specific partnership property is not subject to dower or curtesy, and (5) partnership property can only be attached by creditors for debts of the partnership, not for debts of a partner.

As a form of property ownership, the partnership is a method of combining the capital and expertise of two or more persons. It is equally important to note that the profits and losses of the partnership are taxable directly to each individual partner in proportion to his or her interest in the partnership. Although the partnership files a tax return, it is only for information purposes. The partnership itself does not pay taxes. Negative aspects of this form of ownership center around financial liability, illiquidity, and in some cases, management.

Financial liability means each partner is personally responsible for all the debts of the partnership. Thus, each general partner can lose not only what they have invested in the partnership, but more, up to the full extent of their personal financial worth. If one partner makes a commitment on behalf of the partnership, all partners are responsible for making good on that commitment. If the partnership is sued, each partner is fully responsible, although a recent legislative change requires the creditor to proceed against partnership assets before pursuing the individual partners. **Illiquidity** refers to the possibility that it may be very difficult to sell one's partnership interest on short notice in order to raise cash. **Management** means that each general partner is expected to take an active part in the operation of the partnership.

Texas Partnership Statutes

The nature of the Texas community property laws has generally dictated that a partnership has three distinct interests, which are set out by the Texas partnership statutes. They are as follows:

1. A partner's right to specific partnership property (such as desks, typewriters, machinery, etc.), which is *not* community property.
2. A partner's interest in the partnership (usually determined by a dollar amount), which *may be* community property.
3. A partner's right to management in the partnership, which is *not* community property.

Limited Partnership

Because of unlimited financial liability and management responsibility, an alternative partnership form, the **limited partnership,** has developed. Forty-nine states, plus the District of Columbia, have adopted the **Uniform Limited Partnership Act,** or the newer statute, the **Revised Uniform Limited Partnership Act (RULPA).** In 1987, Texas adopted its own variation of the RULPA, the **Texas Revised Limited Partnership Act.** (The exception is Louisiana, which has its own general and limited partnership laws.) This act recognizes the legality of limited partnerships and requires that a limited partnership be formed by a written document.

A limited partnership is composed of general and limited partners. The general partners organize and operate the partnership, contribute some capital, and agree to accept the full financial liability of the partnership. The **limited partners** provide the bulk of the investment capital, have little say in the day-to-day management of the partnership, share in the profits and losses, and contract with their general partners to limit the financial liability of each limited partner to the amount he or she invests. Additionally, a well-written partnership agreement will allow for the continuity of the partnership in the event of the death of either a general or limited partner.

The advantages of limited liability, minimum management responsibility, and direct pass-through of profits and losses for taxation purposes have made this form of

Before investing in a limited partnership, one should investigate the past record of the general partners, for this is usually a good indication of how the new partnership will be managed. The investigation should include their previous investments, talking to past investors, and checking court records for any legal complaints brought against them. Additionally, the prospective partner should be prepared to stay in for the duration of the partnership as the resale market for limited partnership interests is small.

ownership popular. However, being free of management responsibility is only advantageous to the investors if the general partners are capable and honest. If they are not, the only control open to the limited partners is to vote to replace the general partners.

Limited Liability Partnerships

The Texas legislature also enacted another form of ownership called a **limited liability partnership** . This form of ownership attempts to limit the liability of the general partner from the misconduct of other general partners. For instance, in a law firm or a brokerage firm organized as a general partnership, all the general partners have a right to bind the partnership and all general partners have 100% liability for partnership obligations. The limited liability partnership, however, limits the liability of the partners such that if one partner commits malfeasance or malpractice (for example, a partner in the tax section of a law firm), it would not create a 100% liability for a partner in the real estate section of the law firm. Only the partners who have direct supervisory control over the misconduct will have liability for it. Note that most large law firms now have "L.L.P." behind their names.

To create the limited liability partnership, the firm must register with the Secretary of State and carry a specified amount of malpractice insurance.

Joint Venture

A **joint venture** is a partnership of two or more persons or firms to carry out a single business project. A joint venture is treated as a partnership for tax purposes. However, whereas a general partner can bind her partnership to a contract, a joint venturer cannot bind the other joint venturers to a contract for anything outside the scope of that single business project. Examples of joint ventures in real estate are the purchase of land by two or more persons with the intent of grading it and selling it as lots, the association of a landowner and builder to build and sell, and the association of a lender and builder to purchase land and develop buildings on it to sell to investors. Each member of the joint venture makes a contribution in the form of capital or talent, and all have a strong incentive to make the joint venture succeed. If more than one project is undertaken, the relationship may become a general partnership rather than a joint venture.

LIMITED LIABILITY COMPANIES

There has been legitimate, and probably justified, concern over liabilities of defendants in a business environment. One understands that if a person is harmed, there should be an ability to recover from the wrongdoer, yet many juries are awarding significant sums of money, and attempt to pursue personal liability for officers and directors of corporations because of their duties of care in the business entity (including Real Estate brokers!).

All states (see Table 4.1) have passed laws creating a new form of entity called a **limited liability company,** often referred to as an **"L.C."** or **"L.L.C."** The statutes tend to be lengthy, complicated statutes and only the most general descriptions can be explained here. A lot of case law and perhaps amendments to the statutes will be forthcoming in the coming years.

Formation

Generally, most states allow two or more (Texas apparently allows only one) persons of 18 years of age or older who can act as organizers of a limited liability company by signing the Articles of Organization of such limited liability company and giving the original copy of the Articles to the Secretary of State. The Articles of Organization should include:

1. The name of the limited liability company
2. The period of duration that may have limitations in some states
3. The purpose for which the limited liability company is organized (which may include any or all lawful business)
4. The address of the principal place of business and the name of the initial registered agent in the State
5. The names of the managers or members who are to manage the company

The Secretary of State then issues a Certificate of Organization, and the existence of the limited liability company begins at that time.

In general terms, a member or manager of a limited liability company is not liable for debts, obligations, or liabilities of a limited liability company. A membership interest is considered to be personal property and the member has no interest in specific limited liability company property.

Operations of a Limited Liability Company

The limited liability company name must include the word "Limited" or the abbreviation "Ltd." or "L.C." It must maintain the registered office and registered agent (similar to a corporation), and all real or personal property owned or purchased by the limited liability company shall be held and owned, and the conveyance shall be made, in the name of the limited liability company. All instruments and documents providing for the acquisition, mortgage or disposition of the limited liability company shall be valid and binding upon the company if they are executed by one or more persons acting as a manager or member (if the management of the limited liability company is retained by the members).

Please note that limited liability companies are not corporations, nor partnerships, nor limited partnerships. They borrow attributes from both the general partnership and the corporation but mix them differently than they are mixed in the limited partnership. They are a totally new theory of ownership enacted by the state legislatures and, as stated previously, there is a lot of law yet to be made in this area. A major advantage in using a limited liability company is its classification as a partnership for federal income tax purposes. It is important that the organizers and owners of the limited liability company operate the company other than as a corporation so it will not be taxed as a corporation. Most limited liability companies do not have a continuity of life as a corporation, and the transferability of interest is limited.

The Treasury regulations basically identify six "corporate" characteristics. If the limited liability company is operated too much like a corporation, it could have serious adverse tax consequences, so professional help is critical in establishing and operating the limited liability company, both from a legal and tax perspective.

SYNDICATION

A **syndication** (or **syndicate**) is not a form of ownership; rather, it refers to individuals or firms combining to pursue an investment enterprise too large for any of them to undertake individually. The form of ownership might be a tenancy in common, joint tenancy, partnership, land trust, or a corporation. Applied to real estate investing, the term "syndicate" usually refers to a limited partnership in which the limited partners provide the investment capital and the general partners provide the organizational talent and ongoing management services. The general partners receive compensation for purchasing, managing, and reselling the properties. The limited partners receive both a return of and a return on their investment if the syndicate is successful. Most states require that real estate syndicates be registered with the state before they can be sold to investors. Federal registration may also be necessary. Registration does not relieve an interested investor from investigating carefully and seeking experienced legal direction.

CORPORATIONS

Each state has passed laws to permit groups of people to create **corporations** that can buy, sell, own, and operate in the name of the corporation. The corporation, in turn, is owned by stockholders, who possess shares of stock as evidence of their ownership.

Texas, by statute, gives corporations the right to acquire, purchase, and sell real property. To effect a conveyance, the conveying instrument must be signed by the corporation's president, vice president, or attorney-in-fact and be accompanied by a resolution by the Board of Directors of the corporation. A sale, mortgage, or pledge of substantially all the assets of the corporation must have approval of a majority of the shareholders.

Because the corporation is an entity (or legal being) in the eyes of the law, the corporation must pay income taxes on its profits. What remains after taxes can be used to pay dividends to the stockholders, who, in turn, pay personal income taxes on their dividend income. This double taxation of profits is the most important negative factor in the corporate form of ownership. On the positive side, the entity aspect shields the investor from unlimited liability. Even if the corporation falls on the hardest of financial times and owes more than it owns, the worst that can happen to the stockholder is that the value of her stock will drop to zero. Another advantage is that shares of stock are much more liquid than any previously discussed form of real estate ownership, even sole ownership. Stockbrokers and stock exchanges who specialize in the purchase and sale of corporate stock usually complete a sale in a week or less. Furthermore, shares of stock in most corporations sell for less than $100, thus enabling an investor to operate with small amounts of capital. In a corporation, the stockholders elect a board of directors, who, in turn, hire the management needed to run the day-to-day operations of the company. As a practical matter, however, unless a person is a major shareholder in a corporation, she will have little control over management. Her alternative is to buy stock in firms where she likes the management and sell where she does not.

Subchapter S Corporations

Several large real estate corporations are traded on the New York Stock Exchange, and the corporation is a popular method of organization for real estate brokers and developers. Nevertheless, most real estate investors shun corporations because of the double taxation feature and because the tax benefits of owning real estate are trapped inside the corporation.

In 1958, the Internal Revenue Code first allowed stockholders to organize **Subchapter S corporations** that provided the liability protection of a corporation with the profit-and-loss pass-through of a partnership. Although the initial 10 stockholder maximum was a drawback, the real problem for real estate investors was that no more than 20 percent of a Subchapter S's gross receipts could come from passive income. And rent is passive income. Effective in 1997, Congress revised the rules and increased the maximum number of shareholders to 75. (Regular corporations are now called C Corporations.) The advantages of S corporations were further enhanced by the Internal Revenue Code, which reduced the top personal tax rate below the top rate on corporations.

ASSOCIATIONS

An **association** is an organization that can own property and transact business in its own name. Several examples of associations are the homeowner associations found in condominiums and planned unit developments. There are also professional associations organized for business purposes, such as doctors' associations and architects' associations. If properly incorporated, an association will shield its members from personal liability in the event of lawsuits against the association. In Texas, if it is not properly incorporated, it creates proportional liability for all of its members.

REAL ESTATE INVESTMENT TRUSTS

The idea of creating a trust that in turn carries out the investment objectives of its investors is not new. What has changed is that in 1961 Congress passed a law allowing trusts that specialize in real estate investments to avoid double taxation by following strict rules. Texas has also passed a REIT act that sets forth state guidelines and requirements. These **real estate investment trusts (REITS)** pool the money of many investors for the purchase of real estate, much as mutual funds do with stocks and bonds. Investors in a REIT are called **beneficiaries** and they purchase **beneficial interests** somewhat similar to shares of corporate stock. The trust officers, with the aid of paid advisors, buy, sell, mortgage, and operate real estate investments on behalf of the beneficiaries. If a REIT confines its activities to real estate investments, and if the REIT has at least 100 beneficiaries and distributes at least 95 percent of its net income every year, the Internal Revenue Service will collect tax on the distributed income only once—at the beneficiaries' level. Failure to follow the rules results in double taxation.

The REIT is an attempt to combine the advantages of the corporate form of ownership with single taxation status. Like stock, the beneficial interests are freely transferable and usually sell for $100 each or less, a distinct advantage for the investor with a small amount of money to invest in real estate. Beneficial interests in the larger REITs are sold on a national basis, thus enabling a REIT to have thousands of beneficiaries and millions of dollars of capital for real estate purchases.

INTER VIVOS AND TESTAMENTARY TRUSTS

In all states, the trust form of ownership can be used to provide for the well-being of another person. Basically, this is an arrangement whereby title to real and/or personal property is transferred by its owner (the **trustor**) to a trustee. The **trustee** holds title and manages the property for the benefit of another (the **beneficiary**) in accordance with instructions given by the trustor. Two popular forms are the inter vivos trust, also called a living trust, and the testamentary trust.

FIGURE 4.1
Methods of holding title (Texas).

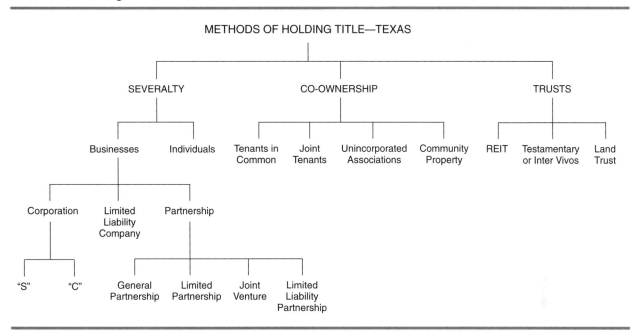

An **inter vivos trust** takes effect during the life of its creator. For example, you can transfer property to a trustee with instructions that it be managed and that income from the trust assets be paid to your children, spouse, relatives, or a charity.

A **testamentary trust** takes effect after death. For example, you could place instructions in your will that upon your death your property is to be placed into a trust. You can name whomever you want as trustee (a bank or trust company or friend, for example) and whom you want as beneficiaries. You can also give instructions as to how the assets are to be managed and how much (and how often) to pay the beneficiaries. Because trusts provide property management and financial control as well as a number of tax and estate planning advantages, this form of property ownership is growing in popularity.

LAND TRUSTS

In several states, an owner of real estate may create a trust wherein he is both the trustor and the beneficiary. Called a **land trust,** the landowner conveys his real property to a trustee, who in turn manages the property according to the beneficiary's (owner's) instructions. Since the beneficial interest created by the trust is considered personal property, the land trust effectively converts real property to personal property. Originally, the land trust gained popularity because true ownership could be cloaked in secrecy behind the name of a bank's trust department. Today, however, its popularity is mainly because it is a useful vehicle for group ownership and may not be subject to legal attachment like real property, which is held in the name of the beneficiary. Land trusts are commonly used in Texas although there is no specific statutory authority for their existence.

CAVEAT

The purpose of this chapter has been to acquaint you with the fundamental aspects of the most commonly used forms of real estate ownership in the United States. You undoubtedly saw instances where you could apply these. Unfortunately, it is not possible in a real estate principles book to discuss each detail of Texas law (many of which change frequently), nor to take into consideration the specific characteristics of a particular transaction. In applying the principles in this book to a particular transaction, you should add competent legal advice regarding legal interpretation of these principles.

REVIEW QUESTIONS

Answers to these questions are found in the Answer Key section at the back of the book.

1. Able, Baker, and Charles are going to purchase an investment property as co-owners and will take title as joint tenants. Which of the following statements are incorrect?
   A. All will acquire their interests at the same moment in time.
   B. Each will receive a separate deed for his share.
   C. All may have equal interest in the property.
   D. All will enjoy equal rights of possession.

2. A married person can hold as separate property
   A. property bought by that person before marriage.
   B. property inherited by that person after marriage.
   C. Both A and B.
   D. Neither A nor B.

3. A tenant in common may NOT
   A. claim a portion of the property for his own use.
   B. convey his interest by will.
   C. use his share of the property as collateral for a mortgage loan.
   D. sell his share without the agreement of the other tenants.

4. All of the following are true of joint tenancy EXCEPT:
   A. Unities of time, title, interest, and possession must be present.
   B. New joint tenants may be added without forming a new joint tenancy.
   C. Survivorship exists among joint tenants.
   D. A husband and wife may hold title as joint tenants.

5. Joint tenants must acquire their interests in jointly held property
   A. at the same time.
   B. from the same source.
   C. in the same instrument.
   D. all of the above.

6. If any unity of joint tenancy is broken, the law will regard the estate as
   A. a tenancy by the entireties.
   B. community property.
   C. a tenancy in common.
   D. an estate in severalty.

7. In Texas, if two or more persons are named as owners and there is no specific indication as to how they are taking title, they are presumed to be
   A. joint tenants.
   B. tenants in common.
   C. separate owners.
   D. joint owners.

8. Community property laws are derived from legal concepts that have their origin in
   A. Spanish and French law.
   B. English common law.
   C. American statutory law.
   D. English parliamentary law.

9. Mr. and Mrs. Marvin live in a community property state. Which of the following would most likely be considered their community property?
   A. Property that is inherited by either spouse.
   B. Property conveyed as a gift to either spouse.
   C. Property purchased after they were married.
   D. Property owned by either spouse prior to their marriage.

10. In community property states, which of the following exists?
    A. Dower.
    B. Curtesy.
    C. Both A and B.
    D. Neither A nor B.

11. The Texas Constitution was amended in 1987 to provide that husbands and wives
    A. could own community property with rights of survivorship.
    B. would no longer own any property with rights of survivorship.
    C. would only be liable for their proportionate share of ownership as in joint tenancy.
    D. Both A and C.
    E. None of the above.

12. A business entity owned by stockholders who possess shares of stock as evidence of their ownership is
    A. a general partnership.
    B. an S corporation.
    C. a C corporation.
    D. All of the above.
    E. Both B and C.

13. The possibility of double taxation on income is a negative factor in
    A. the corporation form of ownership.
    B. the limited partnership form of ownership.
    C. major corporations only.
    D. All of the above.

14. The day-to-day operations of a corporation are the responsibility of its
    A. stockholders.
    B. board of directors.
    C. Both A and B.
    D. Neither A nor B.

15. Before investing in a limited partnership, one should:
    A. determine if the partnership is suitable for his personal objectives.
    B. investigate the past performance of the general partners.
    C. Both A and B.
    D. Neither A nor B.

CHAPTER 5

KEY TERMS

Adverse possession: acquisition of land through prolonged and unauthorized occupation

Bargain and sale deed: a deed that contains no covenants, but does imply that the grantor owns the property being conveyed

Cloud on the title: any claim, lien, or encumbrance that impairs title to property

Color of title: some plausible, but not completely clear-cut indication of ownership rights

Consideration: anything of value given to induce another to enter into a contract

Covenant: a written agreement or promise

Deed: a written document that when properly executed and delivered conveys title to land

Grantee: the person named in a deed who acquires ownership

Grantor: the person named in a deed who conveys ownership

Quitclaim deed: a legal instrument used to convey whatever title the grantor has; it contains no covenants, warranties, nor implication of the grantor's ownership

Warranty: an assurance or guarantee that something is true as stated

Transferring Title

IN THIS CHAPTER *In this chapter you will learn how the ownership of real estate is conveyed from one owner to another. Voluntary conveyance of real estate by deed, conveyance after death and conveyance by occupancy, accession, public grant, dedication, and forfeiture are covered. An important part of this chapter, and a part that you should review very carefully, is the coverage of the essential elements of a deed. Likewise, the various covenants and warranties should be reviewed.*

The previous three chapters emphasized how real estate is described, the rights and interests available for ownership, and how title can be held. In this chapter we shall discuss how ownership of real estate is conveyed from one owner to another. We begin with the voluntary conveyance of real estate by deed, and then continue with conveyance after death, and conveyance by occupancy, accession, public grant, dedication, and forfeiture.

DEEDS

A **deed** is a written legal document by which ownership of real property is conveyed from one party to another. Deeds were not always used to transfer real estate. In early England, when land was sold its title was conveyed by inviting the purchaser onto the land. In the presence of witnesses, the seller picked up a clod of earth and handed it to the purchaser. Simultaneously, the seller stated that he was delivering ownership of the land to the purchaser. In times when land sales were rare, because ownership usually passed from generation to generation, and when witnesses seldom moved from the towns or farms where they were born, this method worked well. However, as transactions became more common and people more mobile, this method of title transfer became less reliable. Furthermore, it was susceptible to fraud if enough people could be bribed or forced to make false statements. In 1677, England passed a law known as the **Statute of Frauds.** This law, subsequently adopted by each of the American states, requires that transfers of real estate ownership be in writing and signed in order to be enforceable in a court of law. Texas has a similar statute that specifically requires deeds to be in writing.

Essential Elements of a Deed

What makes a written document a deed? What special phrases, statements, and actions are necessary to convey the ownership rights one has in land and buildings? First, a deed must identify the **grantor,** who is the person giving up ownership, and the

grantee, the person who is acquiring that ownership. The actual act of conveying ownership is known as a **grant.** To be legally enforceable, the grantor must be of legal age (18 years in Texas) and of sound mind.

Second, the deed must state that **consideration** was given by the grantee to the grantor. In Texas it is common to use the phrase, "For ten dollars ($10.00) and other good and valuable consideration," or the phrase, "For valuable consideration." These meet the legal requirement that consideration be shown, but retain privacy regarding the exact amount paid.

If the conveyance is a gift, the phrase, "For natural love and affection," may be used, provided the gift is not for the purpose of defrauding the grantor's creditors. In these situations, consideration is not required, and the conveyance is still valid.

Third, the deed must contain **words of conveyance.** With these words the grantor clearly states that she is making a grant of real property to the grantee and identifies the quantity of the estate being granted. Usually, this is the fee simple estate, but it may also be a lesser estate (such as a life estate) or an easement.

A land **description** is the fourth requirement. Acceptable legal descriptions are made by the metes and bounds method, by the government survey system, by recorded plat, or by reference to another recorded document that, in turn, uses one of these methods. Street names and numbers are not used because they do not identify the exact boundaries of the land and because street names and numbers can and do change over time. Appraisal district parcel numbers are subject to change, and are not used either. If the deed conveys only an easement or air right, the deed states that fact along with the legal description of the land. The key point is that a deed must clearly specify what the grantor is granting to the grantee.

Fifth, the grantor must execute the deed by signing it. If the grantor is unable to write his name, he may make a mark, usually an X, in the presence of witnesses. They in turn print his name next to the X and sign as witnesses. If the grantor is a corporation, an officer of the corporation with the proper authority signs the deed.

Figure 5.1 illustrates the essential elements that combine to form a deed. Notice that the example includes an identification of the grantor and grantee, fulfills the requirement for consideration, has words of conveyance, a legal description of the land involved, and the grantor's signature. The words of conveyance are "grant" and the phrase, "to have and to hold forever," says that the grantor is conveying all future benefits, not just a life estate or a tenancy for years. Ordinarily, the grantee does not sign the deed.

As a sixth and final requirement, there must also be **delivery and acceptance.** Although a deed may be completed and signed, it does not transfer title to the grantee until the grantor voluntarily delivers it to the grantee and the grantee willingly accepts it. At that moment title passes.

Under Texas law, if a deed has been recorded it is presumed that a proper delivery has been effected. Delivery of the deed into escrow may also constitute delivery. When a deed has been irrevocably delivered into escrow, and the condition of the escrow is thereafter performed, title is said to have passed from the Seller when the deed is deposited into escrow. This is sometimes referred to as the **Relation Back Doctrine,** which effects a full and valid delivery for the grantor. For instance, when a

FIGURE 5.1
Essential elements
of a deed.

Witnesseth, <u>John Stanley</u> *, grantor, for valuable consideration given by* <u>Robert Brenner</u> *, grantee, does hereby grant and release unto the grantee, his heirs and assigns to have and to hold forever, the following described land: [insert legal description here].*

<u>John Stanley</u>
Grantor's signature

grantor delivers title into escrow, but dies before closing of escrow, the conveyance would still be accomplished.

Covenants and Warranties

Although legally adequate, a deed meeting the preceding requirements can still leave a very important question unanswered in the grantee's mind: "Does the grantor possess all the right, title, and interest she is purporting to convey by this deed?" As a protective measure, the grantee can ask the grantor to include certain covenants and warranties in the deed. These are written promises by the grantor that the condition of title is as stated in the deed together with the grantor's guarantee that if title is not as stated she will compensate the grantee for any loss suffered.

Texas law generally recognizes two basic warranties. One warranty is called the **covenant of seizin,** which means that the grantor has not previously conveyed the same estate or any right, title, or interest therein to a person other than the grantee named in the deed. The second warranty is called a **covenant against encumbrances.** This warrants that the estate passed is free from encumbrances other than those therein specified at the time of the execution of the deed. These warranties basically provide that in the event there is a third-party claimant at some later date claiming title to the property, the grantee has the right to recover against the grantor any damages that he may suffer as a result of the failure of the warranties of the grantor in his general warranty deed.

Date and Acknowledgment

Although it is customary to show on the deed the **date** it was executed by the grantor, it is not essential to the deed's validity. Remember that title passes upon **delivery** of the deed to the grantee and that this may not necessarily be the date it was signed.

It is standard practice to have the grantor appear before a notary public or other public officer and formally declare that he signed the deed as a voluntary act. This is known as an **acknowledgment.** An acknowledgment is not necessary in Texas to make the deed a valid conveyance. However, without the acknowledgment the deed is binding only between the parties to the instrument. To protect against third-party claimants, the deed must be recorded in the county clerk's office in the county courthouse in the county in which the land is located. Acknowledgments and the importance of recording deeds will be covered in more detail in Chapter 6. Meanwhile, let's turn our attention to examples of the most commonly used deeds in Texas.

GENERAL WARRANTY DEED

Figure 5.2 illustrates a typical Texas general warranty deed. The name of the deed is shown in **[1]**, although this usually has no effect if the deed is in fact something other than a general warranty deed. An introduction to the deed is usually combined with the location of the property as shown in **[2]**. This is usually the recording jurisdiction, that is, the county where the property is located. The designation of the grantors, as shown in **[3]** and **[4]**, generally shows the marital status of the grantor(s). This helps keep the chain of title intact in the event there are any conflicts or discrepancies regarding the grantor and grantee in future conveyances. Consideration, a requirement for deeds generally, although it need not be valuable consideration, is shown at **[5]**. Consideration is usually stated as "$10.00 and other good and valuable consideration" to show that consideration was in fact paid, but to keep the actual amount of the transaction out of the public record. The granting clause is shown in **[6]**. The use of the word "grant"

FIGURE 5.2
Typical Texas General
Warranty Deed.

[1] **GENERAL WARRANTY DEED**
(Cash)

THE STATE OF TEXAS   §
                                   § KNOW ALL MEN BY THESE PRESENTS:
COUNTY OF HARRIS [2]   §
                                   [3]   [4]

THAT THE UNDERSIGNED, I.M. Seller and wife, Happy Seller, hereinafter referred to as "Grantor", whether one or more, for and in consideration of the sum of TEN DOLLARS ($10.00) [5] cash, and other good and valuable consideration in hand paid by the Grantee, herein named, the receipt and sufficiency of which is hereby fully acknowledged and confessed, has GRANTED, SOLD and [6] CONVEYED, and by these presents does hereby GRANT, SELL and CONVEY unto N. Debted and wife, May B. Debted, herein referred to as "Grantee", whether one or more, the real property described [7] to-wit:

[8]   Lot 1, Block 1, Shakey Acres Subdivision, Harris County, Texas, as shown of record at Volume 7, Page 3, of the Map Records of Harris County, Texas.

This conveyance, however, is made and accepted subject to any and all validly existing encumbrances, conditions and restrictions, relating to the hereinabove described property as now reflected by the records of the County Clerk of Harris County, Texas.

TO HAVE AND TO HOLD the above described premises, together with all and singular the rights and appurtenances thereto in anywise belonging unto the said Grantee, Grantee's heirs, executors, administrators, successors and/or assigns forever; and Grantor does hereby bind Grantor, Grantor's heirs, executors, administrators, successors and/or assigns to WARRANT AND FOREVER [9] DEFEND all and singular the said premises unto the said Grantee, Grantee's heirs, executors, administrators, successors and/or assigns, against every person whomsoever claiming or to claim the same or any part thereof.

Current ad valorem taxes on said property having been prorated, the payment thereof is assumed by Grantee.
                                   [10]
EXECUTED this 28th day of February, 19xx.

_____
I.M. SELLER

Grantee's Address: [11]

_____   _____
                                           HAPPY SELLER

THE STATE OF TEXAS   §
                                   §
COUNTY OF HARRIS   §

The foregoing instrument was acknowledged before me on the 28th day of February, 19xx, by I.M. Seller and Happy Seller.

_____
NOTARY PUBLIC, STATE OF TEXAS

or "convey" in Texas implies general warranty covenants, and unless otherwise stated, Texas law presumes fee simple title. The names of the grantees are shown in **[7]**. If a deed does not have a grantee, it is void because no effective conveyance took place. A legal description, a requirement for all deeds, is shown at **[8]**. The habendum and warranty clauses, which define the obligations of the grantor with respect to the warranties, are shown at **[9]**. Although not legally required, the deed is generally dated, as shown in **[10]**. The important date is not the date of the deed but the date the deed was recorded. The Texas Recording Act provides that priority interests are determined by the first to record, therefore the date of conveyance is not technically as important as the recording date. The final requirement for a deed is that it has the signature of the grantor(s), which are shown at **[11]**. Although not required to convey property, an acknowledgment of the grantors' signatures before a notary public is usually attached so that the deed can be recorded. Texas does not require a seal in order to make the deed valid. However, the acknowledgment must have a seal to be effective.

The exact style or form of a deed is not critical as long as it contains all the essentials clearly stated and in conformity with state law. For example, one commonly used warranty deed format begins with the words "Know all men by these presents," is written in the first person, and has the date at the end. Although a person may prepare his own deed, the writing of deeds should be left to experts in the field. In fact, Texas permits only attorneys to write deeds for other persons. Even the preparation of preprinted deeds from stationery stores and title companies should be left to knowledgeable persons. Preprinted deeds contain several pitfalls for the unwary. First, the form may have been prepared and printed in another state and, as a result, may not meet the requirements of Texas law. Second, if the blanks are incorrectly filled in, the deed may not be legally recognized. This is a particularly difficult problem when neither the grantor nor grantee realizes it until several years after the deed's delivery. Third, the use of a form deed presumes that the grantor's situation can be fitted to the form and that the grantor will be knowledgeable enough to select the correct form.

SPECIAL WARRANTY DEED

In a **special warranty deed,** the grantor covenants and warrants the property's title only against defects occurring during the grantor's ownership and not against defects existing before that time. The special warranty deed is typically used by executors and trustees who convey on behalf of an estate or principal because the executor or trustee has no authority to warrant and defend the acts of previous holders of title. The grantee can protect against the gap in warranty by purchasing title insurance.

BARGAIN AND SALE DEED

The basic **bargain and sale deed** contains no covenants, and only the minimum essentials of a deed (see Figure 5.3). It has a date, identifies the grantor and grantee, recites consideration, describes the property, contains words of conveyance, and has the grantor's signature. But lacking covenants, what assurance does the grantee have that she is acquiring title to anything? Actually, none. In this deed the grantor purports to own the property described in the deed and that he is granting it to the grantee. Logically, then, a grantee will prefer a warranty deed over a bargain and sale deed, or will require title insurance.

QUITCLAIM DEED

A **quitclaim deed** has no covenants or warranties (see Figure 5.4). Moreover, the grantor makes no statement, nor does he even imply that he owns the property he is quitclaiming to the grantee. Whatever rights the grantor possesses at the time the deed is delivered are conveyed to the grantee. If the grantor has no interest, right, or title to the property described in the deed, none is conveyed to the grantee. However, if the grantor possesses fee simple title, fee simple title will be conveyed to the grantee.

The critical wording in a quitclaim deed is the grantor's statement that he does hereby "quitclaim." The word **quitclaim** means to renounce all possession, right, or interest. Sometimes the words "remise" or "release" may also be used. If the grantor subsequently acquires any right or interest in the property, he is not obligated to convey it to the grantee.

FIGURE **5.3**
Bargain and sale
deed.

DEED
(Without Warranties)

THE STATE OF TEXAS	§	
	§	KNOW ALL MEN BY THESE PRESENTS:
COUNTY OF HARRIS	§	

THAT the undersigned, I.M. Seller and wife, Happy Seller, hereinafter referred to as "Grantor", whether one or more, of the County of Harris and State of Texas, for and in consideration of the sum of TEN AND NO/100 DOLLARS ($10.00) and other good and valuable consideration in hand paid by N. Debted and wife, May B. Debted, hereinafter referenced "Grantee", whether one or more, the receipt and sufficiency of which is hereby acknowledged, have granted, sold and quitclaimed, and by these presents do grant, sell and convey unto Grantee, of the County of Harris and State of Texas, the real property described to-wit:

Lot 1, Block 1, Shakey Acres Subdivision, Harris County, Texas, as shown of record at Volume 7, Page 3, of the Map Records of Harris County, Texas.

TO HAVE AND HOLD the above described property and premises unto the said Grantee, Grantee's heirs, administrators, executors, successors and/or assigns forever. This conveyance is made without warranty, express or implied.

EXECUTED this 28th day of February, 19xx.

Grantee's Address:

_____
I.M. SELLER

_____
HAPPY SELLER

THE STATE OF TEXAS	§	
	§	
COUNTY OF HARRIS	§	

The foregoing instrument was acknowledged before me on the 28th day of February, 19xx, by I.M. Seller and Happy Seller.

_____
NOTARY PUBLIC, STATE OF TEXAS

At first glance it may seem strange that such a deed should even exist, but it does serve a very useful purpose. Situations often arise in real estate transactions when a person claims to have a partial or incomplete right or interest in a parcel of land. Such a right or interest, known as a **cloud on the title,** may have been due to an inheritance, a dower, curtesy, or community property right, or to a mortgage or right of redemption due to a court-ordered foreclosure sale. By releasing that claim to the fee simple owner through the use of a quitclaim deed, the cloud on the fee owner's title is removed. A quitclaim deed is also the standard deed format for granting an easement.

After-Acquired Title

The basic bargain and sale deed contains no covenants of warranty. It does purport to pass an interest in real estate, but with no warranties. It is superior to the quitclaim deed in that it passes **after-acquired title.** While generally considered a legal techni-

FIGURE 5.4
Quitclaim deed.

QUITCLAIM DEED

THE STATE OF TEXAS §

§ KNOW ALL MEN BY THESE PRESENTS:

COUNTY OF HARRIS §

That the undersigned, I.M. Seller and wife, Happy Seller, hereinafter referred to as "Grantor", whether one or more, for and in consideration of the sum of TEN AND NO/100 DOLLARS ($10.00) in hand paid by Grantee herein named, and other good and valuable consideration, the receipt and sufficiency of which is hereby acknowledged, has QUITCLAIMED, and by these presents does QUITCLAIM unto N. Debted and wife, May B. Debted, of the County of Harris, State of Texas, herein referred to as "Grantee", whether one or more, the real property described to-wit:

Lot 1, Block 1, Shakey Acres Subdivision, Harris County, Texas, as shown of record at Volume 7, Page 3, of the Map Records of Harris County, Texas.

TO HAVE AND TO HOLD all of Grantor's right, title and interest in and to the above described property and premises unto the Grantee, and Grantee's heirs, administrators, executors, successors and/or assigns forever; so that neither Grantor nor Grantor's heirs, administrators, executors, successors and/or assigns shall have, claim or demand any right or title to the aforesaid property, premises or appurtenances or any part thereof.

EXECUTED this 28th day of February, 19xx.

Grantee's Address:

_____
I.M. SELLER

_____
HAPPY SELLER

THE STATE OF TEXAS §

§

COUNTY OF HARRIS §

The foregoing instrument was acknowledged before me on the 28th day of February, 19xx, by I.M. Seller and Happy Seller.

_____
NOTARY PUBLIC, STATE OF TEXAS

cality, the after-acquired title doctrine generally states that if a grantor conveys an interest in property that the grantor does not own at the time of the conveyance, and if the grantor ever acquires that property subsequent to her initial conveyance, title automatically passes to the initial grantee. A quitclaim deed contains no warranties; the grantor does not claim to own an interest in property. A quitclaim deed is merely a relinquishment of all right, title, and interest that the grantor *may* have. Because of the loose wording of the quitclaim deed, it does not pass after-acquired title. Therefore, for most real estate situations a bargain and sale deed is preferred to a quitclaim deed.

OTHER TYPES OF DEEDS

A **gift deed** is created by simply replacing the recitation or money and other valuable consideration with the statement, "in consideration of his [her, their] natural love and affection." This phrase may be used in a warranty, special warranty, or grant deed.

However, it is most often used in quitclaim or bargain and sale deeds as these permit the grantor to avoid committing himself to any warranties regarding the property.

A **guardian's deed** is used to convey a minor's interest in real property. It contains only one covenant, that the guardian and minor have not encumbered the property. The deed must state the legal authority (usually a court order) that permits the guardian to convey the minor's property.

A **sheriff's deed** or **trustee's deed** in the event of a foreclosure is issued to the new buyer when a person's real estate is sold as the result of a mortgage or other court-ordered foreclosure sale. The deed should state the source of the sheriff's or referee's authority and the amount of consideration paid. Such a deed conveys only the foreclosed party's title, and, at the most, carries only one covenant: that the sheriff or referee has not damaged the property's title.

A **correction deed,** also called a **deed of confirmation,** is used to correct an error in a previously executed and delivered deed. For example, a name may have been misspelled or an error found in the property description. A **tax deed** is used to convey title to property that has been sold by the state or local government because of the nonpayment of real property taxes.

CONVEYANCE AFTER DEATH

If a person dies without leaving a last will and testament (or leaves one that is subsequently ruled void by the courts because it was improperly prepared), he is said to have died **intestate,** which means without a testament. When this happens, state law directs how the deceased's assets shall be distributed. This is known as **title by descent** or **intestate succession.**

Under Texas law, when a person dies, whether testate or intestate, his real or personal property passes immediately upon his death to his heirs or to his beneficiaries, subject to the payments of any debts, except those which are exempted by law. The surviving spouse and children are usually the dominant recipients of the deceased's assets. If there is no spouse or children, the deceased's grandchildren receive the next share. If there are no lineal descendants, the deceased's parents, brothers and sisters, and their children receive the next largest share. These are known as the deceased's **heirs.** The amount each heir receives, if anything, depends on state law and on how many persons with superior positions in the succession are alive. If no heirs can be found, the deceased's property escheats (reverts) to the state.

Testate, Intestate

A person who dies and leaves a valid will is said to have died **testate,** which means that he or she died leaving a testament telling how the property shall be distributed. The person who made the will, now deceased, is known as the **testator** (male) or **testatrix** (female). In the will, the testator names the persons or organizations who are to receive their real and personal property after they die. Real property that is willed is known as a **devise** and the recipient, a **devisee.** Personal property that is willed is known as a **bequest** or **legacy,** and the recipient, a **legatee.** The will usually names an **executor** (male) or **executrix** (female) to carry out its instructions. If one is not named, the court will appoint an **administrator** (male) or **administratrix** (female).

Notice an important difference between the transfer of real estate ownership by deed and by will: once a deed is made and delivered, the ownership transfer is permanent; the grantor cannot change their mind and take back the property. With respect to a will, the devisees, although named, have no rights to the testator's property until the testator dies. Until that time the testator/testatrix can change their mind and their will.

Probate Court

Upon death, the deceased's will must be filed with a court having power to admit and certify wills, called a **probate court** in Texas. In lesser populated Texas counties, the county court performs this function. This court determines if the will meets all the requirements of law: in particular, that it is genuine, properly signed and witnessed, and that the testator was of sound mind when he made it. At this time anyone may step forward and contest the validity of the will. If the court finds the will to be valid, the executor/executrix is permitted to carry out its terms. If the testator owned real property, its ownership is conveyed using an executor's deed prepared and signed by the executor. The executor's deed is used both to transfer title to a devisee and to sell real property to raise cash. The executor's deed is usually a special warranty deed.

Protecting the Deceased's Intentions

Because the deceased are not present to protect their assets, state laws attempt to ensure that fair market value is received for the deceased's real estate by requiring court approval of proposed sales, and in some cases by sponsoring open bidding in the courtroom. To protect one's interests, a purchaser should ascertain that the executor/executrix has the authority to convey title.

For a will to be valid, and subsequently bind the executor to carry out the instructions, it must meet specific legal requirements. All states, including Texas, recognize the **formal** or **witnessed will,** a written document prepared, in most cases, by an attorney. The testator must declare it to be his or her will and sign it in the presence of two witnesses, who, at the testator's request and in his or her presence, sign the will as witnesses. A formal will prepared by an attorney is the preferred method because the will then conforms explicitly to the law. This greatly reduces the likelihood of its being contested after the testator's death. Additionally, an attorney may offer valuable advice on how to word the will to reduce inheritance taxes.

Holographic Wills

Holographic wills are wills that are entirely handwritten, dated, and signed by the testator; but there are no witnesses. Nineteen states, including Texas, recognize holographic wills as legally binding. People selecting this form of will generally do so because it saves the time and expense of seeking professional legal aid, and because it is entirely private. Besides the fact that holographic wills are considered to have no effect in 31 states, they often result in much legal argument in states that do accept them. This can occur when the testator is not fully aware of the law as it pertains to the making of wills. Many otherwise happy families have been torn apart by dissension when a relative dies and they read the will only to find that there is a question as to whether or not it was properly prepared and hence valid. Unfortunately, what follows is not what the deceased intended; those who would receive more from intestate succession will contest that the will be declared void and of no effect. Those with more to gain if the will stands as written will muster legal forces to argue for its acceptance by the probate court.

Oral Will

A **nuncupative will** is an oral will made at the time of the last sickness of the deceased while at home, or where they have resided for ten days or more preceding the date of the will. If the value of the property distributed under a nuncupative will exceeds $30.00, it must be proved by three credible witnesses that the testator called upon a person to take notice of his testimony that this was his last will and testament prior to his death. An oral will can only be used to dispose of personal property. Any real estate belonging to the deceased is disposed of by intestate succession.

Codicil

A **codicil** is a written supplement or amendment made to a previously existing will. It is used to change some aspect of the will or to add a new instruction, without the work of rewriting the entire will. The codicil must be dated, signed, and witnessed in the same manner as the original will. The only valid way to change a will is with a codicil or by writing a completely new will. The law does not recognize cross-outs, notations, or other alterations made on the will itself.

ADVERSE POSSESSION

Through the unauthorized occupation of another person's land for a long enough period of time, it is possible under certain conditions to acquire ownership by **adverse possession.** The historical roots of adverse possession go back many centuries to a time before written deeds were used as evidence of ownership. At that time, in the absence of any claims to the contrary, a person who occupied a parcel of land was presumed to be its owner. Today, adverse possession is, in effect, a statute of limitations that bars a legal owner from claiming title to land when they have done nothing to oust an adverse occupant during the statutory period. From the adverse occupant's standpoint, adverse possession is a method of acquiring title by possessing land for a specified period of time under certain conditions.

Courts of law are quite demanding of proof before they will issue a decree in favor of a person claiming title by virtue of adverse possession. The claimant must have maintained actual, visible, continuous, hostile, exclusive, and notorious possession, and be publicly claiming ownership to the property. These requirements mean that the claimant's use must have been visible and obvious to the legal owner, continuous and not just occasional, and exclusive enough to give notice of the claimant's individual claim. Furthermore, the use must have been without permission and the claimant must have acted as though she were the owner, even in the presence of the actual owner. Finally, the adverse claimant must be able to prove that they have met these requirements for a period ranging from 3 to 30 years.

Adverse possession is statutorily defined in Texas and consists of four types: 3-year, 5-year, 10-year, and 25-year adverse possession.

Under the **3-year possession** statute, the possessor must claim title to the property under "some title" or "color of title," which might even be "irregular." (One or more of the documents of title in the chain of title may be missing.)

Title means a regular chain of transfers from or under the sovereignty of the soil. **Color of title** means a consecutive chain of transfers down to such person in possession, which may be irregular, as long as said defect does not extend to or include the want to intrinsic fairness or honesty.

The **5-year adverse possession** statute requires that the adverse claimant have peaceable and adverse possession of the property; cultivating, using, enjoying, and paying taxes on it; and claiming under a deed or deeds duly registered.

The **10-year adverse possession** statute requires that the adverse claimant have peaceable and adverse possession of the property; cultivating, using, and enjoying the same; and has a restriction of 160 acres unless the property has been fenced off, and unless the claimant has some memorandum of title that fixes the boundaries of the property. The memorandum of title as used in the 10-year statute does not require a deed, but merely a memorandum of title.

The **25-year adverse possession** statute requires peaceable and adverse possession of the real estate for a period of 25 years under a claim of right in good faith under any instrument purporting to convey the same, which has been recorded in the records of the county in which the real estate is located. This type of adverse possession is valid against minors and incompetents.

It is important to realize that any adverse possession in Texas under a fraudulent claim or under a forged document does not comply with the adverse possession requirements as set out by statute. Also, it is easy to understand why the owner of a large ranch would "ride the range" to maintain his fence and boundaries against poachers or other adverse claimants to either maintain his own title or perfect his own adverse possession interest.

Tacking On

In accumulating the required number of years, an adverse claimant may **tack on** her period of possession to that of a prior adverse occupant. This could be done through the purchase of that right. The current adverse occupant could in turn sell her claim to a still later adverse occupant until enough years were accumulated to present a claim in court.

Although the concept of adverse possession often creates the mental picture of a trespasser moving onto someone else's land and living there long enough to acquire title in fee, this is not the usual application. More often, adverse possession is used to extinguish weak or questionable claims to title. For example, if a person buys property at a tax sale, takes possession, and pays the property taxes each year afterward, adverse possession laws act to cut off claims to title by the previous owner. Another source of successful adverse possession claims may arise from encroachments. If a building extends over a property line and nothing is said about it for a long enough period of time, the building might constitute a valid adverse possession claim.

EASEMENT BY PRESCRIPTION

An easement can also be acquired by prolonged adverse use. This is known as acquiring an **easement by prescription.** As with adverse possession, the laws are strict: the usage must be openly visible, continuous, and exclusive, as well as hostile and adverse to the owner. The use must have occurred over a period of 10 years. All these facts must be proved in a court of law before the court will issue the claimant a document legally recognizing ownership of the easement. As an easement is a right to use land for a specific purpose, not ownership of the land itself, Texas courts do not require the payment of property taxes to acquire a prescriptive easement.

As may be seen from the foregoing discussion, a landowner must be given obvious notification *at the location* of his land that someone is attempting to claim ownership or an easement. Since an adverse claim must be continuous and hostile, an owner can break it by ejecting the trespassers or by preventing them from trespassing or by simply giving them permission to be there. Any of these actions would demonstrate the landowner's superior title. Owners of stores and office buildings with private sidewalks or streets used by the public can take action to break any possible claims to a public easement by either periodically barricading the sidewalk or street or by posting signs giving permission to pass. These signs are often seen in the form of brass plaques embedded in the sidewalk or street. In certain states, a landowner may record with the public records office a **notice of consent.** This is evidence that subsequent uses of his land for the purposes stated in the notice are permissive and not adverse. The notice may be revoked later by recording a **notice of revocation.** There is no authority in Texas creating easements by prescription to the public, except for public roads. Federal, state, and local governments protect themselves against adverse claims to their lands by passing laws making themselves immune from adverse possession claims.

OWNERSHIP BY ACCESSION

The extent of one's ownership of land can be altered by the process of **accession.** This can result from natural or man-made causes. With regard to natural causes, the owner of land fronting on a lake, river, or ocean may acquire additional land because of the gradual accumulation of rock, sand, and soil. This process is called **accretion,** and the results are referred to as alluvion and reliction. **Alluvion** is the increase of land that results when waterborne soil is gradually deposited to produce firm dry ground. **Reliction** (or dereliction) results when a lake, sea, or river permanently recedes, exposing dry land. When land is rapidly washed away by the action of water, it is known as **avulsion.** Man-made accession occurs by **annexation** when personal property is permanently attached to the real estate. For example, when lumber, nails, and cement are used to build a house, they alter the extent of one's land ownership.

PUBLIC GRANT OF LAND

A transfer of land by a government body to a private individual is called a **public grant** or **patent.** The Homestead Act passed by the U.S. Congress in 1862 permits persons wishing to settle on otherwise unappropriated federal land to acquire fee simple ownership by paying a small filing charge and occupying and cultivating the land for five years. Similarly, for only a few dollars, a person may file a mining claim to federal land for the purpose of extracting whatever valuable minerals they can find. To retain the claim, a certain amount of work must be performed on the land each year. Otherwise, the government will consider the claim abandoned and another person may claim it. If the claim is worked long enough, a public grant can be sought and fee simple title obtained. In 1976, the U.S. government ended the homesteading program in all states except Alaska.

DEDICATION OF LAND

When an owner makes a voluntary gift of land to the public, it is known as **dedication.** To illustrate, a land developer buys a large parcel of vacant land and develops it into streets and lots. The lots are sold to private buyers, but what about the streets? In all probability they will be dedicated to the town, city, or county. By doing this, the developer, and later the lot buyers, will not have to pay taxes on the streets, and the public will be responsible for maintaining them. The fastest way to accomplish the transfer is by either statutory dedication or dedication by deed. In **statutory dedication,** the developer prepares a map showing the streets, has the map approved by local government officials, and then records it as a public document. In **dedication by deed,** the developer prepares a deed that identifies the streets and grants them to the city.

Common law dedication takes place when landowners, by their acts or words, show that they intend part of their land to be dedicated even though they have never officially made a written dedication. For example, a landowner may encourage the public to travel on his roads in an attempt to convince a local road department to take over maintenance.

REVERSION

Reversion can occur when a deed contains a condition or limitation. For example, a grantor states in his deed that the land conveyed may be used for residential purposes only. If the grantee constructs commercial buildings, the grantor can reacquire title on the grounds that the grantee forfeited his interest by not using the land for the required purpose. Note the discussion on qualified fee estates and life estates in Chapter 3. Similarly, a deed may prohibit certain uses of land. If the land is used for a prohibited purpose, the grantor can claim forfeiture has occurred.

ALIENATION

A change in ownership of any kind is known as an **alienation.** In addition to the forms of alienation discussed in this chapter, alienation can result from court action in connection with escheat, eminent domain, partition, foreclosure, execution sales, quiet title suits, and marriage. These topics are discussed in other chapters.

REVIEW QUESTIONS

Answers to these questions are found in the Answer Key section at the back of the book.

1. A written legal document by which ownership of real property is transferred from one party to another is
   A. a bill of sale.
   B. a lease.
   C. a contract of sale.
   D. a deed.

2. Which of the following is essential to the validity of a deed?
   A. The grantor must be of legal age.
   B. The grantor must be of sound mind.
   C. Both A and B.
   D. Neither A nor B.

3. Which of the following may not be conveyed by deed?
   A. Fee simple estate.
   B. Life estate.
   C. Easements.
   D. Leasehold estate.

4. With the words conveyance in a deed, the grantor
   A. states that he is making a grant of the property to the grantee.
   B. warrants that he has the right to convey title to the property.
   C. Both A and B.
   D. Neither A nor B.

5. In order to convey title to real property, a deed must be signed by the
   A. grantee.
   B. grantor.
   C. agent.
   D. buyer.

6. In order to convey title, a deed must be
   A. delivered by the grantor to the grantee.
   B. accepted by the grantee.
   C. Both A and B.
   D. Neither A nor B.

7. The "Relation Back Doctrine" in Texas applies when
   A. a grantor delivers title directly to the grantee.
   B. a grantor *does not* deliver title to the grantee.
   C. the grantor delivers title into escrow.
   D. the grantee refuses to accept title.

8. Texas law recognizes which two basic deed warranties:
   A. Covenant of seizin and covenant of further assurance.
   B. Covenant of seizin and covenant against encumbrances.
   C. Covenant against encumbrances and covenant of quiet possession.
   D. Covenant of seizin and covenant of warranty forever.

9. The deed considered to be the best deed a grantee can receive is a
   A. general warranty deed.
   B. special warranty deed.
   C. bargain and sale deed.
   D. quitclaim deed.

10. Which of the following are the same?
    A. Grantor—Party conveying title.
    B. Grantee—Party acquiring title.
    C. Both A and B.
    D. Neither A nor B.

11. The phrase "the grantee's heirs and assigns forever" indicates the conveyance of a
    A. fee simple estate.
    B. life estate.
    C. leasehold estate.
    D. less than freehold estate.

12. The most important date on a deed in Texas is the date that the deed is
    A. signed.
    B. conveyed.
    C. recorded.
    D. written.

13. Quitclaim deeds are often used
    A. to remove a cloud from the title.
    B. to convey the grantor's interest without imposing any future obligations to defend the title upon the grantor.
    C. Both A and B.
    D. Neither A nor B.

14. You would expect to find the words "remise" and "release" in a
    A. warranty deed.
    B. special warranty deed.
    C. grant deed.
    D. quitclaim deed.

15. A court of law with the power to admit and certify wills is called a
    A. probate court.
    B. surrogate court.
    C. Both A and B.
    D. Neither A nor B.

16. Title acquired as the result of inheritance from a person who dies intestate is known as
    A. title by descent.
    B. a devise.
    C. title by intestate succession.
    D. Both A and C.
    E. Both B and C.

17. A handwritten will signed by the testator but not witnessed is known as a
    A. nuncupative will.
    B. holographic will.
    C. oral will.
    D. formal will.

18. An easement acquired by prolonged adverse use is acquired by
    A. implied grant.
    B. necessity.
    C. prescription.
    D. condemnation.

19. An owner can break a claim of adverse possession by
    A. ejecting the trespasser.
    B. giving the trespasser permission to trespass.
    C. Both A and B.
    D. Neither A nor B.

20. The process of increasing land due to the gradual deposition of waterborne soil is known as
    A. reliction.
    B. avulsion.
    C. accretion.
    D. alluvion.

CHAPTER 6

KEY TERMS

Abstract: a summary of all recorded documents affecting title to a given parcel of land

Acknowledgment: a formal declaration by a person signing a document that he or she, in fact, did sign the document

Actual notice: knowledge gained from what one has actually seen, heard, read, or observed

Chain of title: the linkage of property ownership that connects the present owner to the original source of title

Constructive notice: notice given by the public records and by visible possession, coupled with the legal presumption that all persons are thereby notified

Marketable title: title that is free from reasonable doubt as to who is the owner

Mechanic's lien: a lien placed against real property by any unpaid workman or supplier who has done work or furnished building materials

Quiet title suit: court-ordered hearings held to determine land ownership

Title insurance: an insurance policy against defects in title not listed in the title report or abstract

Recordation, Abstracts, and Title Insurance

IN THIS CHAPTER *This chapter focuses on (1) the need for a method of determining real property ownership, (2) the process by which current and past ownership is determined from public records, and (3) the availability of insurance against errors made in determining ownership. The chapter also covers the need for public records, requirements for recording, public records organization, chain of title, abstract, title insurance, and quiet title suits.*

NEED FOR PUBLIC RECORDS

Until the enactment of the Statute of Frauds in England in 1677, determining who owned a parcel of land was primarily a matter of observing who was in physical possession. A landowner gave notice to the world of his claim to ownership by visibly occupying his land. After 1677 written deeds were required to show transfers of ownership. The problem then became one of finding the person holding the most current deed to the land. This was easy if the deedholder also occupied the land, but was more difficult if he did not. The solution was to create a government-sponsored public recording service where a person could record his deed. These records would then be open free of charge to anyone. In this fashion, an owner could post notice to all that he claimed ownership of a parcel of land.

Constructive Notice

There are two ways for a person to give notice of a claim or right to land. One is by recording documents in the public records that give written notice to that effect. The other is by visibly occupying or otherwise visibly making use of the land. The law holds the world at large responsible for looking at the public records and looking at the land for this notice of right or claim. This is called **constructive notice.** Constructive notice charges the public with the responsibility of looking in the public records *and* at the property itself to obtain knowledge of all who are claiming a right or interest.

Actual Notice

Actual notice is knowledge that one has actually gained based on what one has seen, heard, read, or observed. For example, if you read a deed from Jones to Smith, you have actual notice of the deed and Smith's claim to the property. If you go to the property and you see someone in possession, you have actual notice of their claim to be there.

Actual notice also includes notice the law presumes you to have when circumstances, appearances, or rumors warrant further inquiry. For example, suppose you are considering the purchase of vacant acreage and upon inspecting it see a dirt road cutting across the land that is not mentioned in the public records. The law expects you to make further inquiry. The road may be a legal easement across the property. Another example is that anytime you buy rental property, you are expected to make inquiry as to the rights of the occupants. They may hold substantial rights you would not know about without asking them.

Remember that anyone claiming an interest or right is expected to make it known either by recorded claim or visible use of the property. Anyone acquiring a right or interest is expected to look in the public records and go to the property to make a visual inspection for claims and inquire as to the extent of those claims.

Recording Acts

All states have passed **recording acts** to provide for the recording of every instrument (i.e., document) by which an estate, interest, or right in land is created, transferred, or encumbered. In Texas, each county has a county clerk's office. Located at the seat of county government, each county clerk's office will record documents submitted to it that pertain to real property in that county. Thus, a deed to property in Tarrant County is recorded with the county clerk in Tarrant County. Similarly, anyone seeking information regarding ownership of land in Tarrant County would go to the county clerk's office in Tarrant County. The recording process itself involves photocopying the documents and filing them for future reference.

To encourage people to use public recording facilities Texas law holds that (1) a deed, mortgage, or other instrument affecting real estate is not effective as far as subsequent purchasers and lenders are concerned if it is not recorded, and (2) prospective purchasers, mortgage lenders, and the public at large are presumed notified when a document is recorded. Figure 6.1 illustrates the concept of public recording.

FIGURE 6.1
The concept of public recording.

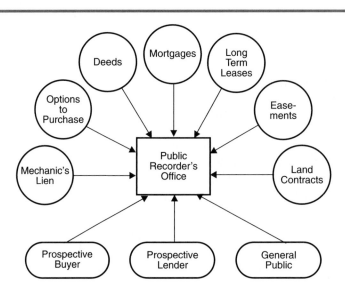

The county clerk's office serves as a central information station for changes in rights, estates, and interests in land.

Example of Notice Laws

To illustrate the effect of constructive and actual notice laws, suppose that Brown offers to sell his land to Carver. Carver then inspects both the land and the public records and finds Brown to be the owner. Satisfied as to Brown's ownership, Carver pays Brown and receives a deed in return. Suppose that Carver does not occupy the land, but he does record his deed with the county clerk's office in the county where the land is located. If Brown now approaches Dawson and attempts to sell the same land, Dawson will find, upon visiting the public records office, that Brown has already conveyed title to Carver.

But what if Dawson assumes that Brown is telling the truth and does not trouble himself to inspect the land or the records? Even though Dawson pays for the land and receives a deed from Brown, the law will not regard Dawson as the rightful owner, even if Dawson records his deed. When Dawson discovers that Carver is the true owner, the only recourse open to Dawson is to sue Brown for the return of his money, presuming he can still locate Brown.

What would the result be if Carver did not record the deed he received and did not occupy the land? If Dawson became interested in buying the land and inspected the public records, he would find Brown to be the owner of the record. Upon inspecting the land, Dawson would find no notice of Carver's ownership either. Having satisfied the law and himself regarding the land's ownership, Dawson would pay Brown and receive a deed to the land. If Dawson records his deed before Carver does, the law will consider Dawson to be the new owner. At this point, the only recourse open to Carver is to try to get his money back from Brown. Even if Carver later records his deed and claims that the date on his deed is earlier than the date on Dawson's deed, it is of no avail. Priority is established by the date of recording, not by the date written on the deed. Failure to record does not invalidate the deed itself. It is still binding between the parties who made it, but it is not valid with respect to the rest of the world.

If Carver does not record the deed he receives, but does occupy the land, the law holds Dawson responsible for visiting the land and asking Carver what his rights are. At that point Dawson would learn of Brown's deed to Carver. Anytime a person buys property knowing that it has been sold before to another and the deed has not been recorded, he will not receive good title.

Although recording acts permit the recording of any estate, right, or interest in land, many lesser rights are rarely recorded because of the cost and effort involved. Month-to-month rentals and leases for a year or less fall into this category. Consequently, only an on-site inspection would reveal their existence, or the existence of any developing adverse possession or prescriptive easement claim.

PUTTING IT TO WORK

With respect to actual and constructive notice, we can draw two important conclusions. First, a prospective purchaser (or lessee or lender) is presumed by law to have inspected both the land itself and the public records to determine the present rights and interests of others. Second, upon receiving a deed, mortgage, or other document relating to an estate, right, or interest in land, one should have it *immediately* recorded in the county in which the land is located so that others will have notice of the recording party's interest in the land.

REQUIREMENTS FOR RECORDING

Texas requires that a document be **acknowledged** before it is eligible to be recorded or it will permit **proper witnessing** or a **jurat** as a substitute.

FIGURE 6.2
A form of jurat.

Subscribed and sworn to before me on this _____ day

of _____, 19_____.

_____

Notary Public in and for

_____ County, Texas

To effect a proper witnessing, the witness must personally appear before some officer authorized to take acknowledgments (notary public) and state under oath that (1) the witness saw the person execute the instrument and that said person executed the instrument for the purposes and consideration therein stated; and (2) that the witness signed the instrument as a witness at the request of the person who executed such instrument.

A jurat is a sworn statement by the person who signed the document that the information contained in the document is true. It is usually sworn to before a notary public or other authorized officer. A form of jurat is shown in Figure 6.2.

The objective of these requirements is to make certain that the person who signs the document is the same person named in the document and that the signing was a free and voluntary act. This is done to ensure the accuracy of the public records and to eliminate the possibility of forgery and fraud. To illustrate, suppose that you own 50 acres of vacant land and someone is intent on stealing it from you. Since the physical removal of your land is an impossibility, an attempt could be made to change the public records. A deed would be typed and the forger would sign your name to it. If he were successful in recording the deed, and then attempted to sell the land, the buyer would, upon searching the records, find a deed conveying the land from you to the forger. A visual inspection of the vacant 50 acres would not show you in actual possession. Although innocent of any wrongdoing and buying in good faith, the buyer would be left with only a worthless piece of paper, as there was no intent on your part to convey title to him.

Acknowledgment

An **acknowledgment** is a formal declaration by a person signing a document that he or she, in fact, did sign the document. Persons authorized to take acknowledgments include notaries public, recording office clerks, commissioners of deeds, judges of courts of record, justices of the peace, and certain others as authorized by Texas law. Commissioned military officers are authorized to take the acknowledgments of persons in the military; foreign ministers and consular agents can take acknowledgments abroad. In Texas, a notary public can take an acknowledgment anywhere in the state. If an acknowledgment is taken outside the state where the document will be recorded, either the recording county must already recognize the out-of-state official's authority or the out-of-state official must provide certification that he or she is qualified to take acknowledgments. The official seal of the notary on the acknowledgment normally fulfills this requirement.

The acknowledgment illustrated in Figure 6.3 is typical of those used by an individual in Texas. In 1997, the legislature amended the form to incorporate a description of the identity card, when one is used. A short form acknowledgment, shown in Figure 6.4, is also used in Texas. Notice that the person signing the document must personally appear before the notary, and that the notary states that he or she knows that person to be the person described in the document. If they are strangers, the notary will require

FIGURE 6.3
An acknowledgment.

THE STATE OF TEXAS   §

                                             §

COUNTY OF   §

BEFORE ME, _____, on this day personally appeared

_____, known to me (or proved to me on the oath of

_____, or through _____, (description

of identity card or other document)) to be the person whose name is subscribed to the

forgoing instrument and acknowledged to me that he executed the same for purposes

and consideration therein expressed.

Given under my hand and seal of office this _____ day of _____,

A.D., _____ .

                    _____

                              NOTARY PUBLIC

FIGURE 6.4
A short form
acknowledgment.

The State of Texas

County of _____ *ss*

*This instrument was acknowledged before me on (date) by (name or names of
person acknowledging).*

> *(Signature of officer)_____*

> *(Title of officer)_____*

> *My commission expires: _____*

proof of identity. The person executing the document states that he or she acknowledges executing the document by signing it in the presence of the notary. Note that it is the signer who does the acknowledging, not the notary. At the completion of the signing, a notation of the event is supposed to be made in a permanent record book kept by the notary.

A 1997 statute also allows a notary public to sign the name of an individual who is physically unable to do so, if authorized to do so by the disabled person in the presence of a disinterested witness.

PUBLIC RECORDS ORGANIZATION

Each document brought to a public recorder's office for recordation is photocopied and then returned to its owner. The photocopy is arranged in chronological order with photocopies of other documents and bound into a book. These books are placed in chronological order on shelves that are open to the public for inspection. References are simply **book** and **page** of the recorded documents.

Filing incoming documents in chronological order makes sense for the recorder's office, but it does not provide an easy means for a person to locate all the documents relevant to a given parcel of land. To illustrate, suppose that you are planning to purchase a parcel of land and want to make certain that the person selling it is the legally recognized owner. Without an index to guide you, you would have to inspect every document in every volume, starting with the most recent book, until you located the current owner's deed. In a heavily populated county, your search might require you to look through hundreds of books, each containing up to 1,000 pages of documents. Consequently, recording offices have developed systems of indexing called grantor and grantee indexes.

In addition to the book and page records that are used in most counties in Texas, the legislature has specifically enacted legislation that provides for the microfilming of records by counties. Rather than record them under mortgage records, deed records, or other similar records, all records relating to or affecting real property are recorded under the heading of "Real Property Records" or "Official Public Records of Real Property." Then, instead of getting a volume and page number, the document is given a Clerk's File Number and a Film Code Number. Texas has also provided for a *fixture* recording system for property, which is personalty but is to become attached to realty. These are commonly termed **UCC liens** or **chattel mortgage liens** (UCC liens are liens that attach pursuant to the provisions of the Uniform Commercial Code, which Texas has adopted as the Texas Business and Commerce Code). As discussed in the fixture portion of this text, there are certain criteria under which the lien created by a supplier of certain fixtures may even be superior to that of a first lien deed of trust. Therefore it is important that the fixture records be searched as well as the lis pendens records, judgment rolls, and mechanics' liens filings in those counties that have those extra records.

Tract Indexes

Of the two indexing systems, the **tract index** is the simplest to use. In it, one page is allocated to either a single parcel of land or to a group of parcels, called a tract. On that page you will find a reference to all the recorded deeds, mortgages, and other documents at the recorder's office that relate to that parcel. Each reference gives the book and page where the original document is recorded. Title companies organize their records this way. The county clerks in Texas do not.

Grantor and Grantee Indexes

Grantor and grantee indexes are alphabetical indexes and are usually bound in book form. There are several variations in use in the United States, but the basic principle is the same. For each calendar year, the **grantor index** lists in alphabetical order all grantors named in the documents recorded that year. Next to each grantor's name is the name of the grantee named in the document, the book and page where a photocopy of the document can be found, and a few words describing the document. The **grantee index** is arranged by grantee names and gives the name of the grantor and the location and description of the document. This type of indexing system is required for county clerk's offices in Texas.

CHAIN OF TITLE

A **chain of title** shows the linkage of property ownership that connects the present owner to the original source of title. In most cases it starts with the original sale or grant of the land from the government to a private citizen. It is used to prove how title came to be **vested** in (i.e., possessed by) the current owner. Figure 6.5 illustrates the chain-of-title concept.

Sometimes, while tracing (running) a chain of title back through time, an apparent break or dead end will occur. This can happen because the grantor is an administrator,

FIGURE 6.5
Chain of title.

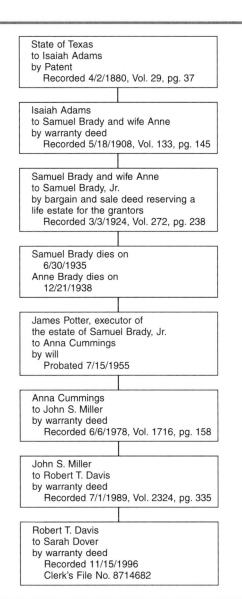

State of Texas
to Isaiah Adams
by Patent
    Recorded 4/2/1880, Vol. 29, pg. 37

Isaiah Adams
to Samuel Brady and wife Anne
by warranty deed
    Recorded 5/18/1908, Vol. 133, pg. 145

Samuel Brady and wife Anne
to Samuel Brady, Jr.
by bargain and sale deed reserving a
life estate for the grantors
    Recorded 3/3/1924, Vol. 272, pg. 238

Samuel Brady dies on
    6/30/1935
Anne Brady dies on
    12/21/1938

James Potter, executor of
the estate of Samuel Brady, Jr.
to Anna Cummings
by will
    Probated 7/15/1955

Anna Cummings
to John S. Miller
by warranty deed
    Recorded 6/6/1978, Vol. 1716, pg. 158

John S. Miller
to Robert T. Davis
by warranty deed
    Recorded 7/1/1989, Vol. 2324, pg. 335

Robert T. Davis
to Sarah Dover
by warranty deed
    Recorded 11/15/1996
    Clerk's File No. 8714682

executor, sheriff, or judge, or because the owner died or because a mortgage against the land was foreclosed. To regain the title sequence, one must search outside the recorder's office by checking probate court records in the case of a death or by checking civil court actions in the case of a foreclosure.

In addition to looking for grantors and grantees, a search must be made for any outstanding mortgages, judgments, actions pending, liens, and unpaid taxes that may affect the title. In Texas, mortgages are placed in the general grantor and grantee indexes, listing the borrower (mortgagor) as the grantor and the lender (mortgagee) as the grantee. The process involves looking for the name of the property owner in each annual **mortgagor index** published while he owned the land. If a mortgage is found, a further check will reveal whether or not it has been satisfied and released. If it has been released, the recorder's office will have noted on the margin of the recorded mortgage the book and page where the release is located. When one knows the lender's name, the mortgage location and its subsequent release can also be found by searching the **mortgagee index.**

Public records must also be checked to learn if any lawsuits have resulted in judgments against recent owners, or if any lawsuits are pending that might later affect title. This information is found, respectively, on the **judgment rolls** and in the **lis pendens**

index at the office of the county clerk. The term "lis pendens" is Latin for pending lawsuits. A separate search must also be made for **mechanics' liens** against the property that may have been filed by unpaid workmen and material suppliers. This step should also include an on-site inspection of the land for any recent construction activity or material deliveries. A visit must also be made to the local tax assessor's office to check the tax rolls for unpaid property taxes. This does not exhaust all possible places that must be visited to do a thorough title search. A title searcher may also research birth, marriage, divorce, and adoption records, probate records, military files, and federal tax liens in an effort to identify all the parties with an interest or potential interest in a given parcel of land and its improvements.

ABSTRACT OF TITLE

Although it is useful for the real estate practitioner to be able to find a name or document in the public records, full-scale title searching should be left to professionals. In a sparsely populated county, title searching is usually done on a part-time basis by an attorney. In more heavily populated counties, a full-time **abstractor** (also spelled **abstracter**) will search the records. These persons are experts in the field of title search, and for a fee they will prepare an abstract of title for a parcel of land.

An **abstract of title** is a complete historical summary of all recorded documents affecting the title of a property. It recites all recorded grants and conveyances and identifies and summarizes recorded easements, mortgages, wills, tax liens, judgments, pending lawsuits, marriages, divorces, etc., that might affect the title. The abstract also includes a list of the public records searched, and not searched, in preparing the abstract.

The abstract is next sent to an attorney. On the basis of her knowledge of law and the abstract she is reading, she renders an **opinion** as to who the fee owner is and names anyone else she feels has a legitimate right or interest in the property. Generally speaking, the seller usually pays the cost of updating the abstract, and the buyer pays his attorney to give the opinion.

TITLE INSURANCE

Despite the diligent efforts of conveyancers, abstracters, and attorneys to give as accurate a picture of land ownership as possible, there is no guarantee that the finished abstract, or its certification, is completely accurate. Persons preparing abstracts and opinions are liable for mistakes due to their own negligence, and they can be sued if that negligence results in a loss to a client. But what if a recorded deed in the title chain is a forgery? Or what if a married person represented himself on a deed as a single person, thus resulting in unextinguished dower rights? Or what if a deed was executed by a minor or an otherwise legally incompetent person? Or what if a document was misfiled, or there were undisclosed heirs, or a missing will later came to light, or there was confusion because of similar names on documents? These situations can result in substantial losses to a property owner, yet the fault may not lie with the conveyancer, abstracter, or attorney. The solution has been the organization of private companies to sell insurance against losses arising from title defects such as these as well as from errors in title examination.

Efforts to insure titles date back to the last century and were primarily organized by and for the benefit of attorneys who wanted protection from errors that they might make in the interpretation of abstracts. As time passed, **title insurance** became available to anyone wishing to purchase it. The basic principle of title insurance is similar to any form of insurance: Many persons pay a small amount into an insurance pool that is then available if any one of them should suffer a loss.

FIGURE 6.6
Title commitment.

TITLE COMMITMENT

The following is a report of the title to the land described in your application for a policy of title insurance.

Land Description: Lot 17, Block M, Atwater's Addition, Jefferson County, State of Texas.

Date and Time of Search: MArch 3, 19xx at 9:00 am

Proposed Insured: Barbara Baker, a single woman

Fee or Interest: Fee simple

Exceptions:

1. *A lien in favor of Jefferson County for property taxes, in the amount of $645.00, due on or before April 30, 19xx.*

2. *A mortgage in favor of the First National Bank in the amount of $30,000, recorded June 2, 1974, in Vol. 2975, Page 245 of the Official County Records.*

3. *An easement in favor of the Southern Telephone Company along the eastern five feet of said land for telephone poles and conduits. Recorded on June 15, 1946, in Vol. 1210, Page 133 of the Official County Records.*

4. *An easement in favor of Coastal States Gas and Electric Company along the north ten feet of said land for underground pipes. Recorded on June 16, 1946, in Vol. 1210, Page 137 of the Official County Records.*

Title Commitment

When a title company receives a request for a title insurance policy, the first step is an examination of the public records. This is done either by an independent abstracter or attorney or by an employee of the title company. A company attorney then reviews the findings and renders an opinion as to who the fee owner is and lists anyone else he feels has a legitimate right or interest in the property such as a mortgage lender or easement holder. This information is typed up and becomes the **title commitment,** which obligates the title insurance company to issue a policy of title when curative requirements, if any, have been satisfied. An example of a title commitment is illustrated in plain language in Figure 6.6. The State Board of Insurance in Texas publishes standard forms for commitments, the use of which is required by all title companies in Texas. They are much longer and in much greater detail than the sample shown.

Notice how a title commitment differs from an abstract of title. Whereas an abstract is a summary of all recorded events that have affected the title to a given parcel of land, a title commitment is more like a snapshot that shows the condition of title at a specific moment in time. A title commitment does not tell who the previous owners were; it only tells who the current owner is. A title commitment does not list all mortgage loans ever made against the land, but only those that have not been removed.

Texas Title Policy

The standard Texas title insurance policy form provides insurance coverage for loss of title. It must be issued on a form promulgated by the State Board of Insurance. Ordinarily, it contains the following exceptions from coverage:

1. Restrictive covenants of record itemized below. (This normally refers to any deed restrictions or covenants that may have been reserved by a prior deed holder, such as those used for land-use control. If there are none, the provision is deleted.)

2. Any discrepancies, conflicts, or shortages in area or boundary lines, or any encroachments, or any overlapping of improvements. (This exception to the title policy may be amended to read "shortages in area" upon request and, in the case of an owner's policy, payment of an additional premium.)

3. Homestead or community property or survivorship rights, if any, of any spouse of any insured

4. Any titles or rights asserted by anyone, including, but not limited to, persons, the public, corporations, governments, or other entities (a) to tidelands, or lands comprising the shores or beds of navigable or parental rivers and streams, lakes, bays, gulf, or oceans, or (b) to land beyond the line of the harbor or boat headlines as established or changed by any government, or (c) to filled-in lands, or artificial islands, or (d) to statutory water rights, including riparian rights, or (e) to the area extending from the line of mean low tide to the line of vegetation, or the right of access to that area or easement along across that area

5. Standby fees and taxes for the current year and subsequent years, and for subsequent years due to changes in usage or ownership. (The title policy only warrants that taxes due prior to the closing have been paid and are up-to-date.)

Texas Residential Owner Policies (Form T-1R) are now required for use on all 1–4 family residential transactions. In all other cases, a Texas Owner Policy Form T-1 is used.

Policy Premium

In Texas, it is generally customary for the seller to pay the cost of the insurance (the title commitment is issued at no cost). However, this is always negotiable between the buyer and the seller. When a property is sold, it is insured for an amount equal to the purchase price. This insurance remains effective as long as the buyer or owner or his heirs have an interest in the property.

The insurance premium consists of a single payment. Title policy rates are set by the Texas Board of Insurance and are the same for all title companies. Each time the property is sold, a new policy must be purchased. The old policy cannot be assigned to the new owner.

Mortgagee's Policy

Thus far our discussion of title insurance has centered on what is called an **owner's policy.** Title insurance companies also offer what is called a **mortgagee's policy.** This protects a lender who has taken real estate as collateral for a loan. There are three significant differences between an owner's and a mortgagee's policy. First, the owner's policy is good for the full amount of coverage stated on the policy for as long as the insured or the insured's heirs have an interest in the property. In contrast, the mortgagee's policy protects only for the amount owed on the mortgage loan. Thus, the coverage on a mortgagee's policy declines and finally terminates when the loan is fully repaid. The second difference is that the mortgagee's policy does not make exceptions for claims to ownership that could have been determined by physically inspecting the property. The third difference is that the mortgagee's title policy provides coverage to subsequent holders of the same mortgage loan.

The cost of a mortgagee's policy (also known as a lender's policy or loan policy) is similar to an owner's policy. Although the insurance company takes added risks by eliminating some exceptions found in the owner's policy, this is balanced by the fact that the liability decreases as the loan is repaid. When an owner's and a mortgagee's policy are purchased at the same time, as in the case of a sale with new financing, the combined cost is only a little more than the cost of the owner's policy alone. The mortgagee's policy covers only title problems. It does not insure that the loan will be repaid by the borrower.

Claims for Losses

When an insured defect arises, the title insurance company reserves the right to either pay the loss or fight the claim in court. If it elects to fight, any legal costs the company incurs are in addition to the amount of coverage stated in the policy. If a loss is paid, the amount of coverage is reduced by that amount and any unused coverage is still in effect. If the company pays a loss, it acquires the right to collect from the party who caused the loss. In Texas, the title policy now provides for payment of actual damages, but if 100% of the title fails, coverage is limited to the face value of the policy.

In comparing title insurance to other forms of insurance (e.g., life, fire, automobile), note that title insurance protects against something that has already happened but has not been discovered. A forged deed may result in a disagreement over ownership: the forgery is a fact of history, the insurance is in the event of its discovery. But in some cases the problem will never be discovered. For example, heirs may be totally unaware of their property rights and fail to timely claim them. If they never claim them, the rights extinguish themselves by limitations, and the intervening property owners will have been unaffected.

Only a small part of the premiums collected by title insurance companies are used to pay claims, largely because they take great pains to maintain on their own premises complete copies of the public records for each county in which they do business. These are called **title plants;** in most cases they are actually more complete and better organized than those available at the public recorder's office. This is because the State Board of Insurance requires that the records be maintained on an **abstract system,** rather than the grantor-grantee system. The philosophy is that the better the quality of the title search, the fewer the claims that must be paid.

The Growth of Title Insurance

The title insurance business has mushroomed due to three important reasons. First, in a warranty deed, the grantor makes several strongly worded covenants. As you will recall, the grantor covenants that he is the owner, that there are no encumbrances except as stated in the deed, and that the grantor will warrant and forever defend the premises. Thus, signing a warranty deed places a great obligation on the grantor. By purchasing title insurance and using only a special warranty, the grantor can transfer a significant portion of that obligation to an insurance company.

Second, a grantee is also motivated to have title insurance. Even with a warranty deed, there is always the lingering question of whether or not the seller would be financially capable of making good on her covenants and warranties. They are useless if one cannot enforce them.

Third, the broad use of title insurance has made mortgage lending more attractive and borrowing a little easier and cheaper for real property owners. This is because title insurance has removed the risk of loss due to defective titles while insuring the lender's lien priority. Secondary market purchasers of loans such as FNMA and FHLMC (Chapter 12) require title insurance on any loan they purchase.

QUIET TITLE SUIT

When a title defect (or **title cloud**) must be removed, it is logical to remove it by using the path of least resistance. For example, if an abstract or title report shows unpaid property taxes, the buyer may require the seller to pay them in full before the deal is completed. Similarly, a distant relative with ownership rights might be willing, upon negotiation, to quitclaim them for a price.

Sometimes a stronger means is necessary to remove title defects. For example, the distant relative may refuse to negotiate, or the lender may refuse to remove a mortgage lien despite pleas from the borrower that it has been paid. The solution is a **quiet title suit** (also called a quiet title action). In Texas, a property owner can ask the courts to hold hearings on the ownership of his land. At these hearings anyone claiming to have an interest or right to the land in question may present verbal or written evidence of that claim. A judge, acting on the evidence presented and the laws of his state, rules on the validity of each claim. The result is to legally recognize those with a genuine right or interest and to "quiet" those without a genuine interest.

REVIEW QUESTIONS

Answers to these questions are found in the Answer Key section at the back of the book.

1. Once a person is aware of another's rights or interest in property, that person is said to have
   A. constructive notice.
   B. legal notice.
   C. inquiry notice.
   D. actual notice.

2. Constructive notice requires that
   A. a landowner give public notice of his or her claim of ownership.
   B. anyone interested in the property inspect the property and the public records.
   C. Both A and B.
   D. Neither A nor B.

3. The public recorder's office
   A. serves as a central information station for documents pertaining to interests in land.
   B. is an agency of the federal government.
   C. Both A and B.
   D. Neither A nor B.

4. Farmer Sorensen leases 320 acres adjacent to his ranch. Sorensen can give notice to the world at large by
   A. plowing the land.
   B. storing his equipment on it.
   C. putting a fence around it.
   D. All of the above.
   E. None of the above.

5. Priority of a recorded instrument is determined by the date of
   A. acknowledgment.
   B. delivery to the grantee.
   C. the instrument.
   D. recordation.

6. Deed and other instruments that affect land titles should be recorded
   A. immediately after delivery or execution.
   B. in order to provide constructive notice.
   C. Both A and B.
   D. Neither A nor B.

7. The purpose of having a person's signature acknowledged is to
   A. make certain the person signing the document is the same person named in the document and that the signing was voluntary.
   B. make the document admissible to the public records.
   C. Both A and B.
   D. Neither A nor B.

8. In a jurisdiction that indexes recorded instruments by grantee and grantor, if one knew the name of the current owner of a property and wished to search the records to verify that ownership, one would look in the
   A. grantee index.
   B. grantor index.
   C. Both A and B.
   D. Neither A nor B.

9. Instruments are recorded in the public records in what order?
   A. Alphabetical order, based on the grantee's last name.
   B. Chronological order, as received for recordation.
   C. According to the date of the instrument.
   D. Alphabetical order, based on the grantor's last name.

10. The name of the borrower would be filed alphabetically in the
    A. mortgagee index.
    B. grantor index.
    C. Lis pendens.
    D. Lender's index.

11. Which of the following would not ordinarily be checked in searching a title to a parcel of land?
    A. Judgment records.
    B. Lien records.
    C. Chattel mortgage records.
    D. Lis pendens index.

12. A lis pendens index is
    A. an index of existing leases on property.
    B. an index of pending lawsuits.
    C. a tract index.
    D. a chain of title.

13. Which of the following are among the provisions of a typical owner's title insurance policy?
    A. The insurer is responsible for having searched the records pertaining to the property and insures its findings.
    B. The insurer is not responsible for pertinent information that is not found in the public records.
    C. The insurer has not make a visual inspection of the land for signs of notice.
    D. All of the above.

14. Summary of all recorded documents affecting title to a given parcel of land is called
    A. a chain of title.
    B. an abstract of title.
    C. a title report.
    D. All of the above.

15. Protection against a loss occasioned by which of the following would not be covered by title insurance?
    A. Forged deeds, or deeds by incompetents.
    B. Unextinguished dower or curtesy rights.
    C. Claims by undisclosed or missing heirs.
    D. Destruction of improvements by a tornado.

16. Should a title insurance company elect to fight a claim in court, the legal expenses incurred will be
    A. deducted from the coverage under the policy.
    B. assumed by the title insurance company without affecting the policy coverage.
    C. shared by the insured and the insurance company.
    D. paid by the insured.

17. The purchase of title insurance eliminates the need for
    A. casualty insurance.
    B. a survey of the property.
    C. constructive notice.
    D. None of the above.
    E. All of the above.

18. All of the following are true of a quiet title suit EXCEPT that it
    A. is a judicial proceeding.
    B. removes all claims to title other than the owner's.
    C. quiets those without a genuine interest in the property.
    D. can be used to clear up a disputed title.

19. The premium for a title insurance policy is
    A. paid annually.
    B. paid semiannually.
    C. a single premium, paid upon issuance.
    D. included in the mortgage payment.

CHAPTER 7

Breach of contract: failure, without legal excuse, to perform as required by a contract

Competent parties: persons considered legally capable of entering into a binding contract

Contract: a legally enforceable agreement to do (or not to do) a particular thing

Duress: the application of force to obtain an agreement

Fraud: an act intended to deceive for the purpose of inducing another to give up something of value

Liquidated damages: an amount of money specified in a contract as compensation to be paid if the contract is not satisfactorily completed

Minor, Infant: a person under the age of legal competence; in most states, under 18 years

Specific performance: contract performance according to the precise terms agreed upon

Void contract: a contract that has no binding effect on the parties who made it

Voidable contract: a contract that is able to be voided by one of its parties

Contract Law

IN THIS CHAPTER *This chapter will introduce you to contract law and how a contract is created. The essentials of a valid contract are also covered in detail. Other topics covered include offer and acceptance, fraud, mistake, lawful objective, consideration, performance, and breach of contract. Although this is a short chapter, it is very important.*

HOW A CONTRACT IS CREATED

A **contract** is a legally enforceable agreement to do or not to do a specific thing. In this chapter we shall see how a contract is created and what makes it legally binding. Topics covered include offer and acceptance, fraud, mistake, lawful objective, consideration, performance, and breach of contract. In Chapter 8 we will turn our attention to the earnest money contract, tax-deferred exchange, and installment contract as they relate to the buying and selling of real estate.

Express Contract

A contract may be either expressed or implied. An **express contract** occurs when the parties to the contract declare their intentions either orally or in writing. The word **party** [plural, **parties**] is a legal term that refers to a person or group involved in a legal proceeding. A lease or rental agreement, for example, is an expressed contract. The lessor landlord expresses the intent to permit the lessee tenant to use the premises, and the lessee agrees to pay the rent. A contract to purchase real estate is also an expressed contract.

Implied Contract

An **implied contract** is created by neither words nor writing but rather by actions of the parties indicating that they intend to create a contract. For example, when you step into a taxicab, you imply that you will pay the fare. The cab driver, by allowing you in the cab, implies that you will be taken where you want to go. The same thing occurs at a restaurant. The presence of tables, silverware, menus, waiters, and waitresses implies that you will be served food. When you order, you imply that you are going to pay when the bill is presented.

PUTTING IT TO WORK

In real estate, certain terms are not included in the listing agreement (exactly how the property will be marketed, advertised, etc.), but it is implied through custom in the industry that certain marketing efforts will be made.

Bilateral Contract

A contract may be either bilateral or unilateral. A **bilateral contract** results when a promise is exchanged for a promise. In the typical real estate sale, the buyer promises to pay the agreed price, and the seller promises to deliver title to the buyer. In a lease contract the lessor promises the use of the premises to the lessee, and the lessee promises to pay rent in return. A bilateral contract is basically an "I will do this *and* you will do that" arrangement.

Unilateral Contract

A **unilateral contract** results when a promise is exchanged for performance. For instance, during a campaign to get more listings, a real estate office manager announces to the firm's sales staff that an extra $100 bonus will be paid for each salable new listing. No promises or agreements are necessary from the salespersons. However, each time a salesperson performs by bringing in a salable listing, he or she is entitled to the promised $100 bonus. An option to purchase is a unilateral contract until it is exercised, at which time it becomes a bilateral contract. A unilateral contract is basically an "I will do this *if* you will do that" arrangement.

Forbearance

Most contract agreements are based on promises by the parties involved to act in some manner (pay money, provide services, or deliver title). However, a contract can contain a promise to **forbear** (not to act) by one or more of its parties. For example, a lender may agree not to foreclose on a delinquent mortgage loan if the borrower agrees to a new payment schedule.

Legal Effect

A contract can be construed by the courts to be valid, void, or unenforceable.

A **valid contract** is one that meets all the requirements of law. It is binding upon its parties and legally enforceable in a court of law. A **void contract** has no legal effect and, in fact, is not a contract at all. Even though the parties may have gone through the motions of attempting to make a contract, no legal rights are created and any party thereto may ignore it at her pleasure. A **voidable contract** binds one party but not the other. An **unenforceable contract** is one that may have been valid, but its enforcement is now barred by the statute of limitations or the doctrine of laches. For instance, if you try to sue on a contract six years after default, the suit would be barred by the four-year statute of limitations. Let's now turn our attention to the requirements of a valid contract.

ESSENTIALS OF A VALID CONTRACT

For a contract to be **legally valid,** and hence binding and enforceable, the following five requirements must be met:

1. Competent parties
2. Mutual agreement
3. Lawful objective
4. Consideration or cause
5. Contract in writing when required by law

If these conditions are met, any party to the contract may, if the need arises, call upon a court of law to either enforce the contract as written or award money damages for nonperformance. In reality, a properly written contract seldom ends up in court because each party knows it will be enforced as written. It is the poorly written and unenforceable contract that ends up in court. A judge must then decide if a contract actually exists and determine the obligations of each party. It is much better if the contract is correctly prepared in the first place. Let's look more closely at the five requirements of an enforceable contract.

COMPETENT PARTIES

For a contract to be legally enforceable, all parties entering into it must be legally competent. In deciding competency, the law provides a mixture of objective and subjective standards. The most objective standard is that of age. A person must reach the age of *majority* to be legally capable of entering into a contract. **Minors** do not have contractual capability. Until the voting age in national elections was reduced from 21 to 18 years by Congress, persons were considered to be minor by most states until the age of 21. Since then most state legislatures (including Texas) have lowered the age for entering into legally binding contracts to 18 years. The purpose of majority laws is to protect minors (also known as "infants" in legal terminology) from entering into contracts that they may not be old enough to understand. Depending on the circumstances, a contract entered into by a minor may be void or voidable.

PUTTING IT TO WORK

In Texas, contracts with minors are voidable. For example, the adult might be bound, but the minor could withdraw. If a contract with a minor is required, it is possible to obtain a binding contract by working through the minor's legal guardian.

Persons of unsound mind who have been declared incompetent by a judge may not make a valid contract, and any attempt to do so results in a void contract. The solution is to contract through the person appointed to act on behalf of the incompetent. If a person has not been judged legally incompetent but nonetheless appears incapable of understanding the transaction in question, that person has no legal power to contract. In some states persons convicted of felonies may not enter into valid contracts without the prior approval of the parole board.

Regarding intoxicated persons, if there was a deliberate attempt to intoxicate a person for the purpose of approving a contract, the intoxicated person, upon sobering up, can call upon the courts to void the contract. If the contracting party was voluntarily drunk to the point of incompetence, when he is sober he may ratify or deny the contract if he does so promptly. However, some courts look at the matter strictly from the standpoint of whether or not the intoxicated person had the capability of formulating the intent to enter into a contract. Obviously, there are some fine and subjective distinctions among these three categories, and a judge may interpret them differently than the parties to the contract. Most other mind-altering drugs are dealt with in the same manner as alcohol.

Power of Attorney

An individual can give another person the power to act on his behalf: for example to buy or sell land, or to sign lease documents. This is called **power of attorney.** The person holding the power of attorney is called an **attorney-in-fact.** With regard to real estate, a power of attorney must be stated in writing because the real estate documents to be signed must be in writing. Any document signed with a power of attorney should be executed as follows: "Paul Jones, principal, by Deborah Smith, agent, his attorney-in-fact." If the agent has power to convey title to land, then the document granting him power of attorney should be acknowledged by the principal and recorded. The agent is legally competent to the extent of the powers granted to him by the principal as long as the principal remains alive. The power of attorney can, of course, be terminated by the principal at any time. A recorded notice of revocation is needed to revoke a recorded power of attorney.

Texas also recognizes a statutory **durable power of attorney.** It does not lapse because of the passage of time unless a time limitation is specifically stated in the instrument creating it. The durable power of attorney has additional requirements, however. To be enforceable, it must:

1. Be in writing, designating another person as attorney-in-fact or agent
2. Be signed by the principal who is an adult
3. Contain the words "this power of attorney is not affected by subsequent disability or incapacity of the principal," or similar words
4. Be acknowledged by a principal before an officer authorized to take acknowledgments to deeds or conveyances and to administer oaths under the laws of this state or any other state

A durable power of attorney can be terminated by express revocation, divorce, annulment, termination by its own terms, the death of the principal, or the appointment of a guardian for the principal. Even those terminations are limited. However, the statute clearly states that the revocation, divorce, annulment, death, or qualification of a guardian of the estate of the principal doesn't revoke or terminate the agency as to the attorney-in-fact who doesn't have actual knowledge of the termination. How does the attorney-in-fact prove he didn't have knowledge? The statute merely requires that he signs an affidavit saying that he did not have at the time, the exercise of his power, actual knowledge of the termination of the power of attorney by revocation, death, or qualification of the guardian, and that the affidavit is "conclusive proof as between the attorney-in-fact or agent and a person other than the principal." The same is true of people's reliance on the durable power of attorney when the principal becomes disabled or incapacitated. The affidavit is, again, "conclusive proof" of a disability or incapacity of the principal at the time.

A revocation to the durable power of attorney is not effective as to a third party relying on the power of attorney until the third party receives *actual notice* of the revocation.

If the durable power of attorney is for a real property transaction, the durable power of attorney is required to be recorded in the office of the County Clerk of the county in which the land is located. The statute even provides a form power of attorney to be used. The form is not exclusive, and other forms of power of attorney can be used. Third parties who rely on good faith of the acts of the agent within the scope of the power of attorney, may do so *without fear of liability to the principal.*

Corporations and Other Entities

Corporations are considered legally competent parties. However, the individual contracting on behalf of the corporation must have authority from the board of directors. Some states also require that the corporate seal be affixed to contracts, although Texas does not. A partnership can contract either in the name of the partnership or in the name of any of its general partners. Trustees, executors, and administrators can legally contract on behalf of trusts and estates, provided that they have proper authorization.

MUTUAL AGREEMENT

The requirement of **mutual agreement** (also called **mutual consent,** or **mutual assent,** or **meeting of the minds**) means that there must be agreement to the provisions of the contract by the parties involved. In other words, there must be a mutual willingness to enter into a contract. This means that their intention is to be bound by the agreement, thus precluding jokes or jests from becoming valid contracts. The existence of mutual agreement is evidenced by the words and acts of the parties indicating that there is a valid offer and an unqualified acceptance. In addition, there must be no fraud, misrepresentation, or mistake, and the agreement must be genuine and freely given. Let us consider each of these points in more detail.

Offer and Acceptance

Offer and acceptance requires that one party (the **offeror**) make an offer to another party (the **offeree**). If the offer is acceptable, the offeree must then communicate that acceptance to the offeror. The means of communication may be spoken or written or an action that implies acceptance. To illustrate, suppose that you own a house and want to sell it. You tell your listing broker that you will accept $100,000 and that you would deliver a general warranty deed and pay the normal closing costs for the area. Within a few days, the broker submits a signed document from a prospective buyer. This constitutes an offer, and the buyer (the offeror) has just communicated it to you (the offeree). One requirement of a valid offer is that the offer be specific in its terms. Mutual agreement cannot exist if the terms of the offer are vague or undisclosed and/or the offer does not clearly state the obligations of each party involved. If the seller were to say to a prospective purchaser "Do you want to buy this house?" without stating the price, and the prospective purchaser said "Yes," the law would not consider this to be a valid offer.

It should also be pointed out that an offer can be revoked by the offeror at any time prior to the offeror hearing of its acceptance. For example, if you submit an offer to purchase a house for $90,000 and while waiting for a response you find another house that you prefer, you can revoke your first offer at any time prior to hearing of its acceptance, then make your contract with the second homeowner. An offeror should be strongly advised, however, not to initiate more than one offer at a time, since considerable confusion can be caused by multiple offers, revocations, and acceptances in one transaction.

Counteroffer

Upon receiving the offer, the offeree has three options: to agree to it, to reject it, or to make a counteroffer. If the offeree agrees, he must agree to every item of the offer. An offer is considered by law to be rejected not only if the offeree rejects it outright but also if any change in the terms is made. Any change in the terms is considered a counteroffer. Although it may appear that the offeree is only amending the offer before she accepts it, the offeree has actually rejected it, and is making a new offer. This now makes the seller the offeror. To illustrate, suppose the prospective purchaser submits an offer to the listing broker to purchase the property for $95,000, but instead of accepting the $95,000 offer, the seller amends the contract to reflect a selling price of $100,000. This is a rejection of the original offer, which creates a counteroffer to the purchaser. The purchaser now has the right to accept or reject this counteroffer. If, however, the original $95,000 offer is agreeable to the offeree (seller), she must communicate the acceptance to the purchaser. A spoken "Yes, I'll take it," would not be legally adequate; a real estate licensee should obtain the signature of the seller on a contract, without any further changes.

Fraud

Mutual agreement requires that there be no fraud, misrepresentation, or mistake in the contract if it is to be valid. A **fraud** is an act intended to deceive for the purpose of inducing another to part with something of value. It can be as blatant as knowingly telling a lie or making a promise with no intention of performance. For example, you are showing your home, and a prospective buyer asks if there is frequent bus service nearby. There isn't, but you say, "Yes," as you sense this is important and you want to sell the home. The prospective tenant, relying on this information from you, buys the home and moves in. The next day he calls and says that there is no public transportation and he wants to break the agreement immediately. Because mutual agreement was lacking, the buyer can **rescind** (cancel) the contract and get his money back.

Fraud can also result from failing to disclose important information, thereby inducing someone to accept an offer. For example, the day you show your apartment to a prospective tenant the weather is dry. But you know that during every rainstorm the tenant's automobile parking space becomes a lake of water six inches deep. This would qualify as fraud if the prospective tenant was not made aware of it before agreeing to the rental contract. Once again, the law will permit the aggrieved party to rescind the contract. However, the tenant does not have to rescind the contract. If he likes the other features of the apartment enough, he can elect to live with the flooded parking space.

PUTTING IT TO WORK

If a real estate agent commits fraud to make a sale and the deceived party later rescinds the sales contract, not only is the commission lost, but explanations will be necessary to the other parties of the contract. Moreover, state license laws provide a suspension or **revocation** of a real estate license for fraudulent acts.

Innocent Misrepresentation

Innocent misrepresentation differs from fraud (intentional misrepresentation) in that the party providing the wrong information is not doing so to deceive another for the purpose of reaching an agreement. To illustrate, suppose that over the past year you have observed that city buses stop near your apartment building. If you tell a prospective tenant that there is bus service, only to learn the day after the tenant moves in that service stopped last week, this is innocent misrepresentation. Although there was no dishonesty involved, the tenant still has the right to rescind the contract. If performance has not begun on the contract (in this case the tenant has not moved in), the injured party may give notice that he **disaffirms** (revokes) the contract. However, if the tenant wants to break the contract, he must do so in a timely manner; otherwise the law will presume that the situation is satisfactory to the tenant.

Mistake

Mistake as applied in contract law has a very narrow meaning. It does not include innocent misrepresentation nor does it include ignorance, inability, or poor judgment. If a person enters into a contract that he later regrets because he did not investigate it thoroughly enough, or because it did not turn out to be beneficial, the law will not grant relief to him on the grounds of mistake, even though he may now consider it a "mistake" to have made the contract in the first place. Mistake as used in contract law arises from ambiguity in negotiations and mistake of material fact. For example, you offer to sell your mountain cabin to an acquaintance. He has never seen your cabin, and you give him instructions on how to get there to look at it. He returns and accepts your offer; however, he made a wrong turn and the cabin he looked at was not your cabin. A week later he discovers his error. The law considers this ambiguity in negotiations. In this case the buyer, in his mind, was purchasing a different cabin than the seller was selling; therefore, there is no mutual agreement and any contract signed is void.

To illustrate a mistake of fact, suppose that you show your apartment to a prospective tenant and tell her that she must let you know by tomorrow whether or not she wants to rent it. The next day she visits you and together you enter into a rental contract. Although neither of you is aware of it, there has just been a serious fire in the apartment. Since a fire-gutted apartment is not what the two of you had in mind when the rental contract was signed, there is no mutual agreement.

Occasionally, "mistake of law" will be claimed as grounds for relief from a contract. However, mistake as to one's legal rights in a contract is not generally accepted by courts of law unless it is coupled with a mistake of fact. Ignorance of the law is not considered a mistake.

Duress

The last requirement of mutual agreement is that the offer and acceptance be genuine and freely given. **Duress** (use of force), **menace** (threat of violence), or **undue influence** (unfair advantage) cannot be used to obtain agreement. The law permits a contract made under any of these conditions to be revoked by the aggrieved party.

LAWFUL OBJECTIVE

To be enforceable, a contract cannot call for performing an illegal act. This is because a court of law cannot be called upon to enforce a contract that requires that a law be broken. Such a contract is void, or if already in operation, it is unenforceable in a court of law. For example, a debt contract requiring interest rates in excess of those allowed by state law would be void. If the borrower had started repaying the debt and then later stopped, the lender would not be able to look to the courts to enforce collection of the balance. Contracts contrary to good morals and general public policy are also unenforceable.

CONSIDERATION

For an agreement to be enforceable, it must be supported by **consideration.** Money is usually thought of as meeting this requirement. Yet in the vast majority of contracts, the consideration requirement is met by a promise for a promise. For example, in selling real estate the promise of a purchaser to buy and the promise of an owner to sell constitute sufficient consideration to support their agreement. No deposit money is necessary.

The purpose of requiring consideration is to demonstrate that a bargain has been struck between the parties to the contract. The size, quantity, nature, or amount of what is being exchanged is irrelevant as long as it is present. Consideration can be money, property, personal services, or a promise to do something. For example, there can be an exchange of a promise for a promise, money for a promise, money for property, goods for services, etc. Forbearance also qualifies as consideration.

PUTTING IT TO WORK

In a typical offer to purchase a home, the consideration is the mutual exchange of promises by the buyer and seller to obligate themselves to do something they were not previously required to do. In other words, the seller agrees to sell on the terms agreed and the buyer agrees to buy the property on those same terms. The earnest money the buyer may put down is not the consideration necessary to make the contract valid. Rather, earnest money is a tangible indication of the buyer's intent and may become a source of compensation (damages) to the seller in the event the buyer does not carry out his promises.

In a deed, which is evidence of a contract, the consideration requirement is usually met with a statement such as "For ten dollars and other good and valuable consideration." In a lease, the periodic payment of rent is the consideration for the use of the premises.

A contract fails to be legally binding if consideration is lacking from any party to the contract. The legal philosophy is that a person cannot promise to do something of value for someone else without receiving in turn some form of consideration. Stated another way, each party must give up something, for example, each must suffer a detriment. For example, if I promise to give you my car, the consideration requirement is not met because you promise nothing in return. But if I promise to give you my car when you quit smoking, that meets the consideration requirement.

As a group, money plus promises, property, legal rights, services, and forbearance are classified as **valuable consideration,** if they are worth money. There is one exception to the requirement that each party must provide valuable consideration. That is the case of a gift. If a person wishes to give something of value to a friend or loved one, courts have ruled that "love and affection" will meet the consideration requirement. Although this is not valuable consideration, it is nonetheless **good consideration** and as such fulfills the legal requirement that consideration be present. The law generally will not inquire as to the adequacy of the consideration unless there is evidence of fraud, mistake, duress, threat, or undue influence. For instance, if a man gave away his property or sold it very cheaply to keep it from his creditors, the creditors could ask the courts to set aside those transfers.

CONTRACT IN WRITING

In each state (including Texas) there is a law that is commonly known as a **statute of frauds.** The purpose of such laws is to prevent frauds by requiring that all contracts for the sale of land, or an interest in land, be in writing and signed in order to be enforceable in a court of law. This includes such things as offers, acceptances, binders, land contracts, deeds, escrows, and options to purchase. Mortgages and trust deeds (and their accompanying bonds and notes) and leases whose obligations cannot be completed within one year must be in writing to be enforceable. In addition, most states (including Texas) have also adopted the **Uniform Commercial Code** that requires, among other things, that the sale of property with a value in excess of $500 be in writing. Texas also requires that real estate employment contracts be expressed in writing in order for the agent to sue the principal for a commission.

The purpose of requiring that a contract be written and signed is to prevent perjury and fraudulent attempts to seek legal enforcement of a contract that never existed. It is not necessary that a contract be a single formal document. It can consist of a series of signed letters or memorandums as long as the essentials of a valid contract are present. Note that the requirement for a written contract relates only to the enforceability of the contract. Thus, if Mr. Cheddar orally agrees to sell his land to Mr. Cheese and they carry out the deal, neither can come back after the contract was performed and ask a court to rescind the deal because the agreement to sell was oral.

The most common real estate contract that does not need to be in writing to be enforceable is a month-to-month rental agreement that can be terminated by either landlord or tenant on one-month notice. Nonetheless, most are in writing, because people tend to forget oral promises. While the unhappy party can go to court, the judge may have a difficult time determining what oral promises were made, particularly if there were no witnesses other than the parties to the agreement. Hence, it is advisable to put all important contracts in writing and for each party to recognize the agreement by signing it. It is also customary to date written contracts, although most can be enforced without showing the date the agreement was reached.

Putting It To Work

A written contract will supersede an oral one. Thus, if two parties orally promise one thing and then write and sign something else, the written contract will prevail. This has been the basis for many complaints against overzealous real estate practitioners who make oral promises that do not appear anywhere in the written contract.

Parol Evidence Rule

Under certain circumstances the **parol evidence rule** permits oral evidence to complete an otherwise incomplete or ambiguous written contract. However, the application of this rule is quite narrow. If a contract is complete and clear in its intent, the courts presume that what the parties put into writing is what they agreed upon.

PERFORMANCE AND DISCHARGE OF CONTRACTS

Most contracts are discharged by being fully performed by the contracting parties in accordance with the contract terms. However, alternatives are open to the parties of the contract. One is to sell or otherwise **assign** the contract to another party. Unless prohibited by the contract, rights, benefits, and obligations under a contract can be assigned to someone else. The original party to the contract, however, still remains ultimately liable for its performance. Note, too, that an assignment is a contract in itself and must meet all the essential contract requirements to be enforceable. A common example of an assignment occurs when a lessee wants to move out and sells his lease to another party. When a contract creates a personal obligation, such as a listing agreement with a broker, an assignment may not be made.

Novation

A contract can also be performed by **novation.** Novation is the substitution of a new contract between the same or new parties. For example, novation occurs when a buyer assumes a seller's loan, *and* the lender releases the seller from the loan contract. With novation the departing party is released from the obligation to complete the contract.

If the objective of a contract becomes legally impossible to accomplish, the law will consider the contract discharged. For example, a new legislative statute may forbid what the contract originally intended. If the parties mutually agree to cancel their contract before it is executed, this too is a form of discharge. For instance, you sign a five-year lease to pay $500 per month for an office. Three years later you find a better location and want to move. Meanwhile, rents for similar offices in your building have increased to $575 per month. Under these conditions the landlord might want to cancel your lease.

If one of the contracting parties dies, a contract is considered discharged if it calls for some specific act that only the dead person could have performed. For example, if you hired a freelance gardener to tend your landscaping and he died, the contract would be discharged. However, if your contract is with a firm that employs other gardeners who can do the job, the contract would still be valid. Damage to the premises may also discharge the agreement. As a case in point, it is common in real estate sales contracts to provide that the contract is deemed canceled if the property is destroyed or substantially damaged before title passes. However, if the damage is minor and promptly repaired by the seller, the contract would still be valid.

If nothing is said in the contract about damage to the premises, then the general rule in Texas is that if neither possession nor title has passed and there is material destruction to the property, the seller cannot enforce the contract and the purchaser is entitled to his money back. If damage is minor and promptly repaired by the seller, the contract would still be enforceable. If either title or possession has passed and destruction occurs, the purchaser is not relieved of his duty to pay the price, nor is he entitled to a refund of money already paid.

BREACH OF CONTRACT

When one party fails to perform as required by a contract and the law does not recognize the reason for failure to be a valid excuse, there is a **breach of contract.** The wronged or innocent party has six alternatives: (1) accept partial performance, (2) rescind the contract unilaterally, (3) sue for specific performance, (4) sue for money damages, (5) accept liquidated money damages, or (6) mutually rescind the contract. Let us consider each of these.

Partial Performance

Partial performance may be acceptable to the innocent party because there may not be a great deal at stake or because the innocent party feels that the time and effort to sue would not be worth the rewards. Suppose that you contracted with a roofing repairman to fix your roof for $400. When he was finished you paid him. A week later you discover a spot that he had agreed to fix, but missed. After many futile phone calls, you accept the breach and consider the contract discharged, because it is easier to fix the spot yourself than to keep pursuing the repairman.

Unilateral Rescission

Under certain circumstances, the innocent party can **unilaterally rescind** a contract. That is, the innocent party can take the position that if the other party is not going to perform his obligations, then the innocent party will not either. An example would be a rent strike in retaliation to a landlord who fails to keep the premises habitable. Unilateral rescission should be resorted to only after consulting an attorney.

Specific Performance

The innocent party may sue in a court of equity to force the breaching party to carry out the remainder of the contract according to the precise terms, price, and conditions agreed upon. For example, you make an offer to purchase a parcel of land and the seller accepts. A written contract is prepared and signed by both of you. If you carry out all your obligations under the contract, but the seller changes his mind and refuses to deliver title to you, you may bring a lawsuit against the seller for **specific performance.** In reviewing your suit, the court will determine if the contract is valid and legal, if you have carried out your duties under the contract, and if the contract is just and reasonable. If you win your lawsuit, the court will force the seller to deliver title to you as specified in the contract.

Money Damages

If the damages to the innocent party can be reasonably expressed in terms of money, the innocent party can sue for **money damages.** For example, you rent an apartment to a tenant. As part of the rental contract you furnish the refrigerator and freezer unit. While the tenant is on vacation, the unit breaks down and $200 worth of frozen meat and other perishables spoil. Since your obligation under the contract is to provide the tenant with a working refrigerator-freezer, the tenant can sue you for $200 in money damages. He can also recover interest on the money awarded to him from the day of the loss to the day you reimburse him.

Comparison of Remedies

Note the difference between suing for money damages and suing for specific performance. When money can be used to restore one's position (such as the tenant who can buy $200 worth of fresh food), a suit for money damages is appropriate. In situations where money cannot provide an adequate remedy, and this is often the case in real estate because no two properties are exactly alike, specific performance is appropriate. Notice, too, that the mere existence of the legal rights of the wronged party is often enough to gain cooperation. In the case of the spoiled food, you would give the tenant the value of the lost food before spending time and money in court to hear a judge tell you to do the same thing. A threat of a lawsuit will often bring the desired results if the defendant knows that the law will side with the wronged party. The cases that do go to court are usually those in which the identity of the wronged party and/or the extent of the damages is not clear.

Liquidated Damages

The parties to a contract may decide in advance the amount of damages to be paid in the event either party breaches the contract. An example is an offer to purchase real estate that includes a statement to the effect that, once the seller accepts the offer, if the buyer fails to complete the purchase, the seller may keep the buyer's deposit (earnest money) as **liquidated damages.** If a broker is involved, the seller and broker usually agree to divide the damages, thus compensating the seller for damages and the broker for time and effort. Another case of liquidated damages occurs when a builder promises to finish a building by a certain date or pay the party that hired him a certain number of dollars per day until it is completed. This impresses upon the builder the need for prompt completion and compensates the property owner for losses due to the delay.

Mutual Rescission

Specific performance, money damages, and liquidated damages are all designed to aid the innocent party in the event of a breach of contract. However, as a practical matter, the time and cost of pursuing a remedy in a court of law may sometimes exceed the benefits to be derived. Moreover, there is the possibility that the judge for your case may not agree with your point of view. Therefore, even though you are the innocent party and you feel you have a legitimate case that can be pursued in the courts, you may find it more practical to agree with the other party (or parties) to simply cancel (i.e., rescind or annul) the contract. To properly protect everyone involved, the agreement to cancel must be in writing and signed by the parties to the original contract. Properly executed, mutual rescission relieves the parties to the contract from their obligations to each other.

An alternative to mutual rescission is novation. As noted earlier, this is the substitution of a new contract for an existing one. Novation provides a middle ground between suing and rescinding. Thus, the breaching party may be willing to complete the contract provided the innocent party will voluntarily make certain changes in it. If this is acceptable, the changes should be put into writing (or the contract redrafted) and then signed by the parties involved.

STATUTE OF LIMITATIONS

The **statute of limitations** limits by law the amount of time a wronged party has to seek the aid of a court in obtaining justice. The aggrieved party must start legal proceedings within a certain period of time or the courts will not help him. The amount of time varies from state to state and by the type of legal action involved. Texas recognizes a four-year limit on written contracts and a two-year limit on oral contracts.

IMPLIED OBLIGATIONS

As was pointed out at the beginning of this chapter, one can incur contractual obligations by implication as well as by oral or written contracts. Home builders and real estate agents provide two timely examples. For many years, if a homeowner discovered poor design or workmanship after he had bought a new home, it was his problem. The philosophy was **caveat emptor,** let the buyer beware *before* he buys. Today, courts of law find that in building a home and offering it for sale, the builder simultaneously implies that it is fit for living. Thus, if a builder installs a toilet in a bathroom, the implication is that it will work. In fact, Texas law now requires builders to guarantee their work for one year.

PUTTING IT TO WORK

Real estate practitioner trade organizations, such as the National Association of REALTORS® and state and local REALTOR® associations, are constantly working to elevate the status of real estate brokers and salespeople to that of competent professionals in the public's mind. And as professional status is gained, there is an implied obligation to dispense professional-quality service. Thus, an individual practitioner will not only be responsible for acting in accordance with written laws, but will also be held responsible for being competent and knowledgeable in the field. Once recognized as a professional by the public, the real estate practitioner will not be able to plead ignorance. In view of the present trend towards consumer protection, it appears that the concept of "Let the buyer beware" is being replaced with "Let the agent beware."

REVIEW QUESTIONS

Answers to these questions are found in the Answer Key section at the back of the book.

1. Which of the following would be defined as a party to a contract?
   A. Buyer.
   B. Seller.
   C. Landlord.
   D. Tenant.
   E. All of the above.

2. A contract based upon a promise exchanged for a promise is a
   A. semilateral contract.
   B. dilateral contract.
   C. binary contract.
   D. bilateral contract.

3. A contract based upon one party's promise in exchange for an act from the other party is classified as
   A. a bilateral contract.
   B. an unenforceable contract.
   C. an executed contract.
   D. a unilateral contract.

4. A unilateral contract is enforceable against
   A. either party.
   B. the offeror.
   C. the offeree.
   D. neither party.

5. A contract binding on one party but not the other is
   A. unenforceable.
   B. void.
   C. voidable.
   D. illegal.

6. A person who has not reached the age of majority is also known as
   A. a minor.
   B. an infant.
   C. Both A and B.
   D. Neither A nor B.

7. As a rule, a contract between an adult and a minor is NOT
   A. voidable by the minor.
   B. enforceable against the adult.
   C. enforceable against either party.
   D. enforceable against the minor.

8. Attorneys-in-fact derive their powers from
   A. the state bar association.
   B. a power of attorney.
   C. judicial appointment.
   D. popular election.

9. A partnership may contract in the name of
   A. its general partners.
   B. the partnership.
   C. Both A and B.
   D. Neither A nor B.

10. When an offeror makes a valid offer and communicates it to the offeree, the offeree may
    A. reject the offer.
    B. accept the offer.
    C. make a counteroffer.
    D. All of the above.

11. An offer may be terminated by
    A. withdrawal of the offer.
    B. refusal from the offeree.
    C. the lapse of time.
    D. All of the above.

12. Mutual agreement is missing when a contract is made under
    A. menace.
    B. undue influence.
    C. duress.
    D. All of the above.

13. An act intended to deceive the other party in a contract is
    A. duress.
    B. menace.
    C. mistake.
    D. fraud.

14. A contract made as a joke or in jest is precluded from becoming a valid contract because it lacks
    A. contractual intent.
    B. mutual agreement.
    C. Both A and B.
    D. Neither A nor B.

15. In Dallas, Texas, Green sold his home to Blue, who took possession prior to settlement. After moving in but before settlement took place, the house was destroyed by a tornado. Which of the following statements is true?
    A. The loss will be borne by Green.
    B. The loss will be borne by Blue.
    C. Blue is entitled to a refund of money already paid.
    D. Blue is relieved of his duty to pay the purchase price.

16. When a lessee in a rented property assigns his lease to another party, he assumes the role of
    A. assignor.
    B. assignee.
    C. sublessee.
    D. None of the above.

17. Substitution of a new contract and a new party for a previous one is known as
    A. innovation.
    B. assignment.
    C. subrogation.
    D. novation.

18. Legal action to force the breaching party to carry out the remainder of a contract is called a suit for
    A. liquidated damages.
    B. specific performance.
    C. partial performance.
    D. breach of contract.

19. The law that limits the time in which a wronged party may file legal action for obtaining justice is the statute of
    A. frauds.
    B. limitations.
    C. novation.
    D. performance.

20. In view of current trends toward consumer protection, the watchwords for real estate salespersons and brokers might well be
    A. caveat emptor.
    B. caveat agent.
    C. Both A and B.
    D. Neither A nor B.

KEY TERMS

"As is": said of property offered for sale in its present condition with no guaranty or warranty of quality provided by the seller

Counter offer: an offer made in response to an offer

Default: failure to perform a legal duty, such as failure to carry out the terms of a contract

Earnest money deposit: money that accompanies an offer to purchase as evidence of good faith

Equitable title: the right to demand that title be conveyed upon payment of the purchase price

Installment contract: a method of selling and financing property whereby the seller retains title but the buyer takes possession while making the payments

Lease-option: allows the tenant to buy the property at a preset price and terms for a given period of time

Right of first refusal: the right to match or better an offer before the property is sold to someone else

Tax deferred exchange: a sale of real property in exchange for another parcel of real estate to affect a nontaxable gain.

"Time is of the essence": a phrase that means that the time limits of a contract must be faithfully observed or the contract is voidable

Real Estate Sales Contracts

IN THIS CHAPTER *Chapter 8 focuses on real estate contracts, especially the purchase contract. Other contracts covered include the installment contract and a lease with the option to buy. The right of first refusal and tax deferred exchange are also discussed. The earnest money contract will be covered in detail.*

PURPOSE OF SALES CONTRACTS

What is the purpose of a real estate sales contract? If a buyer and a seller agree on a price, why can't the buyer hand the seller the necessary money and the seller simultaneously hand the buyer a deed? The main reason is that the buyer needs time to ascertain that the seller is, in fact, legally capable of conveying title. For protection, the buyer enters into a written and signed contract with the seller, promising that the purchase price will be paid only after title has been searched and found to be in satisfactory condition. The seller, in turn, promises to deliver a deed to the buyer when the buyer has paid his money. This exchange of promises forms the legal consideration of the contract. A contract also gives the buyer time to arrange financing and to specify how such matters as taxes, mortgage debts, leases, and property inspections will be handled.

A properly prepared contract commits each party to its terms. Once a sales contract is in writing and signed, the seller cannot suddenly change his mind and sell his property to another person. The seller is obligated to convey title to the buyer when the buyer has performed the requirements of the contract. Likewise, the buyer must carry out his promises, including paying for the property, providing the seller has done everything required by the contract.

EARNEST MONEY CONTRACTS

The **purchase contract,** or as it is commonly called in Texas, the **earnest money contract,** must basically satisfy five requirements in Texas in order for it to be upheld as an enforceable agreement:

1. It must be in writing
2. The instrument must be signed by the parties sought to be charged therewith
3. There must be evidence of an intent to convey an interest at some time in the future
4. There must be an identifiable vendor and vendee
5. The subject matter to be conveyed must be identifiable

For general information purposes, it is also recognized in this state that there is such a thing as an **oral earnest money contract.** However, this is very rare.

All real estate licensees are required to use, when appropriate, one of the standard contract forms and applicable addendums in all real estate transactions. The forms are promulgated by the Texas Real Estate Commission. Copies of two of these TREC contracts are shown in this chapter. If one of the promulgated forms is not used, the licensee is required to use either a form prepared by an attorney at law licensed in this state, or forms prepared by the owner, or forms prepared by an attorney and required by the property owner.

The Real Estate Commission revised all of the earnest money contract forms in 1997, replacing the previously promulgated forms. One of the new purchase contracts, the One to Four Family Contract (Resale) etc. (TREC 20-3) is reprinted here as Figure 8.1 and begins at **[1]** and **[2]** by identifying the buyer and seller by name. This is followed by proper legal description to be filled in at **[3]** and **[4]**, a place for the address of the property. The new contract forms expanded the personal items and has an exception for items that will not be included in the sale at **[5]**. There is now also a place to check whether the property is subject to mandatory membership in the home-owner's association at **[6]**. The cash down payment, payable at closing, is to be filled in at **[7]** with the amount of the note (excluding PMI premium) to be filled in at **[8]**. In Paragraph 3, line C of the contract there is a provision for the total sum, or total selling price, to be filled in at **[9]**.

Paragraph 4 describes the various types of financing that can be used with this form. There are five alternatives (A through E), which can be selected by checking the appropriate box and filling in the corresponding blanks.

If THIRD PARTY FINANCING (A) is involved, provisions for the first lien note are provided at **[10]**, and the second lien note, if any, provided at **[11]**. The TEXAS VETERAN'S HOUSING ASSISTANCE PROGRAM LOAN terms (B), if applicable, are shown at **[12]**.

If the property is to be SELLER FINANCED (C), three different alternatives are provided in the new Seller Financing Addendum, required to be attached. The basic terms of amount and interest rate are specified at **[13]** and **[14]**, respectively.

The ASSUMPTION provision, (D), provides for assuming the first lien note to the proper payee, shown at **[15]**, a provision for the unpaid balance at **[16]** and a place to insert total monthly payments at **[17]**. The contract then provides for the ability to assume a second lien note, showing the payee at **[18]**, the unpaid balance at **[19]**, and total monthly payments at **[20]**. Note that if there is a variation on the assumed loan, the Buyer and Seller need to agree at the time of the Contract whether to adjust the cash payable at closing or the Sales Price at **[21]**. For instance, if the Contract Price is $100,000.00 and the assumed loan balance is indicated to be $91,000.00, but the true amount to be assumed turns out at closing to be $91,200.00, there are two alternatives: (1) the parties can agree to keep the down payment the same (i.e., $9,000.00) which would, in effect, increase the Sales Price; or (2) they could change the down payment (i.e., $8,800.00) and keep the Sales Price the same. Note that the following paragraph provides for the principal balances to vary as much as $350.00. If the variation is greater, either party may terminate the contract. Guidelines for the buyer's assumption terms are outlined in **[22]**.

Under Paragraph 4.E. the Buyer is required to deliver to the Seller a credit report, verification of employment or verification of funds on deposit in financial institutions, and/or current financial statements to establish Buyer's creditworthiness within a specified number of days shown at **[23]**. Note also that the seller has seven days to disapprove buyer's credit. Otherwise, it is deemed approved.

In Paragraph 5 the EARNEST MONEY amount is set out at **[24]**, with the depository, usually a title company, shown at **[25]**. A provision for additional earnest money, if any, is shown at **[26]**. In this newest revision, if the earnest money is not deposited, it is a default by the Buyer.

FIGURE 8.1
Sample of an earnest money contract.

PROMULGATED BY THE TEXAS REAL ESTATE COMMISSION (TREC)   9-22-97

ONE TO FOUR FAMILY RESIDENTIAL CONTRACT (RESALE)
ALL CASH, ASSUMPTION, THIRD PARTY CONVENTIONAL OR SELLER FINANCING

NOTICE: Not For Use For Condominium Transactions

1. **PARTIES:** [1]_____ (Seller) agrees
to sell and convey to [2]_____(Buyer) and Buyer
agrees to buy from Seller the property described below.

2. **PROPERTY:** Lot [3]_____, Block _____, _____
Addition, City of _____, _____ County,
Texas, known as [4]_____
(Address/Zip Code), or as described on attached exhibit, together with the following items, if any: curtains
and rods, draperies and rods, valances, blinds, window shades, screens, shutters, awnings, wall-to-wall
carpeting, mirrors fixed in place, ceiling fans, attic fans, mail boxes, television antennas and satellite dish
system with controls and equipment, permanently installed heating and air-conditioning units, window air-
conditioning units, built-in security and fire detection equipment, plumbing and lighting fixtures including
chandeliers, water softener, stove, built-in kitchen equipment, garage door openers with controls, built-in
cleaning equipment, all swimming pool equipment and maintenance accessories, shrubbery, landscaping,
permanently installed outdoor cooking equipment, built-in fireplace screens, artificial fireplace logs and
all other property owned by Seller and attached to the above described real property except the following
property which is not included: _____
_____[5]_____
_____.
All property sold by this contract is called the "Property." The Property ❑ is ❑ is not subject to mandatory
membership in an owners' association. The TREC Addendum For Property Subject To Mandatory
Membership In An Owners' Association ❑ is ❑ is not attached. [6]

3. **SALES PRICE:**
   A. Cash portion of Sales Price payable by Buyer at closing . . . . $ [7]_____
   B. Sum of all financing described below
      (excluding any private mortgage insurance [PMI] premium) . . . . $ [8]_____
   C. Sales Price (Sum of A and B) . . . . $ [9]_____

4. **FINANCING:** Within _____ days after the effective date of this contract Buyer shall apply for all third party
financing or noteholder's approval of any assumption and make every reasonable effort to obtain financing
or assumption approval. Financing or assumption approval will be deemed to have been obtained when
the lender determines that Buyer has satisfied all of lender's financial requirements (those items relating
to Buyer's net worth, income and creditworthiness). If financing (including any financed PMI premium) or
assumption approval is not obtained within _____ days after the effective date hereof, this contract will
terminate and the earnest money will be refunded to Buyer. Each note to be executed hereunder must be
secured by vendor's and deed of trust liens.
The portion of Sales Price not payable in cash will be paid as follows: (Check applicable boxes below)
❑ A. THIRD PARTY FINANCING:
    ❑ (1)   This contract is subject to approval for Buyer of a third party first mortgage loan having a
           loan-to-value ratio not to exceed _____ % as established by such third party (excluding any
    [10]   financed PMI premium), due in full in _____ year(s), with interest not to exceed _____ %
           per annum for the first _____ year(s) of the loan. The loan will be ❑ with ❑ without PMI.

Initialed for identification by Buyer_____ and Seller_____   **01A**   TREC NO. 20-3

(continued)

There are provisions in the contracts for title policies and surveys. Note at **[27]**, the owner's title policy of title insurance is to be furnished in the amount of the Sales Price, and there is a choice (new to this form) as to who will pay. In most Texas counties, it is customary for the Seller to pay. In other counties it is customary for the Buyer to pay. At other times, a Buyer's employer may pay as a part of the closing costs. Note that the title company is required to deliver to Buyer a commitment for title insurance within twenty days after the title company receives a copy of the contract along with legible copies of restrictive covenants and documents evidencing exceptions (at Buyer's expense). This paragraph also authorizes the title company to deliver the commitment and documents to the Buyer's address shown below. It is very important that

FIGURE **8.1**
Continued.

One to Four Family Residential Contract Concerning_____Page Two   9-22-97
                                    (Address of Property)

☐ (2) This contract is subject to approval for Buyer of a third party second mortgage loan having a loan-to-value ratio not to exceed _____ % as established by such third party (excluding any
[11] financed PMI premium), due in full in _____ year(s), with interest not to exceed _____ % per annum for the first _____ year(s) of the loan. The loan will be ☐ with ☐ without PMI.

☐ B. TEXAS VETERANS' HOUSING ASSISTANCE PROGRAM LOAN: This contract is subject to approval for Buyer of a Texas Veterans' Housing Assistance Program Loan (the Program Loan)
[12] of $_____ for a period of at least _____ years at the interest rate established by the Texas Veterans' Land Board at the time of closing.

☐ C. SELLER FINANCING: A promissory note from Buyer to Seller of $ _[13]_____, bearing _[14]_ % interest per annum, secured by vendor's and deed of trust liens, in accordance with the terms and conditions set forth in the attached TREC Seller Financing Addendum. If an owner policy of title insurance is furnished, Buyer shall furnish Seller with a mortgagee policy of title insurance.

☐ D. ASSUMPTION:

☐ (1) Buyer shall assume the unpaid principal balance of a first lien promissory note payable to _[15]_____ which unpaid balance at closing will be $ _[16]_____ . The total current monthly payment including principal, interest and any reserve deposits is $ _[17]_____ . Buyer's initial payment will be the first payment due after closing.

☐ (2) Buyer shall assume the unpaid principal balance of a second lien promissory note payable to _[18]_____ which unpaid balance at closing will be $ _[19]_____ . The total current monthly payment including principal, interest and any reserve deposits is $ _[20]_____ . Buyer's initial payment will be the first payment due after closing.

Buyer's assumption of an existing note includes all obligations imposed by the deed of trust securing the note.

If the unpaid principal balance(s) of any assumed loan(s) as of the Closing Date varies from the
[21] loan balance(s) stated above, the ☐ cash payable at closing ☐ Sales Price will be adjusted by the amount of any variance; provided, if the total principal balance of all assumed loans varies in an amount greater than $350.00 at closing, either party may terminate this contract and the earnest money will be refunded to Buyer unless the other party elects to eliminate the excess in the variance by an appropriate adjustment at closing. If the noteholder requires (a) payment of an assumption fee in excess of $ _____ in D(1) above or $ _____ in D(2) above and Seller
[22] declines to pay such excess, or (b) an increase in the interest rate to more than _____ % in D(1) above, or _____ % in D(2) above, or (c) any other modification of the loan documents, Buyer may terminate this contract and the earnest money will be refunded to Buyer. A vendor's lien and deed of trust to secure assumption will be required which shall automatically be released on execution and delivery of a release by noteholder. If Seller is released from liability on any assumed note, the vendor's lien and deed of trust to secure assumption will not be required.

NOTICE TO BUYER: The monthly payments, interest rates or other terms of some loans may be adjusted by the lender at or after closing. If you are concerned about the possibility of future adjustments, do not sign the contract without examining the notes and deeds of trust.

NOTICE TO SELLER: Your liability to pay the note assumed by Buyer will continue unless you obtain a release of liability from the lender. If you are concerned about future liability, you should use the TREC Release of Liability Addendum.

☐ E. CREDIT APPROVAL ON ASSUMPTION OR SELLER FINANCING: Within _[23]_ days after the effective date of this contract, Buyer shall deliver to Seller ☐ credit report ☐ verification of employment, including salary ☐ verification of funds on deposit in financial institutions ☐ current financial statement to establish Buyer's creditworthiness for assumption approval or seller financing and ☐ _____
_____

If Buyer's documentation is not delivered within the specified time, Seller may terminate this contract by notice to Buyer within 7 days after expiration of the time for delivery, and the earnest money will

Initialed for identification by Buyer_____and Seller_____   0 1A   TREC NO. 20-3

(continued)

the Buyer's address should be inserted in the contract so that the title company can comply with this provision of the contract. If the title commitment and related documents are not delivered timely, there is an automatic extension for fifteen (15) days.

Surveys have always been a concern at closings. The contract reserves the right of the Buyer to object to the survey provided to a third party at **[28],** or to object to a survey provided directly to the Buyer at **[29].** Note that the specifications to the survey are extensive.

If the Buyer has a specific concern about his ability to use the property for a specific purpose, he has the right to make that a contingency by inserting that contingency at **[30].** For instance, the Buyer may want to insert "launch pad site," so that if the property could not be used for that purpose, the Buyer has no obligation to perform.

One to Four Family Residential Contract Concerning_____Page Three   9-22-97
                                                            (Address of Property)

be paid to Seller. If this contract is not so terminated, Seller will be deemed to have accepted Buyer's credit. If the documentation is timely delivered, and Seller determines in Seller's sole discretion that Buyer's credit is unacceptable, Seller may terminate this contract by notice to Buyer within 7 days after expiration of the time for delivery and the earnest money will be refunded to Buyer. If Seller does not so terminate this contract, Seller will be deemed to have accepted Buyer's credit. Buyer hereby authorizes any credit reporting agency to furnish to Seller at Buyer's sole expense copies of Buyer's credit reports.

5. **EARNEST MONEY:** Buyer shall deposit $__[24]_____ as earnest money with __[25]_____
_____ at _____
(Address), as escrow agent, upon execution of this contract by both parties. Additional earnest money of $_[26]_____ must be deposited by Buyer with escrow agent on or before _____, 19____. If Buyer fails to deposit the earnest money as required by this contract, Buyer will be in default.

6. **TITLE POLICY AND SURVEY:**   **[27]**
 ❑ A. TITLE POLICY: Seller shall furnish to Buyer at ❑ Seller's ❑ Buyer's expense an owner policy of title insurance (the Title Policy) issued by _____(the Title Company) in the amount of the Sales Price, dated at or after closing, insuring Buyer against loss under the provisions of the Title Policy, subject to the promulgated exclusions (including existing building and zoning ordinances) and the following exceptions:
   (1) Restrictive covenants common to the platted subdivision in which the Property is located.
   (2) The standard printed exception for standby fees, taxes and assessments.
   (3) Liens created as part of the financing described in Paragraph 4.
   (4) Utility easements created by the dedication deed or plat of the subdivision in which the Property is located.
   (5) Reservations or exceptions otherwise permitted by this contract or as may be approved by Buyer in writing.
   (6) The standard printed exception as to discrepancies, conflicts, shortages in area or boundary lines, encroachments or protrusions, or overlapping improvements.
   (7) The standard printed exception as to marital rights.
   (8) The standard printed exception as to waters, tidelands, beaches, streams, and related matters.
 Within 20 days after the Title Company receives a copy of this contract, Seller shall furnish to Buyer a commitment for title insurance (the Commitment) and, at Buyer's expense, legible copies of restrictive covenants and documents evidencing exceptions in the Commitment other than the standard printed exceptions. Seller authorizes the Title Company to mail or hand deliver the Commitment and related documents to Buyer at Buyer's address shown below. If the Commitment is not delivered to Buyer within the specified time, the time for delivery will be automatically extended up to 15 days. Buyer will have 7 days after the receipt of the Commitment to object in writing to matters disclosed in the Commitment.
 ❑ B. SURVEY: (Check one box only)
[28] ❑ (1) Within _____ days after Buyer's receipt of a survey furnished to a third-party lender at ❑ Seller's ❑ Buyer's expense, Buyer may object in writing to any matter shown on the survey which constitutes a defect or encumbrance to title.
[29] ❑ (2) Within _____ days after the effective date of this contract, Buyer may object in writing to any matter which constitutes a defect or encumbrance to title shown on a survey obtained by Buyer at Buyer's expense.
 The survey must be made by a Registered Professional Land Surveyor acceptable to the Title Company and any lender. Utility easements created by the dedication deed and plat of the subdivision in which the Property is located will not be a basis for objection.
 Buyer may object to existing building and zoning ordinances, items 6A(1) through (8) above and matters shown on the survey if Buyer determines that any such ordinance, items or matters prohibits the following use or activity: _____**[30]**_____
_____

Initialed for identification by Buyer_____ and Seller_____   01A   TREC NO. 20-3

(continued)

The final provisions of Paragraph 6 advises the Buyer (as required by the Real Estate License Act) to have an attorney of his choice examine the title or to obtain a title policy. There are also warnings included concerning notices as to utility or other specially created taxing districts and advice to the Buyer concerning toxic waste or other environmental hazards, and an agreement that the Seller may continue to market the property.

In general terms, Paragraph 7 gives the Buyer the right to inspect the property and, under certain circumstances, refuse to purchase the property after the inspection. Note that Section 7.A gives the Buyer the right to inspect the property at all reasonable time and that there is virtually no limit on how many inspections the Buyer can perform. Note the language at **[31].**

FIGURE 8.1
Continued.

One to Four Family Residential Contract Concerning_____Page Four   9-22-97
(Address of Property)

Buyer's failure to object under Paragraph 6A or 6B within the time allowed will constitute a waiver of Buyer's right to object; except that the requirements in Schedule C of the Commitment will not be deemed to have been waived. Seller shall cure the timely objections of Buyer or any third party lender within 15 days from the date Seller receives the objections and the Closing Date will be extended as necessary. If objections are not cured by the extended Closing Date, this contract will terminate and the earnest money will be refunded to Buyer unless Buyer elects to waive the objections.

NOTICE TO SELLER AND BUYER:

(1) Broker advises Buyer to have an abstract of title covering the Property examined by an attorney of Buyer's selection, or Buyer should be furnished with or obtain a Title Policy. If a Title Policy is furnished, the Commitment should be promptly reviewed by an attorney of Buyer's choice due to the time limitations on Buyer's right to object.

(2) If the Property is situated in a utility or other statutorily created district providing water, sewer, drainage, or flood control facilities and services, Chapter 49 of the Texas Water Code requires Seller to deliver and Buyer to sign the statutory notice relating to the tax rate, bonded indebtedness, or standby fee of the district prior to final execution of this contract.

(3) If the Property abuts the tidally influenced waters of the state, Section 33.135, Texas Natural Resources Code, requires a notice regarding coastal area property to be included in the contract. An addendum either promulgated by TREC or required by the parties should be used.

(4) Buyer is advised that the presence of wetlands, toxic substances, including asbestos and wastes or other environmental hazards or the presence of a threatened or endangered species or its habitat may affect Buyer's intended use of the Property. If Buyer is concerned about these matters, an addendum either promulgated by TREC or required by the parties should be used.

(5) Unless expressly prohibited in writing by the parties, Seller may continue to show the Property for sale and to receive, negotiate and accept back up offers.

(6) Any residential service contract that is purchased in connection with this transaction should be reviewed for the scope of coverage, exclusions and limitations. **The purchase of a residential service contract is optional. Similar coverage may be purchased from various companies authorized to do business in Texas.**

7. PROPERTY CONDITION:

A. INSPECTIONS, ACCESS AND UTILITIES: Buyer may have the Property inspected by an inspector selected by Buyer, licensed by TREC or otherwise permitted by law to make such inspections. Seller **[31]** shall permit access to the Property at reasonable times for inspection, repairs and treatment and for reinspection after repairs and treatment have been completed. Seller shall pay for turning on utilities for inspection and reinspection.

B. SELLER'S DISCLOSURE NOTICE PURSUANT TO SECTION 5.008, TEXAS PROPERTY CODE (Notice) (check one box only):
   ❑ (1) Buyer has received the Notice.
   ❑ (2) Buyer has not received the Notice. Within _____ days after the effective date of this contract, Seller shall deliver the Notice to Buyer. If Buyer does not receive the Notice, Buyer may terminate this contract at any time prior to the closing. If Seller delivers the Notice, Buyer may terminate this contract for any reason within 7 days after Buyer receives the Notice or prior to the closing, whichever first occurs.
   ❑ (3) The Texas Property Code does not require this Seller to furnish the Notice.

C. SELLER'S DISCLOSURE OF LEAD-BASED PAINT AND LEAD-BASED PAINT HAZARDS is required by Federal law for a residential dwelling constructed prior to 1978. An addendum providing such disclosure ❑ is ❑ is not attached.

D. ACCEPTANCE OF PROPERTY CONDITION: (check one box only):
   ❑ (1) In addition to any earnest money deposited with escrow agent, Buyer has paid Seller **[32]** $_____ (the "Option Fee") for the unrestricted right to terminate this contract by giving notice of termination to Seller within _____ days after the effective date of this contract. If Buyer gives notice of termination within the time specified, the Option Fee will not be refunded, however, any earnest money will be refunded to Buyer. If Buyer does not give notice of

Initialed for identification by Buyer_____ and Seller_____   **01A**   TREC NO. 20-3

(continued)

The Buyer's choices become more critical when he checks box 7.D.1 or 7.D.2, shown at **[32]**. Paragraph 7.D.1 basically converts the earnest money contract into an option contract (discussed later in this chapter). In effect, the Buyer pays the Seller for the privilege of taking the property off the market for a specified number of days, but the Buyer is not obligated to perform under the contract if he gives the specified notice of termination. It is important to note that it is the Buyer who must give that notice of termination.

If the Buyer chooses (Paragraph 7.D.2), the Buyer is basically taking the property "as is" except for certain specified repairs. Paragraph 7.D.2 may give the Buyer a much better bartering position because it effectively waives the Buyer's right to repairs (waives the repair contingency) for which the Buyer may be able to negotiate a lower

FIGURE 8.1
Continued.

One to Four Family Residential Contract Concerning_____Page Five 9-22-97
(Address of Property)

termination within the time specified, Buyer will be deemed to have accepted the Property in its current condition and the Option Fee ❑ will ❑ will not be credited to the Sales Price at closing.

❑ (2) Buyer accepts the Property in its present condition; provided Seller, at Seller's expense, shall complete the following repairs and treatment: _____

_____.

E. LENDER REQUIRED REPAIRS AND TREATMENTS (REPAIRS): Unless otherwise agreed in writing, neither party is obligated to pay for lender required repairs or treatments for wood destroying insects. If the cost of lender required repairs exceeds 5% of the Sales Price, Buyer may terminate this contract.

F. COMPLETION OF REPAIRS AND TREATMENT. Unless otherwise agreed by the parties in writing, Seller shall complete all agreed repairs and treatment prior to the Closing Date. Repairs and treatments must be performed by persons who regularly provide such repairs or treatments. At Buyer's election, any transferable warranties received by Seller with respect to the repairs will be transferred to Buyer at Buyer's expense. If Seller fails to complete any agreed repairs and treatment prior to the Closing Date, Buyer may do so and the Closing Date will be extended up to 15 days, if necessary, to complete repairs and treatment or treatments for wood destroying insects.

8. **BROKERS' FEES:** All obligations of the parties for payment of brokers' fees are contained in separate written agreements.

9. **CLOSING:** The closing of the sale will be on or before _[33]_____, 19___, or within 7 days after objections to matters disclosed in the Commitment or by the survey have been cured, whichever date is later (the Closing Date). *If financing or assumption approval has been obtained pursuant to Paragraph 4,* the Closing Date will be extended up to 15 days if necessary to comply with lender's closing requirements (for example, appraisal, survey, insurance policies, lender-required repairs, closing documents). If either party fails to close this sale by the Closing Date, the non-defaulting party will be entitled to exercise the remedies contained in Paragraph 15. At closing Seller shall furnish tax statements or certificates showing no delinquent taxes and a general warranty deed conveying good and indefeasible title showing no additional exceptions to those permitted in Paragraph 6.

10. **POSSESSION:** Seller shall deliver possession of the Property to Buyer on _[34]_____ in its present or required repaired condition, ordinary wear and tear excepted. Any possession by Buyer prior to closing or by Seller after closing which is not authorized by a temporary lease form promulgated by TREC or required by the parties will establish a tenancy at sufferance relationship between the parties. *Consult your insurance agent prior to change of ownership or possession as insurance coverage may be limited or terminated. The absence of a written lease or appropriate insurance coverage may expose the parties to economic loss.*

11. **SPECIAL PROVISIONS:** (Insert only factual statements and business details applicable to this sale. TREC rules prohibit licensees from adding factual statements or business details for which a contract addendum, lease or other form has been promulgated by TREC for mandatory use.)

Initialed for identification by Buyer_____ and Seller_____   **01A**   TREC NO. 20-3

(continued)

sales price. You may note that the lender-required repairs are also specified under Paragraph 7. If the lender requires repairs, and neither party is obligated to make those repairs, the Buyer will not be able to obtain his financing and therefore will exercise his contingency under Paragraph 4 of the contract.

There is now a provision requiring the seller to complete the repairs prior to the Closing Date. If they are not done, the buyer has a right to deduct the costs of repairs up to the maximum agreed amount from the Sales Proceeds.

Paragraph 8, although titled Brokers' Fees, provides only that the listing broker is to be identified. The amount of his compensation is specified in the listing agreement and is not a part of this contract between the buyer and seller. A new provision in the contract provides for the brokers to designate who they represent. Under the Texas

FIGURE 8.1
Continued.

One to Four Family Residential Contract Concerning_____ Page Six   9-22-97
(Address of Property)

12. SETTLEMENT AND OTHER EXPENSES:

A. The following expenses must be paid at or prior to closing:

(1) Appraisal fees will be paid by _[35]_____.

(2) The total of loan discount fees (including any Texas Veterans' Housing Assistance Program Participation Fee) may not exceed _____% of the loan of which Seller shall pay _____ and Buyer shall pay the remainder. The total of any buydown fees may not exceed _____ which will be paid by _____.

[36] (3) Seller's Expenses: Releases of existing liens, including prepayment penalties and recording fees; release of Seller's loan liability; tax statements or certificates; preparation of deed; one-half of escrow fee; and other expenses stipulated to be paid by Seller under other provisions of this contract.

(4) Buyer's Expenses: Loan application, origination and commitment fees; loan assumption costs; preparation and recording of deed of trust to secure assumption; lender required expenses incident to new loans, including PMI premium, preparation of loan documents, loan related inspection fee, recording fees, tax service and research fees, warehouse or underwriting fees, copies of restrictions and easements, amortization schedule, premiums for mortgagee title policies and endorsements required by lender, credit reports, photos; required premiums for flood and hazard insurance; required reserve deposit for insurance premiums and ad valorem taxes; interest on all monthly installment notes from date of disbursements to one month prior to dates of first monthly payments; customary Program Loan costs for Buyer; one-half of escrow fee; and other expenses stipulated to be paid by Buyer under other provisions of this contract.

B. If any expense exceeds an amount expressly stated in this contract for such expense to be paid by a party, that party may terminate this contract unless the other party agrees to pay such excess. In no event will Buyer pay charges and fees expressly prohibited by the Texas Veterans' Housing Assistance Program or other governmental loan program regulations.

13. PRORATIONS: Taxes for the current year, interest, maintenance fees, assessments, dues and rents will be prorated through the Closing Date. If taxes for the current year vary from the amount prorated at closing, the parties shall adjust the prorations when tax statements for the current year are available. *If a loan is assumed* and the lender maintains an escrow account, the escrow account must be transferred to Buyer without any deficiency. Buyer shall reimburse Seller for the amount in the transferred account. Buyer shall pay the premium for a new insurance policy. If taxes are not paid at or prior to closing, Buyer will be obligated to pay taxes for the current year.

14. CASUALTY LOSS: If any part of the Property is damaged or destroyed by fire or other casualty loss after the effective date of the contract, Seller shall restore the Property to its previous condition as soon as reasonably possible, but in any event by the Closing Date. If Seller fails to do so due to factors beyond Seller's control, Buyer may either (a) terminate this contract and the earnest money will be refunded to Buyer (b) extend the time for performance up to 15 days and the Closing Date will be extended as necessary or (c) accept the Property in its damaged condition and accept an assignment of insurance proceeds. Seller's obligations under this paragraph are independent of any obligations of Seller under Paragraph 7.

15. DEFAULT: If Buyer fails to comply with this contract, Buyer will be in default, and Seller may either (a) enforce specific performance, seek such other relief as may be provided by law, or both, or (b) terminate this contract and receive the earnest money as liquidated damages, thereby releasing both parties from this contract. If, due to factors beyond Seller's control, Seller fails within the time allowed to make any non-casualty repairs or deliver the Commitment, Buyer may either (a) extend the time for performance up to 15 days and the Closing Date will be extended as necessary or (b) terminate this contract as the sole remedy and receive the earnest money. If Seller fails to comply with this contract for any other reason, Seller will be in default and Buyer may either (a) enforce specific performance, seek such other relief as may be provided by law, or both, or (b) terminate this contract and receive the earnest money, thereby releasing both parties from this contract.

Initialed for identification by Buyer_____ and Seller_____   **01A**   TREC NO. 20-3

(continued)

Real Estate Commission Rules and Regulations, this should have been done prior to signing the contract, and the disclosure in the contract should be nothing more than a confirmation of previous disclosed agency relationships.

Provisions and deadlines for closing are set forth at **[33].** Possession date for the buyer is stated at **[34].** This is generally "at closing" or perhaps "upon funding."

A Special Provisions section is provided at Paragraph 11 of the earnest money contract. This particular earnest money contract has very little need for special provisions, except for specifying certain exceptions to the fixtures that the purchaser may expect to be conveyed with the house, because of the all-encompassing type of language set out in Paragraph 2 of the contract. Additional items that are not included in Paragraph 2 may be inserted in Paragraph 11, but the cautious real estate

One to Four Family Residential Contract Concerning_____Page Seven   9-22-97
(Address of Property)

16. **DISPUTE RESOLUTION:** It is the policy of the State of Texas to encourage the peaceable resolution of disputes through alternative dispute resolution procedures. The parties are encouraged to use an addendum approved by TREC to submit to mediation disputes which cannot be resolved in good faith through informal discussion.

17. **ATTORNEY'S FEES:** The prevailing party in any legal proceeding brought under or with respect to the transaction described in this contract is entitled to recover from the non-prevailing party all costs of such proceeding and reasonable attorney's fees.

18. **ESCROW:** The earnest money is deposited with escrow agent with the understanding that escrow agent is not (a) a party to this contract and does not have any liability for the performance or nonperformance of any party to this contract, (b) liable for interest on the earnest money and (c) liable for any loss of earnest money caused by the failure of any financial institution in which the earnest money has been deposited unless the financial institution is acting as escrow agent. At closing, the earnest money must be applied first to any cash down payment, then to Buyer's closing costs and any excess refunded to Buyer. If both parties make written demand for the earnest money, escrow agent may require payment of unpaid expenses incurred on behalf of the parties and a written release of liability of escrow agent from all parties. If one party makes written demand for the earnest money, escrow agent shall give notice of the demand by providing to the other party a copy of the demand. If escrow agent does not receive written objection to the demand from the other party within 30 days after notice to the other party, escrow agent may disburse the earnest money to the party making demand reduced by the amount of unpaid expenses incurred on behalf of the party receiving the earnest money and escrow agent may pay the same to the creditors. If escrow agent complies with the provisions of this paragraph, each party hereby releases escrow agent from all adverse claims related to the disbursal of the earnest money. Escrow agent's notice to the other party will be effective when deposited in the U. S. Mail, postage prepaid, certified mail, return receipt requested, addressed to the other party at such party's address shown below. Notice of objection to the demand will be deemed effective upon receipt by escrow agent.

19. **REPRESENTATIONS:** Seller represents that as of the Closing Date (a) there will be no liens, assessments, or security interests against the Property which will not be satisfied out of the sales proceeds unless securing payment of any loans assumed by Buyer and (b) assumed loans will not be in default. If any representation in this contract is untrue on the Closing Date, this contract may be terminated by Buyer and the earnest money will be refunded to Buyer. All representations contained in this contract will survive closing.

20. **FEDERAL TAX REQUIREMENT:** If Seller is a "foreign person," as defined by applicable law, or if Seller fails to deliver an affidavit that Seller is not a "foreign person," then Buyer shall withhold from the sales proceeds an amount sufficient to comply with applicable tax law and deliver the same to the Internal Revenue Service together with appropriate tax forms. IRS regulations require filing written reports if cash in excess of specified amounts is received in the transaction.

21. **AGREEMENT OF PARTIES:** This contract contains the entire agreement of the parties and cannot be changed except by their written agreement. Addenda which are a part of this contract are (list): _____
_____
_____
_____
_____.

22. **CONSULT YOUR ATTORNEY:** Real estate licensees cannot give legal advice. This contract is intended to be legally binding. READ IT CAREFULLY. If you do not understand the effect of this contract, consult your attorney BEFORE signing.

Buyer's   Seller's
Attorney is: **[37]**_____   Attorney is: **[38]**_____

Initialed for identification by Buyer_____ and Seller_____   **01A**   TREC NO. 20-3

(continued)

licensee should pay close attention to the fact that only business details can be inserted and not anything which otherwise affects the legal obligations of either party. Note that if there is an applicable TREC Addendum, it *must* be utilized by the licensee.

Paragraph 12 deals with various expenses the buyer and seller will be expected to pay at or prior to closing. Responsibility for loan appraisal fees is shown at **[35]**. (These are generally paid by the party obtaining the loan.) Seller's expenses, which may include the dollar amount for points or commitment fees or discount fees to enable the purchaser to secure his loan, are set out at **[36]**, along with certain other expenses that are incidental to selling. Note that if the costs are *less* than expected, the seller gets the benefit of the reduced cost.

FIGURE 8.1
Continued.

One to Four Family Residential Contract Concerning_____ Page Eight   9-22-97
(Address of Property)

23. NOTICES: All notices from one party to the other must be in writing and are effective when mailed to, hand-delivered at, or transmitted by facsimile machine as follows:

To Buyer at: **To Seller at:**

Telephone:(   )_____   Telephone:(   )_____

Facsimile:(   )_____   Facsimile:(   )_____

EXECUTED the _____ day of _____, 19___ (THE EFFECTIVE DATE). (BROKER: FILL IN THE DATE OF FINAL ACCEPTANCE.)

_____   _____
Buyer   Seller

_____   _____
Buyer   Seller

> The form of this contract has been approved by the Texas Real Estate Commission. Such approval relates to this contract form only. No representation is made as to the legal validity or adequacy of any provision in any specific transaction. It is not suitable for complex transactions. Extensive riders or additions are not to be used. Texas Real Estate Commission, P.O. Box 12188, Austin, TX 78711-2188, 1-800-250-8732 or (512) 459-6544 (http://www.trec.state.tx.us) TREC NO. 20-3. This form replaces TREC NO. 20-2.

BROKER INFORMATION AND RATIFICATION OF FEE

Listing Broker has agreed to pay Other Broker _____ of the total sales price when Listing Broker's fee is received. Escrow Agent is authorized and directed to pay Other Broker from Listing Broker's fee at closing.

Other Broker   License No.   Listing Broker   License No.
represents ☐ Seller as Listing Broker's subagent   represents ☐ Seller and Buyer as an intermediary
            ☐ Buyer only as Buyer's agent   ☐ Seller only as Seller's agent

                                                      Listing Associate   Telephone

Associate   Telephone   Selling Associate   Telephone

Broker Address   Broker Address

                                                      Telephone   Facsimile
Telephone   Facsimile

RECEIPT

Receipt of ☐ Contract and ☐ $_____ Earnest Money in the form of_____ is acknowledged.

Escrow Agent: _____   Date: _____, 19___

By:_____

_____   Telephone: (_____)_____
Address

_____   Facsimile: (_____)_____
City   State   Zip Code

                                          01A   TREC NO. 20-3

Paragraphs 13 through 23 are very specific and explanatory provisions that are generally standard to all earnest money contracts. Items generally prorated are taxes, insurance, and rents. Paragraph 14 contains provisions for loss (damage or destruction) of the real estate, penalties in the event of default of buyer or seller, and explanations as to escrow and representations. Paragraph 16 allows for mediation as an alternative method of dispute resolution. Paragraph 21 sets out addenda to be attached, if any. Note that there is an addendum approved by the Texas Real Estate Commission to submit to mediation dispute. Paragraph 22 is the provision that suggests to the purchaser and seller that if they need some legal advice, they should consult an attorney. Those names are inserted at **[37]** and **[38]**. The "Notices" paragraph provides for the use of facsimile machines for notices from one party to the other party.

The brokers' commission agreement is *after* the contractual agreement between the seller and buyer. It is a separate agreement, *negotiated* between the brokers.

Acceptance

For an offer to become binding, the seller must accept everything in it. The rejection of even the smallest portion of the offer is a rejection of the entire offer. If the seller wishes to reject the offer but keep negotiations alive, he can make a counteroffer. This is a written offer to sell to the buyer at a new price and with terms that are closer to the buyer's offer than the seller's original asking price and terms. The agent prepares the counteroffer by either filling out a fresh purchase contract identical in all ways to the buyer's offer except for these changes, or by writing on the back of the offer (or on another sheet of paper) that the seller offers to sell at the terms the buyer had offered except for the stated changes. The counteroffer is then dated and signed by the seller. A time limit may be given to the buyer to accept. The seller keeps a copy, and the counteroffer is delivered to the buyer for a decision. If the counteroffer is acceptable to the buyer, she signs and dates it, and the contract is complete. Another commonly used, but less desirable, practice is to take the buyer's offer, cross out each item unacceptable to the seller, and write above or below it what the seller will accept. Each change is then initialed by the seller and buyer. If the offer is rejected, it is good practice to have the seller write the word *rejected* on the offer followed by his signature.

Federal Clauses

In two instances, the government requires that specific clauses be included in real estate sales contracts. First, an **amendatory language** clause must be included whenever a sales contract is signed by a purchaser prior to the receipt of an FHA Appraised Value or a VA Certificate of Reasonable Value on the property. The purpose is to ensure that the purchaser may terminate the contract without loss when it appears that the agreed purchase price may be significantly above appraised value. The specific clauses, which must be used verbatim, are contained in the TREC promulgated form for FHA-insured or VA-guaranteed financing (TREC No. 21-3). Second, the Federal Trade Commission (FTC) requires that builders and sellers of new houses must include **insulation disclosures** in all earnest money contracts. Disclosures, which may be based upon manufacturer claims, must cite the type, thickness, and R-value of the insulation installed in the home. These disclosures are contained in the TREC promulgated New Home Insulation Addendum (TREC No. 13-0).

Negotiation

One of the most important principles of real estate contracts in general is that everything is negotiable and nearly everything has a price. In preparing or analyzing any contract, consider what the advantages and disadvantages of each condition are to each party to the contract. A solid contract results when the buyer and seller each feel that they have gained more than they have given up. The prime example is the sales price of the property itself. The seller prefers the money over the property, while the buyer prefers the property over the money. Each small negotiable item in the purchase contract has its price too. For example, the seller may agree to include the refrigerator for $200 more. Equally important in negotiating is the relative bargaining power of the buyer and seller. If the seller is confident he will have plenty of buyers at his asking price, he can elect to refuse offers for less money and reject those with numerous conditions or insufficient earnest money. However, if the owner is anxious to sell and has received only one offer in several months, he may be quite willing to accept a lower price and numerous conditions.

Required Disclosures

Rollback Taxes

New Texas laws require other disclosures. Contracts for the sale of vacant land must include a statutory notice about the potential liability for **rollback taxes** if the property has special tax classification, such as agricultural or open space use, discussed in Chapter 13. If the seller fails to include the required notice, the seller is liable to the purchaser for any rollback tax liability.

Pipelines

A seller of unimproved land to be used for residential property must also disclose in writing to the purchaser, on or before the effective date of the contract, the **location of any transportation pipeline** on the property, including a pipeline for the transport of natural gas, natural gas liquids, synthetic gas, liquefied petroleum gas, petroleum, or petroleum product, or hazardous substances. If the seller does not know whether pipelines exist under the property, that fact must be stated. If a contract is entered into without the notice, the purchaser may terminate it for any reason not later than the seventh day after the effective date of the contract. This notice doesn't need to be given if the seller is obligated, under the terms of the earnest money contract, to delivery of title commitment to the purchaser, and if the purchaser has a right to terminate the contract if objections to title are not cured. TREC forms already provide for this approval, but the exception does not apply if the seller is going to supply an abstract of title.

Lead-Based Paint

Federal law now requires that before a buyer or tenant becomes obligated under a contract for sale or lease, the sellers and landlords must disclose known lead-based paint and lead-based paint hazards and provide available reports to buyers or tenants. The sellers and landlords must give a buyer a pamphlet "Protect Your Family From Lead In Your Home." Unless otherwise agreed to, homebuyers are entitled to a ten-day period to conduct a lead-based paint inspection or risk assessment at their own expense. Sales contracts and leasing arrangements must include certain language to ensure that disclosure notification actually takes place. The TREC approved lead-based paint disclosure form is shown as Figure 8.2. There is a special burden on real estate agents, who must ensure that sellers and landlords are aware of their obligations and that they disclose the proper information to buyers and tenants. The agent must comply with the law if the seller or landlord fail to do so.

Water Districts

Texas law also has special requirements for anyone who proposes to sell or convey real property located in the municipal utility district or other drainage or flood control district that utilizes bonds to finance its improvements. The statute requires that any person who proposes to sell or convey real property located in such a district must first give a notice to the purchaser in a separate written document executed and acknowledged by the seller that the property is located in a water, sewer, drainage, and flood control or protection facilities district. The notice must be given to the prospective purchaser prior to the execution of a binding contract of sale and purchase, either separately or as a separate portion or paragraph of a purchase contract. If the contract for purchase and sale is entered into without the seller providing the notice required, the purchaser shall be entitled to terminate the contract. The statute specifies the notice to be given and it must

FIGURE 8.2
Lead-based paint
disclosure form.

APPROVED BY THE
TEXAS REAL ESTATE COMMISSION
02-10-97

**ADDENDUM FOR SELLER'S DISCLOSURE OF INFORMATION
ON LEAD-BASED PAINT AND LEAD-BASED PAINT HAZARDS
AS REQUIRED BY FEDERAL LAW**

CONCERNING THE PROPERTY AT _____
(Street Address and City)

A. **LEAD WARNING STATEMENT:** "Every purchaser of any interest in residential real property on which a residential dwelling was built prior to 1978 is notified that such property may present exposure to lead from lead-based paint that may place young children at risk of developing lead poisoning. Lead poisoning in young children may produce permanent neurological damage, including learning disabilities, reduced intelligence quotient, behavioral problems, and impaired memory. Lead poisoning also poses a particular risk to pregnant women. The seller of any interest in residential real property is required to provide the buyer with any information on lead-based paint hazards from risk assessments or inspections in the seller's possession and notify the buyer of any known lead-based paint hazards. A risk assessment or inspection for possible lead-paint hazards is recommended prior to purchase."

B. **SELLER'S DISCLOSURE:**
   1. PRESENCE OF LEAD-BASED PAINT AND/OR LEAD-BASED PAINT HAZARDS (check one box only):

   ❑ (a) Known lead-based paint and/or lead-based paint hazards are present in the Property (explain): _____
   _____

   ❑ (b) Seller has no actual knowledge of lead-based paint and/or lead-based paint hazards in the Property.
   2. RECORDS AND REPORTS AVAILABLE TO SELLER (check one box only):

   ❑ (a) Seller has provided the purchaser with all available records and reports pertaining to lead-based paint and/or lead-based paint hazards in the Property (list documents): _____
   _____

   ❑ (b) Seller has no reports or records pertaining to lead-based paint and/or lead-based paint hazards in the Property.

C. **BUYER'S RIGHTS** (check one box only):
   ❑ 1. Buyer waives the opportunity to conduct a risk assessment or inspection of the Property for the presence of lead-based paint or lead-based paint hazards.

   ❑ 2. Within ten days after the effective date of this contract, Buyer may have the Property inspected for the presence of lead-based paint and/or lead-based paint hazards. If lead-based paint or lead-based paint hazards are present, Buyer may terminate this contract by giving Seller written notice within 14 days after the effective date of this contract.

D. **BUYER'S ACKNOWLEDGMENT** (check applicable boxes):
   ❑ 1. Buyer has received copies of all information listed above.

   ❑ 2. Buyer has received the pamphlet *Protect Your Family from Lead in Your Home.*

E. **BROKERS' ACKNOWLEDGMENT:** Brokers have informed Seller of Seller's obligations under 42 U.S.C. 4852d to: (a) provide Buyer with the federally approved pamphlet on lead poisoning prevention; (b) complete this addendum; (c) disclose any known lead-based paint and/or lead-based paint hazards in the Property; (d) deliver all records and reports to Buyer pertaining to lead-based paint and/or lead-based paint hazards in the Property; (e) provide Buyer a period of up to 10 days to have the Property inspected; and (f) retain a completed copy of this addendum for at least 3 years following the sale. Brokers are aware of their responsibility to ensure compliance.

F. **CERTIFICATION OF ACCURACY:** The following persons have reviewed the information above and certify, to the best of their knowledge, that the information they have provided is true and accurate.

Seller	Date	Buyer	Date

Seller	Date	Buyer	Date

Listing Broker	Date	Other Broker	Date

The form of this addendum has been approved for voluntary use by the Texas Real Estate Commission for use only with similarly approved or promulgated forms of contracts. No representation is made as to the legal validity or adequacy of any provision in any specific transactions. Texas Real Estate Commission, P.O. Box 12188, Austin, TX 78711-2188, 1-800-250-8732 or (512) 459-6544.

000

be executed, acknowledged, and recorded in the deed records of the county in which the property is located at the closing of the purchase and sale. This statutory provision must also be provided for any executory contract of purchase and sale (i.e., installment land contract) having a performance period of more than six months.

Licensee Benefits

The use of the foregoing contracts will benefit the licensee in his normal residential real estate transactions. Most of the technical legal questions concerning title, default, escrow, inspections, and closing guarantees, as well as representations and warranties of buyer and seller, are contained as a matter of form in these forms. All the licensee has to do is fill in the blanks. Most clients who are parties to a residential earnest money contract find it easy to understand a fill-in-the-blank type form.

Practicing Law

It should be well understood by all real estate brokers and salespersons that they are not permitted to practice law. This is specifically prohibited under Section 16 of the Texas Real Estate Licensing Act, but the nature of the real estate business has led to some confusion and dissension between lawyers and real estate licensees. For instance, it is common practice for real estate practitioners to fill in the blanks of an earnest money contract, yet not fill in the blanks of a deed. To clarify this matter, an Attorney General's opinion issued in 1972 explained that real estate agents, under law, do not have the right to fill in the blanks of an earnest money contract. However, the opinion went on to say that if the Texas Real Estate Commission wished to require the use of a standard form for certain types of transactions, that such forms could be sanctioned by the Texas Real Estate Commission for use by real estate brokers and salespersons. This enables brokers and salespersons to fill in the blanks of earnest money contracts without violating Section 16 of the Texas Real Estate Licensing Act.

INSTALLMENT CONTRACTS

An **installment contract,** also known as a **land contract, conditional sales contract, contract for deed,** or **agreement of sale** combines features from a sales contract, deed, and a mortgage. It is used to sell property in situations where the seller does not wish to convey title until all, or at least a substantial portion, of the purchase price is paid by the buyer. This is different from the purchase contract shown in Figure 8.1 wherein the buyer receives possession and a deed at the closing. With an installment contract, the buyer is given possession and the right to use the property upon signing the contract, but he does not acquire title. Instead, he receives a contract promising that a deed will be delivered at a later date. During the period between signing the contract and the seller delivering the deed, the buyer is said to hold **equitable title** to the property. That is, he has the exclusive right to acquire the title, along with possession of the property. This equitable title can even be sold, usually by the first buyer who can assign his interest on the contract to the second buyer.

A common use of the installment contract occurs when the buyer does not have the full purchase price in cash or he cannot borrow it from a lender. Under these conditions, the seller must be willing to accept a down payment plus monthly payments until the property is paid for. The seller can either deliver a deed to the buyer at closing and simultaneously have the buyer pledge the property as collateral for the balance due (a mortgage) or the seller can agree to deliver title only after the buyer has completed his payments (an installment contract).

Delivering title after payment is advantageous to the seller because if the buyer fails to make her payments, the title to the property is still in the name of the seller. This avoids the time and costs consumed by foreclosure, a requirement if title has already been conveyed to the buyer.

Sample Contract

Figure 8.3 is a simplified illustration of an installment contract. In paragraph **[1]** the buyer and seller are identified, the purchase price is given and dated, and the amount and terms of the balance due are stated. The buyer is sometimes referred to as the **vendee** and the seller as the **vendor.** In paragraph **[2],** the seller promises to deliver a deed to the buyer when the buyer has made all the payments stated in paragraph **[1]**. Paragraph **[2]** also describes the property. Paragraph **[3]** deals with the possibility that the buyer may fail to make the required payments or fail to abide by the other contract terms. The strong wording in this paragraph is typical of the installment contract, particularly when it is utilized to sell vacant land. If you read paragraph **[3]** carefully, you will see that, in the event of the buyer's default, the seller can retain all payments made *and* retake possession of the property. This is the feature that makes the installment contract popular with sellers.

Paragraph **[4]** deals with property taxes. In this example, the buyer agrees to pay them. Sometimes the seller will agree to pay the property taxes until a deed is delivered to the buyer. This is not an act of kindness but protection for the seller. The seller does not want to risk the possibility of the buyer's failure to pay the taxes, thus giving the county tax collector the right to take the property.

In paragraph **[5],** the seller sets construction restrictions. The object is to prevent unsightly structures from being built that would have a negative impact on surround-

---

INSTALLMENT CONTRACT

FIGURE 8.3
Sample installment contract.

[1] *RECEIVED this* 15th *day of* October, 19xx , *from* Cliff Fisher and wife Sandy *(hereafter called the "buyer") of* 7778 Spinner Street, Bridgetown, Anystate *the sum of* $ 200.00 *as down payment toward the sales price of* $ 10,000.00 . *The balance of* $9,800.00 *is to be paid in equal monthly installments of* $ 98.00 *until paid in full. The monthly payment includes principal and interest of* 10% *per annum on the unpaid balance. Payments are to be made on the first of each month to the* Sunrise Lake Land Company *(hereafter called the "seller").*

[2] *BE IT AGREED: if the buyer makes the payments and performs the agreements stated in this contract, the seller agrees to convey to the buyer in fee simple, clear of all encumbrances whatsoever, by special warranty deed, Lot #* 17 , *Block* B-1 , *Sunrise Lakes Tract, situated and recorded in the County of* Sunrise, *State of* Anywhere.

[3] *IF THE BUYER fails to make any of the payments herein designated or fails to perform any of the other agreements made herein, this contract shall be terminated and the buyer shall forfeit all payments made on this contract. Such payments will be retained by the seller as accumulated rent on the property described above, and the seller shall have the right to reenter and take possession of the premises.*

[4] *THE BUYER AGREES to pay all property taxes subsequent to the year* 19xx .

[5] *CONSTRUCTION shall be limited to residences built with new materials. Structures must be located at least twenty feet from the front lot line and five feet from the other lot lines. Shacks or unsightly structures are not permitted.*

[6] *THE BUYER AND SELLER agree that this contract, or any assignment thereof, is not to be recorded without the permission of the seller. To do so shall result in any existing balance on this contract becoming due and payable immediately.*

[7] *THE BUYER AND SELLER agree that prompt payment is an essential part of this contract and that this contract is binding upon their assigns, heirs, executors, and administrators.*

[8] *THE BUYER HAS the right to examine the master abstract.*

BUYER[s]   [9] *SELLER*

  Cliff Fisher   Salem Bigland
                                  Salem Bigland
  Sandy Fisher   *President, Sunrise Lakes Land Company*

ing property values. This enhances the buyer's resale value; for the seller, it means that the property is more valuable if the buyer defaults.

Repossession

In agreement with the provisions in paragraph [3], paragraph [6] provides the seller with a means of smooth recovery of possession and ownership in the event of default by the buyer. If the buyer records his contract with the public recorder, he serves notice that he has an interest in the property. This creates a cloud on the seller's title. If the buyer were to default, the effort necessary to remove this cloud would be inconsistent with the seller's objective of easy recovery. Also, such a cloud makes it more difficult for the seller to borrow against the property. However, a nonrecording provision is definitely not to the advantage of the buyer, as anyone inspecting the public records would not find a record of the buyer's interest. The seller would still be shown as the owner. In view of this, some states outlaw these clauses, but Texas does not.

While repossession and forfeiture in the default of the installment land contract is the same in Texas as it is in most other states, it is important to recognize that the Recording Act in Texas provides that virtually any acknowledged instrument may be recorded. Although there may be a prohibition against recording the land contract itself or of any assignment thereof (provisions that may be legally questionable), it is possible to lease the property, sublet the property, or create some other kind of material interest in the property that can be recorded. The constructive notice will then be effective to show that there is other interest in the property besides that of the owner.

Paragraph [7] reemphasizes that payments must be made promptly and adds that the terms of the contract are binding on anyone to whom the buyer may sell or assign the contract. In the illustrated contract, the buyer does not receive a title report or title insurance for his individual lot when he signs the contract. However, at [8], he is invited to see the abstract; presumably it shows the seller as the owner of the land. The balance of the contract, [9], is for the signatures of the buyer and seller and, when required, witnesses or a notary.

Consumer Criticism

The installment contract has received much consumer criticism because its wording so strongly favors the seller. In numerous instances, buyers, although they have paid a substantial portion of the purchase price, have lost the property and their money due to one or two late payments. Strictly interpreted, that is what the contract says; if the buyer signs it, presumably she agrees. However, the courts and legislatures in several states have found this too harsh.

Texas has provided some statutory relief to this harsh remedy of automatic forfeiture in the installment land contract. The statutes are as follows:

Subchapter D. Executory Contract For Conveyance

A seller may enforce a forfeiture of interest and the acceleration of the indebtedness of a purchaser in default under an executory contract for conveyance of real property used or to be used as the purchaser's residence only after notifying the purchaser of the seller's intent to enforce the forfeiture and acceleration and the expiration of the following periods:

1. If the purchaser has paid less than 10 percent of the purchase price, 15 days after the date notice is given
2. If the purchaser has paid 10 percent or more but less than 20 percent of the purchase price, 30 days after the date notice is given

3. If the purchaser has paid 20 percent or more of the purchase price, 60 days after the date notice is given

§ 5.062. Notice

(a) Notice under Section 5.061 of this code must be in writing. If the notice is mailed, it must be by registered or certified mail. The notice must be conspicuous and printed in 14 point boldface type or uppercase typewritten letters, and must include the statement:

"NOTICE:

YOU ARE NOT COMPLYING WITH THE TERMS OF THE CONTRACT TO BUY YOUR PROPERTY. UNLESS YOU TAKE THE ACTION SPECIFIED IN THIS NOTICE BY (date) THE SELLER HAS A RIGHT TO TAKE POSSESSION OF YOUR PROPERTY."

The notice must also:

(1) identify and explain the remedy the seller intends to enforce;

(2) if the purchaser has failed to make a timely payment, specify:

(a) the delinquent amount, itemized into principal and interest;

(b) any additional charges claimed, such as late charges or attorney's fees; and

(c) the period to which the delinquency and additional charges relate; and

(3) if the purchaser has failed to comply with a term of the contract, identify the term violated and the action required to cure the violation.

§ 5.063. Right to Cure Default

Notwithstanding an agreement to the contrary, a purchaser in default under an executory contract for the conveyance of real property used or to be used as the purchaser's residence may, at any time before expiration of the applicable period provided by Section 5.061 of this code, avoid forfeiture of interest and acceleration of indebtedness by complying with the terms of the contract up to the date of compliance.

These statutes strongly restrict the legal title holder's right of forfeiture and acceleration, and the buyer cannot be summarily evicted without the specified notices.

Other Pitfalls

Another key weak point in the installment sale contract is that the seller does not deed ownership to the buyer until some later date. Thus, a buyer might make payments for several years only to find that the seller cannot deliver title as promised. At that point, unless the seller is willing to give the buyer a refund, the buyer's only recourse is to sue the seller for specific performance or money damages. However, a lawsuit works only if the buyer has the time and money to pursue the matter, if the suit is successful, and if the seller has the money to pay the judgment.

In Chapter 12, the installment contract is discussed as a tool to finance the sale of improved property when other sources of financing are not available.

PUTTING IT TO WORK

If an installment contract is used for the purchase of real estate, it should be done with the help of legal counsel to make certain that it provides adequate safeguards for the buyer as well as the seller.

LEASE WITH OPTION TO BUY

An option is an agreement to keep an offer open for a fixed period of time. One of the most popular option contracts in real estate is the **lease with option to buy.** Often simply referred to as a **lease-option,** it allows the tenant to buy the property at a pre-set price and terms during the option period. For a residential property, the lease is typically for one year, and the option to buy must be exercised during that time. Let's look more closely.

In this lease-option contract all the normal provisions of a lease are present, such as those shown later in Figure 16.1. All the normal provisions of a purchase contract are present, such as those shown in Figure 8.1. In addition, there will be wording stating that the tenant has the option of exercising the purchase contract, provided the tenant notifies the landlord in writing of that intent during the option period. All terms of the purchase contract must be negotiated and in writing when the lease is signed. Both the tenant and the landlord must sign the lease. Only the landlord must sign the purchase contract and option agreement, although both parties often do so. If the tenant wants to buy during the option period, the tenant notifies the landlord in writing that the tenant wishes to exercise the purchase contract. Together they proceed to carry out the purchase contract as in a normal sale.

If the tenant does not exercise the option within the option period, the option expires and the purchase contract is null and void. If the lease also expires at the end of the option period, the tenant must either arrange with the landlord to continue renting or move out. Alternatively, they can negotiate a new purchase contract or a new lease-option contract.

Popularity

Lease-options are particularly popular in soft real estate markets in which a home seller is having difficulty finding a buyer. One solution is to lower the asking price and/or make the financing terms more attractive. However, the seller may wish to hold out in hopes that prices will rise within a year. In the meantime, the seller needs someone to occupy the property and provide some income.

The lease-option is attractive to a tenant because the tenant has a place to rent plus the option of buying any time during the option period for the price in the purchase contract. In other words, the tenant can wait a year and see if she likes the property and if values rise to or above the price in the purchase contract. If the tenant does not like the property and/or the property does not rise in value, the tenant is under no obligation to buy. Once the lease expires, the tenant is also under no obligation to continue renting either.

Examples

To encourage a tenant to exercise the option to buy, the contract may allow the tenant to apply part or all of the rent paid to the purchase price. In fact, quite a bit of flexibility and negotiation can take place in creating a lease-option. For example, take a house that would rent for $750 per month and sell for $100,000 on the open market. Suppose the owner wants $110,000 and won't come down to the market price. Meanwhile the home is vacant and there are mortgage payments to be made. The owner could offer a one-year lease-option with a rental charge of $750 each month and an exercise price of $110,000. Within a year, $110,000 may look good to the tenant, especially if the market value of the property has risen significantly above $110,000. The tenant can exercise the option or, if not prohibited by the contract, sell it to someone who intends to exercise it. The owner receives $10,000.00 more for the property than he could have gotten last year, and the tenant has the benefit of any value increase above that.

Continuing the above example, what if the property rises to $105,000 in value? There is no economic incentive for the tenant to exercise the option at $110,000. The tenant can simply disregard the option and make an offer of $105,000 to the owner. The owner's choice is to sell at that price or continue renting the home, perhaps with another one-year lease-option.

Option Fee

The owner can also charge the tenant extra for the privilege of having the option, but it must make economic sense to a tenant. Suppose in the above example the purchase price is set equal to the current market value—that is, $100,000. This would be a valuable benefit to the tenant, and the owner could charge an up-front cash fee for the option and/or charge above market rent. The amounts would depend on the market's expectations regarding the value of this home a year from now. There is nothing special about a one-year option period, although it is a very popular length of time. The landlord and tenant can agree to a three-month, six-month, or nine-month option if it fits their needs, and the lease can run longer than the option period. Options for longer than one year are generally reserved for commercial properties. For example, a businessperson just starting out, or perhaps expanding, wants to buy a building but needs one or two years to see how successful the business will be and how much space it will need.

Caveats

Be aware that lease-options may create income tax consequences that require professional tax counseling. Legal advice is also very helpful in preparing and reviewing the lease-option papers. This is because the entire deal (lease, option, and purchase contract) must be water-tight from the beginning. One cannot wait until the option is exercised to write the purchase contract or even a material part of it. If a real estate agent puts a lease-option together, the agent is entitled to a leasing commission at the time the lease is signed. If the option is exercised, the agent is due a sales commission on the purchase contract.

Evidence that the option to buy exists should be recorded to establish not only the tenant's rights to purchase the property, but also establish those rights back to the date the option was recorded. An option is an example of a unilateral contract. When it is exercised, it becomes bilateral. The lease portion of a lease-option is a bilateral contract. The party giving the option is called the **optionor** (the owner in a lease-option). The party receiving the option is the **optionee** (tenant in a lease-option). Sometimes an option to buy is referred to as a **call.** You will see how an option can be used by a home builder to buy land in Chapter 14 and how options can be used to renew leases in Chapter 17.

RIGHT OF FIRST REFUSAL

Sometimes a tenant will agree to rent a property only if given an opportunity to purchase it before someone else does. In other words, the tenant is saying, "Ms. Owner, if you get a valid offer from someone else to purchase this property, show it to me and give me an opportunity to match the offer." This is called a **right of first refusal.** If someone presents the owner with a valid offer, the owner must show it to the tenant before accepting it. If the tenant decides not to match it, the owner is free to accept it.

A right of first refusal protects a tenant from having the property sold out from under him when, in fact, if the tenant knew about the offer, he would have been willing to match it. The owner usually does not care who buys, as long as the price and terms are the same. Therefore, an owner may agree to include a right of first refusal clause in a rental contract for little or no additional charge if the tenant requests it. The right of first refusal concept is not limited to just landlord-tenant situations, but that is as deep as we will go here.

Exchange Agreements

Most real estate transactions involve the exchange of real estate for monetary consideration. However, among sophisticated real estate investors, exchanging real property for real property has become popular for two important reasons. First, real estate trades can be accomplished without large amounts of cash by trading a property you presently own for one you want. This sidesteps the intermediate step of converting real estate to cash and then converting cash back to real estate. Second, by using an exchange, you can dispose of one property and acquire another without paying income taxes on the profit in the first property at the time of the transaction. As a result, the phrase *tax-free exchange* is often used when talking about trading.

To illustrate, suppose that you own an apartment building as an investment. The value on your accounting books is $500,000 but its market value today is $750,000. If you sell for cash, you will have to pay income taxes on the difference between the value of the property on your accounting books and the amount you receive for it. If instead of selling for cash, you find another building that you want and can arrange a trade, then for income tax purposes the new building acquires the accounting book value of the old and no income taxes are due at the time of the trade. Taxes will be due, however, if and when you finally sell rather than trade. The **tax-deferred exchange** rules apply to investment properties only. Owner-occupied dwellings are treated differently. The Internal Revenue Service permits a homeowner to sell and exclude all gains with the specified limits (see Chapter 14).

Trading Up

Real estate exchanges need not involve properties of equal value. For example, if you own debt-free a small office building worth $100,000, you could trade it for a building worth $500,000 with $400,000 of mortgage debt against it. Alternatively, if the building you wanted was priced at $600,000 with $400,000 in debt against it, you could offer your building plus $100,000 in cash.

The vast majority of tax-deferred exchanges today consist of three transactions: the two conveyances and an escrow agreement with a **qualified intermediary (QI).** The qualified intermediary can be a title company, an attorney, or in some cases, an independent company providing this service as tax advisors. The QI maintains control over the funds and the closing documents pursuant to the instructions contained in the escrow agreement. This allows the various parties to deposit documents and funds with the QI (often by mail), which makes it much more convenient. As a practical matter, the QI signs all documents relevant to the closing other than the conveyancing documents. The Internal Revenue Service rules allow the conveyancing documents to be executed by the parties to the transaction without involving the formality of the QI's execution. This prevents the QI from becoming "in the chain of title," which could further complicate the transaction.

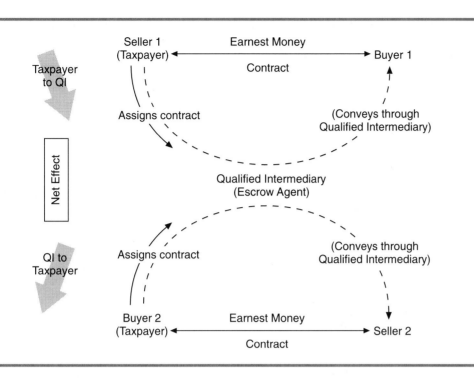

FIGURE 8.4
Possible trading
combinations.

Assume the party who wants to do the tax-deferred exchange is Seller 1, who signs a contract to convey real estate to Buyer 1. After executing a contract of sale, Seller 1 assigns his interest in the contract to the QI, then executes an **escrow agreement** with the QI that defines the QI's role. Seller 1 then locates the property he is interested in purchasing and enters into a purchase contract to acquire that property; he then sends notice of designation of property to the QI, then assigns his interest in the contract as purchaser to the QI. In both transactions, the deed is drafted from Seller to Buyer (so the qualified intermediary owner never takes title to either tract). The QI, who has escrowed the funds from transaction #1, then uses these proceeds to pay Seller 2 to complete transaction #2.

The key factor is that Seller 1 (taxpayer) has no control over the funds held by the qualified intermediary and cannot be deemed to be in receipt of those funds. In effect, the transaction results in Seller 1 conveying his property to the QI and the qualified intermediary conveying the exchange property to the seller. Note Figure 8.4.

Although trading is a complicated business, it can be very lucrative for real estate agents. Whereas an ordinary sale results in one brokerage commission, a two-party exchange results in two commissions, and a four-party exchange in four commissions.

Delayed Exchanges

The Internal Revenue Code allows nonsimultaneous exchanges to be tax-deferred under certain circumstances. Such an exchange, commonly called a **delayed exchange,** occurs when property is exchanged for a right to receive property at a future date. It is a helpful technique when one party is willing to exchange out of a property but has not yet chosen a property to exchange into. Meanwhile the other parties to the exchange are ready and want to close. The delayed exchange allows the closing to take place by giving the party that has not chosen a property the right to designate a property and take title after the closing. The 1984 Act specifically allows this, provided (1) the designated property is identified within 45 days of the original closing, (2) the title to the designated property is acquired within 180 days of the original closing, and (3) the designated property is received before the designating party's tax return is due. If these rules are not met the transaction will be treated as a sale for the designating party, not an exchange.

TYPICAL TRADE CONTRACT

Space does not permit a detailed review of a trade contract. However, very briefly, a typical trade contract identifies the traders involved and their respective properties; names the type of deed and quality of title that will be conveyed; names the real estate brokers involved and how much they are to be paid; discusses prorations, personal property, rights of tenants, and damage to the property; provides a receipt for the deposit that each trader makes; requires each trader to provide an abstract of title; and sets forth the consequences of defaulting on the contract. If the same broker represents more than one trader, he must disclose this to each trader whom he represents.

REVIEW QUESTIONS

Answers to these questions are found in the Answer Key section at the back of the book.

1. A formal real estate sales contract, prepared at the outset by an agent using prepared forms, may be identified as any of the following EXCEPT
   A. a purchase contract
   B. an option contract.
   C. an offer and acceptance.
   D. a purchase offer.

2. Martin purchased real estate from Stevens under an agreement that called for him to pay for the property in installments and to receive a deed upon payment of the entire purchase price. This agreement could properly be identified as a
   A. land contract.
   B. contract for deed.
   C. conditional sales contract.
   D. installment contract.
   E. All of the above.

3. In normal real estate brokerage practice, the amount of earnest money deposit paid by the purchaser is
   A. determined by negotiation.
   B. set by state law.
   C. equal to the agent's commission.
   D. the minimum required to make the contract valid.

4. Property taxes, insurance, loan interest, etc. may be divided between the buyer and seller by the process of
   A. allocation.
   B. appropriation.
   C. proration.
   D. proportioning.

5. In Texas, if a promulgated form is not used, the real estate licensee is required to use a form
   A. prepared by the broker.
   B. prepared by the licensee.
   C. prepared by an attorney at law licensed in Texas.
   D. prepared by the buyer or his agent.

6. Martin is going to purchase a newly built home from the builder. He will finance the purchase by means of a VA-guaranteed loan. The builder must include in the purchase contract
   A. an amendatory clause.
   B. insulation disclosures.
   C. Both A and B.
   D. Neither A nor B.

7. Mr. and Mrs. Silver entered into a real estate contract with Mr. and Mrs. Gold. If Mr. Gold dies before settlement takes place,
   A. Mr. and Mrs. Silver are obligated to carry out the contract.
   B. Mrs. Gold is obligated to carry out the contract.
   C. Mr. Gold's estate is obligated to carry out the contract.
   D. All of the above.

8. According to the 1989 Legislative Statute on selling or conveying property in a municipal utility district or a flood or drainage control district, the seller
   A. does not have to reveal the type of district to the purchaser.
   B. must give separate written notice to the purchaser acknowledging the type of district in which the property is located.
   C. may give oral or written notice of the type of district.
   D. must provide information on the earnest money contract and deed.

9. Currently, Texas brokers are permitted to fill in the blanks on
   A. a real estate deed.
   B. an earnest money contract.
   C. Both A and B.
   D. Neither A nor B.

10. When property is sold by means of an installment contract, the
    A. seller delivers a deed at closing.
    B. buyer is NOT given the right to occupy the property until the contract terms have been fulfilled.
    C. Both A and B.
    D. Neither A nor B.

11. Installment contracts may be used when
    A. the buyer does not have the full purchase price in cash.
    B. the buyer is unable to borrow part of the purchase price from a lender.
    C. Both A and B.
    D. Neither A nor B.

12. The purchaser under an installment contract may protect his interests by requiring that the
    A. seller place a deed in escrow at settlement.
    B. contract be recorded in the land records.
    C. Both A and B.
    D. Neither A nor B.

13. Equitable title can be
    A. transferred by sale.
    B. inherited.
    C. mortgaged.
    D. transferred by deed.
    E. All of the above.

14. The option portion of a lease-option contract can be attached to the lease as
    A. a rider.
    B. an accord.
    C. a binder.
    D. a purchase agreement.

15. Lease-option contracts tend to increase in popularity during a
    A. seller's market
    B. buyer's market.

16. An option to buy is an example of
    A. an executory contract.
    B. a bilateral contract.
    C. a unilateral contract.
    D. Both A and B.
    E. Both A and C.

17. Under the terms of a right of first refusal, the tenant is given the right to
    A. match an offer to purchase the property.
    B. purchase the property at a previously agreed price.
    C. Both A and B.
    D. Neither A nor B.

18. The party with the least amount of flexibility in a lease-option agreement is the
    A. optionor.
    B. optionee.

19. The phrase "time is of the essence" in a sales contract means that
    A. the time limits set by the contract must be faithfully observed or the contract is voidable.
    B. the parties are prohibited from giving each other an extension.
    C. Both A and B.
    D. Neither A nor B.

KEY TERMS

Acceleration clause: allows the lender to demand immediate payment of entire loan if the borrower defaults

Beneficiary: one for whose benefit a trust is created; the lender in a deed of trust arrangement

Deed of Trust: a document that conveys title to a neutral third party trustee as security for a debt

Deficiency judgment: a judgment against a borrower if the foreclosure sale does not bring enough to pay the balance owed

Foreclosure: the procedure by which a person's property can be taken and sold to satisfy an unpaid debt

Junior mortgage: any mortgage on a property that is subordinate to the first mortgage in priority

Mortgage: a document that makes property security for the repayment of a debt

Mortgagee: the party receiving the mortgage; the lender

Mortgagor: the party who gives a mortgage; the borrower

Power of sale: allows a mortgagee to conduct a foreclosure sale without first going to court

Subordination: voluntary acceptance of a lower mortgage priority than one would otherwise be entitled to

Trustee: one who holds property in trust for another

Trustor: one who creates a trust; the borrower in a deed of trusts arrangement

Mortgage Theory and Law

IN THIS CHAPTER *In this chapter we will take a brief look at mortgage theory and law. A mortgage is basically a pledge of property to secure the repayment of a debt. The chapter includes coverage of lien theory and title theory, pledge methods, promissory notes, the mortgage instrument, the "subject to" clause, loan assumption, and debt priorities. The last part of the chapter deals with the foreclosure process, dividing the discussion between judicial and nonjudicial foreclosure.*

EARLY MORTGAGES

A mortgage is a pledge of property to secure the repayment of a debt. If the debt is not repaid as agreed between the lender and borrower, the lender can force the sale of the pledged property and apply the proceeds to repayment of the debt. To better understand present-day mortgage laws, it is helpful to first look at their history.

The concept of pledging property as collateral for a loan is not new. According to historians, the mortgage was in use when the pharaohs ruled Egypt and during the time of the Roman Empire. According to Roman laws, loans could be secured by mortgages on either personal or real property. In the early years of the Empire, nonpayment of a mortgage loan entitled the lender to make the borrower his slave. In the year 326 B.C. Roman law was modified to allow the debtor his freedom while working off his debt. Later, Roman law was again changed, this time to permit an unpaid debt to be satisfied by the sale of the mortgaged property.

Hypothecation

Mortgages were also an important part of English law and, as a result of the English colonization of America, ultimately were incorporated into laws of each state. In England, the concept of pledging real estate by temporarily conveying its title to a lender as security for a debt was in regular use by the eleventh century. However, the Christian church at that time did not allow its members to charge interest. Because of this, the Christian lender took possession of the mortgaged property and collected the rents it produced instead of charging interest.

In contrast, Jewish lenders in England charged interest and left the borrower in possession. It was not until the fourteenth century that charging interest, rather than taking possession, became universal. Leaving the borrower in possession of the pledged property is known as **hypothecation.** The borrower conveys title to the lender, but still has the use of the property. This conveyance of title in the mortgage agreement is conditional. The mortgage states that if the debt it secures is paid on time, the mortgage is defeated and title returns to the borrower. This was and still is known as a **defeasance clause.**

LIEN THEORY VERSUS TITLE THEORY

Although the United States inherited the whole of England's mortgage law, it began to be modified following independence. In 1791 in South Carolina, lawmakers asked the question: "Should a mortgage actually convey title to the lender subject only to the borrower's default? Or does the mortgage, despite its wording, simply create a lien with a right to acquire title only after proper foreclosure?" Their decision was that a mortgage is a lien rather than a conveyance, and South Carolina became the first lien theory state in regard to mortgages. Today, 33 states, including Texas, have adopted this viewpoint.

Fifteen jurisdictions adhere to the older idea that a mortgage is a conveyance of title subject to defeat when the debt it secures is paid. They are classified as **title theory** states. Three states are classified as **intermediate theory** states because they take a position midway between the lien and title theories. In the intermediate states, title does not pass to the lender with the mortgage, but only upon default. In real estate practice, as long as default does not occur, the differences among the three theories are more technical than real.

PLEDGE METHODS

A person can pledge his real estate as collateral for a loan by using any of four methods: the regular mortgage, the equitable mortgage, the deed as security, and the deed of trust.

Regular Mortgage

The **standard** or **regular mortgage** is the mortgage handed down from England and the one commonly found and used in the United States today. In it, the borrower conveys the title to the lender as security for the debt. The mortgage also contains a statement that it will become void if the debt it secures is paid in full and on time. In title theory states, the conveyance feature of the mortgage stands. In lien theory states, such a mortgage is considered to be only a lien against the borrower's property, despite its wording.

Equitable Mortgage

An **equitable mortgage** is a written agreement that, although it does not follow the form of a regular mortgage, is considered by the courts to be one. For example, Black sells his land to Green, with Green paying part of the price now in cash and promising to pay the balance later. Normally, Black would ask Green to execute a regular mortgage as security for the balance due. However, instead of doing this, Black makes a note of the balance due on the deed before handing it to Green. The laws of most states would regard this notation as an equitable mortgage. For all intents and purposes, it is a mortgage, although it is not specifically called one. Another example of an equitable mortgage can arise from the money deposit accompanying an offer to purchase property. If the seller refuses the offer and refuses to return the deposit, the courts will hold that the purchaser has an equitable mortgage in the amount of the deposit against the seller's property.

Deed as Security

Occasionally, a borrower will give a bargain and sale or warranty **deed as security** of a loan. On the face of it, he would appear to be able to do whatever he pleases since he has the title. However, if the borrower can prove that the deed was, in fact, security for a loan, the lender must foreclose as with a regular mortgage if the borrower fails to repay. If the loan is repaid in full and on time, the borrower can force the lender to convey the land back to him. Like the equitable mortgage, a deed used as security is treated according to its intent, not its label.

Deed of Trust

Whereas a mortgage is a two-party arrangement with a borrower and a lender, the **trust deed,** also known as a **deed of trust,** is a three-party arrangement consisting of the borrower (the trustor), the lender (the beneficiary), and a neutral third party (a trustee). The key aspect of this system is that the borrower executes a deed to the trustee rather than to the lender. If the borrower pays the debt in full and on time, the trustee reconveys title back to the borrower. If the borrower defaults on the loan, the lender asks the trustee to sell the property to pay off the debt. In Texas, debts are most often secured by a deed of trust, covered in more detail later in this chapter.

Chattel Mortgage

A mortgage can also be used to pledge personal property as security for a debt. This is a **chattel mortgage.** The word *chattel* is a legal term for personal property and derives from the Old English word for cattle. As with real property mortgages, a chattel mortgage permits the borrower to use mortgaged personal property as long as the loan payments are made. If the borrower defaults, the lender is permitted to take possession and sell the mortgaged goods. In Texas, the use of chattel mortgages is usually in the form of financing statements and security agreements as provided for in the Texas Business and Commerce Code.

PROMISSORY NOTE

Two documents are involved in a standard mortgage loan—the promissory note and the mortgage. Both are contracts. The **promissory note** establishes who the borrower and lender are, the amount of the debt, the terms of repayment, and the interest rate. A sample of the commonly used FNMA/FHLMC promissory note, usually referred to simply as a **note,** or a **real estate lien note,** is shown in Figure 9.1.

To be valid as evidence of debt, a note must (1) be in writing, (2) be between a borrower and lender who both have contractual capacity, (3) state the borrower's promise to pay a certain sum of money, (4) show the terms of payment, (5) be signed by the borrower, and (6) be voluntarily delivered by the borrower and accepted by the lender. If the note is secured by a mortgage or deed of trust or a vendor's lien, it must say so. Otherwise, it is solely a personal obligation of the borrower. Although interest is not required to make the note valid, most loans do carry an interest charge; when they do, the rate of interest must be stated in the note. Finally, in some states it is necessary for the borrower's signature on the note to be acknowledged and/or witnessed.

Borrower–Lender

Referring to Figure 9.1, number **[1]** identifies the document as a note and **[2]** gives the location and date of the note's execution (signing). At **[3],** the borrower states that the receipt of something of value and in turn promises to pay the debt described in the note. Typically, the "value received" is a loan of money in the amount described in the note; it could, however, be services or goods or anything else of value.

The section of the note at **[4]** identifies to whom the obligation is owed and where the payments are to be sent.

Principal and Payments

The **principal** or amount of the obligation, $83,000, is shown at **[5].** Number **[6]** gives the rate of interest on the debt and the date from which it will be charged. The amount of the periodic payment at **[7]** is calculated from the loan tables like those discussed in Chapter 10. In this case, $821.95 each month for 30 years will return the lender's $83,000 plus interest at the rate of $11\frac{1}{2}\%$ per year on the unpaid portion of the principal. Number **[8]** outlines when payments will begin and when subsequent payments will be due. In this example, they are due on the first day of each month until the full $83,000 and interest have been paid. The clause at **[9]** is a **prepayment privilege** for the borrower. It allows the borrower to pay more than the required $821.95 per month and to pay the loan off early without penalty. Without this very important privilege, the note requires the borrower to pay $821.95 per month, no more and no less, until the $83,000 plus interest has been paid.

Acceleration Clause

The clause at **[10]** provides for a late payment fee if payments are not timely made. The provision at **[11]** allows the lender to demand immediate payment of the entire balance remaining on the note if the borrower misses any of the individual payments. This is called an **acceleration clause,** as it "speeds up" the remaining payments due on the note and makes them due immediately. Without this clause, the lender can only foreclose on the payments that have come due and have not been paid. In this example, that could take as long as 30 years. This clause also has a certain psychological value: knowing that the lender has the option of calling the entire loan balance due upon default makes the borrower think twice about being late with payments.

Signature

At **[12],** the borrower agrees to pay any collection costs incurred by the lender if the borrower falls behind in his payments. At **[13],** the promissory note is tied to the mortgage or deed of trust that secures it, making it a secured loan. Without this reference, it would be like a personal loan. At **[14],** the borrower signs the note. A person who signs a note is sometimes referred to as a **maker** of the note. If two or more persons sign the note, it is common to include a statement in the note that the borrowers are "jointly and severally liable" for all provisions in the note. Thus, the terms of the note and the obligations it creates are enforceable upon the makers as a group and upon each maker individually. If the borrower is married, lenders generally require both husband and wife to sign. An acknowledgment is not required, as it is the mortgage rather than the note that is recorded in the public records.

FIGURE **9.1**
Real estate lien note.

NOTE

[Date] [City] [State]

[Property Address]

1. BORROWER'S PROMISE TO PAY

In return for a loan that I have received, I promise to pay U.S. $ (this amount is called "principal"), plus interest, to the order of the Lender. The Lender is

I understand that the Lender may transfer this Note. The Lender or anyone who takes this Note by transfer and who is entitled to receive payments under this Note is called the "Note Holder."

2. INTEREST

Interest will be charged on unpaid principal until the full amount of principal has been paid. I will pay interest at a yearly rate of   %.

The interest rate required by this Section 2 is the rate I will pay both before and after any default described in Section 6(B) of this Note.

3. PAYMENTS

(A) Time and Place of Payments

I will pay principal and interest by making payments every month.

I will make my monthly payments on the   day of each month beginning on   . I will make these payments every month until I have paid all of the principal and interest and any other charges described below that I may owe under this Note. My monthly payments will be applied to interest before principal. If, on   , I still owe amounts under this Note, I will pay those amounts in full on that date, which is called the "Maturity Date."

I will make my monthly payments at
or at a different place if required by the Note Holder.

(B) Amount of Monthly Payments

My monthly payment will be in the amount of U.S. $

4. BORROWER'S RIGHT TO PREPAY

I have the right to make payments of principal at any time before they are due. A payment of principal only is known as a "prepayment." When I make a prepayment, I will tell the Note Holder in writing that I am doing so.

I may make a full prepayment or partial prepayments without paying any prepayment charge. The Note Holder will use all of my prepayments to reduce the amount of principal that I owe under this Note. If I make a partial prepayment, there will be no changes in the due date or in the amount of my monthly payment unless the Note Holder agrees in writing to those changes.

5. LOAN CHARGES

If a law, which applies to this loan and which sets maximum loan charges, is finally interpreted so that the interest or other loan charges collected or to be collected in connection with this loan exceed the permitted limits, then: (i) any such loan charge shall be reduced by the amount necessary to reduce the charge to the permitted limit; and (ii) any sums already collected from me which exceeded permitted limits will be refunded to me. The Note Holder may choose to make this refund by reducing the principal I owe under this Note or by making a direct payment to me. If a refund reduces principal, the reduction will be treated as a partial prepayment.

6. BORROWER'S FAILURE TO PAY AS REQUIRED

(A) Late Charge for Overdue Payments

If the Note Holder has not received the full amount of any monthly payment by the end of   calendar days after the date it is due, I will pay a late charge to the Note Holder. The amount of the charge will be   % of my overdue payment of principal and interest. I will pay this late charge promptly but only once on each late payment.

(B) Default

If I do not pay the full amount of each monthly payment on the date it is due, I will be in default.

(C) Notice of Default

If I am in default, the Note Holder may send me a written notice telling me that if I do not pay the overdue amount by a certain date, the Note Holder may require me to pay immediately the full amount of principal which has not been paid and all the interest that I owe on that amount. That date must be at least 30 days after the date on which the notice is delivered or mailed to me.

(D) No Waiver By Note Holder

Even if, at a time when I am in default, the Note Holder does not require me to pay immediately in full as described above, the Note Holder will still have the right to do so if I am in default at a later time.

(E) Payment of Note Holder's Costs and Expenses

If the Note Holder has required me to pay immediately in full as described above, the Note Holder will have the right to be paid back by me for all of its costs and expenses in enforcing this Note to the extent not prohibited by applicable law. Those expenses include, for example, reasonable attorneys' fees.

FIXED RATE NOTE - Single Family - FNMA/FHLMC Uniform Instrument
N32MU1 05/96

(continued)

FIGURE 9.1
Continued.

7. GIVING OF NOTICES

Unless applicable law requires a different method, any notice that must be given to me under this Note will be given by delivering it or by mailing it by first class mail to me at the Property Address above or at a different address if I give the Note Holder a notice of my different address.

Any notice that must be given to the Note Holder under this Note will be given by mailing it by first class mail to the Note Holder at the address stated in Section 3(A) above or at a different address if I am given a notice of that different address.

8. OBLIGATIONS OF PERSONS UNDER THIS NOTE

If more than one person signs this Note, each person is fully and personally obligated to keep all of the promises made in this Note, including the promise to pay the full amount owed. Any person who is a guarantor, surety or endorser of this Note is also obligated to do these things. Any person who takes over these obligations, including the obligations of a guarantor, surety or endorser of this Note, is also obligated to keep all of the promises made in this Note. The Note Holder may enforce its rights under this Note against each person individually or against all of us together. This means that any one of us may be required to pay all of the amounts owed under this Note.

9. WAIVERS

I and any other person who has obligations under this Note waive notice of intention to accelerate, except as provided in Section 6 (C) above, and the rights of presentment and notice of dishonor. "Presentment" means the right to require the Note Holder to demand payment of amounts due. "Notice of dishonor" means the right to require the Note Holder to give notice to other persons that amounts due have not been paid.

10. UNIFORM SECURED NOTE

This Note is a uniform instrument with limited variations in some jurisdictions. In addition to the protections given to the Note Holder under this Note, a Mortgage, Deed of Trust or Security Deed (the "Security Instrument"), dated the same date as this Note, protects the Note Holder from possible losses which might result if I do not keep the promises which I make in this Note. That Security Instrument describes how and under what conditions I may be required to make immediate payment in full of all amounts I owe under this Note. Some of those conditions are described as follows:

Transfer of the Property or a Beneficial Interest in Borrower. If all or any part of the Property or any interest in it is sold or transferred (or if a beneficial interest in Borrower is sold or transferred and Borrower is not a natural person) without Lender's prior written consent, Lender may, at its option, require immediate payment in full of all sums secured by this Security Instrument. However, this option shall not be exercised by Lender if exercise is prohibited by federal law as of the date of this Security Instrument.

If Lender exercises this option, Lender shall give Borrower notice of acceleration. The notice shall provide a period of not less than 30 days from the date the notice is delivered or mailed within which Borrower must pay all sums secured by this Security Instrument. If Borrower fails to pay these sums prior to the expiration of this period, Lender may invoke any remedies permitted by this Security Instrument without further notice or demand on Borrower.

WITNESS THE HAND(S) AND SEAL(S) OF THE UNDERSIGNED.

_____ (Seal)   _____ (Seal)
                                -Borrower   -Borrower

SSN: SSN:

_____ (Seal)   _____ (Seal)
                                -Borrower   -Borrower

SSN: SSN:

[Sign Original Only]

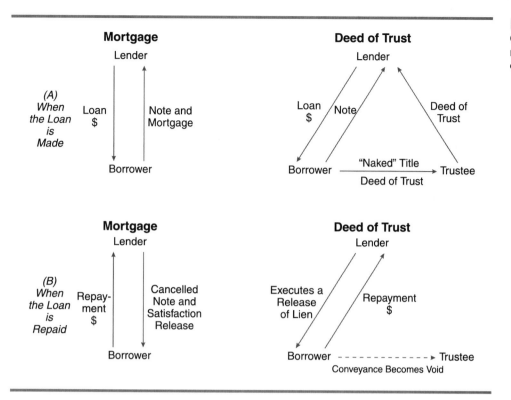

FIGURE 9.2
Comparing a
mortgage with a
deed of trust.

THE DEED OF TRUST

The mortgage is a separate agreement from the promissory note. Whereas the note is evidence of a debt and a promise to pay, the mortgage pledges collateral that the lender can sell if the note is not paid.

In Texas, the **deed of trust** is the same as a mortgage and is almost always used as the mortgage document. Real property is used as security for a debt; if the debt is not repaid, the property is sold and the proceeds are applied to the balance owed. The main legal difference between a deed of trust and a mortgage is diagrammed in Figure 9.2.

Parties to a Deed of Trust

Figure 9.2 shows that when a debt is secured by a mortgage the borrower delivers the promissory note and mortgage to the lender, who keeps them until the debt is paid. But when a note is secured by a deed of trust, three parties are involved: the borrower (the **mortgagor, trustor,** or **grantor**), the lender (the **mortgagee** or **beneficiary**), and a neutral third party (the **trustee**). The lender makes a loan to the borrower, and the borrower gives the lender a promissory note (like the one shown in Figure 9.1) and a deed of trust. In the deed of trust document, the borrower conveys title to the trustee, to be held in trust until the note is paid in full. The deed of trust is recorded in the county in which the property is located and then is usually given to the lender for safekeeping. A variation used in other areas of the country is to deliver the recorded deed of trust to the trustee to be held in a long-term escrow until the note is paid in full. Anyone searching the title records on the borrower's property would find the deed of trust conveying title to the trustee. This would alert the title searcher to the existence of a debt against the property.

In Texas, the title granted to the **trustee** is only a conditional conveyance. The title held by the trustee is limited only to what is necessary to carry out the duty as trustee when requested to do so by the beneficiary (**lender**) under the beneficiary's rights as set out in the deed of trust.

When the note is paid in full, the lender cancels the note and issues the grantor (**borrower**) a **release of lien,** which is recorded in the county records to indicate a full discharge of the previously recorded deed of trust lien. Depending on the terms of the deed of trust instrument, the conveyance to the trustee may become void and of no further force and effect.

If a borrower defaults under a deed of trust, the beneficiary (lender) generally instructs the trustee to post the notice of foreclosure at the courthouse and to hold a public sale of the property according to the requirements of the deed of trust and in accordance with Texas statutes. The deed of trust generally specifies this procedure in its **power of sale** provision, and the borrower agrees to this provision upon signing the deed of trust.

In Texas, an individual is ordinarily named as a trustee in the deed of trust instrument. This person may be the attorney who draws the papers for the lender, or some other agent of the lender. There is normally a provision that allows the lender to appoint a substitute trustee in the event of death or refusal to act by the named trustee. The trustee is supposed to be an impartial third party, although the beneficiary may act as trustee. But because the power of sale remedy is so strict, the instrument and authority of the trustee thereunder is strictly construed to avoid irregularities in the sale. If a person acts as both the trustee and beneficiary, the court may find a conflict of interest or lack of impartiality.

SAMPLE DEED OF TRUST

Figure 9.3 is an example of a deed of trust form that is the standard FNMA/FHLMC uniform instrument commonly used by lenders for residential mortgage documentation. Other deed of trust forms have provisions that may vary. This example shows the agreement between borrower and lender and states the responsibilities of the trustee. Beginning at **[1],** the document is identified as a deed of trust. This is followed by the identification of the grantor (borrower) at **[2].** Conveyance to the trustee is shown at **[3],** and the property is legally described at **[4].** At **[5]** and **[6]** are the habendum and warranty clauses where the borrower states that he will defend the title against claims of others.

At **[7],** it is stated that the conveyance is made *in* TRUST to secure the payment of the promissory note, described at **[8].**

Covenants of Borrower

At **[9]** the borrower agrees to provide a fund for **taxes and insurance** by depositing funds equal to one-twelfth of the yearly taxes and assessments that may attain priority over the deed of trust.

The **covenant of insurance** at **[10]** requires the borrower to carry adequate insurance against damage or destruction of the mortgaged property. This protects the value of the collateral for the loan because without insurance, if the buildings or other improvements on the mortgaged property are damaged or destroyed, the value of the property might fall below the amount owed on the debt. With insurance, the buildings can be repaired or replaced, restoring the value of the borrower's collateral.

The **covenant to repair** shown at **[11]** requires the borrower to keep the mortgaged property in good condition and not to destroy, damage, or substantially change the property. At **[12]** is the condemnation clause. If all or any part of the property is taken by action of eminent domain, any money so received must be paid to the lender.

FIGURE 9.3
Deed of trust.

_____

Company Name

_____

Name of Natural Person

_____

Street Address

_____

City, State ZIP

———————————— [Space Above This Line for Recording Data] ————————————

DEED OF TRUST [1]

[2]   THIS DEED OF TRUST ("Security Instrument") is made on   . The grantor is

("Borrower"). The Trustee is

, whose address is

("Trustee"). The beneficiary is

, which is organized and existing under the laws of   , and whose address is

("Lender"). Borrower owes Lender the principal sum of

Dollars (U.S. $). This debt is evidenced by Borrower's note dated the same date as this Security Instrument
("Note"), which provides for monthly payments, with the full debt, if not paid earlier, due and payable on   , [8]
. This Security Instrument secures to Lender: (a) the repayment of the debt evidenced by the Note, with interest, and all
renewals, extensions and modifications of the Note; (b) the payment of all other sums, with interest, advanced under paragraph 7 to protect
the security of this Security Instrument; and (c) the performance of Borrower's covenants and agreements under this Security Instrument and [3]
the Note. For this purpose, Borrower irrevocably grants and conveys to Trustee, in trust, with power of sale, the following described property
located in   County, Texas:

[7]

[4]

which has the address of

                                        [Street]

            , Texas   ("Property Address");

      [City]   [Zip Code]

[5]   TOGETHER WITH all the improvements now or hereafter erected on the property, and all easements, appurtenances, and fixtures
now or hereafter a part of the property. All replacements and additions shall also be covered by this Security Instrument. All of the foregoing
is referred to in this Security Instrument as the "Property."

[6]   BORROWER COVENANTS that Borrower is lawfully seised of the estate hereby conveyed and has the right to grant and convey
the Property and that the Property is unencumbered, except for encumbrances of record. Borrower warrants and will defend generally the
title to the Property against all claims and demands, subject to any encumbrances of record.

THIS SECURITY INSTRUMENT combines uniform covenants for national use and non-uniform covenants with limited variations
by jurisdiction to constitute a uniform security instrument covering real property.

UNIFORM COVENANTS. Borrower and Lender covenant and agree as follows:
   1. Payment of Principal and Interest; Prepayment and Late Charges. Borrower shall promptly pay when due the principal
of and interest on the debt evidenced by the Note and any prepayment and late charges due under the Note.
   2. Funds for Taxes and Insurance. Subject to applicable law or to a written waiver by Lender, Borrower shall pay to Lender on
[9] the day monthly payments are due under the Note, until the Note is paid in full, a sum ("Funds") for: (a) yearly taxes and assessments which
may attain priority over this Security Instrument as a lien on the Property; (b) yearly leasehold payments or ground rents on the Property, if
any; (c) yearly hazard or property insurance premiums; (d) yearly flood insurance premiums, if any; (e) yearly mortgage insurance premiums,
if any; and (f) any sums payable by Borrower to Lender, in accordance with the provisions of paragraph 8, in lieu of the payment of mortgage
insurance premiums. These items are called "Escrow Items." Lender may, at any time, collect and hold Funds in an amount not to exceed
the maximum amount a lender for a federally related mortgage loan may require for Borrower's escrow account under the federal Real Estate
Settlement Procedures Act of 1974 as amended from time to time, 12 U.S.C. Section 2601 *et seq.* ("RESPA"), unless another law that applies
to the Funds sets a lesser amount. If so, Lender may, at any time, collect and hold Funds in an amount not to exceed the lesser amount. Lender
may estimate the amount of Funds due on the basis of current data and reasonable estimates of expenditures of future Escrow Items or
otherwise in accordance with applicable law.

The Funds shall be held in an institution whose deposits are insured by a federal agency, instrumentality, or entity (including Lender,
if Lender is such an institution) or in any Federal Home Loan Bank. Lender shall apply the Funds to pay the Escrow Items. Lender may not
charge Borrower for holding and applying the Funds, annually analyzing the escrow account, or verifying the Escrow Items, unless Lender
pays Borrower interest on the Funds and applicable law permits Lender to make such a charge. However, Lender may require Borrower to
pay a one-time charge for an independent real estate tax reporting service used by Lender in connection with this loan, unless applicable law
provides otherwise. Unless an agreement is made or applicable law requires interest to be paid, Lender shall not be required to pay Borrower
any interest or earnings on the Funds. Borrower and Lender may agree in writing, however, that interest shall be paid on the Funds. Lender
shall give to Borrower, without charge, an annual accounting of the Funds, showing credits and debits to the Funds and the purpose for which
each debit to the Funds was made. The Funds are pledged as additional security for all sums secured by this Security Instrument.

Initials: _____

Texas Deed of Trust-Single Family-Fannie Mae/Freddie Mac UNIFORM INSTRUMENT
———— THE COMPLIANCE SOURCE, INC. ————
To Order Call: (972) 980-2178•Fax (972) 392-2891
www.compliancesource.com

Form 3044 09/90
(page 1 of 5 pages)
14001TX1.CS 12/97
©1997, All Rights Reserved

(continued)

FIGURE 9.3
Continued.

If the Funds held by Lender exceed the amounts permitted to be held by applicable law, Lender shall account to Borrower for the excess Funds in accordance with the requirements of applicable law. If the amount of the Funds held by Lender at any time is not sufficient to pay the Escrow Items when due, Lender may so notify Borrower in writing, and, in such case Borrower shall pay to Lender the amount necessary to make up the deficiency. Borrower shall make up the deficiency in no more than twelve monthly payments, at Lender's sole discretion.

Upon payment in full of all sums secured by this Security Instrument, Lender shall promptly refund to Borrower any Funds held by Lender. If, under paragraph 21, Lender shall acquire or sell the Property, Lender, prior to the acquisition or sale of the Property, shall apply any Funds held by Lender at the time of acquisition or sale as a credit against the sums secured by this Security Instrument.

3. Application of Payments. Unless applicable law provides otherwise, all payments received by Lender under paragraphs 1 and 2 shall be applied: first, to any prepayment charges due under the Note; second, to amounts payable under paragraph 2; third, to interest due; fourth, to principal due; and last, to any late charges due under the Note.

4. Charges; Liens. Borrower shall pay all taxes, assessments, charges, fines and impositions attributable to the Property which may attain priority over this Security Instrument, and leasehold payments or ground rents, if any. Borrower shall pay these obligations in the manner provided in paragraph 2, or if not paid in that manner, Borrower shall pay them on time directly to the person owed payment. Borrower shall promptly furnish to Lender all notices of amounts to be paid under this paragraph. If Borrower makes these payments directly, Borrower shall promptly furnish to Lender receipts evidencing the payments.

Borrower shall promptly discharge any lien which has priority over this Security Instrument unless Borrower: (a) agrees in writing to the payment of the obligation secured by the lien in a manner acceptable to Lender; (b) contests in good faith the lien by, or defends against enforcement of the lien in, legal proceedings which in the Lender's opinion operate to prevent the enforcement of the lien; or (c) secures from the holder of the lien an agreement satisfactory to Lender subordinating the lien to this Security Instrument. If Lender determines that any part of the Property is subject to a lien which may attain priority over this Security Instrument, Lender may give Borrower a notice identifying the lien. Borrower shall satisfy the lien or take one or more of the actions set forth above within 10 days of the giving of notice.

[10]   **5. Hazard or Property Insurance.** Borrower shall keep the improvements now existing or hereafter erected on the Property insured against loss by fire, hazards included within the term "extended coverage" and any other hazards, including floods or flooding, for which Lender requires insurance. This insurance shall be maintained in the amounts and for the periods that Lender requires. The insurance carrier providing the insurance shall be chosen by Borrower subject to Lender's approval which shall not be unreasonably withheld. If Borrower fails to maintain coverage described above, Lender may, at Lender's option, obtain coverage to protect Lender's rights in the Property in accordance with paragraph 7.

All insurance policies and renewals shall be acceptable to Lender and shall include a standard mortgage clause. Lender shall have the right to hold the policies and renewals. If Lender requires, Borrower shall promptly give to Lender all receipts of paid premiums and renewal notices. In the event of loss, Borrower shall give prompt notice to the insurance carrier and Lender. Lender may make proof of loss if not made promptly by Borrower.

Unless Lender and Borrower otherwise agree in writing, insurance proceeds shall be applied to restoration or repair of the Property damaged, if the restoration or repair is economically feasible and Lender's security is not lessened. If the restoration or repair is not economically feasible or Lender's security would be lessened, the insurance proceeds shall be applied to the sums secured by this Security Instrument, whether or not then due, with any excess paid to Borrower. If Borrower abandons the Property, or does not answer within 30 days a notice from Lender that the insurance carrier has offered to settle a claim, then Lender may collect the insurance proceeds. Lender may use the proceeds to repair or restore the Property or to pay sums secured by this Security Instrument, whether or not then due. The 30-day period will begin when the notice is given.

Unless Lender and Borrower otherwise agree in writing, any application of proceeds to principal shall not extend or postpone the due date of the monthly payments referred to in paragraphs 1 and 2 or change the amount of the payments. If under paragraph 21 the Property is acquired by Lender, Borrower's right to any insurance policies and proceeds resulting from damage to the Property prior to the acquisition shall pass to Lender to the extent of the sums secured by this Security Instrument immediately prior to the acquisition.

[11]   **6. Occupancy, Preservation, Maintenance and Protection of the Property; Borrower's Loan Application; Leaseholds.** Borrower shall occupy, establish, and use the Property as Borrower's principal residence within sixty days after the execution of this Security Instrument and shall continue to occupy the Property as Borrower's principal residence for at least one year after the date of occupancy, unless Lender otherwise agrees in writing, which consent shall not be unreasonably withheld, or unless extenuating circumstances exist which are beyond Borrower's control. Borrower shall not destroy, damage or impair the Property, allow the Property to deteriorate, or commit waste on the Property. Borrower shall be in default if any forfeiture action or proceeding, whether civil or criminal, is begun that in Lender's good faith judgment could result in forfeiture of the Property or otherwise materially impair the lien created by this Security Instrument or Lender's security interest. Borrower may cure such a default and reinstate, as provided in paragraph 18, by causing the action or proceeding to be dismissed with a ruling that, in Lender's good faith determination, precludes forfeiture of the Borrower's interest in the Property or other material impairment of the lien created by this Security Instrument or Lender's security interest. Borrower shall also be in default if Borrower, during the loan application process, gave materially false or inaccurate information or statements to Lender (or failed to provide Lender with any material information) in connection with the loan evidenced by the Note, including, but not limited to, representations concerning Borrower's occupancy of the Property as a principal residence. If this Security Instrument is on a leasehold, Borrower shall comply with all the provisions of the lease. If Borrower acquires fee title to the Property, the leasehold and the fee title shall not merge unless Lender agrees to the merger in writing.

7. Protection of Lender's Rights in the Property. If Borrower fails to perform the covenants and agreements contained in this Security Instrument, or there is a legal proceeding that may significantly affect Lender's rights in the Property (such as a proceeding in bankruptcy, probate, for condemnation or forfeiture or to enforce laws or regulations), then Lender may do and pay for whatever is necessary to protect the value of the Property and Lender's rights in the Property. Lender's actions may include paying any sums secured by a lien which has priority over this Security Instrument, appearing in court, paying reasonable attorneys' fees and entering on the Property to make repairs. Although Lender may take action under this paragraph 7, Lender does not have to do so.

Any amounts disbursed by Lender under this paragraph 7 shall become additional debt of Borrower secured by this Security Instrument. Unless Borrower and Lender agree to other terms of payment, these amounts shall bear interest from the date of disbursement at the Note rate and shall be payable, with interest, upon notice from Lender to Borrower requesting payment.

8. Mortgage Insurance. If Lender required mortgage insurance as a condition of making the loan secured by this Security Instrument, Borrower shall pay the premiums required to maintain the mortgage insurance in effect. If, for any reason, the mortgage insurance coverage required by Lender lapses or ceases to be in effect, Borrower shall pay the premiums required to obtain coverage substantially equivalent to the mortgage insurance previously in effect, at a cost substantially equivalent to the cost to Borrower of the mortgage insurance previously in effect, from an alternate mortgage insurer approved by Lender. If substantially equivalent mortgage insurance coverage is not available, Borrower shall pay to Lender each month a sum equal to one-twelfth of the yearly mortgage insurance premium being paid by Borrower when the insurance coverage lapsed or ceased to be in effect. Lender will accept, use and retain these payments as a loss reserve in lieu of mortgage insurance. Loss reserve payments may no longer be required, at the option of Lender, if mortgage insurance coverage (in the amount and for the period that Lender requires) provided by an insurer approved by Lender again becomes available and is obtained. Borrower shall pay the premiums required to maintain mortgage insurance in effect, or to provide a loss reserve, until the requirement for mortgage insurance ends in accordance with any written agreement between Borrower and Lender or applicable law.

Initials: ____ ____ ____

Texas Deed of Trust-Single Family-**Fannie Mae/Freddie Mac UNIFORM INSTRUMENT**   **Form 3044 09/90**
———— THE COMPLIANCE SOURCE, INC. ————   (page 2 of 5 pages)
To Order Call: (972) 980-2178•Fax (972) 392-2891   14001TX2.CS 12/97
www.compliancesource.com   ©1997, All Rights Reserved

(continued)

FIGURE **9.3**
Continued.

9. Inspection. Lender or its agent may make reasonable entries upon and inspections of the Property. Lender shall give Borrower notice at the time of or prior to an inspection specifying reasonable cause for the inspection.

[12]   **10. Condemnation.** The proceeds of any award or claim for damages, direct or consequential, in connection with any condemnation or other taking of any part of the Property, or for conveyance in lieu of condemnation, are hereby assigned and shall be paid to Lender.

In the event of a total taking of the Property, the proceeds shall be applied to the sums secured by this Security Instrument, whether or not then due, with any excess paid to Borrower. In the event of a partial taking of the Property in which the fair market value of the Property immediately before the taking is equal to or greater than the amount of the sums secured by this Security Instrument immediately before the taking, unless Borrower and Lender otherwise agree in writing, the sums secured by this Security Instrument shall be reduced by the amount of the proceeds multiplied by the following fraction: (a) the total amount of the sums secured immediately before the taking, divided by (b) the fair market value of the Property immediately before the taking. Any balance shall be paid to Borrower. In the event of a partial taking of the Property in which the fair market value of the Property immediately before the taking is less than the amount of the sums secured immediately before the taking, unless Borrower and Lender otherwise agree in writing or unless applicable law otherwise provides, the proceeds shall be applied to the sums secured by this Security instrument whether or not the sums are then due.

If the Property is abandoned by Borrower, or if, after notice by Lender to Borrower that the condemnor offers to make an award or settle a claim for damages, Borrower fails to respond to Lender within 30 days after the date the notice is given, Lender is authorized to collect and apply the proceeds, at its option, either to restoration or repair of the Property or to the sums secured by this Security Instrument, whether or not then due.

Unless Lender and Borrower otherwise agree in writing, any application of proceeds to principal shall not extend or postpone the due date of the monthly payments referred to in paragraphs 1 and 2 or change the amount of such payments.

11. Borrower Not Released; Forbearance By Lender Not a Waiver. Extension of the time for payment or modification of amortization of the sums secured by this Security Instrument granted by Lender to any successor in interest of Borrower shall not operate to release the liability of the original Borrower or Borrower's successors in interest. Lender shall not be required to commence proceedings against any successor in interest or refuse to extend time for payment or otherwise modify amortization of the sums secured by this Security Instrument by reason of any demand made by the original Borrower or Borrower's successors in interest. Any forbearance by Lender in exercising any right or remedy shall not be a waiver of or preclude the exercise of any right or remedy.

12. Successors and Assigns Bound; Joint and Several Liability; Co-signers. The covenants and agreements of this Security Instrument shall bind and benefit the successors and assigns of Lender and Borrower, subject to the provisions of paragraph 17. Borrower's covenants and agreements shall be joint and several. Any Borrower who co-signs this Security Instrument but does not execute the Note: (a) is co-signing this Security Instrument only to mortgage, grant and convey that Borrower's interest in the Property under the terms of this Security Instrument; (b) is not personally obligated to pay the sums secured by this Security Instrument; and (c) agrees that Lender and any other Borrower may agree to extend, modify, forbear or make any accommodations with regard to the terms of this Security Instrument or the Note without that Borrower's consent.

13. Loan Charges. If the loan secured by this Security Instrument is subject to a law which sets maximum loan charges, and that law is finally interpreted so that the interest or other loan charges collected or to be collected in connection with the loan exceed the permitted limits, then: (a) any such loan charge shall be reduced by the amount necessary to reduce the charge to the permitted limit; and (b) any sums already collected from Borrower which exceeded permitted limits will be refunded to Borrower. Lender may choose to make this refund by reducing the principal owed under the Note or by making a direct payment to Borrower. If a refund reduces principal, the reduction will be treated as a partial prepayment without any prepayment charge under the Note.

14. Notices. Any notice to Borrower provided for in this Security Instrument shall be given by delivering it or by mailing it by first class mail unless applicable law requires use of another method. The notice shall be directed to the Property Address or any other address Borrower designates by notice to Lender. Any notice to Lender shall be given by first class mail to Lender's address stated herein or any other address Lender designates by notice to Borrower. Any notice provided for in this Security Instrument shall be deemed to have been given to Borrower or Lender when given as provided in this paragraph.

15. Governing Law; Severability. This Security Instrument shall be governed by federal law and the law of the jurisdiction in which the Property is located. In the event that any provision or clause of this Security Instrument or the Note conflicts with applicable law, such conflict shall not affect other provisions of this Security Instrument or the Note which can be given effect without the conflicting provision. To this end the provisions of this Security Instrument and the Note are declared to be severable.

16. Borrower's Copy. Borrower shall be given one conformed copy of the Note and of this Security Instrument.

[13]   **17. Transfer of the Property or a Beneficial Interest in Borrower.** If all or any part of the Property or any interest in it is sold or transferred (or if a beneficial interest in Borrower is sold or transferred and Borrower is not a natural person) without Lender's prior written consent, Lender may, at its option, require immediate payment in full of all sums secured by this Security Instrument. However, this option shall not be exercised by Lender if exercise is prohibited by federal law as of the date of this Security Instrument.

If Lender exercises this option, Lender shall give Borrower notice of acceleration. The notice shall provide a period of not less than 30 days from the date the notice is delivered or mailed within which Borrower must pay all sums secured by this Security Instrument. If Borrower fails to pay these sums prior to the expiration of this period, Lender may invoke any remedies permitted by this Security Instrument without further notice or demand on Borrower.

18. Borrower's Right to Reinstate. If Borrower meets certain conditions, Borrower shall have the right to have enforcement of this Security Instrument discontinued at any time prior to the earlier of: (a) 5 days (or such other period as applicable law may specify for reinstatement) before sale of the Property pursuant to any power of sale contained in this Security Instrument; or (b) entry of a judgment enforcing this Security Instrument. Those conditions are that Borrower: (a) pays Lender all sums which then would be due under this Security Instrument and the Note as if no acceleration had occurred; (b) cures any default of any other covenants or agreements; (c) pays all expenses incurred in enforcing this Security Instrument, including, but not limited to, reasonable attorneys' fees; and (d) takes such action as Lender may reasonably require to assure that the lien of this Security Instrument, Lender's rights in the Property and Borrower's obligation to pay the sums secured by this Security Instrument shall continue unchanged. Upon reinstatement by Borrower, this Security Instrument and the obligations secured hereby shall remain fully effective as if no acceleration had occurred. However, this right to reinstate shall not apply in the case of acceleration under paragraph 17.

19. Sale of Note; Change of Loan Servicer. The Note or a partial interest in the Note (together with this Security Instrument) may be sold one or more times without prior notice to Borrower. A sale may result in a change in the entity (known as the "Loan Servicer") that collects monthly payments due under the Note and this Security Instrument. There also may be one or more changes of the Loan Servicer unrelated to a sale of the Note. If there is a change of the Loan Servicer, Borrower will be given written notice of the change in accordance with paragraph 14 above and applicable law. The notice will state the name and address of the new Loan Servicer and the address to which payments should be made. The notice will also contain any other information required by applicable law.

20. Hazardous Substances. Borrower shall not cause or permit the presence, use, disposal, storage, or release of any Hazardous Substances on or in the Property. Borrower shall not do, nor allow anyone else to do, anything affecting the Property that is in violation of any Environmental Law. The preceding two sentences shall not apply to the presence, use, or storage on the Property of small quantities of Hazardous Substances that are generally recognized to be appropriate to normal residential uses and to maintenance of the Property.

Borrower shall promptly give Lender written notice of any investigation, claim, demand, lawsuit or other action by any governmental or regulatory agency or private party involving the Property and any Hazardous Substance or Environmental Law of which Borrower has actual knowledge. If Borrower learns, or is notified by any governmental or regulatory authority, that any removal or other remediation of any Hazardous Substance affecting the Property is necessary, Borrower shall promptly take all necessary remedial actions in accordance with Environmental Law.

Initials: ___ ___ ___

Texas Deed of Trust-Single Family-Fannie Mae/Freddie Mac UNIFORM INSTRUMENT
——— THE COMPLIANCE SOURCE, INC. ———
To Order Call: (972) 980-2178•Fax (972) 392-2891
www.compliancesource.com

Form 3044 09/90
(page 3 of 5 pages)
14001TX3.CS 12/97
©1997, All Rights Reserved

(continued)

FIGURE 9.3
Continued.

As used in this paragraph 20, "Hazardous Substances" are those substances defined as toxic or hazardous substances by Environmental Law and the following substances: gasoline, kerosene, other flammable or toxic petroleum products, toxic pesticides and herbicides, volatile solvents, materials containing asbestos or formaldehyde, and radioactive materials. As used in this paragraph 20, "Environmental Law" means federal laws and laws of the jurisdiction where the Property is located that relate to health, safety or environmental protection.

NON-UNIFORM COVENANTS. Borrower and Lender further covenant and agree as follows:

[14]   **21. Acceleration; Remedies. Lender shall give notice to Borrower prior to acceleration following Borrower's breach of any covenant or agreement in this Security Instrument (but not prior to acceleration under paragraph 17 unless applicable law provides otherwise). The notice shall specify: (a) the default; (b) the action required to cure the default; (c) a date, not less than 30 days from the date the notice is given to Borrower, by which the default must be cured; and (d) that failure to cure the default on or before the date specified in the notice will result in acceleration of the sums secured by this Security Instrument and sale of the Property. The notice shall further inform Borrower of the right to reinstate after acceleration and the right to bring a court action to assert the non-existence of a default or any other defense of Borrower to acceleration and sale. If the default is not cured on or before the date specified in the notice, Lender at its option may require immediate payment in full of all sums secured by this Security Instrument without further demand and may invoke the power of sale and any other remedies permitted by applicable law. Lender shall be entitled to collect all expenses incurred in pursuing the remedies provided in this paragraph 21, including, but not limited to, reasonable attorneys' fees and costs of title evidence.**

If Lender invokes the power of sale, Lender or Trustee shall give notice of the time, place and terms of sale by posting and recording the notice at least 21 days prior to sale as provided by applicable law. Lender shall mail a copy of the notice of sale to Borrower in the manner prescribed by applicable law. Sale shall be made at public vendue between the hours of 10 a.m. and 4 p.m. on the first Tuesday of the month. Borrower authorizes Trustee to sell the Property to the highest bidder for cash in one or more parcels and in any order Trustee determines. Lender or its designee may purchase the Property at any sale.

Trustee shall deliver to the purchaser Trustee's deed conveying indefeasible title to the Property with covenants of general warranty. Borrower covenants and agrees to defend generally the purchaser's title to the Property against all claims and demands. The recitals in the Trustee's deed shall be prima facie evidence of the truth of the statements made therein. Trustee shall apply the proceeds of the sale in the following order: (a) to all expenses of the sale, including, but not limited to, reasonable Trustee's and attorneys' fees; (b) to all sums secured by this Security Instrument; and (c) any excess to the person or persons legally entitled to it.

If the Property is sold pursuant to this paragraph 21, Borrower or any person holding possession of the Property through Borrower shall immediately surrender possession of the Property to the purchaser at that sale. If possession is not surrendered, Borrower or such person shall be a tenant at sufferance and may be removed by writ of possession.

[15]   **22. Release.** Upon payment of all sums secured by this Security Instrument, Lender shall release this Security Instrument to Borrower. Borrower shall pay any recordation costs. Lender may charge Borrower a fee for releasing this Security Instrument, but only if the fee is paid to a third party for services rendered and the charging of the fee is permitted under applicable law.

23. Substitute Trustee. Lender, at its option and with or without cause, may from time to time remove Trustee and appoint, by power of attorney or otherwise, a successor trustee to any Trustee appointed hereunder. Without conveyance of the Property, the successor trustee shall succeed to all the title, power and duties conferred upon Trustee herein and by applicable law.

24. Subrogation. Any of the proceeds of the Note used to take up outstanding liens against all or any part of the Property have been advanced by Lender at Borrower's request and upon Borrower's representation that such amounts are due and are secured by valid liens against the Property. Lender shall be subrogated to any and all rights, superior titles, liens and equities owned or claimed by any owner or holder of any outstanding liens and debts, regardless of whether said liens or debts are acquired by Lender by assignment or are released by the holder thereof upon payment.

25. Partial Invalidity. In the event any portion of the sums intended to be secured by this Security Instrument cannot be lawfully secured hereby, payments in reduction of such sums shall be applied first to those portions not secured hereby.

26. Waiver of Notice of Intention to Accelerate. Borrower waives the right to notice of intention to require immediate payment in full of all sums secured by this Security Instrument except as provided in paragraph 21.

27. Riders to this Security Instrument. If one or more riders are executed by Borrower and recorded together with this Security Instrument, the covenants and agreements of each such rider shall be incorporated into and shall amend and supplement the covenants and agreements of this Security Instrument as if the rider(s) were a part of this Security Instrument. [Check applicable box(es)].

☐ Adjustable Rate Rider   ☐ Condominium Rider   ☐ 1-4 Family Rider
☐ Graduated Payment Rider   ☐ Planned Unit Development Rider   ☐ Biweekly Payment Rider
☐ Balloon Rider   ☐ Rate Improvement Rider   ☐ Second Home Rider
☐ Other(s) [specify]

28. Vendor's Lien (Purchase Money); Acknowledgment of Cash Advanced; Renewal and Extension.
[Check applicable box]
☐ **Vendor's Lien (Purchase Money):** The Note secured hereby is primarily secured by the Vendor's Lien retained in the Deed of even date herewith conveying the Property to Borrower, which Vendor's Lien has been assigned to Lender, this Security Instrument being additional security therefor.

☐ **Acknowledgment of Cash Advanced:** The Note herein described represents funds advanced to Borrower on this day at Borrower's request and Borrower acknowledges receipt of such funds.

☐ **Renewal and Extension:** The Note secured hereby is in renewal and extension, but not in extinguishment, of that indebtedness described on the Renewal and Extension Exhibit attached hereto and made a part hereof for all purposes.

BY SIGNING BELOW, Borrower accepts and agrees to the terms and covenants contained in this Security Instrument and in any rider(s) executed by Borrower and recorded with it.

Witnesses:

[16]

_____   _____ (Seal)
                                                                                                               -Borrower

_____   _____ (Seal)
                                                                                                               -Borrower

                                                                    _____ (Seal)
                                                                                                               -Borrower

                                                                    _____ (Seal)
                                                                                                               -Borrower

                                                                    Initials: _____ _____ _____

Texas Deed of Trust-Single Family-Fannie Mae/Freddie Mac UNIFORM INSTRUMENT   Form 3044 09/90
———— THE COMPLIANCE SOURCE, INC. ————   (page 4 of 5 pages)
To Order Call: (972) 980-2178•Fax (972) 392-2891   14001TX4.CS 12/97
www.compliancesource.com   ©1997, All Rights Reserved

(continued)

FIGURE **9.3**
Continued.

———————————————————— [Space Below This Line For Acknowledgment] ————————————————————

State of Texas   §
County of   §

[17]   Before me, a Notary Public, on this day personally appeared

known to me (or proved to me on the oath of   or through
(description of identity card or other document)) to be the person whose name is subscribed to the foregoing instrument and acknowledged
to me that he executed the same for the purposes and consideration therein expressed.
      Given under my hand and seal of office this   day of   , A.D.,

     (Seal)

                                                Notary Public

                                                Title of Officer

                                                My Commission Expires: _____

Initials: _____ _____

Alienation Clause

When used in a mortgage, an **alienation clause** (also called a **due-on-sale clause**) gives the lender the right to call the entire loan balance due if the mortgaged property is sold or otherwise conveyed (alienated) by the borrower. An example is shown at **[13].** The purpose of an alienation clause is two-fold. If the mortgaged property is put up for sale and a buyer proposes to assume the existing loan, the lender can refuse to accept that buyer as a substitute borrower if the buyer's credit is not good. But, more importantly, lenders have been using it as an opportunity to eliminate old loans with low rates of interest. Responding to complaints by consumers, 17 states have taken the attitude that due-on-sale clauses cannot be enforced in order to raise interest rates. However, the U.S. Supreme Court has ruled that a due-on-sale clause can be enforced by the lender in most circumstances. (The due-on-sale issue, from both the borrower's and lender's perspectives is discussed more in Chapter 12.) Texas courts have tended to uphold due-on-sale clauses.

    At **[14]** is the **acceleration clause.** If the borrower breaks any of the mortgage covenants or note agreements, the lender wants the right to terminate the loan. The acceleration clause permits the lender to demand the balance to be paid in full immediately. If the borrower cannot pay, foreclosure takes place and the property is sold.

    At **[15]** we have the **release clause,** which provides that the lender has the obligation to release the lien upon payment in full of the note secured by the deed of trust.

    At **[16],** the mortgagor states that he has made this mortgage. Actually, the execution statement is more a formality than a requirement; the mortgagor's signature alone indicates his execution of the mortgage and agreement to its provisions. At **[17],** the mortgage is acknowledged and/or witnessed as required by state law for placement in the public records. Like deeds, mortgages must be recorded if they are to be effective against any subsequent purchaser, mortgagee, or lessee. The reason the mortgage is recorded, but not the promissory note, is that the mortgage deals with rights and interests in real property, whereas the note represents a personal obligation.

Partial Release

Occasionally, the situation arises wherein the borrower wants the lender to release a portion of the mortgaged property from the mortgage after part of the loan has been repaid. This is known as asking for a **partial release.** For example, a land developer purchases 40 acres of land for a total price of $500,000 and finances the purchase with

$100,000 in cash plus a mortgage and note for $400,000 to the seller. In the mortgage agreement the developer might ask that the seller release 10 acres free and clear of the mortgage encumbrance for each $100,000 paid against the loan.

"Subject To" Clause

If an existing mortgage on a property does not contain a due-on-sale clause, the seller can pass the benefits of that financing along to the buyer. (This can occur when the existing loan carries a lower rate of interest than currently available on new loans.) One method of doing this is for the buyer to purchase the property **subject to the existing loan.** In the purchase contract the buyer states that he is aware of the existence of the loan and the mortgage that secures it, but takes no personal liability for it. Although the buyer may pay the remaining loan payments as they come due, the seller continues to be personally liable to the lender for the loan. As long as the buyer faithfully continues to make the loan payments, which he would normally do as long as the property is worth more than the debts against it, this arrangement presents no problem to the seller. However, if the buyer stops making payments before the loan is fully paid, even though it may be years later, in most states the lender can require the seller to pay the balance due plus interest. This is true even though the seller thought he was free of the loan because he sold the property.

Assumption of the Loan

The seller is on somewhat different ground if he requires the buyer to **assume the loan.** Under this agreement, the buyer promises in writing to the seller that he will pay the loan, thus personally obligating himself. In the event of default on the loan or a breach of the mortgage agreement, the lender will first expect the buyer to remedy the problem. If the buyer does not pay, the lender will look to the seller, because the seller's name is still on the original promissory note.

Deed of Trust to Secure Assumption

In the event the grantor under a deed of trust wants to sell her property and allow the purchaser to assume the obligations of that deed of trust, the TREC promulgated forms require that the proposed purchaser execute a deed of trust in favor of the grantor to secure the assumption. An example of a deed of trust to secure an assumption is shown in Figure 9.4. In this instrument, we will assume that the parties, N. Debted and wife May B. Debted, have conveyed their property to Chuck Roast and wife Berna. The only significant difference between Figure 9.4 and Figure 9.3 is the obligation secured. Instead of securing a real estate lien note, Figure 9.4 secures the assumption of an existing note. The grantors, Mr. and Mrs. Debted, become the beneficiaries under this Deed of Trust to Secure Assumption.

There has been little Texas law to date regarding the use of the Deed of Trust to Secure Assumption form. In practice, if the purchaser defaults, the sellers probably are unaware of it. However, since the Texas statutes for foreclosures under a deed of trust specify that "each debtor" must receive written notice of the proposed sale, it is assumed that the sellers, who are the original debtors on the deed of trust and promissory note, would be given notice of such sale. This would give them the right to pay the obligation or buy the property at the foreclosure sale.

At best, the Assumption form purports to give the seller of the property some tangible equity in the property. Note the paragraph specifying default in the payment of the note being assumed. The seller (the beneficiary) may, at his option, advance and pay the

Figure **9.4**
Deed of trust to secure assumption.

DEED OF TRUST TO SECURE ASSUMPTION

THE STATE OF TEXAS	§	
	§	KNOW ALL MEN BY THESE PRESENTS:
COUNTY OF HARRIS	§	

THAT Chuck Roast and wife, Berna Roast, of Harris County, Texas, hereinafter called Grantor (Whether one or more) for the purpose of securing the indebtedness hereinafter described, and in consideration of the sum of TEN DOLLARS ($10.00) to us in hand paid by the Trustee hereinafter named, the receipt of which is hereby acknowledged, and for the further consideration of the uses, purposes and trusts hereinafter set forth, have granted, sold and conveyed, and by these presents do grant, sell and convey unto Charles J. Jacobus, Trustee, whose address is 1100 Louisiana, Suite 1800, Houston, Harris County, Texas, 77002, and his substitutes or successors, all of the following described property situated in Harris County, Texas, to-wit:

Lot 1, Block 1, Shakey Acres Subdivision, Harris County, Texas, as shown of record at Volume 7, Page 3, of the Map Records of Harris County, Texas.

TO HAVE AND TO HOLD the above described property, together with the rights, privileges and appurtenances thereto belonging, unto the said Trustee and to his substitutes or successors forever. And Grantor does hereby bind Grantor, Grantor's heirs, executors, administrators and assigns to warrant and forever defend the said premises unto the said Trustee, Trustee's substitutes or successors and assigns forever, against the claim or claims, of all persons claiming or to claim the same or any part thereof.

This conveyance, however, is made in TRUST for the following purposes:

WHEREAS, N. Debted and wife, May B. Debted, hereinafter called Beneficiary, by deed of even date herewith conveyed the above described property to Grantor named herein, who, as part of the consideration therefor assumed and promised to pay, according to the terms thereof, all principal and interest remaining unpaid upon that one certain promissory note in the original principal sum of $83,000.00, dated February 1, 19xx, executed by N. Debted and May B. Debted, and payable to the order of Friendly Lender Savings and Loan Association, which said note is secured by a Deed of Trust recorded in Volume 666, Page 444 and/or under Clerk's File No. 99999 of the Official Public Records of Real Property of Harris County, Texas, the obligations and covenants of the Grantor named in said Deed of Trust were also assumed by Grantor named herein, and in said Deed the superior title and a vendor's lien were expressly reserved and retained by Beneficiary until said indebtedness and obligations so assumed are fully paid and satisfied, and should Grantor do and perform all of the obligations and covenants so assumed and make prompt payment of the indebtedness evidenced by said note so assumed as the same shall become due and payable, then this conveyance shall become null and void and of no further force and effect, it being agreed that a

(continued)

FIGURE **9.4**
Continued.

release of such indebtedness so assumed and of the liens securing the same by the legal owner and holder thereof prior to the advancement and payment thereon by Beneficiary of any sum or sums required to cure any default, shall be sufficient to release the lien created by this instrument as well as said vendor's lien so retained, without the joinder of Beneficiary. Unless, prior to the filing of a release of the indebtedness so assumed and of the liens securing the same in the office of the County Clerk of the County where said real property is situated, Beneficiary shall have filed in the office of the County Clerk of said County a sworn statement duly acknowledged and containing a legal description of the property hereinafter described and setting forth any and all sums that Beneficiary may have so advanced and paid, it shall be conclusively presumed that no sum or sums have been advanced and paid thereon by Beneficiary.

Grantor agrees that in the event of default in the payment of any installment, principal or interest, of the note so assumed by Grantors, or in the event of default in the payment of said note when due or declared due, or of a breach of any of the obligations or covenants contained in the Deed of Trust securing said note so assumed, Beneficiary may advance and pay such sum or sums as may be required to cure any such default, and that any and all such sums so advanced and paid by Beneficiary to cure such default shall be paid by Grantors to Beneficiary at Piggy National Bank in the City Houston, Harris County, Texas, within five (5) days after the date of such payment, without notice or demand, which are expressly waived. Grantor covenants to pay promptly to Beneficiary, without notice or demand, within the time and as provided in the foregoing paragraph, any and all sums that may, under the provisions of the foregoing paragraph, be due Beneficiary.

In the event of a breach of the foregoing covenant, it shall thereupon, or at any time thereafter, be the duty of the Trustee, or his successor or substitute as hereinafter provided, at the request of Beneficiary (which request is hereby conclusively presumed), to enforce this Trust, and after advertising the time, place and terms of the sale of the above-described and conveyed property, then subject to the lien hereof and mailing and filing notices, all as required by Section 51.002 Texas Property Code, as then amended, and otherwise complying with that statute, the Trustee shall sell the above-described property, then subject to the lien hereof, at public auction in accordance with such notices on the first Tuesday in any month between the hours of ten o'clock A.M. and four o'clock P.M., to the highest bidder for cash, selling all of the property as an entirety or in such parcels as the Trustee acting may elect, and make due conveyance to the Purchaser or Purchasers, with general warranty binding Grantor, Grantor's executors, administrators, heirs, successors and assigns; and out of the money arising from such sale, the Trustee acting shall pay first, all the expenses of advertising the sale and making the conveyance, including a commission of five percent (5%) to Trustee which commission shall be due and owing in addition to the attorney's fees provided for in said note, and then to Beneficiary the full amount of principal, interest, attorney's fees and other charges due and unpaid on said note and all other indebtedness secured hereby, rendering the balance of the sales price, if any, to Grantor, Grantor's heirs, executors, administrators, successors or assigns; and the recitals in the conveyance to Purchaser or Purchasers shall be full and conclusive evidence of the truth of the matter therein stated, and all prerequisites to said sale shall be presumed to have been performed, and such sale and conveyance shall be conclusive against Grantor, Grantor's heirs, executors, administrators, successors or assigns.

(continued)

FIGURE **9.4**
Continued.

Beneficiary shall have the right to purchase at any sale of the property, being the highest bidder and to have the amount for which such property is sold credited on the total sums owed Beneficiary.

Beneficiary is hereby authorized to appoint a substitute trustee, or a successor trustee, to act instead of the Trustee named herein without other formality than the designation in writing of a substitute or successor trustee; and the authority hereby conferred shall extend to the appointment of other successor and substitute trustees successively until the full and final payment and satisfaction of the indebtedness and obligations so assumed by Grantor; and each substitute and successor trustee shall succeed to all of the rights and powers of the original Trustee named herein.

Beneficiary may institute suit to enforce the provisions of this Deed of trust and for the foreclosure of this Deed of Trust lien.

The term "Grantor" used in this instrument shall also include any and all successors in interest of Grantor to all or any part of the herein described and conveyed property as well as any and all purchasers thereof at any sale made hereunder by the Trustee or Substitute Trustee, and the provisions of this Deed of Trust shall be covenants running with the land.

It is expressly stipulated that the liability of Grantor to Beneficiary, arising by virtue of the assumption by Grantor of the payment of the note herein described and of the obligations of the Deed of Trust securing said note, as well as the liability to Beneficiary of any and all persons hereafter assuming payment of said note and performance of the obligations of said Deed of Trust, shall in no wise be discharged or released by this instrument or by the exercise by Beneficiary of the rights and remedies herein provided for it being agreed that this instrument and all rights and remedies herein accorded Beneficiary are cumulative of any and all other rights and remedies existing at law.

Grantor expressly represents that any indebtedness becoming due and payable under and by virtue of the terms and provisions of this Deed of Trust is in part payment of the purchase price of the herein described and conveyed property and that this Deed of Trust is cumulative and in addition to the Vendor's Lien expressly retained in deed of even date herewith executed by Beneficiary to Grantor, and it is expressly agreed that Beneficiary may foreclose under either or both of said liens as Beneficiary may elect, without waiving the other, said deed hereinbefore mentioned, together with its record, being here referred to and made a part of this instrument.

In the event any sale is made of the above-described property, or any portion thereof, under the terms of this Deed of Trust, Grantor, Grantor's heirs and assigns, shall forthwith upon the making of such sale surrender and deliver possession of the property so sold to the Purchase at such sale, and in the event of their failure to do so they shall thereupon from and after the making of such sale be and continue as tenants at will of such Purchaser, and in the event of their failure to surrender possession of said property upon demand, the Purchaser, his heirs or assigns, shall be entitled to institute and maintain an action for forcible detainer of said property in the Justice of Peace Court in the Justice Precinct in which such property, or any part thereof, is situated.

3 of 4 pages

(continued)

FIGURE **9.4**
Continued.

This Deed of Trust lien shall be subordinate and inferior to any purchase money lien hereafter created.

EXECUTED this First day of February, 19xx.

GRANTOR:

_____

Chuck Roast

_____

Berna Roast

THE STATE OF TEXAS   §
                                    §
COUNTY OF HARRIS   §

This instrument was acknowledged before me on this the First day of February, 19xx, by Chuck Roast.

_____

NOTARY PUBLIC, STATE OF TEXAS

THE STATE OF TEXAS   §
                                    §
COUNTY OF HARRIS   §

This instrument was acknowledged before me on this the First day of February, 19xx, by Berna Roast.

_____

NOTARY PUBLIC, STATE OF TEXAS

AFTER RECORDING RETURN TO: PREPARED IN THE LAW OFFICE OF:

sums required to cure any such default. The grantors (purchasers of the property) must reimburse the beneficiaries (sellers of the property) within five days. If this is not done, the beneficiaries may exercise their right to foreclose under the power of sale clause.

The Deed of Trust to Secure Assumption form is intended to be used in conjunction with an assumption deed. An assumption deed is similar to other deeds, except that for consideration it specifies that the grantee is to assume the obligations of the note and deed of trust signed by the grantor.

NOVATION

The safest arrangement for the seller is to ask the lender to **substitute** the buyer's liability for his. This releases the seller from the personal obligation created by his promissory note, and the lender can now require only the buyer to repay the loan. The seller is also on safe ground if the mortgage agreement or state law prohibits deficiency judgments, a topic that will be explained later in this chapter.

When a buyer is to continue making payments on an existing loan, he will want to know exactly how much is still owing. An **estoppel certificate** (also called a **mortgagee's information letter**) is prepared by the lender to show how much of the loan remains to be paid. If a recorded mortgage states that it secures a loan for $35,000, but the borrower has reduced the amount owed to $25,000, the certificate of reduction will show that $25,000 remains to be paid. This is also used when the holder of a mortgage loan sells it to another investor. In it, the borrower is asked to verify the amount still owed and the rate of interest.

DEBT PRIORITIES

The same property can usually be pledged as collateral for more than one mortgage. This presents no problems to the lenders involved as long as the borrower makes the required payments on each note secured by the property. The difficulty arises when a default occurs on one or more of the loans, and the price the property brings at its foreclosure sale does not cover all the loans against it. As a result, a priority system is necessary. The debt with the highest priority is satisfied first from the foreclosure sale proceeds, and then the next highest priority debt is satisfied, then the next, until either the foreclosure sale proceeds are exhausted or all debts secured by the property are satisfied.

First Lien Mortgage

In the vast majority of foreclosures, the sale proceeds are not sufficient to pay all the outstanding debt against the property; thus, it becomes extremely important that a lender know her priority position before making a loan. Unless there is a compelling reason otherwise, a lender will want to be in the most senior position possible. This is normally accomplished by being the first lender to record a mortgage against a property that is otherwise free and clear of mortgage debt; this lender is said to hold a **first lien mortgage** on the property. If the same property is later used to secure another note before the first is fully satisfied, the new mortgage is a **second lien mortgage,** and so on. The first mortgage is also known as the **senior mortgage.** Any mortgage with a lower priority is a **junior mortgage.** As time passes and higher priority mortgages are satisfied, the lower priority mortgages move up in priority. Thus, if a property is secured by a first and a second mortgage and the first is paid off, the second becomes a first mortgage. Note that nothing is stamped or written on a mortgage document to indicate whether it is a first or second or third mortgage, etc. That priority can only be determined by searching the public records for mortgages recorded against the property that have not been released.

Subordination

Sometimes a lender will voluntarily take a lower priority position than he would otherwise be entitled to by virtue of his recording date. This is known as **subordination** and it allows a junior loan to move up in priority. For example, the holder of a first mortgage can volunteer to become a second mortgagee and allow the second mortgage to move into the first position. Although it seems irrational that a lender would actually volunteer to lower his priority position, it is sometimes done by landowners to encourage developers to buy their land.

Chattel Liens

An interesting situation regarding priority occurs when chattels are bought on credit and then affixed to land that is already mortgaged. If the chattels are not paid for, can the chattel lienholder come onto the land and remove them? If there is default on the mortgage loan against the land, are the chattels sold as fixtures? The solution is for the chattel lienholder to record a **chattel mortgage** or a **financing statement.** This protects the lienholder's interest even though the chattel becomes a fixture when it is affixed to land.

THE FORECLOSURE PROCESS

Although relatively few mortgages are foreclosed, it is important to have a basic understanding of what happens when foreclosure takes place. First, knowledge of what causes foreclosure can help in avoiding it; and, second, if foreclosure does occur, one should know the rights of the parties involved.

Although noncompliance with any part of the mortgage agreement by the borrower can result in the lender calling the entire balance immediately due, in most cases foreclosure occurs because the note is not being repaid on time. When a borrower is behind in payments, the loan is said to be **delinquent** or **nonperforming.** At this stage, rather than presume foreclosure is automatically the next step, the borrower and lender usually meet and attempt to work out an alternative payment program. Contrary to early motion picture plots in which lenders seem anxious to foreclose their mortgages, today's lender considers foreclosure to be the last resort. This is because the foreclosure process is time-consuming, expensive, and unprofitable. The lender would much rather have the borrower make regular payments. Consequently, if a borrower is behind in loan payments, the lender prefers to arrange a new, stretched-out, payment schedule rather than immediately to declare the acceleration clause in effect and move toward foreclosing the borrower's rights to the property.

If a borrower realizes that stretching out payments is not going to solve his financial problem, instead of presuming foreclosure to be inevitable, he can seek a buyer for the property who can make the payments. More than any other reason, this is why relatively few real estate mortgages are foreclosed. The borrower, realizing he is in or is about to be in financial trouble, sells his property. It is only when the borrower cannot find a buyer and when the lender sees no further sense in stretching the payments that the acceleration clause is invoked and the path toward foreclosure taken.

Foreclosure Routes

Basically there are two foreclosure routes: judicial and nonjudicial. **Judicial foreclosure** means taking the matter to a court of law in the form of a lawsuit that asks the judge to foreclose (cut off) the borrower. A **nonjudicial foreclosure** does not go to court and is not heard by a judge. It is conducted by the lender (or by a trustee) in accordance with provisions in the mortgage and in accordance with state law pertaining to nonjudicial foreclosures. Comparing the two, a judicial foreclosure is more costly and more time-consuming, but it does carry the approval of a court of law and it may give the lender rights to collect the full amount of the loan if the property sells for less than the amount owed. It is also the preferred method when the foreclosure case is complicated and involves many parties and interests. The nonjudicial route is usually faster, simpler, and cheaper, and it is preferred by lenders when the case is simple and straightforward.

Except for home equity loans, which require a judicial hearing, almost all loans in Texas are foreclosed nonjudicially because of Texas's wide use of the deed of trust as a mortgage.

NONJUDICIAL FORECLOSURE

Forty-two states, including Texas, permit the use of a **power of sale** as a means of simplifying and shortening the foreclosure proceeding.

The foreclosure process, as set out in the power of sale provision, is pursuant to statutory guidelines that provide for executions by sales under a deed of trust. To be enforceable, the power of sale provisions cannot be in violation of state law.

Texas law states that upon default, sale of real estate under the power conferred by the deed of trust shall be made in the county in which the real estate is located. When the real estate is situated in more than one county, the sale may be held in any of these counties, as long as all notices specify in which county the real estate will be sold. Texas statute now requires that a 20-day notice be given to each debtor to cure their default if it is the borrower's primary residence. If the default is not cured, notice of the proposed sale shall be given by posting written notice of the sale at least 21 days preceding the date of the sale. The notice must be posted at the courthouse door (and most courthouses provide a bulletin board located in close proximity to the court house door). If the real estate is situated in more than one county, the notice is to be posted at the courthouse door of each county in which the real estate is located. The notice must also be filed in the office of the County Clerk. The lender must also serve written notice of the proposed sale at least 21 days preceding the date of the sale (by certified mail) on each debtor obligated to pay such debt, according to the records of the lender or note holder. Service of the notice is considered complete upon deposit of the notice in the United States Mail in a properly addressed post-paid wrapper. The sale is held open to the public at specified time intervals between the hours of 10 a.m. and 4 p.m. on the first Tuesday of the next month after proper notice has been given.

As a practical matter, the mortgagee generally gives the trustee a Request to Act (Figure 9.5). The trustee gives the required notice to cure, then posts the notice of trustee's sale (Figure 9.6) on the courthouse door 21 days prior to the first Tuesday of the following month in which the sale is to take place. The trustee also files a copy of the notice in the county clerk's office. Then, on the day and time specified by statute, a public auction is held at the courthouse door. If there are no other bidders, the sale is normally made to a representative of the mortgage company or the note holder. Upon finalization of the sale and execution of the **trustee's deed,** the trustee executes an affidavit that such notice was properly carried out in compliance with state law. By execution of the deed and signing of this affidavit, the law presumes that the sale was carried out correctly.

Deficiencies

After the foreclosure, the lender is given the right to sue under the Promissory Note for any deficiency. For instance, suppose there is a $100,000.00 Deed of Trust and, at the time of foreclosure, $70,000.00 is still owed on the note. If the foreclosure sale is

FIGURE 9.5
Request to act.

FRIENDLY LENDER SAVINGS and LOAN
000 Sunrise Valley / Anywhere, Texas 00091

REQUEST TO ACT

Mr. Charles J. Jacobus
P. O. Box 1000000
Houston, Texas 77001

                              RE: Deed of Trust, dated February 1, 19xx,
                                    executed by N. Debted and wife, May B.
                                    Debted, to Charles J. Jacobus,
                                    Trustee, recorded in Volume 666 ,
                                    page   444 , Deed of Trust Records of
                                    Harris County, Texas.

Dear Sir:

     Default has occurred in the payment of the indebtedness de-
scribed in and secured by the above mentioned Deed of Trust and
by reason thereof said entire indebtedness is now past due and
unpaid.

     The undersigned, being the holder of said indebtedness and
lien, hereby request you, Charles J. Jacobus, as Trustee, to sell
the property in said Deed of Trust described and as provided
therein, in order to satisfy said indebtedness.

     Please furnish the undersigned several signed copies of the
Notice of the Trustee's Sale so that notice thereof can be served
by certified mail at least twenty-one (21) days preceding the
date of sale on each debtor obligated to pay such indebtedness
according to the records of the undersigned and as required by
law.

                              FRIENDLY LENDER SAVINGS AND LOAN

                              BY: *Mort Gage*
                                    _____
                                              President

held, and the property is sold for $50,000.00, the lender can then sue on the Promissory Note for the $20,000.00 deficiency. Texas has adopted, however, an anti-deficiency statute that allows the homeowner, upon being sued by the lender, to produce evidence in court of the fair market value of the house. If the appraised value of the house (presuming fair market value) is in excess of $50,000.00, the court must allow an offset for the entire appraised value of the house against the deficiency. In the current example, if the house appraised for $80,000.00, the court would require a complete offset against the sales price and the lender could not pursue a deficiency. The anti-deficiency statute also applies to judicial foreclosures and to anyone who may have guaranteed the Note. The anti-deficiency statute does not apply to private mortgage insurance. The mortgage insurer can still sue the borrower if the insurer pays the deficiency. Private mortgage insurance is discussed in Chapter 10.

NOTICE OF TRUSTEE'S SALE

FIGURE 9.6
Notice of trustee's sale.

Pursuant to authority conferred upon me by that certain Deed of Trust executed by N. Debted and wife, Mary B. Debted, of Harris County, Texas, dated February 1, 19xx, and duly recorded in Volume 666 , on page 444 of the Deed of Trust Records of Harris County, Texas, I will as Trustee under said Deed of Trust, in order to satisfy the indebtedness secured thereby and at the request of the holder of said indebtedness, default having been made in the payment thereof, sell on Tuesday, April 4, 19xx, at public auction to the highest bidder for cash before the courthouse door of Harris County, Texas, in Houston, Texas, between the hours of ten o'clock A.M. and four o'clock P.M. of that day, the following described property, to wit:

> *Lot 1, Block 1, Shakey Acres Subdivision, Harris County Texas, as shown of record at Volume 7, Page 3 of the Map Records of Harris County, Texas.*

EXECUTED this 4th day of March, 19xx.

Charles J. Jacobus
Charles J. Jacobus, Trustee

Redemption

Some states provide an **equity of redemption** to redeem the property prior to sale and reinstate the borrower's right to continue to make payments. In Texas, however, once the notice to cure has been sent to the debtor, the only equity of redemption that the debtor has is to pay the full amount owing, or to buy the property at the foreclosure. There is also no statutory **right of redemption** in Texas to reinstate the deed of trust after the foreclosure sale has taken place. The net effect of this is that once the note has been accelerated, the mortgagor has no rights except that of paying the full amount of the note due in cash at or before the foreclosure sale, unless otherwise agreed to by the mortgagee.

The power of sale provision of a deed of trust has consistently been upheld to be constitutional. However, it is important to take into consideration that because the state allows this type of foreclosure, lenders are more ready to make loans and provide money for mortgages, knowing that in the event of default their remedy is reasonably swift and inexpensive. In states that do not allow a quick and swift remedy to foreclosure proceedings, one consistently finds that loan procedures and credit searches become much more intense, to allow the mortgagee to minimize the risk of making a real estate loan. This, coupled with the fact that most mortgagees do not want to foreclose on property, means that mortgagees will generally give the mortgagor an agreed time to redeem, rather than immediately foreclose. The lender is in the business of making money on house payments, not in foreclosing and becoming a homeowner. A consistent string of foreclosures puts the lender into the real estate business, and most mortgagees wish to remain solely in the lending business.

ADVANTAGES OF THE DEED OF TRUST

The popularity of the deed of trust can be traced to the following attributes: (1) the time between default and foreclosure is relatively short, (2) the foreclosure process under the power of sale provision is far less expensive and complex than a court-ordered foreclosure; and (3) once the foreclosure sale takes place, there is no statutory redemption. These are primarily advantages to the lender, but such advantages have attracted lenders and made real estate loans less expensive and easier for borrowers to obtain. Some states prohibit deficiency judgments against borrowers when a deed of trust is used.

Property can be purchased "subject to" an existing deed of trust or it can be "assumed," just as with a regular mortgage. Debt priorities are established as for mortgages: There are the first and second, senior and junior trust deeds. Deeds of trust can be subordinated and partial releases are possible.

DEED IN LIEU OF FORECLOSURE

To avoid the hassle of foreclosure proceedings, a borrower may voluntarily deed the property to the lender. In turn, the borrower should demand cancellation of the unpaid debt and a letter to that effect from the lender. This method relieves the lender of foreclosing and waiting out any required redemption periods, but it also presents the lender with a sensitive situation. With the borrower in financial distress and about to be foreclosed, it is quite easy for the lender to take advantage of the borrower. As a result, courts may side with the borrower if the borrower complains of any unfair dealings. Thus, the lender must be prepared to prove conclusively that the borrower received a fair deal by deeding the property voluntarily to the lender in return for cancellation of his debt. A deed in lieu of foreclosure is a voluntary act by both borrower and lender; if either feels they will fare better in regular foreclosure proceedings, they need not agree to it. Texas has a new statute that gives renewed validity to deeds in lieu, so lenders may start using them more often.

REVIEW QUESTIONS

Answers to these questions are found in the Answer Key section at the back of the book.

1. When a deed of trust is recorded, bare title is conveyed by the
   A. lender to the borrower.
   B. borrower to the lender.
   C. borrower to the trustee.
   D. trustee to the lender.

2. When a deed of trust is foreclosed, title is conveyed by the
   A. borrower to the lender.
   B. trustee to the borrower.
   C. borrower to the trustee.
   D. trustee to the purchaser at foreclosure.

3. Which of the following clauses would be found in a deed of trust but not in a mortgage?
   A. A reconveyance clause.
   B. A power of sale clause.
   C. An acceleration clause.
   D. A defeasance clause.

4. If the trustee should die or be dissolved before the debt secured by a deed of trust is paid off, a successor may be named by the
   A. trustor.
   B. beneficiary.
   C. judge.
   D. Both A and B.

5. Comparing a deed of trust to a mortgage, which of the following would be unique to the deed of trust?
   A. Reconveyance.
   B. Power of Sale.
   C. Statutory redemption.
   D. None of the above.

6. The period of equitable redemption given to a borrower
   A. begins when the loan goes into default.
   B. ends when the property is sold at foreclosure.
   C. Both A and B.
   D. Neither A nor B.

7. When the amount received from a foreclosure sale is insufficient to pay off the mortgage loan and the other expenses of the sale, the lender may sometimes secure
   A. a deficiency judgment.
   B. a mechanic's lien.
   C. an estoppel lien.
   D. a statutory lien.

8. The period of time set by state law after a fore-closure sale, during which the mortgagor may redeem the property, is known as the period of
   A. equitable redemption.
   B. legal redemption.
   C. voluntary redemption.
   D. statutory redemption.

9. A borrower who feels mistreated by a power of sale foreclosure can
   A. obtain a judicial foreclosure.
   B. appeal the issue to the courts.
   C. obtain a judgment.
   D. obtain a lien.

10. By voluntarily giving the lender a deed in lieu of foreclosure, a delinquent borrower might avoid
    A. foreclosure proceedings.
    B. possible deficiency judgments.
    C. Both A and B.
    D. Neither A nor B.

11. A document that for all intents and purposes is a mortgage, although not labeled one, would most likely be
    A. an installment contract.
    B. a deed of trust.
    C. an equitable mortgage.
    D. a deed as security.

12. The borrower under a deed of trust is the
    A. beneficiary.
    B. trustee.
    C. grantor
    D. assignor.

13. The lender under a deed of trust is the
    A. beneficiary.
    B. trustee.
    C. grantor.
    D. assignee.

14. Evidence of the amount and terms of a borrower's debt to a lender is provided by means of a
    A. mortgage.
    B. promissory note.
    C. deed of trust.
    D. first mortgage.

15. A promissory note that fails to state that it is to be secured by a mortgage or deed of trust is
    A. a personal obligation of the borrower.
    B. an unsecured obligation of the borrower.
    C. Both A and B.
    D. Neither A nor B.

16. Should a borrower fail to make payments when due, the lender may demand immediate payment of the entire balance under the terms of the
    A. prepayment clause.
    B. defeasance clause.
    C. acceleration clause.
    D. hypothecation clause.

17. At the time of origination, a mortgage creates a lien on the mortgaged property in states that subscribe to the
    A. lien theory.
    B. title theory.
    C. intermediate theory.
    D. Both A and B.
    E. Both A and C.

18. The clause that gives the lender the right to call in the note if the mortgaged property is sold or otherwise conveyed by the borrower is known as the
    A. due-on-sale clause.
    B. alienation clause.
    C. Both A and B.
    D. Neither A nor B.

19. Who may be held responsible for mortgage loan repayment when a loan is assumed as part of a real estate sale?
    A. The purchaser.
    B. The seller.
    C. Both A and B.
    D. Neither A nor B.

20. When a loan is assumed, the
    A. seller can be relieved of liability by novation.
    B. the buyer should verify the loan balance with the lender.
    C. Both A and B.
    D. Neither A nor B.

CHAPTER 10

KEY TERMS

Amortized loan: a loan requiring periodic payments that include both interest and partial repayment of principal

Balloon loan: any loan in which the final payment is larger than the preceding payments

Conventional loans: real estate loans that are not insured by the FHA or guaranteed by the VA

Equity: the market value of a property less the debt against it

Impound or reserve account: an account into which the lender places monthly tax and insurance payments

Loan origination fee: the expenses a lender incurs in processing a mortgage loan

Loan-to-value ratio: a percentage reflecting what a lender will lend divided by the sale price or market value of the property, whichever is less

Maturity: the end of the life of a loan

OBRA: Omnibus Budget Reconciliation Act

PITI payment: a loan payment that combines principal, interest, taxes, and insurance

PMI: private mortgage insurance—a private mortgage insurance source to insure lenders against foreclosure loss

Point: one percent of the loan amount

Principal: the balance owing on a loan

Section 203(b): FHA's popular mortgage insurance program for houses

UFMIP: up-front mortgage insurance premium—a one-time charge by the FHA for insuring a loan

Lending Practices

IN THIS CHAPTER *Whereas Chapter 9 dealt with the legal aspects of notes, mortgages, and trust deeds, Chapters 10 and 11 deal with the money aspects of these instruments. We begin in this chapter with term loans, amortized loans, balloon loans, partially amortized loans, loan-to-value ratio, equity, and points. These topics are followed by the functions and importance of the FHA and VA and private mortgage insurance. Chapter 11 discusses Truth in Lending and provides a helpful and informative description of the loan application and approval process you (or your buyer) will experience when applying for a real estate loan. In Chapters 12 and 13, we look at sources and types of financing, including where to find mortgage loan money, where mortgage lenders obtain their money, and various types of financing instruments such as the adjustable rate mortgage, equity mortgage, wraparound mortgage, seller financing, and so forth. Note that from here on whatever is said about mortgages applies equally to deeds of trust.*

TERM LOANS

A loan that requires only interest payments until the last day of its life, at which time the full amount borrowed is due, is called a **term loan** (or straight loan). Until 1930, the term loan was the standard method of financing real estate in the United States. These loans were typically made for a period of three to five years. The borrower signed a note or bond agreeing: (1) to pay the lender interest on the loan every six months, and (2) to repay the entire amount of the loan upon **maturity;** that is, at the end of the life of the loan. As security, the borrower mortgaged the property to the lender.

Loan Renewal

In practice, most real estate term loans were not paid off when they matured. Instead, the borrower asked the lender, typically a bank, to renew the loan for another three to five years. The major flaw in this approach to lending was that the borrower might never own the property free and clear of debt. This left the borrower continuously at the mercy of the lender for renewals. As long as the lender was not pressed for funds, the borrower's renewal request was granted. However, if the lender was short of funds, no renewal was granted and the borrower was expected to pay in full.

The inability to renew term loans caused hardship to hundreds of thousands of property owners during the Great Depression that began in 1930 and lasted most of the decade. Banks were unable to accommodate requests for loan renewals and at the same time satisfy unemployed depositors who needed to withdraw their savings to live. As a result, owners of homes, farms, office buildings, factories, and vacant land lost their property as foreclosures reached into the millions. The market was so glutted with properties being offered for sale to satisfy unpaid mortgage loans that real estate prices fell at a sickening pace.

AMORTIZED LOANS

In 1933, a congressionally legislated Home Owner's Loan Corporation (HOLC) was created to assist financially distressed homeowners by acquiring mortgages that were about to be foreclosed. The HOLC then offered monthly repayment plans tailored to fit the homeowner's budget that would repay the loan in full by its maturity date without the need for a balloon payment. The HOLC was terminated in 1951 after rescuing over a million mortgages in its 18-year life. However, the use of this stretched-out payment plan, known as an **amortized loan,** took hold in American real estate, and today it is the accepted method of loan repayment.

Repayment Methods

The amortized loan requires regular equal payments during the life of the loan, of sufficient size and number to pay all interest due on the loan and reduce the amount owed to zero by the loan's maturity date. Figure 10.1 illustrates the contrast between an amortized and a term loan. Figure 10.1A shows a 6-year, $1,000 term loan with interest of $90 due each year of its life. At the end of the sixth year, the entire **principal** (the amount owed) is due in one lump sum payment along with the final interest payment. In Figure 10.1B, the same $1,000 loan is fully amortized by making six equal annual payments of $222.92. From the borrower's standpoint, $222.92 once each year is easier to budget than $90 for 5 years and $1,090 in the sixth year.

Furthermore, the amortized loan shown in Figure 10.1 actually costs the borrower less than the term loan. The total payments made under the term loan are $90 + $90 + $90 + $90 + $90 + $1,090 = $1,540. Amortizing the same loan requires total payments of 6 × $222.92 = $1,337.52. The difference is due to the fact that under the amortized loan the borrower begins to pay back part of the $1,000 principal with the first payment. In the first year, $90 of the $222.92 payment goes to interest and the remaining $132.92 reduces the principal owed. Thus, the borrower starts the second year owing only $867.08. At 9% interest per year, the interest on $867.08 is $78.04; therefore, when the borrower makes the second payment of $222.92, only $78.04 goes to interest. The remaining $144.88 is applied to reduce the loan balance, and the borrower starts the third year owing $722.20. Figure 10.2 charts this repayment program. Notice that the balance owed drops faster as the loan becomes older, that is, as it matures.

Monthly Payments

As you have just seen, calculating the payments on a term loan is relatively simple compared with calculating amortized loan payments. The widespread use of computers has greatly simplified the calculations, however. To illustrate how the amortization works, though, we should note that **amortization tables** are published and used throughout the real estate industry. Table 10.1 shows the monthly payments per $1,000 of loan for interest rates from 5% to 15% for periods ranging from 5 to 40 years. (Amortization tables are also published for quarterly, semiannual, and annual payments.) When you use an amortization table, notice that there are five variables:

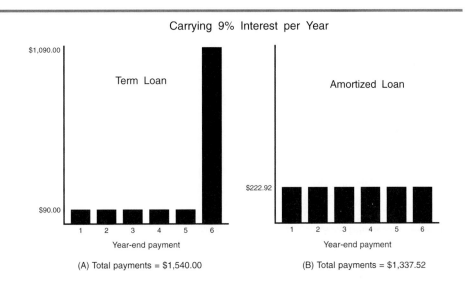

FIGURE 10.1
Repaying a 6-year $1,000 loan.

Carrying 9% Interest per Year

Term Loan

$1,090.00

$90.00

1   2   3   4   5   6

Year-end payment

(A) Total payments = $1,540.00

Amortized Loan

$222.92

1   2   3   4   5   6

Year-end payment

(B) Total payments = $1,337.52

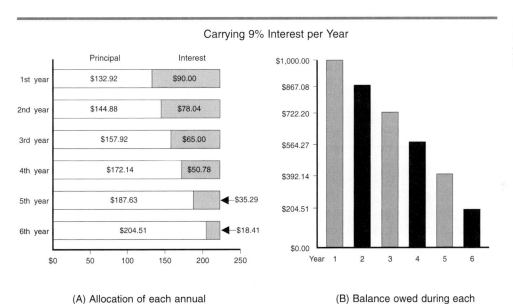

FIGURE 10.2
Repaying a 6-year $1,000 amortized loan.

Carrying 9% Interest per Year

Principal   Interest

1st year $132.92 $90.00
2nd year $144.88 $78.04
3rd year $157.92 $65.00
4th year $172.14 $50.78
5th year $187.63   ◄—$35.29
6th year $204.51   ◄—$18.41

$0   50   100   150   200   250

(A) Allocation of each annual payment to principal and interest

$1,000.00
$867.08
$722.20
$564.27
$392.14
$204.51
$0.00

Year 1   2   3   4   5   6

(B) Balance owed during each year of the loan

(1) frequency of payment, (2) interest rate, (3) maturity, (4) amount of the loan, and (5) amount of the periodic payment. If you know any four of these, you can obtain the fifth variable from the tables. For example, suppose that you want to know the monthly payment necessary to amortize a $60,000 loan over 30 years at $9^{1}/_{2}$% interest. The first step is to look in Table 10.1 for the $9^{1}/_{2}$% line. Then locate the 30-year column. Where they cross, you will find the necessary monthly payment per $1,000: $8.41. Next, multiply $8.41 by 60 to get the monthly payment for a $60,000 loan: $504.60. If the loan is to be $67,500, then multiply $8.41 by 67.5 to get the monthly payment: $567.68.

Continuing the foregoing example, suppose we reduce the repayment period to 15 years. First look for the $9^{1}/_{2}$% line, then go over to the 15-year column. The number there is $10.45. Next, multiply $10.45 by 60 to get the monthly payment for a $60,000 loan: $627.00. If the loan is to be $67,500, then multiply $10.45 by 67.5 to get the monthly payment: $705.38.

TABLE 10.1
Amortization table
monthly payment per
$1,000 of loan

Interest Rate per Year				LIFE OF THE LOAN				
	5 years	10 years	15 years	20 years	25 years	30 years	35 years	40 years
5 %	$18.88	$10.61	$ 7.91	$6.60	$5.85	$5.37	$5.05	$4.83
5 ¹/₂	19.11	10.86	8.18	6.88	6.15	5.68	5.38	5.16
6	19.34	11.11	8.44	7.17	6.45	6.00	5.71	5.51
6 ¹/₂	19.57	11.36	8.72	7.46	6.76	6.32	6.05	5.86
7	19.81	11.62	8.99	7.76	7.07	6.66	6.39	6.22
7 ¹/₂	20.04	11.88	9.28	8.06	7.39	7.00	6.75	6.59
8	20.28	12.14	9.56	8.37	7.72	7.34	7.11	6.96
8 ¹/₂	20.52	12.40	9.85	8.68	8.06	7.69	7.47	7.34
9	20.76	12.67	10.15	9.00	8.40	8.05	7.84	7.72
9 ¹/₂	21.01	12.94	10.45	9.33	8.74	8.41	8.22	8.11
10	21.25	13.22	10.75	9.66	9.09	8.78	8.60	8.50
10 ¹/₂	21.50	13.50	11.06	9.99	9.45	9.15	8.99	8.89
11	21.75	13.78	11.37	10.33	9.81	9.53	9.37	9.29
11 ¹/₂	22.00	14.06	11.69	10.67	10.17	9.91	9.77	9.69
12	22.25	14.35	12.01	11.02	10.54	10.29	10.16	10.09
12 ¹/₂	22.50	14.64	12.33	11.37	10.91	10.68	10.56	10.49
13	22.76	14.94	12.66	11.72	11.28	11.07	10.96	10.90
13 ¹/₂	23.01	15.23	12.99	12.08	11.66	11.46	11.36	11.31
14	23.27	15.53	13.32	12.44	12.04	11.85	11.76	11.72
14 ¹/₂	23.53	15.83	13.66	12.80	12.43	12.25	12.17	12.13
15	23.79	16.14	14.00	13.17	12.81	12.65	12.57	12.54

Loan Size

Amortization tables are also used to determine the amount of loan a borrower can support if you know how much the borrower has available to spend each month on loan payments. Suppose that a prospective home buyer can afford monthly principal and interest payments of $650 and lenders are making 30-year loans at 10%. How large a loan can this buyer afford? In Table 10.1 find where the 10% line and the 30-year column meet. You will see 8.78 there. This means that every $8.78 of monthly payment will support $1,000 of loan. To find how many thousands of dollars $650 per month will support, just divide $650 by $8.78. The answer is 74.031 thousands or $74,031. By adding the buyer's down payment, you know what price property the buyer can afford to purchase. If interest rates are 7¹/₂%, the number from the table is 7.00 and the loan amount is $92,857. (You can begin to see why the level of interest rates is so important to real estate prices.)

As you have noticed, everything in Table 10.1 is on a monthly payment per thousand basis. With a full book of amortization tables rather than one page, it is possible to look up monthly payments for loans from $100 to $100,000 to determine loan maturities for each year from 1 to 40 years and to calculate many more interest rates. Amortization books are available from most local bookstores.

Change in Maturity Date

An amortization table also shows the impact on the size of the monthly payment when the life of a loan is extended. For example, at 11% interest, a 10-year loan requires a monthly payment of $13.78 per thousand of loan. Increasing the life of the loan to 20 years drops the monthly payment to $10.33 per $1,000. Extending the loan payback to 30 years reduces the monthly payment to $9.53 per thousand. The smaller monthly payment is why 30 years is a popular loan term with borrowers. Note, however, that going beyond 30 years does not significantly reduce the monthly payment. Going from 30 to 35 years reduces the monthly payment by only 16¢ per thousand but adds 5 years of monthly payments. Extending the payback period from 35 to 40 years reduces the monthly payment by just 8¢ per $1,000 ($4 per month on a $50,000 loan) and adds another 60 months of payments at $464.50 per month. As a practical matter, amortized real estate loans are seldom made for more than 30 years.

BUDGET MORTGAGE

The **budget mortgage** takes the amortized loan one step further. In addition to collecting the monthly principal and interest payment (often called *P + I*), the lender collects one-twelfth of the estimated cost of the annual property taxes and hazard insurance on the mortgaged property. The money for tax and insurance payments is placed in an **impound account** (also called an **escrow** or **reserve account**). When taxes and insurance payments are due, the lender pays them. Thus, the lender makes certain that the value of the mortgaged property will not be undermined by unpaid property taxes or by uninsured fire or weather damage. This form of mortgage also helps the borrower to budget for property taxes and insurance on a monthly basis. To illustrate, if insurance is $240 per year and property taxes are $1,800 per year, the lender collects an additional $20 and $150 each month along with the regular principal and interest payments. This combined principal, interest, taxes, and insurance payment is often referred to as a **PITI payment.**

BALLOON LOAN

A **balloon loan** is any loan that has a final payment larger than any of the previous payments on the loan. The final payment is called a **balloon payment.** The term loan described at the beginning of this chapter is a type of balloon loan. Partially amortized loans, discussed next, are another type of balloon loan. In tight money markets, the use of balloon loans increased considerably. Balloon loans with maturities as short as three to five years were commonplace. This arrangement gives the buyer (borrower) three to five years to find cheaper and longer-term financing elsewhere. If such financing does not materialize and the loan is not repaid on time, the lender has the right to foreclose. The alternative is for the lender and borrower to agree to an extension of the loan, usually at prevailing interest rates.

PARTIALLY AMORTIZED LOAN

When the repayment schedule of a loan calls for a series of amortized payments followed by a balloon payment at maturity, it is called a **partially amortized loan.** For example, a lender might agree to a 30-year amortization schedule with a provision that at the end of the tenth year all the remaining principal be paid in a single balloon payment. The advantage to the borrower is that for 10 years the monthly payments will be smaller than if the loan was completely amortized in 10 years. (You can verify this in Table 10.1.) However, the disadvantage is that the balloon payment due at the end of the tenth year might be the borrower's financial downfall. Just how large that balloon payment will be can be determined in advance by using a **loan balance table** (also

9 1/2% ANNUAL INTEREST							11 1/2% ANNUAL INTEREST						
Age of Loan	Original Life (years)						Age of Loan	Original Life (years)					
(yrs.)	10	15	20	25	30	35	(yrs.)	10	15	20	25	30	35
2	$868	$934	$963	$978	$987	$992	2	$880	$944	$971	$984	$991	$995
4	708	853	918	952	971	983	4	729	873	935	965	981	989
6	515	756	864	921	953	971	6	539	784	889	940	967	982
8	282	639	799	883	930	957	8	300	672	831	909	950	972
10		497	720	837	902	940	10		531	759	870	929	960
12		326	625	781	869	920	12		354	667	821	902	945
14		119	510	714	828	896	14		132	553	759	868	926
16			371	633	780	866	16			228	585	772	873
18			203	535	721	830	18			409	682	825	903
20				416	650	787	20				462	704	836
22				273	564	735	22				308	620	789
24				100	460	671	24				115	513	729
26					335	595	26					380	655
28					183	503	28					211	561
30						391	30						444
32						256	32						296
34						94	34						110

called a **remaining balance table**). Presuming an interest rate of 11 1/2% and a 30-year loan, at the end of 10 years the loan balance table in Table 10.2 shows that for each $1,000 originally loaned, $929 would still be owed. If the original loan was for $100,000, at the end of 10 years 100 × $929 = $92,900 would be due as one payment. This qualifies it as a balloon loan.

As you can see from this example, when an amortized loan has a long maturity, relatively little of the debt is paid off during the initial years of the loan's life. Nearly all the early payments go for interest, so that little remains for principal reduction. For example, Table 10.2 shows that even after 16 years of payments on a 30-year, 11 1/2% loan, 82 1/2% of the loan is still unpaid. Not until this loan is about 6 years from maturity will half of it have been repaid.

EARLIER PAYOFF

During the late 1970s when inflation rates exceeded interest rates, the popular philosophy was to borrow as much as possible for as long as possible. Then in the early 1980s inflation rates dropped below interest rates and the opposite philosophy became attractive to many borrowers. This was especially true for those who had borrowed (or were contemplating borrowing) at double-digit interest rates. Let us use as an example an $80,000 loan at 11 1/2% interest. If the loan has a maturity of 30 years, from Table 10.1 we can determine the monthly payments to be $792.80. (Follow this example on your own.)

15-Year Loan

Suppose the maturity of the aforementioned loan is changed from 30 to 15 years. Looking at Table 10.1, the monthly payments would now be $935.20. This is $142.40

more per month, but the loan is fully paid in 15 years, not 30 years. The total amount of interest paid on the 15-year loan is $(15 \times 12 \times \$935.20) - \$80,000 = \$88,336$. The total amount of interest paid on the 30-year loan is $(30 \times 12 \times \$792.80) - \$80,000 = \$205,408$. Thus, for an extra $142.40 per month for 180 months (which amounts to $25,632) the borrower saves the difference between $205,408 and $88,336 (which is $117,072). Many borrowers consider this a very good return on their money. (It is, in fact, an $11^1/_2\%$ compounded rate of return.) Lenders are more receptive to making fixed-rate loans for 15 years than for 30 years. This is because the lender is locked into the loan for 15 years, not 30 years. As a result, a lender is usually willing to offer a 15-year loan at a lower rate of interest than a 30-year loan. In view of these benefits to borrower and lender alike, the 15-year loan is becoming a popular home financing tool.

Biweekly Payments

A small but growing number of lenders offer a biweekly repayment plan. The loan is amortized as if it were going to last 30 years. But instead of paying once a month, the borrower makes one-half the monthly payment every two weeks. This may not sound like much of a difference but the results are eye-opening. Assume you borrow $100,000 at 7% interest, paying (see Table 10.1) $666.00 per month. You will retire the loan in 30 years at a cost of $139,509 in interest. If you decide to pay half of $666.00 every two weeks, the loan will be fully paid in just 18 years and will have cost you $105,046 in interest. This happens because biweekly compounding works in your favor and because you make 26 half-size payments a year, not 24.

Existing Loans

Borrowers with existing loans who want to celebrate with an early mortgage burning can simply add a few dollars each month to the required monthly payment. This can be particularly beneficial for people who borrowed at rates of 13%, 14%, and 15% or more. In effect, whatever extra amount is added to the monthly payment will "earn" interest at the loan's interest rate. Thus, if a loan has a 14% rate, early payments "earn" at 14%. If the borrower has no alternative places to invest that will yield 14%, then a few additional dollars each month will work miracles. For example, a 30-year, $100,000 loan at 14% interest requires monthly payments (see Table 10.1) of $1,185. Voluntarily adding an extra $19 per month reduces the maturity (payoff) date from 30 years to 25 years (see Table 10.1 again). If an extra $40 is added to the $19, the maturity date shrinks to 20 years. In other words, an extra $59 per month eliminates 10 years of payments.

You may be wondering why this has not been a popular idea with borrowers. When interest rates are around 6% and 7% (as they were in the 1960s and, more recently, in the 1990s), the mathematics of early payoff are not very impressive.

LOAN-TO-VALUE RATIO

The relationship between the amount of money a lender is willing to loan and the lender's estimate of the market value of the property that will serve as security is called the **loan-to-value ratio** (often abbreviated **L/V** or **LTV ratio**). For example, a prospective home buyer wants to purchase a house priced at $80,000. A local lender appraises the house, finds it has a market value of $80,000 and agrees to make an 80% L/V loan. This means that the lender will loan up to 80% of the $80,000 and the buyer must provide at least 20% in cash. In dollars, the lender will loan up to $64,000, and the buyer must make a cash down payment of at least $16,000. If the lender appraises the home for more than $80,000, the loan will still be $64,000. If the appraisal is for less than $80,000, the loan will be 80% of the appraised value, and the buyer must pay the balance in cash. The rule is that price or value, whichever is lower, is applied to the L/V ratio. This rule exists to prevent the lender from overlending on a property just because the borrower overpaid for it.

EQUITY

The difference between the market value of a property and the debt owed against it is called the owner's **equity.** On a newly purchased $80,000 home with a $16,000 cash down payment, the buyer's equity is $16,000. As the value of the property rises or falls and as the mortgage loan is paid down, the equity changes. For example, if the value of the home rises to $90,000 and the loan is paid down to $62,000, the owner's equity will be $28,000. If the owner completely repays the loan so that there is no debt against the home, the owner's equity is equal to the market value of the property.

LOAN POINTS

Probably no single term in real estate finance causes as much confusion and consternation as the word *points.* In finance, the word **point** means 1% of the loan amount. Thus, on a $60,000 loan, one point is $600. On a $40,000 loan, three points is $1,200. On a $100,000 loan, eight points is $8,000.

The use of points in real estate mortgage finance can be split into two categories: (1) loan origination fees expressed in terms of points and (2) the use of points to change the effective yield of a mortgage loan to a lender. Let us look at these two uses in more detail.

Origination Fee

When a borrower asks for a mortgage loan, the lender incurs a number of expenses, including such things as the time its loan officer spends interviewing the borrower, office overhead, the purchase and review of credit reports on the borrower, an on-site appraisal of the property to be mortgaged, title searches and review, legal and recording fees, and so on. For these, some lenders make an itemized billing, charging so many dollars for the appraisal, credit report, title search, and so on. The total becomes the **loan origination fee,** which the borrower pays to get the loan. Other lenders do not make an itemized bill, but instead simply state the origination fee in terms of a percentage of the loan amount, for example, one point. Thus, a lender quoting a loan origination fee of one point is saying that for a $95,000 loan, its fee to originate the loan will be $950.

Discount Points

Points charged to raise the lender's monetary return on a loan are known as **discount points.** A simplified example illustrates their use and effect. If you are a lender and agree to make a term loan of $100 to a borrower for one year at 10% interest, you would normally expect to give the borrower $100 now (disregard loan origination fees for a moment) and, one year later, the borrower would give you $110. In percentage terms, the **effective yield** on your loan is 10% per annum (year) because you received $10 for your one-year, $100 loan. Now suppose that instead of handing the borrower $100, you handed him $99 but still required him to repay $100 plus $10 in interest at the end of the year. This is a discount of one point ($1 in this case), and the borrower paid it out of the loan funds. The effect of this financial maneuver is to raise the effective yield (yield to maturity) to you without raising the interest rate itself. Therefore, if you loan out $99 and receive $110 at the end of the year, you effectively have a return of $11 for a $99 loan. This gives you an effective yield of $11 / $99 or 11.1%, rather than 10%.

Calculating the effective yield on a discounted 20- or 30-year mortgage loan is more difficult because the amount owed drops over the life of the loan, and because the majority are paid in full ahead of schedule due to refinancing. Computers and calculators usually make these calculations; however, a useful rule of thumb states that on the typical home loan each point of discount raises the effective yield by $1/8$ of 1%. Thus, four discount points would raise the effective yield by approximately $1/2$ of 1% and eight points would raise it by 1%. Discount points are most often charged during periods of **tight money,** that is, when mortgage money is in short supply. During periods of **loose money,** when lenders have adequate funds to lend and are actively seeking borrowers, discount points disappear.

Real estate loans that are not insured by the FHA or guaranteed by the VA are termed **conventional loans.** As previously discussed, the conventional loan market has a growing presence in the marketplace. FHA and VA loans are now only a small fraction of the single-family loan origination market. FHA handles a little over 12%; VA about 2%. Let's discuss the impact of the FHA and VA.

FHA INSURANCE PROGRAMS

The Great Depression caused a major change in the attitude of the federal government toward home financing in the United States. In 1934, one year after the Home Owners Loan Corporation was established, Congress passed the National Housing Act. The Act's most far-reaching provision was to establish the Federal Housing Administration (FHA) for the purpose of encouraging new construction as a means of creating jobs. To accomplish this goal, the FHA offered to insure lenders against losses due to non-repayment when they made loans on both new and existing homes. In turn, the lender had to grant 20-year fully amortized loans with loan-to-value ratios of 80% rather than the 3- to 5-year, 50% to 60% term loans common up to that time.

The FHA did its best to keep from becoming a burden to the American taxpayer. When a prospective borrower approached a lender for an FHA-secured home loan, the FHA reviewed the borrower's income, expenses, assets, and debts. The objective was to determine whether there was adequate room in the borrower's budget for the proposed loan payments. The FHA also sent inspectors to the property to make certain that it was of acceptable construction quality and to determine its fair market value. To offset losses that would still inevitably occur, the FHA charged the borrower an annual insurance fee of approximately $1/2$ of 1% of the balance owed on the loan. The FHA was immensely successful in its task. Not only did it create construction jobs, but it raised the level of housing quality in the nation and, in a pleasant surprise to taxpayers, actually returned annual profits to the U.S. Treasury. In response to its success, in 1946 Congress changed its status from temporary to permanent.

Current FHA Coverage

The FHA has had a marked influence on lending policies in the real estate industry. Foremost among these is the widespread acceptance of the high loan-to-value, fully amortized loan. In the 1930s, lenders required FHA insurance before making 80%

L/V loans. By the 1960s, lenders were readily making 80% L/V loans without FHA insurance. Meanwhile, the FHA insurance program was working so well that the FHA raised the portion it was willing to insure. Congress established a new maximum LTV ratio by passing the **Omnibus Budget Reconciliation Act (OBRA).** The OBRA calculation does not include closing costs, but the maximum L/V ratio is 98.75% for houses with a sales price of less than $50,000, and 97.75% for houses with a sales price in excess of $50,000. FHA now insures a lender for the lesser of: (1) the OBRA value, or (2) the "old rule," which is 97% of the appraised value up to an appraised value of $50,000. If the property's appraised value exceeds $50,000, FHA insures 97% of the first $25,000 plus 95% of the balance of its appraised value up to $125,000, and 90% of such value in excess of $125,000. Utilizing the new OBRA calculations, 100% of the good faith estimate of closing costs can be included in calculating the loan amount. To illustrate, on a $60,000 home the FHA would insure 97% of the first $25,000 and 95% of the remaining $35,000, for a total of $57,500, although new regulations require that seller-paid closing costs be deducted from the value of the property. In our example, this means a cash down payment of only $2,500 for the buyer. The borrower is not permitted to use a second mortgage to raise this $2,500. The FHA requires some down payment; otherwise, it would be too easy for the borrower to walk away from the debt and leave the FHA to pay the lender's insurance claim. The maximum amount the FHA will insure has varied from city to city and changes from time to time. As of 1998, the maximum loan amount in high cost areas was $170, 362. FHA has proposed eliminating loan limits by geographical area to simplify FHA loan underwriting.

Private investors are banned from the FHA single-family program. In addition, no single-family loans can be assumed by investors. Any loan made before December 15, 1989 may be assumed by an investor, but additional restrictions have to be met: (1) the balance due must be no more than 75% of the cost of the property; and (2) if the monthly mortgage payment exceeds the net rental income, the mortgage amount must be reduced so that its payment does not exceed the amount amortized by the net rental income.

Assumability

Traditionally, FHA loans were popular because the 30-year fixed-rate loans could be assumed without any increase in interest. This is still true for loans that were originated prior to December 1, 1986. The assumption procedure can be one of two types, a simple assumption or a formal assumption. In the **simple assumption** procedure, the property is sold and the loan is assumed by the buyer without notification to the FHA or its agent. The seller remains fully liable to the FHA for full repayment. In the **formal assumption,** the property is not conveyed to a new buyer until the new buyer's creditworthiness has been approved by the FHA or its agent. When the creditworthy buyer assumes the loan, the seller may obtain a full release of liability from the FHA.

If the FHA loan was originated between December 1, 1986, and December 15, 1989, the owner-occupant cannot sell the property with a loan assumption during the first 12 months after execution of the mortgage without creditworthiness approval for each person who assumes the loan. If the seller is an investor, the assumption cannot be made without prior approval during the first 24 months after execution of the mortgage. Failure to comply with either requirement results in an acceleration of the loan balance. After the one- or two-year loan period, the loan can be assumed without approval. If the assumption is a simple assumption, the seller remains fully liable for five years after the new mortgage is executed. If the loan is not in default after the five years, the seller is automatically released from liability.

If the loan was originated after December 15, 1989, the FHA requires the creditworthiness approval prior to the conveyance of title on all assumption loans. If the borrower assumes a mortgage loan, the lender cannot refuse to release the original borrower from liability on the loan.

Mortgage Insurance

The FHA charges a one-time **Up Front Mortgage Insurance Premium (UFMIP)** that is paid when the loan is made. The amount of the UFMIP is 2.25% of the loan amount, although there are exceptions. First-time home buyers pay only 1.5% for homes in central cities. If the first-time home buyers are located outside of central cities, the rate is 1.25%. In both cases, the home buyers must take educational programs. FHA mortgages with terms of 15 years or less charge 2%, with no annual premium if the loan-to-value ratio is less than 90%. The premium can be paid in cash or added to the amount borrowed. If borrowed, it can be over and above the FHA ceiling. Thus, if the ceiling is $90,000 and the loan requested is $90,000, the UFMIP will be $3,420 and the total amount financed will be $93,420. The $93,420 becomes the principal amount of the loan, and an amortization table is used to find the monthly payment. If the loan is fully repaid within 7 years, the borrower is entitled to a refund of part of the UFMIP.

The FHA now also charges an annual premium amounting to $\frac{1}{2}$ of 1% of the annual loan balance. One-twelfth of the annual premium is added to the monthly payment and must be included in the proposed monthly housing expense to qualify the borrower for the loan. The amount is calculated each year on the unpaid principal balance without the UFMIP and excluding closing costs. Since 1994, if the down payment exceeds 10%, the term for premium payment is 11 years. If the down payment is 10% or less, the term of the premium is 30 years. Annual premiums are nonrefundable.

Floating Interest Rates

At one time, FHA set interest rate ceilings. Fixed-rate FHA loans are now negotiable and float with the market, and the seller also has a choice in how many points to contribute toward the borrower's loan. This can be none, some, or all the points, and the seller can even pay the borrower's mortgage insurance premium (MIP). Typical purchase contract language is, "The seller will pay X points and the buyer will pay not more than Y points and the agreed-on interest rate is Z%." Thus, X is the contribution the seller will make, and the seller is protected from having to pay more. The buyer will pay any additional points, but not more than Y points. Beyond that, the buyer can cancel the purchase contract. That would happen if the market rates rose quickly while the rate at Z is fixed.

Loan Qualification

Before leaving the topic of the FHA, it is interesting to note that much of what we take for granted as standard loan practice today was the result of FHA innovation years ago. As already noted, before 1934 standard real estate loan practice called for short-term renewable loans. Then the FHA boldly offered 20-year amortized loans. Once these were shown to be successful investments for lenders, loans without FHA insurance were made for 20 years. Later, when the FHA successfully went to 30 years, non–FHA-insured loans followed. The FHA also established loan application review techniques that have been widely accepted and copied throughout the real estate industry. The biggest step in this direction was to analyze a borrower's loan application in terms of earning power.

The U.S. Department of Housing and Urban Development (HUD) announced major revisions in its FHA single-family underwriting guidelines in January 1995, giving lenders more flexibility in considering an applicant's income and savings. The new regulations provide that FHA may now participate in state housing finance agencies and programs to use alternative qualifying methods, such as (1) the applicant's existing housing payments, (2) tax benefits of home ownership, and (3) nonhousing debt history. In addition, FHA now uses a 3-year test for income stability instead of the previous 5-year test. Only debts extending 10 or more months are included into debt-to-income calculations and child care costs are no longer counted as a recurring debt. FHA lenders can now also use a three-repository merged credit report. HUD also gave FHA limited approval for the use of automatic underwriting systems (discussed in Chapter 12).

Construction Regulations

Since its inception, the FHA has imposed its own minimum construction requirements. Often this was essential where local building codes did not exist or were weaker than the FHA wanted. Before issuing a loan, particularly on new construction, the FHA would impose minimum requirements as to the quantity and quality of building materials to be used. Lot size, street access, landscaping, siting, and general house design also were required to fit within broad FHA guidelines. During construction, an FHA inspector would come to the property several times to check on whether or not work was being done correctly.

The reason for such care in building standards was that the FHA recognized that if a building is defective either from a design or construction standpoint, the borrower is more likely to default on the loan and create an insurance claim against the FHA. Furthermore, the same defects will lower the price the property will bring at its foreclosure sale, thus increasing losses to the FHA. Because building codes are now becoming stricter and more standardized in states, counties, and cities, the FHA anticipates eliminating its own minimum property standards. FHA has also softened its standards for property defects. The new FHA standards, which became effective January 1, 1995, advised underwriters to delete "conditions that have little or nothing to do with the safety and soundness of the property" from repair requirements stipulated by an appraiser.

As we leave our discussion of the FHA and go to the Department of Veteran Affairs, keep in mind that the FHA is not a lender. The FHA is an insurance agency. The loan itself is obtained from a savings and loan, bank, mortgage company, or similar lender. In addition to principal and interest payments, the lender collects an insurance premium from the borrower that is forwarded to the FHA. The FHA, in turn, guarantees repayment of the loan to the lender. This arrangement makes lenders much more willing to loan to buyers who are putting only 3% to 5% cash down. Thus, when you hear the phrase "FHA loan" in real estate circles, know that it is an FHA-*insured* loan, not a loan from the FHA.

DEPARTMENT OF VETERAN AFFAIRS

In 1944, to show its appreciation to servicemen returning from World War II, Congress passed far-reaching legislation to aid veterans in education, hospitalization, employment training, and housing. In housing, the popularly named G.I. Bill of Rights empowered the Comptroller General of the United States to guarantee the repayment of a portion of first mortgage real estate loans made to veterans. For this guarantee, no fee would be charged to the veteran. Rather, the government itself would stand the losses. On March 15, 1989, the Veterans Administration was elevated to cabinet level and is now officially called the Department of Veteran Affairs, but still clings to its old initials, the VA.

LOAN AMOUNT	GUARANTEE
Up to $45,000	50% of the Loan Amount
$45,001 to $56,250	$22,500
$56,251 to $144,000	40% of the Loan Amount
$144,001 and higher	$50,750

Some lenders will go higher if the borrower makes a down payment.

TABLE 10.3
VA loan guarantee amounts.

No Down Payment

The original 1944 law provided that lenders would be guaranteed against losses up to 50% of the amount of the loan, but in no case for more than $2,000. The objective was to make it possible for a veteran to buy a home with no cash down payment. Thus, on a house offered for sale at $5,000 (houses were much cheaper in 1944), this guarantee enabled a veteran to borrow the entire $5,000. From the lender's standpoint, having the top $2,000 of the loan guaranteed by the U.S. government offered the same asset protection as a $2,000 cash down payment. If the veteran defaulted and the property went into foreclosure, the lender had to net less than $3,000 before suffering a loss.

To keep up with the increased cost of homes, the guarantee has been increased several times. The VA now uses the sliding-scale system for calculating the applicable guarantee amounts. The guarantee increases with the amount of the loan using fixed dollar amounts and percentages of loan amounts. The current limits are shown in Table 10.3.

In the original G.I. Bill of 1944, eligibility was limited to World War II veterans. However, subsequent legislation has broadened eligibility to include any veteran who served for a period of at least 90 days in the armed forces of the United States or an ally between September 16, 1940 and July 25, 1947, or between June 27, 1950 and January 31, 1955. Any veteran of the United States who has served at least 181 days of continuous active duty from January 31, 1955 to the present is also eligible. If service was during the Vietnam conflict period (August 5, 1964 to May 7, 1975) or the Persian Gulf War, 90 days is sufficient to qualify. The veteran's discharge must be on conditions other than dishonorable, and the guarantee entitlement is good until used. If not remarried, the spouse of a veteran who died as a result of service can also obtain a housing guarantee. Active duty personnel can also qualify. Shorter active duty periods are allowed for service-connected disabilities.

VA Certificates

To determine benefits, a veteran should make application to the Department of Veteran Affairs for a **certificate of eligibility,** which shows whether the veteran is qualified and the amount of guarantee available. This document is necessary to obtain a VA-guaranteed loan.

The VA works diligently to protect veterans and reduce foreclosure losses. When a veteran applies for a VA guarantee, the property is appraised and the VA issues a **certificate of reasonable value.** Often abbreviated **CRV,** it reflects the estimated value of the property as determined by the VA staff appraiser. Similarly, the VA establishes income guidelines to make certain that the veteran can comfortably meet the proposed loan payments. Also, the veteran must agree to occupy the property. Pursuant to the newly enacted Safe Drinking Water Act, if the building was constructed after June 19, 1988, the CRV must now reflect a certification that any solders or fluxes used in construction did not contain more than 0.2% lead in any pipes or that the pipe fittings used did not contain more than 8% lead.

The VA guarantees fixed-rate loans for as long as 30 years on homes, and no pre-payment penalty is charged if the borrower wishes to pay sooner. Moreover, there is no due-on-sale clause that requires the loan to be repaid if the property is sold. The VA guarantees loans for the purchase of townhouses and condominiums, to build or improve a home, and to buy a mobile home as a residence. A veteran wishing to refinance an existing home or farm can obtain a VA-guaranteed loan provided that there is existing debt that will be repaid. The VA also makes direct loans to veterans if there are no private lending institutions nearby.

Financial Liability

No matter what loan guarantee program is elected, the veteran should know that in the event of default and subsequent foreclosure he or she is required eventually to make good any losses suffered by the VA on the loan. (This is not the case with FHA-insured loans, in which the borrower pays for protection against foreclosure losses that may result from the loan.) Even if the veteran sells the property and the buyer assumes the VA loan, the veteran is still financially responsible if the buyer later defaults. To avoid this, the veteran must arrange with the VA to be released from liability. For VA loans underwritten after March 1, 1988, Congress created a new Guarantee and Indemnity Fund that allows a release from liability to the VA in the event of foreclosure, provided that the following requirements are met:

1. The loan payments must be current.
2. The prospective purchasers must meet creditworthiness standards as required by the VA.
3. The prospective purchaser must assume full liability for repayment of the loan, including indemnity liability to the VA.

In the event borrowers are unable to make their mortgage payments, the VA offers an assistance procedure that may be helpful in declining markets. If the borrower can obtain a purchase offer that is insufficient to pay off the existing loan balance, a **compromise agreement** may allow the VA to pay the difference between the sales proceeds and the mortgage balance. To effect the compromise agreement, the borrower must be willing to find a purchaser who will pay fair market value of the house, and the original borrower must agree to remain liable to the government for the amount that the VA pays to the noteholder.

A veteran is permitted a full new guarantee entitlement if complete repayment of a previous VA-guaranteed loan has been made. If a veteran has sold and let the buyer assume the VA loan, the balance of the entitlement is still available. For example, if a veteran has used $15,000 of his or her entitlement to date, the difference between $15,000 and the current VA guarantee amount is still available for use.

Funding Fee

From its inception until October 1, 1982, the VA made loan guarantees on behalf of veterans without a charge. Congress initially enacted a funding fee in 1982, increased it in 1991, and in 1993 established a funding fee with three categories of veterans, each with different fees depending on the veteran status and down payment. Note the new rates set out in Table 10.4. Funding fees for interest-rate-reduction refinancing loans were reduced to $1/2$ of 1%. Funding fees on manufactured homes remain at 1% for all veterans and reservists. The fee still remains at $1/2$ of 1% for assumptions by veterans or reservists. Funding fees can be added to the loan amount for calculating the loan-to-value ratio.

TABLE 10.4.
VA loan funding fees.

Down Payment	Veterans	National Guard & Reservists	Multiple Users
No down payment	2.00%	2.75%	3.00%
Down payment of at least 5%	1.50%	2.25%	1.50%
Down payment of 10% or more	1.25%	2.00%	1.25%

Interest Rates

In 1992, Congress passed an historic change that eliminated the interest rate ceilings on VA loans. The new program allows an interest rate and discount points agreed on by the veteran and the lender. Discount points may not be financed on any loan except interest-rate-reduction refinancing loans (IRRRLs). IRRRLs are limited to two discount points. The two-point limit does not include origination fees, which are limited to one point.

Assumption Requirements

On VA loans assumed prior to March 1, 1988, approval was not required prior to loan assumption. Therefore, sellers could sell their property on assumption without obtaining any approval from the VA, but sellers remained fully liable for repayment. As stated previously, they could be released from liability if the VA approved the creditworthiness of the new purchaser. After March 1, 1988, the VA required prior approval for transfer of the property. Federal law now requires that the mortgage or deed of trust and note for loans carry on the first page in type $2^1/_2$ times larger than the regular type the following statement:

> THIS LOAN IS NOT ASSUMABLE WITHOUT THE PRIOR APPROVAL OF
> THE DEPARTMENT OF VETERAN AFFAIRS OR AUTHORIZED AGENT.

Because Congress frequently changes eligibility and benefits, a person contemplating a VA or FHA loan should make inquiry to the field offices of these two agencies and to mortgage lenders to ascertain the current status and details of the law, as well as the availability of loan money. Field offices also have information on foreclosed properties that are for sale. Additionally, one should query lenders as to the availability of state veteran benefits. A number of states offer special advantages, including mortgage loan assistance, to residents who have served in the armed forces.

Adjustable-Rate Mortgages

The VA can also issue its guarantee for an adjustable-rate mortgage. The approved plan is structured the same as the FHA adjustable-rate mortgages, underwritten at an interest rate 1% above the initial rate agreed on by the veteran and the lender. Increases in the interest rate are limited to an annual adjustment of 1% and capped at 5% over the life of the loan. The index for calculating interest-rate adjustments is the weekly average yield on Treasury securities to a constant maturity of one year as reported by the Federal Reserve Board.

PRIVATE MORTGAGE INSURANCE

In 1957, the Mortgage Guaranty Insurance Corporation (MGIC) was formed in Milwaukee, Wisconsin, as a privately owned business venture to insure home mortgage loans. Demand was slow but steady for the first 10 years and then grew rapidly until today when there are over a dozen private mortgage insurance companies. Like FHA insurance, the object of **private mortgage insurance (PMI)** is to insure lenders against foreclosure losses. But, unlike the FHA, PMI insures only the top 20% to 25% of a loan, not the whole loan. This allows a lender to make 90% and 95% L/V loans with about the same exposure to foreclosure losses as a 70% to 75% L/V loan. The borrower, meanwhile, can purchase a home with a cash down payment of either 10% or 5% rather than the 20% to 30% down required by lenders when mortgage insurance is not purchased. For this privilege the borrower pays a PMI fee of 1% or less when the loan is made plus an annual fee of a fraction of 1%. When the loan is partially repaid (e.g., to a 70% L/V), the premiums and coverage can be terminated. PMI is also available on apartment buildings, offices, stores, warehouses, and leaseholds, but at higher rates than on homes.

Under a 1997 Texas statute, a lender must now provide an annual promulgated notice to each borrower who is required to purchase mortgage guaranty insurance. The notice informs the borrower that if the principal of their loan is 80% or less of the current fair market value of their home, the borrower may have the right to cancel the insurance.

Approval Procedure

Private mortgage insurers work to keep their losses to a minimum by first approving the lenders with whom they do business. Particular emphasis is placed on the lender's operating policy, appraisal procedure, and degree of government regulation. Once approved, a lender simply sends the borrower's loan application, credit report, and property appraisal to the insurer. Based on these documents, the insurer either agrees or refuses to issue a policy. Although the insurer relies on the appraisal prepared by the lender, the insurer sends, on a random basis, its own appraiser to verify the quality of the information being submitted. When an insured loan goes into default, the insurer has the option of either buying the property from the lender for the balance due or letting the lender foreclose and then paying the lender's losses up to the amount of the insurance. As a rule, insurers take the first option because it is more popular with lenders and it leaves the lender with immediate cash to relend. The insurer is then responsible for foreclosing.

RURAL HOUSING SERVICES ADMINISTRATION

The **Rural Housing Sevices Administration** is a federal agency under the U.S. Department of Agriculture. Like the FHA, it came into existence due to the financial crises of the 1930s. The RHSA offers programs to help purchase or operate farms. The RHSA will either guarantee a portion of a loan made by a private lender or it will make the loan itself. RHSA loans can also be used to help finance the purchase of homes in rural areas.

Answers to these questions are found in the Answer Key section at the back of the book.

1. A loan wherein the principal is all repaid in one lump sum payment at the end of the loan's life is known as a (an)
   A. straight or term loan
   B. amortized loan.
   C. budget mortgage.
   D. balloon note.

2. The last day of a loan's life is known as the
   A. settlement date.
   B. maturity date.
   C. sale date.
   D. contract date.

3. To determine the amount of loan payments by using an amortization table, you must know all the following EXCEPT:
   A. loan-to-value ratio.
   B. frequency of payments.
   C. interest rates.
   D. amount of loan.

4. Amortization tables may be used by real estate agents to determine which of the following?
   A. Frequency of payment.
   B. Interest rate.
   C. Maturity.
   D. Amount of loan.
   E. All of the above.

5. A major negative of balloon loan financing is that the borrower may have difficulty
   A. meeting the final payment when it becomes due.
   B. refinancing when the final payment comes due.
   C. Both A and B.
   D. Neither A nor B.

6. Kevin wants to know what portion of a 30-year, fully amortized loan would be paid off by the fourth year of the loan's life. Kevin would consult
   A. an amortization table.
   B. a loan balance table.
   D. a partial amortization table.
   D. the loan-to-value ratio.

7. By the tenth year of a $9^1/_2$ percent 30-year amortization period, how much of the principal balance will have been repaid under a monthly amortization of equal installments? Use Table 10.2 in the text.
   A. One-half.
   B. One-third.
   C. Two-thirds.
   D. None of the above.

8. The FHA has been influential in bringing about acceptance of
   A. long-term amortization of loans.
   B. standardized construction techniques.
   C. Both A and B.
   D. Neither A nor B.

9. Regarding mortgage insurance, which of the following statements are true?
   A. PMI insures only the top 20 or 25 percent of the loan.
   B. FHA insures the entire loan.
   C. Both A and B.
   D. Neither A nor B.

10. Which of the following statements regarding the FmHA are correct?
   A. FmHA guarantees loans on farms and rural homes.
   B. FmHA makes loans on farms and rural homes.
   C. Both A and B.
   D. Neither A nor B.

KEY TERMS

APR: the annual percentage rate as calculated under the federal Truth-in-Lending Act by combining the interest rate with other costs of the loan

Credit report: a report reflecting the creditworthiness of a borrower by showing past credit history

Finance charge: the total amount the credit will cost over the life of the loan

Liquid asset: asset that is in cash or is readily convertible to cash

Redlining: a lender's refusal to make loans in certain neighborhoods

Regulation Z: federal regulations that implement the enforcement of the Truth-in-Lending Act

Truth-in-Lending Act: a federal law that requires certain disclosures when extending or advertising credit

The Loan and the Consumer

IN THIS CHAPTER *The previous chapter discussed lending practices applied to the types of payment arrangements that can be made in retiring debt. Consumer protection was enabled through the Federal Consumer Credit Protection Act, and additional protections have been created through standardized loan procedures. This chapter will discuss the federal Truth-in-Lending Act and standard loan procedures that consumers need to use in order to make application for a loan.*

TRUTH-IN-LENDING ACT

The **Federal Consumer Credit Protection Act,** popularly known as the **Truth-in-Lending Act,** went into effect in 1969. The act, implemented by Federal Reserve Board **Regulation Z,** requires that a borrower be clearly shown, before committing to a loan, how much is being paid for credit in both dollar terms and percentage terms. The borrower is also given the right to rescind (cancel) the transaction in certain instances. The act came into being because it was not uncommon to see loans advertised for rates lower than the borrower actually wound up paying. Once the act took effect, several weaknesses and ambiguities of the act and Regulation Z became apparent. Thus, the **Truth-in-Lending Simplification and Reform Act (TILSRA)** was passed by Congress and became effective October 1, 1982. Concurrently, the Federal Reserve Board issued a **Revised Regulation Z (RRZ)** that details rules and regulations for TILSRA. For purposes of discussion we refer to all of this as the Truth-in-Lending Act, or TIL.

Advertising

Whether you are a real estate practitioner or a property owner acting on your own behalf, TIL rules affect you when you advertise just about anything (including real estate) and include financing terms in the ad.

Trigger Terms

Five specific disclosures must be included in any ad that contains even one of the following trigger terms: (1) the amount of down payment (for example, only 5% down, 10% down, $4,995 down, 95% financing); (2) the amount of any payment (for example, monthly payments only $499, buy for less than $650 a month, payments

PUTTING IT TO WORK

If an advertisement contains any item from the TIL list of financing terms (called **trigger terms** and explained below), the ad must also include other required information. For example, an advertisement that reads: "Bargain! Bargain! Bargain! New 3-bedroom townhouses only $499 per month" may or may not be a bargain depending on other financing information missing from the ad.

only 1% per month); (3) the number of payments (for example, only 36 monthly payments and you own it, all paid up in 10 annual payments); (4) the period of repayment (for example, 30-year financing, owner will carry for 5 years, 10-year second available); and (5) the dollar amount of any finance charge (finance this for only $999) or the statement that there is no charge for credit (pay no interest for 3 years).

If any of the aforementioned trigger terms are used, then the following five disclosures must appear in the ad: (1) the cash price or the amount of the loan; (2) the amount of down payment or a statement that none is required; (3) the number, amount, and frequency of repayments; (4) the annual percentage rate; and (5) the deferred payment price or total payments. Item 5 is not a requirement in the case of the sale of a dwelling or a loan secured by a first lien on the dwelling that is being purchased.

Annual Percentage Rate

The **annual percentage rate (APR)** combines the interest rate with the other costs of the loan into a single figure that shows the true annual cost of borrowing. This is one of the most helpful features of the law as it gives the prospective borrower a standardized yardstick by which to compare financing from different sources.

If the annual percentage rate being offered is subject to increase after the transaction takes place (such as with an adjustable rate mortgage), that fact must be stated, for example, "9% annual percentage rate subject to increase after settlement." If the loan has interest rate changes that follow a predetermined schedule, those terms must be stated, for example, "7% first year, 9% second year, 11% third year, 13% remainder of loan, 12.5% annual percentage rate."

If you wish to say something about financing and avoid triggering full disclosure, you may use general statements. The following would be acceptable: "assumable loan," "financing available," "owner will carry," "terms to fit your budget," "easy monthly payments," or "FHA and VA financing available."

Lending Disclosures

If you are in the business of making loans, the Truth-in-Lending Act requires you to make 18 disclosures to your borrower. Of these, the four that must be most prominently displayed on the papers the borrower signs are: (1) the amount financed, (2) the finance charge, (3) the annual percentage rate, and (4) the total payments.

The **amount financed** is the amount of credit provided to the borrower. The **finance charge** is the total dollar amount the credit will cost the borrower over the life of the loan. This includes interest, *plus* such things as borrower-paid discount points, loan fees, loan finder's fees, loan service fees, required life insurance, and mortgage guarantee premiums. On a long-term mortgage loan, the total finance charge can easily exceed the amount of money being borrowed. For example, the total amount of interest on a 7%, 30-year, $160,000 loan is just over $223,000.

The annual percentage rate was described earlier. The total payment is the amount in dollars the borrower will have paid after making all the payments as scheduled. In the aforementioned 7%, 30-year loan it would be the interest of $223,000 plus the principal of $160,000 for a total of $383,000.

The other 14 disclosures that a lender must make are as follows: (1) the identity of the lender; (2) the payment schedule; (3) prepayment penalties and rebates; (4) late payment charges; (5) any insurance required; (6) any filing fees; (7) any collateral required; (8) any required deposits; (9) whether or not the loan can be assumed; (10) the demand feature, if the note has one; (11) the total sales price of the item being purchased if the seller is also the creditor; (12) any adjustable rate features of the loan; (13) an itemization of the amount financed; and (14) a reference to any terms not shown on the disclosure statement but which are shown on the loan contract.

These disclosures must be delivered or mailed to the credit applicant within three business days after the creditor receives the applicant's written request for credit. The applicant must have this information before the transaction can take place—for example, before the closing.

Who Must Comply?

Any person or firm that regularly extends consumer credit subject to a finance charge (such as interest) or payable by written agreement in more than four installments must comply with the lending disclosures. This includes banks, savings and loans, credit unions, finance companies, and so on, as well as private individuals who extend credit more than five times a year.

Whoever is named on the note as the creditor must make the lending disclosures even if the note is to be resold. A key difference between the old and the new TIL acts is that the new TIL act does not include mortgage brokers or real estate practitioners as creditors just because they brokered a deal containing financing. This is because they do not appear as creditors on the note. But if a broker takes back a note for part of the commission on a deal, that is extension of credit and the lending disclosures must be made.

Exempt Transactions

Certain transactions are exempt from the lending disclosure requirement. The first exemption is for credit extended primarily for business, commercial, or agricultural purposes. This exemption includes dwelling units purchased for rental purposes (unless the property contains four or fewer units and the owner occupies one of them, in which case special rules apply).

The second exemption applies to credit over $25,000 secured by personal property unless the property is the principal residence of the borrower. For example, a mobile home that secures a loan over $25,000 qualifies under this exemption if it is used as a vacation home, but is not exempt if it is used as a principal residence.

Failure to Disclose

If the Federal Trade Commission (FTC) determines that an advertiser has broken the law, it can order the advertiser to cease from further violations. Each violation of that order can result in a $10,000 civil penalty each day the violation continues.

Failure to disclose properly when credit is extended can result in a penalty of twice the amount of the finance charge with a minimum of $100 and a maximum of $1,000 plus court costs, attorney fees, and actual damages. In addition, the FTC can add a fine of up to $5,000 and/or one year imprisonment. If the required disclosures are not made or the borrower is not given the required 3 days to cancel (see the following), the borrower can cancel the transaction at any time within three years following the date of the transaction. In that event the creditor must return all money paid by the borrower, and the borrower returns the property to the creditor.

Right to Cancel

A borrower has a limited **right to rescission** (right to cancel) in a credit transaction. The borrower has three business days (counting Saturdays) to back out after signing the loan papers. This aspect of the law was inserted primarily to protect a homeowner from unscrupulous sellers of home improvements and appliances when the credit to purchase is secured by a lien on the home. Vacant lots for sale on credit to buyers who expect to use them for principal residences are also subject to cancellation privileges.

The right to rescind does not apply to credit used for the acquisition or initial construction of one's principal dwelling.

LOAN APPLICATION AND APPROVAL

When a mortgage lender reviews a real estate loan application, the primary concern for both applicant and lender is to approve loan requests that show a high probability of being repaid in full and on time, and to disapprove requests that are likely to result in default and eventual foreclosure. How is this decision made? Loan analysis varies. However, the five major federal agencies have recently combined their requirements for credit reports. All loans intended for underwriting by Fannie Mae, Freddie Mac, HUD/FHA, VA, or Farmer's Home Administration must comply with the new standards. Figure 11.1 shows the new Uniform Residential Loan Application (a requirement for standardized loan application) and summarizes the key terms that a loan officer considers when making a decision regarding a loan request. Let's review these items and observe how they affect the acceptance of a loan by a lender.

Note that in section **[1]** the borrower is requested to specify the type of mortgage and terms of the loan being sought. This greatly facilitates the lender's ability to determine the availability of the loan that the borrower may be seeking.

In section **[2]** the lender begins the loan analysis procedure by looking at the property and the proposed financing. Using the property address and legal description, an appraiser is assigned to prepare an appraisal of the property and a title search is ordered. These steps are taken to determine the fair market value of the property and the condition of title. In the event of default, the property is the collateral the lender must fall back on to recover the loan. If the loan request is in connection with a purchase rather than the refinancing of an existing property, the lender will know the purchase price. As a rule, loans are made on the basis of the appraised value or purchase price, whichever is lower. If the appraised value is lower than the purchase price, the usual procedure is to require the buyer to make a larger cash down payment. The lender does not want to overloan simply because the buyer overpaid for the property.

Settlement Funds

Next, in section **[2]**, the lender wants to know whether the borrower has adequate funds for settlement. Are these funds presently in a checking or savings account, or are they coming from the sale of the borrower's present property? In the latter case,

FIGURE **11.1**
Uniform residential
loan application.

FIGURE 11.1
Continued.

Borrower *Prestatario*	IV. EMPLOYMENT INFORMATION *INFORMACION SOBRE EMPLEO*		Co-Borrower *Co-Prestatario*
Name & Address of Employer / *Nombre y Dirección del Empleador* ☐ Self Employed / *Empleado por Cuenta Propia* [5]	Yrs. on this job / *Años en este trabajo* Yrs. employed in this line of work/profession / *Años de empleo en este tipo de trabajo/profesión*	Name & Address of Employer / *Nombre y Dirección del Empleador* ☐ Self Employed / *Empleado por Cuenta Propia* [6]	Yrs. on this job / *Años en este trabajo* Yrs. employed in this line of work/profession / *Años de empleo en este tipo de trabajo/profesión*
Position/Title/Type of Business / *Posición/Título/Tipo de Negocio*	Business Phone (incl. area code) / *Teléfono en el lugar de Empleo (incluya código de área)*	Position/Title/Type of Business / *Posición/Título/Tipo de Negocio*	Business Phone (incl. area code) / *Teléfono en el lugar de Empleo (incluya código de área)*

If employed in current position for less than two years or if currently employed in more than one position, complete the following: /
Si ha estado trabajando en la posición actual menos de dos años o si actualmente está empleado en más de una posición, complete lo siguiente:

Name & Address of Employer / *Nombre y Dirección del Empleador* ☐ Self Employed / *Empleado por Cuenta Propia*	Dates (from-to) / *Fechas de empleo (de-hasta)* Monthly Income / *Ingreso Mensual* $	Name & Address of Employer / *Nombre y Dirección del Empleador* ☐ Self Employed / *Empleado por Cuenta Propia*	Dates (from-to) / *Fechas de empleo (de-hasta)* Monthly Income / *Ingreso Mensual* $
Position/Title/Type of Business / *Posición/Título/Tipo de Negocio*	Business Phone (incl. area code) / *Teléfono en el lugar de Empleo (incluya código de área)*	Position/Title/Type of Business / *Posición/Título/Tipo de Negocio*	Business Phone (incl. area code) / *Teléfono en el lugar de Empleo (incluya código de área)*
Name & Address of Employer / *Nombre y Dirección del Empleador* ☐ Self Employed / *Empleado por Cuenta Propia*	Dates (from-to) / *Fechas de empleo (de-hasta)* Monthly Income / *Ingreso Mensual* $	Name & Address of Employer / *Nombre y Dirección del Empleador* ☐ Self Employed / *Empleado por Cuenta Propia*	Dates (from-to) / *Fechas de empleo (de-hasta)* Monthly Income / *Ingreso Mensual* $
Position/Title/Type of Business / *Posición/Título/Tipo de Negocio*	Business Phone (incl. area code) / *Teléfono en el lugar de Empleo (incluya código de área)*	Position/Title/Type of Business / *Posición/Título/Tipo de Negocio*	Business Phone (incl. area code) / *Teléfono en el lugar de Empleo (incluya código de área)*

V. MONTHLY INCOME AND COMBINED HOUSING EXPENSE INFORMATION
INFORMACION SOBRE EL INGRESO Y LOS GASTOS COMBINADOS DE VIVIENDA MENSUAL

[7]

Gross Monthly Income *Ingreso Bruto Mensual*	Borrower *Prestatario*	Co-Borrower *Co-Prestatario*	Total	Combined Monthly Housing Expense *Gastos Combinados de Vivienda Mensual*	Present *Actual*	Proposed *Propuesto*
Base Empl. Income* *Ingreso Básico del Empleado**	$	$	$	Rent *Alquiler*	$	
Overtime *Horas adicionales*				First Mortgage (P&I) *Hipoteca Principal (Principal e Interés (P&I))*		$
Bonuses *Bonos*				Other Financing (P&I) *Otro Financiamiento (P&I)*		
Commissions *Comisiones*				Hazard Insurance *Seguro Contra Riesgos*		
Dividends/Interest *Dividendos/Intereses*				Real Estate Taxes *Impuestos Sobre Bienes Raíces*		
Net Rental Income *Ingreso Neto por Alquiler*				Mortgage Insurance *Seguro de Hipoteca*		
Other (before completing, see the notice in "describe other income," below) *Otros (antes de llenar, vea el aviso en "describa otros ingresos" a continuación)*				Homeowner Assn. Dues *Cuotas de la Asociación de Propietarios* Other: *Otro:*		
Total	$	$	$	Total	$	$

[8] (next to Proposed column header)
[9] (next to Total row)

*Self Employed Borrower(s) may be required to provide additional documentation such as tax returns and financial statements.
Se podrá requerir al Prestatario o Prestatarios que son empleados por cuenta propia que proporcionen documentos adicionales tales como declaraciones y planillas de impuestos y estados financieros.

Describe Other Income **Notice:** Alimony, child support, or separate maintenance income need not be revealed if the Borrower (B) or Co-Borrower (C) does not choose to have it considered for repaying this loan.
Describa Otros Ingresos *Aviso:* *La pensión conyugal, pensión para el sustento de hijos o ingreso de mantenimiento por separación, no tienen que declararse si el Prestatario (B) o Co-Prestatario (C) no desean que se considere para el pago de este préstamo.*

B/C *B/C*		Monthly Amount *Cantidad Mensual*
		$

APPSPAN

Page 2 of 6
Página 2 de 6

Fannie Mae
Form 1003(S) Nov. 96

(continued)

FIGURE 11.1
Continued.

VI. ASSETS AND LIABILITIES *BIENES Y DEUDAS*

This Statement and any applicable supporting schedules may be completed jointly by both married and unmarried Co-Borrowers if their assets and liabilities are sufficiently joined so that the Statement can be meaningfully and fairly presented on a combined basis; otherwise separate Statements and Schedules are required. If the Co-Borrower section was completed about a spouse, this Statement and supporting schedules must be completed about that spouse also. [10]

Esta Declaración y cualquier anexo pertinente pueden llenarse conjuntamente tanto por Co-Prestatarios casados como no casados si sus bienes y deudas están suficientemente unidos de manera que la Declaración pueda presentarse con sentido sobre una base combinada y de una forma fiel; o de lo contrario, se requieren las Declaraciones y anexos por separado. Si en la sección del Co-Prestatario se completó la parte sobre el cónyuge, esta Declaración y los anexos también deben completarse para dicho cónyuge.

Completed / *Completado* ☐ Jointly / *Conjuntamente* ☐ Not Jointly / *Por Separado* ☐

ASSETS / *BIENES* Description / *Descripción*	Cash or Market Value *Valor en Efectivo o Valor en el Mercado*	Liabilities and Pledged Assets. List the creditor's name, address and account number for all outstanding debts, including automobile loans, revolving charge accounts, real estate loans, alimony, child support, stock pledges, etc. Use continuation sheet, if necessary. Indicate by (*) those liabilities which will be satisfied upon sale of real estate owned or upon refinancing of the subject property. *Deudas y Bienes Gravados. Indique el nombre, la dirección y el número de cuenta del acreedor de todas las deudas pendientes, incluyendo préstamos para autos, cuentas de crédito rotativo, préstamos de bienes raíces, pensión conyugal, pensión para el sustento de hijos, valores gravados, etc. Si es necesario, use una hoja adicional. Indique con un (*) aquellas deudas que se satisfarán al venderse o refinanciarse la propiedad inmobiliaria en cuestión.*		
Cash deposit toward purchase held by: / *Depósito en efectivo para la compra en poder de:*	$			

List checking and savings accounts below / *Indique abajo las cuentas de cheques y de ahorros*		LIABILITIES *DEUDAS*	Monthly Payt. & Mos. Left to Pay / *Pago Mensual y Nº de Pagos Mensuales Pendientes*	Unpaid Balance / *Balance Pendiente* [11]
Name and address of Bank, S&L, or Credit Union / *Nombre y dirección del Banco, Asociación de Ahorro y Préstamo o Cooperativa de Crédito*		Name and address of Company / *Nombre y dirección de la Compañía*	$ Payt./Mos. $ *Pago/meses*	$
Acct. no. / *Nº de Cuenta*	$	Acct. no. / *Nº de Cuenta*		
Name and address of Bank, S&L, or Credit Union / *Nombre y dirección del Banco, Asociación de Ahorro y Préstamo o Cooperativa de Crédito*		Name and address of Company / *Nombre y dirección de la Compañía*	$ Payt./Mos. $ *Pago/meses*	$
		Acct. no. / *Nº de Cuenta*		
Acct. no. / *Nº de Cuenta*	$	Name and address of Company / *Nombre y dirección de la Compañía*	$ Payt./Mos. $ *Pago/meses*	$
Name and address of Bank, S&L, or Credit Union / *Nombre y dirección del Banco, Asociación de Ahorro y Préstamo o Cooperativa de Crédito*				
		Acct. no. / *Nº de Cuenta*		
Acct. no. / *Nº de Cuenta*	$	Name and address of Company / *Nombre y dirección de la Compañía*	$ Payt./Mos. $ *Pago/meses*	$
Name and address of Bank, S&L, or Credit Union / *Nombre y dirección del Banco, Asociación de Ahorro y Préstamo o Cooperativa de Crédito*				
		Acct. no. / *Nº de Cuenta*		
Acct. no. / *Nº de Cuenta*	$	Name and address of Company / *Nombre y dirección de la Compañía*	$ Payt./Mos. $ *Pago/meses*	$
Stocks & Bonds (Company name/number & description) / *Valores y Bonos (Nombre de la compañía/número y descripción de los valores y bonos)*	$	Acct. no. / *Nº de Cuenta*		
Life insurance net cash value / *Valor en efectivo neto del seguro de vida* Face amount: / *Cantidad de la póliza:* $	$	Name and address of Company / *Nombre y dirección de la Compañía*	$ Payt./Mos. $ *Pago/meses*	$
Subtotal Liquid Assets / *Subtotal de los Bienes Líquidos*	$			
Real estate owned (enter market value from schedule of real estate owned) / *Propiedad inmobiliaria de la cual es dueño (indique el valor en el mercado según el anexo de la propiedad inmobiliaria)*	$	Acct. no. / *Nº de Cuenta*		
		Name and address of Company / *Nombre y dirección de la Compañía*	$ Payt./Mos. $ *Pago/meses*	$
Vested interest in retirement fund / *Intereses adquiridos en el fondo de retiro*	$			
Net worth of business(es) owned (attach financial statement) / *Valor neto de negocio(s) propio(s) (incluya estados financieros)*	$	Acct. no. / *Nº de Cuenta*		
		Alimony/Child Support/Separate Maintenance Payments Owed to: / *Pagos de Pensión Conyugal/Pensión de Sustento de los Hijos/Mantenimiento por Separación, debidos a:*	$	
Automobiles owned (make and year) / *Autos de los cuales es dueño (fabricante y año)*	$			
		Job Related Expense (child care, union dues, etc.) / *Gastos Relacionados con el Empleo (cuidado de niños, cuotas de uniones, etc.)*	$	
Other Assets (itemize) / *Otros Bienes (detalle)*	$	Total Monthly Payments / *Total de Pagos Mensuales*	$	
Total Assets a. / *Total de Bienes a.*	$	Net Worth (a minus b) / *Valor Neto (a menos b)* $ [12]	Total Liabilities b. / *Total de Deudas b.*	$

Schedule of Real Estate Owned (If additional properties are owned, use continuation sheet.)
Anexo de Propiedades Inmobiliarias (Si es dueño de más propiedades, use la hoja de continuación.)

Property Address (enter S if sold, PS if pending sale or R if rental being held for income) / *Dirección de la Propiedad (Ponga una S por vendida, una PS por venta pendiente o una R si recibe ingreso por alquiler)*	Type of Property / *Tipo de Propiedad*	Present Market Value / *Valor Actual en el Mercado*	Amount of Mortgages & Liens / *Cantidad de Hipotecas y Gravámenes*	Gross Rental Income / *Ingreso Bruto por Alquiler*	Mortgage Payments / *Pagos Hipotecarios*	Insurance, Maintenance, Taxes & Misc. / *Seguro, Mantenimiento, Impuestos y Otros*	Net Rental Income / *Ingreso Neto por Alquiler*
		$	$	$	$	$	$
Totals / *Totales*		$	$	$	$	$	$

List any additional names under which credit has previously been received and indicate appropriate creditor name(s) and account number(s):
Indique otros nombres bajo los cuales ha recibido crédito anteriormente, así como los nombres de los acreedores y el número de las cuentas:

Alternate Name / *Otro Nombre*	Creditor Name / *Nombre del Acreedor*	Account Number / *Número de Cuenta*
		[13]

(continued)

FIGURE 11.1
Continued.

VII. DETAILS OF TRANSACTION *DETALLES DE LA TRANSACCION*

		$
a.	Purchase price / *Precio de compra*	
b.	Alterations, improvements, repairs / *Remodelaciones, mejoras, reparaciones*	
c.	Land (if acquired separately) / *Terreno (si fue adquirido por separado)*	
d.	Refinance (incl. debts to be paid off) / *Refinanciamiento (incluya deudas por pagar)*	
e.	Estimated prepaid items / *Estimado de partidas prepagadas*	
f.	Estimated closing costs / *Estimado de los costos de cierre*	
g.	PMI, MIP, Funding Fee / *Seguro de hipoteca privado (PMI), Primas de seguro de hipoteca (MIP), Costos de Financiamiento*	
h.	Discount (if Borrower will pay) / *Descuento (si el Prestatario lo pagará)*	
i.	**Total costs** (add items a through h) / *Total de costos (sume las líneas "a" hasta la "h")*	
j.	Subordinate financing / *Financiamiento subordinado*	
k.	Borrower's closing costs paid by Seller / *Costos de cierre del Prestatario pagados por el Vendedor*	
l.	Other Credits (explain) / *Otros Créditos (explicar)*	
m.	Loan amount (exclude PMI, MIP, Funding Fee financed) / *Cantidad del Préstamo (excluya PMI, MIP, Costos de Financiamiento Financiados)*	
n.	PMI, MIP, Funding Fee financed / *Seguro de hipoteca privado (PMI), Primas de seguro de hipoteca (MIP), Costos de Financiamiento Financiados*	
o.	Loan amount (add m & n) / *Cantidad del Préstamo (sume líneas "m" y "n")*	
p.	Cash from/to Borrower (subtract j, k, l & o from i) / *Dinero del/para el Prestatario (reste j, k, l & o de i)*	

VIII. DECLARATIONS *DECLARACIONES*

If you answer "yes" to any questions a through i, please use continuation sheet for explanation.
Si responde "sí" a cualquiera de las preguntas de la "a" a la "i", debe utilizar una hoja adicional para dar una explicación.

	Borrower / *Prestatario* Yes / Sí	No	Co-Borrower / *Co-Prestatario* Yes / Sí	No
a. Are there any outstanding judgments against you? *¿Existe alguna sentencia o fallo judicial pendiente en contra suya?*	☐	☐	☐	☐
b. Have you been declared bankrupt within the past 7 years? *¿Se le ha declarado en bancarrota en los últimos 7 años?*	☐	☐	☐	☐
c. Have you had property foreclosed upon or given title or deed in lieu thereof in the last 7 years? *¿Se le ha entablado una ejecución hipotecaria o ha transferido el título de la propiedad en sustitución de una ejecución hipotecaria en los últimos 7 años?*	☐	☐	☐	☐
d. Are you a party to a lawsuit? *¿Es usted una parte en una demanda judicial?*	☐	☐	☐	☐
e. Have you directly or indirectly been obligated on any loan which resulted in foreclosure, transfer of title in lieu of foreclosure, or judgment? (This would include such loans as home mortgage loans, SBA loans, home improvement loans, educational loans, manufactured (mobile) home loans, any mortgage, financial obligation, bond, or loan guarantee. If "Yes," provide details, including date, name and address of Lender, FHA or VA case number, if any, and reasons for the action.) *¿Ha estado usted obligado, directa o indirectamente, en algún préstamo que provocó una ejecución hipotecaria, transferencia de título en sustitución de una ejecución hipotecaria, o alguna sentencia, o fallo en su contra? (Esto incluye préstamos tales como préstamos hipotecarios para vivienda, préstamos SBA, préstamos para mejoras en la casa, préstamos educacionales, préstamos para casas móviles, cualquier hipoteca, obligación financiera, bono o préstamo garantizado. Si la respuesta es "sí", incluya la fecha, el nombre y la dirección del Prestador, o el número de caso de FHA o VA, si lo hubiera, y las razones de la acción.)*	☐	☐	☐	☐
f. Are you presently delinquent or in default on any Federal debt or any other loan, mortgage, financial obligation, bond, or loan guarantee? If "Yes," give details as described in the preceding question. *¿Se encuentra atrasado, moroso, o en incumplimiento con alguna deuda federal o cualquier otro préstamo, hipoteca, obligación financiera, bono o préstamo garantizado? Si la respuesta es "SI", provea detalles según se describe en la pregunta anterior.*	☐	☐	☐	☐
g. Are you obligated to pay alimony, child support, or separate maintenance? *¿Esta obligado a pagar por pensión conyugal, pensión alimenticia, o mantenimiento por separación?*	☐	☐	☐	☐
h. Is any part of the down payment borrowed? *¿Le prestaron alguna parte del pago inicial?*	☐	☐	☐	☐
i. Are you a co-maker or endorser on a note? *¿Es usted co-prestatario o endosante de un pagaré?*	☐	☐	☐	☐
j. Are you a U.S. citizen? *¿Es usted ciudadano de los Estados Unidos?*	☐	☐	☐	☐
k. Are you a permanent resident alien? *¿Es usted un residente permanente de los Estados Unidos?*	☐	☐	☐	☐
l. **Do you intend to occupy the property as your primary residence?** If "Yes," complete question m below. *¿Tiene usted la intención de ocupar la propiedad como su residencia principal? Si la respuesta es "SI", conteste la pregunta "m".*	☐	☐	☐	☐
m. Have you had an ownership interest in a property in the last three years? *¿Ha tenido usted participación como dueño en una propiedad en los últimos tres años?*	☐	☐	☐	☐
(1) What type of property did you own—principal residence (PR), second home (SH), or investment property (IP)? *(1) ¿De qué tipo de propiedad era usted dueño—residencia principal (PR), casa secundaria (SH), o propiedad de inversión (IP)?*				
(2) How did you hold title to the home—solely by yourself (S), jointly with your spouse (SP), or jointly with another person (O)? *¿Cómo estaba registrado el título—únicamente a su favor (S) o conjuntamente con su cónyuge (SP), o conjuntamente con otra persona (O)?*				

(continued)

FIGURE **11.1**
Continued.

IX. ACKNOWLEDGMENT AND AGREEMENT *RECONOCIMIENTO Y ACUERDO*

The undersigned specifically acknowledge(s) and agree(s) that: (1) the loan requested by this application will be secured by a first mortgage or deed of trust on the property described herein; (2) the property will not be used for any illegal or prohibited purpose or use; (3) all statements made in this application are made for the purpose of obtaining the loan indicated herein; (4) occupation of the property will be as indicated above; (5) verification or reverification of any information contained in the application may be made at any time by the Lender, its agents, successors and assigns, either directly or through a credit reporting agency, from any source named in this application, and the original copy of this application will be retained by the Lender, even if the loan is not approved; (6) the Lender, its agents, successors and assigns will rely on the information contained in the application and I/we have a continuing obligation to amend and/or supplement the information provided in this application if any of the material facts which I/we have represented herein should change prior to closing; (7) in the event my/our payments on the loan indicated in this application become delinquent, the Lender, its agents, successors and assigns, may, in addition to all their other rights and remedies, report my/our name(s) and account information to a credit reporting agency; (8) ownership of the loan may be transferred to successor or assign of the Lender without notice to me and/or the administration of the loan account may be transferred to an agent, successor or assign of the Lender with prior notice to me; (9) the Lender, its agents, successors and assigns make no representations or warranties, express or implied, to the Borrower(s) regarding the property, the condition of the property, or the value of the property.
Certification: I/We certify that the information provided in this application is true and correct as of the date set forth opposite my/our signature(s) on this application and acknowledge my/our understanding that any intentional or negligent misrepresentation(s) of the information contained in this application may result in civil liability and/or criminal penalties including, but not limited to, fine or imprisonment or both under the provisions of Title 18, United States Code, Section 1001, et seq. and liability for monetary damages to the Lender, its agents, successors and assigns, insurers and any other person who may suffer any loss due to reliance upon any misrepresentation which I/we have made on this application.

El infrascrito específicamente reconoce y acuerda que: (1) el préstamo que se solicita por medio de esta solicitud estará asegurado por una primera hipoteca o escritura de fideicomiso sobre la propiedad descrita en el presente documento; (2) la propiedad no se utilizará para ningún propósito ilegal o prohibido; (3) todas las declaraciones hechas en esta solicitud se hacen con el fin de obtener el préstamo indicado en la presente solicitud; (4) la propiedad se ocupará según indicado arriba; (5) la verificación o reverificación de cualquier información contenida en esta solicitud puede realizarse en cualquier momento por el Prestador Hipotecario, sus agentes, sucesores y cesionarios, ya sea directamente o a través de una agencia de informes de crédito, de cualquiera de las fuentes mencionadas en esta solicitud, y la copia original de esta solicitud será retenida por el Prestador Hipotecario, aunque el préstamo no se apruebe; (6) el Prestador Hipotecario, sus agentes, sucesores y cesionarios dependerán de la información contenida en la solicitud y yo/nosotros tengo/tenemos una obligación continua de enmendar y/o suplementar la información proporcionada en esta solicitud si alguno de los hechos esenciales que he/hemos expuesto aquí cambiara antes del cierre de esta transacción; (7) en el caso de que no se cumpliera con los pagos del préstamo mencionado en esta solicitud, el Prestador Hipotecario, sus agentes, sucesores y cesionarios pueden, además de ejercer todos sus otros derechos y remedios, dar información sobre mi/nuestros nombre(s) y número de mi/nuestras cuenta(s) a una agencia de informes de crédito; (8) el título del préstamo puede transferirse a un sucesor o cesionario del Prestador Hipotecario sin avisarme/avisarnos, y/o la administración de la cuenta del préstamo puede transferirse a un agente, sucesor o cesionario del Prestador Hipotecario con previo aviso a mí; (9) el Prestador Hipotecario, sus agentes, sucesores y cesionarios no hacen ninguna representación o garantía, expresa o implícita, al Prestatario o Prestatarios respecto a la propiedad, la condición de la propiedad, o el valor de la misma.
Certificación: *Yo/nosotros certifico/certificamos que la información proporcionada en esta solicitud es correcta y conforme a la verdad hasta la fecha que aparece en esta solicitud al lado de mi/nuestras firma(s), y reconozco/reconocemos mi/nuestro entendimiento de que toda tergiversación intencional o negligente de la información contenida en esta solicitud puede resultar en una responsabilidad civil y/o penas criminales que incluyen, pero no se limitan a, multas o encarcelamiento, o ambos, bajo las disposiciones del Título 18 del Código de los Estados Unidos, Artículo 1001, et seq. y responsabilidad por daños monetarios al Prestador Hipotecario, sus agentes, sucesores y cesionarios, aseguradores y cualquier otra persona que pudiera sufrir pérdidas al haber confiado en los datos que tergiverse/tergiversamos en esta solicitud.*

THE SPANISH TRANSLATION IS FOR CONVENIENCE PURPOSES ONLY. IN THE EVENT OF AN INCONSISTENCY BETWEEN THE ENGLISH AND SPANISH LANGUAGE VERSIONS OF THIS FORM, THE ENGLISH LANGUAGE VERSION SHALL PREVAIL.
LA TRADUCCION AL ESPAÑOL ES PARA SU CONVENIENCIA UNICAMENTE. EN CASO DE QUE EXISTA UNA INCONSISTENCIA ENTRE LA VERSION EN INGLES Y LA VERSION EN ESPAÑOL DE ESTE FORMULARIO, PREVALECERA LA VERSION EN INGLES.

LEA ESTO PRIMERO: *Este documento contiene una traducción al español de su texto en inglés.*

Borrower's Signature / *Firma del Prestatario*	Date / *Fecha*	Co-Borrower's Signature / *Firma del Co-Prestatario*	Date / *Fecha*
X		X	

X. INFORMATION FOR GOVERNMENT MONITORING PURPOSES *INFORMACION PARA FINES DE VERIFICACION POR EL GOBIERNO*

The following information is requested by the Federal Government for certain types of loans related to a dwelling, in order to monitor the Lender's compliance with equal credit opportunity, fair housing and home mortgage disclosure laws. You are not required to furnish this information, but are encouraged to do so. The law provides that a Lender may neither discriminate on the basis of this information, nor on whether you choose to furnish it. However, if you choose not to furnish it, under Federal regulations this Lender is required to note race and sex on the basis of visual observation or surname. If you do not wish to furnish the above information please check the box below. (Lender must review the above material to assure that the disclosures satisfy all requirements to which the Lender is subject under applicable state law for the particular type of loan applied for.)

La siguiente información la solicita el Gobierno Federal para ciertos tipos de préstamos relacionados con una vivienda, con el fin de verificar el cumplimiento del Prestador con las leyes de Igualdad de Oportunidades de Crédito, "fair housing" y las leyes de divulgación de los préstamos. Usted no está obligado a proporcionar esta información, pero se le instamos que lo haga. La ley dispone que un Prestador no puede discriminar en base a esta información ni por el hecho de que decida o no proporcionarla. Sin embargo, si usted decide no proporcionarla, bajo reglamentaciones federales el Prestador debe anotar la raza y el sexo basado en una observación visual o por apellido. Si usted no desea proporcionar la información anterior, sírvase marcar el cuadro correspondiente. (El Prestador debe evaluar el material mencionado arriba para asegurarse de que la información proporcionada cumple con todos los requisitos a los que está sujeto el Prestador bajo la ley estatal pertinente para el tipo de préstamo en particular que se ha solicitado.)

BORROWER / *PRESTATARIO*

☐ I do not wish to furnish this information
No deseo proporcionar esta información

Race/National Origin:
Raza/Origen Nacional:

☐ American Indian or Alaskan Native /
Indio Americano o Nativo de Alaska
☐ Black, not of Hispanic origin
Negro, no de origen Hispano
☐ Asian or Pacific Islander / *Asiático o de las Islas del Pacífico*
☐ Hispanic / *Hispano*
☐ White, not of Hispanic Origin / *Blanco, no de origen Hispano*
☐ Other (specify) / *Otro (especificar)* _____

Sex / *Sexo:* ☐ Female / *Femenino* ☐ Male / *Masculino*

CO-BORROWER / *CO-PRESTATARIO*

☐ I do not wish to furnish this information
No deseo proporcionar esta información

Race/National Origin:
Raza/Origen Nacional:

☐ American Indian or Alaskan Native /
Indio Americano o Nativo de Alaska
☐ Black, not of Hispanic origin
Negro, no de origen Hispano
☐ Asian or Pacific Islander / *Asiático o de las Islas del Pacífico*
☐ Hispanic / *Hispano*
☐ White, not of Hispanic Origin / *Blanco, no de origen Hispano*
☐ Other (specify) / *Otro (especificar)* _____

Sex / *Sexo:* ☐ Female / *Femenino* ☐ Male / *Masculino*

To be Completed by Interviewer *A completarse por el Entrevistador* This application was taken by: *Esta solicitud se obtuvo por:* ☐ face-to-face interview *entrevista en persona* ☐ by mail / *correo* ☐ by telephone / *teléfono*	Interviewer's Name (print or type) *Nombre del Entrevistador (use letra de imprenta o a máquina)*	Name and Address of Interviewer's Employer *Nombre y Dirección del Empleador del Entrevistador*
	Interviewer's Signature / *Firma del Entrevistador* Date / *Fecha*	
	Interviewer's Phone Number (incl. area code) *N° de Teléfono del Entrevistador (inc. código de área)*	

(continued)

FIGURE 11.1
Continued.

CONTINUATION SHEET RESIDENTIAL LOAN APPLICATION	HOJA DE CONTINUACION SOLICITUD PARA PRESTAMO HIPOTECARIO RESIDENCIAL	
Use this continuation sheet if you need more space to complete the Residential Loan Application. Mark B for Borrower or C for Co-Borrower. *Utilice esta hoja de continuación si necesita más espacio para completar la Solicitud para Préstamo Hipotecario Residencial. Marque B para Prestatario o C para Co-Prestatario.*	Borrower: / *Prestatario:*	Agency Case Number: / *Número de Préstamo de la Agencia:*
	Co-Borrower: / *Co-Prestatario:*	Lender Case Number: / *Número de Préstamo del Prestador:*

THE SPANISH TRANSLATION IS FOR CONVENIENCE PURPOSES ONLY. IN THE EVENT OF AN INCONSISTENCY BETWEEN THE ENGLISH AND SPANISH LANGUAGE VERSIONS OF THIS FORM, THE ENGLISH LANGUAGE VERSION SHALL PREVAIL.
LA TRADUCCION AL ESPAÑOL ES PARA SU CONVENIENCIA UNICAMENTE. EN CASO DE QUE EXISTA UNA INCONSISTENCIA ENTRE LA VERSION EN INGLES Y LA VERSION EN ESPAÑOL DE ESTE FORMULARIO, PREVALECERA LA VERSION EN INGLES.

I/We fully understand that it is a Federal crime punishable by fine or imprisonment, or both, to knowingly make any false statements concerning any of the above facts as applicable under the provisions of Title 18, United States Code, Section 1001, et seq.
Entiendo/entendemos que es un crimen federal penado con multa o encarcelamiento, o ambos, el hacer declaraciones falsas con respecto a cualquiera de los hechos arriba declarados según sea pertinente de acuerdo con las disposiciones del Título 18 del Código de los Estados Unidos, Artículo 1001, et seq.

LEA ESTO PRIMERO: Este documento contiene una traducción al español de su texto en inglés.

Borrower's Signature: / *Firma del Prestatario:*	Date / *Fecha*	Co-Borrower's Signature: / *Firma del Co-Prestatario:*	Date / *Fecha*
X		X	

APPSPAN

Page 6 of 6
Página 6 de 6

Fannie Mae
Form 1003(S) Nov. 96

the lender knows that the present loan is contingent on closing that escrow. If the down payment and settlement funds are to be borrowed, then the lender needs to be extra cautious as experience has shown that the less money a borrower personally puts into a purchase, the higher is the probability of default and foreclosure.

Purpose of Loan

The lender is also interested in the proposed use of the property. Lenders feel most comfortable when a loan is for the purchase or improvement of a property the loan applicant will actually occupy. This is because owner-occupants usually have pride of ownership in maintaining their property and even during bad economic conditions will continue to make the monthly payments. An owner-occupant also realizes that losing the home still means paying for shelter elsewhere. It is standard practice for lenders to ask loan applicants to sign a statement declaring whether they intend to occupy the property.

If the loan applicant intends to purchase a dwelling to rent out as an investment, the lender will be more cautious because, during periods of high vacancy, the property may not generate enough income to meet the loan payments. At that point, a strapped-for-cash borrower is likely to default. Note too that lenders generally avoid loans secured by purely speculative real estate. If the value of the property drops below the amount owed, the borrower may see no further logic in making the loan payments.

Finally, the lender assesses the borrower's attitude toward the proposed loan. Someone with a casual attitude, such as "I'm buying because real estate always goes up," or an applicant who does not appear to understand the obligation being undertaken, would bring a low rating here. Much more welcome is the applicant who shows a mature attitude and understanding of the loan obligation and who exhibits a strong and logical desire for ownership.

Borrower Analysis

In sections [3] and [4] the lender begins an analysis of the borrower, and, if there is one, the co-borrower. At one time age, sex, and marital status played an important role in the lender's decision to lend or not to lend. Often the young and the old had trouble getting loans, as did women and persons who were single, divorced, or widowed. Today, the federal Equal Credit Opportunity Act prohibits discrimination based on age, sex, race, and marital status. Lenders are no longer permitted to discount income earned by women because a job is part-time or the woman is of childbearing age. If the applicant chooses to disclose it, alimony, separate maintenance, and child support must be counted in full. Young adults and single persons cannot be turned down because the lender feels they have not "put down roots." Seniors cannot be turned down as long as life expectancy exceeds the early risk period of the loan and collateral is adequate. In other words, the emphasis in borrower analysis is now focused on job stability, income adequacy, net worth, and credit rating.

Thus in sections [5] and [6] we see questions directed at how long the applicants have held their present jobs and the stability of the jobs themselves. An applicant who possesses marketable job skills and has been regularly employed with a stable employer is considered the ideal risk. Persons whose income can rise and fall erratically, such as commissioned salespersons, present greater risks. Persons whose skills (or lack of skills) or lack of job seniority result in frequent unemployment are more likely to have difficulty repaying a loan. In these sections the lender also inquires as to the number of dependents the applicant must support from his or her income. This information provides some insight as to how much will be left for monthly house payments.

Monthly Income

In section **[7]** the lender looks at the amount and sources of the applicants' income. Quantity alone is not enough for loan approval since the income sources must be stable too. Thus a lender will look carefully at overtime, bonus, and commission income in order to estimate the levels at which these may be expected to continue. Interest, dividend, and rental income is considered in light of the stability of their sources also. Income from social security and retirement pensions is entered and added to the totals for the applicants. Alimony, child support, and separate maintenance payments received need not be revealed. However, such sums must be listed in order to be considered as a basis for repaying the loan.

In section **[8]** the lender compares what the applicants have been paying for housing with what they will be paying if the loan is approved. Included in the proposed housing expense total are principal, interest, taxes, and insurance along with any assessments or homeowner association dues (such as in a condominium). Some lenders add the monthly cost of utilities to this list.

At **[9]** proposed monthly housing expense is compared with gross monthly income. A general rule of thumb is that monthly housing expense (PITI) should not exceed 25% to 30% of gross monthly income. A second guideline is that total fixed monthly expenses should not exceed 33% to 38% of income. This includes housing payments plus automobile payments, installment loan payments, alimony, child support, and investments with negative cash flows. These are general guidelines, but lenders recognize that food, health care, clothing, transportation, entertainment, and income taxes must also come from the applicants' income.

Assets and Liabilities

In section **[10]** the lender is interested in the applicants' sources of funds for closing and whether, once the loan is granted, the applicants have assets to fall back on in the event of an income decrease (a job layoff) or unexpected expenses (hospital bills). Of particular interest is the portion of those assets that are in cash or are readily convertible into cash in a few days. These are called **liquid assets.** If income drops, they are much more useful in meeting living expenses and loan payments than assets that may require months to sell and convert to cash—that is, assets that are **illiquid.**

Note in section **[10]** that two values are shown for life insurance. **Cash value** is the amount of money the policyholder would receive if the policy were surrendered to the insurance company or, alternatively, the amount the policyholder could borrow against the policy. **Face amount** is the amount that would be paid in the event of the insured's death. Lenders feel most comfortable if the face amount of the policy equals or exceeds the amount of the proposed loan. Obviously a borrower's death is not anticipated before the loan is repaid, but lenders recognize that its possibility increases the probability of default. The likelihood of foreclosure is lessened considerably if the survivors receive life insurance benefits.

In section **[11]** the lender is interested in the applicants' existing debts and liabilities for two reasons. First, each month these items compete against housing expenses for available monthly income. Thus high monthly payments in this section may lower the lender's estimate of what the applicants will be able to repay and, consequently, may influence the lender to reduce the size of the loan. The presence of monthly liabilities is not all negative: It can also show the lender that the applicants are capable of repaying their debts. Second, the applicants' total debts are subtracted from their total assets to obtain their **net worth,** reported at **[12]**. If the result is negative (more owed than owned) the loan request will probably be turned down as too risky. In contrast, a substantial net worth can often offset weaknesses elsewhere in the application, such as too little monthly income in relation to monthly housing expense or an income that can rise and fall erratically.

References

At number **[13]** lenders ask for credit references as an indicator of the future. Applicants with no previous credit experience will have more weight placed on income and employment history. Applicants with a history of collections, adverse judgments, foreclosure, or bankruptcy will have to convince the lender that this loan will be repaid on time. Additionally, the applicants may be considered poorer risks if they have guaranteed the repayment of someone else's debt by acting as a co-maker or endorser.

Redlining

In the past, it was not uncommon for lenders to refuse to make loans in certain neighborhoods regardless of the quality of the structure or the ability of the borrower to repay. This practice was known as **redlining,** and it effectively shut off mortgage loans in many older or so-called "bad risk" neighborhoods across the country. Today a lender cannot refuse to make a loan simply because of the age or location of a property; the neighborhood income level; or the racial, ethnic, or religious composition of the neighborhood.

A lender can refuse to lend on a structure intended for demolition; a property in a known geological hazard area; a single-family dwelling in an area devoted to industrial or commercial use; or a property that is in violation of zoning laws, deed covenants, conditions or restrictions, or significant health, safety, or building codes.

Loan-to-Value Ratios

The lender next looks at the amount of down payment the borrower proposes to make, the size of the loan being requested, and the amount of other financing the borrower plans to use. This information is then converted into loan-to-value ratios. As a rule, the larger the down payment is, the safer the loan is for the lender. On an uninsured loan, the ideal loan-to-value (L/V) ratio for a lender on owner-occupied residential property is 70% or less. This means the value of the property would have to fall more than 30% before the debt owed would exceed the property's value, thus encouraging the borrower to stop making loan payments.

Loan-to-value ratios from 70% through 80% are considered acceptable but do expose the lender to more risk. Lenders sometimes compensate by charging slightly higher interest rates. Loan-to-value ratios above 80% present even more risk of default to the lender, and the lender will either increase the interest rate charged on these loans or require insurance coverage from an outside insurer, such as the FHA or a private mortgage insurer.

Credit Report

As part of the loan application, the lender will order a **credit report** on the applicant(s). The applicant is asked to authorize this and to pay for the report. This provides the lender with an independent means of checking the applicant's credit history. A credit report that shows active use of credit with a good repayment record and no derogatory information is most desirable. The applicant will be asked by the lender to explain any negative information. Because it is possible for inaccurate or untrue information in a credit report to unfairly damage a person's credit reputation, Congress passed the **Fair Credit Reporting Act.** This act gives individuals the right to inspect their file at a credit bureau, correct any errors, and make explanatory statements to supplement the file.

As previously discussed, the major federal agencies have combined their requirements for credit reports, and loans intended for underwriting by federal government agencies must comply with the new credit standards. Under these newly adopted rules, the name of the consumer reporting agency must be clearly identified, as well as who ordered the report and who is paying for it. The information must be obtained from at least two national repositories for each area in which the borrower resided in the past two years, and must be verified for the previous two years. An explanation must be provided if the information is unavailable, and all questions must be responded to, even if the answer must be "unable to verify." A history must be furnished and all missing information must be verified by the lender. The history must have been checked within 90 days of the credit report and the age of information that is not considered obsolete by the Fair Credit Reporting Act (7 years general credit date or 10 years for bankruptcy) must be indicated. If any credit information is incomplete or if undisclosed information is discovered, the lender must have a personal interview with the borrower. The lender is additionally required to warrant that the credit report complies with all of the new standards.

Real estate practitioners should be particularly aware of this law. If an applicant for rental of a property is rejected on the basis of a credit report, there are special disclosures (set out by federal law) the owner, or the owner's agent, must make. If the applicant is rejected for reasons other than a credit report, the reasons must be disclosed. All disclosures must be made even if no request is made by the applicant.

Subprime Loans

There is an expanding market today for what are called **subprime loans.** Subprime loans have risk-based pricing and rates are not quoted. Usually a rate is found, or negotiated, if it fits the risk profile. Interest rates are typically one to five percentage points higher than for good credit risks. With these loans, appraisals are critical and the risk profiles tend to be variable from lender to lender. The lowest risk borrowers are considered prime borrowers and are rated an "A" classification. Higher risk loans fall into lower categories from "A–" to "F." Although exact criteria vary, the "A" to "F" credit scoring has become somewhat standard in the last few years.

REVIEW QUESTIONS

Answers to these questions are found in the Answer Key section at the back of the book.

1. All of the following are exempt from the provisions of the Federal Truth in Lending Act EXCEPT:
   A. commercial loans.
   B. personal property loans in excess of $25,000
   C. financing extended to corporations.
   D. consumer loans to natural persons.

2. Which of the following loans would be exempt from the disclosure requirements of the truth in lending laws?
   A. An unsecured personal loan of $3,000.
   B. An educational loan from a commercial bank.
   C. A second mortgage loan on a residence.
   D. A $30,000 loan for the purchase of a $40,000 automobile.

3. Penalties for violation of the truth in lending laws include
   A. a fine of up to $5,000 and/or imprisonment for up to one year.
   B. civil penalties up to twice the amount of the finance charge up to a maximum of $1,000.
   C. court costs, attorney fees, and actual damages.
   D. All of the above.

4. A borrower does not have the right, under the truth in lending laws, to rescind a credit transaction
   A. for a consumer loan on personal property.
   B. for the acquisition of the borrower's principal dwelling.
   C. Both A and B.
   D. Neither A nor B.

5. Generally, before a lender will approve a loan, the borrower must
   A. have sufficient funds for the down payment.
   B. sign a statement if the borrower intends to occupy the property.
   C. Both A and B.
   D. Neither A nor B.

6. Which of the following is given consideration in evaluation of a loan application?
   A. Race
   B. Marital status
   C. Sex
   D. Income adequacy

7. A lender can legally discriminate in loan terms based on the applicant's
   A. religion.
   B. marital status.
   C. race or skin color.
   D. intention to occupy (or not occupy) the mortgaged property.

8. The right of an individual to inspect his or her file at a credit bureau is found in the
   A. Truth-in-Lending Act.
   B. Fair Credit Reporting Act.
   C. Regulation Z.
   D. Federal Consumer Credit Protection Act.

9. The abbreviation APR stands for
   A. average percentage rate.
   B. allotted percentage rate.
   C. approximate percentage rate.
   D. annual percentage rate.

10. The annual percentage rate is
   A. usually lower than the interest rate.
   B. made up of the interest rate combined with the other costs of the loan.
   C. Both A and B.
   D. Neither A nor B.

KEY TERMS

Alienation clause: requires immediate repayment of the loan if ownership transfers; also called a due-on-sale clause

Automated underwriting systems: computerized systems for loan approval communication between a loan originator and the investor

Computerized loan origination: originating loans through the use of a networked computer system

Disintermediation: the result created when lenders are required to pay high rates of interest for deposits while receiving long-term income from low-interest-rate mortgage loans

Fannie Mae: a real estate industry nickname for the Federal National Mortgage Association

Freddie Mac: a real estate industry nickname for the Federal Home Loan Mortgage Corporation

Mortgage broker: one who brings together borrowers and lenders

Mortgage company: a firm that makes mortgage loans and then sells them to investors

Participation certificates: a certificate representing an undivided interest in a Freddie Mac pool

Primary market: the market in which lenders originate loans and make funds available to borrowers

Secondary mortgage market: a market in which mortgage loans can be sold to investors

Usury: charging an interest rate that is in excess of the legal rate

Sources of Financing

After reading this chapter, you will be able to (1) identify various mortgage lenders (the primary market), (2) describe where these lenders get much of their money (the secondary market), and (3) explain provisions of mortgage loan instruments that have an impact on the cost of funds. Many people feel that understanding the financing market is the most important of all real estate topics because, without financing, real estate profits and commissions would be difficult to achieve.

PRIMARY MARKET

The **primary market** (also called the **primary mortgage market**) is where lenders originate loans—that is, where lenders make funds available to borrowers. The primary market is what the borrower sees as the source of mortgage loan money, the institution with which the borrower has direct and personal contact. It's the place where the loan application is taken, where the loan officer interviews the loan applicant, where the loan check comes from, and the place to which loan payments are sent by the borrower.

These sources of funds can generally be divided into two markets: (1) those markets regulated by the federal government and (2) those markets that are not regulated by the government. The regulated lenders are commercial banks, savings and loan (S&L) associations, and savings banks. The nonregulated lenders are commercial finance companies, investment bankers, life insurance companies, and finance companies. Nonregulated sources of funds are relatively new to the mortgage market and are not subject to the same restrictive regulations that are designed to protect the lender with deposits insured by the federal government. In today's markets, a purchaser is wise to contact both regulated and nonregulated lenders to make an adequate comparison of available loan money. Markets differ widely within states and even within certain urban areas. The regulated lenders are subject to examinations by federal regulators, pay risk-based premiums on their deposit insurance, and are restricted to certain loan-to-value ratios.

Most borrowers assume that the loan they receive comes from depositors who visit the same bank or S&L to leave their excess funds. This is partly true. But this, by itself, is an inadequate source of loan funds in today's market. Thus, primary lenders often sell their loans in what is called the secondary market. Insurance companies, pension funds, and individual investors, as well as other primary lenders with excess deposits, buy these loans for cash. This makes more money available to a primary lender who, in turn, can loan these additional funds to borrowers. The secondary market is so huge that it rivals the entire U.S. corporate bond market in size of annual offerings. We return to the secondary market later in this chapter. Meanwhile, let's discuss the various lenders a borrower will encounter when looking for a real estate loan.

SAVINGS AND LOAN ASSOCIATIONS

Historically, the origin of **savings and loan associations** can be traced to early building societies in England and Germany and to the first American building society, the Oxford Provident Building Association, started in 1831 in Pennsylvania. These early building societies were cooperatives whose savers were also borrowers. As times progressed, savings and loan associations became a primary source of residential real estate loans. To encourage residential lending, the federally chartered savings and loans were required by federal regulation to hold at least 80% of their assets in residential loans. In addition, they were subjected to special tax laws that permitted a savings and loan association to defer payment of income taxes on profits, so long as those profits were held in surplus accounts and not distributed to the savings and loan association's owners. During this same period, there were also limits on the interest rate that could be paid on savings accounts. This provided the savings and loan associations with a dependable source of funds at a fixed interest rate, which gave them the potential for making long-term loans at reasonable rates. For instance, if the passbook savings account was limited to $5\frac{1}{4}\%$ per annum, home loans in the vicinity of $7\frac{1}{2}\%$ to $8\frac{1}{2}\%$ would still allow for reasonable profit margins. Unfortunately, the nature of the finance markets began to change in the late 1970s when an inflationary economy caused interest rates to skyrocket. This created problems that were unforeseen by the savings and loan industry.

Disintermediation

In order to attract depositors, savings and loans offer, in addition to passbook accounts, **certificates of deposit (CDs)** at rates higher than passbook rates. These are necessary to compete with higher yields offered by U.S. Treasury bills, notes, and bonds and to prevent disintermediation. **Disintermediation** results when depositors take money out of their savings accounts and invest directly in government securities, corporate bonds, and money market funds. A major problem, and one that nearly brought the S&L industry to its knees in the late 1970s and early 1980s, was that S&Ls traditionally relied heavily on short-term deposits from savers and then loaned that money on long-term (often 30-year) loans to borrowers. When interest rates rose sharply in the 1970s, S&Ls either had to raise the interest paid to their depositors or watch depositors withdraw their savings and take the money elsewhere for higher returns. Meanwhile, the S&Ls were holding long-term, fixed-rate mortgage loans, and, with interest rates rising, borrowers were not anxious to repay those loans early.

Restructuring the System

Disintermediation was only the beginning of the problems. Loan demand at S&Ls was declining. In 1976, 57% of the residential mortgage loans were held by savings and loan institutions. By 1996, the percentage fell to 13%. There are many reasons for this flow of funds out of the S&L industry. One of the primary reasons, however, appears to be the deregulation of the lending industry. This, coupled with bad investments, inadequately trained executives, and loose government controls on S&L risks and investments, resulted in an industry that could not remain solvent.

In August 1989, President Bush signed into law a sweeping revision of the regulatory authorities governing savings and loans. This law is referred to as the **Financial Institutions Reform, Recovery, and Enforcement Act of 1989,** commonly called **FIRREA.** The law redefined or created seven new regulatory authorities and initiated a system of federally designated real property appraisers, discussed in greater detail in Chapter 17.

COMMERCIAL BANKS

The nation's 15,000 **commercial banks** store far more of the country's money than the S&Ls. However, only one bank dollar in six goes to real estate lending. Of the loans made by banks for real estate, the tendency is to emphasize short-term maturities and adjustable rate mortgages, since the bulk of a bank's deposit money comes from demand deposits (checking accounts) and a much smaller portion from savings and time deposits.

Oddly enough, the same factors that have plagued the S&Ls seem to have helped the commercial banks. During the Deregulation Acts of 1980 and 1982, banks began making more home loans, but they were short-term, with adjustable rates. These types of loans prevent the problem of disintermediation, as the loan rates can rise with the rates that are required by the source of funds. Commercial banks, too, have realized that first-lien residential loans are also very secure, low-risk loans. They have also determined maintaining all of a customer's loan accounts, including a home loan, in the bank's portfolio provides a market advantage. "One-stop banking" has become a very successful marketing tool. The merger of many banks into large multistate national banks has also created a larger source of funds to lend. To accommodate this higher demand and facilitate the organization of sources of funds for the bank's lending purposes, many banks have now organized their own mortgage departments to assist customers in making home loans, even through sources other than bank deposits.

LIFE INSURANCE COMPANIES

As a group, the nation's 2,200 **life insurance companies** have long been active investors in real estate as developers, owners, and long-term lenders. Although not federally regulated, life insurance companies are subject to state regulations. Their source of money is the premiums paid by policyholders. These premiums are invested and ultimately returned to the policyholders. Because premiums are collected in regular amounts on regular dates and because policy payoffs can be calculated from actuarial tables, life insurers are in ideal positions to commit money to long-term investments. Life insurance companies channel their funds primarily into government and corporate bonds and real estate. The dollars allocated to real estate go to buy land and buildings, which are leased to users, and to make loans on commercial, industrial, and residential property. Generally, life insurers specialize in large-scale investments such as shopping centers, office and apartment buildings, and million-dollar blocks of home loans purchased in the **secondary mortgage market**, which is discussed later in this chapter.

Repayment terms on loans made by insurance companies for shopping centers, office buildings, and apartment complexes sometimes call for interest and a percentage of any profits from rentals over a certain level. These **participation loans,** which provide a "piece of the action" for the insurance company, also provide the insurance company with more inflation protection than a fixed rate of interest.

MORTGAGE COMPANIES

A **mortgage company** makes a mortgage loan and then sells it to a long-term investor. The process begins with locating borrowers, qualifying them, preparing the necessary loan papers, and, finally, making the loans. Once a loan is made, it is sold for cash on the secondary market. The mortgage company will usually continue to *service the loan*—that is, collect the monthly payments and handle such matters as insurance and property tax impounds, delinquencies, early payoffs, and mortgage releases.

Mortgage companies, also known as **mortgage bankers,** vary in size from one or two persons to several dozen. As a rule, they close loans in their own names and are locally oriented, finding and making loans within 25 or 50 miles of their offices. This gives them a feel for their market, greatly aids in identifying sound loans, and makes loan servicing much easier. For their efforts, mortgage bankers typically receive 1% to 3% of the amount of the loan when it is originated, and from $^1/_4$ to $^1/_2$ of 1% of the outstanding balance each year thereafter for servicing. Mortgage banking, as this business is called, is not limited to mortgage companies. Commercial banks, savings and loan associations, and mutual savings banks in active real estate areas often originate more real estate loans than they can hold themselves, and these are sold on the secondary market. Mortgage companies often do a large amount of their business in FHA and VA loans. As the shift in mortgage origination continues, it is important to note that the mortgage brokers' share of originations, which increased more than 30% from 1980 to 1995, will probably continue to increase.

MORTGAGE BROKERS

Mortgage brokers, in contrast to mortgage bankers, specialize in bringing together borrowers and lenders, just as real estate brokers bring together buyers and sellers. The mortgage broker does not lend money and usually does not service loans. The mortgage broker's fee is expressed in points and is usually paid by the borrower. Mortgage brokers are locally oriented, often small firms of from 1 to 10 persons. They seldom make loans in their own names as lender.

The mortgage brokering businesses actually felt an explosion during the late 1980s and early 1990s. The secondary market (discussed later in this chapter) has made investors' funds more readily available, and virtually anyone with some expertise in loan qualifications can originate loans and sell to secondary market purchasers. As a result, the field has become crowded with new loan originators such as home builders, finance companies, commercial credit companies, insurance agents, attorneys, and real estate brokers. These have generally been considered nontraditional lenders, but they can originate mortgage loans with their own resources or, through various networks, have the loan funded directly through to the secondary market purchaser. These new loan originators have offered substantial competition to regulated lenders.

PUTTING IT TO WORK

Whether or not a real estate broker may operate as a mortgage broker and collect a fee for placing a loan has been a "gray" area of the law. The concern expressed by some is that the fee retained by the broker (which is in addition to the real estate broker's fee) may be an undisclosed kickback, which violates the Real Estate Settlement Procedures Act (RESPA; see Chapter 15). Agency law also comes into play because a real estate broker may be representing the buyer on a loan while also representing the seller in the sale of the home. This may result in a duty for the listing broker to disclose everything the practitioner knows (including borrower financial information) to the principal (seller). Lenders also have some concern that the real estate agent may "fudge" mortgage qualification criteria to facilitate a lucrative sale. However, changes in RESPA now allow the involvement of a broker in the mortgage process on a very limited basis, provided proper disclosures are made to the borrower.

COMPUTERIZED LOAN ORIGINATION

The growth of computer networks has also enabled many independent loan processors to work under the guidance of large lending institutions and mortgage companies. Using a **computerized loan origination (CLO),** real estate brokers, attorneys, insurance agents, or mortgage companies can arrange to have a computer link installed in their offices, connected to lenders' mainframe computers. By utilizing a series of questions, borrowers can obtain preliminary loan approval immediately from the loan originator with a firm acceptance or rejection from the lending institution within a few days.

A full-featured CLO has three basic functions: (1) It provides information on current mortgage loan terms and loan types available on the market; (2) it conveys loan application information electronically; and (3) it monitors the loan approval process so that the practitioner can check on the progress of the loan application at any time. From the home buyer's perspective, the CLO provides the convenience of seeking home financing alternatives without calling and visiting a large number of local lenders, and in many cases it can increase the number of choices available. A broker should exercise caution, however, as conflicts can exist.

PUTTING IT TO WORK

New RESPA regulations greatly limit the use of CLOs by real estate agents, so legal counsel should be consulted before a practitioner attempts to utilize a CLO as a second source of income.

MUNICIPAL BONDS

In some cities, **municipal bonds** provide a source of mortgage money for home buyers. The special advantage to borrowers is that municipal bonds pay interest that is tax-free from federal income taxes. Knowing this, bond investors will accept a lower rate of interest than they would if the interest were taxable—as it normally is on mortgage loans. This saving is passed on to the home buyer. Those who qualify will typically pay about 2% less than if they had borrowed through conventional channels.

The objective of such programs is to make home ownership more affordable for low- and middle-income households. Also, a city may stipulate that loans be used in neighborhoods the city wants to revitalize. The loans are made by local lenders who are paid a fee for originating and servicing these loans. Although popular with the real estate industry, the U.S. Treasury has been less than enthusiastic about the concept because it bears the cost in lost tax revenues. As a result, federal legislation has been passed to limit the future use of this source of money.

OTHER LENDERS

Pension funds and **trust funds** traditionally have channeled their money to high-grade government and corporate bonds and stocks. However, the trend now is to place more money into real estate loans. Already active buyers on the secondary market, pension and trust funds will likely become a still larger source of real estate financing in the future. In some localities, pension fund members can tap their own pension funds for home mortgages at very reasonable rates. Pension funds are an often overlooked source of primary market financing.

Finance companies that specialize in making business and consumer loans also provide limited financing for real estate. As a rule, finance companies seek second mortgages at interest rates 2% to 5% higher than the rates prevailing on first mortgages. First mortgages are also taken as collateral; however, the lenders already discussed usually charge lower interest rates for these loans and thus are more competitive.

Credit unions normally specialize in consumer loans. However, real estate loans are becoming more and more important as many of the country's 16,000 credit unions have branched out into first and second mortgage loans. Credit unions are an often overlooked but excellent source of home loan money.

Commercial finance companies also have entered the mortgage lending fields. These are private companies, such as General Electric Capital Mortgage Corporation, General Motors Acceptance Corporation, and Ford Motor Company, which are subject to neither banking restrictions nor deposit insurance regulations. They are becoming a more widely used source of finance money, particularly in affordable housing loans, discussed in the next chapter.

Individuals are sometimes a source of cash loans for real estate, with the bulk of these loans made between relatives or friends, often as investments with their IRAs or private pension plans that require a low-risk investment with attractive rates. Generally, loan maturities are shorter than those obtainable from the institutional lenders already described. In some cities, persons can be found who specialize in making or buying second and third mortgage loans of up to 10-year maturities. Individuals are beginning to invest substantial amounts of money in secondary mortgage market securities. Ironically, these investments are often made with money that would have otherwise been deposited in a savings and loan.

Texas Loan Programs

Texas has made its own loan programs available for veterans and low- to middle-income borrowers. All of them have had a very beneficial impact on the Texas housing industry and deserve more detailed discussion.

Texas Veterans Land Fund

The Texas Veterans Land Board has made a program available by which an eligible veteran may buy land from the Veterans Land Board by a contract of sale, installment land contract, or contract for deed at very favorable interest rates determined by the Texas Veterans Land Board. The contract cannot exceed 40 years and the purchase price of the property cannot exceed $20,000. There must be a minimum down payment of 5%, not to exceed $1,000. If the price of the land exceeds the $20,000, the veteran must pay the Board, in cash, a down payment equal to that portion of the sales price in excess of $20,000. The veteran may either purchase land owned by the Board, or the veteran may designate certain land that the Board may purchase in his or her behalf and then resell to him or her under the installment land contract.

Veterans' Housing Assistance Program

Another program that the Texas Veterans Land Board has made available is the Veterans' Housing Assistance Program (VHAP). You will note that the TREC-promulgated contracted forms have special provisions under the "Financing Conditions" section to provide for the Veterans' Housing Assistance Program. The program is made available to eligible veterans who wish to purchase a new or existing home, which must be the primary residence of the veteran for at least three years. The VHAP loan is used in conjunction with any other type of financing, and enables the veteran to borrow up to $20,000 as a first or second lien mortgage. There is a maximum amount of $20,000 on the loan, so if there is going to be a single mortgage of less than $20,000 the Veterans Land Board will be the only noteholder on the loan. If more than $20,000 is borrowed, the Veterans Land Board and the first lien lender share the first lien position, and the first lien lender services and originates the loan.

If the VHAP loan is used in conjunction with another conventional first lien, 5% down payment of the purchase price is required. If it is used in conjunction with a VA loan, there is no down payment if the veteran has full VA eligibility. As with other veteran loans, the veteran can transfer the loan to another veteran or nonveteran as long as the original veteran has lived in the house for a minimum of three years.

Additional information on both of these Veterans Land Board approved loans can be obtained by calling the Texas Veterans Land Board at their toll-free number: 1 (800) 252-VETS.

Texas Department of Housing and Community Affairs

In 1979, the Texas Legislature established the Texas Housing Agency for the purpose of financing the acquisition, construction, or rehabilitation of housing that meets the needs of low- and moderate-income persons and families. In 1991, Texas abolished the Agency, transferring its essential functions to the Texas Department of Housing and Community Affairs.

The programs currently available are the First Time Homebuyer Program and a Down Payment Assistance program. To qualify for the First Time Homebuyer Program, the applicant must not have owned a principal residence in the past three years, must have an annual income in the low to moderate range, must be considered creditworthy, and must agree to buy a residence within the State of Texas. Income limits vary depending upon the area of the state, the number of people in the family, and whether or not the property is within a targeted or nontargeted area. (Targeted areas are federally designated regions defined as being economically depressed. Some program restrictions are waived or reduced to encourage development and housing in these areas).

By periodically selling tax-exempt mortgage revenue bonds (MRBs), the agency raises money in financial markets at the lower interest rates available to state and municipal bonds (the interest paid on such bonds is exempt from federal income tax). By passing the lower rates on to home buyers, mortgage loans can be made at less than conventional market rates.

This program is designed to help low-income buyers with home purchases. The Department offers a program of cash assistance to qualified home buyers, who are entitled to a cash advance of up to $1,5000.00 in the form of a loan at zero interest. The loan can cover up to two-thirds of the down payment and acceptable closing costs on a home purchased through any of the Department's First Item Homebuyer programs. The loan must be repaid when the home is sold or the original mortgage is paid off.

Acceptable closing costs include evidence of title, survey, credit report, FHA appraisal fee, attorney's fee, origination fee, and home inspection fee.

Qualification is limited to the purchase of a home for $65,000.00 or less. Eligibility is confined to low-income, first-time home buyers (those not owning a house in the past three years). "Low-income" is defined as those with incomes 80% or less of the local area median income.

Housing Finance Corporation

Texas also provides a mechanism whereby a local governmental unit can authorize the creation of a Housing Finance Corporation within that governmental unit. This is a nonprofit corporation that can sell bonds and utilize other methods of incurring income to provide financing to local lending institutions for low- and middle-income housing, similar to a state-sponsored program administered by the Texas Housing Agency. There are also similar criteria for providing housing for the elderly. These corporations can only be enabled by the local governing body such as a city council. The determination must be made from town to town as to whether or not a housing financing corporation is available as a source for these types of funds.

SECONDARY MARKET

The **secondary market** (also called the **secondary mortgage market**) provides a way for a lender to sell a loan. It also permits investment in real estate loans without the need for loan origination and servicing facilities. Although not directly encountered by real estate buyers, sellers, and agents, the secondary market plays an important role in getting money from those who want to lend to those who want to borrow. In other words, think of the secondary market as a pipeline for loan money. Visualize that pipeline running via the Wall Street financial district in New York City, as Wall Street is now a major participant in residential mortgage lending. Figure 12.1 illustrates this pipeline and diagrams key differences between the traditional mortgage delivery system and the secondary market system.

Traditional Delivery System

Notice in Figure 12.1 that, in the traditional system, the lender is a local institution gathering deposits from the community and then lending that money as real estate loans in the same community. Traditionally, each lender (S&L, mutual savings bank, commercial bank, credit union) was an independent unit that developed its own appraisal technique, loan application form, loan approval criteria, note and mortgage forms, servicing method, and foreclosure policy. Nonetheless, three major problems needed solving. The first occurred when an institution had an imbalance of depositors and borrowers. Rapidly growing areas of the United States often needed more loan money than their savers were capable of depositing. Stable regions had more depositors than loan opportunities. Thus it was common to see correspondent relationships between lenders, for example, a lender in Los Angeles would sell some of its mortgage loans to a savings bank in Brooklyn. This provided loans for borrowers and interest for savers. The system worked well, but required individual correspondent relationships.

FIGURE 12.1
Mortgage loan delivery systems.

The second problem occurred when depositors wanted to withdraw their money from their accounts and invest it in other sources. Lenders, seeking to attract these depositors, raised their interest rates, which results in loan rates increasing. The third problem was timing. Lenders must borrow "short" (from their deposit relationships) and lend "long" (30-year mortgages). Savers, then, are encouraged to leave their money on deposit for longer periods of time.

The answer to these three problems is relatively simple: Find a market to sell your loans to investors who will pay cash for them and reimburse you, the primary lender. The result, then, is that there is an investor who is willing to hold the loan long-term for its guaranteed rate of return. The primary lender continues to make loans, gambling that he will find another investor in the secondary market to buy that loan for a long term. In effect, the primary lenders can make loans from the secondary market instead of from their deposits.

Secondary Market Delivery Systems

As shown in Figure 12.1, with the secondary market system the borrower obtains a loan from a mortgage originator. This includes mortgage companies, banks, CLOs, and thrifts that originate loans they intend to sell. The mortgage originator packages the loan with other loans and then either sells the package as a whole or keeps the package and sells securities that are backed by the loans in the package. If the originator is not large enough to package its own mortgages, it will sell the loans to someone who can.

There are now two sources for this secondary market. The first is private investors such as commercial banks, savings and loans, pension plans, trust funds, and other investors who are looking for low-risk, long-term returns on their investments. The second group of investors, relatively new in the investment business, is the investment "pools" or "poolers" who are looking for more security in their investments. This results in two primary investors in the secondary market: (1) the pure portfolio purchasers who are looking for the initial investments with an attractive return, and (2) the "poolers" who are looking for the longer term, more stable return.

Standardized Loan Procedures

A major stumbling block to a highly organized and efficient secondary market has been the uniqueness of both lenders and loans. Traditionally, each primary lender developed its own special loan forms and procedures. Moreover, each loan is a unique combination of real estate and borrower. No two are exactly alike. How do you package such diversity into an attractive package for investors? A large part of the answer has come through standardized loan application forms; standardized appraisal forms; standardized credit report forms; standardized closing statements; standardized loan approval criteria; and standardized promissory notes, mortgages, and trust deeds. Loan terms have been standardized into categories, for example, fixed-rate, 30-year loans; fixed-rate, 15-year loans; and various adjustable rate combinations. Additionally, nearly all loans must be insured. This can take the form of FHA or private mortgage insurance, or a VA guarantee on each loan in the package. Additionally, there will be some form of assurance of timely repayment of the mortgage package as a whole. The net result is a mortgage security that is attractive to investors who in the past have not been interested in investing in mortgages.

Let's now look at some of the key secondary market participants including the giants of the industry: the Federal National Mortgage Association, the Government National Mortgage Association, the Federal Home Loan Mortgage Corporation, and Farmer Mac.

FNMA

The **Federal National Mortgage Association (FNMA)** was organized by the federal government in 1938 to buy FHA mortgage loans from lenders. This made it possible for lenders to grant more loans to consumers. Ten years later it began purchasing VA loans. FNMA (fondly known in the real estate business and to itself as "Fannie Mae") was successful in its mission.

In 1968, Congress divided the FNMA into two organizations: the Government National Mortgage Association (to be discussed in the next section) and the FNMA, as we know it today. As part of that division, the FNMA changed from a government agency to a private profit-making corporation, chartered by Congress but owned by its shareholders and managed independently of the government. Some 60 million shares of Fannie Mae stock are in existence, and it is one of the most actively traded issues on the New York Stock Exchange. Fannie Mae buys FHA and VA loans and, since 1972, conventional whole loans from lenders across the United States. Money to buy these loans comes from the sale of FNMA stock plus the sale of FNMA bonds and notes. FNMA bond and note holders look to Fannie Mae for timely payment of principal and interest on these bonds and notes, and Fannie Mae looks to its mortgagors for principal and interest payments on the loans it owns. Thus, Fannie Mae stands in the middle and, although it is very careful to match interest rates and maturities between the loans it buys and the bonds and notes it sells, it still takes the risk of the middleman. In this respect, it is like a giant thrift institution.

Commitments

Fannie Mae's method of operation is to sell commitments to lenders pledging to buy specified dollar amounts of mortgage loans within a fixed period of time and usually at a specified yield. Lenders are not obligated to sell loans to Fannie Mae if they can find better terms elsewhere. However, Fannie Mae must purchase all loans delivered to it under the terms of the commitments. Loans must be made using FNMA-approved forms and loan approval criteria. The largest loan Fannie Mae would buy in 1998 was $227,150 for a single-family unit. This limit is adjusted each year as housing prices change. Fannie Mae also buys loans on duplexes, triplexes, and fourplexes all at larger loan limits. Although the FNMA loan limit may seem inadequate for some houses and neighborhoods, the intention of Congress is that Fannie Mae cater to the mid-range of housing prices and leave the upper end of the market to others.

In addition to purchasing first mortgages, Fannie Mae also purchases second mortgages from lenders. FNMA forms and criteria must be followed and the loan-to-value ratio of the combined first and second mortgages cannot exceed 80% if owner-occupied and 70% if not owner-occupied. This is a very helpful program for those who have watched the value of their homes increase and want to borrow against that increase without first having to repay the existing mortgage loan.

FNMA Pooling

The demand for loans in the primary market could not match the demand that investors required in the secondary market, so Fannie Mae began purchasing large blocks of mortgage loans, and then assigned them to specified pools with an "agency guarantee" certificate that guaranteed long-term return to the pool investors. Fannie Mae guarantees to pass through to the certificate holders whatever principal, interest, and prepayments of principal are generated by the loans into the underlying pool of mortgage investors. Fannie Mae's pooling arrangements undertook the issuance of **mortgage-backed securities (MBS).** Utilizing this system of issuing securities that are backed by mortgages, the securities markets could then be used as a source for investment funds. In the second quarter of 1997, Fannie Mae held $170 billion dollars of loans in portfolio investments. At the same time, however, Fannie Mae had underwritten $673 billion in mortgage pools, totaling 10% of all residential loans. This is an incredible shift in loan procedures since 1982. This is also a strong indication that the government-guaranteed loan pools provide a much better procedure for making funds available in the secondary market. This, in turn, assures funds available for the primary market and long-term mortgage loans for individual home purchasers.

Home Seller Program

Another innovation of Fannie Mae to help real estate is the **home seller program.** This is a secondary market for sellers who carry back mortgages. To qualify, the note and mortgage must be prepared by a FNMA-approved lender using standard FNMA loan qualification procedures. The note and mortgage may be kept by the home seller as an investment or sold to a FNMA-approved lender for possible resale to the FNMA.

In other developments, Fannie Mae has standardized the terms of adjustable rate mortgages it will purchase. This is a major step forward in reducing the proliferation of variety in these loans. Fannie Mae is also test marketing mortgage-backed securities in $1,000 increments to appeal to individuals, particularly for Individual Retirement Accounts. Additionally, Fannie Mae has started a collateralized mortgage obligation program and begun a mortgage pass-through program, both of which will be defined momentarily.

Revised Lending Practices

In 1992, as pressure increased from both Congress and the U.S. Department of Housing and Urban Development to become more socially responsible in lending practices, Congress passed legislation requiring stricter supervision of Fannie Mae by a HUD-appointed oversight committee. In March 1994, Fannie Mae announced a plan to provide one trillion dollars in financing over the rest of the decade to poor families, rural communities, and disabled people. Fannie Mae now cooperates with others in the purchase of 97% of conventional loans, working with local housing authorities, nonprofit associations, nonprofit housing groups, and private mortgage insurance, to spread the risk of some other loans.

GNMA

The **Government National Mortgage Association (GNMA,** popularly known to the industry and to itself as **"Ginnie Mae"**) was created in 1968 when the FNMA was partitioned into two separate corporations. Ginnie Mae is a federal agency entirely within the HUD. Although Ginnie Mae has some low-income housing functions, it is best known for its mortgage-backed securities (MBS) program. Previously discussed, the MBS program attracts additional sources of credit to FHA, VA, and FmHA mortgages. Ginnie Mae does this by guaranteeing timely repayment of privately issued securities backed by pools of these mortgages. Remember that the FNMA MBS program offers "agency guarantees" for their investors. GNMA offers a government guarantee of repayment, backed by the full faith and credit of the U.S. government.

Ginnie Mae Procedures

Ginnie Mae is limited to underwriting only HUD/FHA, VA, and certain Farmer's Home Administration loans. It is not possible to purchase loans as both FNMA and FHLMC (discussed next). Ginnie Mae sets its own requirements for loans that can be accepted into their mortgage pool, then it subsequently approves loan poolers who are committed to comply with those requirements. Ginnie Mae must examine the loans and the loan poolers before it can determine its ability to guarantee those loans into the loan pooler source of funds.

The result is that Ginnie Mae issues guarantee certificates, popularly known as "Ginnie Maes." By the second quarter of 1997, Ginnie Maes accounted for 12% of all residential loans. A Ginnie Mae certificate carries the equivalent of a U.S. government bond guarantee and pays the holder of those certificates, the loan pooler, an interest rate of 1% to $1\frac{1}{2}$% higher than that of a government bond.

FHLMC

The **Federal Home Loan Mortgage Corporation (FHLMC,** also known to the industry and to itself as **"Freddie Mac"** or the "Mortgage Corporation") was created by Congress in 1970. Its goal, like that of the FNMA and GNMA, is to increase the availability of financing for residential mortgages. Where FHLMC differs is that Freddie Mac deals primarily in conventional mortgages.

Freddie Mac was initially established to serve as a secondary market for S&L members of the Federal Home Loan Bank System. The ownership of Freddie Mac was originally held by more than 3,000 savings associations. In 1988, the shares were released and sold publicly by the savings associations. Unlike Ginnie Mae, which guarantees securities issued by others, Freddie Mac issues its own securities against its own mortgage pools. These securities are its participation certificates and collateralized mortgage obligations. By the second quarter of 1997, Freddie Mac held nearly $45 billion in its own loan portfolio, accounting for almost 15.5% (including FHLMC pools) of all outstanding loans in residential lending.

Participation Certificates

Participation certificates (PCs) allow a mortgage originator to deliver to Freddie Mac either whole mortgages or part interest in a pool of whole mortgages. In return, Freddie Mac gives the mortgage originator a PC representing an undivided interest in a pool of investment-quality conventional mortgages created from mortgages and mortgage interests purchased by Freddie Mac. Freddie Mac guarantees that the interest and principal on these PCs will be repaid in full and on time, even if the underlying mortgages are in default. (Freddie Mac reduces its losses by setting strict loan qualification criteria and requiring mortgage insurance on high loan-to-value loans.) The PCs can be kept as investments, sold for cash, or used as collateral for loans. PCs are popular investments for S&Ls, pension funds, and other institutional investors looking for high-yield investments. Individuals who can meet the $25,000 minimum also find PCs attractive. Freddie Mac also has a collateralized mortgage obligation program and plans to offer a trust for investments in mortgages. Both of these programs are designed to deal with the unpredictability of mortgage maturities caused by early repayment by dividing the cash flows from a mortgage pool into separate securities with separate maturities, which are then sold to investors.

As with Fannie Mae, Congress and HUD provide the oversight committee to Freddie Mac. New guidelines provided by HUD call for both Freddie Mac and Fannie Mae to purchase about 30% of their mortgages in inner-city areas and from lower-income home buyers.

Farmer Mac

The newest agency created by Congress to underwrite loan pools is the **Federal Agricultural Mortgage Corporation,** known as **Farmer Mac.** The Agricultural Credit Act of 1987 established Farmer Mac as a separate agency within the Farm Credit System to establish the secondary market needed for farm real estate loans. Farmer Mac started actual operations in 1989.

Originally, Farmer Mac functioned similarly to Ginnie Mae in that it certified loan poolers rather than purchase loans. Farmer Mac guaranteed timely repayment of principal and interest in the loan pool, but did not guarantee any individual loans within that pool.

In 1996, Congress passed the **Farm Credit System Reform Act** allowing Farmer Mac to act as a pooler for qualified loans. Farmer Mac is now permitted to purchase loans directly from originators and to issue its own 100% guaranteed securities backed by the loans. For the first time, Farmer Mac became a true secondary market.

Loan Qualification

To qualify for a pool, a loan must be collateralized by agricultural real estate located in the United States. The real estate can include a home, which can cost no more than $100,000, and must be located in a rural community with a population of 2,500 or less. The maximum loan is $2.5 million or the amount secured by no more than 1,000 acres, whichever is larger. The loan-to-value ratio must be less than 80%, and the borrower must be a United States citizen engaged in agriculture and must demonstrate a capability to repay the loan.

Private Conduits

The financial success of the three giants of the secondary mortgage market (FNMA, GNMA, and FHLMC) has brought private mortgage packagers into the marketplace. These are organizations such as MGIC Investment Corporation (a subsidiary of Mortgage Guaranty Investment Corporation); Residential Funding Corporation (a subsidiary of Norwest Mortgage Corp.); financial subsidiaries of such household-name companies as General Electric, Lockheed Aircraft, and Sears, Roebuck; and mortgage packaging subsidiaries of state realtor associations. These organizations both compete with the big three and specialize in markets not served by them. For example, Residential Funding Corp. will package mortgage loans as large as $500,000, well above the limits imposed by FNMA and FHLMC and on FHA and VA loans. All of these organizations will buy from loan originators who are not large enough to create their own pools.

Computerization

Before leaving the topic of the secondary market, it is important to note that, without electronic data transmission and computers, the programs just described would be severely handicapped. There are currently thousands of mortgage pools, each containing from $1 million to $500 million (and more) in mortgage loans. Each loan in a pool has its own monthly payment schedule, and each payment must be broken down into its principal and interest components and any property tax and insurance impounds. Computers do this work as well as issue receipts and late notices. The pool, in turn, will be owned by several dozen to a hundred or more investors, each with a different fractional interest in the pool. Once a month, incoming mortgage payments are tallied, a small fee is deducted for the operation of the pool, and the balance is allotted among the investors—all by computer. A computer also prints and mails checks to investors and provides them with an accounting of the pool's asset level.

AUTOMATED UNDERWRITING SYSTEMS

The computer age has introduced a whole new system in underwriting procedures as they apply to the relationship between the loan originator and the investor (secondary market). In the "old days," underwriting guidelines would be published and circulated to the primary lenders weekly. As interest rates began to fluctuate wildly in the 1970s, the sheet was updated and circulated more often. In some real estate offices, one person was given the job of calling lenders daily for quotes on loan availability and interest rates.

The entire process is being overhauled by a computerized mortgage loan underwriting system with the introduction of Freddie Mac's Loan Prospector program, which was released for marketing in early 1995. At this time, the program is limited to Freddie Mac's approved sellers and servicers. This process is very streamlined. The regular uniform residential loan application is submitted to the lender and the lender then verifies the applicant's employment, income, and assets. This information is fed into the computer and is promptly analyzed by the computer program. If the borrower is accepted and if the loan-to-value ratio is greater than 80%, the application is then forwarded to a private mortgage insurer. Those that are not accepted are considered as "refer" or "caution." Those classified as "refer" are sent to the underwriting department with at least four reasons stating why the loan is referred. The "caution" category indicates that there are serious issues preventing the loan's purchase. The real estate can be appraised and a loan completely processed in as little as two hours if the lender requests an "expedited" appraisal. A nonexpedited appraisal can take less than 72 hours. Freddie Mac reports that about 60% of all applicants can be accepted in four minutes. It is anticipated that by using this streamlined program, the cost of processing the loan is cut in half.

FNMA now has its own software programs, called Desktop Originator (used by a broker or practitioner to submit information to a lender) and Desktop Underwriter (used by a lender to submit the application directly to FNMA). As with the Freddie Mac program, responses can be confirmed in seconds.

AVAILABILITY AND PRICE OF MORTGAGE MONEY

Thus far we have been concerned with the money pipelines between lenders and borrowers. Ultimately, though, money must have a source. These sources are savings generated by individuals and businesses as a result of their spending less than they earn (**real savings**) and government-created money, called **fiat money** or "printing press money." This second source does not represent unconsumed labor and materials; instead it competes for available goods and services alongside the savings of individuals and businesses.

In the arena of money and capital, real estate borrowers must compete with the needs of government, business, and consumers. Governments, particularly the federal government, compete the hardest when they borrow to finance a deficit. Not to borrow would mean bankruptcy and the inability to pay government employees and provide government programs and services. Strong competition also comes from business and consumer credit sectors. In the face of such strong competition for loan funds, home buyers must either pay higher interest or be outbid.

One "solution" to this problem is for the federal government to create more money, thus making competition for funds easier and interest rates lower. Unfortunately, the net result is often too much money chasing too few goods, and prices are pulled upward by the demand caused by the newly created money. This is followed by rising interest rates as savers demand higher returns to compensate for losses in purchasing power. Many economists feel that the higher price levels and interest rates of the 1970s resulted from applying too much of this "solution" to the economy since 1965.

The alternative solution, from the standpoint of residential loans, is to increase real savings or decrease competing demands for available money. A number of plans and ideas have been put forth by civic, business, and political leaders. They include proposals to simplify income taxes and balance the federal budget, incentives to increase productive output, and incentives to save money in retirement accounts.

USURY

An old idea that has been tried, but is of dubious value for holding down interest rates, is legislation to impose interest rate ceilings. Known as **usury** laws and found in nearly all states, these laws were originally enacted to prohibit lenders from over-charging interest on loans to individuals. Most states raised usury limits in response to higher interest rates. Additionally, the U.S. Congress passed legislation in 1980 that exempts from state usury limits most first-lien home loans made by institutional lenders. Recent Texas legislation has all but eliminated usury issues in Texas for first lien home loans. Low interest rates and the availability of funds for loans has been so competitive that usury is not much of an issue anymore.

PRICE TO THE BORROWER

Ultimately, the rate of interest the borrower must pay to obtain a loan is dependent on the cost of money to the lender, reserves for default, loan servicing costs, and available investment alternatives. For example, go to a savings institution and see what they are paying depositors on various accounts. To this add 2% for the cost of maintaining cash in the tills, office space, personnel, advertising, free gifts for depositors, deposit insurance, loan servicing, loan reserves for defaults, and a $^1/_2$% profit margin. This gives you an idea of how much borrowers must be charged.

Life insurance companies, pension funds, and trust funds do not have to "pay" for their money as do thrift institutions. Nonetheless, they do want to earn the highest possible yields, with safety, on the money in their custody. Thus, if a real estate buyer wants to borrow in order to buy a home, the buyer must compete successfully with the other investment opportunities available on the open market. To determine the rate for yourself, look at the yields on newly issued corporate bonds as shown in the financial section of your daily newspaper. Add $^1/_2$ of 1% to this for the extra work in packaging and servicing mortgage loans and you will have the interest rate home borrowers must pay to attract lenders.

DUE-ON-SALE

From an investment risk standpoint, when a lender makes a loan with a fixed interest rate, the lender recognizes that during the life of the loan interest rates may rise or fall. When they rise, the lender remains locked into a lower rate. Most loans contain a **due-on-sale clause** (also called an **alienation clause** or a **call clause**). In the past, these were inserted by lenders so that if the borrower sold the property to someone considered uncreditworthy by the lender, the lender could call the loan balance due. When interest rates increase, though, lenders can use these clauses to increase the rate of interest on the loan when the property changes hands by threatening to accelerate the balance of the loan unless the new owner accepts a higher rate of interest.

PREPAYMENT

If loan rates drop it becomes worthwhile for a borrower to shop for a new loan and repay the existing one in full. To compensate, loan contracts sometimes call for a **prepayment penalty** in return for giving the borrower the right to repay the loan early. A typical prepayment penalty amounts to the equivalent of six months interest on the amount that is being paid early. However, the penalty varies from loan to loan and from state to state. Some loan contracts permit up to 20% of the unpaid balance to be paid in any one year without penalty. Other contracts make the penalty stiffest when the loan is young. In certain states, laws do not permit prepayment penalties on loans more than five years old. By federal law, prepayment penalties are not allowed on FHA and VA loans.

REVIEW QUESTIONS

Answers to these questions are found in the Answer Key section at the back of the book.

1. The place where a real estate borrower makes a loan application, receives a loan, and makes loan payments describes the
   A. primary mortgage market.
   B. secondary mortgage market.
   C. first loan market.
   D. second loan market.

2. Historically, the foremost single source of funds for residential mortgage loans in this country has been
   A. commercial banks.
   B. insurance companies.
   C. mortgage companies.
   D. savings and loan associations.

3. When savings are removed from thrift institutions in large amounts for investment in Treasury securities,
   A. the real estate market enjoys an increase in activity.
   B. disintermediation occurs.
   C. Both A and B.
   D. Neither A nor B.

4. Reasons for the decline in residential loans made by the S&Ls include all but the following:
   A. Deregulation of the lending industry.
   B. Proliferation of savings and loan organizations.
   C. New laws that allowed higher risk loans.
   D. Placing the Federal Savings and Loan Insurance Corporation under the Federal Depositors Insurance Corporation.

5. A real estate loan that calls for the lender to receive interest plus a percentage of the rental income from a property is
   A. designed to protect the lender from inflation.
   B. known as a participation loan.
   C. Both A and B.
   D. Neither A nor B.

6. Mortgage companies
   A. originate loans.
   B. service loans that they have sold on the secondary mortgage market.
   C. Both A and B.
   D. Neither A nor B.

7. The secondary mortgage market provides
   A. a means for investors to acquire real estate loans with origination and servicing facilities.
   B. a way for a lender to sell real estate loans.
   C. Both A and B.
   D. Neither A nor B.

8. All of the following are true of the Federal National Mortgage Association EXCEPT that it is
   A. a privately owned corporation.
   B. managed by the federal government.
   C. active in buying FHA and VA mortgage loans.
   D. known as Fannie Mae.

9. Participation certificates issued by Freddie Mac can be
   A. sold for cash.
   B. used as collateral for loans.
   C. Both A and B.
   D. Neither A nor B.

10. Collateralized mortgage obligations issued by the FHLMC provide an investor with investments of
   A. predictable maturity.
   B. guaranteed yields.
   C. Both A and B.
   D. Neither A nor B.

KEY TERMS

Adjustable rate mortgage (ARM): a mortgage on which the interest rate rises and falls with changes in prevailing interest rates

Asset integrated mortgage: a mortgage designed to create a savings from the down payment

Blanket mortgage: a mortgage secured by two or more properties

Construction loan: short-term loan for new construction or remodeling of an existing structure

Equity sharing: an arrangement whereby a party providing financing gets a portion of the ownership

Graduated payment mortgage: a mortgage with an interest rate and maturity that are fixed, but the monthly payment gradually rises, because the initial monthly payments are insufficient to fully amortize the loan

Negative amortization: accrual of interest on a loan balance so that, as loan payments are made, the loan balance rises

Option: a right, for a given period of time, to buy, sell, or lease property at specified price and terms

Package mortgage: a mortgage that secures personal property in addition to real property

RAM: reverse-annuity mortgage

Seller financing: a note accepted by a seller instead of cash

Wraparound mortgage: a mortgage that encompasses any existing mortgages and is subordinate to them

Types of Financing

IN THIS CHAPTER *An "alphabet soup" of mortgaging alternatives are now available to a borrower. With computerized loan origination, the expanded secondary market, and the availability of mortgage funds from nonregulated lending sources, a vast array of available mortgaging techniques and types of financing have been created. The documents (discussed in Chapter 9) and the sources of funds (discussed in Chapter 12) still remain the same, but the number of alternative types of financing continues to expand. Only the most fundamental concepts will be discussed in this chapter, including types of financing, including adjustable rate mortgages, other generally accepted types of loans often encountered by a broker in real estate lending, and the newest concepts of the affordable housing programs.*

ADJUSTABLE RATE MORTGAGES

As we have already seen, a major problem for savings institutions is that they are locked into long-term loans while being dependent on short-term savings deposits. As a result, savings institutions now prefer to make mortgage loans that allow the interest rate to rise and fall during the life of the loan. To make this arrangement more attractive to borrowers, these loans are offered at a lower rate of interest than a fixed-rate loan of similar maturity.

The first step toward mortgage loans with adjustable interest rates came in the late 1970s. The loan was called a **variable rate mortgage** and the interest rate could be adjusted up or down by the lender during the 30-year life of the loan to reflect the rise and fall in interest rates paid to savers by the lender.

Current Format

The Office of Thrift Supervision (OTS) authorizes institutions to make the type of adjustable mortgage loan you are most likely to encounter in today's loan marketplace. This loan format is called an **adjustable rate mortgage (ARM).** Other federal agencies followed, but used differing guidelines. The main ARM requirement is that the interest rate on these loans be tied to some publicly available index that is mutually acceptable to the lender and the borrower. As interest rates rise and fall in the open market, the interest rate the lender is entitled to receive from the borrower rises and falls (Figure 13.1). The purpose is to match more closely what the savings institution receives from borrowers to what it must pay savers to attract funds.

FIGURE **13.1**
Adjustable Rate
Mortgage.

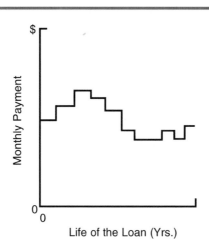

The benefit of an ARM to a borrower is that ARMs carry an initial interest rate that is lower than the rate on a fixed-rate mortgage of similar maturity. This often makes the difference between being able to qualify for a desired home and not qualifying for it. Other advantages to the borrower are that if market interest rates fall, the borrower's monthly payments fall. (This happens without incurring prepayment penalties or new loan origination costs, which could be the case with a fixed-rate loan.) Most ARMs allow assumption by a new buyer at the terms in the ARM, and most allow total prepayment without penalty, particularly if there has been an upward adjustment in the interest rate.

For the borrower, the disadvantage of an ARM is that if interest rates rise, the borrower is going to pay more. During periods of rising interest rates, property values and wages presumably will also rise. But the possibility of progressively larger monthly payments for the family home is still not attractive. As a result, various compromises have been worked out between lenders and borrowers whereby rates can rise on loans, but not by too much. In view of the fact that about one-half of all mortgage loans being originated by thrifts, banks, and mortgage companies are now adjustable, let's take a closer look at what a borrower gets with this loan format.

Interest Rate

The interest rate on an ARM is tied to an **index rate.** As the index rate moves up or down, so do the borrower's payments when adjustment time arrives. Lenders and borrowers alike want a rate that genuinely reflects current market conditions for interest rates and that can be easily verified. By far the most popular index is the interest rate on one-year U.S. Treasury securities. Next most popular is the cost of funds to thrift institutions as measured by the OTS. A few loans use six-month Treasury bills as an index rate.

Margin

To the index rate is added the margin. The **margin** is for the lender's cost of doing business, risk of loss on the loan, and profit. Currently this runs from 2% to 3%, depending on the characteristics of the loan. The margin is a useful comparison device because if two lenders are offering the same loan terms and the same index, but one loan has a margin of 2% and the other 3%, then the one with the 2% margin will have lower loan payments. As a rule, the margin stays constant during the life of the loan. At each adjustment point in the loan's life, the lender takes the index rate and adds the margin. The total becomes the interest the borrower will pay until the next adjustment occurs.

Adjustment Period

The amount of time that elapses between adjustments is called the **adjustment period.** By far the most common adjustment period is one year. Less commonly used are six-month, three-year, and five-year adjustment periods. When market rates are rising, the longer adjustment periods benefit the borrower. When market rates are falling, the shorter periods benefit the borrower because index decreases will show up sooner in their monthly payments.

Interest Rate Cap

Lenders are now required by federal law to disclose an **interest rate cap** or ceiling on how much the interest rate can increase for any one adjustment period during the life of the loan. If the cap is very low, say $1/2$% per year, the lender does not have much more flexibility than if holding a fixed-rate loan. Thus, there would be little reduction of initial rate on the loan compared with a fixed-rate loan. Compromises have prevailed, and the two most popular caps are 1% and 2% per year. In other words, the index rate may rise by 3%, but the cap limits the borrower's rate increase to 1% or 2%. Any unused difference may be added the next year, assuming the index rate has not fallen in the meantime. Since federal law now requires the ceiling, many lenders simply impose a very high ceiling (e.g., 18%) if they choose not to negotiate with the borrower.

Payment Cap

What if a loan's index rate rises so fast that the annual rate cap is reached each year and the lifetime cap is reached soon in the life of the loan? A borrower might be able to handle a modest increase in payments each year, but not big jumps in quick succession. To counteract this possibility, a **payment cap** sets a limit on how much the borrower's monthly payment can increase in any one year. A popular figure now in use is $7^1/2$%. In other words, no matter how high a payment is called for by the index rate, the borrower's monthly payment can rise, at the most, $7^1/2$% per year. For example, given an initial rate of 10% on a 30-year ARM for $100,000, the monthly payment of interest and principal is $878 (see Table 10.1). If the index rate calls for a 2% upward adjustment at the end of one year, the payment on the loan would be $1,029. This is an increase of $151 or 17.2%. A $7^1/2$% payment cap would limit the increase to 107.5% × $878 = $943.85.

Negative Amortization

Although the $7^1/2$% payment cap in the foregoing example protects the borrower against a monthly payment that rises too fast, it does not make the difference between what's called for ($1,029) and what's paid ($943.85) go away. The difference ($85.15) is added to the balance owed on the loan and earns interest just like the original amount borrowed. This is called **negative amortization:** instead of the loan balance dropping each month as loan payments are made, the balance owed rises. This can bring concern to the lender who can visualize the day the loan balance exceeds the value of the property. A popular arrangement is to set a limit of 125% of the original loan balance. At that point, either the lender accrues no more negative amortization or the loan is reamortized depending on the wording of the loan contract. *Reamortized* in this situation means the monthly payments will be adjusted upward by enough to stop the negative amortization.

Disclosures

In response to consumers' concern over adjustable rate mortgages, Regulation Z requires creditors to provide consumers with more extensive information about the variable rate feature of ARMs. The amendments apply only to closed-end credit transactions secured by the consumer's principal dwelling. Transactions secured by the consumer's principal dwelling with a term of one year or less are exempt from the new disclosure. To comply with the amendment, lenders must provide consumers with a historical example that shows how actual changes in index values would have affected payments on a $10,000 loan, as well as provide a statement of initial and maximum interest rates. Lenders must also provide prospective borrowers with an educational brochure about ARMs called " The Consumer Handbook on Adjustable Rate and Mortgages" or a suitable substitute. All the information must be given to the consumer at the time the loan application form is provided or before a nonrefundable fee is paid, whichever is earlier. The maximum interest rate must be stated as a specified amount or stated in a manner in which the consumer may easily ascertain the maximum interest rate at the time of entering the obligation.

Choosing Wisely

When a lender makes an ARM loan, the lender must explain to the borrower, in writing, the *worst-case scenario.* In other words, the lender must explain what will happen to the borrower's payments if the index rises the maximum amount each period up to the lifetime interest cap. If there is a payment cap, that and any possibility of negative amortization must also be explained. If the borrower is uneasy with these possibilities, then a fixed-rate loan should be considered. Most lenders offer fixed-rate loans as well as adjustable rate loans. VA loans are fixed-rate loans, but FHA now provides an adjustable rate loan program.

   "Teaser rate" adjustables have been offered from time to time by a few lenders and are best avoided. This type of loan is an ARM with an enticingly attractive, below-market initial rate. For example, the teaser rate may be offered at 2% below market. A borrower who cannot qualify at the market rate might be able to do so at the teaser rate. However, in a year the loan contract calls for a 2% jump followed by additional annual increases. This overwhelms the borrower who, unable to pay, allows foreclosure to take place.

GRADUATED PAYMENT MORTGAGE

The objective of a **graduated payment mortgage** is to help borrowers qualify for loans by basing repayment schedules on salary expectations. With this type of mortgage, the interest rate and maturity are fixed but the monthly payment gradually rises. For example, a 10%, $60,000, 30-year loan normally requires monthly payments of $527 for complete amortization. Under the graduated payment mortgage, payments could start out as low as $437 per month the first year, then gradually increase to $590 in the eleventh year and then remain at that level until the thirtieth year. Since the interest alone on this $60,000 loan is $500 per month, the amount owed on the loan actually increases during its early years. Only when the monthly payment exceeds the monthly interest does the balance owed on the loan decrease.

EQUITY SHARING

Giving the party that provides the financing a "piece of the action in the deal" is not an innovation. Insurance companies financing shopping centers and office buildings have long used the idea of requiring part of the rental income and/or part of the profits plus interest on the loan itself. In other words, in return for providing financing, the lender wants to share in some of the benefits normally reserved for the equity holder, called **equity sharing.** The equity holder would agree to this either to get a lower rate of interest or to get financing when financing was scarce or where the equity holder was not big enough to handle the deal alone. For example, on a $5 million project, the lender might agree to make a loan of $4 million at a very attractive rate if it can buy a half-interest in the equity for $500,000.

"RICH UNCLE" FINANCING

A second variation of equity sharing is often called **"rich uncle" financing.** The investor may be a parent helping a son or daughter buy a home or a son or daughter buying a parent's present home while giving the parent(s) the right to occupy it. A third variation is for an investor to provide most of the down payment for a home buyer, collect rent from the home buyer, pay the mortgage payments and property taxes, and claim depreciation. Each party has a right to a portion of any appreciation and the right to buy out the other. The FHLMC now recognizes the importance of equity sharing and will buy mortgage loans on shared-equity properties. The FHLMC requires that the owner-occupant contribute at least 5% of the equity, that the owner-occupant and the owner-investor sign the mortgage and note, that both be individuals, and that there be no agreement requiring sale or buy-out within seven years of the loan date. Equity sharing can provide attractive tax benefits; however, you must seek competent tax advice before involving yourself or someone else in such a plan.

PACKAGE MORTGAGE

Normally, we think of real estate mortgage loans as being secured solely by real estate. However, it is possible to include items classed as personal property in a real estate mortgage, thus creating a **package mortgage.** In residential loans (particularly in new construction or remodeling), such items as the refrigerator, clothes washer, and dryer can be pledged along with the house and land in a single mortgage. The purpose is to raise the value of the collateral in order to raise the amount a lender is willing to loan. For the borrower, it offers the opportunity of financing major appliances at the same rate of interest as the real estate itself. This rate is usually lower than if the borrower finances the appliances separately. Once an item of personal property is included in a package mortgage, selling it without the prior consent of the lender is a violation of the mortgage.

BLANKET MORTGAGE

A mortgage secured by two or more properties is called a **blanket mortgage.** Suppose you want to buy a house plus the vacant lot next door, financing the purchase with a single mortgage that covers both properties. The cost of preparing one mortgage instead of two is a savings. Also, by combining the house and the lot, the lot can be financed on better terms than if it were financed separately, as lenders more readily loan on a house and land than on land alone. Note, however, that if the vacant lot is later sold separately from the house before the mortgage loan is fully repaid, it will be necessary to have it released from the blanket mortgage. This is usually accomplished by including in the original mortgage agreement a partial release clause that specifies how much of the loan must be repaid before the lot can be released.

REVERSE MORTGAGE

With a regular mortgage, the lender makes a lump-sum payment to the borrower, who, in turn, repays it through monthly payments to the lender. With a **reverse mortgage,** also known as a **reverse-annuity mortgage** or **RAM,** the lender has two alternatives: (1) payment to the homeowner in a lump sum (sometimes referred to as a "line of credit" RAM) or (2) monthly payments to the homeowner as an annuity for the reverse term of the loan. The reverse mortgage can be particularly valuable for an elderly homeowner who does not want to sell, but whose retirement income is not quite enough for comfortable living. The homeowner receives a monthly check, has full use of the property, and is not required to repay until he or she sells or dies. If the home is sold, money from the sale is taken to repay the loan. If the borrower dies first, the property is sold through the estate and the loan repaid.

In 1997, Fannie Mae introduced another type of reverse annuity mortgage aimed at senior citizens, which is activated at the time the house is purchased. It allows senior citizens (who must be 62 years or older) to obtain a mortgage against the equity in a house if a substantial down payment is made. Repayment of the mortgage is deferred until the borrower no longer occupies the principal residence. If the loan balance exceeds the value of the property, the borrower, or the estate, will never owe more than the value of the property. For instance, if a homeowner sells an existing home for $100,000 and chooses to purchase a retirement home, also costing $100,000, the homeowner would immediately qualify for a $52,000 loan, with a $48,000 down payment. There would be no monthly payments, and the homeowner would have $52,000 in cash!

In addition, Texas passed a new constitutional amendment that allows a reverse mortgage on Texas homesteads. It is valid only under the following conditions: (1) That it is secured by a voluntary lien with the consent of each owner and each owner's spouse; (2) that it is made to a person who is or whose spouse is 55 years or older; (3) that it is made without recourse for personal liability; (4) that advances are provided to a borrower based on the equity in a borrower's homestead; (5) that it cannot permit the lender to reduce the amount or number of advances because of an adjustment in the interest rate if periodic advances are made; (6) that it requires no payment of principal or interest until the homestead is sold or the borrower ceases to occupy the homestead property for more than 180 consecutive days; (7) that documents provide that if the lender fails to make the loan advances as required by the loan documents and if the lender fails to cure the default as required in the loan documents, lender forfeits all principal and interest of the reverse mortgage; and (8) that the loan cannot be made unless the owner of the home attests in writing that the owner received counseling on the advisability and availability of reverse mortgages and other financial alternatives.

CONSTRUCTION LOAN

Under a **construction loan,** also called an **interim loan,** money is advanced as construction takes place. For example, a vacant lot owner arranges to borrow $60,000 to build a house. The lender does not advance all $60,000 at once because the value of the collateral is insufficient to warrant that amount until the house is finished. Instead, the lender will parcel out the loan as the building is being constructed, always holding a portion until the property is ready for occupancy or, in some cases, actually occupied. Some lenders specialize only in construction loans and do not want to wait 20 or 30 years to be repaid. In this case, the buyer will have to obtain a permanent long-term mortgage from another source for the purpose of repaying the construction loan. This is known as a *permanent commitment* or a *take-out loan,* since it takes the construction lender out of the financial picture when construction is completed and allows the lender to recycle its money into new construction projects.

BLENDED-RATE LOAN

Many real estate lenders still hold long-term loans that were made at interest rates below the current market. One way of raising the return on these loans is to offer borrowers who have them a **blended-rate loan.** Suppose you owe $50,000 on your home loan and the interest rate on it is 7%. Suppose further that the current rate on home loans is 12%. Your lender might offer to refinance your home for $70,000 at 9%, presuming the property will appraise high enough and you have the income to qualify. The $70,000 refinance offer would put $20,000 in your pocket (less loan fees), but would increase the interest you pay from 7% to 9% on the original $50,000. This makes the cost of the $20,000 14% per year. The arithmetic is as follows: You will now be paying 9% x $70,000 = $6,300 in interest. Before, you paid 7% x $50,000 = $3,500 in interest. The difference, $2,800, is what you pay to borrow the additional $20,000. This equates to $2,800 / $20,000 = 14% interest. This is the figure you should use in comparing other sources of financing (such as a second mortgage) or deciding whether or not you even want to borrow.

A blended-rate loan can be very attractive in a situation in which you want to sell your home and you do not want to help finance the buyer. Suppose your home is worth $87,500 and you have the aforementioned $50,000, 7% loan. A buyer would normally expect to make a down payment of $17,500 and pay 12% interest on a new $70,000 loan. But, with a blended loan, your lender could offer the buyer the needed $70,000 financing at 9%, a far more attractive rate and one that requires less income in order to qualify. Blended loans are available on FHA, VA, and conventional loans held by the FNMA. Other lenders also offer them on fixed-rate assumable loans they hold.

EQUITY MORTGAGE

An **equity mortgage** is a loan arrangement wherein the lender agrees to make a loan based on the amount of equity in a borrower's home.

It is typically a second mortgage that is used to tap the increase in equity resulting from rising home prices and first loan paydown. It's all done without having to refinance the first loan and uses the home as an asset against which the homeowner can borrow and repay as needed. Equity mortgages are very popular as a source of home improvement loans, money for college expenses, money to start a business, money for a major vacation, and money to buy more real estate.

Since the Internal Revenue Code of 1986 limited personal interest deductions to home mortgages, these loans have become one of the fastest growing areas of real estate lending. For the first time in 1998, Texas has created a mechanism that allows for home equity mortgages. At the time, Texas was the only state that would not allow home equity lending, and the Texas homestead protection (discussed in Chapter 3) was legendary. The new legislation enabling home equity lending is highly restrictive. The loan cannot exceed 80% of the fair market value of the home and must be nonrecourse (no personal liability). It cannot be foreclosed without a judicial hearing, and loan fees cannot exceed 3% of the loan amount. The loans cannot be an open-end account, nor can they be made in order to pay off another debt to the lender, and they cannot be cross-defaulted with other loans. Prepayment penalties are prohibited, and the loan cannot be accelerated if the value of the collateral decreases. In Texas, a consumer can only have one home equity loan at a time.

Before the home equity loan can be made, there must be a 12-day cooling off period and a three day right of rescission after the credit has been extended. The consumer protections built into the legislation make the loans highly technical from a legal standpoint, and if a lender fails to comply with all the equity loan requirements as set out by the statutes and the constitution, the lender must forfeit all principal and interest on the loan to the homeowner. This will unquestionably cause a lot of extended litigation in home equity mortgage foreclosures in Texas.

AFFORDABLE HOUSING LOAN

An **affordable housing loan** is an umbrella term that covers many slightly different loans that target first-time home buyers and low- to moderate-income borrowers. Although there are no fixed standards for measurement, the generally accepted definition of a *low-income borrower* is a person or family with an income of not more than 80% of the median income for the local area. *Moderate income* is 115% of the median income for the area. *Median* means an equal number of people of incomes above or below the number. Funding for the programs is obtained through a commitment from an investor to buy the loans. Freddie Mac and Fannie Mae cooperate with local community, labor union, or trade associations by committing to buy a large block of mortgage loans provided they meet the agreed-on standards. Affordable housing loans can be privately insured through a mortgage guaranty insurance company or GE Capital Mortgage Insurance Corporation.

In 1997, the Texas Legislature provided for the appointment of a **Texas Affordable Housing Task Force,** composed of eleven members, appointed by the Governor, and a Director, who serves as an ex-officio member. The task force must include people from various segments of the real estate industry. The purpose of the task force is to review and evaluate regulations and policies relating to housing to identify those regulations and policies that unnecessarily increase the cost of constructing or rehabilitating affordable housing, that create barriers to affordable housing opportunities for low-income Texans, or that otherwise eliminate the ability of affordable housing. The task force is required to make recommendations designed to increase the availability of affordable housing throughout the state based on this review and evaluation. The task force shall submit their report to the Governor, the presiding officer of each house of the legislature, and appropriate state agencies not later than December 31, 1998. The report is supposed to identify regulations and policies that unnecessarily increase the cost of housing and to develop recommendations to promote the availability of affordable housing.

Credit Criteria

Underwriting standards for affordable housing loans are modified to recognize different forms of credit responsibility. Many low- and moderate-income families do not have checking accounts. Recognizing the lack of payment records, most affordable housing programs accept timely payment of rent and utility bills as credit criteria. Initial cash down payments can be reduced by allowing borrowing or acceptance of grants from housing agencies or local communities, which sometimes offer cash assistance. Studies indicate that lower-income families pay a higher percentage of their income for housing than others, so an affordable housing program allows a higher ratio of income to be applied to housing (33% of gross income instead of 28% found in similar loans; you may recall that the FHA housing guideline is 29%).

Consumer Education

One of the requirements to qualify for an affordable housing loan is for the borrower to take a prepurchase home buyer education course. Many of these first-time home buyers are unaware of real estate brokers, title insurance, or appraisals. These subjects, plus the care and maintenance of a home, are included in the variety of courses now available through community colleges, banks, and mortgage companies. The four major supporting entities of these programs are Fannie Mae, Freddie Mac, MGIC, and GE Capital Mortgage Insurance Corporation. All of these entities provide video tapes and course outlines that are available for these educational purposes.

Licensees should be aware that these programs are most effective if presented to a group of applicants. If there is not a program in your area, one could be started. An agent may want to contact local lenders, as many are still not fully aware of the opportunities available, and some tend to overlook the lower income market for economic reasons. Participation in the program, however, greatly benefits their Community Reinvestment Act rating. Effectively marketing these programs can be very profitable and provide a great amount of personal satisfaction.

97% Conventional Loan

One of the most significant developments in mortgage lending has been the introduction of a 3%-down-payment conventional loan. FIRREA and the Community Reinvestment Act (discussed in Chapter 17) provided strong incentives for private lenders to engage in affordable housing loans to help lower middle-income homeowners. To encourage homeownership among lower- and middle-income people, General Electric Capital Mortgage Insurance Corporation experimented with affordable housing loans, which it calls "community home buyer's program" loans. Results show that the rates of default among their borrowers prove to be as good or better than those of its regular loan portfolio. GE introduced a 97% conventional loan in February of 1994. Fannie Mae agreed to purchase 97% loans as long as the applicant met Fannie Mae guidelines, which include an income limit not to exceed 100% of the local area median income. Another conduit has been established by the investment banker Goldman Sachs to purchase these loans for buyers with up to 115% of area median income.

ASSET INTEGRATED MORTGAGE

The **asset integrated mortgage (AIM)** is designed to create a savings from the down payment and is applicable primarily to borrowers expecting to make at least a 15% to 20% down payment. With this plan, the actual down payment would be about 5% while the rest of the cash is used to purchase a fixed annuity in the name of the borrower and held by the lender as additional collateral. This, in effect, makes a loan with a 95% loan-to-value ratio.

For instance, if a borrower purchased a $100,000 house and wants to make a $20,000 payment and finance $80,000 at 8 1/2% for 30 years, the monthly payment is $615.14. With an AIM, the borrower can make a down payment of $5,000 and deposit the $15,000 difference in a fixed annuity paying a market rate (e.g., 6.25% annually). This would increase the borrower's monthly payment to $730.47, but, over a period of time, the $15,000 fixed annuity accumulates at a compound interest which should offset the higher monthly payments. After seven years, the cost of a regular mortgage with 20% paid down would amount to $71,660, while the asset integrated mortgage would show a net cost of only $58,120. Consider the example in Table 13.1.

	Conventional Mortgage	Asset Integrated Mortgage
Cash down on house	$20,000	$5,000
Cash to annuity	-0-	$15,000
Loan amount	$80,000	$95,000
Monthly payments	$ 615	$ 730
Payments after 7 years	$51,660	$61,320
Initial cash down	$20,000	$20,000
Total cash outlay—7 years	$71,660	$81,320
In 7 years the value of fixed annuity assuming a 6.25% rate annually	-0-	$23,200
Net amount paid after 7 years	$71,660	$58,120
Net after 25 years	$130,723	$113,274
Net after 30 years	$241,408	$184,632

SELLER FINANCING

When a seller is willing to accept part of the property's purchase price in the form of the buyer's promissory note accompanied by a mortgage or deed of trust, it is called **seller financing.** This allows the buyer to substitute a promissory note for cash, and the seller is said to be "taking back paper." Seller financing is popular for land sales (where lenders rarely loan), on property where an existing mortgage is being assumed by the buyer, and on property where the seller prefers to receive the money spread out over a period of time with interest instead of lump-sum cash. For example, a retired couple sells a rental home they own. The home is worth $120,000, and they owe $20,000. If they need only $60,000 in cash, they might be more than happy to take $60,000 down, let the buyer assume the existing mortgage, and accept the remaining $40,000 in monthly payments at current interest rates. Alternatively, the buyer and seller can agree to structure the $40,000 as an adjustable, graduated, partially amortized, or interest-only loan.

If the seller receives the sales price spread out over two or more years, income taxes are calculated using the installment reporting method discussed in Chapter 22. Being able to spread out the taxes on a gain may be an incentive to use seller financing. The seller should be aware, however, that the "paper" may not be convertible to cash without a long wait or without having to sell it at a substantial discount to an investor (although this can be remedied by a "balloon" provision). Additionally, the seller is responsible for servicing the loan and is subject to losses due to default and foreclosure.

Note that some real estate agents and lenders refer to a loan that is carried back by a seller as a **purchase money** loan. Others define a purchase money loan as any loan, carryback or institutional, that is used to finance the purchase of real property.

WRAPAROUND MORTGAGE

An alternative method of financing a real estate sale such as the one just reviewed is to use a **wraparound mortgage** or **wraparound deed of trust.** A *wraparound* encompasses existing mortgages and is subordinate (junior) to them. The existing mortgages stay on the property and the new mortgage wraps around them. Note Figure 13.2.

To illustrate, presume the existing $20,000 loan in the previous example carries an interest rate of 7% and that there are 10 years remaining on the loan. Presume further that current interest rates are 12%, and the current seller chooses to sell for $100,000.

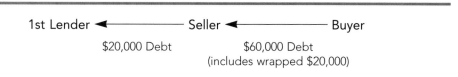

FIGURE 13.2
The wraparound mortgage.

This is done by taking the buyer's $40,000 down payment and then creating a new junior mortgage (for $60,000) that includes not only the $20,000 owed on the existing first mortgage but also the $40,000 the buyer owes the seller. The seller continues to remain liable for payment of the first mortgage. If the interest rate on the wraparound is set at 10%, the buyer saves by not having to pay 12% as he would on an entirely new loan. The advantage to the seller is that she is earning 10%, not only on her $40,000 equity, but also on the $20,000 loan for which she is paying 7% interest. This gives the seller an actual yield of $11\frac{1}{2}\%$ on her $40,000. (The calculation is as follows. The seller receives 10% on $60,000, which amounts to $6,000. She pays 7% on $20,000, which is $1,400. The difference, $4,600, is divided by $40,000 to get the seller's actual yield of $11\frac{1}{2}\%$.) There is an additional point of concern. If the monthly payment on the underlying $20,000 debt includes taxes and insurance (PITI payment), the wraparound mortgage payment amount should also include taxes and insurance so that the monthly payment is sufficient to meet *all* of the underlying debt.

Wraparounds are not limited to seller financing. If the seller in the foregoing example did not want to finance the sale, a third-party lender could provide the needed $40,000 and take a wraparound mortgage. The wraparound concept does not work when the underlying mortgage debt to be "wrapped" contains a due-on-sale clause. One other word of caution. If the seller defaults (and doesn't tell the buyer), the buyer may have an unwelcome surprise.

SUBORDINATION

Another financing technique is **subordination.** For example, a person owns a $200,000 vacant lot suitable for building, and a builder wants to build an $800,000 building on the lot. The builder has only $100,000 cash and the largest construction loan available is $800,000. If the builder can convince the lot owner to take $100,000 in cash and $100,000 later, the buyer would have the $1 million total. However, the lender making the $800,000 loan will want to be the first mortgagee to protect its position in the event of foreclosure. The lot owner must be willing to take a subordinate position, in this case a second mortgage. If the project is successful, the lot owner will receive $100,000, plus interest, either in cash after the building is built and sold, or as monthly payments. If the project goes into foreclosure, the lot owner can be paid only if the $800,000 first mortgage claim is satisfied in full from the sale proceeds. As you can surmise here, the lot owner must be very careful that the money loaned by the lender actually goes into construction and that whatever is built is worth at least $800,000 in addition to the land.

CONTRACT FOR DEED

A **contract for deed,** also called an **installment contract** or **land contract,** enables the seller to finance a buyer by permitting him to make a down payment followed by monthly payments. However, title remains in the name of the seller. In addition to its wide use in financing land sales, it has also been a very effective financing tool in several states as a means of selling homes. For example, a homeowner owes $25,000 on his home and wants to sell it for $85,000. A buyer is found but does not have the $60,000 down payment necessary to assume the existing loan. The buyer does have $8,000, but for one reason or another cannot or chooses not to borrow from an institutional lender. If the seller is agreeable, the buyer can pay the seller $8,000 and enter into an installment contract with the seller for the remaining $77,000. The contract calls for monthly payments by the buyer to the seller that are large enough to allow the seller to meet the payments on the $25,000 loan plus repay the $52,000 owed to the seller, with interest. Unless property taxes and insurance are billed to the buyer, the seller will also collect for these and pay them. When the final payment is made to the seller (or the property refinanced through an institutional lender), title is conveyed to the buyer. Meanwhile, the seller continues to hold title and is responsible for paying the mortgage. In addition to wrapping around a mortgage, an installment contract can also be used to wrap around another installment contract, provided it does not contain an enforceable due-on-sale clause. (Please see Chapter 8 for more about the contractual side of installment contracts.)

OPTION

When viewed as a financing tool, an **option** provides a method by which the need to finance the full price of a property immediately can be postponed. For example, a developer is offered 100 acres of land for a house subdivision but is not sure that the market will absorb that many houses. The solution is to buy 25 acres outright and take three 25-acre options at present prices on the remainder. If the houses on the first 25 acres sell promptly, the builder can exercise the options to buy the remaining land. If sales are not good, the builder can let the remaining options expire and avoid being stuck with unwanted acreage.

A popular variation on the option idea is the **lease with option to buy** combination. Under it, an owner leases to a tenant who, in addition to paying rent and using the property, also obtains the right to purchase it at a present price for a fixed period of time. Homes are often sold this way, particularly when the resale market is sluggish. (Please see Chapter 8 for more about a lease with option to buy.)

Options can provide speculative opportunities to persons with limited amounts of capital. If prices do not rise, the optionee loses only the cost of the option; if prices do rise, the optionee exercises the option and realizes a profit.

OVERLY CREATIVE FINANCING?

One seller-financing arrangement that deserves special attention because of its traps for the unwary is the **overencumbered property.** Institutional lenders are closely regulated regarding the amount of money they can loan against the appraised value of the property. Individuals are not regulated. The following illustrates the potential problem. Suppose a seller owns a house that is realistically worth $100,000 and the mortgage balance is $10,000. A buyer offers to purchase the property, with the condition that she be allowed to obtain an $80,000 loan on the property from a lender. The $80,000 is used to pay off the existing $10,000 loan and to pay the broker's commission, loan fees, and closing costs. The remaining $62,000 is split $30,000 to the seller and $32,000 to the buyer. The buyer also gives the seller a note, secured by a second mortgage against the property, for $80,000. The seller may feel good about getting $30,000 in cash and an $80,000 mortgage, for this is more than the property is worth, or so it seems.

But the $80,000 second mortgage stands junior to the $80,000 first mortgage. That's $160,000 of debt against a $100,000 property. The buyer might be trying to resell the property for $160,000 or more, but the chances of this are slim. More likely the buyer will wind up walking away from the property. This leaves the seller the choice of taking over the payments on the first mortgage or losing the property completely to the holder of the first.

Although such a scheme sounds crazy when viewed from a distance, the reason it can be performed is that the seller wants more for the property than it's worth. Someone then offers a deal showing that price, and the seller looks the other way from the possible consequences. Real estate practitioners who participate in such transactions are likely to find their licenses suspended. State licensing authorities take the position that a real estate practitioner is a professional who should know enough not to take part in a deal that leaves the seller holding a junior lien on an overencumbered property. This, too, seems logical when viewed from a distance. But when sales are slow and commissions thin, it is sometimes easy to put commission income ahead of fiduciary responsibility. If in doubt about the propriety of a transaction, the Golden Rule of doing unto others as you would have them do unto you still applies. (Or, as some restate it: "What goes around, comes around.")

INVESTING IN MORTGAGES

Individuals can invest in mortgages in two ways. One is to invest in mortgage loan pools through certificates guaranteed by Ginnie Mae and Freddie Mac and available from stockbrokers. These yield about $1/2$ of 1% below what FHA and VA borrowers are paying. In 1997, for example, this was approximately 7%, and the certificates are readily convertible to cash at current market prices on the open market if the investor does not want to hold them through maturity.

Individuals can also buy junior mortgages at yields above Ginnie Mae and Freddie Mac certificates. These junior mortgages are seconds, thirds, and fourths offered by mortgage brokers. They yield more because they are riskier as to repayment and much more difficult to convert to cash before maturity. "There is," as the wise old adage says, "no such thing as a free lunch." Thus, it is important to recognize that when an investment of any kind promises above-market returns, there is some kind of added risk attached. With junior mortgages, it is important to realize that when a borrower offers to pay a premium above the best loan rates available from banks and thrift institutions, it is because the borrower and/or the property does not qualify for the best rates.

Before buying a mortgage as an investment, one should have the title to the property searched. This is the only way to know for certain what priority the mortgage will have in the event of foreclosure. There have been cases where investors have purchased what they were told to be first and second mortgages only to find in foreclosure that they were actually holding third and fourth mortgages and the amount of debt exceeded the value of the property.

And how does one find the value of a property? By having it appraised by a professional appraiser who is independent of the party making or selling the mortgage investment. This value is compared to the existing and proposed debt against the property. The investor should also run a credit check on the borrower. The investor's final protection is, however, in making certain that the market value of the property is well in excess of the loans against it and that the property is well constructed, well located, and functional.

RENTAL

Even though tenants do not acquire fee ownership, **rentals** and **leases** are means of financing real estate. Whether the tenant is a bachelor receiving the use of a $30,000 apartment for which he pays $350 rent per month or a large corporation leasing a warehouse for 20 years, leasing is an ideal method of financing when the tenant does not want to buy, cannot raise the funds to buy, or prefers to invest available funds elsewhere.

Similarly, **farming leases** provide for the use of land without the need to purchase it. Some farm leases call for fixed rental payment. Other leases require the farmer to pay the landowner a share of the value of the crop that is actually produced—say 25%—and the landowner shares with the farmer the risks of weather, crop output, and prices.

Under a **sale and leaseback** arrangement, an owner-occupant sells the property and then remains as a tenant. Thus, the buyer acquires an investment and the seller obtains capital for other purposes while retaining the use of the property. A variation is for the tenant to construct a building, sell it to a prearranged buyer, and immediately lease it back.

LAND LEASES

Although **leased land** arrangements are common throughout the United States for both commercial and industrial users and for farmers, anything other than fee owner-ship of residential land is unthinkable in many areas. Yet in some parts of the United States (e.g., Baltimore, Maryland; Orange County, California; throughout Hawaii; and parts of Florida) homes built on leased land are commonplace. Typically, these leases are at least 55 years in length and, barring an agreement to the contrary, the improvements to the land become the property of the fee owner at the end of the lease. Rents may be fixed in advance for the life of the lease, renegotiated at present points during the life of the lease, or a combination of both.

To hedge against inflation, when fixed rents are used in a long-term lease, it is common practice to use **step-up rentals.** For example, under a 55-year house-lot lease, the rent may be set at $400 per year for the first 15 years, $600 per year for the next 10 years, $800 for the next 10 years, and so forth. An alternative is to renegotiate the rent at various points during the life of a lease so that the effects of land value changes are more closely equalized between the lessor and the lessee. For example, a 60-year lease may contain renegotiation points at the fifteenth, thirtieth, and forty-fifth years. At those points, the property would be reappraised and the lease rent adjusted to reflect any changes in the value of the property. Property taxes and any increases in property taxes are paid by the lessee.

FINANCING OVERVIEW

If people always paid cash for real estate, the last several chapters would not have been necessary. But 95% of the time they don't; thus means have been devised to finance their purchases. This has been true since the beginning of recorded history and will continue into the future. The financing methods that evolve will depend on the problems to be solved. For example, long-term fixed-rate amortized loans were the solution to foreclosures in the 1930s, and they worked well as long as interest rates did not fluctuate greatly. Graduated payment loans were devised when housing prices rose faster than buyer's incomes. Adjustable rate loans were developed so that lenders could more closely align the interest they receive from borrowers with the interest they pay their savers. Extensive use of loan assumptions, wraparounds, and seller financing became necessary in the early 1980s because borrowers could not qualify for 16% and 18% loans and sellers were unwilling to drop prices.

With regard to the future, if mortgage money is expensive or in short supply, seller financing will play a large role. With the experience of rapidly fluctuating interest rates fresh in people's minds, loans with adjustable rates will continue to be widely offered. Fixed-rate loans will either have short maturities or carry a premium to compensate the lender for being locked into a fixed rate for a long period. When interest rates are low, borrowers with adjustable loans will benefit from lower monthly payments. If rates stay down long enough, fixed-rate loans will become more popular again.

Answers to these questions are found in the Answer Key section at the back of the book.

1. In order to make adjustable rate mortgage loans more attractive to borrowers, lenders offer
   A. lower initial interest rates.
   B. gifts such as appliances, trips, etc.
   C. lower insurance rates.
   D. lower down payments.

2. Prior to the introduction of adjustable rate mortgages, the FHLBB approved the use of
   A. variable rate mortgages.
   B. renegotiable rate mortgages.
   C. Both A and B.
   D. Neither A nor B.

3. When considering an ARM loan, the lender must explain to the borrower, in writing, the
   A. worst-case scenario.
   B. best-case scenario.
   C. average case scenario.
   D. respective credit report.

4. Equity sharing is based on the concept of someone who has assets sharing those assets in exchange for
   A. a share of the ownership.
   B. tax benefits.
   C. Both A and B.
   D. Neither A nor B.

5. When an existing loan at a low interest rate is refinanced by a new loan at an interest rate between the current market rate and the rate on the old loan, the result is a
   A. combined loan.
   B. blended loan.
   C. wraparound loan.
   D. merged loan.

6. An individual who is contemplating the purchase of a mortgage as an investment should have
   A. the property appraised.
   B. a credit check made on the borrower.
   C. the title searched.
   D. All of the above.

7. Under the terms of a shared appreciation mortgage
   A. the loan is made at a below-market interest rate.
   B. the lender received a portion of the property's appreciation.
   C. Both A and B.
   D. Neither A nor B.

8. ARM loans with teaser rates are avoided by
   A. mortgage insurers.
   B. secondary market buyers.
   C. Both A and B.
   D. Neither A nor B.

9. All of the following statements are true of seller financing EXCEPT:
   A. The seller of the property is the mortgagee under the mortgage.
   B. Mortgage terms and interest rates are negotiable between the seller and buyer.
   C. If repayment is spread over two or more years, income taxes are calculated on the installment reporting method.
   D. Carryback mortgages are usually salable to investors without discount.

10. Which of the following is NOT true of wraparound mortgages?
    A. They are junior mortgages, subordinate to an existing first mortgage.
    B. The interest rate on the buyer's note is usually the same as the market rate.
    C. They are useless when the first mortgage carries a due-on-sale clause.
    D. The yield to the seller (mortgagee) is usually greater than the interest rate specified on the note.

11. A sale may be made and financed under a contract for deed
    A. only when the seller owns the property free and clear.
    B. by combining wraparound financing with an existing mortgage loan on the property, provided the existing mortgage does not contain a due-on-sale clause.
    C. Both A and B.
    D. Neither A nor B.

CHAPTER 14

Adjusted sales price: the sales price of a property less commissions, fix-up, and closing costs

Ad valorem taxes: taxes charged according to the value of a property

Assessed value: a value placed on a property for the purpose of taxation

Assessment appeal board: local governmental body that hears and rules on property owner complaints of overassessment

Basis: the price paid for property; used in calculating income taxes

Documentary tax: a fee or tax on deeds and other documents payable at the time of recordation

Gain: the profit on the sale of an appreciated asset

Installment sale: sale of real estate in which the proceeds of the sale are deferred beyond the year of sale

Mill rate: property tax rate that is expressed in tenths of a cent per dollar of assessed valuation

Tax lien: a charge or hold by the government against property to insure the payment of taxes

Taxes and Assessments

IN THIS CHAPTER *In this chapter we are primarily concerned with ad valorem taxes and various types of property assessments. Determining how much tax the property owner must pay involves these basic steps: appropriation, assessment, and tax rate calculation. The chapter also covers unpaid property taxes, assessment appeal, property tax exemptions and variations, tax limitation measures, and special assessments. In the latter half of the chapter, income taxes on the sale of a residence, including the lifetime exclusion, taxable gain, and installment sales, are covered. The chapter concludes with coverage of property tax and interest deductions and the agent's liability for tax advice.*

PROPERTY TAXES

The largest single source of income in America for local government programs and services is the property tax. Schools (from kindergarten through two-year colleges), fire and police departments, local welfare programs, public libraries, street maintenance, parks, and public hospital facilities are mainly supported by property taxes. Some state governments also obtain a portion of their revenues from this source.

Property taxes are **ad valorem taxes.** This means that they are levied according to the value of one's property; the more valuable the property, the higher the tax, and vice versa. The underlying theory of ad valorem taxation is that those owning the more valuable properties are wealthier and hence able to pay more taxes.

Determining how much tax a property owner will be charged involves three basic steps: (1) local government budget determination and appropriation, (2) appraisal of all taxable property within the taxation district, and (3) allocation among individual property owners of the revenue that needs to be collected.

Appropriation

Each taxing body with the authority to tax prepares its budget for the coming year. Taxing bodies include the State of Texas, counties, cities, towns and villages, school districts, utility districts, water districts, and, in some counties, levee districts, sanitation districts, and other improvement districts. Each budget, along with a list of sources from which the money will be derived, is enacted into law. This is the **appropriation process.** Then estimated sales taxes, state and federal revenue sharing, business licenses, and city income taxes are subtracted from the budget. The balance must come from property taxes.

Assessment

Next, the valuation of the taxable property within each taxing body's district must be determined. To assure uniformity in appraisals, the Texas Property Tax Code provides for an **appraisal district** in each county. All taxing districts are required to use the appraisal district's value in determining the taxes to be paid. The county appraisal district appraises each taxable parcel of land and the improvements thereon. Since 1989, the market value of the land and the total market value of the improvements must be listed separately. The appraised value is the estimated fair market cash value of the property. This is the cash price one would expect a buyer and a seller to agree upon in a normal open market transaction.

The appraised value is converted into an assessed value upon which taxes are based. In Texas, the **assessed value** is set equal to the fair market value; in some other states, it is a percentage of the appraised value. Mathematically, the percentage selected makes no difference as long as each property is treated equally. Consider two houses with appraised values of $60,000 and $120,000, respectively. Whether the assessed values are set equal to appraised values or at a percentage of appraised values, the second house will still bear twice the property tax burden of the first.

Tax Rate Calculation

Certain types of property are exempt from taxation. The assessed values of the remaining taxable properties are then added together in order to calculate the **tax rate** that must be determined by the appropriate elected governing body. To explain this process, suppose that a building lies within the taxation districts of the Westside School District, the city of Rostin, and the county of Pearl River. The school district's budget for the coming year requires $800,000 from property taxes, and the assessed value of taxable property within the district is $20,000,000. By dividing $800,000 by $20,000,000, we see that the school district must collect a tax of 4 cents for every dollar of assessed valuation. This levy can be expressed three ways: (1) as a mill rate, (2) as dollars per hundred, or (3) as dollars per thousand. All three rating methods are found in the United States. The State of Texas uses dollars per hundred.

This tax rate is usually expressed as **dollars per hundred** of assessed value. For instance, a rate would be $4 per hundred of assessed valuation. As **dollars per thousand,** it would be $40 per thousand.

A city calculates its tax rate by dividing its property tax requirements by the assessed value of the property within its boundaries. Suppose that its needs are $300,000 and the city limits enclose property totaling $10,000,000 in assessed valuation. (In this example, the city covers a smaller geographical area than the school district.) Thus the city must collect 3 cents for each dollar of assessed valuation in order to balance its budget.

The county government's budget requires $2,000,000 from property taxes and the county contains $200,000,000 in assessed valuation. This makes the county tax rate 1 cent per dollar of assessed valuation. Table 14.1 shows the school district, city, and county tax rates expressed as dollars per hundred and dollars per thousand.

The final step is to apply the tax rate to each property. Applying the rate on a dollars per hundred basis, divide the $20,000 assessed valuation by $100 and multiply by $8. The result is $1,600. To ensure collection, a lien for this amount is placed by the taxing authority against the property. It is removed when the tax is paid. Property tax liens are superior to other types of liens. Also, a mortgage foreclosure does not clear property tax liens; they still must be paid.

To avoid duplicate tax bill mailings, it is a common practice for all taxing bodies in a given county to have the county collect for them at the same time that the county collects on its own behalf.

	Dollars per Hundred	Dollars per Thousand
School district	$4.00	$40.00
City	3.00	30.00
County	1.00	10.00
Total	$8.00	$80.00

TABLE 14.1
Expressing property tax rates.

The property tax year in Texas for state and county taxes is the calendar year. County and state taxes are billed once a year, are payable on October 1, and become delinquent on February 1 of the following year. Other taxing jurisdictions vary. A small discount is allowed for early payment of state and county taxes. Penalties are charged for late payment in all taxing jurisdictions.

UNPAID PROPERTY TAXES

All **tax liens** in Texas are, by law, superior to any other liens in existence on real estate. When an owner fails to pay **property taxes,** the property is sold at a public tax auction; this extinguishes all other liens. However, unlike most liens in Texas, if foreclosure is due to unpaid taxes, the tax statutes provide a redemption period for the taxpayer to pay the taxes and have the property returned to him.

If the property is used as the residence homestead of the owner, or the land was designated for agricultural use when the suit to collect the taxes was filed, Texas statute provides that the period of redemption for suits brought under the authority of the tax foreclosure statute for the taxpayer's residence homestead or land designated for agricultural use shall be within *two years* from the date of the filing for record of the purchaser's deed, on the following basis:

1. Within the first year of the redemption period, upon the payment of the amount of the bid for the property by the purchaser at such sale, including a One Dollar ($1) tax deed recording fee and all taxes, penalties, interest and costs thereafter paid thereon, plus 25% of the aggregate total.
2. Within the last year of the redemption period, upon the payment of the amount bid for the property at such sale, including a One Dollar ($1) tax deed recording fee and all taxes, penalties, interest and costs thereafter paid thereon, plus 50% of the aggregate total; and no further or additional amount than herein specified shall be required to be paid to effect any such redemption.

All other property must be redeemed on the same basis, but within *six months,* rather than two years.

If the property is not the taxpayer's residence homestead or designated for agricultural use, the redemption period is six months, and the owner must pay a 25% penalty to redeem. Texas does not allow the former owner to reserve possession or receive the benefits of the property during the redemption period. There are other provisions for redemption if the land is sold under a decree and judgment of a court. Title does not pass to the purchaser until the deed is confirmed after the redemption period.

The right of government to foreclose on a property owner for nonpayment of property taxes is well established by law. However, if the sale procedure is not properly followed, the purchaser may later find the property's title successfully challenged in court. Thus, it behooves the purchaser to obtain a title search and title insurance and, if necessary, to conduct a quiet title suit or file a suit to foreclose the rights of anyone previously having a right to the property. Tax liens are barred from enforcement if they are over 20 years old (the statute of limitations).

ASSESSMENT APPEAL

By law, assessment procedures must be uniformly applied to all properties within a taxing jurisdiction. To this end, the values of all lands and buildings, as determined by the tax assessors, are made available for public inspection. These are the **assessment rolls.** They permit property owners to compare the assessed valuation on their property with assessed valuations on similar properties. If an owner feels overassessed, an appeal can be filed before the **Appraisal Review Board.** Texas also permits appeal to a court of law, if the property owner remains dissatisfied with the assessment. Note that the appeal process deals only with the method of assessment and taxation, not with the tax rate or the amount of tax.

PROPERTY TAX EXEMPTIONS

More than half the land in many cities and counties is exempt from real property taxation. This is because governments and their agencies do not tax themselves or each other. Thus, government-owned offices of all types, public roads and parks, schools, military bases, and government-owned utilities are exempt from property taxes. Also exempted are properties owned by religious and charitable organizations (so long as they are used for religious or charitable purposes), hospitals, and cemeteries. In rural areas of Texas, large tracts of land are owned by federal and state governments, and these too are exempt from taxation. Texas also exempts from taxation poorhouses, public libraries, art galleries, property of Boy and Girl Scouts, prison farms, veterans' organizations, fraternal organizations, public charities, certain nonprofit organizations, and volunteer fire departments. There are certain additional property tax exemptions for veterans of the armed forces.

Property tax exemptions are also used to attract industries and to appease voters. In the first instance, a local government agency may buy industrial land and buildings and lease them to industries at a price lower than would be possible if they were privately owned and hence taxed. Alternatively, outright property tax reductions may be granted for a certain length of time to newly established or relocating firms. The rationale is that the cost to the public is outweighed by the economic boost that the new industry brings to the community. In the second instance, a number of states, including Texas, grant assessment reductions to resident homeowners for homestead property. This increases the tax burden for owners of rented houses and owners of households that rent and for commercial properties.

PROPERTY TAX VARIATIONS

Property taxes on similarly priced homes within a city or county can vary widely when prices change faster than the assessor's office can reappraise. As a result, a home worth $90,000 in one neighborhood may receive a tax bill of $1,800 per year, while a $90,000 home in another neighborhood will be billed $2,400. When the appraisal district conducts a reappraisal, taxes in the first neighborhood will suddenly rise 33%, undoubtedly provoking complaints from property owners who were unaware that they were previously underassessed. In times of slow-changing real estate prices, reappraisals were made only once every 10 years. Today, appraisal districts are developing computerized assessment systems that can adjust assessments to the market annually.

As an aid to keeping current on property value changes, some states are enacting laws that require a real estate buyer to advise the assessor's office of the price and terms of his purchase within 90 days after taking title. This information, coupled with building permit records and on-site visits by assessor's office employees, provides the data necessary to regularly update assessments. Such laws have not yet been enacted in Texas.

The amount of property taxes a property owner may expect to pay varies quite widely across the United States. On a home worth $90,000, for example, property taxes range from less than $900 per year to more than $3,600 per year. Why do differences exist and why are they so great? The answers fall into four basic categories: level of services offered, other sources of revenue, type of property, and government efficiency. Generally, cities with low property taxes offer fewer services to their residents. This may be by choice, such as smaller welfare payments, lower school expenditures per student, no subsidized public transportation, fewer parks and libraries, or because the city does not include the cost of some services in the property tax. For example, sewer fees may be added to the water bill and trash may be hauled by private firms. Lower rates can also be due to location. Wage rates are lower in some regions of the country, and a city not subject to ice and snow will have lower street maintenance expenses. Finally, a city may have other sources of revenue, such as oil royalties from wells on city property.

Supplemental Funding

Property tax levels are also influenced by the ability of local tax districts to obtain federal revenue sharing funds and money from state revenues (especially for schools) and to share in collections from sales taxes, license fees, liquor and tobacco taxes, and fines.

The amount and type of taxable property in a community greatly affects local tax rates. Taxable property must bear the burden avoided by tax-exempt property whereas privately owned vacant land, stores, factories, and high-priced homes generally produce more taxes than they consume in local government services thereby helping to keep rates lower. Finally, one must look at the efficiency of the city under review. Has it managed its affairs in prior years so that the current budget is not burdened with large interest payments on debts caused by deficits in previous years? Is the city or county itself laid out in a compact and efficient manner, or does its sheer size make administration expensive? How many employees are required to perform a given service?

TAX LIMITATION MEASURES

Texas restricts increases in property taxes by local taxing units. The statute basically provides that the governing body may not adopt a tax rate that exceeds the rate for the previous year by more than 3 percent until the governing body has (1) given public notice of its intention to adopt a higher rate and (2) held a public hearing on the proposed increase. The hearing must be on a weekday that is not a public holiday and must begin after 5:00 p.m. and before 9:00 p.m. There are also provisions for notice to the property owners if the property value has been increased over the preceding tax year. The governing body of the taxing unit may decrease the official tax rate for the current year at any time.

SPECIAL ASSESSMENTS

Often the need arises to make local municipal improvements that will benefit property owners within a limited area, such as the paving of a street, the installation of street lights, curbs, storm drains, and sanitary sewer lines, or the construction of irrigation and drainage ditches. Such improvements can be provided through special assessments on property.

The theory underlying special assessments is that the improvements must benefit the land against which the cost will be charged, and the value of the benefits must exceed the cost. The area receiving the benefit of an improvement is the **improvement district** or **assessment district,** and the property within that district bears the cost of the improvement. This is different from a **public improvement.** A public improvement, such as reconstruction of the city's sewage plant, benefits the public at large and is financed through the general (ad valorem) property tax. A local improvement, such as extending a sewer line into a street of homes presently using septic tanks or cesspools, does not benefit the public at large and should properly be charged only to those who directly benefit. Similarly, when streets are widened, owners of homes lining a 20-foot-wide street in a strictly residential neighborhood would be expected to bear the cost of widening it to 30 or 40 feet and to donate the needed land from their front yards. But a street widening from two lanes to four to accommodate traffic not generated by the homes on the street is a different situation, as the widening benefits the public at large. In this case the street widening is funded from public monies and the homeowners are compensated for any land taken from them.

Forming an Improvement District

An improvement district can be formed by the action of a group of concerned citizens who want and are willing to pay for an improvement. Property owners desiring the improvement take their proposal to the state legislature, city council, or other similar public body in charge of levying assessments. A public notice showing the proposed improvements, the extent of the improvement district, and the anticipated costs is prepared by the board. This notice is mailed to landowners in the proposed improvement district, posted conspicuously in the district, and published in a local newspaper. The notice also contains the date and place of public hearings on the matter at which property owners within the proposed district are invited to voice their comments and objections.

Texas Homestead Exemption

Special assessments pose a particular problem in Texas because of the constitutional nature of the homestead laws. Therefore, assessments for water districts, street improvements, or any special assessments district may not necessarily operate as a lien on a homestead to force a sale of the home to satisfy the amounts due. In an effort to make these liens more enforceable, lenders often put requirements for maintenance fees, homeowners' association dues, and special district assessments in the homeowner's mortgage. Defaulting in the payment of such special assessments might then be considered to be a default in the payment of the purchase money mortgage. This theory has been successfully enforced in Texas.

Confirmation

If the hearings result in a decision to proceed, then under the authority granted by Texas law regarding special improvements, a local government ordinance is passed that describes the project and its costs and the improvement district boundaries. An assessment roll is also prepared that shows the cost to each parcel in the district. Hearings are held regarding the assessment roll. When everything is in order, the roll is **confirmed** (approved). Then the contract to construct the improvements is awarded and work is started.

The proposal to create an improvement district can also come from a city council, board of trustees, or board of supervisors. Whenever this happens, notices are distributed and hearings held to hear objections from affected parties. Objections are ruled upon by a court of law and if found to have merit, the assessment plans must be revised or dropped. Once approved, assessment rolls are prepared, more hearings are held, the roll is confirmed, and the contract is awarded.

Bond Issues

Upon completion of the improvement, each landowner receives a bill for their portion of the cost. If the cost to a landowner is less than $100, the landowner either pays the amount in full to the contractor directly or to a designated public official who, in turn, pays the contractor. If the assessment is larger, the landowner can immediately pay it in full or let it **go to bond.** If let go to bond, local government officials prepare a bond issue that totals all the unpaid assessments in the improvement district. These bonds are either given to the contractor as payment for the work or sold to the public through a securities dealer and the proceeds are used to pay the contractor. The collateral for the bonds is the land in the district upon which assessments have not been paid.

The bonds spread the cost of the improvements over a period of 5 to 10 years and are payable in equal annual (or semiannual) installments plus accumulated interest. Thus, a $2,000 sewer and street-widening assessment on a 10-year bond would be charged to a property owner at the rate of $200 per year (or $100 each 6 months) plus interest. As the bond is gradually retired, the amount of interest added to the regular principal payment declines.

Apportionment

Special assessments are apportioned according to benefits received, rather than by the value of the land and buildings being assessed. In fact, the presence of buildings in an improvement district is not usually considered in preparing the assessment roll; the theory is that the land receives all the benefit of the improvement. Several illustrations can best explain how assessments are apportioned. In a residential neighborhood, the assessment for installation of storm drains, curbs, and gutters is made on a **front-foot basis.** A property owner is charged for each foot of lot that abuts the street being improved.

In the case of a sanitary sewer line assessment, the charge per lot can either be based on front footage or on a simple count of the lots in the district. In the latter case, if there are 100 lots on the new sewer line, each would pay 1% of the cost. In the case of a park or playground, lots nearest the new facility are deemed to benefit more and thus are assessed more than lots located farther away. This form of allocation is very subjective and usually results in spirited objections at public hearings from those who do not feel they will use the facility in proportion to the assessment that their lots will bear.

INCOME TAXES ON THE SALE OF A RESIDENCE

We now turn to the income taxes that are due if a home is sold for more than it cost. Income taxes are levied by the federal government, by 44 states (the exceptions are Florida, Nevada, South Dakota, Texas, Washington, and Wyoming), and by 48 cities, including New York City, Baltimore, Pittsburgh, Philadelphia, Cincinnati, Cleveland, and Detroit. The discussion here centers on the federal income tax and includes key provisions of the Internal Revenue Code as it applies to owner-occupied residences. Aspects of this code that apply to real estate investments are located in Chapter 24.

Calculating a Home's Basis

The first step in determining the amount of taxable gain upon the sale of an owner-occupied residence is to calculate the home's **basis.** This is the price originally paid for the home plus any fees paid for closing services and legal counsel and any fee or commission paid to help find the property. If the home was built rather than purchased, the basis is the cost of the land plus the cost of construction, such as the cost of materials and construction labor, architect's fees, building permit fees, planning and zoning commission approval costs, utility connection charges, and legal fees. The value of labor contributed by the homeowner and free labor from friends and relatives cannot be added. If the home was received as compensation, a gift, an inheritance, or in a trade, or if a portion of the home was depreciated for business purposes, special rules apply that will not be covered here, and the seller should consult the **Internal Revenue Service (IRS).**

Assessments for local improvements and any improvements made by the seller during occupancy are added to the original cost of the home. An improvement is a permanent betterment that materially adds to the value of a home, prolongs its life, or changes it use. For example, finishing an unfinished basement or upper floor, building a swimming pool, adding a bedroom or bathroom, installing new plumbing or wiring, installing a new roof, erecting a new fence, and paving a new driveway are classed as improvements and are added to the home's basis. Maintenance and repairs are not added as they merely maintain the property in ordinary operating condition. Fixing gutters, mending leaks in plumbing, replacing broken windowpanes, and painting the inside or outside of the home are considered maintenance and repair items. However, repairs, when done as part of an extensive remodeling or restoration job, may be added to the basis.

Calculating the Amount Realized

The next step in determining taxable gain is to calculate the **amount realized** from the sale. This is the selling price of the home less selling expenses. Selling expenses include brokerage commissions, advertising, legal fees, title services, escrow or closing fees, and mortgage points paid by the seller. If the sale includes furnishings, the value of those furnishings is deducted from the selling price and reported separately as personal property. If the seller takes back a note and mortgage that is immediately sold at a discount, the discounted value of the note is used, not its face amount.

Calculating Gain on the Sale

The **gain on the sale** is the difference between the amount realized and the basis. Table 14.2 illustrates this with an example. Unless the seller qualifies for tax postponement or tax exclusion as discussed next, this is the amount he reports as gain on his annual income tax forms.

Income Tax Exclusion

A new rule applies to the sale or exchange of a taxpayer's principal residence after May 7, 1997. Under the new rule, a taxpayer can exclude $250,000 of gain from the

TABLE 14.2
Calculation of gain.

May 1, 1982	Buy home for $90,000; closing costs are $500	Basis is	$90,500
July 1, 1983	Add landscaping and fencing for $3,500	Basis is	$94,000
Dec. 1, 1985	Add extra bedroom and bathroom for $15,000	Basis is	$109,000
June 1, 1986	Sell home for $125,000; sales commissions and closing costs are $8,000	Amount realized is	$117,000
	Calculation of gain:	Amount realized is	$117,000
		Less basis	−109,000
		Equals gain	$8,000

sale of the taxpayer's principal residence. If the taxpayer is married, there is a $500,000 exclusion for married individuals filing jointly, if: (1) either spouse meets the ownership test, (2) both spouses meet the use test, (3) the taxpayer has resided there for at least two of five years, and (4) neither spouse is ineligible for exclusion by virtue of sale or exchange of the residence within the last two years. This new rule *eliminates* taxable gain on the sale of the residence up to these limits. This exclusion is allowable each time the homeowner meets the eligibility requirement but generally no more frequently than once every two years.

There is still a need to keep records for home improvements, however. The gain is calculated as the sales price, less the home's basis, or adjusted basis, whichever is applicable. If one owns a house that will *never* exceed the allowable gain, then there is no need to keep a record of requirements.

Starting with sales after May 6, 1997, the IRS will not receive notification of any home sales of $250,000 or under ($500,000 for married taxpayers) provided that the homebuyer provides to the escrow agent assurances that (1) the home was a "principle residence," (2) there was no federally subsidized mortgage financing assistance, (3) the final gain is excludable from gross income *(Internal Revenue Code 6045(e)(5))*.

The new rules are even applicable if the "once in a lifetime" exclusion was used, so long as the two-year ownership requirement is met.

CAPITAL GAINS

Significant savings of capital gains also have been reinstated under the Taxpayer Relief Act of 1997. For income reported after May 6, 1997, the maximum capital gains rate is 20 % (10% for individuals in the 15% tax bracket). A lower rate of 18% (8% for individuals in the 15% tax bracket) applies to transactions after December 31, 2000, if the asset was held more than five years. The holding period for real estate assets has been extended, however, to 18 months.

The key date for long-term capital assets is July 2, 1997. If an asset is sold before July 29, 1997, and the asset has been held more than 12 months, the old 28% capital gains rate applies.

INSTALLMENT METHOD

When a gain cannot be postponed by purchasing a more expensive home, or excluded using the lifetime exclusion, the seller can spread out the payment of taxes on the gain by selling on the **installment method.** This means the seller accepts a note or an installment contract for part (or all) of the purchase price, and receives one or more payments in later taxable years. When this occurs, the seller reports that proportion of the gain that is received in each year as it is received. We will not go through the calculations (which are different for homes versus investment property) as these are available on IRS forms should you be involved in an installment sale. The point to know for now is that a seller can postpone some of the taxes due on a gain by agreeing with the buyer to accept some of the purchase price in subsequent taxable years. If a taxpayer is classed as a "dealer" in real property, however, the taxpayer must report all of the income in the first year, regardless of when it is received.

PROPERTY TAX AND INTEREST DEDUCTIONS

The Internal Revenue Code of 1986 retains the deductibility of state and local real estate taxes. A homeowner can deduct real property taxes and personal property taxes from other income when calculating income taxes. This applies to single-family residences, condominiums, and cooperatives. The deduction does not extend to special assessment taxes for improvement districts.

The Internal Revenue Code of 1986 also retains the deductibility of interest, but subject to two limitations that will be discussed momentarily. The basic rule is that interest paid to finance the purchase of a home is deductible against a homeowner's other income. Also deductible are interest paid on improvement district bonds, loan prepayment penalties, and the deduction of points on new loans that are clearly distinguishable as interest and not service fees for making the loan. Loan points paid by a seller to help a buyer obtain an FHA or VA loan are not deductible as interest (it is not the seller's debt), but can be deducted from the home's selling price in computing a gain or loss on the sale. FHA mortgage insurance premiums are not deductible, nor are those paid to private mortgage insurers.

From an individual taxpayer's standpoint, the ability to deduct property taxes and mortgage interest on a personal residence becomes more valuable in successively higher tax brackets. At the 28% bracket, every dollar spent for something tax-deductible costs the taxpayer only 72¢ in after-tax money. Or seen from another viewpoint, the taxpayer obtains the full enjoyment of the money he spends on interest and property taxes without having to first pay income taxes on it. Although progressively less dramatic, the same argument applies to persons in the 15% tax bracket. As viewed from a national standpoint, the deductibility of interest and property taxes encourages widespread ownership of the country's land and buildings.

BELOW-MARKET INTEREST

In 1984 and 1985, Congress enacted legislation requiring sellers to charge market rates of interest or be taxed as if they had. This legislation requires minimum rates tied to prevailing rates on federal securities, that is, U.S. Treasury notes and bonds. Effective July 1, 1985, if the amount of seller financing in a transaction is $2.8 million or less, the seller must charge no less than 9% interest or a rate equal to the applicable federal rate (AFR). If the amount of seller financing in a transaction is greater than $2.8 million, the seller must charge a rate equal to or greater than the AFR. This rule applied to home sellers as well as investors. Investing in real estate and its tax implications are discussed in Chapter 24.

Because tax rules for real estate are continually changing, only the major rules are reported and discussed here and in Chapter 24. As a real estate owner or agent you need a source of more frequent and more detailed information such as the annual income tax guide published by the Internal Revenue Service (free) or the privately published guides available in most bookstores. Additionally, you may wish to subscribe to a tax newsletter for up-to-the-minute tax information.

AGENT'S LIABILITY FOR TAX ADVICE

The real estate industry's desire for professional recognition coupled with the results of several key court cases strongly suggests that a real estate practitioner ought to be reasonably knowledgeable about taxes. This does not mean the practitioner must have knowledge of tax laws at the level of an accountant or tax attorney. Neither does it mean a practitioner can plead ignorance of tax laws. Rather it means a real estate practitioner is now liable for tax advice (or lack of it) if the advice is material to the transaction—and giving such advice is common in the brokerage business. What this means is that a practitioner should have enough general knowledge of real estate tax laws to be able to answer basic questions accurately and to warn clients and recommend tax counsel if the questions posed by the transaction are beyond the agent's knowledge. Note that the obligation to inform exists even when a client fails to ask about tax consequences. This is to avoid situations where after the deed has been recorded the client says, "Gee, I didn't know I'd have to pay all these taxes, my agent should have warned me," and then sues the agent. Lastly, if the agent tries to fill the role of accountant or tax attorney for the client, then the agent will be held liable to the standards of an accountant or tax attorney.

To summarize, a real estate practitioner must be aware of tax laws that affect the properties the practitioner is handling. A real estate agent has a responsibility to alert clients to potential tax consequences, liabilities, and advantages whether they ask for it or not. Lastly, an agent is responsible for the quality and accuracy of tax information given out by the agent.

REVIEW QUESTIONS

Answers to these questions are found in the Answer Key section at the back of the book.

1. Local government programs and services are financed primarily through
   A. property taxes.
   B. federal income taxes.
   C. state income taxes.
   D. states sales taxes.

2. Taxes on real property are levied
   A. on an ad valorem basis.
   B. according to the value of the property.
   C. Both A and B.
   D. Neither A nor B.

3. The assessment ratio of real property in a community may be
   A. 100% of its appraised value.
   B. more than its fair market value.
   C. more than its appraised value.
   D. All of the above.

4. Which of the following properties has the highest assessed value?
   A. Market value $75,000, assessed at 75% of value.
   B. Market value $50,000, assessed at 100% of value.
   C. Market value $90,000, assessed at 50% of value.
   D. Market value $130,000, assessed at 35% of value.

5. Tax rates may be expressed as
   A. a millage rate.
   B. dollars of tax per hundred dollars of valuation.
   C. dollars of tax per thousand dollars of valuation.
   D. All of the above.

6. Which of the following would be the highest tax rate?
   A. 38 mills.
   B. $3.80/$100.
   C. $38/$1,000.
   D. No difference.

7. Jeff plans to bid on real estate being offered at a tax auction. Before bidding on a parcel he would be wise to
   A. conduct a title search.
   B. purchase title insurance.
   C. sign a contract.
   D. obtain a tax receipt.

8. Which of the following liens holds the highest degree of lien priority?
   A. Federal income tax liens.
   B. Mechanics' liens.
   C. Ad valorem tax liens.
   D. First mortgage liens.

9. Records of the assessed valuations of all properties within a jurisdiction are known as
   A. appraisal rolls.
   B. allocation rolls.
   C. appropriation rolls.
   D. assessment rolls.

10. In Texas, the assessed value of real property is set
    A. equal to its fair market value.
    B. greater than its fair market value.
    C. at a percentage of its appraised value.
    D. less than its appraised value.

11. Land and buildings may be exempted from property taxation
    A. as a means of attracting industry to a community.
    B. if they are used for religious or educational purposes.
    C. Both A and B.
    D. Neither A nor B.

12. All of the following types of property are usually exempt from taxation EXCEPT:
    A. government-owned utilities.
    B. residences owned by elderly homeowners.
    C. property owned by charitable organizations.
    D. hospitals.

13. Real property taxes are sometimes limited by laws that limit
    A. the amount of taxes that can be collected.
    B. how much a government can spend.
    C. Both A and B.
    D. Neither A nor B.

14. An improvement district may be created as a result of action originated by
    A. a group of concerned citizens.
    B. local governing bodies.
    C. Both A and B.
    D. Neither A nor B.

15. Which of the following statements is correct?
    A. There is no redemption period in Texas when foreclosure due to taxes has occurred.
    B. All tax liens in Texas are superior to any other liens.
    C. The redemption period in Texas is one year when foreclosure due to taxes has occurred.
    D. Properties in Texas, when tax foreclosure has occurred, may not be sold at public auction.

16. When a person sells land for more than she paid for it
    A. there is no federal tax applicable to the gain.
    B. the gain is taxed by all state governments.
    C. Both A and B.
    D. Neither A nor B.

17. Which of the following would NOT be considered an improvement to a home in determining its cost basis?
    A. Repairs to a leaky roof.
    B. Construction of a new fence.
    C. Repairs done as part of an extensive remodeling project.
    D. None of the above.

18. Which of the following liens holds the highest degree of lien priority?
    A. Federal income tax liens.
    B. Mechanics' liens.
    C. Ad valorem tax liens.
    D. First mortgage liens.

19. Sources of information on income tax laws and rules include
    A. tax guides published by the Internal Revenue Service.
    B. privately published tax guides sold in bookstores.
    C. privately published tax newsletters.
    D. All of the above.

20. In 1979, the Texas legislature voted to restrict increases in property taxes by local taxing units. An increase, without public hearing, may not exceed the previous year by more than
    A. 3 percent.
    B. 2 percent.
    C. 5 percent.
    D. 10 percent.

CHAPTER 15

KEY TERMS

Closing meeting: a meeting at which the buyer pays for the property and receives a deed to it and all other matters pertaining to the sale are concluded

Closing statement: an accounting of funds to the buyer and the seller at the completion of a real estate transaction

Escrow agent: the person placed in charge of an escrow

Escrow closing: the deposit of documents and funds with a neutral third party along with instructions as to how to conduct the closing

Prorating: the division of ongoing expenses and income items between the buyer and the seller

Real Estate Settlement Procedures Act (RESPA): a federal law that deals with procedures to be followed in certain types of real estate closings

Title closing: the process of completing a real estate transaction

Walk-through: a final inspection of the property just prior to settlement

Title Closing and Escrow

Once the title has been searched, a decision should have been made as to how to take title, prepare a deed, make loan arrangements, check property tax records, and begin the final steps in the process. In this chapter you will learn how the process evolves from the buyer's walk-through to the closing meeting or escrow. You will also become familiar with the calculations or at least the procedures to determine prorations and complete the final settlement statement.

Numerous details must be handled between the time a buyer and seller sign a sales contract and the day title is conveyed to the buyer. Title must be searched (Chapter 6), a decision made as to how to take title (Chapter 4), a deed prepared (Chapter 5), loan arrangements made (Chapters 9 through 13), property tax records checked (Chapter 14) and so forth. In this chapter we will look at the final steps in the process, in particular the buyer's walk-through, the closing meeting or escrow, prorations, and the settlement statement.

BUYER'S WALK-THROUGH

To protect both the buyer and the seller, it is good practice for a buyer to make a **walk-through.** This is a final inspection of the property just prior to the settlement date. It is quite possible the buyer has not been on the parcel or inside the structure since the initial offer and acceptance. Now, several weeks later, the buyer wants to make certain that the premises have been vacated, that no damage has occurred, that the seller has left behind personal property agreed upon, and that the seller has not removed and taken any real property. If the sales contract requires all mechanical items to be in normal working order, then the buyer will want to test the heating and air-conditioning systems, dishwasher, disposal, stove, garage door opener, etc., and the refrigerator, washer, and dryer if included. The buyer will also want to test all the plumbing to be certain the hot water heater works, faucets and showers run, toilets flush, and sinks drain. A final inspection of the structure is made, including walls, roof, gutters, driveway, decks, patios, etc., as well as the land and landscaping.

Note that a walk-through is not the time for the buyer to make the initial inspection of the property. That is done before the contract is signed, and if there are questions in the buyer's mind regarding the structural soundness of the property, a thorough inspection (possibly with the aid of a professional real estate inspector) should be conducted within ten days of signing the purchase contract. The walk-through is for the purpose of giving the buyer the opportunity to make certain that agreements regarding the condition of the premises have been kept. If during the walk-through the buyer notes the walls were damaged when the seller moved out, or the furnace does not function, the buyer (or the buyer's agent) notes these items and asks that funds be withheld at the closing to pay for repairs.

TITLE CLOSING

Title closing refers to the completion of a real estate transaction. This is when the buyer pays for the property and the seller delivers the deed. The day on which this occurs is called the **closing date.** Depending on where one resides in the United States, the title closing process is referred to as a **closing, settlement,** or **escrow.** All accomplish the same basic goal, but the method of reaching that goal can follow one of two paths.

In some parts of the United States, particularly in the East, and to a certain extent in the Mountain states, the Midwest, and the South, the title closing process is concluded at a meeting at which each party to the transaction, or his/her representative, is present. Elsewhere, title closing is conducted by an escrow agent, who is a neutral third party mutually selected by the buyer and seller to carry out the closing. With an escrow, there is no necessity for a closing meeting; in fact, most of the closing process is conducted by mail. In Texas, the escrow closing is the fastest, safest, and most convenient method of carrying out the title closing process. The escrow agent is usually a title company. Let's look at the operation of each method.

CLOSING OR SETTLEMENT MEETING

When a meeting is used to close a real estate transaction, the seller (or the seller's representative) meets in person with the buyer and delivers the deed. At the same time, the buyer pays the seller for the property. To ascertain that everything promised in the sales contract has been properly carried out, it is customary for the buyer and seller to each have an attorney present. The real estate practitioners who brought the buyer and seller together are also present, along with a representative of the firm that conducted the title search. If a new loan is being made or an existing one is being paid off at the closing, a representative of the lender will be present.

The location of the meeting and the selection of the person responsible for conducting the closing will depend on local custom and the nature of the closing. It is the custom in some states for the real estate agent to conduct the closing at his office. In other localities, the attorney for the seller conducts it in the attorney's office. An alternative is to have the title company responsible for the title search and title policy conduct the closing at its office.

Seller's Responsibilities at Closing

To ensure a smooth closing, each person attending is responsible for bringing certain documents. The seller and his attorney are responsible for preparing and bringing the deed, together with the most recent property tax bill (and receipt if it has been paid). If required by the sales contract, they also bring the insurance policy for the property, the termite and wood-rot inspection report, documents showing the removal of unacceptable liens and encumbrances, a title insurance policy, a bill of sale for personal property, a survey map, and a statement showing the remaining balance on any loan that the buyer will assume. The loan payment booklet, keys to the property, garage door opener, and the like are also brought to the meeting. If the property produces income, existing leases, rent schedules, current expenditures, and letters advising the tenants of the new owner must also be furnished.

Buyer's Responsibilities at Closing

The buyer's responsibilities include having adequate settlement funds ready, having an attorney present to protect his interests, and, if borrowing, obtaining the loan commitment and advising the lender of the meeting's time and place. The real estate agent is present because it is the custom in some localities that the agent be in charge of the closing and prepare the proration calculations, although this is not generally done in Texas. The agent also receives a commission check at the time and, as a matter of good business, will make certain that all goes well.

If a new loan is involved, the lender provides the required funds along with a note and mortgage for the borrower to sign. If an existing loan is to be paid off as part of the transaction, the lender is present to receive a check and release the mortgage held on the property. If a lender elects not to attend, the check and/or loan papers are given to the person in charge of the closing, along with instructions for their distribution and signing. A title insurance representative is also present to provide the latest status of title and the title insurance policy. If title insurance is not used, the seller is responsible for bringing an abstract or asking the abstracter to be present.

Real Estate Agent's Duties

The seller and the seller's attorney may be unaware of all the things expected of them at the closing. Therefore, it is the duty of the agent who listed the property to make certain that they are prepared. Similarly, it is the duty of the agent who found the buyer to make certain that the buyer and the buyer's attorney are prepared for the closing. If the agent both lists and sells the property, the agent assists both the buyer and seller. If more than one agent is involved in the transaction, each should keep the other(s) fully informed so the transaction will go as smoothly as possible. At all times the buyer and seller are to be kept informed as to the status of the closing. An agent should provide them with a preview of all actions that will take place, explain the amounts of money involved and the purpose served by each payment or receipt, and in general prepare the parties for informed participation at the closing.

The Transaction

When everyone concerned has arrived at the meeting place, the closing begins. The various documents called for by the sales contract are exchanged for inspection. The buyer and his attorney inspect the deed the seller is offering, the title search and/or title policy, the mortgage papers, survey, leases, removals of encumbrances, and proration calculations. The lender also inspects the deed, survey, title search, and title policy. This continues until each party has a chance to inspect each document of interest.

As the title search will usually have been prepared before the closing, the buyer and lender both want protection against any changes in title condition since then. A common solution is for the seller to sign a **seller's affidavit.** In this affidavit, the seller states that he is the true owner of the property, that there are no liens or proceedings currently against him, and that he has done nothing to damage the quality of title since the title search. If a defect caused by the seller later appears, he may be sued for damages. Furthermore, he may be liable for criminal charges if it can be shown that he was attempting to obtain money under false pretenses by signing the affidavit. Another solution is to require the person in charge of the closing to hold the money being paid to the seller until a final title search is made and the new deed recorded.

A settlement statement (discussed later in this chapter) is given to the buyer and seller to summarize the financial aspects of their transaction. It is prepared by the person in charge of the closing either just before or at the meeting. It provides a clear picture of where the buyer's and seller's monies are going at the closing by identifying each party to whom money is being paid.

If everyone involved in the closing has done his or her homework and comes to the meeting prepared, the closing usually goes smoothly. When everything is in order, the seller hands a completed deed to the buyer. The buyer then gives the seller a check that combines the down payment and net result of the prorations. The lender has the buyer sign the mortgage and note and hands checks to the seller and the existing lender if one is involved. The seller writes a check to his real estate broker, attorney, and the abstracter. The buyer writes a check to his attorney for his services. This continues until every document is signed and everyone is paid. The deed, new mortgage, and release of the old mortgage are then recorded, and the transaction is complete.

Closing Into Escrow

Occasionally an unavoidable circumstance can cause delays in a closing. Perhaps an important document, known to be in the mail, has not arrived. Yet it will be difficult to reschedule the meeting. In such a situation, the parties concerned may agree to **close into escrow.** In such a closing, all parties sign their documents and entrust them to the escrow agent for safekeeping. No money is disbursed and the deed is not delivered until the missing paperwork has arrived. When it does, the escrow agent completes the transaction and delivers the money and documents by mail or messenger. The use of escrow to close a real estate transaction involves a neutral third party, called an **escrow agent,** escrow holder, or escrowee, who acts as a trusted stakeholder for all the parties to the transaction. Instead of delivering the deed directly to the buyer at a closing meeting, the seller gives the deed to the escrow agent with instructions that it be delivered only after the buyer has completed all his promises in the sales contract. Similarly, the buyer hands the escrow agent the money for the purchase price plus instructions that it be given to the seller only after fulfillment of the seller's promises. Let us look closer at this arrangement.

A typical real estate escrow closing starts when a sales contract is signed by the buyer and seller. They select a neutral escrow agent to handle the closing. This may be the escrow department of a bank or savings and loan or other lending agency, an attorney, or a title insurance company. Sometimes real estate brokers offer escrow services. However, if the broker is earning a sales commission in the transaction, the broker cannot be neutral and disinterested. Because escrow agents are entrusted with valuable documents and large sums of money, Texas title companies have licensing and bonding requirements that escrow agents must meet and, therefore, handle most closings in Texas.

Escrow Agent's Duties

The escrow agent's task begins with the deposit of the buyer's earnest money in a special bank trust account. In most commercial closings and almost all residential closings in Texas, the escrow agent's duties are very seldom written out as formal escrow instructions. An exception to this is the lender who furnishes a **mortgagee's information letter (MIL)** to direct the escrow agent as to how to disburse the funds for the loan proceeds.

When the title search is completed, the escrow agent forwards it to the buyer or his attorney for approval. The property insurance and tax papers the seller would otherwise bring to the closing meeting are sent to the escrow agent for proration. Leases, service contracts, and notices to tenants are also sent to the escrow agent for proration and delivery to the buyer. The deed conveying title to the buyer is prepared, signed by the seller, and given to the escrow agent. Once delivered into escrow, even if the seller dies, marries, or is declared legally incompetent before the close of escrow, the deed will still pass title to the buyer.

The Closing

As the closing date draws near, if all the instructions are otherwise complete, the escrow agent requests any additional money the buyer and lender must deposit in order to close. The day before closing the escrow agent orders a last minute check on the title. If no changes have occurred since the first (preliminary) title search, the deed, mortgage, mortgage release, and other documents to be recorded as part of the transaction are recorded first thing the following morning. As soon as the recording is confirmed and **good funds** (cash, wired funds, cashier check) have been deposited in the escrow agent's trust account, the escrow agent hands or mails a check to every party to whom funds are due from the escrow (usually the seller, real estate broker, and previous lender), along with any papers or documents that must be delivered through escrow (such as the fire insurance policy, copy of the property tax bill, and tenant leases). Several days later the buyer and lender will receive a title insurance policy in the mail from the title company. The public recorder's office also mails the documents it recorded to each party. The deed is sent to the buyer, the mortgage release to the seller, and the new mortgage to the lender.

In the escrow closing method, the closing, delivery of title, and recordation are considered to all take place at the same moment. Technically, the seller does not physically hand a deed to the buyer on the closing day. However, once all the conditions of the escrow are met, the escrow agent, as a disinterested third party, represents neither party but fulfills the escrow requirements as set out by both parties. Thus, a buyer, through the escrow agent, receives the deed, and the law regarding delivery is fulfilled.

PUTTING IT TO WORK

With an escrow closing, it is not necessary for the buyer and seller to meet face-to-face during the escrow period or at the closing. This can eliminate personality conflicts that might be detrimental to an otherwise sound transaction. The escrow agent, having previously accumulated all the documents, approvals, deeds, and monies prior to the closing date, does the closing alone.

In a brokered transaction, the real estate agent may be the only person who actually meets the escrow agent. All communication can be handled through the broker, by mail, or by telephone. If a real estate agent is not involved, the buyer and/or seller can open the escrow, either in person or by mail. The use of an escrow agent does not eliminate the need for an attorney. Although there might be no closing meeting for the attorneys to attend, they play a vital role in advising the buyer and seller on each document sent by the escrow agent for approval and signature.

DELAYS AND FAILURE TO CLOSE

When a real estate purchase contract is written, a closing date is also negotiated and placed in the contract. The choice of closing date will depend on when the buyer wants possession, when the seller wants to move out, and how long it will take to obtain a loan, title search, and termite report and otherwise fulfill the contract requirements. In a typical residential sale this is 30 to 60 days, with 45 days being a popular choice when new financing is involved. The Texas Real Estate Commission (TREC)-promulgated earnest money form simply states that the closing will be "on or before" a specified date.

Delays along the way are sometimes encountered and may cause a delay in the closing. This is usually not a problem as long as the buyer still intends to buy, the seller still intends to sell, and the delay is for a reasonable cause and a justifiable length of time. Note that the TREC form provides for extensions beyond the specified closing date to cure title objections or to complete loan requirements. These are common delays that are often beyond the control of either buyer or seller. This allows for some reasonable flexibility when these problems occur without requiring extensive or stress-filled renegotiation.

The delay might be quite lengthy, however. For example, there may be a previously undisclosed title defect that will take months to clear, or perhaps there are unusual problems in financing, or there has been major damage to the premises. In such cases, relieving all parties from further obligation to each other may be the wisest choice for all involved. This is one of the remedies provided for in Paragraph 16 of the TREC promulgated form. If so, it is essential that the buyer and seller sign mutual release papers. These are necessary to rescind the purchase contract and cancel the escrow if one has been opened. The buyer's deposit is also returned. Without release papers, the buyer still has a vaguely defined liability to buy and the seller can still be required to convey the property, so the escrow agent will refuse to disburse to either party. A mutual release gives the buyer the freedom to choose another property and the seller the chance to fix the problem and remarket the property later.

A stickier problem occurs when one party wants out of the contract and attempts to use any delay in closing as grounds for contract termination. (For example, the buyer may have found a preferable property for less money and better terms. Or, the seller may have received a higher offer since signing the purchase contract.) Although the party wishing to cancel may threaten with a lawsuit, courts might not enforce cancellation of valuable contract rights because of reasonable delays that are not the fault of the other party. Conversely, courts might not go along with a reluctant buyer or seller who manufactures delays so as to delay the closing and then claim default and cancellation of the contract. If the reluctance continues and negotiations to end it fail, the performing party may choose to complete its requirements and then ask the courts to force the reluctant party to the closing table.

LOAN ESCROWS

Escrows can be used for purposes other than real estate or sales transactions. For example, a homeowner who is refinancing his property could enter into an escrow with the lender. The conditions of the escrow would be that the homeowner deliver a properly executed note and mortgage to the escrow agent and that the lender deposit the loan money. Upon closing, the escrow agent delivers the documents to the lender and the money to the homeowner. Or, in reverse, an escrow could be used to pay off the balance of a loan. The conditions would be the borrower's deposit of the balance due and the lender's deposit of the mortgage release and note. Even the weekly office sports pool is an escrow—with the person holding the pool money acting as escrow agent for the participants.

REPORTING REQUIREMENTS

The Internal Revenue Code now requires that the seller's proceeds from all sales of real estate must be reported to the Internal Revenue Service on their Form 1099. The responsibility for filing Form 1099 goes in the following order: the person responsible for the closing, the mortgage lender, the seller's broker, the buyer's broker, and any person designated by the U.S. Treasury. It is important to determine at the closing who needs to file the Form 1099. These forms must be filed at no charge to the taxpayer.

PRORATING AT THE CLOSING

Ongoing expenses and income items must be prorated between the seller and buyer when property ownership changes hands. Items subject to proration include property insurance premiums, property taxes, accrued interest on assumed loans, and rents and operating expenses if the property produces income. If heating is done by oil and the oil tank is partially filled when title transfers, that oil can be prorated, as can utility bills when service is not shut off between owners. The TREC promulgated forms state that all prorations are made "through the closing date," indicating that for the day of closing, the seller is responsible for payments, and is entitled to income prorations also. The prorating process has long been a source of considerable mystery to real estate newcomers. Several sample prorations common to most closings are set out below to help clarify the process.

Hazard Insurance

Hazard insurance policies for such things as fire, wind, storm, and flood damage are paid for in advance. At the beginning of each year of the policy's life, the premium for that year's coverage must be paid. When real estate is sold, the buyer may ask the seller to transfer the remaining coverage to him. The seller usually agrees if the buyer reimburses him for the value of the remaining coverage on a prorated basis.

The first step in prorating hazard insurance is to find out how often the premium is paid, how much it is, and what period of time it covers. Suppose that the seller has a one-year policy that cost $180 and started on January 1 of the current year. If the property is sold and the closing date is June 30, the policy is half used up. Therefore, if the buyer wants the policy transferred to him, he must pay the seller $90 for the remaining six months of coverage.

Because closing dates do not always occur on neat, evenly divided portions of the year, nor do most items that need prorating, it is usually necessary to break the year into months and the months into days to make proration calculations. Suppose, in the previous hazard insurance example, that prorations are to be made on June 29 instead of June 30. This would give the buyer six months and one day of coverage. How much does he owe the seller? The first step is to calculate the monthly and daily rates for the policy: $180 divided by 12 is $15 per month. Dividing the monthly rate of $15 by 30 days gives a daily rate of 50¢. The second step is to add 6 months at $15 and 1 day at 50¢. Thus, the buyer owes the seller $90.50 for the unused portion of the policy.

Loan Interest

When a buyer agrees to assume an existing loan from the seller, an interest proration is necessary. For example, a sales contract calls for the buyer to assume a 9% mortgage loan with a principal balance of $31,111 at the time of closing. Loan payments are due the tenth of each month, and the sales contract calls for a July 3 closing date, with interest on the loan to be prorated through the closing date. How much is to be prorated and to whom?

First, we must recognize that interest is normally paid in arrears. On a loan that is payable monthly, the borrower pays interest for the use of the loan at the end of each month of the loan. Thus, the July 10 monthly loan payment includes the interest due for the use of $31,111 from June 10 through July 9. However, the seller owned the property through July 3, and from June 10 through July 3 is 24 days. At the closing the seller must give the buyer enough money to pay for 24 days interest on the $31,111. If the annual interest rate is 9% one month's interest is $31,111 times 9% divided by 12, which is $233.33. Divide this by 30 days to get a daily interest rate of $7.7777. Multiply the daily rate by 24 to obtain the interest for 24 days, $186.66.

30-Day Month

In Texas, it is the custom when prorating interest, property taxes, water bills, and insurance to use a 30-day month because it simplifies proration calculations. Naturally, using a 30-day month produces some inaccuracy when dealing with months that do not have 30 days. If this inaccuracy is significant to the buyer and seller, they can agree to prorate either by using the exact number of days in the closing month or by dividing the yearly rate by 365 to find a daily rate.

Rents

It is the custom in Texas to prorate rents on the basis of the actual number of days in the month, however. Using the July 3 closing date again, if the property is currently rented for $450 per month, paid in advance on the first of each month, what would the proration be? If the seller has already collected the rent for the month of July, he is obligated to hand over to the buyer that portion of the rent earned between July 4 and July 31, inclusive, a period of 28 days. To determine how many dollars this is, divide $450 by the number of days in July. This gives $14.516 as the rent per day. Then multiply the daily rate by 28 days to get $406.45, the portion of the July rent that the seller must hand over to the buyer. If the renter has not paid the July rent by the July 3 closing date, no proration is made. If the buyer later collects the July rent, he must return three days rent to the seller.

Property Taxes

Prorated property taxes are common to nearly all real estate transactions. The amount of proration depends on when the property taxes are due, what portion has already been paid, and what period of time they cover. Property taxes are levied on an annual basis, but depending on the locality, they may be due at the beginning, middle, or end of the tax year. In Texas, property owners are permitted to pay half their property taxes during the first six months of the tax year and the other half during the second six months. Although this is seldom done, prorations are usually made on an annual basis. The state and county tax year is concurrent with the calendar year. Property bills are sent out in early October and are due October 1, but are not delinquent until February 1 of the following year. If a transaction calls for property taxes to be prorated to September 4, how is the calculation made?

Our problem is complicated by the fact that the new property tax bill will not have been issued by the September 4 closing date. The solution is to use the previous year's tax bill as the best estimate available. Suppose that it was $1,080 for the year. The proration would be from January 1 through September 4, a period of 8 months and 4 days. One month's taxes would be one-twelfth of $1,080, or $90. Dividing $90 by 30 gives a daily rate of $3. If you take 8 months at $90 each and 4 days at $3 each, the total is $732. The seller pays the buyer $732 because he owned the property through September 4; yet the buyer will later receive a property tax bill for the period starting January

1. If there is a possibility that the October property tax bill will change substantially from the previous year, the buyer and seller can agree to make another adjustment between themselves when the new bill is available.

In the event there is a miscalculation of the taxes, most title companies and escrow agents require the buyer and seller to settle their differences between themselves.

Let us work one more property tax proration example. Presume that the annual property taxes are $1,350, the tax year runs from January 1 through the following December 31, the closing and proration date is December 28, and the day of closing belongs to the seller. First, determine how much of the annual property tax bill has been paid by the seller. If the seller has paid the taxes for January 1 through December 31, the buyer must reimburse the seller for the taxes from December 29 through December 31, a period of 3 days. The amount is calculated by taking one-twelfth of $1,350 to find the monthly tax rate of $112.50, and dividing by 30 to get the daily rate of $3.75. Then by multiplying the daily rate by 3 days we get $11.25, the amount that the buyer must give the seller.

Homeowners' Association

If the property being sold is a condominium unit or in a cooperative or a planned unit development, there will be a monthly homeowners' association payment to be prorated. Suppose the monthly fee is $120 and is paid in advance on the first of the month. If the closing takes place two-thirds of the way through the month, the buyer owes the seller $40 for the unused portion of the month.

Proration Date

Prorations need not be calculated as of the closing date. In the sales contract, the buyer and seller can mutually agree to a different proration date if they wish. If nothing is said, local law and custom will prevail. As stated previously, this means the seller pays for the day of closing in Texas.

Special assessments for such things as street improvements, water mains, and sewer lines are not usually prorated. As a rule, the selling price of the property reflects the added value of the improvements, and the seller pays any assessments in full before closing. This is not an ironclad rule, however; the buyer and seller in their sales contract can agree to do whatever they want about the assessment.

Proration Summary

Figure 15.1 summarizes the most commonly found proration situations found in real estate closings. The table also shows who is to be charged and who is to be credited and whether the proration is to be worked forward from the closing date or backward. As a rule, items that are paid in advance by the seller are prorated forward from the closing date; for example, prepaid fire insurance. Items that are paid in arrears, such as interest on an existing loan, are prorated backward from the closing date.

SAMPLE CLOSING

To illustrate the arithmetic involved, let us work through a residential closing situation. Note that this example is not particular to any region of the United States, but is rather a composite that shows you how the most commonly encountered residential closing items are handled.

FIGURE 15.1
Common prorations.

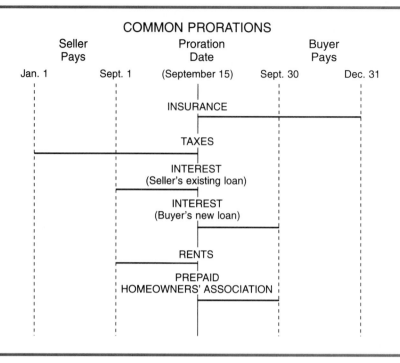

COMMON PRORATIONS

Homer Leavitt has listed his home for sale with List-Rite Realty for $125,000, and the sales commission is to be 6% of the selling price. A salesperson from Quick-Sale Realty learns about the property through the multiple listing service and produces a buyer willing to pay $123,000 with $33,000 down. The offer is conditioned on the seller paying off the existing $48,000, 12% interest mortgage loan and the buyer obtaining a new loan for $90,000. Property taxes, hazard insurance, and heating oil in the home's oil tank are to be prorated as of the closing date. The buyer also asks the seller to pay for a termite inspection and repairs if necessary, a title search, an owner's title insurance policy, and one-half of the closing fee. The seller accepts this offer on August 15, and they agree to close on September 15.

The property-tax year for this home runs from January 1 through December 31. Mr. Leavitt has paid the taxes for last year, but not for the current year. Newly issued tax bills show that $1,680 will be due on October 1 for the current year. The hazard insurance policy (fire, windstorm, etc.) that the buyer wishes to assume was purchased by the seller for $240 and covers the period June 15 through the following June 14. The Charter Title Insurance Company will charge the seller $400 for a combined title search, title examination, and owner's title policy package.

The buyer obtains a loan commitment from the Park Tower National Bank for $90,000. To make this loan, the bank will charge a $900 loan origination fee, $100 for an appraisal, and $25 for a credit report on the buyer. The bank also requires a lender's title policy in the amount of $90,000 (added cost $90), 6 months of property tax reserves, and 4 months of hazard insurance reserves. The loan is to be repaid in equal monthly installments beginning November 1. The termite inspection by Dead-Bug Pest Company costs $39, and recording fees are $5 for deeds and mortgage releases and $10 for mortgages. The title company charges the buyer and the seller $110 each to conduct the closing and an attorney charges $60 to prepare a deed for the seller, although this may be prepared by one of the party's attorneys and included in their fees for representation. The seller is leaving $130 worth of fuel oil for the buyer.

The buyer and seller have each hired an attorney to advise them on legal matters in connection with the sales contract and closing. They are to be paid $250 and $300 respectively, out of the settlement. List-Rite Realty and Quick-Sale Realty have advised the closing agent that they are splitting the $7,380 sales commission equally.

FIGURE 15.2.
Transaction summary.

	Amount	Comments
Sale Price	$123,000	
Down Payment	$ 33,000	
Deposit (Earnest Money)	$ 3,000	Credit to buyer's down payment.
Existing Loan	$ 48,000	Seller to pay off through settlement. Interest rate is 12%.
New Loan	$ 90,000	Monthly payments begin Nov. 1. Interest rate is 9.6%.
Loan Origination Fee	$ 900	
Appraisal Fee	$ 100	Paid by buyer in connection with obtaining $90,000 loan.
Credit Report	$ 25	
Owner's Title Policy	$ 400	Seller pays Charter Title Co.
Lender's Title Policy	$ 90	Buyer pays Charter Title Co.
County Property Taxes	$1,680/yr	Not yet paid.
Hazard Insurance	$ 240/yr	Existing policy with 9 months to run. Transfer to buyer.
Heating Oil	$ 130	Remaining heating oil in tank. Transfer to buyer.
Pest Inspection	$ 39	Seller pays Dead-Bug Pest Co.
Property Tax Reserves	$ 840	6 months at $140 for lender.
Hazard Insurance Reserves	$ 80	4 months at $20 for lender.
Buyer's Attorney	$ 250	
Seller's Attorney	$ 300	
Closing Fee	$ 220	Charter Title Company; buyer & seller each pay $110.
Deed Preparation	$ 60	Seller pays attorney.
Record Deed	$ 5	Buyer pays.
Record Mortgage Release	$ 5	Seller pays.
Record Mortgage	$ 10	Buyer pays.
Brokerage Commission	$ 7,380	Seller pays; to be split equally between List-Rite Realty and Quick-Sale Realty.

Settlement and Proration date is September 15. All prorations are to be based on a 30-day banker's month.

Finally, the $3,000 earnest money deposit that the buyer made with the offer is to be credited toward the down payment. Using this information, which is summarized in Figure 15.2 for your convenience, let us see exactly how a settlement statement is prepared.

RESIDENTIAL SETTLEMENT STATEMENT

Figure 15.3 is the most widely used residential settlement form in the United States, and it is filled out to reflect the transaction outlined in Figure 15.2. Let us work through this sample transaction in order to see where each item is placed on the settlement statement. (You will notice that the buyer is referred to as the borrower throughout Figure 15.3. This is not important for the moment and will be explained at the end of the chapter.)

Buyers Side

Lines 101 (Section J) and 401 (Section K) of the settlement statement show identically the price the buyer is paying and the seller is receiving for the property. On line 103 is the $3,512 total of the buyer's settlement charges from the reverse side of this form. (The reverse side will be discussed in a moment.) On lines 109 and 409 we find the hazard insurance proration. The existing policy cost the seller $240 and has 9 months to run. For these 9 months the buyer is being charged $180 on line 109 and the seller is being credited the same amount on line 409. The heating oil remaining in the heating system tank is charged to the buyer on line 110 and credited to the seller on line 410. The gross amount of $126,822 that is due from the buyer is tallied on line 120.

On line 201 the buyer is credited with the $3,000 earnest money paid at the time the purchase contract was written. On the next line, the buyer is credited with the principal amount of the new $90,000 loan. On line 211 there is a property tax proration credit for the buyer; on line 511 the same proration is shown as a charge to the seller. This is because $1,680 in property taxes are due on October 1 for the period January 1 through December 31. Not yet paid for the year, the buyer must pay these taxes on October 1. However, the seller owned the property from January 1 to September 15, a period of 8 months. At the rate of $140 per month, this means the seller must give the buyer $1,190 as part of the closing costs.

On line 220 we see the $94,190 total of the buyer's credits. Line 301 shows the gross amount that is due from the buyer for this transaction. The difference, on line 303, is the amount of cash that is needed from the buyer (borrower) to close the transaction.

Seller's Side

On the seller's side of the settlement statement (Section K) at line 420 we have the gross amount due to the seller from the sales price and proration credits. On line 502 is the $8,189 total of the seller's settlement costs from the reverse side of the form (line 1400). Continuing, on line 504 the seller is charged for the existing mortgage loan that is being paid off as part of the closing. Accrued interest of $240 on that loan for the first half of September is charged to the seller on line 506. On line 520 the $57,619 total is what must come out of the seller's funds at the closing. This is subtracted from the gross amount due to the seller on line 601. The difference, on line 603, is the $65,691 cash the seller will receive at the closing.

Settlement Charges

Continuing on the next page of Figure 15.3 (reverse side of the actual form), the real estate commission is detailed on lines 700, 701, and 702. Note that if a closing agent makes the commission split shown here, that closing agent must have written instructions to do so from the real estate broker who is being paid by the seller. Otherwise, all the commission goes to the seller's broker and the seller's broker pays the cooperating broker according to whatever agreement they have.

Lines 801, 803, and 804 show the charges incurred by the buyer in connection with obtaining the new $90,000 loan. Line 901 carries the interest on the $90,000 loan as it is calculated from the date of closing to September's end. This charge brings the loan up to the first day of the next month and simplifies future bookkeeping for the monthly loan payments. At 9.6% the interest on $90,000 is $24.00 a day, and the buyer is charged $360 for 15 days.

As a condition for the loan, the lender requires impound accounts for hazard insurance and property taxes. In order to have enough on hand to make the property tax payment on October 1, the lender requires an immediate reserve of $1,680 (line 1004). Beginning November 1, one-twelfth of the estimated taxes for next year will be added to the buyer's monthly payment so as to have money in the impound account from which to pay taxes next year. The same concept applies to the hazard insurance. It comes due in 8 months, therefore the lender requires 4 months worth of reserves in advance (line 1001).

FIGURE **15.3**
Residential
settlement form.

A.		B. TYPE OF LOAN		
U.S. DEPARTMENT OF HOUSING AND URBAN DEVELOPMENT		1. ☐ FHA 2. ☐ FmHA 3. ☐ CONV. UNINS.		
		4. ☐ VA 5. ☐ CONV. INS.		
SETTLEMENT STATEMENT		6. FILE NUMBER:		7. LOAN NUMBER:
		8. MORTGAGE INSURANCE CASE NUMBER:		

C. NOTE: *This form is furnished to give you a statement of actual settlement costs. Amounts paid to and by the settlement agent are shown. Items marked "(p.o.c.)" were paid outside the closing; they are shown here for informational purposes and are not included in the totals.*

D. NAME OF BORROWER:	E. NAME OF SELLER:	F. NAME OF LENDER:
Neidi Delone 2424 Newpaige Lane City, State 00000	Homer Leavitt 1654 West 12th Street City, State 00000	Acme National Bank 1111 West 1st Street City, State 00000

G. PROPERTY LOCATION:	H. SETTLEMENT AGENT:	I. SETTLEMENT DATE:
1654 West 12th Street City, State 00000	Acme National Bank PLACE OF SETTLEMENT: Acme National Bank	Sept. 15, 19xx

J. SUMMARY OF BORROWER'S TRANSACTION		K. SUMMARY OF SELLER'S TRANSACTION	
100. GROSS AMOUNT DUE FROM BORROWER:		*400. GROSS AMOUNT DUE TO SELLER:*	
101. Contract sales price	$123,000	401. Contract sales price	$123,000
102. Personal property		402. Personal property	
103. Settlement charges to borrower *(line 1400)*	3,512	403.	
104.		404.	
105.		405.	
Adjustments for items paid by seller in advance		*Adjustments for items paid by seller in advance*	
106. City/town taxes to		406. City/town taxes to	
107. County taxes to		407. County taxes to	
108. Assessments to		408. Assessments to	
109. Hazard insurance 9/15 to 6/15	180	409. Hazard insurance 9/15 to 6/15	180
110. Heating oil	130	410. Heating oil	130
111.		411.	
112.		412.	
120. GROSS AMOUNT DUE FROM BORROWER	$126,822	420. GROSS AMOUNT DUE TO SELLER	$123,310
200. AMOUNTS PAID BY OR IN BEHALF OF BORROWER:		*500. REDUCTIONS IN AMOUNT DUE TO SELLER:*	
201. Deposit or earnest money	$ 3,000	501. Excess deposit *(see instructions)*	
202. Principal amount of new loan(s)	90,000	502. Settlement charges to seller *(line 1400)*	8,189
203. Existing loan(s) taken subject to		503. Existing loan(s) taken subject to	
204.		504. Payoff of first mortgage loan	48,000
205.		505. Payoff of second mortgage loan	
206.		506. Accrued interest 9/1 to 9/15	240
207.		507.	
208.		508.	
209.		509.	
Adjustments for items unpaid by seller		*Adjustments for items unpaid by seller*	
210. City/town taxes to		510. City/town taxes to	
211. County taxes 1/1 to 9/15	1,190	511. County taxes 1/1 to 9/15	1,190
212. Assessments to		512. Assessments to	
213.		513.	
214.		514.	
215.		515.	
216.		516.	
217.		517.	
218.		518.	
219.		519.	
220. TOTAL PAID BY/FOR BORROWER	$ 94,190	520. TOTAL REDUCTION AMOUNT DUE SELLER	$ 57,619
300. CASH AT SETTLEMENT FROM/TO BORROWER		*600. CASH AT SETTLEMENT TO/FROM SELLER*	
301. Gross amount due from borrower *(line 120)*	$126,822	601. Gross amount due to seller *(line 420)*	$123,310
302. Less amounts paid by/for borrower *(line 220)*	(94,190)	602. Less reductions in amount due seller *(line 520)*	(57,619)
303. CASH (☑ FROM)/(☐ TO) BORROWER	$ 32,632	603. CASH (☑ TO)/(☐ FROM) SELLER	$ 65,691

(continued)

Lines 1101, 1105, and 1106 show the settlement (closing fee), and the document preparation fee associated with this closing. Title insurance charges of $400 to the seller for the owner's policy and $90 to the buyer for the lender's policy are itemized on line 1108. Lines 1109 and 1110 show the coverage for each. The amounts paid from settlement funds to the attorneys of the buyer and seller are listed on lines 1111 and 1112 ($90,000 and $123,000 respectively). Note that the buyer and seller can

FIGURE 15.3
Continued.

L. SETTLEMENT CHARGES		PAID FROM BORROWER'S FUNDS AT SETTLEMENT	PAID FROM SELLER'S FUNDS AT SETTLEMENT
700. TOTAL SALES/BROKER'S COMMISSION based on price $ 123,000 @ 6 % = $7380			
Division of Commission (line 700) as follows:			
701. $ 3,690 to List-Rite Realty			
702. $ 3,690 to Quick-Sale Realty			
703. Commission paid at Settlement			$7,380
704.			
800. ITEMS PAYABLE IN CONNECTION WITH LOAN			
801. Loan Origination Fee %		$ 900	
802. Loan Discount %			
803. Appraisal Fee to		100	
804. Credit Report to		25	
805. Lender's Inspection Fee			
806. Mortgage Insurance Application Fee to			
807. Assumption Fee			
808.			
809.			
810.			
811.			
900. ITEMS REQUIRED BY LENDER TO BE PAID IN ADVANCE			
901. Interest from Sept 15 to Sept 30 @ $ 24.00 /day		360	
902. Mortgage Insurance Premium for months to			
903. Hazard Insurance Premium for years to			
904. years to			
905.			
1000. RESERVES DEPOSITED WITH LENDER			
1001. Hazard insurance 4 months @ $ 20 per month		80	
1002. Mortgage insurance months @ $ per month			
1003. City property taxes months @ $ per month			
1004. County property taxes 12 months @ $ 140 per month		1,680	
1005. Annual assessments months @ $ per month			
1006. months @ $ per month			
1007. months @ $ per month			
1008. months @ $ per month			
1100. TITLE CHARGES			
1101. Settlement or closing fee to Acme National Bank		110	110
1102. Abstract or title search to			
1103. Title examination to			
1104. Title insurance binder to			
1105. Document preparation to Acme National Bank			10
1106. Notary fees to Acme National Bank		2	2
1107. Attorney's fees to			
(includes above items numbers;			
1108. Title insurance to Safety Title Insurance Company		90	400
(includes above items numbers;			
1109. Lender's coverage $ 90,000			
1110. Owner's coverage $ 123,000			
1111. Buyer's attorney		150	
1112. Seller's attorney			120
1113.			
1200. GOVERNMENT RECORDING AND TRANSFER CHARGES			
1201. Recording fees: Deed $ 5 ; Mortgage $ 10 ; Releases $ 5		15	5
1202. City/county tax/stamps: Deed $; Mortgage $			
1203. State tax/stamps: Deed $ 123 ; Mortgage $			123
1204.			
1205.			
1300. ADDITIONAL SETTLEMENT CHARGES			
1301. Survey to			
1302. Pest inspection to Dead-Bug Pest Company			39
1303.			
1304.			
1305.			
1400. TOTAL SETTLEMENT CHARGES (enter on lines 103, Section J and 502, Section K)		$3,512	$8,189

choose to pay their attorneys outside of the closing. **Outside of the closing** or **outside of escrow** means a party to the closing has paid someone directly and not through the closing agent.

Government recording fees and conveyance taxes necessary to complete this transaction are itemized on lines 1201 and 1203 and are charged to the buyer and seller as shown. On line 1302 the settlement agent pays the pest inspection company $39 on behalf of the seller. This is another item that is sometimes paid outside of the closing, that is, the seller can write a check directly to the termite company once the inspection has been made. On line 1400, the totals for both the buyer (borrower) and seller are entered. The same totals ($3,512 and $8,189) are transferred to page 1 or obverse of the settlement statement on lines 103 and 502 respectively.

Note that Figure 15.3 shows both the buyer's side of the transaction and the seller's side. In actual practice, the seller will receive this settlement statement with lines 101 through 303 (Section J) blacked out, and the buyer will receive this statement with lines 401 through 603 (Section K) blacked out.

REAL ESTATE SETTLEMENT PROCEDURES ACT

In response to consumer complaints regarding real estate closing costs and procedures, Congress passed the Real Estate Settlement Procedures Act (RESPA) effective June 20, 1975 throughout the United States. The purpose of RESPA, which is administered by the U.S. Department of Housing and Urban Development (HUD), is to regulate and standardize real estate settlement practices when "federally related" first mortgage loans are made on one- to four-family residences, condominiums, and cooperatives. RESPA now also applies to closings involving subordinate liens and refinancings. Federally related is defined to include FHA or VA or other government-backed or assisted loans, loans from lenders with federally insured deposits, loans that are to be purchased by FNMA, GNMA, FHLMC, or other federally controlled secondary mortgage market institutions, and loans made by lenders who make or invest more than $1 million per year in residential loans. As the bulk of all home loans now made fall into one of these categories, the impact of this law is far-reaching.

Restrictions

RESPA prohibits kickbacks and fees for services not performed during the closing process. For example, in some regions of the United States prior to this act, it was common practice for attorneys and closing agents to channel title business to certain title companies in return for a fee. This increased settlement costs without adding services. Now there must be a justifiable service rendered for each closing fee charge. The act also prohibits the seller from requiring that the buyer purchase title insurance from a particular title company. RESPA underwent major revisions in 1996. You might recall the discussion in Chapter 11 as to how disclosures must now be made for business referrals and origination fees.

The Real Estate Settlement Procedures Act also contains restrictions on the amount of advance property tax and insurance payments a lender can collect and place in an impound or reserve account. The amount is limited to the property owner's share of taxes and insurance accrued prior to settlement, plus one-sixth of the estimated amount that will come due for these items in the twelve-month period beginning at settlement. This requirement assures that the lender has an adequate but not excessive amount of money impounded when taxes and insurance payments fall due. If the amount in the reserve account is not sufficient to pay an item when it comes due, the lender must temporarily use its own funds to make up the difference. Then the lender bills the borrower or increases the monthly reserve payment. If there is a drop in the amount the lender must pay out, then the monthly reserve requirement can be reduced.

Considerable criticism and debate have raged over the topic of reserves. Traditionally, lenders have not been required to pay interest to borrowers on money held as reserves, effectively creating an interest-free loan to themselves. This, in turn, tempted many lenders to require overly adequate reserves. HUD's RESPA sets a reasonable limit on reserve requirements, and some states now require that interest be paid on reserves. Although not always required to do so, some lenders now voluntarily pay interest on reserves.

Benefits

To the typical home buyer who is applying for a first mortgage loan the most obvious benefits of RESPA are that (1) the borrower will receive from the lender a special HUD information booklet explaining RESPA, (2) the borrower will receive a good faith estimate of closing costs from the lender, (3) the lender will use the HUD Uniform Settlement Statement, and (4) the buyer as borrower has the right to inspect the Uniform Settlement Statement one business day before the day of closing.

The primary reason lenders are required to promptly give loan applicants an estimate of closing costs is to allow the loan applicant an opportunity to compare prices for the various services the transaction will require. Additionally, these estimates help the borrower calculate how much the total closing costs will be. Figure 15.4

FIGURE 15.4
Good faith estimate.

GOOD FAITH ESTIMATE OF CLOSING COSTS

The charges listed below are our Good Faith Estimate of some of the settlement charges you will need to pay at settlement of the loan for which you have applied. These charges will be paid to the title or escrow company that conducts the settlement. This form does not cover all items you will be required to pay in cash at settlement, for example, deposit in escrow for real estate taxes and insurance. You may wish to inquire as to the amounts of such other items. You may be required to pay other additional amounts at settlement. This is not a commitment to make a loan.

SERVICES		ESTIMATED FEES
801. Loan Origination Fee _____ % + $ _____		$
802. Loan Discount		$
803. Appraisal Fee		$
804. Credit Report		$
806. Mortgage Insurance Application Fee		$
807. Assumption Fee		$
808. Tax Service Fee		$
901. Interest		$
902. Mortgage Insurance Premium		$
1101. Settlement or Closing Fee		$
1106. Notary Fees		$
1109. Title Insurance, Lender's Coverage	List only those items borrower will pay	$
1109. Title Insurance, Owner's Coverage		$
1201. Recording Fees		$
1202. County Tax/Stamps		$
1203. City Tax/ Stamps		$
1302. Pest Inspection		$
1303. Building Inspection		$
These numbers correspond to the HUD Settlement Statement	TOTAL	$

illustrates a good faith estimate form. Note that it is primarily concerned with settlement services.

RESPA does not require estimates of escrow impounds for property taxes and insurance, although the lender can voluntarily add these items to the form. Note also that RESPA allows lenders to make estimates in terms of ranges. For example, escrow fees may be stated as $150 to $175 to reflect the range of rates being charged by local escrow companies for that service.

HUD SETTLEMENT STATEMENT

The HUD Settlement Statement you saw in Figure 15.3 is required of all federally related real estate lenders. There is also a new form, HUD-1A, that is widely used. Because it is actually a lender requirement, it uses the word *borrower* instead of *buyer*. However, if the loan is in connection with a sale, and most are, the buyer and the borrower are one and the same person. This is not true when an owner is refinancing a property, however.

The HUD Settlement Statement has become so widely accepted that it is now used even when it is not required. Closing agents who handle high volumes of closings use computers with special HUD Settlement Statement programs to fill out these forms. Typically, the closing agent types the numbers onto a video screen and a tractor-fed printer with continuous-feed HUD forms takes over the rest of the typing task.

REVIEW QUESTIONS

Answers to these questions are found in the Answer Key section at the back of the book.

1. Details that must be handled between the time a purchase contract is signed and the closing typically include
   A. title search.
   B. deed preparation.
   C. loan arrangements.
   D. checking the property taxes.
   E. All of the above.

2. A buyer's walk-through is conducted for the purpose of
   A. appraising the property in order to get a loan on it.
   B. inspecting the property for major structural defects.
   C. meeting the seller and obtaining the keys to the property.
   D. making a final inspection just prior to closing.

3. At which of the following are the buyer and seller more likely to shake hands upon completing the real estate transaction?
   A. Escrow closing.
   B. Settlement meeting.

4. A settlement meeting may take place in the offices of
   A. the real estate agent.
   B. an attorney.
   C. a title company.
   D. a lender's office.
   E. All of the above.

5. When a real estate settlement is held in escrow,
   A. there is no closing meeting.
   B. the closing process may be conducted by mail.
   C. Both A and B.
   D. Neither A nor B.

6. The purpose of a settlement statement is to
   A. provide an accounting of all funds involved in the transaction.
   B. identify all parties who receive funds from the transaction.
   C. Both A and B.
   D. Neither A nor B.

7. Rents in Texas are customarily prorated on the basis of
   A. 30-day months.
   B. the actual number of days in the month.
   C. a 360-day year.
   D. None of the above.

8. Which of the following may serve as an escrow agent?
   A. A title company.
   B. A bank.
   C. An independent escrow company.
   D. All of the above.

9. Barnes sold his home to Hyatt through broker Quinn. The sale is to be settled through escrow. The escrow agent would be selected by
   A. Barnes.
   B. Hyatt.
   C. Quinn.
   D. Mutual agreement between Barnes and Hyatt.

10. In Texas, when title transfers are handled in escrow by a title company, the escrow agent must be
    A. bonded.
    B. licensed.
    C. Both A and B.
    D. Neither A nor B.

11. In an escrow closing, funds are disbursed
    A. when all escrow papers have been signed.
    B. as soon as the buyer brings his money in.
    C. after necessary recordings take place.
    D. None of the above.

12. In an escrow closing, the escrow agent serves as agent for
    A. the buyer.
    B. the seller.
    C. Both A and B.
    D. Neither A nor B.

13. One advantage of the escrow closing method is that it can eliminate
    A. personal confrontation between buyer and seller
    B. the need for an attorney.
    C. Both A and B.
    D. Neither A nor B.

14. In addition to the closing of sales of real property through standard purchase agreements, escrows can be used when a
    A. property is being refinanced.
    B. mortgage loan is being paid off.
    C. property is being sold under an installment contract.
    D. All of the above.

15. RESPA
    A. prohibits the seller from requiring that the buyer purchase title insurance from a particular title company.
    B. requires that each settlement fee charged be for a justifiable service rendered.
    C. Both A and B.
    D. Neither A nor B.

16. When a home is sold and a new loan by an institutional lender is required to complete the transaction, the typical time between purchase contract signing and settlement will most likely be
    A. 0–29 days.
    B. 30–60 days.
    C. 61–120 days.
    D. over 120 days.

17. Which of the following statements is true?
    A. The buyer always pays for the day of closing in Texas.
    B. Local law prohibits negotiation of the proration date.
    C. Special assessments are part of the tax proration in Texas.
    D. In Texas, the seller usually pays for the day of closing.

18. Prorations of items in a real estate closing are made usually as of the date of
    A. signing of the sales contract.
    B. title transfer.
    C. buyers' walk-through.
    D. the mortgage payment.

19. In a typical closing, insurance prorations will usually be
    A. a credit to the seller and an expense to the buyer.
    B. a credit to the buyer and an expense to the seller.
    C. a credit to the seller and a credit to the buyer.
    D. an expense to the buyer and an expense to the seller.

20. Under the provisions of RESPA,
    A. the buyer must be given an estimate of closing charges and costs in advance of closing.
    B. payments outside of escrow are prohibited.
    C. Both A and B.
    D. Neither A nor B.

CHAPTER 16

KEY TERMS

Escalation clause: provision in a lease for upward and downward rent adjustments

Ground rent: rent paid to occupy a plot of land

Lessee: the tenant

Lessor: the landlord

Option clause: the right at some future time to purchase or lease a property at a predetermined price

Quiet enjoyment: the right of possession and use of property without undue disturbance by others

Reversionary interest: the right to retake possession of a leased property at some future time

Sublease: a lease that is given by a lessee

Sublessee: a lessee who rents from another lessee

Sublessor: a lessee who rents to another lessee

Real Estate Leases

IN THIS CHAPTER *In this chapter you will look at leases from the standpoint of the tenant, owner, and property manager. First, we will cover some of the important terminology and explain a sample lease. Landlord-tenant laws, Statute of Frauds, setting rents, ground leases, lease termination, fair housing laws, and rent controls are also covered in this chapter. Specific terminology and concepts covered include assignment and subletting.*

Earlier chapters of this book discussed leases as estates in land (Chapter 3) and as a means of financing (Chapter 12). This chapter looks at leases from the standpoint of the tenant, the property owner, and the property manager. (During your lifetime you may be in any one of these roles, and perhaps all three.) Our discussion begins with some important terminology. Then comes a sample lease form with explanation, information on locating, qualifying, and keeping tenants and finally, some information on job opportunities available in professional property management. Emphasis is on residential property, although a number of key points regarding commercial property leases are also included.

THE LEASEHOLD ESTATE

A lease conveys to the **lessee** (tenant) the right to possess and use another's property for a period of time. During this time, the **lessor** (the landlord or fee owner) possesses a **reversion** that entitles the landlord to retake possession at the end of the lease period. This is also called a **reversionary right** or **reversionary interest.**

The tenant's right to occupy land is called a leasehold estate. There are four categories of leasehold estates: estate for years, periodic estate, estate at will, and tenancy at sufferance. An **estate for years** must have a specific starting time and a specific ending time. It can be for any length of time, and it does not automatically renew itself. A **periodic estate** has an original lease period of fixed length that continually renews itself for like periods of time until the tenant or landlord acts to terminate it. A month-to-month lease is an example. In an **estate at will** all the normal landlord-tenant rights and duties exist except that the estate can be terminated by either party at any time. A **tenancy at sufferance** occurs when a tenant stays beyond the legal tenancy without the consent of the landlord. The tenant is commonly called a **holdover tenant** and no advance notice is required for eviction. The holdover tenant differs from a trespasser in that his original entry onto the property was legal.

CREATING A VALID LEASE

A lease is both a conveyance and a contract. As a conveyance it transfers or conveys rights of possession to the tenant in the form of a leasehold estate. As a contract it establishes legally enforceable provisions for the payment of rent and any other obligations the landlord and tenant have to each other.

For a valid lease to exist, it must meet the usual requirements of a contract as described in Chapter 7. That is to say, the parties involved must be legally competent, and there must be mutual agreement, lawful objective, and sufficient consideration. The main elements of a lease are (1) the names of the lessee and lessor, (2) a description of the premises, (3) an agreement to convey (let) the premises by the lessor and to accept possession by the lessee, (4) provisions for the payment of rent, (5) the starting date and duration of the lease, and (6) signatures of the parties to the lease.

Statute of Frauds

The **Statute of Frauds** in Texas provides that a lease of real estate for a term that cannot be performed within one year must be in writing. This implies that a lease of one year or less need not be in writing to be enforceable.

PUTTING IT TO WORK

A lease for one year or less or a month-to-month lease could be oral and still be valid, but as a matter of good business practice, all leases should be written and signed. This gives all parties a written reminder of their obligations under the lease and reduces chances for dispute. A real estate practitioner should remember, however, that there is no promulgated form for a lease. An agent should not use another lease form without seeking legal assistance.

THE LEASE DOCUMENT

Figure 16.1 illustrates a lease document that contains provisions typically found in a residential lease. These provisions are presented in simplified language to help you more easily grasp the rights and responsibilities created by a lease.

Conveyance

The first paragraph is the conveyance portion of the lease. At **[1]** and **[2]** the lessor and lessee are identified. At **[3]**, the lessor conveys to the lessee and the lessee accepts the property. A description of the property follows at **[4]**, and the **term** of the conveyance at **[5]**. The property must be described so that there is no question as to the extent of the premises the lessee is renting. If the lease illustrated here were a month-to-month lease instead, the term of the lease would be changed to read, "commencing April 15, 19xx and continuing on a month-to-month basis until terminated by either the lessee or the lessor." During the tenancy the lessee is entitled to **quiet enjoyment** of the property. This means uninterrupted use of the property without interference from the owner, lessor, or other third party.

A month-to-month rental is the most flexible arrangement. It allows the owner to recover possession of the property on one-month notice and the tenant to leave on one-month notice with no further obligation to the owner. In rental agreements for longer

FIGURE 16.1
Lease document.

LEASE

This lease agreement is entered into the 10th day of April , 19 xx between John and Sally Land-lord **[1]** *(hereinafter called the Lessor) and Gary and Barbara Tenant* **[2]** *(hereinafter called the Lessee). The Lessor hereby leases to the Lessee* **[3]** *and the Lessee hereby leases from the Lessor the premises known as Apartment 24, 1234 Maple St., City, State* **[4]** *for the term of one* **[5]** *year beginning 12:00 noon on April 15, 19xx and ending 12:00 noon on April 15, 19xx unless sooner terminated as herein set forth.*

    The rent for the term of this lease is $ 6,000.00 **[6]** *payable in equal monthly installments of $ 500.00* **[7]** *on the 15th day of each month beginning on April 15, 19xx . Receipt of the first monthly installment and $ 500.00* **[8]** *as a security, damage, and clean-up deposit is hereby acknowledged. It is furthermore agreed that:*

[9] *The use of the premises shall be as a residential dwelling for the above named Lessee only.*

[10] *The Lessee may not assign this lease or sublet any portion of the premises without written permission from the Lessor.*

[11] *The Lessee agrees to abide by the house rules as posted. A current copy is attached to this lease.*

[12] *The Lessor shall furnish water, sewer, and heat as part of the rent. Electricity and telephone shall be paid for by the Lessee.*

[13] *The Lessor agrees to keep the premises structure maintained and in habitable condition.*

[14] *The Lessee agrees to maintain the interior of said premises and at the termination of this lease to return said premises to the Lessor in as good condition as it is now except for ordinary wear and tear.*

[15] *The Lessee shall not make any alterations or improvements to the premises without the Lessor's prior written consent. Any alterations or improvements become the property of the Lessor at the end of this lease.*

[16] *If the premises are not ready for occupancy on the date herein provided, the Lessee may cancel this agreement and the Lessor shall return in full all money paid by the Lessee.*

[17] *If the Lessee defaults on this lease agreement, the Lessor may give the Lessee three days notice of intention to terminate the lease. At the end of those three days the lease shall terminate and the Lessee shall vacate and surrender the premises to the Lessor.*

[18] *If the Lessee holds over after the expiration of this lease without the Lessor's consent, the tenancy shall be month to month at twice the monthly rate indicated herein.*

[19] *If the premises are destroyed or rendered uninhabitable by fire or other cause, this lease shall terminate as of the date of the casualty.*

[20] *The Lessor shall have access to the premises for the purpose of inspecting for damage, making repairs, and showing to prospective tenants or buyers.*

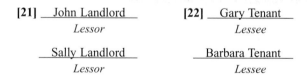

[21] John Landlord	**[22]** Gary Tenant
Lessor	*Lessee*
Sally Landlord	Barbara Tenant
Lessor	*Lessee*

periods of time, each party gives up some flexibility to gain commitment from the other. Under a one-year lease, a tenant has the property committed to him for a year. This means that the tenant is committed to paying rent for a full year, even though the tenant may want to move out before the year is over. Similarly, the owner has the tenant's commitment to pay rent for a year, but loses the flexibility of being able to regain possession of the property until the year is over.

    The balance of the lease document is concerned with contract aspects of the lease. At number **[6]**, the amount of rent that the lessee will pay for the use of the property is set forth. In a lease for years it is the usual practice to state the total rent for the entire lease period. This is the total number of dollars the lessee is obligated to pay to the lessor. If the lessee wants to leave the premises before the lease period expires, there is still liability for the full amount of the contract. The method of payment of the obligation is shown at number **[7]**. Unless the contract calls for rent to be paid in advance, under common law it is not due until the end of the rental period. At number **[8]**, the lessor has taken a deposit in the form of the first monthly installment and acknowledges receipt of it. The lessor has also taken additional money as security against the possibility of uncollected rent or damage to the premises and for clean-up expenses. (The tenant is supposed to leave the premises clean.) The deposit is refunded, less legitimate charges, when the tenant leaves.

Items **[9]** through **[20]** summarize commonly found lease clauses. At **[9]** and **[10]**, the lessor wants to maintain control over the use and occupancy of the premises. Without this the lessor might find the premises used for an entirely different purpose by people to whom the lessor did not rent. At **[11]**, the tenant agrees to abide by the house rules. These normally cover such things as use of laundry and trash facilities, swimming pool rules, noise rules, etc. Number **[12]** states the responsibility of the lessee and lessor with regard to the payment of utilities.

The strict legal interpretation of a lease as a conveyance means the lessee is responsible for upkeep and repairs during the tenancy unless the lessor promises to do so in the lease contract. The paragraph at number **[13]** is that promise. Note however that with regard to residential properties, Texas courts and the Texas legislature now take the position that the landlord is obligated to keep a residential property repaired and habitable even if this is not specifically stated in the contract. Commercial property still goes by the traditional lease interpretation.

Number **[14]** is the lessee's promise to maintain the interior of the dwelling. If the lessee damages the property, that individual is to repair it. Normal wear and tear are considered to be part of the rent. At paragraph **[15]**, the lessor protects against unauthorized alterations and improvements and then goes on to point out that anything the tenant affixes to the building becomes realty. As realty it remains a part of the building when the tenant leaves.

Paragraphs **[16]** through **[19]** deal with the rights of both parties if the premises are not ready for occupancy, if the lessee defaults after moving in, if the lessee holds over, or if the premises are destroyed. The lessor also retains the right (paragraph **[20]**) to enter the leased premises from time to time for business purposes.

Finally, at **[21]** and **[22]**, the lessor and lessee sign. It is not necessary to have these signatures notarized. That is done only if the lease is to be recorded. The purpose of recording is to give constructive notice that the lessee has an estate in the property. Recording is usually done only when the lessee's rights are not apparent from inspection of the property for actual notice or where the lease is to run many years. From the property owner's standpoint, the lease is an encumbrance on the property. If the owner should subsequently sell the property or mortgage it, the lessee's tenancy remains undisturbed. The buyer or lender must accept the property subject to the lease.

If one of the lessors dies, the lease is still binding on the remaining lessor(s) and upon the estate of the deceased lessor. Similarly, if one of the lessees dies, the lease is still binding on the remaining lessee(s) and upon the estate of the deceased lessee. This is based on common law doctrine that applies to contracts in general. The lessee and lessor can, however, agree to do otherwise. The lessee could ask the lessor to **waive** (give up) the right to hold the lessee's estate to the lease in the event of the lessee's death. For example, an elderly tenant about to sign a lease might want to add wording to the lease whereby the tenant's death would allow the estate to terminate the lease early.

LANDLORD–TENANT LAWS

Traditionally, a lease was enforceable in court based solely on what it contained. This philosophy still prevails with regard to leases on commercial property. However, with regard to residential rental property, the trend today is for the legislature to establish special landlord-tenant laws. The intent is to strike a reasonable balance between the responsibilities of landlords to tenants and vice versa. Typically, these laws limit the amount of security deposit a landlord can require, tell the tenant how many days' notice need to be given before vacating a periodic tenancy, and require the landlord to deliver possession on the date agreed. The landlord must maintain the premises in a fit condition for living, and the tenant is to keep the unit clean and not damage it. The tenant is to obey the house rules and the landlord must give advance notice before entering an apartment except in legitimate emergencies. Additionally the laws set forth such things as the procedure for accounting for any deposit money not returned, the right of the tenant to make needed repairs and bill the landlord, the right of the landlord to file court actions for unpaid rent, and the proper procedure for evicting a tenant.

Since 1967, a number of statutes have been passed to provide protection to the tenant in residential leasehold situations.

These laws, very generally summarized, specify:

1. **Notice must be provided before a tenancy may be terminated.** This is generally 30 days on a month-to-month tenancy. This does not apply to eviction proceedings, but rather to termination of tenancies.

2. **Interruption and exclusion by the landlord of the tenant's right to the premises.** This basically provides that the landlord may not exclude the tenant from the premises, but may only change the door locks to the tenant's premises, after proper notice is given. If the landlord does change the door locks to the tenant's premises, a written notice must be posted on the tenant's door indicating that the tenant may pick up the new key to the premises at any time upon request, 24 hours a day. The tenant can also exercise a right to re-enter, under certain circumstances, by filing a sworn affidavit. In a commercial tenancy, the landlord has the right to demand rent prior to providing the key.

3. **Landlord's lien for rent.** However, the exemptions provided under this statute are very extensive and ultimately allow very little of the furniture and household goods as those on which the landlord may obtain a lien as security for his rent.

4. **Security deposits.** There are very strict provisions now for the landlord's retaining security deposits. Basically, the landlord must return the security deposit within 30 days or give the tenant an explanation of why the security deposit was not returned and what the funds were used to repair. There are some strict provisions for the landlord's failure to comply with the statute.

5. **Habitable premises.** The landlord must provide habitable premises and may not evict a tenant for the purposes of retaliation for tenant's notice to repair the premises. The term habitable is determined by the facts in any given situation and varies from case to case.

6. **Installation of security devices.** The landlord has an obligation, upon request of tenant, to install security devices. The law defines security devices as window latches, deadbolt locks, pen locks, and night latches. The initial installation of these devices must be at the landlord's expense. Any installation of additional security devices will be at the tenant's expense. There is also a time limit for the landlord's responses for repairs to the security devices.

7. **Disclosure of ownership and management of dwelling unit.** The landlord has the duty to disclose to the tenant the name and address of the owner of the dwelling unit in the manner specified in the statute. The same is true of the name and address of any property management company that is currently managing the dwelling unit.

8. **Smoke detectors in dwelling units.** At least one smoke detector must be installed in dwelling units by the landlord outside of each separate bedroom in the immediate vicinity of the bedroom, with certain specified exceptions.

9. **Occupying limits.** There is now a maximum limit of three adults per bedroom.

Note that these statutes apply to *all* landlord-tenant residential situations. Even when the TREC-promulgated leases are used, these rights (except for the security device requirements) exist, *regardless of the term of the tenancy* .

Methods for Setting Rents

There are several methods for setting rents. The first is the **fixed rental fee,** also called a **flat rent** or **gross lease.** The tenant agrees to pay a specified amount of money for the use of the premises. A tenant paying $600 per month on a month-to-month apartment lease or a dentist paying $13,000 per year for office space are both examples of fixed rents. A second method of setting rents is called the **step-up** or **graduated rental.** For example, a five-year office lease might call for monthly rents of 85¢ per square foot of floor space the first year, 89¢ the second year, 95¢ the third year, $1.00 the fourth year, and $1.05 the fifth.

Because of inflation, most lessors (particularly in office buildings) add an **escalation clause.** This allows the landlord to pass along to the tenant increases in such items as property taxes, utility charges, or janitorial fees.

Another variation is to have the tenant pay for all property taxes, insurance, repairs, utilities, etc., in addition to the base rent. This arrangement is called a **net lease** (since the tenant pays all expenses, the rent is *net* to the landlord), and it is commonly used when an entire building is being leased.

Another system for setting rents is the **percentage basis** wherein the owner receives a percentage of the tenant's gross receipts as rent. For example, a farmer who leases land may give the landowner 20% of the value of the crop when it is sold. The monthly rent for a small hardware store might be $600 plus 6% of gross sales above $10,000. A supermarket may pay $7,500 plus $1\frac{1}{2}\%$ of gross above $50,000 per month. By setting rents this way, the tenant shares some of the business risk with the property owner. Also, there is a built-in inflation hedge to the extent that inflation causes the tenant's receipts to increase.

Option Clauses

Option clauses give the tenant the right at some future time to lease the property at a predetermined price. This gives a tenant flexibility. For example, suppose that a prospective tenant is starting a new business and is not certain how successful it will be. Thus, in looking for space to rent, the prospective tenant will want a lease that allows an "out" if the new venture does not succeed but will permit staying if the venture is successful. The solution is a lease with options. The landlord could offer a one-year lease, plus an option to stay for two more years at a higher rent plus a second option for an additional five years at a still higher rent. If the venture is not successful, the tenant is obligated for only one year. But if successful, he has the option of staying two more years, and if still successful, for five years after that.

Another option possibility offers the tenant a lease that also contains an option to buy the property for a fixed period of time at a preset price. This is called a **lease with option to buy** and is discussed in Chapter 8.

Assignment and Subletting

In Texas, the tenant may not assign the lease or sublet the premises without the landlord's prior written consent unless provision was made in the lease contract. An **assignment** is the total transfer of the tenant's rights to another person. These parties are referred to as the **assignor** and the **assignee** respectively. The assignee acquires all the right, title, and interest of the assignor, no more and no less. However, the assignor remains liable for the performance of the contract unless release is given by the landlord. To **sublet** means to transfer only a portion of the rights held under a lease. The sublease thereby created may be for a portion of the premises or for part of the lease term. The party acquiring those rights is called the **sublessee.** The original lessee is the **sublessor** with respect to the sublessee. The sublessee pays rent to the lessee who in turn remains liable to the landlord for rent on the entire premises.

GROUND LEASE

A **ground lease** is a lease of land alone. The lessor is the fee simple owner of the land and conveys to the lessee an estate for years, typically lasting from 25 to 99 years. The lessee pays for and owns the improvements. Thus a ground lease separates the ownership of land from the ownership of buildings on that land. The lease rent, called the **ground rent,** is on a net lease basis. As a hedge against inflation, the rent is usually increased every 5 to 10 years. This is done either by a graduated lease or by requiring a reappraisal of the land and then by charging a new rent based on that valuation.

A lease need not be restricted to the use of the earth's surface. In Chapter 2 it was shown that land extends from the center of the earth skyward. Consequently, it is possible for one person to own the mineral rights, another the surface rights, and a third the air rights. This can also be done with leases. A landowner can lease to an oil company the right to explore and extract minerals, oil, and gas below the land and, at the same time, lease the surface rights to a farmer. In Chicago and New York City railroads have leased surface and air rights above their downtown tracks for the purpose of constructing office buildings.

CONTRACT RENT, ECONOMIC RENT

The amount specified in the lease is the rent that the tenant must pay the landlord for the use of the premises and is called the **contract rent.** The rent which the same property can command in the competitive open market is called the **economic rent.** When a lease contract is negotiated, the contract rent and economic rent are nearly always the same. However, as time passes the market value of the right to use the premises may increase while the contract rent stays the same. When this occurs the lease itself becomes valuable. That value is determined by the difference between the contract rent and the economic rent, and how long the lease has to run. An example would be a 5 year lease with 3 years left at a contract rent of $900 per month where the current rental value of the premises is now $1,200 per month. If the lease is assignable, the fact that it offers a $300 per month savings for 3 years makes it valuable. Similarly, an oil lease obtained for $50 per acre before oil was discovered might be worth millions after its discovery. Conversely, when contract rent exceeds economic rent, the lease takes on a negative value.

LEASE TERMINATION

Most leases terminate because of the expiration of the term of the lease. The tenant has received the use of the premises and the landlord has received rent in return. However, a lease can be terminated if the landlord and the tenant mutually agree. The tenant surrenders the premises and the landlord releases him from the contract. Under certain conditions, destruction of the premises is cause for lease termination. Abandonment of the premises by the tenant can be grounds for lease termination provided the tenant's intention to do so is clear.

If either the tenant or the landlord fails to live up to the lease contract, termination can occur. Where the tenant is at fault, the landlord can evict him and recover possession of the premises. If the premises are unfit for occupancy, the tenant can claim constructive **eviction** as the reason for leaving. The government, under its right of eminent domain, can also terminate a lease, but must provide just compensation. An example of this would be construction of a new highway that requires the demolition of a building rented to tenants. The property owner and the tenants would both be entitled to compensation.

A mortgage foreclosure can also bring about lease termination. It all depends on priority. If the mortgage was recorded before the lease was signed, then foreclosure of the mortgage also forecloses the lease. If the lease was recorded first, then the lease still stands. Because a lease can cloud a lender's title, wording is sometimes inserted in leases that makes them subordinate to any future financing of the property. This is a highly technical, but nonetheless very significant matter for long-term shopping center, office building, and industrial leases.

Eviction Process

Under Texas law, the Forcible Entry and Detainer statutes provide for eviction proceedings. "Forcible Entry and Detainer" is a legal term referring to a tenant who takes possession of the premises without the consent of the landlord and then refuses to give up possession after demand is made by the landlord. According to the statutes, the landlord must give the tenant a minimum of three days' written notice to vacate the premises before filing an action for Forcible Entry and Detainer. A person cannot be guilty of Forcible Entry and Detainer until he has been so adjudged by the Justice of the Peace Court in the precinct where the real estate is situated. The lawsuit must be heard within ten days after the filing. As in all other legal proceedings, there are additional procedural laws pertaining to the Forcible Entry and Detainer statutes, which could provide for quite a lengthy tenancy while eviction proceedings are in process.

REVIEW QUESTIONS

Answers to these questions are found in the Answer Key section at the back of the book.

1. A lease for a definite period of time, which terminates when that time has expired, is an estate
   A. for years.
   B. periodic estate.
   C. at will.
   D. at sufferance.

2. A lease of fixed length that continually renews itself for the like periods of time until the lessor or lessee acts to terminate it is
   A. a holdover estate.
   B. a periodic estate.
   C. an estate at will.
   D. an estate at sufferance.

3. A lease is a
   A. conveyance.
   B. contract.
   C. Both A and B.
   D. Neither A nor B.

4. To be valid, which of the following must be in writing and signed?
   A. A month-to-month lease.
   B. A 14-month lease.
   C. A three-month lease.
   D. All of the above.

5. The right of the lessee to uninterrupted use of the leased premises is called
   A. quiet possession.
   B. quiet enjoyment.
   C. quiet rights.
   D. tenant rights.

6. A written lease agreement is still legal even though it fails to include
   A. the terms of the lease.
   B. a property description.
   C. Both A and B.
   D. Neither A not B.

7. As compared to a lease for years, a month-to-month lease gives flexibility to the
   A. landlord.
   B. tenant.
   C. Both A and B.
   D. Neither A nor B.

8. Bob Short and Bill Tall rent an apartment unit from owner Haf High. Bill dies during the lease term. The lease is still binding upon
   A. Bob.
   B. Haf.
   C. Bill's estate.
   D. All of the above.

9. The word "waive" means to
   A. say "goodbye."
   B. demand.
   C. relinquish.
   D. die naturally.

10. A lease that calls for specified rental increases at predetermined intervals is known as a
    A. step-up lease.
    B. graduated lease.
    C. Both A and B.
    D. Neither A nor B.

11. The clause in a lease that allows the landlord to pass along to the tenant certain increases in operating expenses is called
    A. an escalator clause.
    B. a participation clause.
    C. Both A and B.
    D. Neither A nor B.

12. When the tenant pays a base rent plus some or all of the operating expenses of a property, the result is a
    A. gross lease.
    B. net lease.
    C. percentage lease.
    D. graduated lease.

13. A lease in which the tenant pays a rent based upon the gross sales made from the rented premises is known as a
    A. percentage lease.
    B. participation lease.
    C. net lease.
    D. gross lease.

14. Which of the following is NOT specifically designed to protect against rising operating costs?
    A. A net lease.
    B. An escalator clause.
    C. An index clause.
    D. A gross lease.

15. A lease for years may be terminated by
    A. constructive eviction.
    B. eminent domain.
    C. mutual agreement.
    D. actual eviction.
    E. All of the above.

16. A written lease agreement is still legal even though it fails to include
    A. the amount of rent to be paid.
    B. a security deposit.
    C. Both A and B.
    D. Neither A nor B.

17. Flint leased a building to Newton under an agreement that gave Newton the right to occupy the premises for two years, with an option to renew for an additional one-year period. In order to be enforceable, must this lease be in writing and signed by both Flint and Newton?
    A. Yes, because all contracts dealing with real property must be in writing in order to be enforceable.
    B. Yes, because the lease is for a period of time in excess of one year.
    C. No, because oral leases for five years or less are enforceable.
    D. No, because a 2-year oral lease is enforceable.

18. Under the Forcible Entry and Detainer statutes in Texas, the landlord must give the tenant
    A. 3 days written notice to vacate the premises.
    B. 3 days notice to vacate the premises.
    C. 10 days written notice to vacate the premises.
    D. 10 days written or oral notice to vacate the premises.

19. The best defense against losses from uncollected rent is
    A. a threat of legal action against the delinquent tenant.
    B. careful tenant selection, good service, and a businesslike policy on rent collections.

20. Regarding residential rentals, Texas courts and the Texas legislature now take the position that
    A. the landlord and tenant are jointly responsible for all repairs.
    B. without a contract, the tenant is responsible for repairs.
    C. without a contract, the landlord is obligated to keep the property repaired.
    D. without a contract, the cost of repairs must be negotiated.

KEY TERMS

Appraise: to estimate the value of something

Capitalize: to convert future income to current value

Comparables: properties similar to the subject property that have sold recently

Cost approach: land value plus current construction costs minus depreciation

Depreciation: loss in value due to deterioration and obsolescence

FIRREA: the Financial Institution's Reform, Recovery, and Enforcement Act of 1989

Gross rent multiplier (GRM): a number that is multiplied by a property's gross rents to produce an estimate of the property's worth

Highest and best use: that use of a parcel of land that will produce the greatest current value

Income approach: a method of valuing a property based on the monetary returns it can be expected to produce

Market approach: a method of valuing property based on recent sales of similar properties

Market value: the cash price that a willing buyer and a willing seller would agree upon, given reasonable exposure of the property to the marketplace, full information as to the potential uses of the property, and no undue compulsion to act

Operating expenses: expenditures necessary to maintain the production of income

Scheduled gross, Projected gross: the estimated rent a fully occupied property can be expected to produce on an annual basis

Real Estate Appraisal

IN THIS CHAPTER *This chapter deals with the three approaches to estimating value—the market approach, the cost approach, and the income approach. The market approach is sometimes referred to as the market comparison approach, which provides an estimate of market or fair market value. The market approach is also used in estimating values of condominiums and townhouses. Other topics covered include competitive market analysis and gross rent multipliers. The cost and income approaches lead into a discussion of income forecasting, depreciation, construction costs, operating expense ratio, and capitalizing income. The chapter concludes with coverage of the appraisal report, principles of value, and the multiple meanings of the word "value."*

To **appraise** real estate, in general terms, means to estimate its value. An **appraisal** is defined under federal law as "a written statement used in connection with a federally-related transaction that is independent and impartially prepared by a licensed, certified appraiser that states an opinion of the defined value of an adequately described property as of a specific date that is supported by the presentation, and analysis of relevant market information." In more generic terms, an appraisal is defined in applying the Uniform Standard of Professional Appraisal Practice as "the act or process of estimating the value."

There are three approaches to making this estimate. The first is to locate similar properties that have sold recently and use them as bench marks in estimating the value of the property you are appraising. This is the **market approach,** also called the market-data approach or market comparison approach. The second approach is to add together the cost of the individual components that make up the property being appraised. This is the **cost approach;** it starts with the cost of a similar parcel of vacant land and adds the cost of the lumber, concrete, plumbing, wiring, labor, etc., necessary to build a similar building. Depreciation is then subtracted. The third approach is to consider only the amount of net income that the property can reasonably be expected to produce for its owner plus any anticipated price increase or decrease. This is the **income approach.**

PUTTING IT TO WORK

For the person who owns or plans to own real estate, knowing how much a property is worth is a crucial part of the buying or selling decision. For the real estate practitioner, being able to estimate the value of a property is an essential part of taking a listing and conducting negotiations.

MARKET VALUE

In this chapter you will see demonstrations of the market, cost, and income approaches and how they are used in determining market value. **Market value,** also called **fair market value,** is the highest price in terms of money that a property will bring if (1) payment is made in cash or its equivalent, (2) the property is exposed on the open market for a reasonable length of time, (3) the buyer and seller are fully informed as to market conditions and the uses to which the property may be put, (4) neither is under abnormal pressure to conclude a transaction, and (5) the seller is capable of conveying marketable title. Market value is at the heart of nearly all real estate transactions.

MARKET COMPARISON APPROACH

Let's begin by demonstrating the application of the **market comparison approach** to a single-family residence. The residence to be appraised is called the **subject property** and is described as follows:

> The subject property is a one-story, wood-frame house of 1,520 square feet containing three bedrooms, two bathrooms, a living room, dining room, kitchen, and utility room. There is a two-car garage with concrete driveway to the street, a 300-square-foot concrete patio in the backyard, and an average amount of landscaping. The house is located on a 10,200-square-foot, level lot that measures 85 by 120 feet. The house is 12 years old, in good repair, and located in a well-maintained neighborhood of houses of similar construction and age.

Comparables

After becoming familiar with the physical features and amenities of the subject property, the next step in the market approach is to locate houses with similar physical features and amenities that have sold recently under market value conditions. These are known as **comparables** or "comps." The more similar they are to the subject property, the fewer and smaller the adjustments that must be made in the comparison process, and hence the less room for error. As a rule it is best to use comparable sales no more than six months old. During periods of relatively stable prices, this can be extended to one year. However, during periods of rapidly changing prices even a sale six months old may be out of date.

Sales Records

To apply the market comparison approach, the following information must be collected for each comparable sale: date of sale, sales price, financing terms, location of the property, and a description of its physical characteristics and amenities. Recorded deeds at public records offices can provide dates and locations of recent sales. Although a deed seldom states the purchase price, nearly all states levy a deed transfer fee or conveyance tax, the amount of which is shown on the recorded deed. This tax can sometimes provide a clue as to the purchase price.

Records of past sales can often be obtained from title and abstract companies. Property tax assessors keep records on changes in ownership as well as property values. Where these records are kept up-to-date and are available to the public, they can provide information on what has sold recently and for how much. Assessors also keep detailed records of improvements made to land. This can be quite helpful in making adjustments between the subject property and the comparables. For real estate sales-people, locally operated multiple listing services provide asking prices and descriptions of properties currently offered for sale by member brokers along with descriptions, sales prices, and dates for properties that have been sold. In some cities, commercially operated financial services publish information on local real estate transactions and sell it on a subscription basis.

Verification

To produce the most accurate appraisal possible, each sale used as a comparable should be inspected and the price and terms verified. An agent who specializes in a given neighborhood will have already visited the comparables when they were still for sale. The agent can verify price and terms with the selling broker or from multiple listing service sales records.

Number of Comparables

Three to five comparables usually provide enough basis for reliable comparison. To use more than five, the additional accuracy must be weighed against the extra effort involved. When the supply of comparable sales is more than adequate, one should choose the sales that require the fewest adjustments.

It is also important that the comparables selected represent current market conditions. Sales between relatives or close friends may result in an advantageous price to the buyer or seller, and sales prices that for some other reason appear to be out of line with the general market should not be used. Listings and offers to buy should not be used in place of actual sales. They do not represent a meeting of minds between a buyer and a seller. Listing prices do indicate the upper limit of prices, whereas offers to buy indicate lower limits. Thus, if a property is listed for sale at $80,000 and there have been offers as high as $76,000, it is reasonable to presume the market price lies somewhere between $76,000 and $80,000.

Adjustment Process

Let us now work through the example shown in Table 17.1 to demonstrate the application of the market comparison approach to a house. We begin at lines 1 and 2 by entering the address and sale price of each comparable property. For convenience, we shall refer to these as comparables A, B, and C. On lines 3 through 10, we make time adjustments to the sale price of each comparable to make it equivalent to the subject property today. **Adjustments** are made for price changes since each comparable was sold, as well as for differences in physical features, amenities, and financial terms. The result indicates the market value of the subject property.

Time Adjustments

Returning to line 3 in Table 17.1, let us assume that house prices in the neighborhood where the subject property and comparables are located have risen 5% during the six months that have elapsed since comparable A was sold. If it were for sale today, comparable A would bring 5% or $4,590 more. Therefore, we must add $4,590 to bring it up to the present. Comparable B was sold three months ago, and to bring it up to the present we need to add $2^{1}/_{2}$% or $2,200 to its sales price. Comparable C was just sold and needs no time correction as its price reflects today's market.

TABLE 17.1
Valuing a house by the market comparison approach.

Line	Item	Comparable Sale A		Comparable Sale B		Comparable Sale C	
1	Address	1702 Brookside Ave.		1912 Brookside Ave.		1501 18th Street	
2	Sales price		$91,800		$88,000		$89,000
3	Time adjustment	sold 6 mos. ago, add 5%	+4,590	sold 3 mos. ago, add 2 1/2%	+2,200	just sold	0
4	House size	160 sq ft larger at $40/sq ft	-6,400	20 sq ft smaller at $40/sq ft	+800	same size	0
5	Garage/carport	carport	+$4,000	3-car garage	-2,000	2-car garage	0
6	Other	larger patio	-300	no patio	+600	built-in bookcases	-500
7	Age, upkeep, and overall quality of house	superior	-2,000	inferior	+400	equal	0
8	Landscaping	inferior	+1,000	equal	0	superior	-700
9	Lot size, features, and location	superior	-3,890	inferior	+900	equal	0
10	Terms & conditions of sale	equal	0	special financing	-1,500	equal	0
11	Total adjustments		-3,000		+1,400		-1,200
12	Adjusted Market Price		$88,800		$89,400		$87,800

13	Correlation process:				
	Comparable A	$88,800 x 20% = $17,760			
	Comparable B	$89,400 x 30% = $26,820			
	Comparable C	$87,800 x 50% = $43,000			
14	Indicated Value	$88,480			
	Round to	$88,500			

When using the market comparison approach, all adjustments are made to the comparable properties, not to the subject property. This is because we cannot adjust the value of something for which we do not yet know the value.

House Size

Because house A is 160 square feet larger than the subject house, it is logical to expect that the subject property would sell for less money. Hence a deduction is made from the sales price of comparable A on line 4. The amount of this deduction is based on the difference in floor area and the current cost of similar construction, minus an allowance for depreciation. If we value the extra 160 square feet at $40 per square foot, we must subtract $6,400. For comparable B, the house is 20 square feet smaller than the subject house. At $40 per square foot, we add $800 to comparable B, as it is reasonable to expect that the subject property would sell for that much more because it is that much larger. Comparable C is the same-sized house as the subject property, so no adjustment is needed.

Garage and Patio Adjustments

Next, the parking facilities (line 5) are adjusted. We first look at the current cost of garage and carport construction and the condition of these structures. Assume that the value of a carport is $2,000; a one-car garage, $4,000; a two-car garage, $6,000; and a three-car garage, $8,000. Adjustments would be made as follows. The subject property has a two-car garage worth $6,000 and comparable A has a carport worth $2,000. Therefore, based on the difference in garage facilities, we can reasonably expect the subject property to command $4,000 more than comparable A. By adding $4,000 to comparable A, we effectively equalize this difference. Comparable B has a garage worth $2,000 more than the subject property's garage. Therefore, $2,000 must be subtracted from comparable B to equalize it with the subject property. For comparable C, no adjustment is required, as comparable C and the subject property have similar garage facilities.

At line 6, the subject property has a 300-square-foot patio in the backyard worth $600. Comparable A has a patio worth $900; therefore, $300 is deducted from comparable A's selling price. Comparable B has no patio. As it would have sold for $600 more if it had one, a +$600 adjustment is required. The patio at comparable C is the same as the subject property's. However, comparable C has $500 worth of custom built-in living room bookcases that the subject property does not have. Therefore, $500 is subtracted from comparable C's sales price. Any other differences between the comparables and the subject property such as swimming pools, fireplaces, carpeting, drapes, roofing materials, and kitchen appliances would be adjusted in a similar manner.

Building Age, Condition, and Quality

On line 7 we recognize differences in building age, wear and tear, construction quality, and design usefulness. Where the difference between the subject property and a comparable can be measured in terms of material and labor, the adjustment is the cost of that material and labor. For example, the $400 adjustment for comparable B reflects the cost of needed roof repair at the time B was sold. The adjustment of $2,000 for comparable A reflects the fact it has better-quality plumbing and electrical fixtures than the subject property. Differences that cannot be quantified in terms of labor and materials are usually dealt with as lump-sum judgments. Thus, one might allow $1,000 for each year of age difference between the subject and a comparable, or make a lump-sum adjustment of $2,000 for an inconvenient kitchen design.

Keep in mind that adjustments are made on the basis of what each comparable property was like on the day it was sold. Thus, if an extra bedroom was added or the house was painted after its sale date, these items are not included in the adjustment process.

Landscaping

Line 8 shows the landscaping at comparable A to be inferior to the subject property. A positive correction is necessary here to equalize it with the subject. The landscaping at comparable B is similar and requires no correction; that at comparable C is better and thus requires a negative adjustment. The dollar amount of each adjustment is based on the market value of lawn, bushes, trees, and the like.

Lot Features and Location

Line 9 deals with any differences in lot size, slope, view, and neighborhood. In this example, all comparables are in the same neighborhood as the subject property, thus eliminating the need to judge, in dollar terms, the relative merit of one neighborhood over another. However, comparable A has a slightly larger lot and a better view than the subject property. Based on recent lot sales in the area, the difference is judged to be $890 for the larger lot and $3,000 for the better view. Comparable B has a slightly smaller lot judged to be worth $900 less, and comparable C is similar in all respects.

Terms and Conditions of Sale

Line 10 in Table 17.1 accounts for differences in financing. As a rule, the more accommodating the terms of the sale to the buyer, the higher the sales price, and vice versa. We are looking for the highest cash price the subject property may reasonably be expected to bring, given adequate exposure to the marketplace and a knowledgeable buyer and seller not under undue pressure. If the comparables were sold under these conditions, no corrections would be needed in this category. However, if it can be determined that a comparable was sold under different conditions, an adjustment is necessary. For example, if the going rate of interest on home mortgages is 10% per year and the seller offers to finance the buyer at 7% interest, it is reasonable to expect that the seller can charge a higher selling price. Similarly, the seller can get a higher price if he has a low-interest loan that can be assumed by the buyer. Favorable financing terms offered by the seller of comparable B enabled him to obtain an extra $1,500 in selling price. Therefore, we must subtract $1,500 from comparable B. Another situation that requires an adjustment on line 10 is if a comparable was sold on a rush basis. If a seller is in a hurry to sell, a lower selling price usually must be accepted than if the property can be given more time in the marketplace.

Adjusted Market Price

Adjustments for each comparable are totaled and either added or subtracted from its sale price. The result is the **adjusted market price** shown at line 12. This is the dollar value of each comparable sale after it has gone through an adjustment process to make it the same as the subject property. If it were possible to precisely evaluate every adjustment, and if the buyers of comparables A, B, and C had paid exactly what their properties were worth at the time they purchased them, the three prices shown on line 12 would be the same. However, buyers are not that precise, particularly in purchasing a home where amenity value influences price and varies considerably from one person to the next.

Correlation Process

While comparing the properties, it will usually become apparent that some comparables are more like the subject property than others. The **correlation** step gives the appraiser the opportunity to assign more weight to the more similar comparables and less to the others. At 13, comparable C is given a weight of 50% since it is more like the subject and required fewer adjustments. Moreover, this sameness is in areas where adjustments tend to be the hardest to estimate accurately: time, age, quality, location, view, and financial conditions. Of the remaining two comparables, comparable B is weighted slightly higher than comparable A because it is a more recent sale and required fewer adjustments overall.

In the correlation process, the adjusted market price of each comparable is multiplied by its weighting factor and totaled at line 14. The result is the **indicated value** of the subject property. It is customary to round off to the nearest $50 or $100 for properties under $10,000; to the nearest $250 or $500 for properties between $10,000 and $100,000; to the nearest $1,000 or $2,500 for properties between $100,000 and $250,000; and to the nearest $2,500 or $5,000 above that.

Unique Issues

Condominium, Townhouse, and Cooperative Appraisal

The process for estimating the market value of a condominium, townhouse, or cooperative living unit by the market approach is similar to the process for houses except that fewer steps are involved. For example, in a condominium complex with a large number of two-bedroom units of identical floor plan, data on a sufficient number of comparable sales may be available within the building. This would eliminate adjustments for differences in unit floor plan, neighborhood, lot size and features, age and upkeep of the building, and landscaping. The only corrections needed would be those that make one unit different from another. This would include the location of the individual unit within the building (end units and units with better views sell for more), the upkeep and interior decoration of the unit, a time adjustment, and an adjustment for terms and conditions of the sale.

When there are not enough comparable sales of the same floor plan within the same building and it is necessary to use different-sized units, an adjustment must be made for floor area. If the number of comparables is still inadequate and units in different condominium buildings must be used, adjustments will be necessary for neighborhood, lot features, management, upkeep, age, and overall condition of the building.

Vacant Land Valuation

Subdivided lots zoned for commercial, industrial, or apartment buildings are usually appraised and sold on a square foot basis. Thus, if apartment land is currently selling for $3.00 per square foot, a 100,000-square-foot parcel of comparable zoning and usefulness would be appraised at $300,000. Another method is to value on a front-foot basis. For example, if a lot has 70 feet of street frontage and if similar lots are selling for $300 per front foot, that lot would be appraised at $21,000. Storefront land is often sold this way. House lots can be valued either by the square foot, front foot, or lot method. The lot method is useful when one is comparing lots of similar size and zoning in the same neighborhood. For example, recent sales of 100-foot by 100-foot house lots in the $18,000 to $20,000 range would establish the value of similar lots in the same neighborhood.

Rural land and large parcels that have not been subdivided are usually valued and sold by the acre. For example, how would you value 21 acres of vacant land when the only comparables available are 16-acre and 25-acre sales? The method is to establish a per acre value from comparables and apply it to the subject land. Thus, if 16- and 25-acre parcels sold for $32,000 and $50,000 respectively and are similar in all other respects to the 21-acre subject property, it would be reasonable to conclude that land is selling for $2,000 per acre. Therefore, the subject property is worth $42,000.

4-3-2-1 Rule

The **4-3-2-1 rule** is a depth adjustment that appraisers sometimes use when valuing vacant lots. It states that the land at the back of the lot is worth less than the land at the front. To illustrate, consider a single-family residential lot that has 75 feet of frontage on a street and is 200 feet deep. Across the street and in an equally desirable location are two lots for sale that are each 75 feet on the street and 100 feet deep. Would you pay as much for the single 75' x 200' lot as you would for two 75' x 100' lots? Let us omit the arithmetic and just remember the principle: The land at the back of a lot is worth less than the land at the front.

Competitive Market Analysis

A variation of the market comparison approach and one that is very popular with agents who list and sell residential property is the **competitive market analysis**

(CMA). This method is based on the principle that value can be estimated not only by looking at similar homes that have sold recently but also by taking into account homes presently on the market plus homes that were listed for sale but did not sell. The CMA is a listing tool that a sales agent prepares in order to show a seller what the home is likely to sell for, and the CMA helps the agent decide whether or not to accept the listing.

Figure 17.1 shows a competitive market analysis form published by the National Association of Realtors. The procedure in preparing a CMA is to select homes that are comparable to the subject property. The greater the similarity, the more accurate the appraisal will be and the more likely it is that the client will accept the agent's estimate of value and counsel. It is usually best to use only properties in the same neighborhood; this is easier for the seller to relate to and removes the need to compensate for neighborhood differences. The comparables should also be similar in size, age, and quality. Although a CMA does not require that individual adjustments be shown as in Table 17.1, it does depend on the agent's understanding of the process that takes place in that table. That is why Table 17.1 and its explanation are important. A residential agent may not be called upon to make a presentation as is done in Table 17.1; nonetheless, all those steps are considered and consolidated in the practitioner's mind before entering a probable final sales price on the CMA.

Homes for sale.   In section **[1]** of the CMA shown in Figure 17.1, similar homes presently offered for sale are listed. This information is usually taken directly from the practitioner's multiple listing service (MLS) book, and ideally the agent will already have toured these properties and have first-hand knowledge of their condition. These are the homes the seller's property will compete against in the marketplace.

In section **[2]** the agent lists similar properties that have sold in the past several months. Ideally, the agent will have toured the properties when they were for sale. Sale prices are usually available through MLS sales records. Section **[3]** is for listing homes that were offered for sale but did not sell. In other words, buyers were unwilling to take these homes at the prices offered.

In section **[4]** recent FHA and VA appraisals of comparable homes can be included if it is felt that they will be useful in determining the price at which to list. Two words of caution are in order here. First, using someone else's opinion of value is risky. It is better to determine your own opinion based on actual facts. Second, FHA and VA appraisals often tend to lag behind the market. This means in a rising market they will be too low; in a declining market they will be too high.

Buyer appeal.   In section **[5],** buyer appeal, and in section **[6],** market position, the agent evaluates the subject property from the standpoint of whether or not it will sell if placed on the market. It is important to make the right decision to take or not to take a listing. Once taken, the agent knows that valuable time and money must be committed to get a property sold. Factors that make a property more appealing to a buyer include good location, extra features, small down payment, low interest, meticulous maintenance, and a price below market. Similarly, a property is more saleable if the sellers are motivated to sell, want to sell soon, will help with financing, and will list at or below market. A busy practitioner will want to avoid spending time on overpriced listings, listings for which no financing is available, and listings where the sellers have no motivation to sell. Under the rating systems in sections **[5]** and **[6],** the closer the total is to zero, the less desirable the listing; the closer to 100%, the more desirable the listing.

Section **[7]** provides space to list the property's high and low points, current market conditions, and recommended terms of sale. Section **[8]** shows the seller how much to expect in selling costs. Section **[9]** shows the seller what to expect in the way of a sales price and the amount of cash that can be expected from the sale.

The emphasis in CMA is on a visual inspection of the data on the form in order to arrive at market value directly. No pencil and paper adjustments are made. Instead,

FIGURE 17.1
Competitive market analysis.

COMPETITIVE MARKET ANALYSIS

Property Address_____   Date_____

For Sale Now: [1]	Bed-rms.	Baths	Den	Sq. Ft.	1st Loan	List Price	Days on Market	Terms

Sold Past 12 Mos. [2]	Bed-rms.	Baths	Den	Sq. Ft.	1st Loan	List Price	Days on Market	Date Sold	Sale Price	Terms

Expired Past 12 Mos. [3]	Bed-rms.	Baths	Den	Sq. Ft.	1st Loan	List Price	Days on Market	Terms

[4]   **F.H.A. – V.A. Appraisals**

Address	Appraisal	Address	Appraisal

[5]   **Buyer Appeal**   [6]   **Marketing Position**

(Grade each item 0 to 20% on the basis of desirability or urgency)

1 Fine Location _____ %
2 Exciting Extras _____ %
3 Extra Special Financing _____ %
4 Exceptional Appeal _____ %
5 Under Market Price _____Yes ____No ____ %

1 Why Are They Selling _____ %
2 How Soon Must They Sell_____ %
3 Will They Help Finance .... Yes____No_____ %
4 Will They List at Competitive Market Value .... Yes ____No_____ %
5 Will They Pay for Appraisal .... Yes ____No_____ %

Rating Total_____ %   Rating Total_____ %

[7]

Assets _____
Drawbacks _____
Area Market Conditions _____

Recommended Terms _____

[8]   **Selling Costs**

Brokerage	$
Loan Payoff	$
Prepayment Privilege	$
FHA – VA Points	$
Title and Escrow Fees: IRS Stamps Recons Recording	$
Termite Clearance	$
Misc. Payoffs: 2nd T.D., Pool, Patio, Water Softener, Fence, Improvement Bond.	$
	$
	$
Total	$

Top Competitive Market Value $_____

[9]

Probable Final Sales Price $_____

Total Selling Costs $_____

Net Proceeds $_____   Plus or Minus $_____

The statements and figures presented herein, while not guaranteed, are secured from sources we believe authoritative.   Prepared by_____

adjustments are made in a generalized fashion in the minds of the agent and the seller. In addition to its application to single-family houses, CMA can also be used on condominiums, cooperative apartments, townhouses, and vacant lots—provided sufficient comparables are available.

Gross Rent Multipliers

A popular market comparison method that is used when a property produces income is the **gross rent multiplier,** or **GRM.** The GRM is an economic comparison factor that relates the gross rent a property can produce to its purchase price. For apartment

TABLE 17.2
Calculating gross rent
multipliers.

Building	Sales Price		Gross Annual Rents		Gross Rent Multiplier
No. 1	$245,000	÷	$34,900	=	7.02
No. 2	$160,000	÷	$22,988	=	6.96
No. 3	$204,000	÷	$29,352	=	6.95
No. 4	$196,000	÷	$27,762	=	7.06
As a Group:	$805,000	÷	$115,002	=	7.00

buildings and commercial and industrial properties, the GRM is computed by dividing the sales price of the property by its gross annual rent. For example, if an apartment building grosses $100,000 per year in rents and has just sold for $700,000, it is said to have a GRM of 7. The use of a GRM to value single-family houses is questionable since they are usually sold as owner-occupied residences rather than as income properties. Note that if you do work a GRM for a house, it is customary to use the monthly (not yearly) rent.

Where comparable properties have been sold at fairly consistent gross rent multiples, the GRM technique presumes the subject property can be valued by multiplying its gross rent by that multiplier. To illustrate, suppose that apartment buildings were recently sold in your community as shown in Table 17.2. These sales indicate that the market is currently paying seven times gross. Therefore, to find the value of a similar apartment building grossing $24,000 per year, multiply by 7.00 to get an indicated value of $168,000.

The GRM method is popular because it is simple to apply. Having once established what multiplier the market is paying, one need only know the gross rents of a building to set a value. However, this simplicity is also the weakness of the GRM method because the GRM takes into account only the gross rent a property produces. Gross rent does not allow for variations in vacancies, uncollectible rents, property taxes, maintenance, management, insurance, utilities, or reserves for replacements.

Weakness of GRM.   To illustrate the problem, suppose that two apartment buildings each gross $100,000 per year. However, the first has expenses amounting to $40,000 per year and the second, expenses of $50,000 per year. Using the same GRM, the buildings would be valued the same, yet the first produces $10,000 more in net income for its owner. The GRM also overlooks the expected economic life span of a property. For example, a building with an expected remaining life span of 30 years would be valued exactly the same as one expected to last 20 years, if both currently produce the same rents. One method of partially offsetting these errors is to use different GRMs under different circumstances. Thus, a property with low operating expenses and a long expected economic life span might call for a GRM of 7 or more, whereas a property with high operating expenses or a shorter expected life span would be valued using a GRM of 6 or 5 or even less.

COST APPROACH

There are times when the market approach is an inappropriate valuation tool. For example, the market approach is of limited usefulness in valuing a fire station, school building, courthouse, or highway bridge. These properties are rarely placed on the market and comparables are rarely found. Even with properties that are well-suited to the market approach, there may be times when it is valuable to apply another valuation approach. For example, a real estate agent may find that comparables indicate a certain style and size of house is selling in a particular neighborhood for $150,000. Yet

Step 1:	Estimate land as vacant		$30,000	**TABLE 17.3** Cost approach to value.
Step 2:	Estimate new construction cost of similar building	$120,000		
Step 3:	Less estimated depreciation	−12,000		
Step 4:	Indicated value of building		$108,000	
Step 5:	Appraised property value by the cost approach		$138,000	

the astute agent discovers through the cost approach that the same house can be built from scratch, including land, for $125,000. The agent builds and sells ten of these and concludes that, yes, there really is money to be made in real estate. Let us take a closer look at the cost approach.

Table 17.3 demonstrates the **cost approach.** Step 1 is to estimate the value of the land upon which the building is located. The land is valued as though vacant using the market comparison approach described earlier. In Step 2, the cost of constructing a similar building at today's costs is estimated. These costs include the current prices of building materials, construction wages, architect's fees, contractor's services, building permits, utility hookups, etc., plus the cost of financing during the construction stage and the cost of construction equipment used at the project site. Step 3 is the calculation of the amount of money that represents the subject building's wear and tear, lack of usefulness, and obsolescence when compared to the new building of Step 2. In Step 4, depreciation is subtracted from today's construction cost to give the current value of the subject building on a used basis. Step 5 is to add this amount to the land value. Let us work through these steps.

Estimating New Construction Costs

In order to choose a method of estimating construction costs, one must decide whether cost will be approached on a reproduction or on a replacement basis. **Reproduction cost** is the cost at today's prices of constructing an *exact replica* of the subject improvements using the same or very similar materials. **Replacement cost** is the cost, at today's prices and using today's methods of construction, for an improvement having the same or *equivalent usefulness* as the subject property. Replacement cost is the more practical choice of the two as it eliminates nonessential or obsolete features and takes full advantage of current construction materials and techniques. It is the approach that will be described here.

Square-Foot Method

The most widely used approach for estimating construction costs is the **square-foot method.** It provides reasonably accurate estimates that are fast and simple to prepare.

The square-foot method is based on finding a newly constructed building that is similar to the subject building in size, type of occupancy, design, materials, and construction quality. The cost of this building is converted to cost per square foot by dividing its current construction cost by the number of square feet in the building.

Cost Handbooks

Cost information is also available from construction cost hand books. Using a **cost handbook** starts with selecting a handbook appropriate to the type of building being appraised. From photographs of houses included in the handbook along with brief

FIGURE 17.2
Square-foot method
of cost estimating.

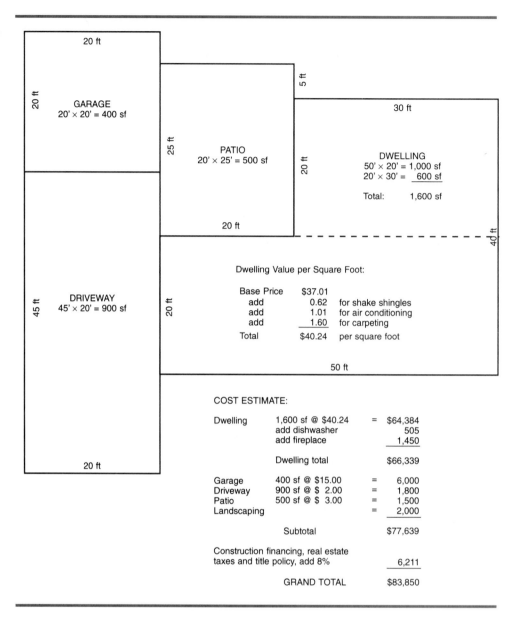

descriptions of the buildings' features, the appraiser finds a house that most nearly fits the description of the subject house. Next to pictures of the house is the current cost per square foot to construct it. If the subject house has a better quality roof, floor covering, or heating system; greater or fewer built-in appliances, or plumbing fixtures; or a garage, basement, porch, or swimming pool, the handbook provides costs for each of these. Figure 17.2 illustrates the calculations involved in the square-foot method.

Estimating Depreciation

Having estimated the current cost of constructing the subject improvements, the next step in the cost approach is to estimate the loss in value due to depreciation since they were built. In making this estimate we look for three kinds of **depreciation:** physical deterioration, functional obsolescence, and economic obsolescence.

   Physical deterioration results from wear and tear through use, such as wall-to-wall carpet that has been worn thin or a dishwasher, garbage disposal, or water heater that must be replaced. Physical deterioration also results from the action of nature in the form of sun, rain, heat, cold, and wind, and from damage due to plants and animal life such as tree roots breaking sidewalks and termites eating wood. Physical deterioration can also result from neglect (an overflowing bathtub) and from vandalism.

Functional obsolescence results from outmoded equipment (old-fashioned plumbing fixtures in the bathrooms and kitchen), faulty or outdated design (a single bathroom in a three- or four-bedroom house or an illogical room layout), inadequate structural facilities (inadequate wiring to handle today's household appliance loads), and overadequate structural facilities (high ceilings in a home). Functional and physical obsolescence can be separated into curable and incurable components. **Curable** is something that can be fixed at reasonable cost such as worn carpeting, a leaky roof, or outdated faucets in bathrooms. **Incurable** is something that cannot be reasonably fixed and must simply be lived with, for example, an illogical room layout.

Economic obsolescence is the loss of value due to external forces or events. For example, a once-popular neighborhood becomes undesirable because of air or noise pollution or because surrounding property owners fail to maintain their properties. Or, a city that is dependent on a military base finds the base closed and with it a big drop in demand for real estate. Or, the motel district in town loses customers because a new interstate highway has been built several miles away. Far more often, however, properties experience economic appreciation and not economic obsolescence. The appreciation can come from new industries moving into town, city growth in a new direction, a shortage of land in beach or waterfront areas, etc. Thus it is quite possible for the economic appreciation of a property to more than offset the depreciation it experiences. The result is a building that is physically and functionally depreciating and at the same time appreciating in value. Consequently, while the chronological age of a building is important to value, what is more important is the remaining economic life of the building and whether or not it is functionally adequate for use in the future. This is what real estate investors look for.

Final Steps in the Cost Approach

After calculating the current construction cost of the subject improvements and estimating the amount of depreciation, the next step is to subtract the amount of depreciation from the current construction cost to get the depreciated value of the improvements. This is added to the value of the land upon which the subject improvements rest. The total is the value of the property by the cost approach.

INCOME APPROACH

The market approach is very useful in connection with the sale or purchase of a home. The cost approach is very useful for someone planning to build. But what about someone planning to invest? For investors the income approach is the most popular method of valuing a property. The **income approach** considers the monetary returns a property can be expected to produce and converts that into a value the property should sell for if placed on the market today. This is called capitalizing the income stream. To **capitalize** means to convert future income to current value. To illustrate, suppose that an available apartment building is expected to return, after expenses, $18,000 per year. How much would you, as an investor, pay for the building? The answer depends on the return you require on each dollar you invest. Suppose you will accept a return of 9% per year. In that case you will pay $200,000 for this building. The calculation is as follows:

$$\frac{\text{Income}}{\text{Rate}} = \text{Value} \qquad \frac{\$18,000}{0.09} = \$200,000$$

This is the basic principle of capitalization. The appraisal work comes in estimating the net income a property will produce and looking at recent sales of similar properties to see what capitalization rates are currently acceptable to investors. Let us look at the techniques one would use in estimating a property's income. Pay close attention because each $1 error in projected annual income or expenses can make a difference of from $8 to $15 in the market value of the property.

Income and Expense Forecasting

The best starting point is to look at the actual record of income and expenses for the subject property over the past three to five years. Although the future will not be an exact repetition of the past, the past record of a property is usually the best guide to future performance. These historical data are blended with the current operating experience of similar buildings in order to estimate what the future will bring. The result is a projected operating statement, such as the one shown in Table 17.4, which begins with the estimated rents that the property can be expected to produce on an annual basis. This is the **projected gross,** or **scheduled gross,** and represents expected rentals from the subject property on a fully occupied basis. From this, vacancy and collection losses are subtracted. These are based partly on the building's past experience and partly on the operating experience of similar buildings.

Operating Expenses

The next step is to itemize anticipated **operating expenses** for the subject property. These are expenses necessary to maintain the production of income. For an apartment building without recreational facilities or an elevator, the list in Table 17.4 is typical.

TABLE 17.4
Projected annual operating statement (also called a pro forma statement).

Scheduled gross annual income	$84,000	
Vacancy allowance and collection losses	4,200	
Effective Gross Income		$79,800
Operating Expenses		
Property taxes	9,600	
Hazard and liability insurance	1,240	
Property management	5,040	
Janitorial services	1,500	
Gardener	1,200	
Utilities	3,940	
Trash pickup	600	
Repairs and maintenance	5,000	
Other	1,330	
Reserves for replacement		
Furniture & furnishings	1,200	
Stoves & refrigerators	600	
Furnace &/or air-conditioning	700	
Plumbing & electrical	800	
Roof	750	
Exterior painting	900	
Total Operating Expenses		$34,400
Net Operating Income		$45,400
Operating Expense Ratio: $34,400 / $79,800 = 43.1%		

Again, we must consider both the property's past operating expenses and what we expect those expenses to be in the future. For example, even though a property is currently being managed by its owner and no management fee is being paid, a typical management fee, say 6% of the gross rents, is included.

Not included as operating expenses are outlays for capital improvements, such as the construction of a new swimming pool, the expansion of parking facilities, and assessments for street improvements. Improvements are not classified as expenses because they increase the usefulness of the property, which increases the rent the property will generate and therefore the property's value.

Reserves

Reserves for replacement are established for items that do not require an expenditure of cash each year. To illustrate, lobby furniture (and furniture in apartments rented as "furnished") wears out a little each year, eventually requiring replacement. Suppose that these items cost $7,200 and are expected to last six years, at which time they must be replaced. An annual $1,200 reserve for replacement not only reflects wear and tear of the furniture during the year, but also reminds us that to avoid having to meet the entire furniture and furnishings replacement cost out of one year's income, money should be set aside for this purpose each year. In a similar manner, reserves are established for other items that must be replaced or repaired more than once during the life of the building, but not yearly.

Net Operating Income

The operating expense total is then subtracted from the effective gross income. The balance that remains is the **net operating income.** From the net operating income the property owner receives both a return *on* and a return *of* investment. The return *on* investment is the interest received for investing money in the property. The return *of* investment is compensation for the fact that the building is wearing out.

Operating Expense Ratio

At this point, the **operating expense ratio** can be calculated. It is obtained by dividing the total operating expenses by the effective gross income. The resulting ratio provides a handy yardstick against which similar properties can be compared. If the operating expense ratio is out of step compared to similar properties, it signals the need for further investigation. A range of 25% to 45% is typical for apartment buildings. The Institute of Real Estate Management of the National Association of Realtors publishes books and articles that give typical operating ratios for various types of income properties across the United States. Local inquiry to appraisers and brokers who specialize in income properties will also provide typical ratios for buildings in a community.

Capitalizing Income

The final step in the income approach is to capitalize the net operating income. In other words, what price should an investor offer to pay for a property that produces a given net income per year? The solution is: income / rate = value. If the annual net operating income is $45,400 and if the investor intends to pay all cash, expects to receive a 10% return on this investment, and anticipates no change in the value of the

TABLE 17.5
Overall rates—
10-year holding
period, 25-year loan
for 75% of the pur-
chase price, 10%
investor return

Appreciation, Depreciation	Loan Interest Rate			
	9%	10%	11%	12%
+100%	0.07251	0.07935	0.08631	0.09338
+ 50%	**0.09376**	0.10060	0.10756	0.11463
+ 25%	0.10439	0.11123	0.11819	0.12526
+ 15%	0.10864	0.11548	0.12244	0.12951
+ 10%	0.11077	0.11761	0.12457	0.13164
+ 5%	0.11289	0.11973	0.12669	0.13376
0	0.11502	0.12186	0.12882	0.13589
− 5%	0.11715	0.12399	0.13095	0.13802
− 10%	0.11927	0.12611	0.13307	0.14014
− 15%	0.12140	0.12824	0.13520	0.14227
− 25%	0.12565	0.13249	0.13945	0.14652
− 50%	0.13628	0.14312	0.15008	0.15715
−100%	0.15753	0.16437	0.17133	0.17840

Source: *Financial Capitalization Rate Tables,* Financial Publishing Company, Boston, Mass. By permission.

property while owning it, the solution is to divide $45,400 by 10%. However, most investors today borrow much of the purchase price and usually expect an increase in property value. Under these conditions, how much should the investor pay?

The best known method for solving this type of investment question involves using the Ellwood Tables, published in 1959 by L. W. Ellwood, MAI. However, for the person who does not use these tables regularly, the arithmetic involved can prove confusing. As a result **mortgage-equity tables** are now available from bookstores. These allow the user to look up a single number, called an **overall rate,** and divide it into the net operating income to find a value for the property.

For example, suppose an investor who is interested in buying the above property can obtain a 9%, fully amortized 25-year mortgage loan for 75% of the purchase price. He wants a 10% return on his equity in the property, plans to hold it 10 years, and expects it will increase 50% in value (after selling costs) during that time. How much should he offer to pay the seller? In Table 17.5, we look for an interest rate of 9% and for appreciation of 50%. This gives an overall rate of 0.09376 and the solution is:

$$\frac{\text{Income}}{\text{Overall rate}} = \text{Value} \qquad \frac{\$45,400}{0.09376} = \$484,215$$

Further exploration of the numbers in Table 17.5 shows that as loan money becomes more costly, the overall rate rises, and as interest rates fall, so does the overall rate. If the investor can anticipate appreciation in value, the overall rate drops; if she can't, the overall rate climbs. You can experiment by dividing some of the other overall rates in this table into $45,400 to see how the value of this property changes under different circumstances.

Depreciation

The pro forma in Table 17.4 provides reserves for replacement of such items as the roof, furnace, air conditioning, plumbing, electrical and exterior paint, and so forth. Nonetheless, as the building ages the style of the building will become dated, the neighborhood will change, and the structure will experience physical deterioration. Allowance for this is usually accounted for in the selection of the capitalization rate.

The less functional, economic, and physical obsolescence that is expected to take place, the lower the acceptable "cap" rate and vice versa.

Fictional Depreciation

In contrast to actual depreciation, there is the **fictional depreciation** that the U.S. Treasury allows income property owners to deduct as an expense when calculating income taxes. The Internal Revenue Service allows a purchaser of a commercial building to completely depreciate the structure over a period of $27^1/_2$ years regardless of the age or condition of the structure. This figure may be an understatement of the remaining life of the structure, but it was chosen by Congress to create an incentive to invest in real estate, not as an accurate gauge of a property's life. Thus it is quite common to see depreciation claimed on buildings that are in reality appreciating because of rising income from rents and/or falling capitalization rates.

CHOICE OF APPROACHES

For certain types of real property, some approaches are more suitable than others. This is especially true for single-family residences. Here you must rely almost entirely on the market and cost approaches as very few houses are sold on their ability to generate cash rent. Unless you can develop a measure of the "psychic income" in home ownership, relying heavily on rental value will lead to a property value below the market and cost approaches. Applying all three approaches to special-purpose buildings may also prove to be impractical. For example, in valuing a college or university campus or a state capitol building, the income and market approaches have only limited applicability.

When appraising a property that is bought for investment purposes such as an apartment building, shopping center, office building, or warehouse, the income approach is the primary method of valuation. As a cross-check on the income approach, an apartment building should be compared to other apartment buildings on a price per apartment unit basis or price per square foot basis. Similarly, an office, store, or warehouse can be compared to other recent office, store, or warehouse sales on a price per square foot basis. Additionally, the cost approach can be used to determine whether or not it would be cheaper to buy land and build rather than to buy an existing building.

APPRAISER'S BEST ESTIMATE

It is important to realize that the appraised value is the appraiser's best *estimate* of the subject property's worth. Thus, no matter how painstakingly it is done, property valuation requires the appraiser to make many subjective judgments. Because of this, it is not unusual for three highly qualified appraisers to look at the same property and produce three different appraised values. It is also important to recognize that an appraisal is made as of a specific date. It is not a certificate of value, good forever until used. If a property was valued at $115,000 on January 5th of this year, the more time that has elapsed since that date, the less accurate that value is as an indication of the property's current worth.

An appraisal does not take into consideration the financial condition of the owner, the owner's health, sentimental attachment, or any other personal matter. An appraisal does not guarantee that the property will sell for the appraised market value. (The buyer and the seller determine the actual selling price.) Nor does buying at the appraised market value guarantee a future profit for the purchaser. (The real estate market can change.) An appraisal is not a guarantee that the roof will not leak, that there are no termites, or that everything in the building works. An appraisal is not an offer to buy, although a buyer can order one made so as to know how much to offer. An appraisal is not a loan commitment, although a lender can order one made so as to apply a loan-to-value ratio when making a loan.

APPRAISAL REGULATION

The Appraisal Foundation

When the country was suffering from harsh economic times, standards of appraisals came under extremely close scrutiny by many lenders. For instance, two appraisers may appraise the same property for significantly different values while using the same data, both acting in good faith. It is hard to draw a distinction, however, between an error in judgment and a fraudulent appraisal. The more difficult question is: How can a lender, in reviewing an appraisal, distinguish between good and bad appraisals? At least part of the answer is being addressed by an organization called the Appraisal Foundation. It is a private organization whose purpose is (1) to establish and approve uniform appraisal standards, (2) to set appropriate criteria for the certification and recertification of qualified appraisers, and (3) to maintain appropriate systems for the certification and recertification of qualified appraisers.

To effect this result, the Appraisal Foundation has established two subcommittees, the Appraiser Qualifications Board and the Appraisal Standards Board. The first establishes criteria for appraisers. The second sets standards for the appraisal to be performed. The Foundation's aim is to disseminate such qualification criteria to the various states, governmental entities, and others to assist them in establishing and maintaining an appropriate system for the certification and recertification of qualified appraisers.

Federal Regulation

Congress addressed the appraisal issue by enacting Title XI of the Financial Institution's Reform, Recovery, and Enforcement Act of 1989 **(FIRREA).** The Act, for the first time in history, established standards that will have a far-reaching impact on the appraisal industry.

Congress also created the Appraisal Subcommittee of the Federal Financial Institution's Examination Council to establish standards. The Subcommittee looks exclusively to the Appraisal Foundation for establishing standards under FIRREA for both appraiser qualifications as well as appraisal standards and has proven to be an excellent effort by leaders in the appraisal industry, coupled with the governmental enforcement powers, to establish standards that ultimately benefit the lenders and public in general.

Developing the Appraisal

FIRREA created mandatory requirements for real estate appraisals. These requirements are known as the **Uniform Standards of Professional Appraisal Practice,** commonly referred to as the **USPAP standards.**

In developing an appraisal, the Act requires that the appraiser must be aware of, understand, and correctly employ those recognized methods and techniques that are necessary to produce a credible appraisal. There are specific requirements for an appraiser's analysis, requiring consideration of current sales, options, or listings within certain time periods prior to the date of the appraisal. Specifically, this analysis of market data must consider all sales, options, or listings within: (1) one year for a one- to four-family residential property and (2) within three years for all other property types. The Act further requires that the appraiser must consider and reconcile the quality and quantity of data available and analyze within the approaches used, the applicability or suitability of the approaches used as it pertains to the subject parcel of real estate.

Departure Provisions

There were significant changes to the USPAP in 1994. The Uniform Standards now provide for a Departure Provision that permits limited departures from the standards that are classified as specific guidelines rather than binding requirements.

Before entering into an agreement to perform an appraisal that contains a departure, (1) the appraiser must have determined that the appraisal or consulting process to be performed is not so limited that the resulting assignment would tend to mislead or confuse the client or the intended users of the report; (2) the appraiser must have advised the client that the assignment calls for something less than, or different from, the work required by the specific guidelines and that the report will clearly identify and explain the departures(s); and (3) the client must have agreed that the performance of a limited appraisal or consulting service would be appropriate.

The Definition Section of the USPAP defines "appraisal" as "the act or process of estimating value; an estimate of value" and then defines two types of appraisals:

1. A **complete appraisal,** which is defined as the act or process of estimating value without invoking the Departure Provision. A complete appraisal report may not depart from Specific USPAP Guidelines;
2. A **limited appraisal,** defined as the act or process of estimating value performed under and resulting from invoking the Departure Provision.

Reporting Options

In addition, the revised USPAP now define three optional levels of reporting.

1. The **self-contained appraisal report,** which is the most detailed and encompassing of the report options. The length and descriptive detail in such a report should fully support (in a self-contained format) the conclusions of the appraiser.
2. The **summary report,** which is less detailed than a self-contained report. The information obtained and the appraisal procedures that were followed may be summarized in this report rather than describing the information in detail.
3. The **restrictive report** is the least detailed of the reporting options. There is only a minimal presentation of information and it is intended for use only by the client. This level of report must contain a prominent use restriction that limits the reliance on the report to the client and warns the report cannot be properly understood without additional information from the workfile of the appraiser.

Reporting Standards

USPAP also sets forth required standards for the appraisal report. Each self-contained appraisal report must (1) identify and describe the real estate being appraised; (2) state the real property interest being appraised; (3) state the purpose and intended use of the appraisal; (4) define the value to be estimated; (5) state the effective date of the appraisal and the date of the report; (6) state the extent of the process of collecting, confirming, and reporting data; (7) state all assumptions and limiting conditions that affect the analyses, opinions, and conclusions; (8) describe the information considered, the appraisal procedures followed, and the reasoning that supports the analyses, opinions, and conclusions; (9) describe the appraiser's opinion of the highest and best use of the real estate, when such an opinion is necessary and appropriate; (10) explain and support the exclusion of any of the usual valuation approaches; (11) describe any additional information that may be appropriate to show compliance with, or clearly identify and explain permitted departures from the specific guidelines of Standard 1 (on developing an appraisal); and (12) include a signed certification.

Each appraisal report must also (1) clearly and accurately set forth the appraisal in a manner that will not be misleading; (2) contain sufficient information to enable person(s) who are expected to receive or rely on the report to understand it properly; and (3) clearly and accurately disclose any extraordinary assumption or limiting condition that directly affects the appraisal and indicate its impact on value.

USPAP requires that each written real property appraisal report include a signed certification similar in content to the following form:

I certify that, to the best of my knowledge and belief:

- The statements of fact contained in this report are true and correct.
- The reported analyses, opinions, and conclusions are limited only by the reported assumptions and limiting conditions and are my personal, unbiased professional analyses, opinions, and conclusions.
- I have no (or the specified) present or prospective interest in the property that is the subject of this report, and I have no (or the specified) personal interest or bias with respect to the parties involved.
- My compensation is not contingent upon the reporting of a predetermined value or direction in value that favors the cause of the client, the amount of the value estimate, the attainment of a stipulated result, or the occurrence of a subsequent event.
- My analyses, opinions and conclusions were developed, and this report has been prepared, in conformity with the Uniform Standards of Professional Appraisal Practice.
- I have (or have not) made a personal inspection of the property that is the subject of this report. (If more than one person signs the report, this certification must clearly specify which individuals did and which individuals did not make a personal inspection of the appraised property).
- No one provided significant professional assistance to the person signing this report. (If there are exceptions, the name of each individual providing significant professional assistance must be stated.)

FORMATS OF APPRAISAL REPORTS

There are three traditional formats for written reports. The choice depends on the amount of detail required by the client, the intended use of the report, and the appraisal standards to be met. The format to be used also depends on the reporting option (self-contained, summary, or restricted). A brief description of reporting formats follows.

The Letter Report

The least formal letter report is usually only one to five pages long. It contains the conditions of the assignment, a summary of the nature and scope of the appraiser's investigation, and an opinion of value. While brief, the letter report must describe the extent of the appraisal process performed and clearly state its detail. Whether reporting a complete or limited appraisal, the letter format is most suited to the restricted appraisal report. It is used most often when the client is familiar with the property and appraisal details are not needed.

The Form Report

The form report is an appraisal made on a preprinted form. A checklist is often used for describing and rating property characteristics. This makes the appraisal form a logical choice for the summary report option.

Institutions and government agencies use forms designed to suit their special needs. Standard forms are usually available for single-family residential, multifamily residential, commercial, and industrial properties. This is the most common type of report used for real estate loan appraisals.

The Narrative Report

The narrative appraisal is the longest and most formal of the appraisal reports. It is a step-by-step presentation of the facts used by the appraiser to arrive at a value. This report also contains a detailed discussion of the methods used to interpret the data presented. Narrative appraisal reports are used when the client needs to review each logical step taken by the appraiser. They are the preferred format for self-contained appraisal reports.

Review Appraisal

FIRREA also developed standards for reviewing appraisals and reporting their adequacy and appropriateness. In reviewing the appraisal, the appraiser must observe specific guidelines that identify the report being reviewed and the real property being appraised, the effective date of the report, and the date of the review. The review appraiser must also identify the scope of the review process to be conducted and form an opinion as to the adequacy and relevance of the data and propriety of any adjustments to the data. The opinion must also reflect the appropriateness of the appraisal and the methods and techniques used to develop the reasons for any disagreement with the appraiser.

Real Estate Analysis

An **analysis** is the act or process of providing information, recommendations, and/or conclusions on diversified problems in real estate other than estimating the value and can include a number of different forms of analysis, such as cash flow analysis, feasibility analysis, investment analysis, or market analysis. This differs from an *appraisal,* which, under USPAP standards, is defined as the act or process of estimating value.

In developing the real estate analysis, the analyst must be aware of, understand, and correctly employ those recognized methods and techniques that are necessary to produce a credible analysis. The analyst must not commit a substantial error of omission or commission that significantly affects the analysis and must not render services in a careless or negligent manner which, when considering the results of the analysis would consider to be misleading. The analyst must also observe the following specific guidelines; (1) clearly identify the client's objective; (2) define the problem to be considered and the purpose and intended use of the analysis, consider the scope of the assignment, adequately identify the real estate under consideration, and describe any special limiting condition; (3) collect, verify, and reconcile such data as may be required to complete the assignment and withhold no pertinent information; (4) apply the appropriate tools and techniques of analysis to data collected; and (5) base all projections of the analysis on reasonably clear and appropriate evidence. There are additional requirements established and separate criteria for each type of analysis being utilized by the analyst.

In reporting the results of the real estate analysis, the analyst must communicate each analysis, opinion, and conclusion in a manner that is not misleading, and the report must contain sufficient information to enable the persons who receive it to understand it properly, and clearly and accurately disclose any extraordinary assumptions that would indicate any impact on the final conclusions or recommendation of the analysis.

The analysis report must contain a certification that is similar in content to that of the appraisal certification.

APPRAISER QUALIFICATIONS

To comply with federal regulations established by the Appraisal Subcommittee, the Appraiser Qualifications Board of the Appraisal Foundation has established federal standards for certification and licensing of appraisers. Texas has adopted these standards in their entirety and has established four categories of appraisers: (1) a certified general real estate appraiser; (2) a certified residential real estate appraiser; (3) a state licensed real estate appraiser; and (4) an appraiser trainee. The respective qualifications are set out in Table 17.6.

Texas Regulations

In Texas, the Appraiser Licensing and Certification Board (TALCB) was created to recommend education, experience, and continuing education requirements for applications for certification and renewal of certification, specifications of any examination to be required, standards for the development of communication of real estate appraisal by certified appraisers, and a code of professional responsibility for certified real estate appraisers. The Governor appoints eight of the members, four of which must be appraiser members and four of which must be public members. The ninth member will be the executive secretary of the Texas Veterans Land Board. The TALCB is an "independent subdivision of the Texas Real Estate Commission."

The Texas Real Estate Commission has responded to the Appraisal Foundation's USPAP by passing new rules and regulations governing appraisals and property analyses to be made by all licensees and to bring Texas into compliance with the new federal rules.

There are two major exceptions. The new regulations do not apply to: (1) a statement of opinion of value of real property (commonly known as a broker's opinion of value) given by a licensee in connection with seeking or obtaining a listing contract; or (2) a price comparison of similar properties (commonly known as a comparative market analysis) provided as part of other brokerage business for the purpose of determining a listing, selling, or rental price for a specific property. These exceptions provide that a real estate licensee can provide information and determine an estimate of value without having to comply with all the technical regulations required for formal real estate appraisals, if the licensee provides the person for whom the opinion or analysis is prepared with a written statement containing the following language:

> THIS IS AN OPINION OF VALUE OR COMPARATIVE MARKET ANALYSIS AND SHOULD NOT BE CONSIDERED AN APPRAISAL. In making any decision that relies upon my work, you should know that I have not followed the guidelines for development of an appraisal or analysis contained in the Uniform Standards of Professional Appraisal Practice of the Appraisal Foundation.

CHARACTERISTICS OF VALUE

Up to this point we have been concerned primarily with value based on evidence found in the marketplace and how to report it. Before concluding this chapter, let us briefly

Classification	Education	Experience	Examination	
Certified General Real Estate Appraiser	180 classroom hours of acceptable real estate appraisal-related courses, including at least 30 hours of actual appraisal courses 15 hours of the Uniform Standards of Professional Appraisal Practice (USPAP).	3,000 hours of acceptable real estate appraisal experience with a minimum of 2 years (30 months) and may be acquired any time during one's career A minimum of 1,500 hours must be in non-residential appraising.	Appraiser Qualifications Board (AQB)-approved TALCB general certification examination.	**TABLE 17.6** Texas appraiser licensing and certification board.
Certified Residential Real Estate Appraiser	120 classroom hours of acceptable real estate appraisal-related courses, including at least 30 hours of actual appraisal courses and 15 hours of USPAP.	2,500 hours of acceptable real estate appraisal experience with a minimum of 2 years (24 months) and may be acquired any time during one's career.	AQB-approved TALCB residential certification examination.	
State Licensed Real Estate Appraiser	90 classroom hours of acceptable real estate appraisal-related courses, including at least 30 hours of actual appraisal courses and 15 hours of USPAP.	2,000 hours of acceptable real estate appraisal experience.	AQB-approved TALCB "State Licensed" exam.	
Appraiser Trainee	None	None	None	

touch on what creates value, the principles of real property valuation, and appraisal for purposes other than market value.

For a good or service to have value in the marketplace it must possess four characteristics: demand, utility, scarcity, and transferability. **Demand** is a need or desire coupled with the purchasing power to fill it, whereas **utility** is the ability of a good or service to fill that need. **Scarcity** means there must be a short supply relative to demand. Air, for example, has utility and is in demand, but it is not scarce. Finally, a good or service must be **transferable** to have value to anyone other than the person possessing it.

PRINCIPLES OF VALUE

The **principle of anticipation** reflects the fact that what a person will pay for a property depends on the expected benefits from the property in the future. Thus, the buyer of a home anticipates receiving shelter plus the investment and psychic benefits of home ownership. The investor buys property in anticipation of future income.

The **principle of substitution** states that the maximum value of a property in the marketplace tends to be set by the cost of purchasing an equally desirable substitute property provided no costly delay is encountered in making the substitution. In other words, substitution sets an upper limit on price. Thus, if there are two similar houses for sale, or two similar apartments for rent, the lower priced one will generally be purchased or rented first. In the same manner, the cost of buying land and constructing a new building sets a limit on the value of existing buildings.

Highest and Best Use

The **highest and best use** of a property is that use which will give the property its greatest current value. This means you must be alert to the possibility that the present use of a parcel of land may not be the one that makes the land the most valuable. Consider a 30-year-old house located at a busy intersection in a shopping area. To place a value on that property based on its continued use as a residence would be misleading if the property would be worth more with the house removed and shopping or commercial facilities built on the land instead.

The **principle of competition** recognizes that where substantial profits are being made, competition will be encouraged. For example, if apartment rents increase to the point where owners of existing apartment buildings are making substantial profits, builders and investors will be encouraged to build more apartment buildings.

Supply and Demand

Applied to real estate, the **principle of supply and demand** refers to the ability of people to pay for land coupled with the relative scarcity of land. This means that attention must be given to such matters on the demand side as population growth, personal income, and preferences of people. On the supply side, you must look at the available supply of land and its relative scarcity. When the supply of land is limited and demand is great, the result is rising land prices. Conversely, where land is abundant and there are relatively few buyers, supply and demand will be in balance at only a few cents per square foot.

The **principle of change** reminds us that real property uses are always in a state of change. Although it may be imperceptible on a day-to-day basis, change can easily be seen over longer periods of time. Because the present value of a property is related to its future uses, the more potential changes that can be identified, the more accurate the estimate of its present worth will be.

Diminishing Marginal Returns

The **principle of diminishing marginal returns,** also called the **principle of contribution,** refers to the relationship between added cost and the value it returns. It tells us that we should invest dollars whenever they will return to us more than $1 of value and we should stop when each dollar invested returns less than $1 in value.

The **principle of conformity** holds that maximum value is realized when there is a reasonable degree of homogeneity in a neighborhood. This is the basis for zoning laws across the country; certain tracts in a community are zoned for single-family houses, others for apartment buildings, stores, and industry. Within a tract there should also be a reasonable amount of homogeneity. For example, a $200,000 house would be out of place in a neighborhood of $90,000 houses.

MULTIPLE MEANINGS OF THE WORD "VALUE"

When we hear the word *value,* we tend to think of market value. However, at any given moment in time, a single property can have other values too. This is because value or worth is very much affected by the purpose for which the valuation was performed. For example, **assessed value** is the value given a property by the county tax assessor for purposes of property taxation. **Estate tax value** is the value that federal and state taxation authorities establish for a deceased person's property; it is used to calculate the amount of estate taxes that must be paid. **Insurance value** is concerned with the cost of replacing damaged property. It differs from market value in two major respects: (1) the value of the land is not included, as it is presumed that only the structures are destructible, and (2) the amount of coverage is based on the replacement cost of the structures. **Loan value** is the value set on a property for the purpose of making a loan.

Plottage Value

When two or more adjoining parcels are combined into one large parcel it is called **assemblage.** The increased value of the large parcel over and above the sum of the smaller parcels is called **plottage value.** For example, local zoning laws may permit a six-unit apartment building on a single 10,000-square-foot lot. However, if two of these lots can be combined, zoning laws permit 15 units. This makes the lots more valuable if sold together.

Rental Value

Rental value is the value of a property expressed in terms of the right to its use for a specific period of time. The fee simple interest in a house may have a market value of $80,000, where as the market value of one month's occupancy might be $600.

Replacement Value

Replacement value is value as measured by the current cost of building a structure of equivalent utility. **Salvage value** is what a structure is worth if it has to be removed and taken elsewhere, either in whole or dismantled for parts. Because salvage operations require much labor the salvage value of most buildings is usually very low.

This list of values is not exhaustive, but it points out that the word *value* has many meanings. When reading an appraisal report, always read the first paragraph to see why the appraisal was prepared. Before preparing an appraisal, make certain you know its purpose and then state it at the beginning of your report.

BUYER'S AND SELLER'S MARKETS

Whenever supply and demand are unbalanced because of excess supply, a **buyer's market** exists. This means a buyer can negotiate prices and terms more to his liking, and a seller who wants to sell must accept them. When the imbalance occurs because demand exceeds supply it is a **seller's market;** sellers are able to negotiate prices and terms more to their liking as buyers compete for the available merchandise.

A **broad market** means that many buyers and sellers are in the market at the same time. This makes it relatively easy to establish the price of a property and for a seller to find a buyer quickly, and vice versa. A **thin market** is said to exist when there are only a few buyers and a few sellers in the market at the same time. It is oftentimes difficult to appraise a property in a thin market because there are so few sales to use as comparables.

REVIEW QUESTIONS

Answers to these questions are found in the Answer Key section at the back of the book.

1. Which of the following is NOT one of the three standard approaches to the appraisal of real property?
   A. Income approach.
   B. Cost approach.
   C. Assessment approach.
   D. Market approach.

2. To apply the market data approach, a real estate appraiser must collect all the following data on each comparable sale EXCEPT:
   A. date of sale.
   B. marketability of title.
   C. financing terms.
   D. sale price.

3. Adjustments for advantageous financing would be made in the
   A. market comparison approach to appraisal.
   B. cost approach to appraisal.
   C. income approach to appraisal.
   D. capitalization approach to appraisal.

4. After all adjustments are made to a comparable property, its comparative value for appraisal purposes is known as its
   A. adjusted market price.
   B. indicated market value.
   C. amended market price.
   D. revised market price.

5. The value of vacant land is commonly stated in any of the following terms EXCEPT value per
   A. square foot.
   B. acre.
   C. front foot.
   D. square yard.

6. To evaluate a home in order to list it for sale, a real estate agent could use the
   A. standard market comparison method.
   B. competitive market analysis method.
   C. Both A and B.
   D. Neither A nor B.

7. Seller motivation is considered most in the
   A. income approach.
   B. cost approach.
   C. gross rent multiplier method.
   D. competitive market analysis.

8. Which of the following approaches is most likely to provide only a rough estimate of the value of a rental property?
   A. Cost approach.
   B. Income approach.
   C. Market comparison approach.
   D. Gross rent multiplier.

9. In appraising an historically significant residence built in the Victorian era using the cost approach, an appraiser will probably appraise it on the basis of its
   A. reproduction cost.
   B. restoration cost.
   C. replacement cost.
   D. reconstruction cost.

10. Which of the following results from factors outside the property?
    A. Functional obsolescence.
    B. Physical deterioration.
    C. Economic obsolescence.
    D. None of the above.

11. The conversion of future income into present value is known as
    A. capitalization.
    B. amortization.
    C. hypothecation.
    D. appreciation.

12. The rents that a property can be expected to produce on an annual basis may be referred to as the
    A. projected gross.
    B. scheduled gross.
    C. Both A and B.
    D. Neither A nor B.

13. The operating expense ratio of a building is determined by dividing the total operating expenses by the
    A. effective net income.
    B. net operating income.
    C. effective gross income.
    D. actual gross income.

14. From the viewpoint of a qualified real estate appraiser, the value of the subject property is NOT affected by
    A. demand.
    B. scarcity.
    C. highest and best use.
    D. transferability.

15. The use of a property that will give it its greatest current value is its
    A. highest use.
    B. best use.
    C. highest and best use.
    D. maximum use.

16. The relationship between added cost and the value it returns is known as the principle of
    A. diminishing marginal returns.
    B. contribution.
    C. Both A and B.
    D. Neither A nor B.

17. The principle that holds that maximum value is realized when a reasonable degree of homogeneity is present in a neighborhood is known as the principle of
    A. harmony.
    B. homogeneity.
    C. similarity.
    D. conformity.

18. The process of combining two or more parcels of land into one larger parcel is called
    A. assemblage.
    B. plottage.
    C. salvage.
    D. reproduction.

19. A market where there is an excess of supply over demand is known as a
    A. buyer's market.
    B. broad market.
    C. seller's market.
    D. thin market.

20. Which of the following is not a classification of an appraiser in Texas?
    A. State licensed real estate appraiser.
    B. Certified general real estate appraiser.
    C. Certified licensed real estate appraiser.
    D. Certified residential real estate appraiser.

KEY TERMS

Broker: a person or legal entity licensed to act independently in conducting a real estate brokerage business

Independent contractor: one who contracts to do work according to personal methods and is responsible to the employer only for the results of that work

License revocation: to recall and make void a license

License suspension: to temporarily make a license ineffective

Licensee: one who holds a license

Principal broker: the broker in charge of a real estate office

Real estate commission: a state board that advises and sets policies regarding real estate licensees and transaction procedures

Realtor: a registered trademark owned by the National Association of Realtors for use by its members

Recovery fund: a state-operated fund that can be tapped to pay for uncollectible judgments against real estate licensees

Sales associate: a salesperson or broker employed by a broker

Salesperson: a person employed by a broker to list, negotiate, sell, or lease real property for others

Licensing Laws and Professional Affiliation

IN THIS CHAPTER *In this chapter we will cover the various licensing law requirements, emphasizing the provisions of the state real estate license acts. A license act defines the licensees, explains the licensing procedure, and describes the obligations of the licensees with special emphasis on license suspension and revocation as applicable. A license act also covers the purpose and function of the real estate commission recovery fund, securities licensing, affiliating with a broker, franchise offices, and the independent contractor issue. The chapter concludes with coverage of professional real estate associations.*

For most owners of real estate the decision to sell means hiring a broker to find a buyer. Although some owners choose to market their properties themselves, most find it advantageous to turn the job over to a real estate broker and pay a commission for the service of finding a buyer and carrying the deal through closing. The next three chapters are for the owner who plans to use a broker and for the person who plans to be a real estate salesperson or broker. First, Chapter 18 discusses examination and licensing requirements and an overview of how states regulate the real estate profession, including a section on how to choose a broker with whom to affiliate and professional real estate associations, in particular the National Association of Realtors. In Chapter 19, we begin with a simplified real estate listing contract. Next we take a close look at the agency responsibilities a broker has toward a seller together with the seller's obligations toward the broker. Then we discuss seller and broker responsibilities toward persons who are interested in purchasing the listed property, and buyer brokerage.

RATIONALE FOR REAL ESTATE LICENSING

Does the public have a vested interest in seeing that real estate salespersons and brokers have the qualifications of honesty, truthfulness, good reputation, and real estate knowledge before they are allowed to negotiate real estate transactions on behalf of others? It was this concern that brought about real estate licensing laws as we know them today. Until 1917, no state required real estate agents to be licensed. Anyone who wanted to be an agent could simply hang up a sign stating that he or she was an agent. In larger cities there were persons and firms who specialized in bringing buyers and sellers together. In smaller towns, a local banker, attorney, or barber would know who had what for sale and be the person a buyer would ask for property information.

The first attempt to require that persons acting as real estate agents be licensed was made by the California legislature in 1917. That law was declared unconstitutional, with the main opposition being that the state was unreasonably interfering with the right of every citizen to engage in a useful and legitimate occupation. Two years later, in 1919, the California legislature passed a second real estate licensing act. This time it was upheld by the Supreme Court. That same year, Michigan, Oregon, and Tennessee also passed real estate licensing acts. Today, all 50 states and the District of Columbia require that persons who offer their services as real estate agents be licensed.

The Real Estate License Act (the "Act") of Texas (Art. 6573a, V.A.T.S.) was first passed in 1939. The Act clearly defines the functions and duties of a broker and establishes explicit provisions for license revocation and suspension. It is anticipated that the interpretation of the Act will be administered literally, requiring a higher standard of care from the licensee.

The licensing laws prevent complete freedom of entry into the profession. The public has a vested interest in seeing that salespersons and brokers have the qualifications of honesty, truthfulness, and good reputation. This was the intent of the first license laws. Some years later the additional requirements of license examinations and real estate education were added in the belief that a person who wants to be a real estate agent should meet special knowledge qualifications. To further protect consumers, the Texas Real Estate Commission requires that each active real estate broker display a Consumer Information Form in a prominent location in each place of business the broker maintains. The form informs the consumer of the broker's recovery fund (discussed later) and how to direct complaints to the Texas Real Estate Commission.

Experience to date clearly indicates that the Texas Real Estate License Act has helped to upgrade technical competency and has increased public confidence in brokers and salespersons. Moreover, the Act is an important and powerful tool in reducing fraudulent real estate practices because a state can suspend or revoke a person's license to operate. A complete copy of the Act is shown in Appendix A. It is suggested that it be read several times, in detail. It is a primary basis for test questions at every level, and there is no excuse for not knowing it.

BROKER DEFINED

There are currently two levels of licensure under the Act. A real estate **broker,** as statutorily defined in Texas, means a person (*person* is defined as an "individual or any other entity including but not limited to a governmental body, limited liability company, limited liability partnership, partnership, or corporation, foreign or domestic") who, for another person and for a fee, commission, or other valuable consideration, or with the intention or in the expectation or on the promise of receiving or collecting a fee, commission, or other valuable consideration from another person:

1. sells, exchanges, purchases, rents, or leases real estate
2. offers to sell, exchange, purchase, rent, or lease real estate
3. negotiates, or attempts to negotiate, the listing, sale, exchange, purchase, rental, or leasing of real estate
4. lists, or offers or attempts or agrees to list, real estate for sale, rental, lease, exchange, or trade
5. appraises, or offers or attempts or agrees to auction, real estate
6. auctions, or offers or attempts or agrees to auction, real estate
7. buys or sells, or offers to buy or sell, or otherwise deals in options on real estate
8. aids, attempts, or offers to aid, in locating or obtaining for purchase, rent, or lease any real estate
9. procures, or assists in the procuring of, prospects for the purpose of effecting the sale, exchange, lease, or rental of real estate
10. procures, or assists in the procuring of, properties for the purpose of effecting the sale, exchange, lease, or rental of real estate

In addition to the foregoing, clarification of certain licensing provisions has been set out in recent amendments to the Rules pertaining to the provisions of The Texas Real Estate Licensing Act. These amendments state that an office sales manager who deals only with licensees and office personnel does not have to be licensed, nor does an officer of a corporation acting in behalf of the Board of Directors of the corporation, provided no special compensation is received.

The statutory definition of **broker** in Texas also includes a person employed by, or on behalf of, the owner or owners of lots or other parcels of real estate, at a salary, fee, commission, or any other valuable consideration, employed to sell real estate in lots or parcels, or any other disposition thereof. Broker also includes a person who charges an advance fee, or contracts for collection of a fee in connection with a contract, whereby he undertakes primarily to promote the sale of real estate either through its listing in a publication issued primarily for such purpose, or for referral of information concerning the real estate to brokers, or both.

Salesperson Defined

The definition of **real estate salesperson** means a person associated with a Texas-licensed real estate broker for the purposes of performing acts or transactions comprehended by the term of **real estate broker** as defined in the Act. It is specifically provided that a salesperson shall not accept compensation for real estate transactions from any person other than the broker under whom the salesperson is licensed at the time that the salesperson is paid, or under whom the salesperson was licensed when the salesperson earned the right to compensation. Thus, a salesperson who takes a listing on a property does so in the name of the salesperson's broker. In the event of a legal dispute caused by a salesperson, the dispute would be between the principal and the broker. Thus, some brokers take considerable care to oversee the documents that their salespeople prepare and sign. Other brokers do not, relying instead on the knowledge and sensibility of their salespeople, and accepting a certain amount of risk in the process.

The above definitions are intended to be all-inclusive so that almost any act affecting real property is construed to be one that constitutes brokerage. The objective is to maintain higher standards in the real estate industry through licensing. The only people not required to be licensed are specifically exempted from the Act and are persons operating in unique capacities, such as:

Exemptions from Licensing

1. an attorney-at-law licensed in this state or in any other state
2. an attorney in fact under a duly-executed power of attorney authorizing the consummation of a real estate transaction (however not to circumvent the licensing requirements of the Act)
3. a public official in the conduct of official duties
4. a person conducting an auction under the authority of a license issued by this state provided the person does not perform any other act of a real estate broker or salesman as defined by this Act
5. a person acting under a court order or under the authority of a will or a written trust instrument
6. a salesperson employed by an owner in the sale of structures and land on which said structures are situated, provided such structures are erected by the owner in the due course of his business (such as a builder)
7. an on-site manager of an apartment complex

8. transactions involving the sale, lease, or transfer of any mineral or mining interest in real property

9. an owner or his employees in renting or leasing his own real estate whether improved or unimproved

10. transactions involving the sale, lease, or transfer of cemetery lots

11. transactions involving the renting, leasing, or management of hotels or motels

12. a partnership or limited liability partnership performing an act constituting an act of a broker or salesperson, as defined by the Act, through a partner who is duly licensed as a real estate broker

13. a person registered under Section 9A of the Act who sells, buys, leases, or transfers an easement or right-of-way for use in connection with telecommunication, utility, railroad, or pipeline services.

Sales Associate

The term **sales associate** is not a license category. It merely refers to anyone with a real estate license who is employed by and "associated" with a broker. Most often this associate will be a real estate salesperson. However, a person who holds a broker license can work for another broker. Such a person is a regular member of the employing broker's sales force just like someone with a salesperson license. The salesperson and brokers who work for a broker are known collectively as the broker's sales associates or sales force or sales staff. You will also hear the term *real estate agent* used in a general sense. Correctly speaking, the broker is a special agent of the property owner and the sales associate is a general agent of the broker. In nontechnical language, real estate agent today means anyone, broker or salesperson, who negotiates real estate transactions for others.

License Eligibility

To be eligible for a real estate salesperson's license in Texas, an individual must be a resident of Texas and be at least 18 years of age. An applicant for a brokerage license shall additionally have not less than two years active experience as a licensed real estate practitioner. He or she must further satisfy the Commission, through its application procedures, as to honesty, trustworthiness, integrity, and competency. Competency is determined by passing the licensing examination.

The Act further requires that any applicant for broker licensure shall furnish the Commission satisfactory evidence: (1) that the applicant has satisfied the educational requirements required by the Act; (2) that the applicant has satisfied the requirements for broker licensure; (3) that the applicant was a licensed real estate broker in another state and that the applicant has had not less than two years active experience in that other state as a licensed real estate broker or salesperson during the 36-month period immediately preceding the filing of the application and that the applicant satisfied the educational requirements for broker licensure provided for by the Act; or (4) the applicant has within one year previous to the filing of the application been licensed in the state as a broker.

Education Requirements—Brokers

In recent years, the education requirements have also become an increasingly important part of license qualifications. Nearly all states (including Texas) require that applicants take real estate education courses at community colleges, universities, private real estate schools, or through adult education programs at high schools.

TABLE 18.1
Additional educational requirements.

Annual Certification	Semester Hours That Must Be Completed	Hours of Required Real Estate Core Courses	Classroom Hours Equivalent*
2nd	14	8	210
3rd	16	10	240
4th	18	12	270

*The Texas Real Estate Commission currently considers each semester hour to be equivalent to 15 classroom hours, and each quarter hour to be equivalent to 10 classroom hours.

An applicant for a Texas real estate brokerage license must furnish evidence of successful completion of 60 semester hours (900 classroom hours) of real estate core courses or related courses accepted by the Real Estate Commission.

Education Requirements—Salespersons

An applicant for real estate salesperson license must furnish evidence of successful completion of 12 semester hours (180 classroom hours) of post secondary education. Six hours of these 12 hours must be in real estate core courses as defined by the Act. At least two of the six hours must be completed in a course described as Principles of Real Estate as defined by the Act, which must include at least three classroom hours of instruction on federal, state, and local laws relating to housing discrimination, housing credit discrimination, and community reinvestment. Applicants must also show evidence of completion of 2 hours (30 classroom hours) of a course in the Law of Agency, as defined by the Act, and a minimum of two hours in the Law of Contracts, as described by the Act. Additional educational requirements for the subsequent certifications are as shown in Table 18.1.

Continuing Education

Once the minimum education requirements have been satisfied, the licensee must provide the commission proof of attendance of at least 15 classroom hours of continuing education courses approved by the commission during the term of the current license. At least 6 hours of the instruction must be devoted to the rules of the commission, fair housing laws, agency laws, antitrust laws, the Deceptive Trade Practices-Consumer Protection Act, disclosures to buyers and sellers, current contract and addendum forms, the unauthorized practice of law, and case studies involving violations of laws and regulations, current federal housing administration, veterans administration regulations, tax laws, and other legal topics approved by the commission. The commission may not require examinations except for correspondence courses. Daily course segments must be at least 1 hour long, but not more than 10 hours long.

If a license is renewed for less than two years, the licensee must provide the commission proof of attendance of at least eight classroom hours of continuing education within the term of the current license, three classroom hours of which must have been devoted to the legal topics specified in the previous paragraph.

Table 18.2 shows the education and experience requirements in effect in the United States at the time this book was printed. The table is included to give you an overview of the emphasis currently being placed on education and experience by the various states. For up-to-the-minute information on education and experience requirements in Texas, you should contact the Texas Real Estate Commission, Education Division, in Austin.

TABLE 18.2
Real estate education and experience requirements.

| State | SALESPERSON LICENSE | | BROKER LICENSE (TOTAL HOURS) | | |
	Education Requirement	Continuing Education	Education Requirement	Experience Requirement	Continuing Education
Alabama	60 hours	Yes	N/A	2 years	Yes
Alaska	20 hours	Yes	35 hours	2 years	Yes
Arizona	90 hours	Yes	180 hours	3 years	Yes
Arkansas	60 hours	Yes	None	2 years	Yes
California	135 hours	Yes	360 hours	2 years	Yes
Colorado	N/A	Yes	192 hours	N/A	Yes
Connecticut	30 hours	Yes	60 hours	2 years	Yes
Delaware	99 hours	Yes	189 hours	5 years	Yes
Dist. of Col.	90 hours	Yes	135 hours	2 years	Yes
Florida	63 hours	Yes	135 hours	1 years	Yes
Georgia	75 hours	Yes	135 hours	3 years	Yes
Hawaii	45 hours	Yes	91 hours	2 years	Yes
Idaho	90 hours	Yes	180 hours	2 years	Yes
Illinois	30 hours	Yes	90 hours	1 years	Yes
Indiana	54 hours	Yes	108 hours	1 years	Yes
Iowa	30 hours	Yes	120 hours	2 years	Yes
Kansas	30 hours	Yes	54 hours	2 years	Yes
Kentucky	96 hours	Yes	33 hours	2 years	Yes
Louisiana	90 hours	Yes	240 hours	2 years	Yes
Maine	39 hours	Yes	168 hours	1 or 2 years	Yes
Maryland	90 hours	Yes	135 hours	3 years	Yes
Massachusetts	24 hours	Yes	54 hours	1 years	Yes
Michigan	40 hours	Yes	130 hours	3 years	Yes
Minnesota	90 hours	Yes	120 hours	2 years	Yes
Mississippi	60 hours	Yes	150 hours	1 yr + 60 hrs	Yes

(continued)

Explanation: Hours are clock-hours in the classroom; experience requirement is experience as a licensed real estate salesperson; continuing education refers to education required for license renewal. Some states credit completed salesperson education toward the broker education requirement.

LICENSING PROCEDURE

When a license applicant has completed or is close to completing the education and experience requirements, formal application for licensure is begun by filling out a license application form furnished by the Texas Real Estate Commission. When the application is completed, it is returned to the commission along with a fee to cover application processing and the examination charge. After the commission receives the application, an examination authorization letter is issued that gives the applicant one year in which to take and pass the exam.

Examination

Effective July 1, 1996, license examinations in Texas are now administered by the National Assessment Institute (NAI). NAI contracts with fifteen Sylvan Technology Centers across Texas. Applicants can make reservations with Sylvan via a toll free

TABLE 18.2
Continued.

| State | SALESPERSON LICENSE | | BROKER LICENSE (TOTAL HOURS) | | |
	Education Requirement	Continuing Education	Education Requirement	Experience Requirement	Continuing Education
Missouri	60 hours	Yes	108 hours *or*	2 years	Yes
Montana	60 hours	Yes	120 hours	2 years	Yes
Nebraska	60 hours	Yes	180 hours	2 years	Yes
Nevada	90 hours	Yes	1050 hours	8 years	Yes
New Hampshire	None	Yes	None	1 year	Yes
New Jersey	75 hours	No	150 hours	3 years	No
New Mexico	60 hours	Yes	150 hours	2 years	Yes
New York	45 hours	Yes	80 hours	2 years	Yes
North Carolina	30 hours	Yes	120 hours *or*	2 years	Yes
North Dakota	30 hours	Yes	90 hours	2 years	Yes
Ohio	120 hours	Yes	N/A		Yes
Oklahoma	45 hours	Yes	120 hours	2 years	Yes
Oregon	90 hours	Yes	150 hours	3 years	Yes
Pennsylvania	60 hours	Yes	300 hours	3 years	Yes
Rhode Island	None	No	90 hours	1 year	No
South Carolina	30 hours	No	90 hours	3 years	No
South Dakota	60 hours	Yes	100 hours	N/A	Yes
Tennessee	60 hours	Yes	120 hours	3 years	No
Texas	180 hours	Yes	900 hours	2 years	Yes
Utah	90 hours	Yes	120 hours	3 years	Yes
Vermont	None	Yes	8 hours	1 year	Yes
Virginia	60 hours	Yes	240 hours	3 years	Yes
Washington	30 hours	Yes	120 hours	2 years	No
West Virginia	90 hours	Yes	180 hours	2 years	Yes
Wisconsin	72 hours	Yes	108 hours	None	Yes
Wyoming	30 hours	Yes	60 hours	2 years	Yes

Source: National Association of Real Estate License Law Officials, 563 West 500 South, Bountiful, Utah 84010. Check with your state for any subsequent changes.

number, and seats are scheduled on a first-come first-serve basis. There is a fee charge for each time the exam is taken. An applicant may reschedule an appointment without forfeiting the fee; if a reservation is not kept however, the applicant forfeits the fee.

The examination consists of two parts: a theory portion (based on general principles) and a Texas law portion. The theory portion contains 70 questions. The law portion is 20 questions on a salesperson's exam, and 30 questions on the broker's exam. Two hours are allowed to complete the salesperson's exam; three hours are allowed for the broker's exam, which also includes questions on closing statements, which are not on the salesperson's exam. Each applicant must take both parts the first time; if one part is passed it need not be retaken. Test results are provided immediately following the exam. Each test differs and another fee is required each time the exam is taken. Retaking the exam immediately is not a good idea, because you may not see any of the same questions on the second exam that you experienced on the first exam. A word of caution: The exam tests knowledge of the subject matter, not how to take a test. Study hard and often!

Renewal

Once licensed, as long as a person remains active in real estate the license may be renewed by paying the required annual certification fee. If the licensee has met all of the educational requirements, license renewal is put on a biennial renewal (every two years). No additional exam is required.

If a license expires, the Real Estate Commission must waive the examination of an applicant for a broker or salesperson license who has, within one year previous to the filing of the application, been licensed in Texas as a broker or salesperson. The Commission may, at its discretion, also provide for a waiver of some or all of the requirements for a license under the Act for an applicant who was licensed under the Act within six years preceding the date of filing the renewal application.

The Act also allows a nonresident who was formerly licensed in Texas as a salesperson or broker to apply for licensure in Texas not later than the first anniversary of the date of the expiration of the previous license. The nonresident is subject to the same requirements as a resident applicant, however.

Inactive Status

When the association of a salesperson with the sponsoring broker is terminated, the broker must immediately return the salesperson's license to the Commission. The Real Estate Commission Regulations provide that if the sponsorship has ended because the broker terminated the sponsorship, the broker *must* immediately notify the salespeople *in writing.* If the sponsorship has ended because the salesperson has left the sponsorship, the salesperson *must* immediately notify the broker *in writing.* The salesperson is then placed on "inactive" status by the Commission. That salesperson's license may be activated if, within the calendar year, a request, accompanied by the required fee, is filed with the Commission by a licensed broker advising that she assumes sponsorship of the salesperson. A salesperson may also elect to remain inactive indefinitely so long as the salesperson continues to pay the annual fee to the Commission.

A real estate broker who is not acting as a broker or sponsoring a salesperson may apply to the Commission in writing to be placed on the inactive status list maintained by the Commission and must do so before the expiration of the broker's license. The broker must terminate the broker's association with any salesperson sponsored by the broker by getting written notice to the salesperson before the thirtieth day before the date the broker applies for inactive status. A broker on inactive status is still required to pay the annual renewal fees. If the broker has been on inactive status, the Commission must remove the person from the inactive list on application and proof of attendance of at least 15 classroom hours of continuing education as specified under the Act.

NONRESIDENT LICENSING

The general rule regarding license requirements is that a person must be licensed in the state within which he negotiates. Thus, if a broker or one of his salespeople sells an out-of-state property, but conducts the negotiations entirely within the borders of his own state, he does not need to be licensed to sell in the state where the land is actually located. State laws also permit the broker of one state to split a commission with the broker of another state provided each conducts negotiations only within the state where he is licensed. Therefore, if Broker B, licensed in State B, takes a listing at his office on a parcel of land located in State B, and Broker C in State C sells it to one of his clients, conducting the sale negotiations within State C, then Brokers B and C can split the commission. If, however, Broker C comes to State B to negotiate a contract, then a license in State B is necessary. The standard practice has been to apply for a **nonresident license** and meet substantially the same exam and experience requirements as demanded of resident brokers.

The Texas Real Estate Licensing Act allows a licensed real estate broker in another state to apply for broker licensure if he has been a licensed real estate broker in another state with not less than 2 years' active experience during the 36-month period immediately preceding the filing of his application, and the educational requirements for broker licensure in the state of Texas are satisfied.

License Reciprocity

In recent years, there has been considerable effort to design real estate licensing systems that permit a broker and the broker's sales staff to conduct negotiations in other states without having to obtain nonresident licenses. The result is **license reciprocity** and it applies when one state honors another's license. In permitting reciprocity, state officials are primarily concerned with the nonresident's knowledge of real estate law and practice as it applies to the state in which the applicant wishes to operate.

A few states accept real estate licenses issued by other states. This is called **full reciprocity** and means that a licensee can operate in another state without having to take that state's examination and meet its education and experience requirements. More commonly, most states have **partial reciprocity** that gives credit to the licensees of another state for experience, education, and examination. The 1979 amendment to the Real Estate License Act discarded the term *reciprocity* and technically, Texas does not reciprocate with any state. Instead, the Texas Real Estate License Act provides that a resident broker in another state may apply for a nonresident Texas broker license by meeting the nonresident broker requirements.

Notice of Consent

When a broker operates outside of his home state, he may be required to file a **notice of consent** in each state in which he intends to operate, usually with the secretary of state. This permits the secretary of state to receive legal summonses on behalf of the nonresident broker and provides a state resident an avenue by which he can sue a broker who is a resident of another state. Texas has this requirement.

LICENSING THE BUSINESS FIRM

When a real estate broker wishes to establish a brokerage business, the simplest method is a sole proprietorship under the broker's own name, such as, Kathleen B. Jones, Real Estate Broker. Some states, including Texas, permit a broker to operate out of his residence. However, operating a business in a residential neighborhood can be bothersome to neighbors, and many states require brokers to maintain a place of business in a location that is zoned for businesses.

Assumed Name

When a person operates under a name other than his own, he must register that name by filing an **assumed name certificate** with his county clerk and the state real estate licensing authority. Thus, if John B. Jones wishes to call his brokerage business Great Texas Realty, his business certificate would show "John B. Jones, doing business as Great Texas Realty." (Sometimes "doing business as" is shortened to dba or d/b/a.)

A sole proprietorship, whether operated under the broker's name or an assumed name, offers a broker advantages in the form of absolute control, flexibility, ease of organization, personal independence, ownership of all the profits and losses, and the freedom to expand by sponsoring all the salespeople and staff he can manage and afford. Against this the sole proprietor must recognize that he is the sole source of capital for the business and the only owner available to manage it.

Recognizing the need to accumulate capital and management expertise within a single brokerage operation, Texas also permits corporations, limited liability companies, and partnerships to be licensed. Since a corporation is an artificial being (not an individual), it cannot take a real estate examination. Therefore, Texas laws require that an officer of the corporation be a Texas-licensed real estate broker and qualified to act as the designated person for a corporation holding Texas broker licensure. A corporation incorporated in a state other than Texas may be accepted as a Texas resident for purposes of licensure if it is qualified to do business in Texas; its corporate officers, its principal place of business, and all of its assets are located in Texas; and all of its officers and directors are Texas residents. Similarly, a limited liability company must have a manager as a designated broker. Texas law does not require that a partnership be licensed, provided that each individual partner or non-partner employee who acts as a real estate agent in the partnership's name is licensed as a real estate broker or salesperson. The partnership must also file an assumed name certificate showing the names of the partners and the name of the partnership.

Branch Offices

If a broker expands by establishing branch offices that are geographically separate from the main or home office, each branch must have a branch office license.

LICENSING REAL ESTATE INSPECTORS

A common problem for real estate purchasers, and an area of continuing liability for real estate agents, has been that of defective property. Purchasers frequently feel that the expertise of real estate agents should shield them from the duty to investigate too closely, since the agent sees and inspects property all the time. The agent also has a duty to disclose material defects in the property under the License Act. The difficulty in relying on the agent is that the agent often doesn't have the expertise, and in many cases the defect is too technical or complicated to be discovered by the agent.

In an effort to alleviate this situation, Texas provides for the licensing of **real estate inspectors.** The statute now provides that a person may not act as a real estate inspector for a buyer or seller unless the person possesses a real estate inspector license issued by the Texas Real Estate Commission. The statute further provides for minimum standards of education and a recovery fund, similar to that required of real estate salespersons or brokers. The law is also designed to eliminate certain potential for conflicts of interest, specifically prohibiting the inspector from:

1. accepting an assignment if the employment is contingent on the reporting of a specific, predetermined condition or on reporting findings other than those known to the inspector to be facts at the time of accepting the assignment; or
2. acting in a manner or engaging in a practice that is dishonest or fraudulent or that involves deceit or misrepresentation; or
3. performing the inspection in a negligent or incompetent manner; or
4. acting in the dual capacity of inspector and undisclosed principal; or
5. acting in the dual capacity of real estate inspector and real estate broker or salesperson; or

6. performing any repairs in connection with the real estate inspection.

There are additional prohibitions and specific references to prohibiting the inspector's violations of the Deceptive Trade Practices Act. The statute also provides for recovery of attorney's fees, at the discretion of the court, if they are incurred in obtaining a recovery from a licensed inspector for a violation of the Act.

PUTTING IT TO WORK

Since the statute has been in effect, it has opened a whole new industry in the real estate profession. In addition, it has given the home purchaser a licensed, competent person for protection against defects in the property. The real estate licensee, too, has a person to recommend for the inspections of a more technical nature, which may help to eliminate another potential liability.

REGISTRATION

A new change in the Texas Real Estate License Act now provides for **registration** for those who sell, buy, lease, or transfer an easement or a right-of-way for compensation, or with the intention or in the expectation, or on the promise of receiving or collecting compensation, for use and connection with telecommunication, utility, railroad, or pipeline service. These people, as a part of their daily business, engage in the transfer or sale of real estate for others, but there has been a "gray" area as to whether they needed to be licensed. They don't market real estate for consumers in the regular course of business. Most of their activities are specialized in right-of-way acquisitions. To eliminate this confusion, we now have a registration procedure under Section 9A of the Texas Real Estate License Act. It does not require the same educational requirements of real estate licensing, and has Commission procedures for investigating complaints for revoking or suspending the registration if a registrant had engaged in conduct that violates the Act.

TEXAS REAL ESTATE COMMISSION

The administration of the provisions of the Texas Real Estate License Act is vested in the Texas Real Estate Commission. The Commission consists of nine members appointed by the Governor with the consent of two-thirds of the Senate present. The commissioners hold office for staggered terms of six years, with the terms of three members expiring January 31 of each odd-numbered year. The governor designates one of the licensed broker members as the chairperson.

Commission Membership

Six members of the Commission must have been engaged in the real estate brokerage business as licensed real estate brokers as their major occupation for at least five years preceding their appointments to the Commission, although a broker appointee cannot hold an office in a real estate industry trade association. The other three members must be representatives of the general public who are not licensed under the Texas Real Estate License Act and who do not have a financial interest in the practice of real estate broker or real estate salesperson, other than as consumers, and who are not acting for anyone holding such an interest.

An existing commissioner can be removed from the commission if as broker member he or she ceases to be a licensed real estate broker; or if as a public member he or she acquires a real estate license or financial interest in the practice of real estate; or if that commissioner becomes an employee or paid consultant of any real estate trade association or an officer in a state wide real estate trade association; or if a commissioner misses more than one-half of the regularly scheduled meetings. All appointments to the Commission must be made without regard to the race, creed, sex, religion, or national origin of the appointee.

The Commission has a regular meeting in October of each year, although it usually meets at least once per month. It has the power to make and enforce all rules and regulations in performance of its duties and institute actions to enjoin any violation of any provision of the Texas Real Estate License Act.

Any rule promulgated by the Commission may be blocked or rescinded by a majority vote of the standing committee of the Texas House or Texas Senate having jurisdiction over the affairs of the Texas Real Estate Commission.

Commissioners' Duties

The duties of the commissioners do not normally include the daily operation of the Real Estate Commission. Their compensation as commissioners is only token compensation for time actually spent on their duties, and they are not employees of the Commission. Therefore, to administer the day-to-day activities of the Commission, the Commission selects an Administrator, who has the complete authority to exercise the powers, rights, and duties of the Commission. The Administrator and his or her staff are salaried employees of the Commission and all business of the Commission, service of process, notices, and applications are considered filed with the Administrator or Assistant Administrator.

LICENSE SUSPENSION AND REVOCATION

The most important control a state has over its real estate salespersons and brokers is that it can **suspend** (temporarily make ineffective) or **revoke** (recall and make void) a real estate license. Without one, it is unlawful for a person to engage in real estate activities for the purpose of earning a commission or fee. Unless an agent has a valid license, a court of law will not uphold the agent's claim for a commission from a client.

The Texas Real Estate Licensing Act gives certain reasons for which a license can be revoked or suspended:

1. The licensee has entered a plea of guilty or nolo contendere, or been found guilty or been convicted of, a felony, in which fraud is an essential element, and the time for appeal has elapsed or the judgment or conviction has been affirmed on appeal, irrespective of an order granting probation following such conviction, suspending the imposition of sentence.

2. The licensee has procured, or attempted to procure, a real estate license for himself or herself or a salesperson, by fraud, misrepresentation or deceit, or by making a material misstatement of fact in an application for a real estate license.

3. The licensee, when selling, trading, or renting real property in his or her own name, engaged in misrepresentation or dishonest or fraudulent action.

4. The licensee has failed within a reasonable time to make good a check issued to the commission after the commission has mailed a request for payment by certified mail to the licensee's last known business address as reflected by the Commission's records.

5. The licensee has disregarded or violated a provision of this Act.

6. The licensee, while performing an act constituting a broker or salesperson, as defined by this Act, has been guilty of:

(A)   making a material misrepresentation, or failing to disclose to a potential purchaser any latent structural defect or any other defect known to the broker or salesperson. Latent structural defects and other defects do not refer to trivial or insignificant defects, but refer to those defects that would be significant factors to a reasonable and prudent purchaser in making a decision to purchase;

(B)   making a false promise of a character likely to influence, persuade, or induce any person to enter into a contract or agreement when the licensee could not or did not intend to keep such promise;

(C)   pursuing a continued and flagrant course of misrepresentation or making false promises through agents, salespersons, advertising, or otherwise;

(D)   failing to make clear, to all parties to a transaction, which party the licensee is acting for, or receiving compensation from more than one party except with the full knowledge and consent of all parties;

(E)   failing within a reasonable time to properly account for or remit money coming into his or her possession that belongs to others or commingling money belonging to others with the licensee's own funds;

(F)   paying a commission or fees to, or dividing a commission or fee with, anyone not licensed as a real estate broker or salesperson in this state or in any other state, for compensation for services as a real estate agent;
Note: This provision (coupled with sec. 14A) now subjects a real estate licensee to license revocation for splitting a fee with an attorney who is not a principal in the transaction.

(G)   failing to specify a definite termination date that is not subject to prior notice in a contract, other than a contract to perform property management services, in which the licensee agrees to perform services for which a license is required under this Act;

(H)   accepting, receiving, or charging an undisclosed commission, rebate, or direct profit on expenditures made for a principal;

(I)   soliciting, selling, or offering for sale real property under scheme or program that constitutes a lottery or deceptive practice;

(J)   acting in the dual capacity of broker and undisclosed principal in a transaction;

(K)   guaranteeing, authorizing, or permitting a person to guarantee that future profits will result from a resale of real property;

(L)   placing a sign on real property offering it for sale, lease, or rent without the written consent of the owner or his authorized agent;

(M)   inducing or attempting to induce a party to a contract of sale or lease to break the contract for the purpose of substituting in lieu thereof a new contract;

(N)   negotiating or attempting to negotiate the sale, exchange, lease, or rental of real property with an owner or lessor, knowing that the owner or lessor had a written outstanding contract, granting exclusive agency in connection with the property to another real estate broker;

(O)   offering real property for sale or for lease without the knowledge and consent of the owner or his or her authorized agent, or on terms other than those authorized by the owner or the owner's authorized agent;

(P)   publishing, or causing to be published, an advertisement including, but not limited to, advertising by newspaper, radio, television, or display that is misleading, or which is likely to deceive the public, or which in any manner tends to create a misleading impression, or which fails to identify the person causing the advertisement to be published as a licensed real estate broker or agent;

(Q)   having knowingly withheld from or inserted in a statement of account or invoice, a statement that made it inaccurate in a material particular;

(R)   publishing or circulating an unjustified or unwarranted threat of legal proceedings, or other action;

(S)   establishing an association, by employment or otherwise, with an unlicensed person who is expected or required to act as a real estate licensee, or aiding or abetting or conspiring with a person to circumvent the requirements of this Act;

(T)   failing or refusing on demand to furnish copies of a document pertaining to a transaction dealing with real estate to a person whose signature is affixed to the document;

(U)   failing to advise a purchaser in writing before the closing of a transaction that the purchaser should either have the abstract covering the real estate which is the subject of the contract examined by an attorney of the purchaser's own selection, or be furnished with or obtain a policy of title insurance;

(V)   conduct which constitutes dishonest dealings, bad faith, or untrustworthiness;

(W) acting negligently or incompetently in performing an act for which a person is required to hold a real estate license;

(X)   disregarding or violating a provision of this Act;

(Y)   failing within a reasonable time to deposit money received as escrow agent in a real estate transaction, either in trust with a title company authorized to do business in this state, or in a custodial, trust, or escrow account maintained for that purpose in a banking institution authorized to do business in this state;

(Z)   disbursing money deposited in a custodial, trust, or escrow account, as provided in Subsection (y) before the transaction concerned has been consummated or finally otherwise terminated;

(AA) discriminating against an owner, potential purchaser, lessor, or potential lessee on the basis of race, color, religion, sex, national origin, or ancestry including directing prospective home buyers or lessees interested in equivalent properties to different areas according to the race, color, religion, sex, national origin, or ancestry of the potential owner or lessee.

7. Failing or refusing on demand to produce a document, book, or record in his or her possession concerning a real estate transaction conducted by him or her for inspection by the Real Estate Commission or its authorized personnel or representative.

8. Failing within a reasonable time to provide information requested by the Commission as a result of a formal or informal complaint to the Commission that would indicate a violation of the Act.

9. Failing without just cause to surrender to the rightful owner, on demand, a document or instrument coming into his possession.

Recovery Fund

The Texas Real Estate Commission has established a recovery fund, with specified limits, to pay damages in the event a judgment is obtained against the licensee and there are no other funds recoverable from the licensee. The recovery fund is funded solely from fees paid by licensees. It is important to note that in order to proceed against the recovery fund the complainant must have received a final judgment in a court of competent jurisdiction. The amounts to be recovered are limited to $50,000 per transaction or $100,000 against any one licensed real estate broker or salesperson. The complainant must also prove that there were no attachable assets belonging to the broker or salesperson.

The Texas Real Estate License Act provides that if a person files a complaint with the Commission relating to a real estate broker or salesperson, the Commission shall furnish to that complainant an explanation of the remedies that are available to that person under the Act. The Commission must also provide information about appropriate state or local agencies or officials with which the person may file a complaint. The Commission shall furnish the same explanatory information to the person against whom the complaint is filed. The Commission is required to keep an information file about each complaint filed with the Commission, and it shall inform the complainant and person against whom the complaint is filed as to the status of the complaint at least as often as every three months. If the Commission revokes a person's license issued under the Act, the Commission may not issue another license to that person for one year after the revocation.

The requirement for bonds and the establishment of the recovery funds are not perfect solutions to the problem of uncollectible judgments because the wronged party must expend considerable effort to recover the loss, and it is quite possible that the maximum amount available per transaction or licensee will not fully compensate for the losses suffered. However, either system is better than none at all, which is still the case in some states.

SECURITIES LICENSE

Be aware that there may be times when a real estate licensee also needs a securities license. This is so whenever the property being sold is an investment contract in real estate rather than real estate itself. A prime example is a real estate partnership. Timeshare units and rental pools where condominium owners put their units into a pool for a percentage of the pool's income may also fall into this category. Securities licenses are issued by the National Association of Securities Dealers based on successful completion of their examination. Legal counsel is advised if there is the possibility you may be selling securities. Counsel will also advise on state and federal laws requiring the registration of real estate securities before they are sold.

AFFILIATING WITH A BROKER

If you plan to enter real estate sales, selecting a broker to work for is one of the most important decisions you must make. The best way to approach it is to stop and carefully consider what you have to offer the real estate business and what you expect in return. And look at it in that order! It is easy to become captivated by the big commission income you visualize coming your way. But if that is your only perspective, you will meet with disappointment. People are willing to pay you money because they expect to receive some product or service in return. That is their viewpoint and it would probably be yours if you were in their position. Your clients are not concerned with your income goal; it is only incidental to their goals. If you help them attain their goals, you will reach yours.

Before applying for a real estate license ask yourself if the working hours and conditions of a real estate agent are suitable to you. Specifically, are you prepared to work on a commission-only basis? Evenings and weekends? On your own? With people you've never met before? If you can comfortably answer yes to these questions, then start looking for a broker to sponsor you. (Salesperson license educational requirements can be completed without broker sponsorship, but a salesperson must have a sponsoring broker in order to make application for a salesperson license.)

Training

Your next step is to look for those features and qualities in a broker that will complement, enhance, and encourage your personal development in real estate. If you are new to the industry, training and education will most likely be at the top of your list.

PUTTING IT TO WORK

Real estate franchise operations and large brokerage offices usually offer extensive training. In smaller offices, the broker in charge is usually responsible for seeing that newcomers receive training. An office that offers no training to a newcomer should be avoided.

Therefore, in looking for a broker you will want to find one who will in one fashion or another teach you the trade. (What you have learned to date from books, classes, and license examination preparation will be helpful, but you will need additional specific training.)

Compensation

Another question high on your list will be compensation. Compensation for salespersons is usually a percentage of the commissions they earn for the broker. How much each receives is open to negotiation between the broker and each salesperson working for him. A broker who offers the sales staff office space, extensive secretarial help, a large advertising budget, a mailing program, and generous long-distance telephone privileges might take 40% to 50% of each incoming commission dollar for office overhead. A broker who provides fewer services might take 25% or 30%.

PUTTING IT TO WORK

Many brokers feel that one must produce to be paid and the hungrier the salesperson, the quicker that salesperson will produce. A broker who pays salespersons regardless of sales produced simply must siphon the money from those who are producing. The old saying, "There's no such thing as a free lunch" applies to sales commissions.

Salespersons with proven sales records can sometimes reduce the portion of each earned commission dollar that must go to the broker. This is because the broker may feel that with an outstanding sales performer, a high volume of sales will offset a smaller percentage for overhead. Conversely, a new and untried salesperson, or one with a mediocre past sales record, may have to give up a larger portion of each dollar for the broker's overhead.

When one brokerage agency lists a property and another locates the buyer, the commission is split according to any agreement the two brokers wish to make. After splitting, each broker pays a portion of the money received to the salesperson involved in accordance with the commission agreements.

While investigating commission arrangements, one should also inquire about incentive and bonus plans, automobile expense reimbursement, health insurance, life insurance, and retirement plans.

An alternative commission arrangement is the **100% commission** wherein the salesperson does not share the commission with the broker. Instead the salesperson is charged a fee for office space, advertising, telephone, multiple listings, and any other expenses the broker incurs on behalf of the salesperson. Generally speaking, 100% arrangements are more popular with proven performers than with newcomers.

Broker Support

Broker support will have an impact on any salesperson's success. Specifically: Will you have your own desk to work from? Are office facilities efficient and modern? Does the broker provide secretarial services? What is the broker's advertising policy and who pays for ads? Does the broker have sources of financing for clients? Does the broker allow his salespersons to invest in real estate? Does the broker have a good reputation in the community? Who pays for signs, business cards, franchise fees, and realty board dues?

Finding a Broker

Many salespersons associate with a particular broker as a result of a friendship or word-of-mouth information. However, there are other ways to find a suitable position. An excellent way to start your search is to decide what geographical area you want to work in. If you choose the same community or neighborhood in which you live, you will already possess a valuable sense and feel for that area.

Having selected a geographical area to specialize in, look in the Sunday newspaper real estate advertisements section and the telephone book Yellow Pages for names of brokers. Hold interviews with several brokers and as you do, remember that you are interviewing them just as intensively as they are interviewing you. At your visits with brokers be particularly alert to your feelings. Intuition can be as valuable a guide to a sound working relationship as a list of questions and answers regarding the job.

As you narrow your choices, revisit the offices of brokers who particularly impressed you. Talk with some of the salespersons who have worked or are working there. They can be very candid and valuable sources of information. Be wary of individuals who are extreme in their opinions: Rely instead on the consensus of opinion. Locate clients who have used the firm's services and ask them their opinions of the firm. You might also talk to local appraisers, lenders, and escrow agents for candid opinions. If you do all this advance work, the benefits to you will be greater enjoyment of your work, more money in your pocket, and less likelihood of wanting to quit or move to another office.

Employment Contract

Having selected a broker with whom to associate, your next step is to make an employment contract. An **employment contract** formalizes the working arrangement between the broker and the salespersons. An oral contract may be satisfactory, but a written one is preferred because it sets forth the relationship with a higher degree of precision. This greatly reduces the potential for future controversy and litigation.

The employment contract will cover such matters as compensation (how much and under what circumstances), training (how often and if required), hours of work (including assigned office hours and open houses), company identification (distinctive articles of clothing and name tags), fees and dues (license and realty board), expenses (automobile, advertising, telephone), fringe benefits (health and life insurance, pension and profit-sharing plans), withholding (income taxes and social security), territory (assigned area of the community), termination of employment (quitting and firing), federal tax obligations, and general office policies and procedures (office manual).

INDEPENDENT CONTRACTOR STATUS

Is the real estate sales associate an employee of the broker or an independent contractor? The answer is both. On one hand, the sales associate acts like an **employee** because the associate works for the broker, usually at the broker's place of business. There the associate prepares listings and sales documents on forms specified by the broker and upon closing receives payment from the broker. On the other hand, the sales associate acts like an **independent contractor** because the associate is paid only if the associate brings about a sale that produces a commission. An important distinction between the two is whether or not the broker must withhold income taxes and social security from the associate's commission checks. If the sales associate is considered by the Internal Revenue Service (IRS) to be an employee for tax purposes, the broker must withhold. If classed as an independent contractor for tax purposes, the sales associate is responsible for personal income taxes and social security. The IRS prefers employee status because it is easier to collect taxes from an employer than from an employee.

As a result of federal legislation that took effect January 1, 1983, the IRS will treat real estate sales associates as independent contractors if they meet all of the following three requirements. First, the associate must be a licensed real estate agent. Second, virtually all of the associate's payment for services as a real estate agent must be directly related to sales and not to hours worked. Third, a written agreement must exist between the associate and the broker stating that the associate will be treated as an independent contractor for tax purposes. If an agent and that agent's sponsoring broker do not comply with this statute, they run the risk of losing their independent contractor status, and the sponsoring broker would be subject to the same filing requirements as any other employer in the normal course of business.

These are highlights of the issue. If you plan to work for a broker, you may find it valuable to have this matter as well as your entire employment contract reviewed by an attorney before you sign it.

FRANCHISED OFFICES

Prior to the early 1970s, a real estate brokerage was typically a small business. In fact, most brokerages were one office firms. A brokerage was considered large if it had four or five branch offices, handling perhaps 200 properties a year. Then real estate franchise organizations entered the real estate business in a big way. By offering **franchises,** large organizations such as Century-21, Prudential, ReMax, and Gallery of Homes offered national identification, large-scale advertising, sales staff training programs, management advice, customer referrals, financing help for buyers, and guaranteed sales plans to small brokerage offices. In return, the brokerage firm (the **franchisee**) paid a fee to the national organization of from 3% to 8% of its gross commission income. The new marketing system flourished, and by the mid-1980s approximately half of the real estate licensees affiliated with the National Association of Realtors were working as franchised offices. Meanwhile, the number of franchisers grew to more than 60 large organizations including Realty World, ERA, International Real Estate Network, Better Homes and Gardens Realty, and REMAX offering attractive franchises to the small firms.

Statistics show that franchising appeals mostly to middle-sized firms with 10 to 50 sales associates. Larger firms are able to provide the advantages of a franchise for themselves, while the smallest firms tend to occupy special market niches and often consist of one or two licensees who do not bring in additional sales associates. For a newly licensed salesperson wishing to affiliate with a firm, a franchised firm can offer immediate public recognition, extensive training opportunities, established office routines, regular sales meetings, and access to a nationwide referral system. Franchise affiliation is not magic however. Success still depends on the individual who makes sales calls, values property, gets listings, advertises, shows property, qualifies, negotiates, and closes transactions.

National Real Estate Firms

During the late 1970s a large real estate firm in California—Coldwell Banker—began an expansion program by purchasing multi-branch real estate firms in other states. Today, a number of national franchises have several hundred offices across the United States. Cendant Corp. (formerly HFS, Inc.) has acquired three major franchises to create a huge network of firms that may offer a number of other services to complement their brokerage services—some refer to it as "full service." The additional services can include access to auto dealers, interior decorators, contractors, and other commonly used services by home buyers. Between the national firms and the local firms in size are several well-established regional firms such as Ebby Halliday in Dallas, and Trione & Gordon in Houston.

For a newcomer, affiliation with a national or regional real estate firm offers benefits like those of a franchised firm (recognition, training, routines, etc.). The main difference is who owns the firm. A franchised firm will be locally owned and locally managed; that is, it is an independent firm. Regional and national firms are locally managed but not locally owned. The sales associates will only occasionally, if ever, meet the owner(s).

PROFESSIONAL REAL ESTATE ASSOCIATIONS

Even before laws required real estate agents to have licenses, there were professional real estate organizations. Called real estate boards, they joined together agents within a city or county on a voluntary basis. The push to organize came from real estate people who saw the need for some sort of controlling organization that could supervise the activities of individual agents and elevate real estate licensees to professional status in the public's mind. Next came the gradual grouping of local boards into state associations, and finally, in 1908, the National Association of Real Estate Boards (NAREB) was formed. In 1914, the NAREB developed a model license law that became the basis for real estate license laws in many states.

National Association of Realtors® (NAR)

Today the local boards are still the fundamental units of the **National Association of Realtors® (NAR).** Local board membership is open to anyone holding a real estate license. Called boards of Realtors, real estate boards, and realty boards, they promote fair dealing among their members and with the public and protect members from dishonest and irresponsible licensees. They also promote legislation that protects property rights, offer short seminars to keep members up-to-date with current laws and practices, and, in general, do whatever is necessary to build the dignity, stability, and professionalization of the industry. Local boards often operate the local multiple listing service, although in some communities it is a privately owned and operated business.

State associations are composed of the members of local boards plus salespeople and brokers who live in areas where no local board exists. The purposes of the state associations are to unite members statewide, to encourage legislation that benefits and protects the real estate industry and safeguards the public in their real estate transactions, and to promote economic growth and development in the state. Also, state associations hold conventions to educate members and foster contacts among them.

Texas Association of Realtors® (TAR)

The **Texas Association of Realtors® (TAR),** with approximately 45,000 members, is the Texas organization of Realtors® authorized to use the Realtor® emblem. They maintain an active program of continuing education throughout the NAR Institute and its Real Estate Institute. They publish and distribute information on state legislation (material legislation), licensing laws, and professional standards.

A great deal of information is available through the TAR library of tapes and books. Standardized legal forms are available through the Texas Association of Realtors. The mailing address is

Texas Association of Realtors®

P.O. Box 14488

Austin, Texas 78761

Realtor® and NAR

The NAR is made up of local boards and state associations in the United States. The term **Realtor®** is a registered trade name that belongs to the NAR. Realtor® is not synonymous with real estate agent. It is reserved for the exclusive use of members of the National Association of Realtors®, who as part of their membership pledge themselves to abide by the Association's Code of Ethics. The term *Realtor®* cannot be used by nonmembers, and in some states the unauthorized use of the term is a violation of the real estate law. Prior to 1974, the use of the term *Realtor®* was primarily reserved for principal brokers. Then in November of that year, by a national membership vote, the decision was made to create an additional membership class, the **Realtor-Associate®**, for salespersons working for member Realtors®.

Code of Ethics

The **Code of Ethics** has been revised several times since it was developed in 1913, and it now contains 17 articles that pertain to the Realtor's® relationship to clients, to other real estate agents, and to the public as a whole. The full Code is reproduced below.

Although a complete review of each article is beyond the scope of this chapter, it can be seen in the Code that some articles parallel existing laws. For example, Article 10 speaks against racial discrimination and Article 2 speaks for full disclosure. However, as a whole the Code of Ethics addresses itself to the aspirations and obligations of a Realtor® that may be beyond the written law. In other words, to be recognized as a Realtor®, one must not only comply with the letter of the law, but also observe the ethical standards by which the industry operates.

In some states, ethical standards such as those in the NAR Code of Ethics have been legislated into law. Called **canons,** their intent is to promote ethical practices by all brokers and salespersons, not just by those who join the National Association of Realtors®. The Texas Real Estate Commission promulgates its own Canons of Professional Ethics, set out in Appendix B. Read it. It is almost as important as the License Act, and all licensees should familiarize themselves with it.

In addition to its emphasis on real estate brokerage, the National Association of Realtors® also contains a number of specialized professional groups within itself. These include the American Institute of Real Estate Appraisers, the Farm and Land Institute, the Institute of Real Estate Management, the Realtors® National Marketing Institute, the Society of Industrial Realtors®, the Real Estate Securities and Syndication Institute, the American Society of Real Estate Counselors, the American Chapter of the International Real Estate Federation, and the Women's Council of Realtors®. In each case, membership is open to Realtors® interested in these specialties.

FIGURE 18.1
Code of ethics

Code of Ethics and Standards of Practice
of the NATIONAL ASSOCIATION OF REALTORS®
Effective January 1, 1998

Where the word REALTORS® is used in this Code and Preamble, it shall be deemed to include REALTOR-ASSOCIATE®s.

While the Code of Ethics establishes obligations that may be higher than those mandated by law, in any instance where the Code of Ethics and the law conflict, the obligations of the law must take precedence.

Preamble...

Under all is the land. Upon its wise utilization and widely allocated ownership depend the survival and growth of free institutions and of our civilization. REALTORS® should recognize that the interests of the nation and its citizens require the highest and best use of the land and the widest distribution of land ownership. They require the creation of adequate housing, the building of functioning cities, the development of productive industries and farms, and the preservation of a healthful environment.

Such interests impose obligations beyond those of ordinary commerce. They impose grave social responsibility and a patriotic duty to which REALTORS® should dedicate themselves, and for which they should be diligent in preparing themselves. REALTORS®, therefore, are zealous to maintain and improve the standards of their calling and share with their fellow REALTORS® a common responsibility for its integrity and honor.

In recognition and appreciation of their obligations to clients, customers, the public, and each other, REALTORS® continuously strive to become and remain informed on issues affecting real estate and, as knowledgeable professionals, they willingly share the fruit of their experience and study with others. They identify and take steps, through enforcement of this Code of Ethics and by assisting appropriate regulatory bodies, to eliminate practices which may damage the public or which might discredit or bring dishonor to the real estate profession.

Realizing that cooperation with other real estate professionals promotes the best interests of those who utilize their services, REALTORS® urge exclusive representation of clients; do not attempt to gain any unfair advantage over their competitors; and they refrain from making unsolicited comments about other practitioners. In instances where their opinion is sought, or where REALTORS® believe that comment is necessary, their opinion is offered in an objective, professional manner, uninfluenced by any personal motivation or potential advantage or gain.

The term REALTOR® has come to connote competency, fairness, and high integrity resulting from adherence to a lofty ideal of moral conduct in business relations. No inducement of profit and no instruction from clients ever can justify departure from this ideal.

In the interpretation of this obligation, REALTORS® can take no safer guide than that which has been handed down through the centuries, embodied in the Golden Rule, "Whatsoever ye would that others should do to you, do ye even so to them."

Accepting this standard as their own, REALTORS® pledge to observe its spirit in all of their activities and to conduct their business in accordance with the tenets set forth below.

Duties to Clients and Customers

Article 1

When representing a buyer, seller, landlord, tenant, or other client as an agent, REALTORS® pledge themselves to protect and promote the interests of their client. This obligation of absolute fidelity to the client's interests is primary, but it does not relieve REALTORS® of their obligation to treat all parties honestly. When serving a buyer, seller, landlord, tenant or other party in a non-agency capacity, REALTORS® remain obligated to treat all parties honestly. *(Amended 1/93)*

- **Standard of Practice 1-1**
  REALTORS®, when acting as principals in a real estate transaction, remain obligated by the duties imposed by the Code of Ethics. *(Amended 1/93)*

- **Standard of Practice 1-2**
  The duties the Code of Ethics imposes are applicable whether REALTORS® are acting as agents or in legally recognized non-agency capacities except that any duty imposed exclusively on agents by law or regulation shall not be imposed by this Code of Ethics on REALTORS® acting in non-agency capacities.

  As used in this Code of Ethics, "client" means the person(s) or entity(ies) with whom a REALTOR® or a REALTOR®'s firm has an agency or legally recognized non-agency relationship; "customer" means a party to a real estate transaction who receives information, services, or benefits but has no contractual relationship with the REALTOR® or the REALTOR®'s firm; and "agent" means a real estate licensee acting in an agency relationship as defined by state law or regulation. *(Adopted 1/95, Amended 1/98)*

- **Standard of Practice 1-3**
  REALTORS®, in attempting to secure a listing, shall not deliberately mislead the owner as to market value.

(continued)

FIGURE **18.1**
Continued.

- **Standard of Practice 1-4**
  REALTORS®, when seeking to become a buyer/tenant representative, shall not mislead buyers or tenants as to savings or other benefits that might be realized through use of the REALTOR®'s services. *(Amended 1/93)*

- **Standard of Practice 1-5**
  REALTORS® may represent the seller/landlord and buyer/tenant in the same transaction only after full disclosure to and with informed consent of both parties. *(Adopted 1/93)*

- **Standard of Practice 1-6**
  REALTORS® shall submit offers and counter-offers objectively and as quickly as possible. *(Adopted 1/93, Amended 1/95)*

- **Standard of Practice 1-7**
  When acting as listing brokers, REALTORS® shall continue to submit to the seller/landlord all offers and counter-offers until closing or execution of a lease unless the seller/landlord has waived this obligation in writing. REALTORS® shall not be obligated to continue to market the property after an offer has been accepted by the seller/landlord. REALTORS® shall recommend that sellers/landlords obtain the advice of legal counsel prior to acceptance of a subsequent offer except where the acceptance is contingent on the termination of the pre-existing purchase contract or lease. *(Amended 1/93)*

- **Standard of Practice 1-8**
  REALTORS® acting as agents of buyers/tenants shall submit to buyers/tenants all offers and counter-offers until acceptance but have no obligation to continue to show properties to their clients after an offer has been accepted unless otherwise agreed in writing. REALTORS® acting as agents of buyers/tenants shall recommend that buyers/tenants obtain the advice of legal counsel if there is a question as to whether a pre-existing contract has been terminated. *(Adopted 1/93)*

- **Standard of Practice 1-9**
  The obligation of REALTORS® to preserve confidential information provided by their clients continues after the termination of the agency relationship. REALTORS® shall not knowingly, during or following the termination of a professional relationship with their client:
  1) reveal confidential information of the client; or
  2) use confidential information of the client to the disadvantage of the client; or
  3) use confidential information of the client for the REALTOR®'s advantage or the advantage of a third party unless:
     a) the client consents after full disclosure; or
     b) the REALTOR® is required by court order; or

c) it is the intention of the client to commit a crime and the information is necessary to prevent the crime; or
d) it is necessary to defend the REALTOR® or the REALTOR®'s employees or associates against an accusation of wrongful conduct. *(Adopted 1/93, Amended 1/97)*

- **Standard of Practice 1-10**
  REALTORS® shall, consistent with the terms and conditions of their property management agreement, competently manage the property of clients with due regard for the rights, responsibilities, benefits, safety and health of tenants and others lawfully on the premises. *(Adopted 1/95)*

- **Standard of Practice 1-11**
  REALTORS® who are employed to maintain or manage a client's property shall exercise due diligence and make reasonable efforts to protect it against reasonably foreseeable contingencies and losses. *(Adopted 1/95)*

- **Standard of Practice 1-12**
  When entering into listing contracts, REALTORS® must advise sellers/landlords of:
  1) the REALTOR®'s general company policies regarding cooperation with subagents, buyer/tenant agents, or both;
  2) the fact that buyer/tenant agents, even if compensated by the listing broker, or by the seller/landlord will represent the interests of buyers/tenants; and
  3) any potential for the listing broker to act as a disclosed dual agent, e.g. buyer/tenant agent. *(Adopted 1/93, Renumbered 1/98)*

- **Standard of Practice 1-13**
  When entering into contracts to represent buyers/tenants, REALTORS® must advise potential clients of:
  1) the REALTOR®'s general company policies regarding cooperation with other firms; and
  2) any potential for the buyer/tenant representative to act as a disclosed dual agent, e.g. listing broker, subagent, landlord's agent, etc. *(Adopted 1/93, Renumbered 1/98)*

Article 2

REALTORS® shall avoid exaggeration, misrepresentation, or concealment of pertinent facts relating to the property or the transaction. REALTORS® shall not, however, be obligated to discover latent defects in the property, to advise on matters outside the scope of their real estate license, or to disclose facts which are confidential under the scope of agency duties owed to their clients. *(Amended 1/93)*

- **Standard of Practice 2-1**
  REALTORS® shall only be obligated to discover and disclose adverse factors reasonably apparent to someone with expertise in those areas required by their real estate licensing authority. Article 2 does not impose upon the

(continued)

FIGURE 18.1
Continued.

REALTOR® the obligation of expertise in other professional or technical disciplines. *(Amended 1/96)*

- **Standard of Practice 2-2**
  (Renumbered as Standard of Practice 1-12 1/98)

- **Standard of Practice 2-3**
  (Renumbered as Standard of Practice 1-13 1/98)

- **Standard of Practice 2-4**
  REALTORS® shall not be parties to the naming of a false consideration in any document, unless it be the naming of an obviously nominal consideration.

- **Standard of Practice 2-5**
  Factors defined as "non-material" by law or regulation or which are expressly referenced in law or regulation as not being subject to disclosure are considered not "pertinent" for purposes of Article 2. *(Adopted 1/93)*

Article 3

REALTORS® shall cooperate with other brokers except when cooperation is not in the client's best interest. The obligation to cooperate does not include the obligation to share commissions, fees, or to otherwise compensate another broker. *(Amended 1/95)*

- **Standard of Practice 3-1**
  REALTORS®, acting as exclusive agents of sellers/landlords, establish the terms and conditions of offers to cooperate. Unless expressly indicated in offers to cooperate, cooperating brokers may not assume that the offer of cooperation includes an offer of compensation. Terms of compensation, if any, shall be ascertained by cooperating brokers before beginning efforts to accept the offer of cooperation. *(Amended 1/94)*

- **Standard of Practice 3-2**
  REALTORS® shall, with respect to offers of compensation to another REALTOR®, timely communicate any change of compensation for cooperative services to the other REALTOR® prior to the time such REALTOR® produces an offer to purchase/lease the property. *(Amended 1/94)*

- **Standard of Practice 3-3**
  Standard of Practice 3-2 does not preclude the listing broker and cooperating broker from entering into an agreement to change cooperative compensation. *(Adopted 1/94)*

- **Standard of Practice 3-4**
  REALTORS®, acting as listing brokers, have an affirmative obligation to disclose the existence of dual or variable rate commission arrangements (i.e., listings where one amount of commission is payable if the listing broker's firm is the procuring cause of sale/lease and a different amount of commission is payable if the sale/lease results through the efforts of the seller/landlord or a cooperating broker). The listing broker shall, as soon as practical, disclose the existence of such arrangements to potential cooperating brokers and shall, in response to inquiries from cooperating brokers, disclose the differential that would result in a cooperative transaction or in a sale/lease that results through the efforts of the seller/landlord. If the cooperating broker is a buyer/tenant representative, the buyer/tenant representative must disclose such information to their client. *(Amended 1/94)*

- **Standard of Practice 3-5**
  It is the obligation of subagents to promptly disclose all pertinent facts to the principal's agent prior to as well as after a purchase or lease agreement is executed. *(Amended 1/93)*

- **Standard of Practice 3-6**
  REALTORS® shall disclose the existence of an accepted offer to any broker seeking cooperation. *(Adopted 5/86)*

- **Standard of Practice 3-7**
  When seeking information from another REALTOR® concerning property under a management or listing agreement, REALTORS® shall disclose their REALTOR® status and whether their interest is personal or on behalf of a client and, if on behalf of a client, their representational status. *(Amended 1/95)*

- **Standard of Practice 3-8**
  REALTORS® shall not misrepresent the availability of access to show or inspect a listed property. *(Amended 11/87)*

Article 4

REALTORS® shall not acquire an interest in or buy or present offers from themselves, any member of their immediate families, their firms or any member thereof, or any entities in which they have any ownership interest, any real property without making their true position known to the owner or the owner's agent. In selling property they own, or in which they have any interest, REALTORS® shall reveal their ownership or interest in writing to the purchaser or the purchaser's representative. *(Amended 1/91)*

- **Standard of Practice 4-1**
  For the protection of all parties, the disclosures required by Article 4 shall be in writing and provided by REALTORS® prior to the signing of any contract. *(Adopted 2/86)*

Article 5

REALTORS® shall not undertake to provide professional services concerning a property or its value where they have a present or contemplated interest unless such interest is specifically disclosed to all affected parties.

(continued)

FIGURE **18.1**
Continued.

Article 6

When acting as agents, REALTORS® shall not accept any commission, rebate, or profit on expenditures made for their principal, without the principal's knowledge and consent. *(Amended 1/92)*

- **Standard of Practice 6-1**

  REALTORS® shall not recommend or suggest to a client or a customer the use of services of another organization or business entity in which they have a direct interest without disclosing such interest at the time of the recommendation or suggestion. *(Amended 5/88)*

- **Standard of Practice 6-2**

  When acting as agents or subagents, REALTORS® shall disclose to a client or customer if there is any financial benefit or fee the REALTOR® or the REALTOR®'s firm may receive as a direct result of having recommended real estate products or services (e.g., homeowner's insurance, warranty programs, mortgage financing, title insurance, etc.) other than real estate referral fees. *(Adopted 5/88)*

Article 7

In a transaction, REALTORS® shall not accept compensation from more than one party, even if permitted by law, without disclosure to all parties and the informed consent of the REALTOR®'s client or clients. *(Amended 1/93)*

Article 8

REALTORS® shall keep in a special account in an appropriate financial institution, separated from their own funds, monies coming into their possession in trust for other persons, such as escrows, trust funds, clients' monies, and other like items.

Article 9

REALTORS®, for the protection of all parties, shall assure whenever possible that agreements shall be in writing, and shall be in clear and understandable language expressing the specific terms, conditions, obligations and commitments of the parties. A copy of each agreement shall be furnished to each party upon their signing or initialing. *(Amended 1/95)*

- **Standard of Practice 9-1**

  For the protection of all parties, REALTORS® shall use reasonable care to ensure that documents pertaining to the purchase, sale, or lease of real estate are kept current through the use of written extensions or amendments. *(Amended 1/93)*

Duties to the Public

Article 10

REALTORS® shall not deny equal professional services to any person for reasons of race, color, religion, sex, handicap, familial status, or national origin. REALTORS® shall not be parties to any plan or agreement to discriminate against a person or persons on the basis of race, color, religion, sex, handicap, familial status, or national origin. *(Amended 1/90)*

- **Standard of Practice 10-1**

  REALTORS® shall not volunteer information regarding the racial, religious or ethnic composition of any neighborhood and shall not engage in any activity which may result in panic selling. REALTORS® shall not print, display or circulate any statement or advertisement with respect to the selling or renting of a property that indicates any preference, limitations or discrimination based on race, color, religion, sex, handicap, familial status or national origin. *(Adopted 1/94)*

Article 11

The services which REALTORS® provide to their clients and customers shall conform to the standards of practice and competence which are reasonably expected in the specific real estate disciplines in which they engage; specifically, residential real estate brokerage, real property management, commercial and industrial real estate brokerage, real estate appraisal, real estate counseling, real estate syndication, real estate auction, and international real estate.

REALTORS® shall not undertake to provide specialized professional services concerning a type of property or service that is outside their field of competence unless they engage the assistance of one who is competent on such types of property or service, or unless the facts are fully disclosed to the client. Any persons engaged to provide such assistance shall be so identified to the client and their contribution to the assignment should be set forth. *(Amended 1/95)*

- **Standard of Practice 11-1**

  The obligations of the Code of Ethics shall be supplemented by and construed in a manner consistent with the Uniform Standards of Professional Appraisal Practice (USPAP) promulgated by the Appraisal Standards Board of the Appraisal Foundation.

  The obligations of the Code of Ethics shall not be supplemented by the USPAP where an opinion or recommendation of price or pricing is provided in pursuit of a listing, to assist a potential purchaser in formulating a purchase offer, or to provide a broker's price opinion, whether for a fee or not. *(Amended 1/96)*

- **Standard of Practice 11-2**

  The obligations of the Code of Ethics in respect of real estate disciplines other than appraisal shall be interpreted and applied in accordance with the standards of competence and practice which clients and the public reasonably require to protect their rights and interests considering the complexity of the transaction, the availability of expert assistance, and, where the REALTOR® is an agent or subagent, the obligations of a fiduciary. *(Adopted 1/95)*

(continued)

FIGURE 18.1
Continued.

- **Standard of Practice 11-3**

  When REALTORS® provide consultive services to clients which involve advice or counsel for a fee (not a commission), such advice shall be rendered in an objective manner and the fee shall not be contingent on the substance of the advice or counsel given. If brokerage or transaction services are to be provided in addition to consultive services, a separate compensation may be paid with prior agreement between the client and REALTOR®. *(Adopted 1/96)*

Article 12

REALTORS® shall be careful at all times to present a true picture in their advertising and representations to the public. REALTORS® shall also ensure that their professional status (e.g., broker, appraiser, property manager, etc.) or status as REALTORS® is clearly identifiable in any such advertising. *(Amended 1/93)*

- **Standard of Practice 12-1**

  REALTORS® may use the term "free" and similar terms in their advertising and in other representations provided that all terms governing availability of the offered product or service are clearly disclosed at the same time. *(Amended 1/97)*

- **Standard of Practice 12-2**

  REALTORS® may represent their services as "free" or without cost even if they expect to receive compensation from a source other than their client provided that the potential for the REALTOR® to obtain a benefit from a third party is clearly disclosed at the same time. *(Amended 1/97)*

- **Standard of Practice 12-3**

  The offering of premiums, prizes, merchandise discounts or other inducements to list, sell, purchase, or lease is not, in itself, unethical even if receipt of the benefit is contingent on listing, selling, purchasing, or leasing through the REALTOR® making the offer. However, REALTORS® must exercise care and candor in any such advertising or other public or private representations so that any party interested in receiving or otherwise benefiting from the REALTOR®'s offer will have clear, thorough, advance understanding of all the terms and conditions of the offer. The offering of any inducements to do business is subject to the limitations and restrictions of state law and the ethical obligations established by any applicable Standard of Practice. *(Amended 1/95)*

- **Standard of Practice 12-4**

  REALTORS® shall not offer for sale/lease or advertise property without authority. When acting as listing brokers or as subagents, REALTORS® shall not quote a price different from that agreed upon with the seller/landlord. *(Amended 1/93)*

- **Standard of Practice 12-5**

  REALTORS® shall not advertise nor permit any person employed by or affiliated with them to advertise listed property without disclosing the name of the firm. *(Adopted 11/86)*

- **Standard of Practice 12-6**

  REALTORS®, when advertising unlisted real property for sale/lease in which they have an ownership interest, shall disclose their status as both owners/landlords and as REALTORS® or real estate licensees. *(Amended 1/93)*

- **Standard of Practice 12-7**

  Only REALTORS® who participated in the transaction as the listing broker or cooperating broker (selling broker) may claim to have "sold" the property. Prior to closing, a cooperating broker may post a "sold" sign only with the consent of the listing broker. *(Amended 1/96)*

Article 13

REALTORS® shall not engage in activities that constitute the unauthorized practice of law and shall recommend that legal counsel be obtained when the interest of any party to the transaction requires it.

Article 14

If charged with unethical practice or asked to present evidence or to cooperate in any other way, in any disciplinary proceeding or investigation, REALTORS® shall place all pertinent facts before the proper tribunals of the Member Board or affiliated institute, society, or council in which membership is held and shall take no action to disrupt or obstruct such processes. *(Amended 1/90)*

- **Standard of Practice 14-1**

  REALTORS® shall not be subject to disciplinary proceedings in more than one Board of REALTORS® or affiliated institute, society or council in which they hold membership with respect to alleged violations of the Code of Ethics relating to the same transaction or event. *(Amended 1/95)*

- **Standard of Practice 14-2**

  REALTORS® shall not make any unauthorized disclosure or dissemination of the allegations, findings, or decision developed in connection with an ethics hearing or appeal or in connection with an arbitration hearing or procedural review. *(Amended 1/92)*

- **Standard of Practice 14-3**

  REALTORS® shall not obstruct the Board's investigative or disciplinary proceedings by instituting or threatening to institute actions for libel, slander or defamation against any party to a professional standards proceeding or their witnesses. *(Adopted 11/87)*

(continued)

FIGURE **18.1**
Continued.

- **Standard of Practice 14-4**
REALTORS® shall not intentionally impede the Board's investigative or disciplinary proceedings by filing multiple ethics complaints based on the same event or transaction. *(Adopted 11/88)*

Duties to REALTORS®

Article 15

REALTORS® shall not knowingly or recklessly make false or misleading statements about competitors, their businesses, or their business practices. *(Amended 1/92)*

Article 16

REALTORS® shall not engage in any practice or take any action inconsistent with the agency or other exclusive relationship recognized by law that other REALTORS® have with clients. *(Amended 1/98)*

- **Standard of Practice 16-1**
Article 16 is not intended to prohibit aggressive or innovative business practices which are otherwise ethical and does not prohibit disagreements with other REALTORS® involving commission, fees, compensation or other forms of payment or expenses. *(Adopted 1/93, Amended 1/95)*

- **Standard of Practice 16-2**
Article 16 does not preclude REALTORS® from making general announcements to prospective clients describing their services and the terms of their availability even though some recipients may have entered into agency agreements or other exclusive relationships with another REALTOR®. A general telephone canvass, general mailing or distribution addressed to all prospective clients in a given geographical area or in a given profession, business, club, or organization, or other classification or group is deemed "general" for purposes of this standard. *(Amended 1/98)*

Article 16 is intended to recognize as unethical two basic types of solicitations:

First, telephone or personal solicitations of property owners who have been identified by a real estate sign, multiple listing compilation, or other information service as having exclusively listed their property with another REALTOR®; and

Second, mail or other forms of written solicitations of prospective clients whose properties are exclusively listed with another REALTOR® when such solicitations are not part of a general mailing but are directed specifically to property owners identified through compilations of current listings, "for sale" or "for rent" signs, or other sources of information required by Article 3 and Multiple Listing Service rules to be made available to other REALTORS®

under offers of subagency or cooperation. *(Amended 1/93)*

- **Standard of Practice 16-3**
Article 16 does not preclude REALTORS® from contacting the client of another broker for the purpose of offering to provide, or entering into a contract to provide, a different type of real estate service unrelated to the type of service currently being provided (e.g., property management as opposed to brokerage). However, information received through a Multiple Listing Service or any other offer of cooperation may not be used to target clients of other REALTORS® to whom such offers to provide services may be made. *(Amended 1/93)*

- **Standard of Practice 16-4**
REALTORS® shall not solicit a listing which is currently listed exclusively with another broker. However, if the listing broker, when asked by the REALTOR®, refuses to disclose the expiration date and nature of such listing; i.e., an exclusive right to sell, an exclusive agency, open listing, or other form of contractual agreement between the listing broker and the client, the REALTOR® may contact the owner to secure such information and may discuss the terms upon which the REALTOR® might take a future listing or, alternatively, may take a listing to become effective upon expiration of any existing exclusive listing. *(Amended 1/94)*

- **Standard of Practice 16-5**
REALTORS® shall not solicit buyer/tenant agreements from buyers/tenants who are subject to exclusive buyer/tenant agreements. However, if asked by a REALTOR®, the broker refuses to disclose the expiration date of the exclusive buyer/tenant agreement, the REALTOR® may contact the buyer/tenant to secure such information and may discuss the terms upon which the REALTOR® might enter into a future buyer/tenant agreement or, alternatively, may enter into a buyer/tenant agreement to become effective upon the expiration of any existing exclusive buyer/tenant agreement.
(Adopted 1/94, Amended 1/98)

- **Standard of Practice 16-6**
When REALTORS® are contacted by the client of another REALTOR® regarding the creation of an exclusive relationship to provide the same type of service, and REALTORS® have not directly or indirectly initiated such discussions, they may discuss the terms upon which they might enter into a future agreement or, alternatively, may enter into an agreement which becomes effective upon expiration of any existing exclusive agreement. *(Amended 1/98)*

- **Standard of Practice 16-7**
The fact that a client has retained a REALTOR® as an agent or in another exclusive relationship in one or more past transactions does not preclude other REALTORS® from seeking such former client's future business. *(Amended 1/98)*

(continued)

FIGURE 18.1
Continued.

• **Standard of Practice 16-8**

The fact that an exclusive agreement has been entered into with a REALTOR® shall not preclude or inhibit any other REALTOR® from entering into a similar agreement after the expiration of the prior agreement. *(Amended 1/98)*

• **Standard of Practice 16-9**

REALTORS®, prior to entering into an agency agreement or other exclusive relationship, have an affirmative obligation to make reasonable efforts to determine whether the client is subject to a current, valid exclusive agreement to provide the same type of real estate service. *(Amended 1/98)*

• **Standard of Practice 16-10**

REALTORS®, acting as agents of, or in another relationship with, buyers or tenants, shall disclose that relationship to the seller/landlord's agent or broker at first contact and shall provide written confirmation of that disclosure to the seller/landlord's agent or broker not later than execution of a purchase agreement or lease. *(Amended 1/98)*

• **Standard of Practice 16-11**

On unlisted property, REALTORS® acting as buyer/tenant agents or brokers shall disclose that relationship to the seller/landlord at first contact for that client and shall provide written confirmation of such disclosure to the seller/landlord not later than execution of any purchase or lease agreement.

REALTORS® shall make any request for anticipated compensation from the seller/landlord at first contact. *(Amended 1/98)*

• **Standard of Practice 16-12**

REALTORS®, acting as agents or brokers of sellers/landlords or as subagents of listing brokers, shall disclose that relationship to buyers/tenants as soon as practicable and shall provide written confirmation of such disclosure to buyers/tenants not later than execution of any purchase or lease agreement. *(Amended 1/98)*

• **Standard of Practice 16-13**

All dealings concerning property exclusively listed, or with buyer/tenants who are subject to an exclusive agreement shall be carried on with the client's agent or broker, and not with the client, except with the consent of the client's agent or broker or except where such dealings are initiated by the client. *(Adopted 1/93, Amended 1/98)*

• **Standard of Practice 16-14**

REALTORS® are free to enter into contractual relationships or to negotiate with sellers/landlords, buyers/tenants or others who are not subject to an exclusive agreement but shall not knowingly obligate them to pay more than one commission except with their informed consent. *(Amended 1/98)*

• **Standard of Practice 16-15**

In cooperative transactions REALTORS® shall compensate cooperating REALTORS® (principal brokers) and shall not compensate nor offer to compensate, directly or indirectly, any of the sales licensees employed by or affiliated with other REALTORS® without the prior express knowledge and consent of the cooperating broker.

• **Standard of Practice 16-16**

REALTORS®, acting as subagents or buyer/tenant agents or brokers, shall not use the terms of an offer to purchase/lease to attempt to modify the listing broker's offer of compensation to subagents or buyer's agents or brokers nor make the submission of an executed offer to purchase/lease contingent on the listing broker's agreement to modify the offer of compensation. *(Amended 1/98)*

• **Standard of Practice 16-17**

REALTORS® acting as subagents or as buyer/tenant agents or brokers, shall not attempt to extend a listing broker's offer of cooperation and/or compensation to other brokers without the consent of the listing broker. *(Amended 1/98)*

• **Standard of Practice 16-18**

REALTORS® shall not use information obtained by them from the listing broker, through offers to cooperate received through Multiple Listing Services or other sources authorized by the listing broker, for the purpose of creating a referral prospect to a third broker, or for creating a buyer/tenant prospect unless such use is authorized by the listing broker. *(Amended 1/93)*

• **Standard of Practice 16-19**

Signs giving notice of property for sale, rent, lease, or exchange shall not be placed on property without consent of the seller/landlord. *(Amended 1/93)*

• **Standard of Practice 16-20**

REALTORS®, prior to or after terminating their relationship with their current firm, shall not induce clients of their current firm to cancel exclusive contractual agreements between the client and that firm. This does not preclude REALTORS® (principals) from establishing agreements with their associated licensees governing assignability of exclusive agreements. *(Adopted 1/98)*

Article 17

In the event of contractual disputes or specific non-contractual disputes as defined in Standard of Practice 17-4 between REALTORS® associated with different firms, arising out of their relationship as REALTORS®, the REALTORS® shall submit the dispute to arbitration in accordance with the regulations of their Board or Boards rather than litigate the matter.

In the event clients of REALTORS® wish to arbitrate contractual disputes arising out of real estate transactions, REALTORS® shall arbitrate those disputes in accordance with the regulations of their Board, provided the clients agree to be bound by the decision. *(Amended 1/97)*

(continued)

Figure **18.1**
Continued.

- **Standard of Practice 17-1**
  The filing of litigation and refusal to withdraw from it by REALTORS® in an arbitrable matter constitutes a refusal to arbitrate. *(Adopted 2/86)*

- **Standard of Practice 17-2**
  Article 17 does not require REALTORS® to arbitrate in those circumstances when all parties to the dispute advise the Board in writing that they choose not to arbitrate before the Board. *(Amended 1/93)*

- **Standard of Practice 17-3**
  REALTORS®, when acting solely as principals in a real estate transaction, are not obligated to arbitrate disputes with other REALTORS® absent a specific written agreement to the contrary. *(Adopted 1/96)*

- **Standard of Practice 17-4**
  Specific non-contractual disputes that are subject to arbitration pursuant to Article 17 are:

  1) Where a listing broker has compensated a cooperating broker and another cooperating broker subsequently claims to be the procuring cause of the sale or lease. In such cases the complainant may name the first cooperating broker as respondent and arbitration may proceed without the listing broker being named as a respondent. Alternatively, if the complaint is brought against the listing broker, the listing broker may name the first cooperating broker as a third-party respondent. In either instance the decision of the hearing panel as to procuring cause shall be conclusive with respect to all current or subsequent claims of the parties for compensation arising out of the underlying cooperative transaction. *(Adopted 1/97)*

  2) Where a buyer or tenant representative is compensated by the seller or landlord, and not by the listing broker, and the listing broker, as a result, reduces the commission owed by the seller or landlord and, subsequent to such actions, another cooperating broker claims to be the procuring cause of sale or lease. In such cases the complainant may name the first cooperating broker as respondent and arbitration may proceed without the listing broker being named as a respondent. Alternatively, if the complaint is brought against the listing broker, the listing broker may name the first cooperating broker as a third-party respondent. In either instance the decision of the hearing panel as to procuring cause shall be conclusive with respect to all current or subsequent claims of the parties for compensation arising out of the underlying cooperative transaction. *(Adopted 1/97)*

  3) Where a buyer or tenant representative is compensated by the buyer or tenant and, as a result, the listing broker reduces the commission owed by the seller or landlord and, subsequent to such actions, another cooperating broker claims to be the procuring cause of sale or lease. In such cases the complainant may name the first cooperating broker as respondent and arbitration may proceed without the listing broker being named as a respondent. Alternatively, if the complaint is brought against the listing broker, the listing broker may name the first cooperating broker as a third-party respondent. In either instance the decision of the hearing panel as to procuring cause shall be conclusive with respect to all current or subsequent claims of the parties for compensation arising out of the underlying cooperative transaction. *(Adopted 1/97)*

  4) Where two or more listing brokers claim entitlement to compensation pursuant to open listings with a seller or landlord who agrees to participate in arbitration (or who requests arbitration) and who agrees to be bound by the decision. In cases where one of the listing brokers has been compensated by the seller or landlord, the other listing broker, as complainant, may name the first listing broker as respondent and arbitration may proceed between the brokers. *(Adopted 1/97)*

The Code of Ethics was adopted in 1913. Amended at the Annual Convention in 1924, 1928, 1950, 1951, 1952, 1955, 1956, 1961, 1962, 1974, 1982, 1986, 1987, 1989, 1990, 1991, 1992, 1993, 1994, 1995, 1996 and 1997.

Explanatory Notes

The reader should be aware of the following policies which have been approved by the Board of Directors of the National Association:

In filing a charge of an alleged violation of the Code of Ethics by a REALTOR®, the charge must read as an alleged violation of one or more Articles of the Code. Standards of Practice may be cited in support of the charge.

The Standards of Practice serve to clarify the ethical obligations imposed by the various Articles and supplement, and do not substitute for, the Case Interpretations in *Interpretations of the Code of Ethics.*

Modifications to existing Standards of Practice and additional new Standards of Practice are approved from time to time. Readers are cautioned to ensure that the most recent publications are utilized.

NATIONAL ASSOCIATION OF REALTORS®
430 North Michigan Avenue
Chicago, Illinois 60611

Realtist and NAREB

The National Association of Real Estate Brokers (NAREB) is a national trade association representing minority real estate professionals actively engaged in the industry. Founded in 1947, its 5,000 members use the trade name **Realtist.** The organization extends through 14 regions across the country with more than 60 active local boards. NAREB education and certification programs include the Real Estate Management Brokers Institute, National Society of Real Estate Appraisers, Real Estate Brokerage Institute, and United Developers Council. The organization's purposes are to promote high standards of service and conduct and to protect the public against unethical, improper, or fraudulent real estate practices.

REVIEW QUESTIONS

Answers to these questions are found in the Answer Key section at the back of the book.

1. Real estate licensing laws represent a government's effort to ascertain that real estate brokers and salespersons
   A. are persons of good reputation as to honesty and truthfulness.
   B. are competent.
   C. Both A and B.
   D. Neither A nor B.

2. The two levels of license under the Texas Real Estate License Act are:
   A. broker and appraiser.
   B. salesman and appraiser.
   C. salesman and agent.
   D. broker and salesperson.

3. Which of the following may conduct a real estate brokerage business without a proper license?
   A. Members of the state bar.
   B. Attorneys-in-fact.
   C. Both A and B.
   D. Neither A nor B.

4. A real estate broker differs from a real estate salesperson under the law in that
   A. the broker may act independently in conducting a brokerage business.
   B. a salesperson may operate in the brokerage business only under the supervision of a real estate broker.
   C. Both A and B.
   D. Neither A nor B.

5. Which of the following could be licensed as a real estate broker?
   A. A corporation.
   B. A partnership.
   C. An actual person.
   D. A sole proprietorship.
   E. All of the above.

6. A person who holds a real estate license is a
   A. licensor.
   B. licensee.
   C. vestee.
   D. vestor.

7. Which of the following is NOT a real estate license category?
   A. Salesperson.
   B. Broker.
   C. Attorney-in-fact.
   D. Both A and C.

8. A real estate salesperson, under the Texas Real Estate License Act, may
   A. take a listing in the name of the broker.
   B. accept compensation from real estate owners.
   C. Both A and B.
   D. Neither A nor B.

9. A real estate listing is a contract between
   A. the owner and the listing broker.
   B. the owner, the broker, and the listing salesperson.
   C. the owner and the listing salesperson.
   D. the broker and the listing salesperson.

10. The ultimate responsibility for a mistake in a document prepared by a real estate salesperson rests

   A. equally upon the salesperson and the employing broker.
   B. upon the employing broker.
   C. Both A and B.
   D. Neither A nor B.

11. The term "sales associate" may refer to

   A. a licensed salesperson employed by a real estate broker.
   B. a licensed real estate broker employed by another licensed broker.
   C. Both A and B.
   D. Neither A nor B.

12. As of January 1, 1985, an applicant for a Texas real estate brokerage license must complete

   A. 60 clockhours of real estate core courses.
   B. 900 clockhours of real estate related courses.
   C. 20 clockhours of real estate core courses.
   D. 900 clockhours of real estate core and related courses.

13. An applicant for a salesperson's license in Texas must complete how may clockhours in real estate core courses?

   A. 90
   B. 180
   C. 12
   D. 30

14. Before being granted an original salesperson's license, an applicant must

   A. pass the examination for salesperson licensure.
   B. name the broker with whom the applicant will be associated.
   C. complete any state-mandated education requirements.
   D. All of the above.

15. After licensure as a real estate broker or salesperson, a licensee must, in order to maintain the license, do all the following EXCEPT:

   A. meet any continuing education requirements.
   B. retake the original license examination and pass it.
   C. pay license renewal fees.
   D. renew the license prior to the expiration of any allowable grace period.

16. A real estate broker may share a commission on a real estate sale with any of the following EXCEPT:

   A. a salesperson licensed in his employ.
   B. a broker licensed in another state.
   C. another broker licensed in his state of licensure.
   D. a salesperson licensed with another broker in the state of licensure.

17. Real estate brokers may operate their businesses as sole proprietorships under

   A. their own name.
   B. a fictitious name.
   C. Both A and B.
   D. Neither A nor B.

18. For a corporation to be granted a license as a real estate broker,

   A. all officers must be licensed as real estate brokers.
   B. all stockholders must be licensees.
   C. the chief executive officer must be a licensed broker.
   D. salespersons may NOT hold office in the corporation.

19. In Texas, the requirement that a real estate agent hold a real estate license is set by the

   A. real estate commission.
   B. legislature.
   C. real estate director or commissioner.
   D. governor.

20. The composition of the Texas Real Estate Commission includes

   A. six representatives of the general public.
   B. six real estate brokers.
   C. three real estate brokers and three public representatives.
   D. four representatives of the public.

19

Broker: one who, for a fee, acts as an agent for others in negotiating contracts or sales

Exclusive authority to purchase: listing utilized by buyer's brokers

Exclusive right to sell: a listing that gives the broker the right to collect a commission no matter who sells the property during the listing period

Listing: a contract wherein a broker is employed to find a buyer or tenant

Multiple listing service: organization of member brokers agreeing to share listing information and share commissions

Net listing: a listing agreement that pays the broker an uncertain amount of commission, generating the principal net proceeds from the sale

Ready, willing, and able buyer: a buyer who is ready to buy at the seller's price and terms and who has the financial capability to do so

The Principal–Broker Relationship: Employment

IN THIS CHAPTER *This chapter covers the employment relationship between a broker and his principal. The main topics of the chapter include the listing agreement, exclusive right to sell listing, the exclusive agency listing, open listing, net listing, and the listing period. The chapter also covers the multiple listing service and broker compensation. A discussion of procuring cause, listing contract termination, and bargain brokers is also included.*

Chapter 18 discussed licensure requirements and professional affiliations. This chapter will discuss the principal-broker relationship as it relates to employment, listing agreements, buyer representation agreements, and compensation of real estate brokers. Chapter 20 will then expand into theories of agency relationships and duties of care that result from the laws of agency. Note that the formalities of employment are not necessarily required to establish an agency relationship, so the licensee may be responsible as an agent without the benefits of formal employment!

LISTING AGREEMENT

A **real estate listing** is an *employment contract* between a property owner (the seller) and a real estate broker. Through it the property owner appoints the broker as the owner's agent for the specific purpose of finding a buyer or tenant who is willing to meet the conditions set forth in the listing. It does not authorize the broker to sell or convey title to the property or to sign contracts.

Although persons licensed as real estate salespersons perform listing and sales functions, they are actually extensions of the broker. A seller may conduct all aspects of a listing and sale through a salesperson licensee, but it is the broker behind the salesperson with whom the seller has the listing contract and who is legally liable for its proper execution. If you plan to be a salesperson for a broker, be aware of what is legally and ethically required of a broker because you are the broker's eyes, ears, hands, and mouth. If your interest is in listing your property with a broker, know that it is the broker with whom you have the listing contract even though your day-to-day contact is with the broker's sales associates. **Sales associates** are the licensed salespersons or brokers who work for a broker.

When a property owner signs a listing, all the essential elements of a valid contract must be present. The owner and broker must be legally capable of contracting, there must be mutual assent, and the agreement must be for a lawful purpose. Nearly all states require that a listing be in writing and signed to be valid and thereby enforceable in a court of law.

Figure 19.1 illustrates a simplified **exclusive right to sell listing** agreement. Actual listing contracts tend to be longer and more complex and vary in detail from one contract to the next. The listing in Figure 19.1 is an educational introduction to listings that provides in plain English commonly found listing contract provisions. Beginning at **[1]**, there is a description of the property plus the price and terms at which the broker is instructed to find a buyer. At **[2]**, the broker promises to make a reasonable effort to find a buyer. The period of time that the listing is to be in effect is shown at **[3]**. It is usually to the broker's advantage to make the listing period for as long as possible as this provides more time to find a buyer. Sometimes even an over-priced property will become salable if the listing period is long enough and prices rise fast enough. However, most owners want a balance between their flexibility and the amount of time necessary for a broker to conduct a sales campaign. In residential sales, three to four months is a popular compromise; farm, ranch, commercial, and industrial listings are usually made for six months to one year.

At **[4]**, the owner agrees not to list the property with any other brokers, permit other brokers to have a sign on the property, or advertise it during the listing period. Also, the owner agrees not to revoke the broker's exclusive right to find a buyer as set forth by this contract.

The broker recognizes that the owner may later accept price and terms that are different from those in the listing. The wording at **[5]** states that the broker will earn a commission no matter what price and terms the owner ultimately accepts.

Brokerage Commission

At **[6]**, the amount of compensation the owner agrees to pay the broker is established. The usual arrangement is to express the amount as a percentage of the sale or exchange price, although a stated dollar amount could be used if the owner and broker agreed. In any event, the amount of the fee is negotiable between the owner and the broker. An owner who feels the fee is too high can list with someone who charges less or sell the property himself. The broker recognizes that if the fee is too low it will not be worthwhile spending time and effort finding a buyer. The typical commission fee in the United States at present is 5% to 7% of the selling price for houses, condominiums, and small apartment buildings, and 6% to 10% on farms, ranches, and vacant land. On multimillion-dollar improved properties, commissions usually drop to the 1% to 4% range. Brokerage commissions are not set by a state regulatory agency or by local real estate boards. In fact, any effort by brokers to set commission rates among themselves is a violation of federal and state anti-trust laws. The penalty can be as much as triple damages and criminal liability.

The conditions under which a commission must be paid by the owner to the broker appear next. At **[7]**, a commission is deemed to be earned if the owner agrees to a sale or exchange of the property no matter who finds the buyer. In other words, even if the owner finds a buyer, or a friend of the owner finds a buyer, the broker is entitled to a full commission fee. If the owner disregards the promise at **[4]** and lists with another broker who then sells the property, the owner is liable for two full commissions.

Protecting the Broker

The wording at **[8]** is included to protect the broker against the possibility that the owner may refuse to sell after the broker has expended time and effort to find a buyer at the price and terms of the listing contract. The listing itself is not an offer to sell property. It is strictly a contract whereby the owner employs the broker to find a buyer. Thus, even though a buyer offers to pay the exact price and terms shown in the listing, the buyer does not have a binding sales contract until the offer is accepted in writing

FIGURE 19.1
Exclusive Right To Sell Listing Contract.

EXCLUSIVE RIGHT TO SELL
LISTING CONTRACT

Property Description: <u>A single-family house at 2424 E. **[1]**
Main Street, City, State, Legally
described as Lot 17, Tract 191,
County, State</u>

Price: <u>$105,000</u>
Terms: <u>Cash</u>

In consideration of the services of <u>ABC Realty Company</u> *(herein called the "Broker"),* **[2]**
to be rendered to <u>Roger Leeving and Mary Leeving</u> *(herein called the "Owner"), and
the promise of said Broker to make reasonable efforts to obtain a purchaser, therefore,
the Owner hereby grants to the Broker for the period of time from noon on* <u>April 1,</u> **[3]**
<u>19xx</u> *to noon on* <u>July 1, 19xx</u> *(herein called the "listing period") the exclusive and* **[4]**
*irrevocable right to advertise and find a purchaser for the above described property at
the price and terms shown or for such sum and terms or exchange as the owner later* **[5]**
agrees to accept.

The Owner hereby agrees to pay Broker a cash fee of <u>6%</u> *of the selling or exchange* **[6]**
price:

(A) in case of any sale or exchange of the above property within the listing period **[7]**
either by the Broker, the Owner, or any other person, or

(B) upon the Broker finding a purchase who is ready, willing, and about to complete **[8]**
the purchase as proposed by the owner, or

(C) in the event of a sale or exchange within 60 days of the expiration of the listing **[9]**
*period to any party shown the above property during the listing period by the Broker
or his representative and where the name was disclosed to the Owner.*

The Owner agrees to give the Broker access to the buildings on the property for the **[10]**
*purposes of showing them at reasonable hours, and allows the Broker to post a "For
Sale" sign on the premises.*

The Owner agrees to allow the Broker to place this listing information in any multiple **[11]**
*listing organization of which he is a member and to engage the cooperation of other
brokers as subagents to bring about a sale.*

The Owner agrees to refer to the Broker all inquiries regarding this property during **[12]**
the listing period.

Accepted: <u>ABC Realty Company</u>

By: <u>Kurt Kwiklister</u>   Owner: <u>Roger Leeving</u>   **[13]**

Date: <u>April 1, 19xx</u>   Owner: <u>Mary Leeving</u>

by the owner. However, if the owner refuses to sell at the listed price and terms, the broker is still entitled to a commission. If the owner does not pay the broker voluntarily, the broker can file a lawsuit against the owner to collect.

Protecting the Owner

At **[9],** the broker is protected against the possibility that the listing period will expire while still working with a prospective purchaser. In fairness to the owner, however, two limitations are placed on the broker. First, a sales contract must be concluded within a reasonable time after the listing expires, and second, the name of the purchaser must have been given to the owner before the listing period expires.

Continuing at **[10],** the owner agrees to let the broker enter the property at reasonable hours to show it and put a "For Sale" sign on the property. At **[11],** the property owner gives the broker specific permission to enter the property into a multiple listing service and to engage the cooperation of other brokers as subagents to bring about a sale.

At **[12],** the owner agrees to refer all inquiries regarding the availability of the property to the broker. The purpose is to discourage the owner from thinking that she might be able to save a commission by personally selling it during the listing period and to provide sales leads for the broker. Finally, at **[13],** the owner and the broker (or the broker's sales associate if authorized to do so) sign and date the agreement.

EXCLUSIVE RIGHT TO SELL LISTING

The listing illustrated in Figure 19.1 is called an **exclusive right to sell** or **exclusive authorization to sell** the listing. Its distinguishing characteristic is that no matter who sells the property during the listing period, the listing broker is entitled to a commission. This is the most widely used type of listing in the United States. Once signed by the owner and accepted by the broker, the primary advantage to the broker is that the money and effort the broker expends on advertising and showing the property will be to the broker's benefit. The advantage to the owner is that the broker will usually put more effort into selling a property if the broker holds an exclusive right to sell than if the broker has an exclusive agency or an open listing.

EXCLUSIVE AGENCY LISTING

The **exclusive agency listing** is similar to the listing shown in Figure 19.1, except that the owner may sell the property himself during the listing period and not owe a commission to the broker. The broker, however, is the only broker who can act as an agent during the listing period; hence the term *exclusive agency.* For an owner, this type of listing may seem like the best of two worlds: the owner has a broker looking for a buyer, but if the owner finds a buyer first, the owner can save a commission fee. The broker is less enthusiastic because the broker's efforts can too easily be undermined by the owner. Consequently, the broker may not expend as much effort on advertising and showing the property as with an exclusive right to sell.

OPEN LISTING

Open listings carry no exclusive rights. An owner can give an open listing to any number of brokers at the same time, and the owner can still find a buyer and avoid a commission. This gives the owner the greatest freedom of any listing form, but there is little incentive for the broker to expend time and money showing the property as the broker has little control over who will be compensated if the property is sold. The broker's only protection is that if the broker does find a buyer at the listing price and terms, the broker is entitled to a commission. This reluctance to develop a sales effort usually means that few, if any, offers will be received and the result may be no sale or a sale below market price. Yet, if a broker does find a buyer, the commission earned may be the same as with an exclusive right to sell.

Net Listing

A **net listing** is created when an owner states the price she wants for her property and then agrees to pay the broker anything above that price as the commission. It can be written in the form of an exclusive right to sell, an exclusive agency, or an open listing. If a homeowner asks for a "net $60,000" and the broker sells the home for $75,000, the commission would be $15,000. By using the net listing method, many owners feel that they are forcing the broker to look to the buyer for the commission by marking up the price of the property. In reality though, would a buyer pay $75,000 for a home that is worth $60,000? Because of widespread misunderstanding regarding net listings, some states prohibit them outright (Texas does not), and most brokers strenuously avoid them even when requested by property owners. There is no law that says a broker must accept a listing; a broker is free to accept only those listings for which the broker can perform a valuable service and earn an honest profit.

Exclusive Authority to Purchase

Previous portions of this chapter have presumed the general rule that the real estate broker represents the seller. Historically, it has been the seller who has hired brokers to assist in marketing property. Consumers, though, are far more sophisticated and informed today. They are aware of the complexities of the market, property condition, and consumer protection laws. They need, and want, advice from a real estate professional. The Real Estate Buyer Agent Council (REBAC), a division of the National Association of Realtors®, has increased its membership from 5,000 to 15,000 in only one year, reflecting buyers' requests for an agent to help them to locate property, or to assist them in negotiating the acquisition of a specified property.

In such cases, the broker's primary responsibility is to the purchaser rather than to the seller. In this circumstance, the purchaser can reveal confidential information to the broker and rely on the broker's expertise and competence. This may be particularly helpful in situations where a real estate transaction is complex, or there are peculiar concerns unique to certain regions of the country (termites in Houston, radon in Maine, soil conditions in California) about which a buyer wants to be adequately advised before buying real estate in that area.

In these situations, the principal (now the buyer) needs to be assured as to the scope of employment of the broker (i.e., locating the property) and, similar to a listing contract, the broker needs to be assured that he is protected, and that the buyer does not "go around" the broker and cut the broker out of a commission once the property has been identified. This is a major concern for buyer's brokers, as an agent can educate the buyer, then have the buyer cut out the broker in hope of a better sales price (with a lower commission paid). Buyers, then, need to be committed to their agent, and building that level of trust and confidence is not easy. A good employment contract, coupled with good service, develops this trust.

Figure 19.2 shows a simplified version of an Exclusive Authority to Purchase contract. Note at [1] the parties are named. The real difference in this contract, versus the Listing Agreement, occurs at [2], designating the property to be required in general terms, so that the broker has guidance as to what type of property to be looking for. Compensation is different also. Most buyer's brokers would anticipate being able to access commission splits through the traditional MLS system. If, however, a seller or listing broker refuses to split a commission, there must be an alternative for compensation at [3] for that buyer's broker. Note at [4], there is an expiration date for the term of the agreement, at [5] a requirement by the owner to referral inquiries to the broker, and at [6] a signature provision for both the buyer's broker and the purchaser.

FIGURE 19.2
Exclusive authority to purchase contract.

EXCLUSIVE AUTHORITY TO PURCHASE CONTRACT

This Agreement is made in _____ on this _____ day of _____, 19__, whereby _____ (hereinafter referred to as "Buyer") hereby appoints Buyer's Broker (hereinafter referred to as "Broker") as Buyer's exclusive agent for the purposes set forth in Section 2 hereof and under the terms specified herein. **[1]**

<u>Section 1</u>. Buyer agrees to conduct all negotiations for property of the type described in Section 2 hereof through Broker, and to refer to Broker all inquiries received in any form from real estate brokers, salespersons, prospective sellers, or any other source, during the time this Agreement is in effect. **[5]**

<u>Section 2</u>. Buyer desires to purchase or lease real property (which may include items of personal property described as follows:

Type: _____ Residential _____ Residential Income _____ Other

 _____ Commercial _____ Industrial _____ Vacant Land **[2]**

General Description: _____

Approximate price range: $_____ to $_____, or any other amount which Buyer ultimately decides to spend.

Preferred Terms: _____

<u>Section 3</u>. Broker's authority as Buyer's exclusive agent shall begin upon Buyer's signing this Agreement, and shall continue until _____, 19__, unless sooner terminated or by completion for the purpose(s) of the agency as set forth in Section 2 hereof. **[4]**

<u>Section 4</u>. Broker represents that Broker is duly licenses as a real estate broker, and agrees that Broker will use Broker's best efforts as Buyer's agent to locate property as described in Section 2 hereof, and to negotiate acceptance of any offer to purchase or lease such property. Broker shall submit to Buyer for the Buyer's consideration, properties appearing to Broker to substantially meet the criteria set forth in Section 2.

<u>Section 5</u>. In consideration of the services to be performed by Broker, Buyer agrees to pay Broker an amount equal to the greater of:

(a) (__) Retainer Fee. Buyer will pay Broker a non-refundable retainer fee of $_____ due and **[3]** payable upon signing of this Agreement. (__) Retainer fee shall be credited against commission, IF ANY as set forth in Sub Section 5(c) herein or Retainer Fee shall be retained by Broker in addition to commission; or

(b) (__) Hourly Fee. Buyer will pay Broker at the rate of $_____ per hour for the time spent by Broker pursuant to this Agreement, to be paid to Broker when billed to Buyer. (__) Fee shall be credited against commission, IF ANY or (__) Fee shall be considered full payment of Broker's compensation; or

(c) (__) Commission. Parties hereby agree that Broker shall first seek compensation out of the transaction. Should the fee so obtained by greater than that listed in subsection (c)(1) or (2) below, Broker shall pay Buyer the difference at closing. Should the fee so obtained by less than that listed in subsection (1) or (2) hereof, Buyer shall pay Broker the difference at closing.

<u>Section 6</u>. If a seller in an agreement made on behalf of Buyer fails to close such agreement, with no fault on the part of Buyer, the commission provided in Section 5, subsection (c), shall be waived. If such transaction fails to close because of any fault on the part of the Buyer, such commission will not be waived, but will be due and payable immediately in an amount no less than that referred to in Paragraph 6, said amount to be agreed upon by the parties to be liquidated damages. In no case shall Broker be obligated to advance funds for the benefit of Buyer in order to complete a closing.

<u>Section 7</u>. (__) Broker does (__) Does Not have Buyer's permission to disclose Buyer's identity to third parties without prior written consent of Buyer.

<u>Section 8</u>. Buyer understands that other potential buyers may consider, make offers on, or purchase through, Broker the same or similar properties as Buyer is seeking to acquire. Buyer consents to Broker's representation of such other potential buyers before, during and after the expiration of this Agreement.

<u>Section 9</u>. The parties agree not to discriminate against any prospective seller or lessor because of the race, creed, color, sex, marital status, national origin, familial or handicapped status of such person.

Accepted:

_____ _____
Buyer's Broker Buyer

By:_____ _____
      Title Buyer

REHOU:6982.1 99999-00001

MULTIPLE LISTING SERVICE

Multiple listing service (MLS) organizations enable a broker with a listing to make a blanket offering of subagency and/or compensation to other member brokers, thus broadening the market exposure for a given property. Member brokers are authorized to show each other's properties to their prospects. If a sale results, the commission is divided between the broker who found the buyer and the broker who obtained the listing.

Market Exposure

A property listed with a broker who is a multiple listing service member receives the advantage of greater sales exposure which, in turn, means a better price and a quicker sale. For the buyer it means learning about what is for sale at many offices without having to visit each individually. For a broker or salesperson with a prospect but not a suitable property listed in that office, the opportunity to make a sale is not lost because the prospect can be shown the listings of other brokers.

To give a property the widest possible market exposure and to maintain fairness among its members, most multiple listing organizations obligate each member broker to provide information to the organization on each new listing within three to seven days after the listing is taken. To facilitate the exchange of information, multiple listing organizations have developed customized listing forms. These forms are a combination of an exclusive right-to-sell listing agreement (with authority to place the listing into multiple) plus a data sheet on the property. The data sheet, which describes all the physical and financial characteristics of the property, and a photograph of the property are published weekly in a multiple listing book that is distributed to MLS members. Then, if Broker B has a prospect interested in a property listed by Broker A, Broker B telephones Broker A and arranges to show the property. If Broker B's prospect makes an offer on the property, Broker B contacts Broker A and together they call on the seller with the offer.

MLS by-laws allow for buyer brokerage. The MLS profile sheets provide the listing broker the opportunity to make an offer to compensate the buyer's brokers through a feature of MLS called **MLS Plus.** It allows the buyer's broker, who is a member of MLS, to access all the benefits of MLS, but to reject the automatic offer of subagency. In effect, the buyer's broker can access the commission split, but maintain a fiduciary duty to the purchaser, rather than to the seller of the property.

MLS organizations have been taken to court for being open only to members of local real estate boards. The role that multiple listing services play directly or indirectly in commission splitting is also being tested in the courts. Another idea that has been tested in courts is that an MLS be open to anyone who wants to list a property, broker or owner. It is generally held, though, that owners lacking real estate sophistication would place much inaccurate information in the MLS and this would do considerable harm to MLS members who must rely on that information when describing and showing properties. It is also important to note that the sharing of MLS information to nonmembers violates federal copyright laws.

Computerized MLS

In addition to publishing MLS books, a number of multiple listing services store their listing information in computers. A salesperson with a briefcase-sized MLS terminal can use any telephone, dial the MLS computer, place the hand piece on the terminal, and request up-to-the minute information for any property in the computer. This is a popular system with sales people who are constantly in the field showing property or in their cars (where they can link up by cellular telephone). It is also quicker than waiting for updated printed MLS information.

Video Disc and Camcorders

Electronic advances now make it possible to give a prospective buyer a visual tour through a neighborhood without leaving the broker's office. A single video disc can store over 100,000 still photographs of individual properties, neighborhoods, schools, shopping centers, recreation facilities, etc. The discs are professionally shot and duplicated and made available to real estate offices for a fee. In the real estate office a salesperson can play back any image on the disc onto a television screen. With an MLS book in hand, the salesperson can show a prospect a color picture of each property for sale along with pictures of the street and neighborhood, plus nearby schools and shopping facilities. Realty offices with computerized access to MLS files can interface the video disc with the MLS computer.

The web has entered into the market for both practitioners and individual buyers and sellers. Not only can individual sellers post on many internet services (alternate sources are available for buyers and buyer's brokers), but the MLS is also on the internet (at realtor.com).

BROKER COMPENSATION

Listing Brokers

To be legally eligible for compensation, the listing broker must be able to clearly show that he was employed. Usually, this requirement is fulfilled by using a preprinted listing form approved for use by the local multiple listing service. The broker fills in the blank spaces with the information that applies to the property he is listing. If listings come in the letter form from property owners, the broker must make certain that all the essential requirements of a valid listing are present and clearly stated. If they are not, the broker may expend time and money finding a buyer only to be denied a commission because he was not properly employed. To guard against this, the broker should transfer the owner's request to the preprinted listing form he uses and then have the owner sign it.

"Ready, Willing, and Able"

There is considerable authority in Texas for the view that once a real estate broker has met the foregoing statutory requirements and produces a **ready, willing, and able buyer,** the broker, at that time, has earned his commission and is owed that commission even if the listing agreement says that the commission is contingent upon the closing of the transaction. The theory is that a listing is usually a unilateral contract (I'll pay you if you perform the agency objective). Once the broker has produced a ready, willing, and able buyer, the broker has performed as required in the contract; if the seller chooses not to close the transaction, the seller still owes the broker the commission. There is further authority that in the event a broker must sue for his commission, he may also recover his attorney's fees in pursuing this cause of action against his principal.

The difference between the two arrangements becomes important when a buyer is found at the price and terms acceptable to the owner, but no sale results. The "ready, willing, and able" contract provides more protection for the broker, since his commission does not depend on the deal reaching settlement. The no sale, no commission approach is to the owner's advantage, for he is not required to pay a commission unless there is a completed sale. However, with the passage of time, court decisions have tended to blur the clear-cut distinction between the two. For example, if the owner has a no sale, no commission agreement, it would appear that if the broker brought a ready, willing, and able buyer at the listing price and terms and the owner refused to sell, the owner would owe no commission, for there was no sale. However, a court of law would find in favor of the broker for the full amount of the commission if the refusal to sell was arbitrary and without reasonable cause or in bad faith.

Buyer's Brokers

Buyer's broker issues are a little more complicated. As previously stated, buyers might have an incentive to "go around" the broker to achieve a lower sales price. In addition, the buyer's brokers agreement cannot specify the property to be purchased, as it hasn't been identified yet. Most agreements provide that the buyer's broker will be compensated by the seller's broker, but should contain provisions that if the seller or seller's broker refuses to pay the buyer's agent, the buyer is obligated to pay.

License Act Requirements

In Texas, the Real Estate Licensing Act sets specific requirements that the broker must comply with to maintain an action for a commission. Section 20(a) specifies that a broker may not file a lawsuit for the collection of compensation for her performance without alleging and proving that she is a duly licensed real estate broker or salesperson. Section 20(b) states that an action may not be brought in a court of this state for recovery of a commission unless the promise for such commission is in writing and signed by the party to be charged, or by a person lawfully authorized to sign the commission agreement. This provision does *not*, however, apply to an agreement to share compensation between licensees. These agreements can be verbal. Section 20(c) requires that the licensee shall advise the purchaser, in writing, that the purchaser should have the abstract examined by an attorney of the purchaser selection, or that the purchaser should be furnished with or obtain a policy of title insurance. Section 20(d) allows brokers to sue each other for commissions (or tortious interference) even if nothing is in writing. So licensees need to be very careful when casually involving other licensees. It may result in a law suit! Was this created for buyer's brokers? Maybe!

PUTTING IT TO WORK

Under a ready, willing, and able listing, traditionally, if a broker produced a buyer, it was up to the owner to decide if the buyer was, in fact, financially able to buy. If the owner accepted the buyer's offer and subsequently the buyer did not have the money to complete the deal, the owner still owed the broker a commission. The legal thinking today is that the broker should be responsible, being in a much better position to analyze the buyer's financial ability than the owner.

In today's marketplace, buyers are usually prequalified for financial ability. Increased competition among lenders has made this quick, inexpensive, and easy. Licensees should be careful to only pass on information, though, and not make representations about a buyer's financial ability.

PROCURING CAUSE

A broker who possesses an employment agreement (either with the seller or the buyer) is entitled to a commission if he can prove that the resulting sale was primarily due to his efforts. That is, he has to have been the **procuring cause,** the one whose efforts originated procurement of the sale. Suppose that a broker shows an open-listed property to a prospect and, during the listing period or an extension, that prospect goes directly to the owner and concludes a deal. Even though the owner negotiates her own transaction and prepares her own sales contract, the broker is entitled to a full commission for finding the buyer. This would also be true if the owner and the buyer used a subterfuge or strawman to purchase the property to avoid paying a commission. Texas law protects the broker who has in good faith produced a buyer at the request of an owner.

When an open listing is given to two or more brokers, the first one who produces a buyer is entitled to the commission. For example, Broker 1 shows a property to Prospect P but no sale is made. Later P goes to Broker 2 and makes an offer, which is accepted by the owner. Although two brokers have attempted to sell the property, only one has succeeded, and that one is entitled to the commission. The fact that Broker 1 receives nothing, even though he may have expended considerable effort, is an important reason why brokers dislike open listings.

TERMINATING THE EMPLOYMENT CONTRACT

The usual situation in an employment contract is that the broker produces a buyer acceptable to the owner. Thus, in most employment contracts the agency terminates because the objective of the contract has been completed. In the bulk of the transactions in which a buyer is not produced, the agency is terminated because the employment period expires. Remember that if no termination date is specified in the listing agreement, the Texas Real Estate License Act provides that the agent's license can be suspended or revoked.

Even when an employment contract calls for mutual consideration and has a specific termination date, it is still possible to revoke the agency aspect of the listing before the termination date. However, liability for breach of contract still remains, and money damages may result. Thus, an owner who has listed his property may tell the broker not to bring any more offers, but the owner still remains liable to the broker for payment for the effort expended by the broker up to that time. Depending on how far advanced the broker is at that point, the amount could be as much as a full commission. Similarly, if a buyer's agent finds the product that meets the buyer's criteria and the buyer refuses to purchase, the broker is entitled to be compensated. In these situations, however, there is very little legal precedent for pursuing compensation through the courts. Buyer brokerage is a little riskier in pursuing compensation.

Mutual Agreement

An employment agreement can be terminated by mutual agreement of both the owner and broker without money damage. Because these agreements are the stock in trade of the brokerage business, brokers do not like to lose them, but sometimes this is the only logical alternative since the time and effort in setting and collecting damages can be very expensive. Suppose, however, that a broker has an employment agreement and suspects that the owner (or buyer) wants to cancel because he wants to avoid the commission. The listing broker can stop showing the property, but the owner is still obligated to pay a commission if the property is sold before the listing period expires. Whatever the broker and seller decide, it is best to put the agreement into writing and sign it.

With regard to open listings, once the property is sold by anyone, broker or owner, all listing agreements pertaining to the property are automatically terminated; the objective has been completed, there is no further need for the agency to exist. Similarly, with an exclusive agency listing, if the owner sells the property himself, the agency with the exclusive broker is terminated.

Abandonment, Etc.

Agency can also be terminated by improper performance or abandonment by the agent. Thus, if a broker acts counter to her principal's best financial interests, the agency is terminated, no commission is payable, and the broker may be subject to a lawsuit for any damages suffered by the principal. If a broker accepts an employment opportunity and then does nothing to promote it, the principal can assume that the broker abandoned it and has grounds for revocation. The principal should keep written documentation in the event the matter ever goes to court.

An agency is automatically terminated by the death of either the principal or the agent, or if either is judged legally incompetent by virtue of insanity, and might also be terminated if the principal becomes bankrupt.

BARGAIN BROKERS

The full-service real estate broker who takes a listing and places it in multiple listing, advertises the property at his expense, holds open house, qualifies prospects, shows property, obtains offers, negotiates, opens escrow, and follows through until closing is the mainstay of the real estate selling industry. The vast majority of all open-market sales are handled that way. The remainder are sold by owners, some handling everything themselves and some using flat-fee brokers who oversee the transaction but do not do the actual showing and selling.

Flat-Fee Brokers

For a fee that typically ranges from $400 to $1,500, a **flat-fee broker** will list a property, suggest a market price, write advertising, assist with negotiations, draw up a sales contract, and turn the signed papers over to an escrow company for closing. The homeowner is responsible for paying for advertising, answering inquiries, setting appointments with prospects, showing the property, and applying whatever salesmanship is necessary to induce the prospect to make an offer. Under the flat-fee arrangement, also called self-help brokerage, the homeowner is effectively buying real estate services on an à la carte basis. Some brokerage firms have been very successful in this—offering sellers a choice of à la carte or full service.

Discount Broker

A **discount broker** is a full-service broker who charges less than the prevailing commission rates in the community. In a seller's market a real estate agent's major problem is finding salable property to list, not finding buyers. The discount broker attracts sellers by offering to do the job for less money, for example, 3% or 4% instead of 5% to 7%. Charging less means a discount broker must sell more properties to be successful. Consequently, most discount brokers may be careful to take listings only on property that will sell quickly, and to reject those that won't.

Answers to these questions are found in the Answer Key section at the back of the book.

1. A real estate listing
   A. is an employment contract between a property owner and a real estate broker.
   B. authorizes a real estate broker to sell and convey title to an owner's real property.
   C. Both A and B.
   D. Neither A nor B.

2. All of the following statements are true EXCEPT:
   A. a listing is a contract between an owner and the listing salesperson.
   B. the broker is legally liable for the proper execution of a listing contract.
   C. sales associates are licensed salespersons or brokers who work for a broker.
   D. sales associates operate under the authority of an employing broker's license.

3. A listing to find a buyer for each of the following types of properties will usually be for a period of time ranging from six months to one year EXCEPT:
   A. farms.
   B. commercial properties.
   C. residential properties.
   D. industrial properties.

4. A typical exclusive right to sell listing requires the owner to
   A. exclude other brokers from advertising or placing a sign on the property.
   B. pay a commission if a purchaser is found who agrees to buy at the price and terms stipulated in the listing.
   C. Both A and B.
   D. Neither A nor B.

5. The amount of commission to be paid the broker for selling a property is
   A. set by state law.
   B. negotiated at the time a buyer is found.
   C. set forth in the rules of the state real estate commission.
   D. stated in the listing contract.

6. Under the terms of an exclusive right to sell listing, a commission is due the listing broker if a buyer is found by
   A. the listing broker.
   B. a sales associated employed by the listing broker.
   C. the owner, through his own efforts.
   D. another broker.
   E. All of the above.

7. Broker Kim secured a written listing on a property. Kim later located a buyer who was ready, willing, and able to buy at the price and terms stated in the listing contract, but the owner refused to sign a sales agreement because of animosity toward the buyer. Is Kim entitled to a commission even though no sale was consummated?
   A. Yes, because a commission was earned when the listing was signed.
   B. Yes, because Kim produced a ready, willing, and able buyer at the price and terms requested in the listing.
   C. No, because no sales contract was signed by the owner.
   D. No, because there was not an offer and acceptance.

8. An exclusive agency listing
   A. permits the owner to sell of his own efforts without liability to pay a commission to the listing broker.
   B. allows the owner to list concurrently with other brokers.
   C. Both A and B.
   D. Neither A nor B.

9. All of the following are true of net listings EXCEPT:
   A. many states prohibit a broker from accepting a net listing.
   B. most brokers are reluctant to accept them, even when permitted to do so.
   C. all net listings are open listings.
   D. the commission is the excess above the seller's net price.

10. In regard to net listings,
    A. Texas prohibits them.
    B. most brokers avoid them.
    C. Both A and B.
    D. Neither A nor B.

11. To be valid in Texas, a listing contract must be
    A. written.
    B. signed.
    C. Both A and B.
    D. Neither A nor B.

12. Multiple listing services are open
    A. only to members of real estate boards.
    B. to any licensed broker.
    C. to anyone who wants to join.
    D. to sales agents belonging to the Texas Association of Realtors (TAR).

13. Under the terms of a multiple listing agreement, if a broker other than the listing broker sells the property, the owner
    A. may be liable for two commissions on the sale.
    B. may sell of his own efforts without any obligation to pay a commission.
    C. Both A and B.
    D. Neither A nor B.

14. The advantages of a multiple listing arrangement include
    A. greater market exposure of the property.
    B. the possibility of a higher sales price.
    C. quicker sale.
    D. All of the above.

15. Recent innovations for marketing properties through multiple listing services include
    A. computerized listings.
    B. videodisc display of listings.
    C. Both A and B.
    D. Neither A nor B.

16. When a property under an open listing is shown to a prospect by two different brokers and a sale results, the commission is
    A. payable to the broker who first showed the property to the buyer.
    B. divided between the two brokers.
    C. payable to the broker who made the sale.
    D. payable in full to each broker.

17. An exclusive listing contract with a definite termination date is NOT terminable by
    A. sale of the property.
    B. death of the listing salesperson.
    C. expiration.
    D. mutual agreement.

18. An open listing may be terminated by which of the following means?
    A. Sale of the property.
    B. Abandonment by the broker.
    C. Destruction of the property by casualty.
    D. Death of the owner.
    E. All of the above.

19. If a purchaser arbitrarily defaults on a purchase contract, any earnest money previously paid, in the absence of an agreement to the contrary, will be
    A. paid to the broker as compensation for his efforts.
    B. divided between the broker and the owner/seller.
    C. returned to the purchaser.
    D. paid to the owner/seller.

20. Which of the following is most likely to accept only listings that he thinks will sell quickly?
    A. Flat-fee brokers.
    B. Full-service brokers.
    C. Discount brokers.
    D. Self-help brokers.

KEY TERMS

Agent: the person empowered to act by and on behalf of the principal

Boycotting: two or more people conspiring to restrain competition

Commingling: the mixing of clients' or customers' funds with an agent's personal funds

Dual agency: representation of two or more principals in a transaction by the same agent

Intermediary: a broker who is employed to negotiate a transaction between the parties

Middleman: a person who brings two or more parties together but does not represent either party

Ostensible authority: an agency relationship created by the conduct of the principal

Price fixing: two or more people conspiring to charge a fixed fee, having an anti-competitive effect

Principal: a person who authorizes another to act

Puffing: statements a reasonable person would recognize as nonfactual or extravagant

Third parties: persons who are not parties to a contract but who may be affected by it

The Principal–Broker Relationship: Agency

IN THIS CHAPTER *This chapter covers the principal and agent relationship, and the law of agency in general. Creation of the agency relationship and obligations of the broker to his or her principal and to third parties are discussed. The new concepts of owner disclosure statements and buyer agency are also discussed. The final portions of the chapter deal with dual agency and anti-trust laws.*

The previous chapter has stressed the mechanics of real estate listings. Let us now take a close look at the agency aspects of the principal-broker relationship, that is, the legal responsibilities of the broker toward the principal and vice versa.

AGENCY

When a property owner gives a real estate broker a listing authorizing the broker to find a buyer or a tenant and promising compensation if he does, an **agency relationship** is created. For an agency to exist, there must be a principal and an agent. The **principal** is the person who empowers another to act as their representative; the **agent** is the person who is empowered to act. When someone speaks about the laws of agency, she refers to those laws that govern the rights and duties of the principal, agent, and the persons (called third parties) with whom they deal.

Agencies are divided into three categories: universal, general, and specific. A **universal agency** is very broad in scope, as the principal gives the agent the legal power to transact matters of all types. A **general agency** gives the agent the power to bind the principal in a particular trade or business. For example, the relationship between a real estate broker (principal) and the salesperson (agent) is considered a general agency. With a **special agency** the principal empowers this agent to perform only specific acts and no others. The special agent may not bind the principal by his actions. Applications of special agency include real estate listings, the topic we shall discuss next.

The principal in an agency relationship can be either a natural person or a legal person such as a corporation. Likewise, an agent can be either a natural person or a corporation such as a real estate brokerage company. The persons and firms with whom the principal and agent negotiate are called **third parties.** You will also hear these third parties referred to as the broker's **customers** and the principal referred to as the broker's **client.** Sometimes you will see the phrase "principals only" in real estate advertisements where property is offered for sale by its owner without the aid of a broker. This means the owner wants to be contacted by persons who want to buy and not by real estate agents who want to list the property.

Establishing the Agent's Authority

A written employment agreement outlines the broker's authority to act on behalf of the principal and the principal's obligations to the agent. A written agreement is the preferred method of creating an agency because it provides a document to readily establish the existence of the agency relationship.

Agency authority may also arise from custom in the industry, common usage, and conduct of the parties involved. For example, the right of an agent to post a "For Sale" sign on the listed property may not be expressly stated in the listing. However, if it is the custom in the industry to do so, and presuming there are no deed restrictions or city ordinances to the contrary, the agent has **implied authority** to post the sign. A similar situation exists with regard to showing a listed property to prospects. The seller of a home can expect to have it shown on weekends and evenings whereas a commercial property owner might expect showings only during business hours.

Ostensible authority is conferred when a principal gives a third party reason to believe that another person is his agent even though that person is unaware of the appointment. If the third party accepts this as true, the principal may well be bound by the acts of his agent. For example, as a seller's agent, one may show a home one time, with the seller's permission, to a potential buyer. Even though there may not be an enforceable listing agreement, the agent (with the principal's approval) gives the impression that he represents the seller. The buyer could communicate with the agent, relying on that agent's **apparent authority.** Similarly, if a buyer and a buyer's agent spend weeks looking for a property and have established communication with various seller's agents concerning properties available, the seller's agent can rely on the buyer's agent's apparent authority to act on behalf of the buyer.

An **agency by ratification** is one established after the fact. For example, if an agent secures a contract on behalf of a principal and the principal subsequently ratifies or agrees to it, a court may hold that an agency was created at the time the initial negotiations started. An **agency by estoppel** can result when a principal fails to maintain due diligence over his agent and the agent exercises powers not granted to him. If this causes a third party to believe the agent has these powers, an agency by estoppel has been created. An **agency coupled with an interest** exists when an agent holds an interest in the property he is representing. For example, a broker is a part-owner in a property he has listed for sale.

Remember, all these methods of establishing an agent's authority work for the buyer's agent as well as the seller's agent.

Broker's Obligations to the Principal

When a real estate broker accepts a listing, a **fiduciary relationship** is created. This requires that the agent exhibit trust and honesty and exercise good business judgment when working on behalf of the principal. Specifically, the broker must faithfully perform the agency agreement, be loyal to the principal, exercise competence, and account for all funds handled in performing the agency. The broker also has certain obligations toward the third parties involved. Let's look at these requirements more closely.

Broker responsibility in the State of Texas has mainly been guided by the Canons of Professional Ethics and Conduct for Brokers and Salesmen as established by the Texas Real Estate Commission, the Texas Real Estate Licensing Act, and by regulations adopted by the Texas Real Estate Commission. Some of the more important provisions will be specifically addressed in this chapter.

Faithful Performance

Faithful performance (also referred to as **obedience**) means that the agent is to obey all legal instructions given by the principal and to apply best efforts and diligence to carry out the objectives of the agency. For a real estate broker this means performance as promised in the broker's employment contract. A broker who promises to make a "reasonable effort" or apply "diligence" in finding a buyer and then does nothing to promote the listing gives the owner legal grounds for terminating the listing. Similarly, a broker who represents a buyer but makes no efforts to pursue an acquisition, or to take heed of the buyer's requirements, may also give the buyer grounds to terminate the buyer's representation agreement. Faithful performance also means not departing from the principal's instructions. If the agent does so (except in extreme emergencies not foreseen by the principal), it is at the agent's own risk. If the principal thereby suffers a loss, the agent is responsible for that loss. For example, a broker accepts a personal note from a buyer as an earnest money deposit, but fails to tell the seller that the deposit is not in cash. If the seller accepts the offer and the note is later found to be worthless, the broker may be liable for the amount of the note.

Another aspect of faithful performance is that the agent must personally perform the tasks delegated to that agent. This protects the principal who has selected an agent on the basis of trust and confidence from finding that the agent has delegated that responsibility to another person. However, a major question arises on this point in real estate brokerage, as a large part of the success in finding a buyer for a property results from the cooperative efforts of other brokers and their salespeople. Therefore, employment agreements usually include a statement that the listing broker is authorized to secure the cooperation of other brokers and pay them part of the commission from the sale.

A genuine concern arises over how much information a real estate broker is free to disclose to other real estate brokers or other industry members who rely on this information in determining statistical data, market values, and other pertinent real estate related information. For instance, can a real estate agent maintain a confidential relationship with the principal, yet disclose pertinent details of sales prices and financing terms related to the principal's business? The Texas Real Estate License Act (Section 15D) specifically relieves a broker from liability for providing information about real property sales prices or terms for the purposes of facilitating the listing, selling, leasing, financing, or appraisal of real property unless this disclosure is specifically prohibited by statute or written contract. Any licensee would be well advised to make this provision clear to the principal so that the principal can make an informed decision as to whether or not to disclose this information.

Loyalty to Principal

Probably no other area of agency is as fertile ground for lawsuits as the requirement that, once an agency is created, the agent must be loyal to the principal. The law is clear in all states that in an employment agreement the broker (and the broker's sales staff) occupy a position of trust, confidence, and responsibility. As such, the agent is legally bound to keep their principal (buyer *or* seller) fully informed as to all matters that might affect the sale of the listed property and to promote and protect the owner's interests.

Unfortunately, greed and expediency sometimes get in the way. As a result, numerous laws have been enacted for the purpose of protecting the principal and threatening the agent with court action for misplaced loyalty. For example, an out-of-town landowner who is not fully up-to-date on the value of his land visits a local broker and wants to list it for $30,000. The broker is much more knowledgeable of local land prices and is aware of a recent city council decision to extend roads and utilities to the area of this property. As a result, the broker knows the land is now worth $50,000. The broker remains silent on the matter, and the property is listed for sale at $30,000. At this price the broker can find a buyer before the day is over and have a commission on the sale. However, the opportunity for a quick $20,000 is too tempting to let pass. He buys the property (or to cover up, buys in the name of his wife or a friend) and shortly thereafter resells it for $50,000. Whether he sold the property to a buyer for $30,000 or bought it and resold it for $50,000, the broker did not exhibit loyalty to the principal. A similar breach can occur if a buyer's agent knows that the buyer will pay up to $100,000 for a property, and the agent finds a similar property for $50,000, buys it himself, and sells it to the buyer for $100,000. Laws and penalties for breach of loyalty are stiff: The broker can be sued for recovery of the price difference and the commission paid, his real estate license can be suspended or revoked, and he may be required to pay additional fines and money damages.

If a licensee intends to purchase a property listed for sale by his agency or through a cooperating broker, he is under both a moral and a legal obligation to make certain that the price paid is the fair market value and that the seller knows who the buyer is, and that the buyer is a licensee.

Protecting the Owner's Interest

Loyalty to the principal also means that when seeking a buyer or negotiating a sale, the broker must continue to protect the owner's financial interests. Suppose that an owner lists her home at $82,000 but confides in the broker, "If I cannot get $82,000, anything over $79,000 will be fine." The broker shows the home to a prospect who says, "Eighty-two thousand is too much. What will the owner really take?" or "Will he take seventy-nine thousand?" Loyalty to the principal requires the broker to say that the owner will take $82,000, for that is the price in the listing agreement. If the buyer balks, the broker can suggest that the buyer submit an offer for the seller's consideration. State laws require that all offers be submitted to the owner, no matter what the offering price and terms. This prevents the agent from rejecting an offer that the owner might have accepted if she had known about it. If the seller really intends for the broker to quote $79,000 as an acceptable price, the listing price should be changed; then the broker can say, "The property was previously listed for $82,000, but is now priced at $79,000." When representing a buyer, an agent can have the same conflict. The buyer acknowledges that she will pay up to $100,000, and the agent knows it could be purchased for $80,000, but the commission would be *less*. The buyer's broker has the duty to obtain the cheaper price.

A broker's loyalty to his principal also includes keeping the principal informed of changes in market conditions during the listing period. If after an adjacent landowner is successful in rezoning his land to a higher use and the listed property becomes more valuable, the broker's responsibility is to inform the seller. Similarly, if a buyer is looking at a property and the adjacent property is purchased for a nuclear waste disposal site, it is the duty of the broker to report this to the buyer. If the broker does not keep the principal fully informed, he is not properly fulfilling his duties as the principal's agent.

The Texas Real Estate Licensing Act specifically prohibits certain misplaced loyalties, such as:

1. "*. . . conduct which constitutes dishonest dealings, bad faith, or untrustworthiness [Section 15.a.(6)(V)].* "
2. "*. . . the offering of real property for sale or lease without the knowledge and consent of the owner, or on terms other than those authorized by the owner or his agent [Section 15.a.(6)(O)].*"
3. "*. . . accepting, receiving, or charging an undisclosed commission rebate or making a direct profit on expenditures made for the principal [Section 15.a.(6)(H)].*"
4. "*. . . failing to make clear to all parties to a transaction which party the agent is acting for, or receiving compensation from more than one party, except with the full knowledge and consent of all parties [Section 15.a.(6)(D)].*"

Many licensees take fiduciary duty somewhat lightly, not understanding how consumers truly rely on them and trust their judgment. These principals feel truly cheated when they get less than complete loyalty from their real estate agent.

Reasonable Care

The duty of **reasonable care** implies competence and expertise on the part of the broker. It is the broker's responsibility to disclose all knowledge and material facts concerning a property to the principal. Also, the broker must not become a party to any fraud or misrepresentation likely to affect the sound judgment of the principal.

Although the broker has a duty to disclose all material facts of a transaction, legal interpretations are to be avoided. Giving legal interpretations of documents involved in a transaction can be construed as practicing law without a license, an act specifically prohibited by real estate licensing acts. Moreover, the broker can be held financially responsible for any wrong legal information given to a client.

The duty of reasonable care also requires an agent to take proper care of property entrusted to him by the principal. For example, if a broker is entrusted with a key to an owner's building to show it to prospects, it is the broker's responsibility to see that it is used for only that purpose and that the building is locked upon leaving. Similarly, if a broker receives a check as an earnest money deposit, it must be properly deposited it in a bank and not carried around for several weeks.

Accounting for Funds Received

The earnest money that accompanies an offer on a property does not belong to the broker, even if the broker's name is on the check. For the purpose of holding clients' and customers' money, the law requires a broker to maintain a **trust account.** All monies received by a broker as agent for the principal are to be promptly deposited in this account or in the trust account of the attorney, escrow, or title company handling the transaction. Texas requires that a trust account be a demand deposit (checking account) at a bank or a trust account at a trust company. The broker's trust account must be separate from the broker's personal bank account, and the broker is required by law to accurately account for all funds received into and paid out of the trust account. As a rule, a broker will have one trust account for properties listed for sale and another trust account for rental properties managed by the broker. Failure to comply with trust fund requirements can result in the loss of one's real estate license.

Several provisions in the Texas Real Estate Licensing Act specifically address the broker's obligations to account for funds received. Section 15(6)(E) of the Act states that the broker could have his license revoked or suspended for:

> ". . . failing within a reasonable time to properly account for or remit money coming into his possession that belongs to others, or commingling money belonging to others with his own funds."

Section 15.a.(6)(Y) of the act provides the same penalties for:

> ". . . failing within a reasonable time to deposit money received as escrow agent in a real estate transaction, either in trust with a title company authorized to do business in this state, or in a custodial, trust, or escrow account maintained for that purpose."

Section 15.a.(6)(Z) of the act further specifies the same penalties for:

> ". . . disbursing money deposited in the custodial, trust, or escrow account . . . before the transaction has been consummated or finally otherwise terminated."

Commingling

If a broker places money belonging to a client or customer in a personal account, it is called **commingling** and is grounds for suspension or revocation of the broker's real estate license. The reason for such severe action is that from commingling, it is a very short step to **conversion,** that is, the agent's personal use of money belonging to others. Also, clients' and customers' money placed in a personal bank account can be attached by a court of law to pay personal claims against the broker.

If a broker receives a check as an earnest money deposit, along with instructions from the buyer that it remain uncashed, the broker may comply with the buyer's request as long as the seller is informed of this fact when the offer is presented. Similarly, the broker can accept a promissory note if he informs the seller. The objective is to disclose all material facts to the seller that might influence the decision to accept or reject the offer. The fact that the deposit accompanying the offer is not cash is a material fact. If the broker withholds this information, there is a violation of the agent's duty of care.

Broker's Obligations to Third Parties

A broker's fiduciary obligations are to the principal who has employed him. State law nonetheless makes certain demands on the broker in relation to the third parties the broker deals with on behalf of the principal. Foremost among these are honesty, integrity, and fair business dealing. This includes the proper care of deposit money and offers, as well as responsibility for written or verbal statements. Misrepresenting a property by omitting vital information is as wrong as giving false information. Disclosure of such misconduct usually results in a broker losing the right to a commission. Also possible are loss of the broker's real estate license and a lawsuit by any party to the transaction who suffered a financial loss because of the misrepresentation.

In guarding against misrepresentation, a broker must be careful not to make statements not known to be true. For example, a potential buyer looks at a house listed for sale and asks if it is connected to the city sewer system. The broker does not know the answer, but sensing it is important to making a sale, says, yes. If the prospect relies on this statement, purchases the house and finds out that there is no sewer connection, the broker may be at the center of litigation regarding sale cancellation, commission loss, money damages, and state license discipline. The answer should be, "I don't know, but I will find out for you." This is *very* important when representing a buyer. If a seller asks pertinent questions about the buyer, they must be answered truthfully.

Suppose the seller has told the broker that the house is connected to the city sewer system, and the broker, having no reason to doubt the statement, accepts it in good faith and gives that information to prospective buyers. If this statement is not true, the owner is at fault, owes the broker a commission, and both the owner *and* the broker may be subject to legal action for sale cancellation and money damages. When a broker must rely on information supplied by their principal (buyer *or* seller), it is best to have it in writing and verify its accuracy. However, relying on the principal for information does not completely relieve the broker's responsibility to third parties. If a seller says her house is connected to the city sewer system and the broker knows that is impossible because there is no sewer line on that street, it is the broker's responsibility to correct the erroneous statement.

Disclosure to Third Parties— License Act Requirements

In addition to fair and honest business dealings, Texas law requires real estate licensees to disclose latent defects in the property, to disclose any interest in the real estate held by the licensee, to disclose any additional commissions received from someone other than the principal, and to advise the purchaser, in writing, to obtain title insurance or have an abstract examined. In addition, there are certain contractual obligations to disclose, such as municipal utility districts, lead-based paint, and tax rollbacks (discussed in Chapter 8). Although the licensee owes a duty of confidence and loyalty to his principal, he cannot be a part of any fraud on the principal's behalf. If his principal should request that he make any misrepresentations, the licensee should terminate his employment and refuse to engage in any such acts.

Section 15(a)(6)(A) of the Texas Real Estate Licensing Act states that a licensee may have his license revoked or suspended for failing to disclose to a potential purchaser any latent structural defect that would be a significant factor to a reasonable and prudent purchaser in making a decision to purchase. This may seem to conflict with the licensee's fiduciary obligation to his principal not to disclose information entrusted to him. However, the licensee must remember that if the principal requires him to do anything that is in violation of the Licensing Act, it would be illegal. Therefore, it is assumed that the prudent licensee, when in doubt, would prefer to disclose a potential defect rather than risk the chance of performing an illegal act.

Section 15(a)(6)(D) of the Licensing Act subjects the licensee to penalties for failing to make clear whom he represents. It is not uncommon for a purchaser who has asked a licensee to help him in locating a house to think that the licensee is working for him. The purchaser should be informed that the licensee is working for the seller and the listing agent. Thus, the purchaser remains a third party and the agent should treat him as such. (Note: If a buyer employs a broker, the arrangement should be in writing and disclosed to the seller.)

Section 15(a)(6)(U) subjects a licensee to penalties for failing to advise the purchaser in writing before the closing of a transaction that she should (1) have the property abstract examined by an attorney of her own choosing or (2) be furnished with or obtain a policy of title insurance.

Puffing

Puffing refers to nonfactual or extravagant statements that a reasonable person would recognize as exaggeration. Thus, a buyer may have no legal complaint against a broker who told him that a certain hillside lot had the most beautiful view in the world or that a listed property had the finest landscaping in the county. Usually a reasonable buyer can see these things and make up his own mind. However, if a broker in showing a rural property says it has the world's purest well water, there had better be plenty of good water when the buyer moves in. If a consumer believes the broker and relies on the representation, the broker may have a potential liability. The line between puffing and misrepresentation is subjective. Avoid puffing.

Nondisclosures

Section 15E makes a significant exception to the disclosure presumption. A licensee has no duty to inquire about, make a disclosure related to, or release information related to whether a previous or current occupant had, may have had, has or may have AIDS or an HIV-related illness.

Similar to the HIV-related illnesses, the Act now provides that a licensee has no duty to inquire about, or make disclosure related to, or release information related to whether a death occurred on a property by: (1) natural causes; (2) suicide; or (3) accident unrelated to the condition of the property.

The foregoing obligations to third parties are a part of a constantly growing list in this age of consumerism. When coupled with the provisions of the Deceptive Trade Practices-Consumer Protection Act and Texas statutes relating to real estate fraud, they illustrate the increasing concern for Texas real estate brokers and salespeople regarding their obligations to those they serve.

Since a broker is a special agent of the principal rather than a general agent, there is no power to bind this principal. Therefore, if there is an aggrieved third party who feels damaged because of a material misrepresentation, the third party may not be able to sue the principal and recover. The third party can, however, sue the broker.

At least one court case typifies current legal thinking that facts not known by the buyer must be disclosed to him by the seller, or the broker representing him, if they materially affect the desirability of the property. Even the use of an **"as is" clause** in the purchase contract does not excuse a broker from disclosing material facts regarding a property. The court went on to say that a buyer of real estate has every right to rescind a contract when the agent by his silence has allowed the transaction to proceed without informing the buyer of all facts relevant to the property.

Putting It To Work

Today, courts look upon real estate licensees as professionals who possess superior knowledge or special information regarding real property to which their clients are legally entitled. (This is especially significant in that professional status is what the real estate industry has been working hard to achieve in recent years.)

OWNER DISCLOSURE STATEMENT

Seller disclosure statements are a detailed disclosure of house defects (or lack thereof) on a form often produced by a real estate trade association. The seller needs to fill out the forms, which are then presented to the buyer as a representation of the seller's statement of condition of the property. The seller is the most likely person to fill out the disclosure because the seller simply knows more about the property than anybody else. The risks of using the form are nominal and the benefits are great.

In the last fifteen years there has been extensive litigation on the sales of real property based on misrepresentations and material omissions. When the buyer sues, the broker has often found himself as a defendant, because the seller is gone, and the broker marketed the property. This creates a burden on a broker who may have no knowledge of the defect, nor the expertise to investigate the potential for defects.

For the seller's benefit, the seller disclosure form gives the opportunity for the seller to reinvestigate the house. None of us have perfect homes. Many sellers simply overlook the defects (we all learn to live with them or forget about them, particularly when it's our house). This failure to disclose, however, results in misrepresentation on the part of seller because of negligence or perhaps because he innocently overlooked it. In the worst case scenario, he may intentionally misrepresent, or intentionally fail to mention, a defect in order to induce the buyer to purchase. In all circumstances, the seller's disclosure form yields these benefits: (1) it informs the buyer as to which defects exist, (2) it provides a basis from which the buyer can conduct further investigation on the property, (3) it allows the buyer to make an informed decision as to whether or not to purchase, and (4) it may provide a more concrete basis for litigation if the buyer can determine that the seller filled out the disclosure statement incorrectly or failed to disclose a defect that the seller knew was material.

Similarly, brokers can find the disclosure statement beneficial because they now have written proof as to what disclosures were made to them (which should be compared with their listing agreement and the MLS disclosures) to ensure consistency in marketing their product. In addition, knowing that there is a defect allows the broker to effectively market the property, disclosing the defects and therefore limiting liability for both the seller (they sometimes overlook potential liability in their eagerness to sell) and the broker.

Texas Requirements

In 1993, the Texas legislature added a new section to the Property Code that now requires the seller of residential real property, comprising not more than one dwelling unit, to give the purchaser of the property a written notice in a form substantially similar to the one set out in Figure 20.1.

The notice is to be completed with the best of the seller's knowledge and belief as of the date the notice is completed and signed. If the information required is unknown to the seller, the seller should indicate that fact on the notice to stay in compliance with the Statute.

The Statute does not apply to any transfers: (1) pursuant to a court order; (2) by a trustee in bankruptcy; (3) to a mortgage by a mortgagor or successor in interest; (4) by a mortgagee or a beneficiary under a deed of trust who has acquired the real property of sale conducted pursuant to a power of sale under a deed of trust or a sale pursuant to a court ordered foreclosure or has acquired the real property by deed in lieu of foreclosure; (5) by a fiduciary in the course of the administration of a decedent's estate, guardianship, conservatorship, or trust; (6) from one co-owner to one or more other co-owners; (7) made to a spouse or to a person or persons in the initial line of consanguinity of one or more of the transferrers; (8) between the spouses resulting from a decree of dissolution of marriage or a decree of legal separation or from a property settlement agreement incident to such a decree; (9) to or from any governmental entity; (10) transfers of new residences of not more than one dwelling unit that have not previously been occupied for essential purposes; or (11) transfers of real property where the value of any dwelling does not exceed 5% of the value of the property.

The notice must be delivered by the seller to the purchaser on or before the effective date of an executory contract (signing the earnest money contract) binding the purchaser to purchase the property. If the contract is entered into without the seller providing this required notice, the purchaser may terminate the contract for any reason within seven days after receiving the notice.

BUYER REPRESENTATION

It has long been recognized under Texas law that a real estate agent can represent the purchaser. Buyer's brokerage is a common topic in real estate seminars and is often touted as the solution to the dual agency/intermediary conflict of interest (discussed next). It gives the buyer representation, which some people feel the buyer is entitled to, or needs, in many circumstances. Buyer brokerage may even ease the duty of a listing broker because some duties to the buyer may be performed by the buyer's broker. In cases of office building leasing and more sophisticated commercial property acquisitions, parties frequently seek the assistance of a real estate broker to represent them in making prudent purchases when they lack the expertise to do their own investigations. This has now become more common in residential real estate.

Buyer representation shifts the entire agency theory in the opposite direction of our traditional seller representation. When representing a seller, a real estate agent (and the resulting fiduciary duty) focuses on the marketing of the product for the benefit of the owner. This involves "getting the highest price in the marketplace," maintaining the confidentiality of information, and trying to effect a sale within the shortest period of time for the benefit of the seller. This is the same focus of our traditional MLS subagency concept for cooperating brokers. Historically, the MLS system and most state laws on agency encouraged agents to be trained as seller's brokers or cooperating brokers, so few agents have training as a buyer's broker. To further complicate matters, there is little case law on buyer's brokerage and little comfort in projecting potential outcomes of these more unusual fact situations.

The buyer's broker has a different focus. The emphasis in buyer's brokerage is to help the buyer make informed decisions and obtain the desired product at a fair price, giving the buyer's interests the highest priority. This emphasis would apparently include getting the lowest price in the market place, or at least a "fast deal" for the buyer, to facilitate resale or investment potential (a main reason why relocation companies are concerned about buyer's brokerage), and finding a "safe" purchase of a product without

FIGURE **20.1**
Disclosure notice.

SELLER'S DISCLOSURE NOTICE

Concerning the property at _____
(Street Address and City)

THIS NOTICE IS A DISCLOSURE OF SELLER'S KNOWLEDGE OF THE CONDITION OF THE PROPERTY AS OF THE DATE SIGNED BY SELLER AND IS NOT A SUBSTITUTE FOR ANY INSPECTIONS OR WARRANTIES THE PURCHASER MAY WISH TO OBTAIN. IT IS NOT A WARRANTY OF ANY KIND BY SELLER OR SELLER'S AGENTS.

Seller ____ is ____ is not occupying the Property. If unoccupied, how long since Seller has occupied the Property? _____

1. The Property has the items checked below:
    Write Yes (Y), No (N), or Unknown (U).

____ Range	____ Oven	____ Microwave
____ Dishwasher	____ Trash Compactor	____ Disposal
____ Washer/Dryer Hookups	____ Window Screens	____ Rain Gutters
____ Security System	____ Fire Detection Equipment	____ Intercom System
____ TV Antenna	____ Cable TV Wiring	____ Satellite Dish
____ Ceiling Fans (2)	____ Attic Fan(s)	____ Exhaust Fan(s)
____ Central A/C	____ Central Heating	____ Wall/Window Air Conditioning
____ Plumbing System	____ Septic System	____ Public Sewer System
____ Patio/Decking	____ Outdoor Grill	____ Fences
____ Pool	____ Sauna	____ Spa ____ Hot Tub
____ Pool Equipment	____ Pool Heater	____ Automatic Lawn Sprinkler System
____ Fireplace(s) & Chimney (Wood Burning)		____ Fireplace(s) & Chimney (Mock)
____ Gas Lines (Nat./LP)	____ Gas Fixtures	
____ Garage: Attached	____ Not Attached	____ Carport
____ Garage Door Opener(s):	____ Electronic	____ Control(s)
____ Water Heater:	____ Gas	____ Electric
____ Water Supply:	____ City	____ Well
	____ MUD	____ Co-op

    Roof Type: _____

    Age: _____[approx]
    Are you (Seller) aware of any of the above items that are not in working condition, that have known defects, or that are in need of repair?

    ____ yes   ____ no   ____ unknown

    If yes, then describe. (Attach additional sheets if necessary):

    _____
    _____
    _____

2. Are you (Seller) aware of any known defects/malfunctions in any of the following:
    Write Yes (Y) if you are aware, write No (N) if you are not aware.

____ Interior Walls	____ Ceilings	____ Floors
____ Exterior Walls	____ Doors	____ Windows
____ Roof	____ Foundation/Slab(s)	____ Basement
____ Walls/Fences	____ Driveways	____ Sidewalks
____ Plumbing/Sewers/Septics	____ Electrical Systems	____ Lighting Fixtures

    ____ Other Structural Components (Describe):

(continued)

FIGURE **20.1**
Continued.

If the answer to any of the above is yes, explain. (Attach additional sheets if necessary):

_____

_____

_____

3. Are you (Seller) aware of any of the following conditions?
   Write Yes (Y) if you are aware, write No (N) if you are not aware.

_____	Active Termites (includes wood-destroying insects)	_____	Previous Structural or Roof Repair
_____	Termite or Wood Rot Damage Needing Repair	_____	Hazardous or Toxic Waste
_____	Previous Termite Damage	_____	Asbestos Components
_____	Previous Termite Treatment	_____	Urea Formaldehyde Insulation
_____	Previous Flooding	_____	Radon Gas
_____	Improper Drainage	_____	Lead-Based Paint
_____	Water Penetration	_____	Aluminum Wiring
_____	Located in 100-Year Floodplain	_____	Previous Fires
_____	Present Flood Insurance Coverage	_____	Unplatted Easements
_____	Landfill, Settling, Soil Movement, Fault Lines	_____	Subsurface Structure or Pits

If the answer to any of the above is yes, explain. (Attach additional sheets if necessary):

_____

_____

_____

4. Are you (Seller) aware of any item, equipment, or system in or on the property that is in need of repair?

_____ Yes (if you are aware)   _____ No (if you are not aware).

If yes, explain (attach additional sheets as necessary).

_____

_____

_____

5. Are you (Seller) aware of any of the following?
   Write Yes (Y) if you are aware, write No (N) if you are not aware.

_____ Room additions, structural modifications, or other alterations or repairs made without necessary permits or not in compliance with building codes in effect at that time.

_____ Homeowners' Association or maintenance fees or assessments.

_____ Any "common area" (facilities such as pools, tennis courts, walkways, or other areas) co-owned in undivided interest with others.

_____ Any notices of violations of deed restrictions or governmental ordinances affecting the condition or use of the Property.

_____ Any lawsuits directly or indirectly affecting the Property.

_____ Any condition on the Property that materially affects the physical health or safety of an individual.

If the answer to any of the above is yes, explain. (Attach additional sheets if necessary):

_____

_____

_____

_____	_____
Date	*Signature of Seller*

The undersigned purchaser hereby acknowledges receipt of the foregoing notice.

_____	_____
Date	*Signature of Seller*

latent defects. There is also a shift of focus against effecting the sale of the property, because the buyer's broker is more concerned with a satisfactory purchase for the buyer than just making a sale. This may create a conflict between the seller's and the buyer's brokers. The end result may end up being the same, but the means to achieve the sale may be somewhat different. The buyer's broker may be expected to be more protective of the buyer (the primary focus) than focused on effecting the sale (the main focus of the listing broker). Although buyer brokerage is still a new concept, it's gaining wide acceptance. There is a growing niche in the agency marketplace created by consumers moving into a new area and relocation companies that may want to utilize the services of a buyer's broker. Brokers perceive it as both beneficial and cost-effective given that a home buyer may be a home seller in a few years.

DUAL AGENCY

If a broker represents a seller, it is the broker's duty to obtain the highest price and the best terms possible for the seller. If a broker represents a buyer, the broker's duty may be to obtain the lowest price (or at least a fair price) and best terms for the buyer. When the same broker represents two or more principals in the same transaction, it is a **dual agency** and a conflict of interest results. If the broker represents both principals in the same transaction, to whom is the broker loyal? Does she work equally hard for each principal? This is a difficult question; therefore, the law requires that each principal be told not to expect the broker's full allegiance and thus each principal is responsible for looking after his own interest. If a broker represents more than one principal and does not obtain their consent, the broker cannot claim a commission and the defrauded principal(s) may be able to rescind the transaction. Moreover, the broker's real estate license may be suspended or revoked. This is true even though the broker does her best to be equally fair to each principal.

A dual agency also develops when a buyer agrees to pay a broker a fee for finding a property and the broker finds one, lists it, and earns a fee from the seller as well as the buyer. Again, both the buyer and seller must be informed of the dual agency in advance of negotiations. If either principal does not approve of the dual agency, he can refuse to participate. Texas recognized dual agency in the License Act for a few years, then it was removed in favor of intermediary status (discussed next). Texas still recognizes common law dual agency, though.

The Texas Real Estate Licensing Act provides that a license may be revoked if the broker or salesperson fails to make clear to all parties to a transaction which party he is acting for, or if he receives compensation from more than one party, except with the full knowledge and consent of all parties [Section 15(a)(6)(D)]. If he acts in the dual capacity of broker and undisclosed principal in a transaction [Section 15(a)(6)(J)] (for instance, if the broker is also the purchaser, and takes advantage of a client by making a purchase below market value), he would violate this provision of the Act.

INTERMEDIARIES

The 1995 Texas legislature introduced a new concept of agency representation into Texas real estate brokerage law called an **intermediary.** An intermediary is defined under the License Act as a "broker who is employed to negotiate a transaction between the parties . . . and for that purpose may be an agent to the parties to the transaction." In most circumstances, the sponsoring broker acts as the intermediary.

The statute provides that a real estate broker may act as an intermediary between the parties if: (1) the real estate broker obtains written consent from each party to the transaction for the real estate broker to act as an intermediary in the transaction and (2) the written consent of the parties states the source of any expected compensation to the real estate broker. A written employment agreement, which also authorizes the real estate broker to act as an intermediary, is sufficient to establish that written consent if the written agreement sets forth the real estate broker's obligations in conspicuous bold or underlined print.

A real estate broker who acts as an intermediary between the parties:

1. May not disclose to the buyer or tenant that the seller or landlord will accept a price less than the asking price unless otherwise instructed in a separate writing by the seller or landlord

2. May not disclose to the seller or landlord that the buyer or tenant will pay a price greater than the price submitted in a written offer to the seller or landlord unless otherwise instructed in a separate writing by the buyer or tenant

3. May not disclose any confidential information or any other information a party specifically instructs the real estate broker in writing not to disclose unless otherwise instructed in a separate writing by the prospective party or is required or disclose unless otherwise instructed in a separate writing by the prospective party or is required to disclose such information by this Act [the Real Estate License Act] or a court order, or if the information materially relates to the condition of the property

4. Shall treat all parties to the transaction honestly. Section 15C(j). Note that another amendment also requires that the intermediary be required to

5. "Act fairly so as not to favor one party over the other." See Section 15C(m)(2).

If a real estate broker obtains the consent of the parties to act as an intermediary, the broker may appoint, by providing written notice to the parties, one or more licensees associated with the broker to communicate with and carry out instructions of one party and one or more other licensees associated with the broker to communicate with and carry out instructions of the other party or parties.

In effect, one may say that the intermediary status is nothing more than the old dual agency. The duties and responsibilities of an intermediary are very similar, if not the same, as the dual agent under the old dual agency statute. If the sponsoring broker is an intermediary, however, an appointed licensee **can give advice and opinions,** which is more than can be provided as a dual agent. To properly create intermediary status, the intermediary "check list" should work as follows:

1. Provide the required written information to any party you are working with (or to a party that is not represented) at your first face-to-face meeting (it would be prudent to have it executed to acknowledge receipt)

2. When engaging employment either as a buyer's representative or as a listing broker, the listing broker should be sure that the possibility for intermediary status is disclosed and authorized by the principal

3. Inform everyone else in the transaction (parties and licensees) who you represent at first contact (while the statute doesn't require this disclosure to be in writing, it is good business practice)

4. If the real estate firm (and your employment contract) authorizes an intermediary relationship, the agent should:

    a. remind parties that the firm will act as an intermediary when an in-house is apparent

    b. the firm should choose whether or not to make appointments of its associated licensees at the time the in-house sale becomes apparent

    c. if appointments are made, provide written notice to the parties. Should the sponsoring broker inform the parties that the intermediary appointments are not made, so that the parties shouldn't expect advice? It may be prudent to do so, but does it them create a dual agency? In the intermediary situation, the complications of presentation that we have under the single agency concept don't arise because both parties have agreed and consented to the intermediary status

If the foregoing steps are not complied with exactly, does it result in an undisclosed dual agent? Questions still abound, with few answers.

Agency Disclosure Rules

How do we sort all of these agency relationships out? The 1995 legislation created a disclosure process under §15C of the Texas Real Estate License Act. The disclosure is made in two stages: (1) when meeting a party for the first time and (2) while representing a party. When meeting the party for the first time, the licensee is required to furnish a party in a real estate transaction at the time of the first face-to-face meeting with a party with the written statement shown in Figure 20.2.

What is a "face-to-face" meeting? A face-to-face meeting is defined by the Real Estate License Act as a meeting at which a substantive discussion occurs with respect to specific real property. It does not include a meeting that occurs at a property held open for prospective purchasers or tenants or a meeting that occurs after the parties of the transaction have signed the contract to sell, buy, rent, or lease the real property concerned.

Exemptions

A licensee is not required to provide this written information if (1) the proposed transaction for a residential lease is not more than one year and no sale is being considered or (2) the licensee meets with the party who is represented by another licensee.

If the Licensee Represents a Party

The 1995 legislature also has modified the disclosure process under §15C of the Texas Real Estate License Act. The Statute now provides that a licensee who represents a party in a proposed real estate transaction must disclose that representation at the time of the licensee's first contact with (1) another party to the transaction or (2) another licensee who represents another party to the transaction. The disclosure may be orally or in writing. It would seem to be a prudent business practice, however, to do it in writing so that the agent could confirm that the disclosure was property made.

Middleman Principle

The broker may also operate as a middleman who represents neither party. He simply brings the parties together and neither party expects the middleman's loyalty. This middleman principle can work in some sophisticated real estate transactions. The problem with this theory though is that if either party thinks that the broker represents him, an agency relationship could be created and fiduciary duties established, resulting in potential liability for the broker. It is very difficult, in most situations, to represent neither party, yet still be an effective agent.

Principal's Obligations

The principal also has certain obligations to the agent. Although these do not receive much statutory attention in most states, they are important when the principal fails to live up to those obligations. The principal's primary obligation is **compensation.** Addition-

FIGURE 20.2
Agency disclosure statement.

Before working with a real estate broker, you should know that the duties of a broker depend on whom the broker represents. If you are a prospective seller or landlord (owner) or a prospective buyer or tenant (buyer), you should know that the broker who lists the property for sale or lease is the owner's agent. A broker who acts as a subagent represents the owner in cooperation with the listing broker. A broker who acts as a buyer's agent represents the buyer. A broker may act as an intermediary between the parties if the parties consent in writing. A broker can assist you in locating a property, preparing a contract or lease, or obtaining financing without representing you. A broker is obligated by law to treat you honestly.

IF THE BROKER REPRESENTS THE OWNER: The broker becomes the owner's agent by entering into an agreement with the owner, usually through a written listing agreement, or by agreeing to act as a subagent by accepting an offer of subagency from the listing broker. A subagent may work in a different real estate office. A listing broker or subagent can assist the buyer but does not represent the buyer and must place the interests of the owner first. The buyer should not tell the owner's agent anything the buyer would not want the owner to know because an owner's agent must disclose to the owner any material information known to the agent.

IF THE BROKER REPRESENTS THE BUYER: The broker becomes the buyer's agent by entering into an agreement to represent the buyer, usually through a written buyer representation agreement. A buyer's agent can assist the owner but does not represent the owner and must place the interests of the buyer first. The owner should not tell a buyer's agent anything the owner would not want the buyer to know because the buyer's agent must disclose to the buyer any material information known to the agent.

IF THE BROKER ACTS AS AN INTERMEDIARY: A broker may act as an intermediary between the parties if the broker complies with The Texas Real Estate License Act. The broker must obtain intermediary. The written consent must state who will pay the broker and, in conspicuous bold or underlined print, set forth the broker's obligations as an intermediary. The broker is required to treat each party honestly and fairly and to comply with the Texas Real Estate License Act. A broker who acts as an intermediary in a transaction: (1) shall treat all parties honestly; (2) may not disclose that the owner will accept a price less than the asking price unless authorized in writing to do so by the owner; (3) may not disclose that the buyer will pay a price greater than the price submitted in a written offer unless authorized in writing to do so by the buyer; and (4) may not disclose any confidential information or any information that a party specifically instructs the broker in writing not to disclose unless authorized in writing to disclose the information or is required to do so by the Texas Real Estate License Act or a court order or if the information materially relates to the condition of the property. With the parties' consent, a broker acting as an intermediary between the parties may appoint a person who is licensed under the Texas Real Estate License Act and associated with the broker to communicate with and carry out instructions of one party and another person who is licensed under that Act and associated with the broker to communicate with and carry out instructions of the other party.

If you choose to have a broker represent you, you should enter into a written agreement with the broker that clearly establishes the broker's obligations and your obligations. The agreement should state how and by whom the broker will be paid. You have the right to choose the type of representation, if any, you wish to receive. Your payment of a fee to a broker does not necessarily establish that the broker represents you. If you have any questions regarding the duties and responsibilities of the broker, you should resolve those questions before proceeding.

ally, the agent is eligible for **reimbursement** for expenses not related to the sale itself. For example, if an agent had to pay a plumber to fix a broken pipe for the owner, the agent could expect reimbursement from the owner over and above the sales commission.

The other two obligations of the principal are indemnification and performance. An agent is entitled to **indemnification** upon suffering a loss through no fault of her own, such as when a misrepresentation by the principal to the agent was passed on in good faith to the buyer. The duty of **performance** means the principal is expected to do whatever he reasonably can to accomplish the purpose of the agency such as referring inquiries by prospective buyers to the broker.

ANTITRUST LAWS

Federal antitrust laws, particularly the Sherman Antitrust Act, have made a major impact on the real estate brokerage industry. The purpose of federal antitrust laws is to promote competition in an open marketplace. To some people not familiar with the real estate business, it could appear that all real estate brokers charge the same fee (i.e., 6%). In fact and in practice, nothing is further from the truth. Real estate brokers establish their fees from a complex integration of market factors, and all real estate brokerage fees are a result of a negotiated agreement between the owner and the broker. In tougher markets a broker may charge a much higher fee (10% to 12% of the gross sales price). Very expensive property, in a good market, may be listed by a broker for an amount that is substantially less (2% to 5% of the gross sales price).

Price Fixing

Price fixing in any industry is so grossly anti-competitive and contrary to the free enterprise form of government, that price fixing is construed to be "per se" illegal. This means that the conduct of price fixing is, in itself, so illegal that no series of mitigating circumstances can correct it. While a brokerage company can establish a policy on fees, they should be acutely aware that any hint, or any perceived hint, of price fixing between brokers can result in both civil and criminal penalties. That is, if the court determines that a broker has engaged in price fixing with another broker or group of brokers, the licensee could serve time in the federal penitentiary in addition to paying a substantial fine. Consequently, brokers are well advised *never* to discuss their fees, under *any* circumstances, except with the owner of the property.

Boycotting

Another aspect of antitrust laws that has affected brokers has been boycotting of other brokers in the marketplace. This, too, is a violation of the Sherman Antitrust Act. In some circumstances, realtor trade associations have established rules for membership that have resulted in some brokers being unfairly excluded (unreasonably high fees, part-time employment, "discount" brokers, etc.). Standards for membership are usually an attempt to upgrade the professionalism of the industry and maintain high standards. The difficulty that is encountered, however, is that when high quality real estate brokers are excluded from competing with members of broker trade associations an unfair market advantage results. Antitrust cases involving boycotting have tended to recognize the procompetitive efforts of Boards of Realtors, MLS systems, and other similar trade associations, however. Therefore, Boards of Realtors and other trade associations can establish reasonable fees, residency requirements, and other pertinent requirements for membership. However, no membership requirements can be established that may arbitrarily exclude licensed real estate brokers from participation.

ERRORS AND OMISSION INSURANCE

Because of the trend in recent years to a more consumer-oriented and more litigious society, the possibility of a broker being sued has risen to the point that **errors and omission insurance (E&O)** has become very popular. The broker pays an annual fee to an insurance company that in turn will defend the broker and pay legal costs and judgments. Most "E&O" policies, as they are sometimes called, do not cover intentional acts of a broker to deceive, do not cover punitive damages or fraud, and do not cover negligence or misrepresentation when buying or selling for one's own account. Other than that, E&O offers quite broad coverage. This includes defending so-called "nuisance cases" in which the broker may not be at fault but must defend anyway. Moreover, E&O covers not only courtroom costs and judgments, but pre-trial conferences and negotiations and out-of-court settlements. Today E&O is simply a cost of the real estate business just like rent, telephone, and automobile expenses.

REVIEW QUESTIONS

Answers to these questions are found in the Answer Key section at the back of the book.

1. All of the following statements are true EXCEPT:
   A. the Statute of Frauds requires all agency agreements to be made in writing in order to be enforceable.
   B. a real estate listing is an agency contract.
   C. in a real estate listing, the property owner is the principal.
   D. a real estate broker is the agent under a real estate listing.

2. When an agent is given the right to transact all types of matters on behalf of the principal, the agent serves as a
   A. notary public.
   B. third party.
   C. universal agent.
   D. special agent.

3. An agent who is authorized to bind an employer in a trade or business is
   A. a special agent.
   B. a general agent.
   C. an exclusive agent.
   D. a principal agent.

4. The relationship of a real estate broker to the owner of property listed for sale with the broker is that of a(n)
   A. general agent.
   B. universal agent.
   C. limited agent.
   D. special agent.

5. Which of the following is NOT true of a listing contract?
   A. A corporation may be a principal.
   B. A natural person may be an agent.
   C. A sales associate may be an agent.
   D. Purchasers are third parties to the contract.

6. An agent's authority may be granted by
   A. written agreement.
   B. custom in the industry.
   C. Both A and B.
   D. Neither A nor B.

7. When an agent's authority arises from custom in the industry, it is identified as
   A. implied authority.
   B. ostensible authority.
   C. customary authority.
   D. conventional authority.

8. An agency may be created by
   A. ratification.
   B. estoppel.
   C. Both A and B.
   D. Neither A nor B.

9. Broker Gomez was part owner of an apartment building along with two co-owners. When they decided to sell the building, broker Gomez was named as the agent in the listing agreement. Broker Gomez thus held an agency

A. by ratification.

B. coupled with an interest.

C. by estoppel.

D. by implication.

10. A broker has fiduciary responsibilities to

A. the owner of property listed by the broker.

B. third parties with whom the broker deals.

C. Both A and B.

D. Neither A nor B.

11. Fiduciary responsibilities of an agent to the principal include all of the following EXCEPT:

A. faithful performance.

B. loyalty.

C. accounting for funds or property received.

D. provision of legal advice.

12. When a broker acts as an agent for both purchaser and seller in a transaction, this is identified as

A. an agency by estoppel.

B. a dual agency.

C. an agency coupled with an interest.

D. an agency by ratification.

13. A broker may act as an agent for both parties in a transaction only with the permission of

A. the property owner.

B. the real estate commission.

C. both parties.

D. the purchaser.

14. Isaacs introduced owner DiVita to prospect Park. DiVita and Park conducted negotiations among themselves without assistance from Isaacs. The role of Isaacs was that of a

A. dual agent.

B. middleman.

C. single agent.

D. cooperating broker.

15. Any earnest money deposits paid by the purchaser

A. belong to the broker.

B. must be placed in a proper trust account.

C. Both A and B.

D. Neither A nor B.

16. The placing of funds belonging to others in a broker's personal bank account constitutes

A. commingling.

B. grounds for revocation of the broker's license.

C. Both A and B.

D. Neither A nor B.

17. A broker who misrepresents a property to a prospect may be subject to all of the following EXCEPT:

A. loss of rights to the commission.

B. revocation of broker's license.

C. criminal prosecution.

D. civil action for damages.

18. The Texas Real Estate License Act provides that a license may be revoked if, without consent of all parties,

A. the broker fails to make it clear for which party he is acting.

B. the broker receives compensation from more than one party.

C. Both A and B.

D. Neither A nor B.

19. A broker who intentionally misleads a prospect by making an incorrect statement that is knowingly untrue is

A. guilty of fraud.

B. subject to license revocation.

C. subject to litigation.

D. All of the above.

E. None of the above.

20. An agent who fails to investigate the cause of an apparent underlying defect in a property that he is selling may be found

A. criminally liable.

B. liable for civil damages.

C. guilty of a felony.

D. Both A and C.

21. When an agent engages someone to look into a question raised by a purchaser, the agent

A. should make certain of the competency of the person so engaged.

B. may be liable for civil damages if the person is not professionally competent.

C. Both A and B.

D. Neither A nor B.

22. Can an agent protect himself from liability to disclose defects in a property by stating in writing that the property is being sold "as is"?

    A. Yes, because the statement makes it clear that the purchaser is aware of all problems that might arise.

    B. Yes, because of the rule of caveat emptor.

    C. No, because he may still be liable for having withheld material facts about the property.

    D. No, because the purchaser waives any right to future claims by accepting the property "as is."

23. If a principal asks an agent to participate in an illegal or unethical act in selling a property, the agent should do all the following EXCEPT:

    A. advise against it.

    B. have no part of it.

    C. discourage the principal from doing it.

    D. report the principal to the real estate department.

24. A broker can indemnify herself against legal actions by those with whom she deals by purchasing

    A. errors and omissions insurance.

    B. middleman insurance.

    C. property insurance.

    D. employee insurance.

KEY TERMS

Americans with Disabilities Act (ADA): a federal law giving disabled individuals the right to access to commercial facilities open to the public

Block busting: The illegal practice inducing panic selling in a neighborhood for financial gain

Community Reinvestment Act: federal statute encouraging federally regulated lenders to encourage their participation in low-income areas

Fair Credit Reporting Act: federal law giving an individual the right to inspect his or her file with the credit bureau and correct any errors

Familial status: one or more individuals under the age of eighteen who are domiciled with a parent or other person having custody

Handicapped: having a physical or mental impairment that substantially limits one or more life activities, or having a record of such impairment

Protected class: a class of people that by law are protected from discrimination

Steering: practice of directing home seekers to particular neighborhoods based on race, color, religion, sex, national origin, or handicapped or adults-only status

Tester: an individual or organization that responds to or tests for compliance with fair housing laws

Texas Fair Housing Act: Texas statute enforcing federal and state guidelines against discrimination

Fair Housing, ADA, Equal Credit, and Community Reinvestment

IN THIS CHAPTER *This chapter concentrates on federal legislation that has had a strong impact on expanding the ability of individuals to own real estate. The concept of fair housing prohibits discrimination in the purchase of real property. Equal credit has made lending sources available for thousands who could not previously qualify for loans. The Community Reinvestment Act encourages lenders to make loans in disadvantaged areas.*

It is almost impossible to fully explain the effects of federal legislation on real estate over the last 30 years. The scope and effect of the changes resulting from federal legislation is felt daily and has touched virtually every aspect of the real estate business. The federal government's emphasis on protection of individual rights was imposed because many states found this goal politically difficult to pursue, and in many cases a long history of prejudice was an overwhelming obstacle.

FAIR HOUSING

Federal legislation has been liberally applied to virtually all areas of discrimination—race, color, creed, national origin, alienage, sex, marital status, age, familial status, and handicapped status. The theories supporting these federal laws are applied differently though, depending on the source of the law and enforcement of the applicable statute. Let's review these theories in greater detail.

CONSTITUTIONAL IMPACT ON OWNERSHIP OF REAL PROPERTY

The most fundamental rights in real property are obtained in the U.S. Constitution. These rights are so firmly established and so broadly affect real estate that they deserve discussion at the outset. The Declaration of Independence declared that all [people] are created equal and set the stage for an attitude of the government that we enjoy in the United States. It was with this forethought that our founders wrote the United States Constitution that instilled in all citizens certain inalienable rights of which they can never be deprived. As far as real property ownership is concerned, the most significant of these rights are stated in the Fifth, Fourteenth, and Thirteenth Amendments to the Constitution.

The Fifth Amendment clearly states that no person shall ". . . be deprived of life, liberty, or property without due process of law. . . ." It was from this fundamental statement that we have developed the inherent right that nobody can have their property taken from them without court proceedings. This concept has been expanded over the last 25 years or so to include the prohibition of certain types of discrimination, creating certain "protected classes" of people who may not be discriminated against.

To date, the types of discrimination that have been deemed "suspect" by the United States Supreme Court have included discrimination on the basis of race, color, religion, national origin, and alienage. This is logical in that a citizen of the United States cannot alter his race, color, national origin, or alienage, and is entitled to practice the religion of his choice. Therefore, very strict constitutional prohibitions have been established by the courts to eliminate this type of discrimination for any other citizen in the United States. It should be emphasized that there is no *constitutional* prohibition of discrimination on the basis of sex, age, or marital status.

One of the most significant areas of litigation has been based on racial discrimination. This has been applied to all federal activity through the Fifth Amendment and to state and individual actions through enforcement of interpretation of the Thirteenth and Fourteenth Amendments to the Constitution.

The Fourteenth Amendment prohibits any state (as distinguished from the federal government) from depriving a person of life, liberty, or property without due process of law, and prohibits any state from denying any person within its jurisdiction the equal protection of the laws. The significant case in interpreting the Fourteenth Amendment as it applies to the states was *Shelley* v. *Kraemer.* In this Supreme Court case, some white property owners were attempting to enforce a deed restriction that required that all property owners must be Caucasian. The state courts granted the relief sought. The Supreme Court, however, reversed the case, stating that the action of state courts in imposing penalties deprive parties of other substantive rights without providing adequate notice. The opportunity to defend has long been regarded as a denial of due process of law as guaranteed by the Fourteenth Amendment. The court stated that equality and the enjoyment of property rights were regarded by the framers of the Fourteenth Amendment as an essential precondition to realization of other basic civil rights and liberties which the Fourteenth Amendment was intended to guaranty. Therefore, it was concluded that the "equal protection" clause of the Fourteenth Amendment should prohibit the judicial enforcement by state courts of restrictive covenants based on race or color.

The Thirteenth Amendment to the United States Constitution prohibits slavery and involuntary servitude. This amendment formed the basis for the most significant landmark case on discrimination, *Jones* v. *Alfred H. Mayer Company.* That case basically held that any form of discrimination, even by individuals, creates a "badge of slavery" which in turn results in the violation of the Thirteenth Amendment. The Supreme Court stated that in enforcing the Civil Rights Act of 1866, Congress is empowered under the Thirteenth Amendment to secure to all citizens the right to buy whatever a white man can buy and the right to live wherever a white man can live. The court further stated, "If Congress cannot say that being a free man means at least this much, then the Thirteenth Amendment has a promise the Nation cannot keep." This case effectively prohibits discrimination of all types and is applicable to real estate transactions.

FAIR HOUSING LAWS

In addition to the constitutional issues, two major federal laws prohibit discrimination in housing. The first is the **Civil Rights Act of 1866.** It states that, "All citizens of the United States shall have the same right in every State and Territory, as is enjoyed by the white citizens thereof to inherit, purchase, lease, sell, hold, and convey real and personal property." In 1968, the Supreme Court affirmed that the 1866 Act prohibits "all racial discrimination, private as well as public, in the sale of real property." The second is the **Fair Housing Law,** officially known as Title VIII of the Civil Rights Act of 1968, as amended. This law makes it illegal to discriminate on the basis of race, color, religion, sex, national origin, physical handicap, or familial status in connection with the sale or rental of housing and any vacant land offered for residential construction or use.

Newest Amendments to the Act

In 1988, the president signed an amendment to the Civil Rights Act of 1968. It expands the Act to provide for housing for the handicapped as well as people with children under the age of 18. The Act now provides protection for any form of discrimination based on race, color, religion, national origin, sex, familial status, or handicapped status. The law's application may be very broad, and needs to be discussed in more detail.

Handicapped

The amendment defines *handicapped* as:

1. having a physical or mental impairment that substantially limits one or more major life activities; or
2. having a record of having such an impairment; or
3. being regarded as having such an impairment.

The Act apparently includes recovered mental patients as well as those who are presently suffering from a mental handicap.

The full extent of how the discrimination against handicapped will affect us is still not known. It changed our attitude about certain restrictions. It is assumed, for instance, that a blind person can live with a guide dog in a housing project that prohibits pets. The handicapped are also allowed to make reasonable modifications to existing units, as long as it is at the handicapped's expense. The handicapped renter must also restore the unit to its original use upon termination of occupancy. The law also makes it unlawful for a landlord or owner to refuse to make reasonable accommodations, rules, policies, practices, or services when it is necessary to afford a handicapped person an equal opportunity to use and enjoy the dwelling. In addition, all new multifamily dwellings with four or more units must be constructed to allow access and use by handicapped persons. If the building has no elevators, only first floor units are covered by this provision. Doors and hallways in the buildings must be wide enough to accommodate wheelchairs. Light switches and other controls must be in convenient locations. Most rooms and spaces must be on an accessible route, and special accommodations such as grab bars in the bathrooms must be provided.

There are some exceptions under the handicapped person provision. The term *handicapped* for instance, does not include current illegal use of or addiction to a controlled substance, but it *does* include recovering addicts. Handicapped status also does not include any person whose tenancy imposes a direct threat to the health, safety, and property of others.

Since the statute was enacted, some cases have held that recovering drug addicts and alcoholics are handicapped, as are people infected with the HIV virus. Therefore, they cannot be discriminated against and denial of housing as a result of this "handicap" is a violation of the Fair Housing Act. This may result in unusual situations in which recovering drug addicts (perhaps criminals) could be moving into a neighborhood and the neighbors are prohibited from discriminating against them or denying them housing (by enforcing deed restrictions or zoning ordinances) because it would have a discriminatory effect on the handicapped.

Familial Status

Familial status is defined as one or more individuals (who have not obtained the age of 18 years) being domiciled with a parent or another person having legal custody of such individual or individuals or the designee of such parent or other person having such custody, with the written permission of such parent or other person. These protections also apply to any person who is pregnant or is in the process of securing legal custody of any individual who has not obtained the age of 18 years.

The most significant effect of this amendment is that all homeowner association property, apartment projects, and condominiums now have to have facilities adapted for children and cannot discriminate against anyone on the basis of familial status when leasing, selling, or renting property.

There are specific exemptions to this portion of the Act also. A building can qualify for an exemption if: (1) it provides housing under the state or federal program that the Secretary of Housing and Urban Development determines is specifically designed and operated to assist elderly persons; (2) it provides housing intended for, and is generally occupied only by, persons 62 years of age or older; or (3) it provides housing generally intended and operated for at least one person 55 years of age or older per unit and meets certain regulations that are adopted by the Secretary of Housing and Urban Development. There is often confusion over whether or not housing for the elderly is truly that. There are a large number of housing projects that primarily house the elderly, but do not qualify under the two exemptions under the Fair Housing Act. If a person is genuinely concerned about not having children around they need to be sure that the housing project qualifies as an exemption under familial bill status. They need to make the inquiry to determine whether or not it qualifies under the familial status exemption.

The penalties for violation of the Act are severe. The first violation of the Act results in a fine of not more than $50,000, and for subsequent violations a fine of not more than $100,000. The fines are in addition to other civil damages, potential injunctions, reasonable attorney's fees, and costs.

These amendments to the Fair Housing Law have a significant impact for all licensees attempting to sell, list, lease, or rent real estate. It is unlawful to refuse to sell or rent or to refuse to negotiate the sale or rental of any property based on familial status or handicapped status. Any printing and advertising cannot make any reference to preference based on handicapped or familial status. As stated previously, the landlord cannot deny the right of a handicapped tenant to make any changes in the physical structure of the building provided that the tenant agrees to reinstate the building back to its original form when leaving.

It is safe to say that many circumstances that may occur have not been specifically addressed by the statute. It is critically important that licensees recognize these two new prohibitions against discrimination and deem them just as serious violations of an individual's civil rights as are more traditional theories of race, color, religion, national origin, and sex. The difficulty, though, is that a real estate agent cannot tell if a person is handicapped (a recovering drug addict, for instance) or has children, unless the agent inquires. So it is prudent to inquire, *then* handle their requests. Otherwise one could violate the Act without knowing it.

Specifically, what do these two federal statutes prohibit, and what do they allow? The 1968 Fair Housing Law provides protection against the following acts if they discriminate against one or more of the protected classes:

1. Refusing to sell or rent to, deal or negotiate with any person;
2. Discriminating in the terms or conditions for buying or renting housing;
3. Discriminating by advertising that housing is available only to persons of a certain race, color, religion, sex, or national origin, those who are not handicapped, or adults only;
4. Denying that housing is available for inspection, sale, or rent when it really is available;
5. Denying or making different terms or conditions for home loans by commercial lenders;

6. Denying to anyone the use of or participation in any real estate services, such as brokers' organizations, multiple listing services, or other facilities related to the selling or renting of housing;

7. Steering or block busting.

Steering

Steering is the practice of directing home seekers to particular neighborhoods based on race, color, religion, sex, national origin, nonhandicapped, or adult-only housing. Steering includes efforts to exclude minority members from one area of a city as well as to direct them to minority or changing areas. Examples include showing only certain neighborhoods, slanting property descriptions, and downgrading neighborhoods. Steering is often subtle, sometimes no more than a word, phrase, or facial expression. Nonetheless, steering accounts for the bulk of the complaints filed against real estate licensees under the Fair Housing Act.

Block Busting

Block busting is the illegal practice of inducing panic selling in a neighborhood for financial gain. Block busting typically starts when one person induces another to sell property cheaply by stating that an impending change in the racial or religious composition of the neighborhood will cause property values to fall, school quality to decline, and crime to increase. The first home thus acquired is sold (at a mark-up) to a minority member. This event is used to reinforce fears that the neighborhood is indeed changing. The process quickly snowballs as residents panic and sell at progressively lower prices. The homes are then resold at higher prices to incoming residents.

Note that block busting is not limited to fears over people moving into a neighborhood. In a Virginia case, a real estate firm attempted to gain listings in a certain neighborhood by playing upon residents' fears regarding an upcoming expressway project.

Housing Covered by the Fair Housing Law

The Fair Housing Law applies to the following types of housing:

Single-family houses owned by private individuals when (1) a real estate broker or other person in the business of selling or renting dwellings is used and/or (2) discriminatory advertising is used;

Single-family houses not owned by private individuals;

Single-family houses owned by a private individual who owns more than three such houses or who, in any two-year period, sells more than one in which the individual was not the most recent resident;

Multifamily dwellings of five or more units;

Multifamily dwellings containing four or fewer units, if the owner does not reside in one of the units.

Acts Not Prohibited by the Fair Housing Law

Not covered by the Fair Housing Law are the sale or rental of single-family houses owned by a private individual who owns three or fewer such single-family houses if (1) a broker is not used, (2) discriminatory advertising is not used, and (3) no more than one house in which the owner was not the most recent resident is sold during any two-year period. Not covered by the 1968 Act are rentals of rooms or units in owner-occupied multidwellings for two to four families, if discriminatory advertising is not used. The Act also does not cover the sale, rental, or occupancy of dwellings that a religious organization owns or operates for other than a commercial purpose to persons of the same religion, if membership in that religion is not restricted on account of race, color, or national origin. It also does not cover the rental or occupancy of lodgings that a private club owns or operates for its members for other than a commercial purpose. Housing for the elderly may also allow discrimination in not permitting children or young adult occupants in the development or building, provided that the housing is primarily intended for the elderly, has minimum age requirements (55 or 62), and meets certain HUD guidelines.

Note, however, that the above listed acts *not* prohibited by the Fair Housing Law *are* prohibited by the 1866 Civil Rights Act when discrimination based on race occurs in connection with such acts.

Fair Housing Enforcement

Adherence to the 1968 Act can be enforced in any of three ways by someone who feels discriminated against. The first is to file a written complaint with the Department of Housing and Urban Development in Washington, D.C. The second is to file court action directly in a U.S. District Court or state or local court. The third is to file a complaint with the U.S. Attorney General. If a complaint is filed with HUD, HUD may investigate to see if the law has been broken, may attempt to resolve the problem by conference, conciliation, or persuasion, may refer the matter to a state or local fair housing authority, or may recommend that the complaint be filed in court. A person seeking enforcement of the 1866 Act must file a suit in a federal court.

No matter which route is taken, the burden of proving illegal discrimination under the 1968 Act is the responsibility of the person filing the complaint. If successful, the following remedies are available: (1) an injunction to stop the sale or rental of the property to someone else making it available to the complainant, (2) money for actual damages caused by the discrimination, (3) punitive damages, and (4) court costs. There are also criminal penalties for those who coerce, intimidate, threaten, or interfere with a person's buying, renting, or selling of housing.

Agent's Duties

A real estate agent's duties are to uphold the Fair Housing Law and the 1866 Civil Rights Act. If a property owner asks an agent to discriminate, the agent must refuse to accept the listing. An agent is in violation of fair housing laws by giving a minority buyer or seller less than favorable treatment or by ignoring or referring this individual to an agent of the same minority. Violation also occurs when an agent fails to use best efforts or does not submit an offer because of race, color, religion, sex, national origin, physical handicap, or occupancy by children.

Testers

From time to time a licensee may be approached by fair housing testers. These are individuals or organizations that respond to advertising and visit real estate offices to test for compliance with fair housing laws. The tester does not announce himself or herself as such or ask if the office follows fair housing practices. Rather, the tester plays the role of a person looking for housing to buy or rent and observes whether or not fair housing laws are being followed. If not followed, the tester lodges a complaint with the appropriate fair housing agency.

TEXAS FAIR HOUSING LAW

In 1989, Texas passed the Texas Fair Housing Act which, in most respects, parallels the Federal Fair Housing Law. The statute creates a Commission on Human Rights that is authorized to receive, investigate, and seek to conciliate any active complaints violating the Texas Fair Housing Act. The Commission must investigate discriminatory housing practices if the complaints filed are: (1) in writing, (2) under oath, and (3) in the form prescribed by the Commission, not later than one year after the discriminatory housing practice has occurred or terminated, whichever is later. On the filing of a complaint, the Commission shall give the aggrieved person notice that the complaint has been received, and notify the respondent of the alleged discriminatory housing practice. The respondent may then file an answer which must also be: (1) in writing, (2) under oath, and (3) in the form prescribed by the Commission. The Commission is then required to investigate the complaint and to encourage conciliation if possible. If the Commission concludes that prompt judicial action is necessary, it shall file an investigative report to the Attorney General, who shall then file an action on behalf of the aggrieved person in district court and seek relief from the alleged discriminatory housing practice which has occurred.

Enforcement by Private Persons

A person may also file a civil action in district court not later than the second year after the occurrence or the termination of an alleged discriminatory housing practice; or the breach of a conciliation agreement entered into under the Texas Fair Housing Act, whichever occurs last; or to obtain relief of the breach or discriminatory housing practice. If the court finds that discriminatory practice has occurred or is about to occur, the court may award to the plaintiff: actual and punitive damages, reasonable attorney's fees and court costs, and a permanent or temporary injunction.

Criminal Penalties

The Texas Fair Housing Act also provides criminal penalties for a person who commits an offense under the Act by force or threat of force, or who intentionally intimidates or interferes with a person because of race, color, religion, sex, handicap, familial status, or national origin. The offense is a Class A misdemeanor.

THE AMERICANS WITH DISABILITIES ACT

The **Americans with Disabilities Act (ADA)** was enacted in 1992 and deals primarily with commercial property. Generally stated, it provides access requirements and prohibits discrimination against people with disabilities in public accommodations, state and local government, transportation, telecommunications, and employment. Anyone that has had a physical or mental handicap or that is "perceived" as having such that interferes with a "major life activity" is covered by the Act.

The Act specifically affects the real estate brokerage industry in that real estate licensees need to determine whether or not the product the licensee is selling, managing, or leasing is in compliance with the Act. A licensee should always be cautioned, however, that the statute is very detailed and that there are a number of gray areas in the statute that still lack clear interpretation.

Scope

The antidiscrimination and the removal of barrier requirements of the ADA apply to "places of public accommodations," and the accessibility requirements of the ADA with respect to new construction and alterations apply to public accommodations and "commercial facilities."

"Places of public accommodations" encompasses 12 categories of retail and service businesses, including places of lodging; food and drink establishments; places of exhibitionary entertainment; places of public gathering; sales and rental establishments; services establishments such as law firms, accounting firms, and banks; public transportation stations; places of public display or collection; places of recreation, educational facilities; social service center establishments; and exercise clubs. It is presumed that this definition includes brokerage offices, even if they are located in private homes.

"Commercial facility" is defined as a facility (1) whose operations affect commerce; (2) that is intended for nonresidential use; and (3) that is not a facility expressly exempted from coverage under the Fair Housing Act of 1968.

The ADA contains a broad prohibition affecting public accommodations; it prohibits discriminating against those with disabilities by denying them the full and equal enjoyment of goods, services, facilities, privileges, advantages, and the accommodations of any place of public accommodation. Facilities need to be usable by those with disabilities.

All commercial facilities must also be accessible to the maximum extent feasible whenever alterations are being performed on the facility. Alteration is defined as any change that affects the usability of a facility. If the alterations are made to a lobby or work area of the public accommodation, a path of travel to the altered area and to the bathrooms, telephones, and drinking fountains serving that area must be made accessible to the extent that the added accessibility costs are not disproportionate to the overall cost of the original alteration. Disproportionate cost is defined for the purposes of the Act as costs which exceed 20% of the original alteration. The cost of alteration means all costs and renovating in particular proportion to the facility in a three-year period.

The Act requires modifications to procedures so that disabled individuals are not excluded from regular programs. Places of public accommodations must make reasonable modifications to the policies and procedures in order to accommodate individuals with disabilities and not create restrictions that tend to screen out individuals with disabilities, such as requiring a person to produce a driver's license or not allowing more than one person in a clothes changing area when a disabled person needs the assistance of another. The Act also requires auxiliary aids and services to ensure effective communication with individuals with hearing, vision, or speech impairments. These requirements would include interpreters, listening headsets, television closed caption decoders, telecommunication devices for the deaf, video tech displays, braille materials, and large print materials.

Several defenses and exclusions are available under the Act, but most are extremely narrow in scope. In addition, there are few court precedents to help us with interpretation of the ADA. Problems in compliance will occur. Examples: If a water fountain is placed low enough for someone in a wheel chair to use, what happens to the tall person who has difficulty in bending? Lowering a fire extinguisher for easier access to the person in the wheelchair also gives easier access to small children. Something that is "child proof" will also be inaccessible to someone with limited use of their hands.

Both the Department of Justice and private individuals may maintain a cause of action to enforce Title III against commercial building owners. The Department may seek monetary damages or injunctive relief, but private individuals are entitled only to seek injunctive relief under the statute. Apparently a tort claim may create a cause of action for monetary damages.

EQUAL CREDIT OPPORTUNITY ACT

The Equal Credit Opportunity Act was originally passed to provide for equal credit for borrowers by making it unlawful to discriminate against an applicant for credit based on sex or marital status. In 1976, the Act was amended to prohibit discrimination in any credit transaction based on race, color, religion, national origin, age (not including minors), receipt of income from a public assistance program, and the good faith exercise of rights under the Consumer Credit Protection Act.

Prohibited Requests

To effect this prohibition on discrimination, a creditor is prohibited from requiring certain information from the borrower:

1. Information concerning a spouse or former spouse, except when that spouse will be contractually obligated for repayment or if the spouse resides in a community property state
2. Information regarding the applicant's marital status unless the credit requested is for an individual's unsecured account, or unless the applicant resides in a community property state and the community property is to be relied upon to repay the credit. Inquiries as to the applicant's marital status are limited, however, to categories of "married," "unmarried" and "separated." "Unmarried" includes single, divorced, and widowed persons and may be specified in the application
3. Information concerning the source of an applicant's income without disclosing that information regarding alimony, child support, or separate maintenance is to be furnished only at the option of the applicant. The big exception to the rule is when the applicant expects to use any of those sources of income for repayment. If so, the lender may request this information
4. Information regarding an applicant's birth control practices or any intentions concerning the bearing or rearing of children, although a lender still has the right to ask an applicant about the number and ages of any dependents or about dependent-related financial obligations
5. Questions regarding race, color, religion, or national origin of the applicant.

There are minor exceptions when a real estate loan is involved. These exceptions are allowed in order to provide certain information that may be used by the federal government for the purposes of monitoring conformance with the Equal Credit Opportunity Act. When the information is requested, the lender is required to advise the applicants that the furnishing of the specific information is for purposes of monitoring the lender's compliance and is requested on a voluntary basis only. If the applicant does not wish to answer the questions, the lender simply notes the refusal on the application form. The refusal to give the information requested cannot be used in any way in considering whether or not credit is granted to the applicant. If the applicant agrees to provide the information on a voluntary basis, the following information can be furnished:

1. Race or national origin
2. Sex, relating to gender only (not sexual preference)

3. Marital status (using the categories of married, unmarried, or separated)

When considering race and national origin only the following categories can be used: American Indian or Alaskan Native, Asian or Pacific Islander, Black, White, Hispanic or "other."

Evaluating Credit Applications

As previously stated, the lender cannot use information obtained from an applicant that might be considered to be discriminatory. Each applicant has to be evaluated on the same basic information as any other individual person. Lenders can't refuse credit based on individual category, such as newlyweds, recent divorcees, etc. The lender's rules must be applied uniformly to all applicants. The areas in which there can be no discrimination have already been discussed (sex, marital status, race, color, religion, national origin, age, public assistance) but some of these areas need to be discussed in greater detail.

Age

A lender is prohibited from taking an applicant's age into account in determining their ability to repay, as well as income from any public assistance program. The only exception to this prohibition is minors, who lack contractual capacity and cannot enter into real estate transactions.

Children

As discussed in the previous sections on fair housing, the Equal Credit Opportunity Act has always provided that there can be no assumptions or statistics relating to the likelihood that a group of persons may bear children. In prior years, lenders required nonpregnancy affidavits and other indications that a young newly married couple would not endanger the income-producing capacity of the wife.

Part-Time Income

Income from part-time employment or retirement income cannot be discounted because of the basis of its source. However, the creditor may still consider the amount and probability of continuance of such income.

Alimony and Child Support

Alimony and child support and separate maintenance cannot be considered in evaluating a loan application unless the creditor determines that such payments are not likely to be made consistently. In such cases the lender has the right to determine whether or not the applicant has the ability to compel payment and the creditworthiness of the party who is obligated to make such payments.

Credit History

The Equal Credit Opportunity Act requires a creditor to consider the separate record of the applicant. This prohibits the lender from tying the applicant's credit history to the past record of the spouse or former spouse.

Immigration Residency

A creditor may consider an applicant's immigration status and whether or not he or she is a permanent resident of the United States.

Credit Denial

If an applicant is denied credit the lender must give notice to the applicant and advise the rejected applicant of the federal agency that administers compliance with the Equal Credit Opportunity Act for that particular loan transaction. The statement of specific reasons must give the precise reason or reasons for the denial of credit. There are suggested guidelines for giving reasons for credit denial including:

1. unable to verify credit references;
2. temporary or irregular employment;
3. insufficient length of employment;
4. insufficient income;
5. excessive obligations;
6. inadequate collateral;
7. too short a period of residency;
8. delinquent credit obligation.

Penalties

Failure to comply with the Equal Credit Opportunity Act or the accompanying federal regulations makes a creditor subject to a civil liability for damages limited to $10,000 in individual actions and the lesser of $500,000 or 1% of the creditor's net worth in class actions. The court may also award court costs and reasonable attorney's fees to an aggrieved applicant.

COMMUNITY REINVESTMENT ACT

The Community Reinvestment Act expands the concept that regulated financial institutions must serve the needs of their communities. Whenever a financing institution regulated by the federal government applies for a charter, branch facility, office relocation, or acquisition of another financing institution, the record of the institution's help in meeting local credit needs must be one of the factors considered by the federal supervising agencies.*

The basic requirements of the Community Reinvestment Act (CRA) for any institution applying for recognition are the following:

1. The institution must define its community by drawing a map that shows the areas served by the lender. This is essentially the area in which it does business and may overlap the area of another institution
2. The institution must submit a list of types of credit it offers in that community. This list must also be made available to the public. The decision as to what types of loans an institution makes is still left to the institution, but the information must be made available to the public
3. The lender must provide notice in its lobby that its performance is being evaluated by federal regulators. The notice must advise that a CRA statement and a File of Public Comments are available

CRA Statement

The CRA Statement, which must be made available to the public as well as the federal regulators, calls for mandatory information and some optional information that the statement should contain. The mandatory information consists of the following:

*The supervising agencies include the Office of the Controller of the Currency, the Board of Governors of the Federal Reserve System, the Federal Deposit Insurance Corporation, and the Office of Thrift Supervision.

1. A map of the lender's definition of its community
2. A list of credit services it offers
3. Copy of the public notice
4. A File of Public Comments received in the past two years that relate to the CRA Statement

The optional information that should be contained in the CRA Statement consists of:

1. A description of how current efforts help meet community needs and standards
2. A periodic report of the institution's record in helping to meet community credit needs
3. A description of efforts made to ascertain credit needs of the community

Part of the enforcement procedure of the Community Reinvestment Act calls for open hearings to be held on an application for a branch or any other internal expansions should a protest be lodged against that expansion. Anyone may be asked to be placed on the list for notification of all pending applications. The federal regulating authority must determine whether or not a protest is "substantial" and could therefore justify a hearing within ten days of the protest filing.

Federal Guidelines

The supervising agencies have listed the following guidelines that various federal examiners look for when assessing CRA performances. Three major areas that require examination fall under Section 563e.7 of the Insurance of Accounts Regulations and are numbered (b), (h), and (j) of the Community Reinvestment Act.

Subsection (b) concerns the extent of the institution's marketing and special credit-related programs to make members of the community aware of the credit services offered by the institution, such as public seminars, direct mailings or media campaigns, foreign language advertising, financial counseling, cooperative efforts with local governments or community groups seeking code compliance, technical assistance for revitalization of their neighborhoods.

Subsection (h) deals with the institution's participation including investments and local community development or redevelopment projects or programs. This includes HUD programs, economic development strategies, neighborhood reinvestment corporations, and neighborhood preservation projects.

Subsection (j) relates to the institution's participation in government insured, guaranteed, or subsidized loan programs for housing, small businesses, or small farms. This includes the lending institution's participation in government HUD programs, Veterans Administration programs, Department of Agriculture programs for rural housing loans guaranteed by the Farmer's Home Administration, or Small Business Administration loans. Other participation that can help to satisfy both Subsections (h) and (j) involve community development block grants established by HUD, housing finance agency development, rehabilitation, or home improvement programs for lower and moderate income residents and local development company loan programs.

Minorities

Most statutes and constitutions prohibit discrimination against **minorities.** Minorities are defined as any group, or any member of a group that can be identified either: (1) by race, color, religion, sex, or national origin or (2) by any other characteristic on the basis of which discrimination is prohibited by federal, state, or local fair housing law. It is not always a small group; it refers to any group that can be distinguished in a particular situation from some other group on a basis of race, sex, national origin, or so forth. It has nothing to do with numbers or size of the group. Whenever whites are discriminated against, they too are a minority group.

It is very difficult to ascertain what impact the Community Reinvestment Act has on lending institutions and practices of lenders generally. Many areas of the statute are vague, and it is difficult for the federal regulators to establish hard and fast rules because of the variety of different needs the lending institutions generally serve in different communities. As with a lot of other federal legislation, it may take some time before the full impact of this act is felt.

REVIEW QUESTIONS

Answers to these questions are found in the Answer Key section at the back of the book.

1. Discrimination in the availability of housing on the basis of race is prohibited by the
   A. Civil Rights Act of 1866.
   B. Fair Housing Act of 1968.
   C. Both A and B.
   D. Neither A nor B.

2. Vera, a real estate broker, was offered a rental listing by a homeowner who stated that he would not rent the property to a person of certain religious beliefs. Vera should
   A. refuse to accept the listing on these terms.
   B. accept the listing and leave it up to the owner to refuse any offers received from persons of that religion.
   C. accept the listing and steer persons of that religion to other properties.
   D. file a complaint of discrimination against the owner.

3. Under federal law, the owner of one single-family dwelling, in which he has resided for ten years, who does not employ an agent and does not use discriminatory advertising, may discriminate in the sale or rental of the property on any of the following bases EXCEPT:
   A. religion.
   B. race.
   C. color.
   D. national origin.

4. State and local laws that restrict or prohibit discrimination in the availability of rental housing may
   A. be more restrictive than federal statutes.
   B. prohibit additional forms of discrimination.
   C. Both A and B.
   D. Neither A nor B.

5. The Civil Rights Act of 1866 prohibits
   A. racial discrimination.
   B. steering.
   C. block busting.
   D. discrimination for any reason.

6. All of the following are prohibited by the Fair Housing Act of 1968, as amended, EXCEPT:
   A. discrimination in advertising.
   B. denial of availability of housing on the basis of religion.
   C. discrimination in terms or conditions for sale or rent.
   D. discrimination on the basis of age.

7. An amendment to the Fair Housing Act of 1968, signed by the president in 1988 prohibits:
   A. discrimination on the basis of physical handicap.
   B. the offering of different loan terms by commercial lenders based on race or religion of the loan applicant.
   C. refusal to sell, rent, or negotiate with any person.
   D. steering and block busting.

8. The practice of directing homeseekers to particular neighborhoods based on race, color, religion, sex, or national origin
   A. is known as steering.
   B. is prohibited by the Civil Rights Act of 1866.
   C. constitutes block busting.
   D. None of the above.
   E. All of the above.

9. All of the following are true for the inducement of panic selling in a neighborhood for financial gain EXCEPT:

    A. it is prohibited by the Fair Housing Act of 1968.

    B. it is limited to fear of loss of value because of the changing of the racial composition of a neighborhood.

    C. it is known as block busting.

    D. the prohibition applies to licensed real estate agents.

10. The Fair Housing Act of 1968 applies to

    A. single-family housing.

    B. multiple dwellings.

    C. Both A and B.

    D. Neither A nor B.

11. A church that operates housing for the elderly may restrict occupancy to members of the church if

    A. membership in the church is open to all persons.

    B. the units are to be rented, but not if they are being offered for sale.

    C. Both A and B.

    D. Neither A nor B.

12. A victim of discrimination in housing may seek enforcement of the 1968 Fair Housing Act by any of the following means EXCEPT:

    A. filing a complaint with HUD.

    B. filing action in federal court.

    C. filing a complaint with the U.S. Attorney General.

    D. filing a complaint with the state real estate department.

13. A person seeking enforcement of the Civil Rights Act of 1866 may do so by filing

    A. an action in federal court.

    B. a complaint with the U.S. Attorney General.

    C. an action in county court.

    D. a complaint with HUD.

14. A licensed real estate agent is offered a listing by an owner who stipulates that she will not sell to any person of a certain national origin. The agent should

    A. accept the listing and leave it up to the owner to reject offers from these persons.

    B. refuse to accept the listing.

    C. report the owner to the real estate department.

    D. file a complaint against the owner with HUD.

15. The Sunset Hills Country Club has several guest bedrooms that are made available to members and guests for a nominal charge, but are not available to the general public. Does this constitute a violation of the federal fair housing laws?

    A. Yes, because rental housing of this nature must be open to the public.

    B. Yes, because the charging of a fee constitutes a commercial purpose.

    C. No, because the club is exempt under the provisions of the Fair Housing Act of 1968.

    D. No, because this does not constitute steering or block busting.

KEY TERMS

Bylaws: rules that govern how an owners' association will be run

CC&Rs: covenants, conditions, and restrictions by which a property owner agrees to abide

Common elements: those parts of a condominium that are owned by all the unit owners

Condominium: individual ownership of a space of air plus undivided ownership of the common elements

Condominium declaration: a document that converts a given parcel of land into a condominium subdivision

Cooperative: land and building owned or leased by a corporation which, in turn, leases space to its shareholders

Limited common elements: common elements whose use is limited to certain owners

Planned Unit Development (PUD): individually owned lots and houses with community ownership of common areas

Proprietary lease: a lease issued by a cooperative corporation to its shareholders

Timesharing: the exclusive use of a property for a specified number of days each year

Condominiums, Cooperatives, PUDs, and Timeshares

IN THIS CHAPTER *This chapter covers U.S. housing laws and methods of dividing the land. The condominium declaration is covered in some detail. Other topics include management, maintenance fees, taxes, insurance, and financing. The advantages and disadvantages of condominium living are listed along with a list of things to check before buying. Other condo topics include a discussion of legislation, condo conversions, and physical appearance. Cooperative apartments, PUDs, and Timesharing are also covered.*

U.S. HOUSING LAW

Puerto Rican laws and experience became the basis for the passage by the U.S. Congress in 1961 of Section 234 of the National Housing Act. This section provides a legal model for condominium ownership and makes available FHA mortgage loan insurance on condominium units. Currently, one in four new residences being built in the United States is a condominium. Additionally, many existing apartment buildings are being converted to condominium ownership.

Condominium ownership is not the only legal framework available that combines community living with community ownership, although it is currently the best known. Prior to the enactment of condominium legislation, cooperative ownership of multi-family residential buildings was popular in the United States, particularly in the states of Florida, New York, and Hawaii. A more recent variation is the individually owned house combined with community ownership of common areas in what is called a planned unit development or PUD.

Of the forces responsible for creating the need for condominiums, cooperatives, and PUDs, the most important are land scarcity in desirable areas, continuing escalation in construction costs, disenchantment with the work of maintaining the grounds around a house, and the desire to own rather than rent.

Land-Use Efficiency

When constructing single-family houses on separate lots, a builder can usually average four to five houses per acre of land. In a growing number of cities, the sheer physical space necessary to continue building detached houses either does not exist or, if it does, it is a long distance from employment centers or is so expensive as to eliminate all but a small portion of the population from building there. As in ancient Roman times, the solution is to build more dwellings on the same parcel of land. Instead of four or five dwellings, build 25 or 100 on an acre of land. That way not only is the land more efficiently used, but the cost is divided among more owners. From the standpoint of construction costs, the builder does not have the miles of streets, sewers, or utility lines that would be necessary to reach every house in a subdivision. Furthermore, the facts that there are shared walls, that one dwelling unit's ceiling is often another's floor, and that one roof can cover many vertically stacked units can produce savings in construction materials and labor.

Amenities

For some householders, the lure of "carefree living," wherein such chores as lawn mowing, watering, weeding, snow shoveling, and building maintenance are provided, is the major attraction. For others, it is the security often associated with clustered dwellings or the extensive recreational and social facilities that are not economically possible on a single-dwelling-unit basis. It is commonplace to find swimming pools, recreation halls, tennis and volleyball courts, gymnasiums, and even social directors at some condominium, cooperative, and PUD projects.

A large rental apartment project can also produce the same advantages of land and construction economy and amenities. Nevertheless, we cannot overlook the preference of most American households to own rather than rent their dwellings. This preference is typically based on a desire for a savings program, observation of inflation in real estate prices, and advantageous income tax laws that allow owners, but not renters, to deduct property taxes and mortgage interest.

Dividing the Land of an Estate

Figure 22.1 illustrates the estate in land created by a condominium, cooperative, and planned unit development and compares each with the estate held by the owner of a house. Notice in Figure 22.1 that the ownership of house A extends from lot line B across to lot line C. Except where limited by zoning or other legal restrictions, the owner of house A has full control over and full right to use the land between the lot lines from the center of the earth to the limits of the sky. Within the law, the owner can choose how to use the land, what to build on it or add to it, what color to paint the house and garage, how many people and animals will live there, what type of landscaping to have, from whom to purchase property insurance, and so on. The owner of house D has the same control over the land between lot lines C and E.

The owner of A cannot dictate to a neighbor what color to paint the neighbor's house, what kind of shrubs and trees to grow, or from whom to buy hazard insurance if any at all. (Occasionally, one will find deed restrictions in housing subdivisions that give the owners a limited amount of control over each other's land uses in the subdivision.)

Condominium

In a **condominium,** each dwelling unit owner owns as his fee estate the cubicle of air space that his unit occupies. This is the space lying between the interior surfaces of the unit sides and between the floor and the ceiling. The remainder of the building and the land are called the **common elements** or common areas. Each unit owner holds an undivided interest in the common elements.

In Figure 22.1, the owner of dwelling unit F owns as her fee property the air space enclosed by the lines. Except for the individual unit owners' air spaces, F, G, H, I, and J each owns an undivided interest in everything between lot lines K and L. This includes the land and the shell of the building, plus such things as the manager's apart-

FIGURE 22.1
Comparison of estates.

(Presume fee simple ownership in each case)

1. House

2. Condominium

3. Planned Unit Development

4. Cooperative

ment, lobby, hallways, stairways, elevators, and recreation facilities. In Texas, the Condominium Act also recognizes **limited common elements.** These are common elements reserved for the use of a certain number of apartments to the exclusion of other apartments, such as special corridors, stairways, elevators, and services common to apartments of a particular floor.

Planned Unit Development Estate

In a **planned unit development** each owner owns as his individual property the land that his dwelling unit occupies. For example, the owner of house M in Figure 22.1 owns the land between lot lines P and Q from the center of the earth skyward. A homeowners' association consisting of M, N, and O owns the land at R and S and any improvements thereon, such as recreation facilities or parking lots. The most distinguishing feature of a PUD is the ownership of land by the unit owner, and the PUD concept is often used for townhouse development. In both condominiums and cooperatives, there is no land attributable to the unit owner.

Cooperative Estate

In a **cooperative estate** there is no individually owned property at all. Rather, the owners hold shares of stock in a cooperative corporation, which, in turn, owns the land and building and issues proprietary leases to the owners to use specific apartments. A **pro-**

prietary lease differs from the usual landlord-tenant lease in that the "tenant" is also an owner of the building. In the cooperative in Figure 22.1, all the land and the building lying between lot lines Y and Z are owned by a corporation that is owned by shareholders T, U, V, W, and X. Ownership of the corporation's shares carries the right to occupy apartment units in the building.

Having now briefly illustrated the estates created by the condominium, cooperative, and PUD forms of real estate ownership, let us take a closer look at their organization, financing, and management.

Overview of Condominiums

The Condominium Declaration

In Texas, a condominium is created when a person, usually a real estate developer, files a **condominium declaration** with the county clerk that converts a parcel of land held under a single deed into a number of individual condominium estates, plus an estate that includes the common elements. Included in the declaration is a description of the location of each individual unit with respect to the land, identification of the common elements to be shared, and the percentage interest each unit owner will have in the common elements. If the condominium is to be on leasehold land, the declaration converts the single leasehold interest into individual leases or subleases. The right of a person to file a condominium declaration is outlined in the Texas Uniform Condominium Act. As a general rule, the declaration can only be amended at a meeting of the unit owners, and at least 67% of the ownership must approve the change, although there are exceptions.

Owners' Association

In addition to filing the condominium declaration, also known as the **master deed,** the developer must provide a legal framework by which the unit owners can govern themselves. Often, a nonprofit condominium **unit owners' association** is incorporated, and each unit purchaser automatically becomes a member. The association can also be organized as a trust or unincorporated association. However, in the event of a lawsuit against the association, these may not offer the members the legal protection normally provided by a corporation. The main purpose of the owners' association is to control, regulate, and maintain the common elements.

Finally, the developer must file in the declaration a list of regulations by which anyone purchasing a unit in the condominium must abide. These are known as **covenants, conditions, and restrictions** in the declaration and tell a unit owner such things as the color of the exterior or her living room drapes, whether children or pets can live in the apartment. Typically, these also govern such things as when the swimming pool and other recreation facilities will be open for use and when quiet hours will be observed in the building.

Bylaws

Bylaws may also be recorded with the declaration. They provide the rules by which the association's board of directors or executive committee is elected from among the association members and set the standards by which the board must rule. They also set forth how association dues (maintenance fees) will be established and collected, how contracts will be let for maintenance, management, and repair work, and how personnel will be hired.

Unit Deed

Each purchaser of a condominium unit receives a deed to the unit from the developer. The deed describes the size and location of the unit, both in terms of the unit number in the building and its surveyed airspace. Usually this is done by referring to the parcel map that was filed with the declaration. The deed will also recite the percentage interest in the common elements that the grantee is receiving. The deed is recorded upon closing just as one would record a deed to a house.

Condominium Management

For condominium owners to enjoy maintenance-free living, the association usually employs the services of a building manager. If the project contains only a few units, the association may elect to employ one of its members on a part-time basis. The manager takes care of the landscaping, hallways, trash, and the like and keeps records of expenses needed to do this. For major maintenance items such as painting, roof repairs, and pool refurbishing, independent contractors are hired.

The resident manager is also usually responsible for enforcing the house rules, handling complaints or problems regarding maintenance, and supervising such matters as the handling of the mail and the use of the swimming pool and recreation areas. The extent of the manager's duties and responsibilities is set by the owners' association. The association should also retain the right to fire the resident manager and the management firm if their services are not satisfactory.

Maintenance Fees

The costs of maintaining the common elements in a condominium are allocated among the unit owners in accordance with percentages set forth in the enabling declaration. These **maintenance fees** or **association dues** are collected monthly. Failure to pay creates a lien against the delinquent owner's unit. The amount collected is based on the association's budget. This in turn is based on the association's estimate of the cost of month-to-month maintenance, insurance, legal counsel, and accounting services, plus reserves for expenses that do not occur monthly.

Property Taxes and Insurance

Since condominium law recognizes each condominium dwelling unit as a separate legal ownership, property taxes are assessed on each unit separately. Property taxes are based on the assessed value of the unit, which is based on its market value. As a rule, it is not necessary for the taxing authority to assess and tax the common elements separately. The reason is that the market value of each unit reflects not only the value of the unit itself, but also the value of the fractional ownership in the common elements that accompany the unit.

The association is responsible for purchasing hazard and liability insurance covering the common elements. Each dwelling unit owner is responsible for purchasing hazard and liability insurance for the interior of his or her dwelling. Owners should be cautioned to be sure the association has insurance in force and in sufficient amounts. If damages exceed the policy coverage in Texas, the unit owners are proportionally liable for the damage.

Thus, if a visitor slips on a banana peel in the lobby or a hallway of the building, the association is responsible. If the accident occurs in an individual's unit, the unit owner is responsible. In a high-rise condominium, if the roof breaks during a heavy rainstorm and floods several apartments below, the association is responsible. If an apartment owner's dishwasher overflows and soaks the apartments below that owner is responsible.

If the condominium unit is being rented, the owner will want to have landlord insurance, and the tenant, for protection, will want a tenant's hazard and liability policy.

Condominium Financing

Because each condominium unit can be separately owned, each can be separately financed. Thus, a condominium purchaser can choose whether or not to borrow against his unit. If he borrows, he can choose a large or small down payment and a long or short amortization period. Once in his unit, if he wants to repay early or refinance, this is his option too. When he sells, the buyer can elect to assume the loan, pay it off, or obtain new financing. In other words, while association bylaws, restrictions, and house rules may regulate how an owner may use his unit, in no way does the association control how a unit may be financed.

Since each unit is a separate ownership, if a lender needs to foreclose against a delinquent borrower in the building, the remaining unit owners are not involved. They are neither responsible for the delinquent borrower's mortgage debt, nor are they parties to the foreclosure.

Legislation Against Abuses

The legal documents involved in purchasing a house are few in comparison to those involved in purchasing a condominium. Because the master deed, bylaws, and restrictions often total 100 or more pages of legal language, unit purchasers who are not concerned with "details" often do not read them. As a result, in numerous cases developers have buried in these documents the fact that they are retaining substantial rights and title in their projects, even after all the units have been sold. The 1997 Texas legislature added meeting notice requirements, in addition to general notice and rights for a unit owner who may be assessed a fine.

Two specific areas of abuse have been recreation and management. Some developers retain title to recreation areas and then charge unit owners escalating monthly-use fees that are far more than actual costs. The developer then keeps the difference. If a unit owner protests by refusing to pay, the developer can place a lien against the unit and ultimately have it sold at foreclosure. In the second area of abuse, the fine print appoints the developer as manager of the project for 25 years. When the unit owners find their management fees out of proportion to the level of services received, the developer points out the clause appointing her manager and reminds them that she cannot be fired.

In adopting the Uniform Condominium Act, Texas created a Purchaser's Right To Cancel. In the event a purchaser buys a unit from a unit owner other than the declarant, and has not received from the seller, the declaration, bylaws and association rules before the purchaser executes the contract for sale, or if the contract does not contain an underlined or bold-printed provision acknowledging the person's receipt of those documents and recommending that the purchaser read those documents before executing the contract, the purchaser may cancel the contract before the sixth day after the date the purchaser receives those documents. If the purchaser has not received a resale certificate before executing a contract of sale, the purchaser may cancel the contract before the sixth day after the date the purchaser receives a retail certificate. Similar safeguards are allowed if the purchaser purchases the condominium unit from the original developer and has not received the condominium information. In the event an existing building is converted to condominium use (discussed next), the original declarant of the condominium must give each residential tenant or a subtenant in possession of a portion of the conversion building notice of the conversion at least sixty days before the date the declarant will require the tenant or subtenant in possession to vacate.

Federal law has also addressed the subject when congress passed the Condominium and Cooperative Abuse Relief Act, which applies to all condominium and cooperative projects where the real estate has five or more residential units in each residential structure. The Condominium and Cooperative Abuse Relief Act allows unit owners to terminate certain management contracts or portions thereof that were created while the developer was in control of the project. The statute has a very limited impact, however, because it only provides protection for condominiums that are conversion projects.

Condominium Conversions

Enterprising developers have found that existing apartment buildings can be converted to condominiums. Compared to new construction, a condominium conversion is often simpler, faster, and more profitable for the developer. The procedure involves finding an attractively built existing building that is well-located and has good floor plans. The developer does a facelift on the outside, adds more landscaping, paints the interior, and replaces carpets and appliances. The developer also files the necessary legal paperwork to convert the building and land into condominium units and common elements.

There are, however, some significant problems that have surfaced. One of these is the plight of the tenants who are forced to move out when a building is converted. In a few cities, there have been moratoriums on conversions.

Another potential problem area with condominium conversions, and one that a prospective buyer should be aware of, is that converted buildings are used buildings that were not intended as condominiums when built. As used buildings, there may be considerable deferred maintenance, and the building may have thermal insulation suitable to a time when energy costs were lower. If the building was originally built for rental purposes, sound-deadening insulation in the walls, floors, and ceilings may be inadequate. Fire protection between units may also be less than satisfactory. In contrast, newly built condominiums must meet current building code requirements regarding thermal and sound insulation, fire-wall construction, and so forth.

Lastly, it is worth noting that not all condominium conversions are carried out by developers. Enterprising tenants have successfully converted their own buildings and saved considerable sums of money. It is not uncommon for the value of a building to double when it is converted to a condominium. Tenants who are willing to hire the legal, architectural, and construction help they need can create valuable condominium homes for themselves in the same building where they were previously renters.

Physical Appearance of Condominiums

Before we turn our attention from condominiums, let it be reemphasized that a condominium is first and foremost a legal concept. It tells how title to real property is owned. It does not, by itself, tell us what a condominium looks like. Physically, a condominium can take the shape of a two-story garden apartment building, a 20-story tower, row houses, or four or more clustered houses. You will hear them called low-rise and high-rise condominiums, townhomes, garden-rises, walled garden apartments, villas, and cluster housing.

Condominiums are not restricted to residential uses. In recent years, a number of developers across the nation have built office buildings and sold individual suites to doctors, dentists, and lawyers. The same idea has been applied to shopping centers and industrial space. A condominium does not have to be a new building. Many existing apartment houses have been converted from rental status to condominium ownership with only a few physical changes to the building.

COOPERATIVE APARTMENTS

Prior to the availability of condominium enabling legislation in the United States, owner-occupied community housing took the form of the cooperative housing corporation. Although the condominium is dominant today, there are still substantial numbers of cooperative apartments in New York City, Miami, Chicago, San Francisco, and Honolulu. They are rarely found in Texas.

A **cooperative apartment** is organized by forming a nonprofit corporation. This is usually done by a developer who is either planning to convert an existing rental building to cooperative ownership or to build a new structure. Sometimes, the tenants in a rental building will organize a cooperative corporation to buy their building from the owner. To raise the funds necessary to pay for the building, the corporation borrows as much as it can by mortgaging the building. The balance is raised by selling shares of stock in the corporation.

The Cooperator

The shareholder, or **cooperator,** receives a proprietary lease from the corporation to occupy a certain apartment in the building. The more desirable apartments require the purchase of more shares than the less desirable ones.

In return for this lease, the cooperator does not pay rent; instead, she agrees to pay to the corporation her share of the cost of maintaining the building and her share of the monthly mortgage payments and annual property taxes. This sharing of expenses is a unique and crucial feature of this form of ownership. If one or more cooperators fail to pay their pro rata share, the remaining cooperators must make up the difference. Suppose that the monthly loan payment on a 10-unit cooperative building is $4,000 and it is shared equally by its 10 cooperators, each contributing $400 per month. If one shareholder fails to contribute his $400, only $3,600 is available for the required payment. If the lender is paid $3,600 rather than $4,000, the loan is delinquent and subject to foreclosure. The lender does not take the position that, since 9 of the 10 cooperators made their payments, nine-tenths of the building is free from foreclosure threat. Therefore, it is the responsibility of the remaining nine to continue making the $4,000 monthly payments or lose the building. They can seek voluntary reimbursement by the tardy cooperator, or, if that does not work, terminate him as a shareholder.

Refinancing Methods

Since the entire building serves as collateral for the loan, it is impossible to obtain new financing on an individual apartment unit in a cooperative building. So, if there is to be new mortgage financing, it must be on the entire building. When the original mortgage loan is substantially reduced and/or apartment prices have risen, as evidenced by a rise in the value of shares, this can be a severe handicap if a cooperator wants to sell. To illustrate, suppose that a family buys into a cooperative for $15,000. Several years later the family wants to sell, and is offered $80,000 for its shares. Unlike the purchaser of a house or a condominium who can obtain most of the money he needs by mortgaging the dwelling he is buying, the cooperative purchaser cannot mortgage his unit. Consequently, if the buyer does not have $80,000 in cash, he would be forced to mortgage other assets or seek an unsecured personal loan at an interest rate higher than for regular home mortgage loans.

Board of Directors

How a cooperative will be run is set forth in its articles of incorporation, bylaws, covenants and restrictions, and house rules. The governing body is a board of directors elected by a vote of the cooperators, and voting can either be based on shares held or on a one-vote-per-apartment basis. The board hires the services needed to maintain and operate the building and decides on how cooperative facilities will be used by shareholders. The annual budget and other matters of importance are submitted to all shareholders for a vote. Between shareholder meetings, normally scheduled annually, unhappy cooperators can approach board members and ask that a desired change be made. Or, at election time, they can vote for more sympathetic contenders for board membership or can run for board positions themselves.

Owners' Association

In two very significant areas, the authority of a cooperative owners' association and its board differs from that found in a condominium. First, as the interior of a cooperator's apartment is not her separate property, the association can control how she uses it. This right is based on the principle that the entire building is owned jointly by all cooperators for their mutual benefit. Thus, if a cooperator damages her apartment or is a constant nuisance, her lease can be terminated. As a rule, this requires at least a two-thirds vote of the shareholders and a return of the cooperator's investment.

Second, in a cooperative, the owners' association has the right to accept or reject new shareholders and sublessees. (The latter occurs when a shareholder rents his apartment to another.) If there is much turnover in the building, the association will delegate this right to the board. Thus, whenever a shareholder wishes to sell or rent, the transaction is subject to approval by the board. Except in cases of unlawful discrimination, this feature has been upheld by the courts. The legal basis is that cooperators share not only mutual ownership in their building, but also a joint financial responsibility. However, the board cannot be capricious or inconsistent.

Other Cooperative Forms

Most cooperatives are organized as corporations. It is a practical way to take title, select and control management, administer the day-to-day affairs of the cooperative, and at the same time insulate the individual members from direct liability for the obligations of the corporation. It is also possible to form a cooperative as a general or limited partnership, as a trust arrangement with the cooperators as trust beneficiaries, or as a tenancy in common. None of these has been widely used, primarily because partnerships and trusts do not provide the legal protection of a corporation, and because the tenancy in common idea has now been replaced by the condominium concept.

Low-cost cooperatives can be found in a number of United States cities. Sponsored by the FHA or by the city itself, these cooperatives are subsidized by public tax revenues and provide low- and moderate-income families with an opportunity for home ownership. Leases in these buildings are usually written for only one to three years and are not automatically renewable by the cooperator. This feature reflects the possibility that public funds may be cut back in the future. Also, when a cooperator sells, she is not permitted to retain any profits made upon resale. Rather, she is restricted to recovering only the money actually invested (i.e., down payment, mortgage amortization, and improvements).

PLANNED UNIT DEVELOPMENT

As illustrated in Figure 22.1, each owner in a planned unit development (PUD) owns as separate property the land beneath his dwelling. In addition, each unit owner is a shareholder in a nonprofit, incorporated owners' association that holds title to the common areas surrounding the dwelling units. The common areas can be as minimal as a few green spaces or might include parks, pools, golf courses, clubhouses, and jogging trails.

Since each owner in a planned unit development owns his land and dwelling as separate property, presumably he may use and maintain it as he wishes. However, there may be mutual restrictions upon all separately owned lots and dwellings. The right to establish and enforce these restrictions is usually vested in the owners' association. The association can dictate what color an owner can paint his window shutters, how he can landscape the front of his lot, and how many children and pets can reside in his dwelling. Additionally, the association maintains the common areas and governs how these areas shall be used by the residents and their guests.

Such thoughtful planning is not limited to single-family PUDs. Some of the most attractive planned residential developments in the United States combine natural surroundings with detached houses, row houses, clustered houses, apartment buildings, condominiums, and stores for shopping. So skillfully has this been done that residents are far more aware of the project's green vistas and lakes than they are of neighboring buildings. Reston in Virginia and Columbia in Maryland are city-sized examples of the planned unit development concept. A PUD can also consist of just one or two dozen homes on six acres in suburbia.

RESORT TIMESHARING

Resort **timesharing** is a method of dividing up and selling private occupancy of a living unit at a vacation facility for specified lengths of time each year. The idea started in Europe in the 1960s when groups of people jointly purchased ski resort lodgings and summer vacation villas so each individual owner could enjoy a week or two of exclusive occupancy. U.S. resort developers quickly recognized the market potential of the idea, and in 1969 the first resort timeshare opened in the United States. Since then hotels, motels, condominiums, townhouses, lodges, villas, recreational vehicle parks, campgrounds, houseboats, and even a cruise ship have been timeshared.

Benefits of Timesharing

The appeal of timesharing to developers is that a resort or condominium complex that can be bought and furnished for $100,000 per unit can, typically, be resold in 50 timeshare slices of $6,000 each; that is, $300,000 a unit. The primary appeal of timesharing to consumers is they have a resort to go to every year at a prepaid price. This is particularly appealing during inflationary times, although the annual maintenance fee can change upwards. There may be certain tax benefits if the timeshare is financed and for property taxes on fee simple timeshares. There may also be appreciation of the timeshare unit if it is in a particularly popular and well-run resort.

Then again, some or all of these benefits may not materialize. First, the lump sum paid for a timeshare week is usually much lower than hotel bills added up year after year. However, the timeshare buyer must pay in full in advance (or finance at interest), whereas the vacationer at a hotel pays only for what is used each year. Also, for timesharing there is a maintenance fee of approximately $20 to $40 per day that goes for clerk and maid service, linen laundry and replacement, structural maintenance and repairs, swimming pool service, hazard and liability insurance, reservations, collections and accounting services, general management, etc.

Second, going to the same resort for the same week every year for the next 30 or 40 years may become wearisome for some people. Yet that is what a timeshare buyer is agreeing to do. And, if the week is unused because of schedule problems, the maintenance fee must still be paid. To offset this, two large resort exchange services and several smaller ones and some of the larger timeshare developers help their buyers exchange weeks among their various projects. There is a cost, however, to exchanging. There may be as many as three fees to pay: an initial fee, an annual membership fee, and a fee when an exchange is made. These can amount to $100 or more for each exchange. Moreover, someone else with an unwanted timeshare week that you do want must also be in the exchange bank at the right time of the year. Satisfaction is usually achieved in exchanging by being flexible in accepting an exchange. Note too that if you own an off-season week at Lake Conroe, do not count on exchanging it for a peak-season vacation in Hawaii. Exchange banks usually require members to accept periods of equal or lesser popularity.

Third, tax laws allow deductions for interest expense on financed timeshares and for property taxes on fee timeshares. Timeshares have occasionally been touted as tax shelter vehicles, since the current rules allow for these deductions if the timeshare qualifies as a dwelling unit and is used as a secondary residence. However this has already aroused the ire of the Internal Revenue Service.

Fourth, although there have been several reported instances of timeshare appreciation, it is generally agreed in the timeshare industry and by consumer groups that the primary reason to purchase a resort timeshare is to obtain a vacation, not price appreciation. In fact, a timeshare industry rule-of-thumb is that one-third of the retail price of a timeshare unit goes to marketing costs. This acts as a damper on timeshare resale prices and even suggests that a prospective buyer might be able to purchase a timeshare on the resale market for less than from a developer.

Texas Timeshare Act

All transaction interests under the Texas Timeshare Act are defined as an interest in land within the meaning of the Texas Real Estate License Act. Therefore all brokers and salespeople who market timeshares must be licensed, unless they are otherwise exempt from licensure under the Real Estate License Act. The Timeshare Act further requires that all timeshare properties must be registered with the Texas Real Estate Commission before they can be offered for sale, although a developer can accept a reservation request from a prospective purchaser if the reservation deposit is placed in an escrow account that is fully refundable at any time at the request of the purchaser. A timeshare registration requires extensive disclosures to the Commission. The Commission has the power to investigate all aspects of the development and to suspend the registration (stopping sales) for any violation of the Timeshare Act.

Contracts to Purchase

The contract to purchase the timeshare must include the following: (1) the name and address of the seller and the address of the timeshare unit; (2) whether the purchaser visited the location of the timeshare unit before signing the contract; (3) an agreement by the seller that if the purchaser exercises the right of cancellation under the contract within a specified time, all payments made by the purchaser or the seller in connection with the contract shall be returned to such purchaser before the twenty-first day after the seller receives notice of cancellation; (4) the name of the person or persons actively involved in the sales presentation on behalf of the seller; (5) a warranty that the timeshare common properties are not mortgaged, unless the mortgage contains a nondisturbance clause that protects the timeshare owner in the event of foreclosure; and (6) in the event that such timeshare interests are sold under a lease, right to use, or membership agreement where free and clear title to the timeshare unit is not passed to the buyer, then the contract must contain a warranty that the timeshare is free and clear, or if subject to a mortgage, the mortgage must contain a nondisturbance clause that protects the timeshare owner in the event of foreclosure.

Each contract must have attached to it a separate page identified as Exhibit "A," containing information concerning the Purchaser's Right To Cancel, a statement disclosing the amount of the timeshare fees on a monthly or annual basis that are being accessed currently against or collected from the owners of a timeshare interest, and informing the owner that the owner has a right to request a written annual timeshare fee and expense statement.

Annual Timeshare Fee and Expense Statement

The Timeshare Act also provides that the managing entity of a timeshare must make available to each owner a written annual accounting of the operation of the timeshare property or timeshare system not later than the sixtieth day after the last day of each fiscal year. The managing entity must also post prominently in the registration area of each timeshare property a notice that the timeshare owner has the right to request a written annual timeshare fee and expense statement. The new Act also provides that the managing entity that manages two or more timeshare properties that are not participants in the same timeshare system may not commingle the timeshare fees. Upon request of the owner, the managing entity must make available for examination his registered office or principal place of business at any reasonable time or times and relevant books and records relating to the collection of expenditure and timeshare fees.

Promotion and Advertising

The Timeshare Act requires that a specific promotional disclosure statement be given before the use of any promotion in connection with the offering of a timeshare interest. The person who intends to use the promotion has to include the following information in its advertisements to the prospective purchaser: (1) a statement to the effect that the promotion is intended to solicit purchasers of timeshare interests; (2) if applicable, a statement to the effect that any person whose name is obtained during the promotion may be solicited to purchase a timeshare interest; (3) the full name of the developer and seller of the timeshare property; (4) if applicable, the full name and address of any marketing company involved in the promotion of the timeshare property; (5) the complete rules of the promotion; and (6) the method of awarding, the odds of winning, and a statement of the retail value of prizes, gifts, or other benefits under the promotion as set forth.

In addition to the disclosures listed above, the developer has a new emphasis on its awards. The developer must also give a statement of the retail value of the gift, prize, or award. The retail value of the items is the price at which substantial sales of the exact item have been made to members of the general public by at least two principal retail outlets of the state of Texas during the six months immediately preceding the offering of the prize or gift described in the promotion. If a substantial number of sales of the particular prize have not occurred in the state of Texas in the six months immediately preceding the offering of the prize or gift in the promotion, or if the developer elects, then the retail value of the prize or gift is the actual unit cost, net of any discounts or rebates to the developer, plus 200%. This new regulation may at least limit some of the "come ons" that have occurred in Texas such as the 12-inch "solid oak" grandfather clocks, "recliners" made of canvas and sticks, and similar phony scams. Some of these developers are pretty crafty characters, however. We will have to wait and see.

Exchange Programs

Prior to the signing of any agreement or contract to acquire a timeshare interest in which a prospective purchaser is also offered participation in any exchange program, the developer shall also deliver to the prospective purchaser the exchange disclosure statement of any exchange company whose service is advertised or offered by the developer or other person in connection with the disposition. If participation in an exchange program is offered for the first time after a disposition has occurred, any person offering such participation shall also deliver an exchange disclosure statement to the purchaser prior to the execution by the purchaser of any instrument relating to participation in the exchange program. In all cases, the person offering such participation shall obtain from the purchaser a written acknowledgment of receipt of the exchange disclosure statement. The exchange disclosure statement shall include the following information:

1. The name and address of the exchange company
2. If the exchange company is not the developer, a statement describing the legal relationship, if any between the exchange company and the developer
3. A statement indicating the conditions under which the exchange program might terminate or become unavailable
4. Whether membership or participation or both in the exchange program is voluntary or mandatory
5. A complete description of the required procedure for executing an exchange of timeshare periods
6. The fee required for membership or participation or both in the program and whether such fee is subject to change
7. A statement to the effect that participation in the exchange program is conditioned upon compliance with the terms of a contract between the exchange company and the purchaser
8. A statement in conspicuous and bold-faced print to the effect that all exchanges are arranged on a space-available basis and that neither the developer nor the exchange company guarantees that a particular timeshare period can be exchanged
9. A description of seasonal demand and unit occupancy restrictions employed in the exchange program

All disclosure statements require that the developer obtain written acknowledgment of their receipt from the purchaser.

Right to Cancel

Any purchaser can cancel her contract to purchase a timeshare interest before the sixth day after the date her contract is signed. The purchaser may not waive the right of cancellation. Any contract containing such a waiver is voidable at the option of the purchaser. The following statement must be provided to each purchaser at the time her contract is signed and must be on a separate page and attached to the contract as Exhibit A and must contain the following language.

PURCHASER'S RIGHT TO CANCEL

"(A) BY SIGNING THIS CONTRACT YOU ARE INCURRING AN OBLIGATION TO PURCHASE A TIMESHARE INTEREST. YOU MAY, HOWEVER, CANCEL THIS CONTRACT WITHOUT PENALTY OR OBLIGATION BEFORE THE SIXTH DAY AFTER THE DATE YOU SIGNED THE CONTRACT. IF YOU DO NOT RECEIVE A COPY OF THE CONTRACT AT THE TIME THE CONTRACT IS SIGNED, YOU MAY CANCEL THIS CONTRACT WITHOUT PENALTY OR OBLIGATION BEFORE THE SIXTH DAY AFTER THE DATE YOU RECEIVE A COPY OF THE CONTRACT.

(B) IF YOU DECIDE TO CANCEL THIS CONTRACT, YOU MAY DO SO BY EITHER HAND-DELIVERING NOTICE OF CANCELLATION TO THE SELLER, OR BY MAILING NOTICE BY PREPAID UNITED STATES MAIL TO THE SELLER OR THE SELLER'S AGENT FOR SERVICE OF PROCESS. YOUR

NOTICE OF CANCELLATION IS EFFECTIVE ON THE DATE SENT, OR DELIVERED TO, (INSERT NAME OF SELLER) AT (INSERT ADDRESS OF SELLER). FOR YOUR PROTECTION, SHOULD YOU DECIDE TO CANCEL YOU SHOULD EITHER SEND YOUR NOTICE OF CANCELLATION BY CERTIFIED MAIL WITH A RETURN RECEIPT REQUESTED OR OBTAIN A SIGNED AND DATED RECEIPT IF DELIVERING IT IN PERSON.

(C) A PURCHASER SHOULD NOT RELY ON STATEMENTS OTHER THAN THOSE INCLUDED IN THIS CONTRACT AND THE DISCLOSURE STATEMENT."

"AS A TIMESHARE OWNER, YOU HAVE A RIGHT TO REQUEST A WRITTEN ANNUAL TIMESHARE FEE AND EXPENSE STATEMENT. THIS STATEMENT IS PREPARED ANNUALLY BY THE MANAGING ENTITY AND WILL BE AVAILABLE NO LATER THAN THE 90TH DAY FOLLOWING (INSERT THE DATE OF THE LAST DAY OF THE FISCAL YEAR). YOU MAY REQUEST THE STATEMENT BY WRITING TO (INSERT ADDRESS OF THE MANAGING ENTITY)."

The seller must obtain the purchaser's signature on Exhibit A at the time the contract is signed.

A developer who violates the Timeshare Act is now guilty of a Class A misdemeanor.

If the managing entity is late in filing their statements concerning timeshare fees and expense statements, they are also subject to civil penalty up to $1,000.00 per day.

REVIEW QUESTIONS

Answers to these questions are found in the Answer Key section at the back of the book.

1. Condominium developments are restricted to
   A. residential dwelling units.
   B. multiple unit buildings.
   C. Both A and B.
   D. Neither A nor B.

2. In order to create a condominium development, a developer may
   A. construct a new building.
   B. convert an existing building.
   C. Both A and B.
   D. Neither A nor B.

3. Individual units in a condominium development are
   A. individually owned.
   B. common elements.
   C. cooperative elements.
   D. limited common elements.

4. Within a condominium development, common elements are owned by
   A. the owners' association.
   B. all unit owners, who hold undivided interests in the elements.
   C. the condominium developer.
   D. individual unit owners as community property.

5. Which of the following would be classified as limited common elements in a condominium development?
   A. Elevators.
   B. Hallways.
   C. Assigned parking spaces.
   D. The manager's apartment.

6. The plan for a condominium development that converts a single parcel of land into individual separate property estates and an estate composed of all common elements may be referred to as
   A. an enabling declaration.
   B. a master deed.
   C. Both A and B.
   D. Neither A nor B.

7. The rules by which an owner's association operates are known as
   A. bylaws.
   B. covenants, conditions, and restrictions.
   C. house rules.
   D. ordinances.

8. If the purchaser of a condominium has not received a resale certificate before executing a contract for sale in Texas, the purchaser may

   A. request a certificate from the Texas Association of Realtors.

   B. take possession and then cancel the contract within 30 days.

   C. cancel the contract within 15 days of the date of purchase.

   D. cancel the contract before the sixth day after the date the purchaser receives a resale certificate.

9. In a condominium, the authority to raise homeowner fees (association dues) rests with the

   A. board of directors.

   B. management company.

   C. condominium act.

   D. city and county.

10. The guest of a unit owner was injured by stepping on broker glass in the swimming pool at the Sunset Hills condominium. Liability for this injury would probably initially fall upon

    A. the unit owner.

    B. the condominium association.

    C. the management company.

    D. the developers.

11. The purchaser of a condominium unit

    A. surrenders personal freedoms to community rule.

    B. exchanges freedom of choice for freedom from responsibility.

    C. Both A and B.

    D. Neither A nor B.

12. Ownership of the interior space of your home and garage and an undivided interest in the building structures, common areas, and land area of the entire project describes a

    A. condominium.

    B. cooperative.

    C. PUD.

    D. corporate form of ownership.

13. Traditionally, the resale of cooperative shares have been financed by means of

    A. installment sales agreements.

    B. second mortgages on the seller's unit.

    C. bonds.

    D. government securities.

14. The 1985 Timeshare Act passed by the Texas Legislature required disclosure to the purchaser

    A. prior to the use of any promotion and advertising.

    B. prior to the signing of any agreement or contract.

    C. prior to the signing of any agreement or contract to participate in an exchange program.

    D. All of the above.

15. The owner of a unit in a planned unit development holds title to all of the following EXCEPT:

    A. the air above his unit.

    B. the land beneath his unit.

    C. a share of the common area.

    D. fee simple title to his unit.

16. In a planned unit development, the owners' association can dictate all the following EXCEPT:

    A. exterior paint colors.

    B. exterior landscaping.

    C. use of common areas.

    D. interior paint colors.

17. Under the right-to-use plan of timesharing, the purchaser

    A. holds title to real property.

    B. is a tenant in common with other users of the unit.

    C. Both A and B.

    D. Neither A nor B.

18. In Texas, all timeshare properties must be registered with

    A. the State legislature.

    B. the county clerk.

    C. the Texas Real Estate Commission.

    D. the Veterans Land Board.

KEY TERMS

Building codes: local and state laws that set minimum construction standards

Certificate of occupancy: a government-issued document that states a structure meets local zoning and building code requirements and is ready for use

Downzoning: rezoning of land from a higher-density use to a lower-density use

Environmental impact statement: a report that contains information regarding the effect of a proposed project on the environment of an area

Land-use control: a broad term that describes any legal restriction that controls how a parcel of land may be used

Nonconforming use: an improvement that is inconsistent with current zoning regulations

Restrictive covenants: clauses placed in deeds and leases to control how future owners and lessees may or may not use the property

Variance: allows an individual landowner to vary from zoning requirements

Zoning: public regulations that control the specific use of land

Land-Use Control

IN THIS CHAPTER *Land-use control describes any legal restriction that controls how a parcel of land may be used. There are both public controls and private controls. Public controls include zoning, building codes, subdivision regulations, and master plans. Private controls come in the form of deed restrictions. This chapter covers all those topics and concludes with a brief discussion of environmental impact statements.*

Land-use control is a broad term that describes any legal restriction that controls how a parcel of land may be used. Land-use controls can be divided by origin into two broad categories: public controls and private controls. Examples of public controls are zoning, building codes, subdivision regulations, and master plans. Private controls come in the form of deed restrictions.

ZONING

Zoning laws divide land into zones (districts) and within each zone regulate the purpose for which buildings may be constructed, the height and bulk of the buildings, the area of the lot that they may occupy, and the number of persons that they can accommodate. Through zoning, a community can protect existing land users from encroachment by undesirable uses; ensure that future land uses in the community will be compatible with each other; and control development so that each parcel of land will be adequately serviced by streets, sanitary and storm sewers, schools, parks, and utilities.

The authority to control land use is derived from the basic police power each state has in order to protect the public health, safety, morals, and general welfare of its citizens. Through an enabling act passed by the Texas legislature, the authority to control land use is also given to individual towns, cities, and counties. These local government units then pass zoning ordinances that establish the boundaries of the various land-use zones and determine the type of development that will be permitted in each of them according to a comprehensive plan. By going to his local government offices, a landowner can see on a map how his land is zoned. Once he knows the zoning for his land, he can consult the zoning ordinance to see how he will be allowed to use it.

In Texas it has often been said that the planning and zoning commission does not zone, but only plans. It is the local governing body or city council that does the actual zoning because of the procedures that the zoning statutes and enabling acts have established.

Zoning Symbols

For convenience, zones are usually identified by code abbreviations such as R (residential), C (commercial), I or M (industrial-manufacturing), and A (agriculture). Within each general category there are subcategories, such as R-1 (single-family residence), R-2 (two-family residence), R-3 (low-density, garden-type apartments), R-4 (high-density, high-rise apartments), PUD (multi-use, planned use development), and RPD (residential planned development). Similarly, there are usually three or four manufacturing zones ranging from light, smoke-free industry (I-1 or M-1) to heavy industry (I-4 or M-4). However, there is no mandatory uniformity in zoning classifications in the United States. One city may use R-4 to designate high-rise apartments, while another uses R-4 to designate single-family homes on 4,000-square-foot lots and the letter A to designate apartments.

Land-Use Restrictions

Besides specifying how landowners may use their land, the zoning ordinance includes additional rules. For example, land zoned for low-density apartments may require 1,500 square feet of land per living unit, a minimum of 600 square feet of living space per unit for one bedroom, 800 square feet for two bedrooms, and 1,000 square feet for three bedrooms. The zoning ordinance may also contain a set-back requirement that states that a building must be placed at least 25 feet back from the street, 10 feet from the sides of the lot, and 15 feet from the rear lot line. The ordinance may also limit the building's height to two stories and require that the lot be a minimum of 10,000 square feet in size. As can be seen, zoning encourages uniformity, as it serves the common good.

Enforcement of Zoning Laws

Zoning laws are enforced by virtue of the fact that in order to build upon his land a person must obtain a building permit from his city or county government. Before a permit is issued, the proposed structure must conform with government-imposed structural standards and comply with the zoning on the land. If a landowner builds without a permit, he can be forced to tear down his building.

Nonconforming Use

When an existing structure does not conform with a new zoning law, it is "grandfathered-in" as a **nonconforming use.** Thus, the owner can continue to use the structure even though it does not conform to the new zoning. However, the owner is not permitted to enlarge or remodel the structure or to extend its life. When the structure is ultimately demolished, any new use of the land must be then in accordance with the zoning law. If you are driving through a residential neighborhood and see an old store or service station that looks very much out of place, it is probably a nonconforming use that was allowed to stay because it was built before the current zoning on the property went into effect.

Zoning Changes

Once an area has been zoned for a specific land use, changes are made by **amending the zoning ordinance** or by obtaining a variance. The amendment approach is taken when a change in zoning is necessary. An amendment can be initiated by a property owner in the area to be rezoned or by local government. Either way, if there is a proposed change in the zoning ordinance, the zoning commission, after giving proper public notice, holds a public hearing to provide a forum for public input and response. After the public hearing, the zoning commission makes a recommendation to the city council. The city council, after posting proper public notices, holds its own public hearing. After the city council's public hearing, the city council does the actual enactment of the zoning ordinance or zoning change legislation, which ultimately becomes of record in the municipal ordinances. The city council has the right to accept or reject any recommendation of the planning and zoning commission.

Variances

By comparison, **variances** allow an individual landowner to deviate somewhat from zoning code requirements and do not involve a zoning change. For example, a variance might be granted to the owner of an odd-shaped lot to reduce the setback requirements slightly so that he can fit a building on it. Variances usually are granted where strict compliance with the zoning ordinance or code would cause undue hardship. However, the variance must not change the basic character of the neighborhood, and it must be consistent with the general objectives of zoning as they apply to that neighborhood.

Conditional-Use Permit

A **conditional-use permit** allows a land use that does not conform with existing zoning provided the use is within the limitations imposed by the permit. A conditional use permit is usually quite restrictive, and if the conditions of the permit are violated the permit is no longer valid. For example, a neighborhood grocery store operating under a conditional use permit can only be a neighborhood grocery. The structure cannot be used as an auto parts store.

Spot Zoning

Spot zoning refers to the rezoning of a small area of land in an existing neighborhood. For example, a neighborhood convenience center (grocery, laundry, barbershop) might be allowed in a residential neighborhood provided it serves a useful purpose for neighborhood residents and is not a nuisance.

Downzoning

Downzoning means that land previously zoned for higher-density uses (or more active uses) is rezoned for lower-density uses (or less active uses). Examples are downzoning from high-rise commercial to low-rise commercial, apartment zoning to single-family, and single-family to agriculture. Although a landowner's property value may fall as a result of downzoning, there is no compensation to the landowner as there is no taking of land as with eminent domain.

Taking

Taking is a concept wherein the municipality regulates the property to where it has no value or, in some cases, has no remaining economic value. The U.S. Supreme Court, in several cases, has determined that a municipality can regulate land use to where it becomes a "taking" and results in condemnation. In those instances, the municipality must pay the fair market value of the property to the landowner. Texas even has legislation that allows for certain governmental entities (cities are excluded) to pay the landowner in the event the land is regulated to a less intense use, such that if the fair market value of the land is decreased by 25%, that governmental entity must pay the landowner for the reduction in value. This area of the law is clearly becoming more protective of the private landowner's rights.

Buffer Zone

A **buffer zone** is a strip of land that separates one land use from another. Thus, between a large shopping center and a neighborhood of single-family homes, there may be a row of garden apartments. Alternatively, between an industrial park and a residential subdivision, a developer may leave a strip of land in grass and trees rather than build homes immediately adjacent to the industrial buildings. Note that *buffer zone* is a generic term and not necessarily a zoning law category.

A zoning law can be changed or struck down if it can be proved in court that it is unclear; discriminatory; unreasonable; not for the protection of the public health, safety, and general welfare; or not applied to all property in a similar manner.

It must be recognized that zoning alone does not create land value. For example, zoning a hundred square miles of lonely desert or mountain land for stores and offices would not appreciably change its value. Value is created by the concerted effort of a number of people who want to use a particular parcel of land for a specific purpose. To the extent that zoning channels demand to certain parcels of land and away from others, zoning does have an important impact on property value.

PRECAUTIONS

Because zoning can greatly influence the value of a property, it is absolutely essential that you be aware of the zoning for that parcel when you purchase any real estate. You will need to know what the zoning will allow and what it will not; whether the parcel is under a restrictive or temporary permit; and what the zoning and planning departments might allow on the property in the future. Where there is any uncertainty or where a zone change or variance will be necessary in order to use the property the way you want to, a conservative approach is to make the offer to buy contingent on obtaining planning and zoning approval before going to settlement.

If you are a real estate agent (particularly as a buyer's agent) you must stay abreast of zoning and planning and building matters regarding the properties you list and sell. A particularly sensitive issue that occurs regularly is a property listed for sale that does not meet zoning and/or building code requirements. For example, suppose the current (or previous) owner of a house has converted the garage to a den or bedroom without obtaining building permits and without providing space for parking elsewhere on the parcel. Legally this makes the property unmarketable. If you, as agent, sell this property without telling the buyer about the lack of permits, you've given the buyer grounds to sue you for misrepresentation and the seller for rescission. When faced with a situation like this you should ask the seller to obtain the necessary permits. If the seller refuses, and the buyer still wants to buy, make the problem very clear to the buyer and have the buyer sign a statement indicating acceptance of title under these conditions. You can also refuse to accept the listing if it looks as though it will create more trouble than it's worth.

Professional Obligations Toward Property Zoning

The point here is that the public has a right to expect real estate agents to be professionals in their field. Thus the agent is expected to be fully aware of the permitted uses for a property and whether or not current uses comply. This is necessary to properly value the property for listing and to provide accurate information to prospective buyers. Note too that even if the seller in the above example was unaware of the zoning and building violations, it is the agent's responsibility to recognize the problem and inform the seller. An agent cannot take the position that if the seller didn't mention it, then the agent needn't worry about it *and* if the buyer later complains, it's the seller's problem, not the agent's. Recent court decisions clearly indicate that the agent has a responsibility to inform the seller of a problem so that the seller cannot later complain to the agent, "You should have told me about that when I listed the property with you and certainly before I accepted the buyer's offer."

SUBDIVISION REGULATIONS

Before a building lot can be sold, a subdivider must comply with local government regulations concerning street construction, curbs, sidewalks, street lighting, fire hydrants, storm and sanitary sewers, grading and compacting of soil, water and utility lines, minimum lot size, and so on. In addition, the subdivider may be required to either set aside land for schools and parks or provide money so that land may be purchased nearby for that purpose. Until he has complied with all state and local regulations, the subdivider cannot receive his subdivision approval. Without approval he cannot record his plat map, which in turn means he cannot sell his lots to the public. If he tries to sell his lots without approval, he can be stopped by a government court order and in some states fined. Moreover, permits to build will be refused to lot owners, and anyone who bought from the subdivider is entitled to a refund.

BUILDING CODES

Recognizing the need to protect public health and safety against slipshod construction practices, state and local governments have enacted building codes. These establish minimum acceptable material and construction standards for such things as structural load and stress, windows and ventilation, size and location of rooms, fire protection, exits, electrical installation, plumbing, heating, lighting, and so forth.

Before a building permit is granted, the design of a proposed structure must meet the building-code requirements. During construction, local building department inspectors visit the construction site to make certain that the codes are being observed. Finally, when the building is completed, a **certificate of occupancy** is issued to the building owner to show that the structure meets the code. Without this certificate, the building cannot be legally occupied.

DEED RESTRICTIONS

Although property owners tend to think of land-use controls as being strictly a product of government, it is possible to achieve land-use control through private means. In fact, Houston, Texas, with a population of more than 4 million persons, operates without zoning and relies almost entirely upon private land-use controls and building permits to achieve a similar effect.

Private land-use controls take the form of deed and lease restrictions. In the United States, it has long been recognized that the ownership of land includes the right to sell or lease it on whatever legally acceptable conditions the owner establishes, including the right to dictate to the buyer or lessee how he shall or shall not use it. For example, a developer can sell the lots in his subdivision subject to a restriction written into each deed that the land cannot be used for anything but a single-family residence containing at least 1,200 square feet of living area. The legal theory is that, if the buyer or lessee agrees to the restrictions, he is bound by them. If they are not obeyed, any lot owner in the subdivision can obtain a court order to enforce compliance. The only limit to the number of restrictions that an owner may place on his land is economic. If there are too many restrictions, the landowner may find that no one wants his land.

Deed restrictions, also known as **restrictive covenants,** can be used to dictate such matters as the purpose of the structure to be built, architectural requirements, setbacks, size of the structure, and aesthetics. In neighborhoods with view lots, they are often used to limit the height to which trees may be permitted to grow. In Texas, and particularly Houston, **deed restrictions** have been one of the mainstays of land-use control. Deed restrictions cannot be used to discriminate on the basis of sex, race, color, or creed; if they do they are unenforceable by the courts.

Since deed restrictions are enforced pursuant to contract law, only those who benefit from that contract (i.e., previous owners who may have reserved restrictions or subsequent purchasers in the property affected by the deed restrictions), have the right to enforce these deed restrictions. They must be enforced judicially, since judicial interpretation is generally required for proper construction of the deed restrictions and normally involve lawsuits and expensive litigation. To help facilitate the enforcement of deed restrictions, the Texas legislature passed a statute that enabled incorporated cities, towns, or villages who do not have zoning ordinances to enforce deed restrictions on behalf of the people affected by those deed restrictions.

The City of Houston, pursuant to this enabling act, has made some attempt at enforcing deed restrictions pursuant to its municipal authority. It is an attempt to enforce deed restrictions through the municipal power without the necessity of the homeowners or other beneficiaries of the deed restrictions having to go to court to enforce same, using their own personal funds. Some counties, too, have this authority. Since 1997, county attorneys in counties in excess of 2,000,000 people are authorized to enforce deed restrictions. Since 1997, a suit to enforce restrictive covenants can now be maintained in justice of the peace courts, making enforcement cheaper and easier.

Restrictive covenants normally carry a time limit so that they can be subject to periodic review. However, there has been a judicial interpretation that deed restrictions can run forever, providing that the limitation on the use is not unreasonable. Once the deed restrictions have been filed and are of record, they may not be subsequently modified without the consent of all the property owners, unless the power to amend the restrictions has been reserved or some other procedure for amending the property restrictions is contained in those restrictions.

Deed restrictions can be more functional than zoning restrictions because there is no control over what provisions can be contained in deed restrictions. Virtually anything, providing that it is not unconstitutional or illegal, can be in deed restrictions, and can provide a very tight land-use control. Zoning ordinances, on the other hand, generally have to promote the public health, safety, and welfare and cannot deal with more detailed aspects of land-use control, such as types of shingles and wood fences, or other aspects of architectural style that could be comfortably enforced through the deed restriction mechanism of land-use control.

ENVIRONMENTAL IMPACT STATEMENTS

The purpose of an **environmental impact statement (EIS),** also called an **environmental impact report (EIR),** is to gather into one document enough information about the effect of a proposed project on the total environment so that a neutral decision maker can judge the environmental benefits and costs of the project. For example, a city zoning commission that has been asked to approve a zone change can request an

EIS that will show the expected impact of the change on such things as population density, automobile traffic, noise, air quality, water and sewage facilities, drainage, energy consumption, school enrollments, employment, public health and safety, recreation facilities, wildlife, and vegetation. The idea is that with this information at hand better decisions can be made about land uses. When problems can be anticipated in advance, it is easier to make modifications or explore alternatives.

The EIS requirement has the greatest effect on private development at the city and county level. Usually the EIS accompanies the development application that is submitted to the planning or zoning commission. Where applicable, copies are also sent to affected school districts, water and sanitation districts, and highway and flood control departments. The EIS is then made available for public inspection as part of the hearing process on the development application. This gives concerned civic groups and the public at large an opportunity to voice their opinions regarding the anticipated benefits and costs of the proposed development. If the proposed development is partially or wholly funded by state or federal funds, state or federal hearings are also held.

Content of an EIS

Typically, an EIS will contain a description of present conditions at the proposed development site, plus information on the following five points: (1) the probable impact of the proposed project on the physical, economic, and social environment of the area, (2) any unavoidable adverse environmental effects, (3) any alternatives to the proposed project, (4) the short-term versus long-term effects of the proposed project on the environment, and (5) a listing of any irreversible commitment of resources if the project is implemented. For a government-initiated project, the EIS is prepared by a government agency, sometimes with the help of private consultants. In the case of a private development, it may be prepared by the developer, a local government agency for a fee, or by a private firm specializing in the preparation of impact statements.

Environmental Laws

Since 1982, the number of environmental laws that have affected real estate development has expanded tremendously and has had a definite and profound effect on land-use control. In 1982, Congress passed a **Comprehensive Environmental Response, Compensation, and Liability Act** (commonly referred to as **CERCLA**) that imposed upon (1) the owners, (2) operators of facilities, and (3) any person who, at the time of disposal of any hazardous substance, owned or operated the facility at which such hazardous substances were disposed of, and any person who arranged for disposal, or (4) any persons who have accepted hazardous substances for transport to disposal or treatment sites, joint and several, 100 percent liability for damages resulting from that disposal. Subsequent legislation involved changes in the Clean Water Act that provide for a prohibition against storm water discharges. Similar federal statutes have been passed affecting asbestos, radon gas, lead poisoning, wetland areas, endangered species, and underground storage tanks. This has resulted in purchasers being required to exercise a level of "due diligence" in investigating sites prior to acquisition. A licensee should also note, and be particularly careful, that pertinent questions concerning environmental hazards may be directed to the broker and the broker may be on a "should have known" duty of care to know whether or not any of these incidents may have occurred.

The net result of all this federal legislation has resulted in **environmental site assessments.** Environmental site assessments have basically been divided into Phase I,

Phase II, or Phase III Assessments. While none of these terms are specifically defined by statute or common law, the consensus among environmental consultants seems to be that the principal elements of a Phase I Assessment include an on-site visual inspection of the property, interviews with owners and area residents as to the use and possession of the property, and review of historical aerial photographs and public records to determine past use and possession of the property. A Phase II Assessment typically involves sampling of the soil and water for the presence of hazardous substances. A Phase III Assessment involves further sampling and establishing limits of the contamination and developing a plan for remedial action and clean up.

The horror stories involving environmental clean air pollution are legion. The liability is unlimited, while many of the concerns are real. Some areas of environmental legislation involve enormous expense with very little result. One can be assured this will remain a hot area of litigation, controversy, and federal legislation for the coming years.

REVIEW QUESTIONS

Answers to these questions are found in the Answer Key section at the back of the book.

1. Through zoning, a community can protect existing land users from all of the following, EXCEPT:
   A. encroachment by undesirable uses.
   B. uncontrolled development.
   C. incompatible uses of land.
   D. competitive business establishments.

2. Through an enabling act passed by the Texas legislature, authority to control land use is given to
   A. counties.
   B. towns and cities.
   C. local governments.
   D. All of the above.

3. Land-use controls may be imposed by
   A. state governments.
   B. local governments.
   C. subdivision developers.
   D. All of the above.

4. Zoning laws may NOT be used to regulate which of the following?
   A. The purpose for which a building may be constructed.
   B. The number of persons a building may accommodate.
   C. The placement of interior partitions.
   D. The height and bulk of a building.

5. The basic authority for zoning laws is derived from a state's
   A. powers of eminent domain.
   B. right of taxation.
   C. Both A and B.
   D. Neither A nor B.

6. Zoning laws
   A. tell a landowner the use to which she may put her land.
   B. compensate an owner for loss of property value due to zoning.
   C. Both A and B.
   D. Neither A nor B.

7. Applied to land use, zoning laws may do all of the following EXCEPT:
   A. encourage uniformity in land usage.
   B. set minimum square footage requirements for buildings.
   C. determine the location of a building on a lot.
   D. dictate construction standards for buildings.

8. A use of property that is not in agreement with present zoning laws
   A. is called a nonconforming use.
   B. may be permitted under a so-called "grandfather clause."
   C. Both A and B.
   D. Neither A nor B.

9. Permission to use a building for a nonconforming use may be accomplished by
    A. amendment of the zoning ordinance.
    B. obtaining a zoning variance.
    C. Both A and B.
    D. Neither A nor B.

10. A zoning variance
    A. allows an owner to deviate from existing zoning law.
    B. involves a change in the zoning law.
    C. Both A and B.
    D. Neither A nor B.

11. When a small area of land in an existing neighborhood is rezoned, this is known as
    A. downzoning.
    B. spot zoning.
    C. conditional zoning.
    D. a zoning variance.

12. A garden apartment development is situated between an office park and a subdivision of single-family residences. These apartments are in a
    A. buffer zone.
    B. down zone.
    C. spot zone.
    D. commercial zone.

13. Minimum standards for materials and construction of buildings are set by
    A. zoning laws.
    B. building codes.
    C. deed restrictions.
    D. subdivision regulations.

14. Before a newly constructed building may be utilized by tenants, the owner must secure a certificate of
    A. inspection.
    B. utilization.
    C. approval.
    D. occupancy.

15. Building codes may be enacted
    A. by local governments.
    B. at the state level of government.
    C. Both A and B.
    D. Neither A nor B.

16. A subdivider wants to limit the height to which trees can grow so as to preserve views. He would most likely do this with a
    A. zoning amendment.
    B. conditional use permit.
    C. buffer zone.
    D. deed restriction.

17. The effect of a proposed development on a community is determined by the preparation of
    A. a property disclosure report.
    B. an environmental impact statement.
    C. a prospectus.
    D. the community's master plan.

18. An environmental impact statement will NOT reveal the effect of a planned development on
    A. air quality.
    B. automobile traffic.
    C. property values.
    D. school enrollments.

KEY TERMS

Cash flow: the number of dollars remaining each year after collecting rents and paying operating expenses and mortgage payments

Cash-on-cash: the cash flow produced by a property divided by the amount of cash necessary to purchase it

Downside risk: the possibility that an investor will lose money in an investment

Equity build-up: the increase of one's equity in a property due to mortgage balance reduction and price appreciation

Investment strategy: a plan that balances returns available with risks that must be taken in order to enhance the investor's overall welfare

Leverage: the impact that borrowed funds have on investment return

Negative cash flow: a condition wherein the cash paid out exceeds the cash received

Prospectus: a disclosure statement that describes an investment opportunity

Straight-line depreciation: depreciation in equal amounts each year over the life of the asset

Tax shelter: the income tax savings that an investment can produce for its owner

Investing in Real Estate

IN THIS CHAPTER *This chapter introduces you to the benefits and dangers of investing. Cash flow, tax shelters, loss limitations, capital gain, tax law changes, equity build-up, and leverage are just a few of the topics covered. The chapter also deals with property selection, investment timing, developing a personal investment strategy, valuing an investment, limited partnership, and disclosure laws. The chapter concludes with a brief discussion on the effort and courage it takes to be an investor.*

The monetary returns that are possible from real estate ownership make it a very attractive investment. However, at the same time the real estate investor takes two risks: He may never obtain a return on his investment and he may never recover his investment. There are no simple answers as to what is a "sure-fire" real estate investment. Rather, success depends on intelligently made decisions. With that in mind, we shall consider investment benefits, tax consequences, property selection, investment timing, investment strategy, and limited partnerships.

BENEFITS OF REAL ESTATE INVESTING

The monetary benefits of investing in real estate come from cash flow, tax shelter, mortgage reduction, and appreciation.

Appreciation is the increase in property value that the owner hopes will occur while owning it. Enough appreciation can offset underestimated expenses, overestimated rents, and a rising adjustable rate loan. Without appreciation, a property must produce enough rental income to pay the operating expenses and loan interest, cover wear and obsolescence, and give the investor a decent return.

Mortgage reduction occurs when an investor uses a portion of a property's rental income to reduce the balance owing on the mortgage. At first, the reduction may be quite small because most of the loan payments might be applied more to payments of interest rather than the reduction of principal. But, eventually the balance owing begins to fall at a more rapid rate. Some investors invest with the idea that if they hold a rental property for the entire life of the loan, the tenants will have paid for the property. This presumes the investor is patient, and that the other elements of cash flow and income tax consequences are conducive to holding the property. Let's look at cash flow, tax shelter, depreciation, taxation of gains, and other real estate tax topics.

CASH FLOW

Cash flow refers to the number of dollars remaining each year after you collect rents and pay operating expenses and mortgage payments. For example, suppose you own a small apartment building that generates $30,500 per year in rents. The operating expenses (including reserves) are $10,000 per year and mortgage payments are $20,000 per year. Given these facts, your cash flow picture is shown in Figure 24.1.

The purpose of calculating cash flow is to show the cash-in-the-pocket effect of owning a particular property. In Figure 24.1, $500 per year is going into your pocket. When money is flowing to you it is called a **positive cash flow.** If you must dip into your pocketbook to keep the property going, you have a **negative cash flow.** For example, if in Figure 24.1 the mortgage payments were $21,000 per year, there would be a negative cash flow. A negative cash flow does not automatically mean a property is a poor investment. There may be mortgage reduction, tax benefits, and appreciation that more than offset this.

Two terms that are related to cash flow are net spendable and cash-on-cash. **Net spendable** is the same thing as cash flow and refers to the amount of spendable income a property produces for its owner. **Cash-on-cash** is the cash flow (or net spendable) that a property produces in a given year divided by the amount of cash required to buy the property. For example, if a property has a cash flow of $5,000 per year and can be purchased with a $50,000 down payment (including closing costs), the cash-on-cash figure for that property is 10. For many real estate investors, this is the heart of the investment decision, namely, "How much do I have to put down and how much will I have in my pocket at the end of each year?"

Tax Shelter

Broadly defined, **tax shelter** describes any tax-deductible expense generated by an investment property. Examples most often utilized for real estate investment are interest, maintenance, insurance, property taxes, and depreciation. More narrowly defined, tax shelter refers only to **depreciation** (a non-cash expense, discussed later in this chapter) that a taxpayer can report as a taxable deduction against other income.

The United States Congress has a decades-long history of tinkering with depreciation rules for income tax calculation. In 1993, the depreciation period for commercial real estate was extended to 39 years for property placed in service after December 31, 1993. (Property already owned and being depreciated before that date continues to use whatever rules were in effect when its depreciation was started, that is, they were **grandfathered-in.**) Also, as of January 1, 1987, accelerated depreciation is repealed and only straight-line can be used. (Again, existing investments continue to use whatever depreciation method they started with.)

Loss Limitations

Another aspect of the tax rules is that there are now stricter limits on how much loss can be deducted from a person's other income. This is now a major consideration in whether to buy or sell or hold real estate as an investment and in choosing what types of real estate to own. Using our investment example, suppose that the $20,000 mortgage payment consists of $19,500 in interest (which is an expense for tax purposes) and $500 in loan reduction (which is not an expense for tax purposes). Suppose also

Figure 24.1
Cash flow picture.

Rent receipts for the year	$ 30,500
Less operating expenses	10,000
Less mortgage loan payments	20,000
Equals cash flow	$ 500

FIGURE 24.2
Example of taxable loss.

Rent receipts for the year	$ 30,500
Less operating expenses	10,000
Less interest on loan	19,500
Less depreciation	8,000
Equals taxable income	$ (7,000)*

* In accounting language, parentheses indicate a negative or minus amount.

that tax law allows $8,000 in depreciation on the property for the year. The result is a taxable loss as shown in Figure 24.2.

There are substantial restrictions, and a distinction is made between passive investors and active investors. If you are a **passive investor,** you can deduct your loss only against income from other passive investments. A passive investor is one who does not materially participate on a "regular, substantial, and continuous basis," for example, a limited partner.

If you are an **active investor** (e.g., you manage the rentals you own), it is possible to use as much as $25,000 of your losses to offset your other income (such as your job income). However, this only applies to taxpayers with up to $100,000 of adjusted gross income (as defined on one's annual IRS Form 1040). For those with higher adjusted gross incomes, the loss deduction is gradually reduced, and is eliminated at $150,000 of adjusted gross income. This aspect of the tax law change will have little effect on the middle-income person who owns a rental house or two, or a small apartment building, and has a hand in managing them. But, for persons with larger income who are affected by the new Internal Revenue Code, one can expect to see some restructuring of investments and more investor participation. For example, non-active investors with passive losses will look for properties with passive income, such as parking lots. Those who do not actively manage their real estate holdings may take a more active role so as to qualify as an active investor. Loss-producing partnerships may be attractive acquisitions only for income-producing investors.

Congress recently created another class of tax payers who have the ability to offset their active income with passive losses. These are referred to as **eligible taxpayers.** Eligible taxpayers are individuals in closely held C corporations that must materially participate in rental real estate activities. To satisfy the eligibility requirements, the individual must have performed: (1) more than 50% of the individual's personal services during the tax year in real property trades or businesses in which the individual materially participates, and (2) more than 750 hours of service in real property trades or businesses in which the individual materially participates.

DEPRECIATION CALCULATION

As noted several paragraphs earlier, under tax rules effective January 1, 1987, depreciation is to be straight-line. **Straight-line depreciation** is calculated by taking the total amount of anticipated depreciation and dividing by the number of years. For example, a building valued at $275,000 for depreciation purposes and depreciated over $27 \frac{1}{2}$ years using straight-line will have $10,000 in depreciation each year. (Note that only improvements are depreciable, land is not. Therefore, when buying investment real estate, it is necessary to subtract the value of the land from the purchase price before calculating depreciation.)

In contrast to straight-line depreciation, **accelerated depreciation** is any method of depreciation that allows depreciation at a rate faster than straight-line during the first several years of ownership. Although this is not allowed for real property placed in service starting January 1, 1987, it is retained for certain types of personal property used in business (such as a real estate agent's automobile) and for real property started under accelerated depreciation before 1987.

Passive losses (including depreciation) that are unusable in any given year can be carried forward from year-to-year and used later. Any losses carried forward into the year of sale can be deducted in full at that time.

CAPITAL GAINS

Congress reinstated capital gains as a major tax benefit in 1997. Prior to that time, the maximum capital gains tax rate was 28%. The new maximum tax rates were cut to 20% for sales made after May 6, 1997. For individuals in the 15% tax bracket, the capital gains rate has been lowered to 10%. There is a difference, though, in the holding period for assets sold after July 28, 1997; the asset must be held more than 18 months. Another rate for property held longer than five years will become effective on December 31, 2000. An asset that qualifies for the five-year period will be lowered to 18% and 8% for individuals in the 15% tax bracket.

There was no rate reduction for corporations with capital gains. A corporation's top rate stays at 35% and their holding period remains 12 months.

AT-RISK RULES

Over the past several years, Congress has enacted **at-risk rules** for investors. The issue was that an investor could invest $1, borrow $4 that did not require personal repayment, and take tax write-offs on the full $5. Congress passed rules that limited write-off to the amount actually invested plus **recourse financing,** that is, the investor is personally obligated to repay. Under the old rules, this applied to nearly every investment, except real estate. Under the new rules, it applies to real estate. But real estate sales nearly always require financing, and it is often **nonrecourse financing,** that is, there is no personal obligation, only the value of the property secures the debt. Therefore, Congress considers the amount at risk in real estate to be the sum of third-party financing (note that this does not include seller financing), recourse indebtedness, and cash.

INSTALLMENT SALES

In the past, a seller of real estate who had a substantial gain might choose to sell on the **installment method** to spread out receipt of the gain and therefore the taxes on it. The new rules limit the benefits of using installment sales. The wise seller will seek competent tax advice before agreeing to carry back a mortgage. **Dealers** in real property may not utilize the installment sales benefit.

CONSTRUCTION-PERIOD EXPENSES

In past years, Congress has set various policies as to whether or not interest paid during construction could be taken as an immediate expense or had to be added to the cost of the building and amortized. Beginning January 1, 1987, the rule changed from amortization over 10 years to amortization over the depreciable life of the asset, even though the interest is an actual, paid expense during the construction period.

REHABILITATION TAX CREDITS

In an effort to encourage individuals to rebuild older structures rather than tear them down or let them decay, Congress has had a policy of giving rehabilitation tax credits. Historic structures are allowed a credit of 20%. (This effectively means the federal government will pick up 20% of the cost of rehabilitating an historic structure.) Nonhistoric structures constructed prior to 1935 receive a 10% tax credit. (The investor needs to have other income against which to claim the credit, and the passive loss rules apply.)

LOW-INCOME HOUSING CREDIT

There is one area of tax law that has loosened: low-income housing. A number of inducements such as tax-exempt bond financing, accelerated depreciation, and five-year amortization have been used in the past. The rules now allow a tax credit to owners of buildings that provide low-income rental housing. On new and newly rehabilitated housing the credit is a maximum of 9% per year for 10 years. (Effectively, the government pays for most of the building.) On existing housing the credit is a maximum of 4% for 10 years.

WATCH LIST

Tax law changes have been made in the past decades with increasing frequency and impact. In fact, one of the biggest risks in real estate has been, and continues to be, tax law changes. The values of land and buildings can, and do, go up and down with changes in tax rules. (This is in addition to the marketplace risks that an investor must take.) Therefore, it is of great importance that you stay abreast of tax law changes, impending tax law changes, and even swings in the mood of Congress toward real estate. Keep this in mind as you continue to read this chapter. Also keep in mind that because approximately two out of three households in the United States own their homes, home ownership is likely to continue its favored tax status.

EQUITY BUILD-UP

An owner's **equity** in a property is defined as the market value of the property less all liens or other charges against the property. Thus, if you own a property worth $125,000 and owe $75,000, your equity is $50,000. If you own that property with your brother or sister, each with a one-half interest, your equity is $25,000 and his/her equity is $25,000.

    Equity build-up is the change in your equity over a period of time. Suppose you purchase a small apartment building for $200,000, placing $60,000 down and borrowing the balance. Your beginning equity is your down payment of $60,000. If after five years you have paid the loan down to $120,000 and you can sell the property for $220,000, your equity is now $100,000. Since you started with $60,000, your equity build-up is $40,000. Figure 24.3 recaps this calculation.

LEVERAGE

Leverage is the impact that borrowed funds have on investment return. The purpose of borrowing is to earn more on the borrowed funds than the funds cost. For example, suppose you are an investor and you have $250,000 to invest in an apartment building.

FIGURE 24.3
Calculating equity
build-up.

Equity at Time of Purchase		Equity 5 Years Later		Equity Build-up	
Purchase price	$200,000	Market value	$220,000	Current equity	$100,000
Mortgage loan	−140,000	Less loan balance	−120,000	Less beginning equity	−60,000
Down payment (equity)	$ 60,000	Equals current equity	$100,000	Equals equity build-up	$ 40,000

If you use all your money to buy a $250,000 building there is zero leverage. If you use your $250,000 to buy a $500,000 building, there is 50% leverage. If you use your $250,000 to buy a $2,500,000 building there is 90% leverage.

Whether or not to try leverage depends on whether the property can reasonably be expected to produce cash flow, tax benefits, mortgage reduction, and appreciation in excess of the cost of the borrowed funds. The decision also depends on your willingness to take risk. For example, the $250,000 building would have to fall to zero value before you lost all your money. Moreover, the building could experience a vacancy rate on the order of 60% and there would still be enough cash to meet out-of-pocket operating expenses. In other words, with zero leverage there is very little likelihood of a total financial wipe-out.

In contrast, if you buy the $2,500,000 building, a 10% drop in the property's value to $2,250,000 wipes out your entire equity. Moreover, even the slightest drop-off in occupancy from 95% down to 85% will cause great strain on your ability to meet mortgage loan payments and out-of-pocket operating expenses.

But, suppose apartment building values increase by 10. If you had bought the $250,000 building with borrowed funds, it will now be worth $275,000, an increase of $25,000 on your investment of $250,000. Similarly, if you had bought the $2,500,000 building it will now be worth $2,750,000, an increase of $250,000 on your investment of $250,000. As you can see, leverage can work both against you and for you. If the benefits from borrowing exceed the costs of borrowing, it is called **positive leverage.** If the borrowed funds cost more than they are producing, it is called **negative leverage.**

PROPERTY SELECTION

The real estate market offers a wide selection of properties for investments, including vacant land, houses, condominiums, small, medium, and large apartment buildings, office buildings, stores, industrial property, and so forth. Selecting a suitable type of property is a matter of matching an investor's capital with her attitudes toward risk taking and the amount of time she is willing to spend on management. Let's begin by looking at the ownership of vacant land.

Vacant Land

The major risk of owning vacant land as an investment is that one will have to wait too long for an increase in value. Vacant land produces no income, yet it consumes the investor's dollars in the form of interest, property taxes, insurance, and eventually selling costs. The rule of thumb is that the market value of vacant land must double every five years for the investor to break even. If this increase does not occur, the owner will have spent more on interest, insurance, property taxes, brokerage fees, and closing costs than is made on the price increase.

The key to successful land speculating is in outguessing the general public. If the public feels that development of a vacant parcel to a higher use is 10 years in the future, the market price will reflect the discounted cost at current interest rates and property taxes for that waiting period. If the land speculator buys at these prices, and the higher use occurs in five years, there is a good chance the purchase will be profitable. However, the speculator will lose money if the public expects the higher use to occur in five years and it actually takes ten years.

Finally, land speculators expose themselves to an extra risk that owners of improved property can usually avoid. When it comes time to sell, unless buildings will immediately be placed upon the land by the purchaser, very few lenders will loan the purchaser money to buy the land. This may force the seller to accept the purchase price in the form of a down payment plus periodic payments for the balance. If the interest rate on the balance is below prevailing mortgage rates, as often happens in land sales, the seller is effectively subsidizing the buyer. Furthermore, if the payments are made over several years, the seller takes the risk that the money he receives will buy less because of inflation.

Houses and Condominiums

Houses and condominiums are the smallest properties available in income-producing real estate and as such are within the financial reach of more prospective investors than apartment buildings, stores, or offices. Moreover, they can usually be purchased with lower down payments and interest rates because lenders feel that loans on houses and condominiums are less prone to default than those on larger buildings. With a small property, the investor can fall back upon salary and other income to meet loan payments in the event rents fall short. With larger buildings, the lender knows he must rely more on the rental success of the property and less on the owner's other sources of income.

Houses and condominiums are usually overpriced in relation to the monthly rent they can generate. This is because their prices are influenced both by the value of the shelter they provide and the amenity value of home ownership. Thus, an investor must pay what prospective owner-occupants are willing to pay, yet when the property is rented, a tenant will pay only for the shelter value. However, when the investor sells, the sale price will be higher than would be justified by rents alone. What this means is that the investor can usually expect a negative cash flow during ownership. Consequently, there must be a substantial increase in property value to offset the monthly negative cash flow and give the investor a good return on investment.

Small Apartment Buildings

Because considerable appreciation must occur to make house and condominium investments profitable, many investors who start with these move to more income-oriented properties as their capital grows. Particularly popular with investors who have modest amounts of investment capital are duplexes (two unit), triplexes (three units), and fourplexes (four units).

If it were necessary to hire professional management, such small buildings would be uneconomical to own. However, for most owners of two- to four-unit apartment buildings, management is on a do-it-yourself basis. Moreover, it is possible for the owner to live on the premises. This eliminates a cash outlay for management and allows the owner to reduce repair and maintenance expenses by handling them himself. Also, with the owner living on the property, tenants are encouraged to take better care of the premises and discouraged from moving out without paying their rent. Finally, the ownership of a residential rental property provides the owner with a wealth of experience and education in property management.

Medium-Size Buildings

Apartment buildings containing 5 to 24 units also present good investment opportunities for those with sufficient down payment. However, in addition to analyzing the building, rents, and neighborhood, thought must be given to the matter of property management before a purchase is made. An apartment building of this size is not large enough for a full-time manager; therefore, the owner must either do the job or hire a part-time manager to live on the property. An owner who does the job should be willing to live on the property and devote a substantial amount of time to management, maintenance, and upkeep activities. If a part-time manager is hired, the task is to find one who is knowledgeable and capable of maintaining property, showing vacant units, interviewing tenants, collecting rents on time, and handling landlord-tenant relations in accordance with local landlord-tenant laws. As the size of an apartment building increases, so does its efficiency. As a rule of thumb, when a building reaches 25 units, it will generate enough rent so that a full-time professional manager can be hired to live on the premises. With a live-in manager, the property owner need not reside on the property nor be involved in day-to-day management chores. This is very advantageous if the owner has another occupation where time is better spent.

Larger Apartment Buildings

As the number of apartment units increases, the cost of management per unit drops. Beyond 60 units, assistant managers can be hired. This makes it possible to have a representative of the owner on the premises more hours of the day to look after the investment and keep the tenants happy. Size also means it is possible to add recreational facilities and other amenities that are not possible on a small scale. The cost of having a swimming pool in a 10-unit building might add so much to apartment rents that they would be priced out of the market. The same pool in a 50- or 100-unit building would make relatively little difference in rent. As buildings reach 200 or more units in size, it becomes economical to add such things as a children's pool, gymnasium, game room, lounge, and a social director.

Since larger apartment buildings cost less to manage per unit and compete very effectively in the market for tenants, they tend to produce larger cash flows per invested dollar. However, errors in location selection, building design, and management policy are magnified as the building grows in size. Also, many lenders, particularly small- and medium-size banks and savings associations, are simply not large enough to lend on big projects. Finally, the number of investors who can single-handedly invest a down payment of $500,000 or more is limited. This has caused the widespread growth of the limited partnership as a means of making the economies of large-scale ownership available to investors with as little as $2,000 to invest.

Office Buildings

Office buildings offer the prospective investor not only a higher rent per square foot of floor space than any of the investments discussed thus far, but also larger cash flows per dollar of property worth. This is because office buildings are costlier to build and operate than residential structures, and because they expose the owner to more risk.

The higher construction and operating costs of an office building reflect the amenities and services office users demand. To be competitive today, an office building must offer air-conditioning to all tenants on a room-by-room basis, thus adding to construction and operating costs. Office users also expect and pay for daily cleaning services, such as emptying wastebaskets, cleaning ashtrays, dusting, and vacuuming. Apartment dwellers neither expect these services nor pay for them.

Tenant turnover is more expensive in an office building than an apartment building because a change in office tenants usually requires more extensive remodeling. To offset this, building owners include the cost of remodeling in the tenant's rent. Another consideration is that it is not unusual for office space to remain vacant for long periods of time. Also, if a building is rented to a single tenant, a single vacancy means there is no income at all. To reduce tenant turnover, incentives such as lower rent may be offered if a tenant agrees to sign a longer lease, such as five years instead of one or two years. Care must be taken on longer leases however, so that the owner does not become locked into a fixed monthly rent while operating costs escalate.

The risk in properly locating an office building is greater than with a residential property since office users are very particular about where they locate. If a residential building is not well located, the owner can usually drop rents a little and still fill the building. To do the same with an office building may require a much larger drop; then, even with the building full, it may not generate enough rent to pay the operating expenses and mortgage payments. Finally, the tax shelter benefits available from offices may not be as attractive as comparably priced apartments. This is because compared to office buildings, residential properties tend to have a higher percentage of their value in depreciable improvements and less in nondepreciable land.

INVESTMENT TIMING

The potential risks and rewards available from owning improved real estate depend to a great extent on the point in the life of a property at which an investment is made. Should one invest while a project is still an idea? Or is it better to wait until it is finished and fully rented? That depends on the risks one can afford and the potential rewards.

Land Purchase

The riskiest point at which to invest in a project is when it is still an idea in someone's head. At this point, money is needed to purchase land. But beyond the cost of the land, there are many unknowns, including the geological suitability of the land to support buildings, the ability to obtain the needed zoning, the cost of construction, the availability of a loan, the rents the market will pay, how quickly the property will find tenants, the expenses of operating the property, and finally, the return the investor will obtain. Even though the investor may have a feasibility study that predicts success for the project, such a report is still only an educated guess. Therefore, the anticipated returns to an investor entering a project at this point must be high to offset the risks he takes. As the project clears such hurdles as zoning approval, obtaining construction cost bids, and finding a lender, it becomes less risky. Therefore, a person who invests after these hurdles are cleared would expect somewhat less potential reward. Nonetheless, the investor is buying into the project at a relatively low price; if it is successful, he will enjoy a developer's profit upon which no income tax must be paid until the property is finally sold. Against this, he takes the risk that the project may stall along the way or that, once completed, it will lose money.

Project Completion

Another major milestone is reached when the project is completed and opens its doors for business. At this point, the finished cost of the building is known, and during the first 12 months of operations the property owners learn what rents the market will pay, what level of occupancy will be achieved, and what actual operating expenses will be.

As estimates are replaced with actual operating experience, the risk to the investor decreases. As a result, the investor entering at this stage receives a smaller dollar return on her investment, but is more certain of her return than if she had invested earlier.

First Decade

A building is new only once, and after its first year it begins to face competition from newer buildings. However, if an inflationary economy forces up the construction cost of newer buildings, existing buildings will be able to charge less rent. Furthermore, newer buildings may be forced to use less desirable sites. During the first 10 years, occupancy rates are stable, operating expenses are well established, tax benefits are good, and the building is relatively free of major repairs or replacements.

Second Decade

As a building passes its tenth birthday, the costs and risks it presents to a prospective investor change. Before buying, he must ask whether or not the neighborhood is expected to remain desirable to tenants and whether or not the building's location will increase enough in value to offset wear and tear and obsolescence. A careful inspection must be made of the structure to determine whether poor construction quality will soon result in costly repairs. Also, the investor must be prepared for normal replacements and expenses such as new appliances, water heaters, and a fresh coat of paint. As a result, an investor buying a 10-year-old building will seek a larger return than the buyer of a younger building.

Third and Fourth Decades

Larger returns are particularly important as a building reaches its twentieth year and major expense items such as a new roof, replacement of plumbing fixtures, repair of parking areas, and remodeling become necessary. As a building approaches and passes its thirtieth year, investors must consider carefully the remaining economic life of the property and whether rents permit a return on investment as well as a return of investment. Also, maintenance costs climb as a building becomes older, and decisions will be necessary regarding whether or not major restoration and remodeling should be undertaken. If it is, the cost must be recovered during the balance of the building's life. The alternative is to add little or no money to the building, a decision the surrounding neighborhood may already be forcing upon the property owner. Older properties may offer attractive tax benefits and have been a strong magnet to real estate investors who hope to find properties that can be fixed up for a profit. However, care must be taken not to overpay for this privilege.

Building Recycling

More buildings are torn down than fall down, and this phase in a building's life also represents an investment opportunity. However, as with the first stage in the development cycle, raw land, the risks are high. In effect, when the decision is made to purchase a structure with the intention of demolishing it, the investor is counting on the value of the land being worth more in another use. That use may be a government-sponsored renewal program, or the investor may be accumulating adjoining properties with the ultimate intention of creating plottage value by demolishing the structures and joining the lots. Because the risks of capital loss in this phase are high, the potential returns should be too.

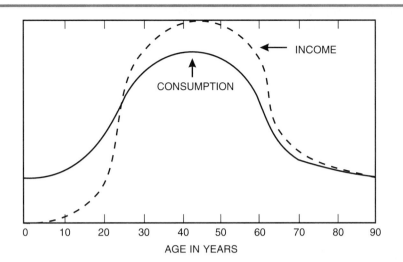

FIGURE 24.4
Lifetime income and consumption patterns.

DEVELOPING A PERSONAL INVESTMENT STRATEGY

The objective in developing a personal investment strategy is to balance the returns available with the risks that must be taken so that the overall welfare of the investor is enhanced. To accomplish this, it is very helpful to look at lifetime income and consumption patterns.

In Figure 24.4 the broken line represents the income that a person can typically expect to receive at various ages during his or her life. It includes income from wages, pensions, and investments. The solid line represents a person's lifetime consumption pattern. Taken together, the two lines show that during the first 20 to 25 years, consumption exceeds income. Then the situation reverses itself and income outpaces consumption. If one is planning an investment program, these are the years to carry it out.

Risk Taking

Figure 24.4 shows that an investment opportunity offering a high risk of loss is better suited for a person under the age of 45. Then, even if the investment does turn sour, the investor still has a substantial amount of working life remaining to recover financially. An investor between 45 and 55 years of age should be somewhat more cautious in terms of risk taking, since there is less time to make a financial recovery if the need arises. Above the age of 55, high-risk investments are even less appropriate for the same reason. Therefore, as a person reaches 55, 60, and 65, there should be a program of moving toward relatively risk-free investments, even though the returns will be smaller. Upon retirement, the investor can live off the investments he or she made when younger.

Debt Repayment

Mortgage debt commitments that require a portion of the investor's personal income should also be considered in light of one's position on the lifetime income and consumption curves. This is done to ascertain whether or not there will be sufficient income in the future to meet the loan payments. Not to consider the future may force a premature sale, perhaps in the midst of a very sluggish market at a distressed price. For the investor who has passed his income peak, financing with less debt and more equity means a higher probability that the properties will generate enough income to meet monthly loan payments. Also, with fewer dollars going to debt repayment, more can be kept by the investor for living expenses. By comparison, a relatively young investor may be handicapped by the lack of starting capital; however, she has the advantages of time and increasing income on her side.

The same points made here in connection with investments can also be applied to one's home. If a homeowner can purchase a home with a mortgage and then pay down the mortgage during those years in life when income substantially exceeds consumption, the home can be carried debt free into retirement to provide a place to live without mortgage payments. The home then becomes an investment in every sense of the word.

VALUING AN INVESTMENT

Chapter 17, "Real Estate Appraisal," discussed value from the standpoint of an appraiser or listing agent who uses current marketplace facts to estimate the value of a property. An investor's valuation problem is somewhat different. An investor knows the seller's asking price, can find information relating to the current income and expenses of a property, and can project future income based on these. Additionally, an investor will have information on how the property can be financed and will have some figure in mind as to how much appreciation to expect. From these, the investor calculates the anticipated return on investment. If this return is more appealing than alternative investments, the property is purchased. If not, no sale results. Figure 24.5 illustrates the different viewpoints of the appraiser and the investor.

LIMITED PARTNERSHIPS

As discussed earlier in this chapter, large investment properties have a number of economic advantages over small ones. Yet the vast majority of investors in the United States do not have the capital to buy a large project single-handedly. Moreover, many persons who would like to own real estate do not do so because they wish to avoid the work and responsibilities of property management. As a result, the United States has witnessed the widespread use of limited partnerships for real estate investment. This popular form of investment offers investors the following advantages:

1. Management of the property and financial affairs of the partnership by the general partner
2. Financial liability limited to the amount invested
3. The opportunity for a small investor to own a part of large projects and to diversify

The organizers of a limited partnership are responsible for selecting properties, putting them into a financial package, and making it available to investors. As a rule, the organizers are the general partners and the investors are the limited partners. For

FIGURE 24.5
Contrasting an appraiser's vs. an investor's viewpoint.

Appraiser's viewpoint	Investor's viewpoint
$\text{Value} = \dfrac{\text{Net Income}}{\text{Return}}$	$\text{Return} = \dfrac{\text{Net income}}{\text{Price}}$
The appraiser solves for value.	The investor solves for return.

their efforts in organizing the partnership, the general partners receive a cash fee from the limited partners and/or a promotional interest in the partnership.

Property Purchase Methods

Property is purchased by one of two methods. The organizers can either buy properties first and then seek limited partners, or they can find limited partners first and then buy properties. The first approach is a **specific property offering.** The second is a **blind pool.** The advantage of the specific property offering is that the prospective limited partner knows in advance precisely what properties will be owned. However, this approach requires the organizers either to find a seller who is willing to wait for a partnership to be formed or to buy the property in their own names using their own capital. If they use their own capital, the organizers risk the chance of financial loss if limited partners cannot be found.

The advantage of the blind pool is that the organizers do not buy until money has been raised from the limited partners. This requires less capital from the organizers and avoids the problem of holding property but not being able to find sufficient investors. Also, the organizers can negotiate better prices from sellers when they have cash in hand. However, if the organizers are poor judges of property, the investors may wind up owning property that they would not have otherwise purchased.

Property Management

Once property is purchased, the general partners are responsible for managing the property themselves or selecting a management firm to do the job. In addition, the general partners must maintain the accounting books and at least once a year remit to each investor his portion of the cash flow, an accounting of the partnership's performance for the year, and profit or loss data for income tax purposes. With regard to selling partnership property, the partnership agreement usually gives the limited partners the right to vote on when to sell, to whom to sell, and for how much. In practice, the general partners decide when to put the matter up to a vote, and the limited partners usually follow their advice.

Financial Liability

The word *limited* in limited partnership refers to the limited financial liability of the limited partner. In a properly drawn agreement, limited partners cannot lose more than they have invested. By comparison, the general partners are legally liable for all the debts of the partnership, up to the full extent of their entire personal worth. Being a limited partner does not eliminate the possibility of being asked at a later date for more investment money if the properties in the partnership are not financially successful. When this happens, each limited partner must decide between adding more money in hopes the partnership will soon make a financial turnaround, or refusing to do so and being eliminated from the partnership. By way of comparison, an individual investor who buys real estate in his own name takes the risks of both the limited and general partner.

Investment Diversification

Investing with others can provide diversification. For example, a limited partnership of 200 members each contributing $5,000 would raise $1,000,000. This could be used as a down payment on one property worth $4,000,000 or on four different properties priced at $1,000,000 each. If the $4,000,000 property is purchased, the entire success or failure of the partnership rides on that one property. With four $1,000,000 properties, the failure of one can be balanced by the success of the others. Even greater diversification can be achieved by purchasing properties in different rental price ranges, in different parts of the same city, and in different cities in the country. Regarding income tax benefits, a very important advantage of the limited partnership is that it allows the investor to be taxed as though she is the sole owner of the property, because the partnership itself is not subject to taxation. All income and loss items, including any tax shelter generated by the property, are proportioned to each investor directly.

Service Fees

The prospective investor should carefully look at the price the organizers are charging for their services. Is it adequate, but not excessive? To expect good performance from capable people, they must be compensated adequately, but to overpay reduces the returns from the investment that properly belong to those who provide the capital. When is the compensation to be paid? If management fees are paid in advance, there is less incentive for the organizers to provide quality management for the limited partners after the partnership is formed. The preferred arrangement is to pay for management services as they are received, and for the limited partners to reserve the right to vote for new management. Similarly, it is preferable to base a substantial portion of the fee for organizing the partnership on the success of the investment. By giving the organizers a percentage of the partnership's profits instead of a fixed fee, the organizers have a direct stake in the success of the partnership.

Pitfalls

Although the limited partnership form of real estate ownership offers investors many advantages, experience has shown that there are numerous pitfalls that can separate investors from their money. Most importantly, a limited partner should recognize that the success or failure of a limited partnership is dependent on the organizers. Do they have a good record in selecting, organizing, and managing real estate investments in the past? Are they respected in the community for prompt and honest dealings? Will local banks and building suppliers offer them credit? What is their rating with credit bureaus? Are they permanent residents of the community in which they operate? Do the county court records show pending lawsuits or other legal complaints against them?

With reference to the properties in the partnership, are the income projections reasonable, and have adequate allowances been made for vacancies, maintenance, and management? Overoptimism, sloppy income and expense projections, and outright shading of the truth will ultimately be costly to the investor. Unless there is absolute confidence in the promoters, one should personally visit the properties in the partnership and verify the rent schedules, vacancy levels, operating expenses, and physical condition of the improvements. Consideration should also be given to the partnership's **downside risk** (i.e., the risk of losing one's money).

The careful investor will consult with a lawyer to make certain that the partnership agreement does limit liability to the amount invested and that the tax benefits will be as advertised. He will also want to know what to expect if the partnership suffers financial setbacks. Are the partnership's properties to be sold at a loss or at a foreclosure sale, or do the general partners stand ready to provide the needed money? Will the limited partners be asked to contribute? The prospective investor should also investigate to see if the properties are overpriced. Far too many partnerships organized to date have placed so much emphasis on tax shelter benefits that the entire matter of whether the investment was economically feasible has been overlooked. Even to a 28% bracket taxpayer, a dollar wasted before taxes is still 72¢ wasted after taxes.

Finally, to receive maximum benefits from his investment, the investor must be prepared to stay with the partnership until the properties are refinanced or sold. The resale market for limited partnership interests is almost nonexistent, and when a buyer is found, the price is usually below the proportional worth of the investor's interest in the partnership. Moreover, the partnership agreement may place restrictions on limited partners who want to sell their interests.

Master Limited Partnerships

One major problem with limited partnerships has been that they are illiquid. Once an investor invests, the commitment is to stay in until the partnership dissolves, and this can be 5, 10, or even 15+ years later. Until then, the limited partner can convert to cash only by selling to someone else or sometimes back to the partnership. This is usually done at a substantial discount to the value of the property in the partnership, assuming a sale can even be arranged. Into this need has come the **master limited partnership (MLP).** MLPs are limited partnerships that can be traded on a stock exchange nearly as easily as corporate stock. Thus, an investor can buy into a partnership after it has been formed and sell out of it before it is dissolved. Meanwhile, the investor receives the available tax advantages of a limited partnership. However, if the underlying partnership is not well run, has poorly operating properties, or is uneconomic, simply making the partnership easily traded is no magic. MLPs do offer liquidity, but you must still carefully analyze the partnership's ability to perform before investing in it.

DISCLOSURE LAWS

Because investors are vulnerable to unsound investments and exploitation at the hands of limited partnership organizers, state and federal disclosure laws have been passed to protect them if the investment qualifies as a "security." Administered by the Securities & Exchange Commission at the federal level and by the Texas Securities Board at the state level, these laws require organizers and sales staff to disclose all pertinent facts surrounding the partnership offering. Prospective investors must be told how much money the organizers wish to raise, what portion will go for promotional expenses and organizers' fees, what properties have been (or will be) purchased, from whom they were bought, and for how much. Also, prospective investors must be provided with a copy of the partnership agreement and given property income and expense records for past years. They must be told how long the partnership expects to hold its properties until selling, the partnership's policy on cash flow distribution, the right of limited partners to a voice in management, the names of those responsible for managing the partnership properties, and how profits (or losses) will be split when the properties are sold.

The Prospectus

The amount of disclosure detail required by state and federal laws varies with the number of properties and the partners' relationship. For a handful of friends forming a partnership among themselves, there would be little in the way of formal disclosure requirements. However, as the number of investors increases and the partnership is offered to investors across state lines, disclosure requirements increase dramatically. It is not unusual for a disclosure statement, called a **prospectus,** to be 50 to 100 pages long.

Blue-Sky Laws

The philosophy of disclosure laws is to make information available to prospective investors and let them make their own decisions. Thus, an investor is free to invest in an unsound investment so long as the facts are explained to him in advance. An alternative point of view is that many investors do not read nor understand disclosure statements; therefore, it is the duty of government to determine the economic soundness of an investment before it can be offered to the public. The result has been the passage of **blue-sky laws** in several states. The first of these was passed by the Kansas legislature in 1911 to protect purchasers from buying into dubious investment schemes that sold them nothing more than a piece of the blue sky. Texas has retained these laws and applies them to limited partnerships and other securities offered within its borders.

EFFORT AND COURAGE

As the opening paragraph of this chapter suggested, you can become rich by investing in real estate. It should be pointed out, however, that success won't drop in your lap; it takes effort and courage. Good properties and good opportunities are always available, but you will look at many opportunities to find one good investment. You will also need to know which ones you don't want, and why. That is the part that takes effort. All investors need to know what a good opportunity looks like, and this book is a step in that direction. After you finish this text, start reading articles and books on real estate investing, and take courses on the subject as well. But most importantly, get out and start looking at properties right away if you have not already done so. Begin to get a sense in the field for what you are learning from your books and classes. Always ask questions as you go along, and demand straight, reasonable answers. After you've viewed several dozen properties and talked to appraisers, lenders, brokers, property managers, etc., you will begin to get a feel for the market—what's for sale, what a property can earn, how much mortgage money costs, etc. As you do this you will see everything you've learned in this book come to life.

As you continue you will recognize what a good investment property looks like. At this point your next big step is to muster the courage to acquire it. All the real estate investment education you've received will not translate into money in your pocket until you make an offer—until you put your money, reputation, and good judgment on the line. There is no "get rich quick" formula, so don't expect one. If you have a good, informed investment strategy and the courage to take the risks, the rewards are certainly attainable.

REVIEW QUESTIONS

Answers to these questions are found in the Answer Key section at the back of the book.

1. ABZ Realty offers you a four-unit residential building in which each unit rents for $500 per month. Given a 5% vacancy rate, operating expenses of $700 per month, and mortgage payments of $1,500 per month, you can anticipate a monthly

   A. net spendable of $200.

   B. net spendable of $300.

   C. negative cash flow of $200.

   D. negative cash flow of $300.

2. Monetary benefits of investing in real estate come from

   A. cash flow.

   B. tax shelter.

   C. mortgage reduction.

   D. All of the above.

3. A negative cash flow may be offset by
   A. tax shelter.
   B. appreciation.
   C. Both A and B.
   D. Neither A nor B.

4. Mortgage balance reduction
   A. is an out-of-pocket expense.
   B. is a deduction for tax purposes.
   C. is tax exempted.
   D. is quite large at the beginning of the loan period.

5. The value of depreciation on an investment property is
   A. inversely proportional to the investor's tax bracket.
   B. the same to all investors, regardless of their tax bracket.
   C. directly proportional to the investor's tax bracket.
   D. not a factor in the investment decision.

6. Tax laws allow depreciation on a building to be
   A. started over each time the property is sold.
   B. more than its value.
   C. Both A and B.
   D. Neither A nor B.

7. Equity build-up in a property can be the result of
   A. mortgage reduction.
   B. appreciation.
   C. Both A and B.
   D. Neither A nor B.

8. Negative leverage occurs when
   A. borrowed funds cost more than they produce in benefits.
   B. an investment property depreciates in value.
   C. Both A and B.
   D. Neither A nor B.

9. What is the cash-on-cash ratio for a property that has a cash flow of $16,900 and could be purchased with a down payment of $130,000?
   A. 7.69%.
   B. 0.219.
   C. 0.12.
   D. 0.13.

10. To be considered a good investment, when a property that generates a negative cash flow is sold,
    A. there must be a substantial increase in property value.
    B. there need be a little increase in property value.
    C. the investor is best off if the property has decreased in value.

11. Tax shelter in real estate
    A. refers to the income tax savings that an investor can realize.
    B. is possible because depreciation is deductible as a cost of doing business.
    C. Both A and B.
    D. Neither A nor B.

12. For most people, when is the best time in life to undertake high-risk investments?
    A. Under age 25.
    B. Age 25 to 45.
    C. Age 55 to 65.
    D. Over age 65.

13. In a typical limited partnership, the
    A. organizers are the limited partners.
    B. investors are the general partners.
    C. Both A and B.
    D. Neither A nor B.

14. In a limited partnership, which cannot lose more than the amount they have invested?
    A. General partners.
    B. Limited partners.
    C. Organizers.
    D. Managers.

15. A disclosure statement given to prospective investors in a limited partnership, outlining the plans and prospects for the partnership, is called a
    A. prospectus.
    B. forecast statement.
    C. cash flow.
    D. binder.

THE REAL ESTATE LICENSE ACT

Article 6573a, V.T.C.S.

SECTION 1. (a) This Act shall be known and may be cited as "The Real Estate License Act."

(b) It is unlawful for a person to act in the capacity of, engage in the business of, or advertise or hold that person out as engaging in or conducting the business of a real estate broker or a real estate salesperson within this state without first obtaining a real estate license from the Texas Real Estate Commission. It is unlawful for a person licensed as a real estate salesperson to act or attempt to act as a real estate broker or salesperson unless that person is, at such time, associated with a licensed Texas real estate broker and acting for the licensed real estate broker.

(c) Each real estate broker licensed pursuant to this Act is responsible to the commission, members of the public, and the broker's clients for all acts and conduct performed under this Act by the broker or by a real estate salesperson associated with or acting for the broker.

(d) No real estate salesperson shall accept compensation for real estate sales and transactions from any person other than the broker under whom the salesperson is at the time licensed or under whom the salesperson was licensed when the salesperson earned the right to compensation.

(e) No real estate salesperson shall pay a commission to any person except through the broker under whom the salesperson is at the time licensed.

SECTION 2. As used in this Act:

(1) "Real estate" means a leasehold, as well as any other interest or estate in land, whether corporeal, incorporeal, freehold, or nonfreehold, and whether the real estate is situated in this state or elsewhere. The term does not include an interest given as security for the performance of an obligation.

(2) "Real estate broker" means a person who, for another person and for a fee, commission, or other valuable consideration, or with the intention or in the expectation or on the promise of receiving or collecting a fee, commission, or other valuable consideration from another person:

(A) sells, exchanges, purchases, rents, or leases real estate;

(B) offers to sell, exchange, purchase, rent, or lease real estate;

(C) negotiates or attempts to negotiate the listing, sale, exchange, purchase, rental, or leasing of real estate;

(D) lists or offers or attempts or agrees to list real estate for sale, rental, lease, exchange, or trade;

(E) appraises or offers or attempts or agrees to appraise real estate;

(F) auctions, or offers or attempts or agrees to auction, real estate;

(G) buys or sells or offers to buy or sell, or otherwise deals in options on real estate;

(H) aids, attempts, or offers to aid in locating or obtaining for purchase, rent, or lease any real estate;

(I) procures or assists in the procuring of prospects for the purpose of effecting the sale, exchange, lease, or rental of real estate; or

(J) procures or assists in the procuring of properties for the purpose of effecting the sale, exchange, lease, or rental of real estate.

(3) "Broker" also includes a person employed by or on behalf of the owner or owners of lots or other parcels of real estate, at a salary, fee, commission, or any other valuable consideration, to sell the real estate or any part thereof, in lots or parcels or other disposition thereof. It also includes a person who engages in the business of charging an advance fee or contracting for collection of a fee in connection with a contract whereby he undertakes primarily to promote the sale of real estate either through its listing in a publication issued primarily for such purpose, or for referral of information concerning the real estate to brokers, or both.

(4) "Real estate salesperson or salesman" means a person associated with a Texas licensed real estate

broker for the purposes of performing acts or transactions comprehended by the definition of "real estate broker" as defined in this Act.

(5) "Person" means an individual or any other entity including a government or governmental subdivision or agency, a limited liability company, a limited liability partnership, a partnership, or a corporation, foreign or domestic.

(6) "Commission" means the Texas Real Estate Commission.

(7) If the sense requires it, words in the present tense include the future tense; in the masculine gender, include the feminine or neuter gender; in the singular number, include the plural number; in the plural number, include the singular number; the word "and" may be read "or"; and the word "or" may be read "and". This Act is substantive in character and is intended to be applied prospectively only.

SECTION 3. EXEMPTIONS.

The provisions of this Act shall not apply to any of the following persons and transactions, and each and all of the following persons and transactions are hereby exempted from the provisions of this Act:

(1) an attorney at law licensed in this state or in any other state;

(2) an attorney in fact under a duly executed power of attorney authorizing the consummation of a real estate transaction;

(3) a public official in the conduct of that person's official duties;

(4) a person calling the sale of real estate by auction under the authority of a license issued by this state provided the person does not perform any other act of a real estate broker or salesperson as defined by this Act;

(5) a person acting under a court order or under the authority of a will or a written trust instrument;

(6) a salesperson employed by an owner in the sale of structures and land on which said structures are situated, provided such structures are erected by the owner in the due course of the owner's business;

(7) an on-site manager of an apartment complex;

(8) transactions involving the sale, lease, or transfer of any mineral or mining interest in real property;

(9) an owner or the owner's employees in renting or leasing the owner's own real estate whether improved or unimproved;

(10) transactions involving the sale, lease, or transfer of cemetery lots;

(11) transactions involving the renting, leasing, or management of hotels or motels; or

(12) a partnership or limited liability partnership acting as a broker or real estate salesman through a partner who is a licensed real estate broker ; or

(13) a person registered under Section 9A of this Act who sells, buys, leases, or transfers an easement or right-of-way for use in connection with telecommunication, utility, railroad, or pipeline service..

SECTION 4.   A person who, directly or indirectly for another, with the intention or on the promise of receiving any valuable consideration, offers, attempts, or agrees to perform, or performs, a single act defined in Subdivisions 2 and 3, Section 2 of this Act, whether as a part of a transaction, or as an entire transaction, is deemed to be acting as a real estate broker or salesperson within the meaning of this Act. The commission of a single such act by a person required to be licensed or registered under this Act and not so licensed or registered shall constitute a violation of this Act.

SECTION 5. (a) The administration of the provisions of this Act is vested in a commission, to be known as the "Texas Real Estate Commission," consisting of nine members to be appointed by the governor with the advice and consent of two-thirds of the senate present. The commissioners hold office for staggered terms of six years with the terms of three members expiring January 31 of each odd-numbered year. Each member holds office until the member's successor is appointed and has qualified. Within 15 days after appointment, each member shall qualify by taking the constitutional oath of office and furnishing a bond payable to the Governor of Texas in the penal sum of $10,000, conditional on the faithful performance of the member's duties as prescribed by law. A vacancy for any cause shall be filled by the governor for the unexpired term. The governor shall designate as chairperson of the commission one member of the commission who is a licensed real estate broker. The chairperson serves in that capacity at the pleasure of the governor. At a regular meeting in February of each year, the commission shall elect from its own membership a vice-chairperson and secretary. A quorum of the commission consists of five members.

(b) (1) All members, officers, employees, and agents of the commission are subject to the code of ethics and standards of conduct imposed by Chapter 421, Acts of the 63rd Legislature, Regular Session, 1973 (Article 6252-9b, Vernon's Texas Civil Statutes). A state elected president, president-elect, vice-president, or secretary-treasurer, employee, or paid consultant of a Texas trade association in the real estate industry may not be a member of the commission or an employee of the commission who is exempt from the state's position classification plan or compensated at or above the amount prescribed by the General Appropriations Act for step 1, salary group 17, of the state position classification salary schedule. A person who is the spouse of an officer, manager, or paid consultant of a Texas trade association in the real estate industry may not be a commission member and may not be a commission employee who is exempt from the state's position classification plan or compensated at or above the amount prescribed by the General Appropriations Act for step 1, salary group 17, of the state position classification salary schedule. For the purposes of this section, a Texas trade association is a nonprofit, cooperative, and voluntarily joined statewide association of business or professional competitors in this state designed to assist its members and its industry or profession in dealing with mutual business or professional problems and in promoting their common interest.

(2) A person may not serve as a member of the commission or act as the general counsel to the commission if the person is required to register as a lobbyist under Chapter 305, Government Code, because of the person's activities for compensation on behalf of a profession related to the operation of the commission.

(c) Appointments to the commission shall be made without regard to the race, color, handicap, sex, religion, age, or national origin of the appointees. Each member of the commission shall be a citizen of Texas and a qualified voter. Six members shall have been engaged in the real estate brokerage business as licensed real estate brokers as their major occupations for at least five years next immediately preceding their appointments. Three members must be representatives of the general public. A person is not eligible for appointment as a public

member of the commission if the person or the person's spouse:

(1) is registered, certified, or licensed by an occupational regulatory agency in the real estate industry;

(2) is employed by or participates in the management of a business entity or other organization regulated by the commission or receiving funds from the commission;

(3) owns or controls, directly or indirectly, more than a 10 percent interest in a business entity or other organization regulated by the commission or receiving funds from the commission; or

(4) uses or receives a substantial amount of tangible goods, services, or funds from the commission, other than compensation or reimbursement authorized by law for commission membership, attendance, or expenses.

(d) It is a ground for removal from the commission if a member:

(1) does not have at the time of appointment the qualifications required by Subsection (c) of this section for appointment to the commission;

(2) does not maintain during service on the commission the qualifications required by Subsection (c) of this section;

(3) violates a prohibition established by Subsection (b) of this section;

(4) cannot discharge the member's duties for a substantial part of the term for which the member is appointed because of illness or disability; or

(5) is absent from more than half of the regularly scheduled commission meetings that the member is eligible to attend during each calendar year, unless the absence is excused by majority vote of the commission.

(e) The validity of an action of the commission is not affected by the fact that it was taken when a ground for removal of a commission member existed.

(f) If the administrator has knowledge that a potential ground for removal exists, the administrator shall notify the chairperson of the commission of the ground. The chairperson shall then notify the governor that a potential ground for removal exists.

(g) Each member of the commission shall receive as compensation for each day actually spent on the member's official duties the sum of $75 and the actual and necessary expenses incurred in the performance of the member's official duties.

(h) The commission shall have the authority and power to make and enforce all rules and regulations necessary for the performance of its duties, to establish standards of conduct and ethics for its licensees in keeping with the purposes and intent of this Act or to insure compliance with the provisions of this Act. In addition to any other action, proceeding, or remedy authorized by law, the commission shall have the right to institute an action in its own name to enjoin any violation of any provision of this Act or any rule or regulation of the commission and in order for the commission to sustain such action it shall not be necessary to allege or prove, either that an adequate remedy at law does not exist, or that substantial or irreparable damage would result from the continued violation thereof. Either party to such action may appeal to the appellate court having jurisdiction of said cause. The commission shall not be required to give any appeal bond in any action or proceeding to enforce the provisions of this Act.

(i) The commission is empowered to select and name an administrator and to select and employ such other subordinate officers and employees as are necessary to administer this Act. The salaries of the administrator and the officers and employees shall be fixed by the commission not to exceed such amounts as are fixed by the applicable general appropriations bill. The commission may designate a subordinate officer as assistant administrator who shall be authorized to act for the administrator in the administrator's absence. The administrator or the administrator's designee shall develop a system of annual performance evaluations. All merit pay for commission employees must be based on the system established under this subsection. The administrator or the administrator's designee shall develop an intraagency career ladder program. The program shall require intraagency postings of all nonentry level positions concurrently with any public posting.

(j) The commission shall adopt a seal of a design which it shall prescribe. Copies of all records and papers in the office of the commission, duly certified and authenticated by the seal of the commission, shall be received in evidence in all courts with like effect as the original.

(k) Except as provided in Subsections (l) and (m) of this section, all money derived from fees, assessments, or charges under this Act, shall be paid by the commission into the State Treasury for safekeeping, and shall be placed by the Comptroller in a separate fund to be available for the use of the commission in the administration of this Act on requisition by the commission. A necessary amount of the money so paid into the State Treasury is hereby specifically appropriated to the commission for the purpose of paying the salaries and expenses necessary and proper for the administration of this Act, including equipment and maintenance of supplies for the offices or quarters occupied by the commission, and necessary travel expenses for the commission or persons authorized to act for it when performing duties under this Act. The comptroller shall, on requisition of the commission, draw warrants from time to time on the State Treasury for the amount specified in the requisition, not exceeding, however, the amount in the fund at the time of making a requisition. However, all money expended in the administration of this Act shall be specified and determined by itemized appropriation in the general departmental appropriation bill for the Texas Real Estate Commission, and not otherwise. The commission shall file annually with the governor and the presiding officer of each house of the legislature a complete and detailed written report accounting for all funds received and disbursed by the commission during the preceding fiscal year. The annual report must be in the form and reported in the time provided by the General Appropriations Act.

(l) In the event that fees collected under the Residential Service Company Act (Article 6573b, Vernon's Texas Civil Statutes), are insufficient to fund the legislative appropriation for that activity, funds from the real estate license fund are hereby authorized to be used for the administration of that Act. In no event, however, will the total expenditures for that activity exceed the legislative appropriation therefor.

(m) The commission shall charge and collect as a condition for issuance and for renewal of a real estate broker license the fee under Section 11(a)(14) of this Act. The commission shall charge and collect as a condition for issuance and for renewal of a registration under Section 9A of this Act the fee under Section

11(a)(14) of this Act. The commission shall charge and collect as a condition for issuance and for renewal of a real estate salesperson license the fee under Section 11(a)(15) of this Act. The commission shall transmit the fees under this subsection quarterly to Texas A&M University for deposit in a separate banking account. The money in the separate account shall be expended for the support and maintenance of the Texas Real Estate Research Center and for carrying out the purposes, objectives, and duties of the center. However, all money expended from the separate account shall be as determined by legislative appropriation.

(n)   The Texas Real Estate Commission is subject to Chapter 325, Government Code (Texas Sunset Act). Unless continued in existence as provided by that chapter, the commission is abolished and this Act expires September 1, 2003.

(o)   The commission is subject to the open meetings law, Chapter 271, Acts of the 60th Legislature, Regular Session, 1967, as amended (Article 6252-17, Vernon's Texas Civil Statutes), and the Administrative Procedure and Texas Register Act, as amended (Article 6252-13a, Vernon's Texas Civil Statutes).

(p)   The commission shall develop and implement policies that provide the public with a reasonable opportunity to appear before the commission and to speak on any issue under the jurisdiction of the commission.

(q)   The commission by rule shall establish methods by which consumers and service recipients are notified of the name, mailing address, and telephone number of the commission for the purpose of directing complaints to the commission. The commission may provide for that notification to be provided with the notification required by Section 8(q) of this Act or:

(1) on each registration form, application, or written contract for services of an individual or entity regulated under this Act;

(2) on a sign prominently displayed in the place of business of each individual or entity regulated under this Act; or

(3) in a bill for service provided by an individual or entity regulated under this Act.

(r)   The commission shall prepare information of public interest describing the functions of the commission and the procedures by which complaints are filed with and resolved by the commission. The commission shall make the information available to the general public and appropriate state agencies.

(s)   The commission shall develop and implement polices that clearly define the respective responsibilities of the governing body of the commission and the staff of the commission.

(t)   The commission may authorize specific employees to conduct hearings and render final decisions in contested cases. The commission may employ a general counsel, attorneys, investigators, and support staff to administer and enforce this Act.

(u)   The administrator or the administrator's designee shall prepare and maintain a written policy statement to assure implementation of a program of equal employment opportunity under which all personnel transactions are made without regard to race, color, handicap, sex, religion, age, or national origin. The policy statement must include:

(1) personnel policies, including policies relating to recruitment, evaluation, selection, appointment, training, and promotion of personnel;

(2) a comprehensive analysis of the commission work force that meets federal and state guidelines;

(3) procedures by which a determination can be made of significant underutilization in the commission work force of all persons for whom federal or state guidelines encourage a more equitable balance; and

(4) reasonable methods to appropriately address those areas of significant underutilization.

(v)   A policy statement prepared under Subsection (u) must cover an annual period, be updated at least annually, and be filed with the governor's office.

(w) The governor's office shall deliver a biennial report to the legislature based on the information received under Subsection (v). The report may be made separately or as a part of other biennial reports made to the legislature.

(x)   The commission shall provide to its members and employees, as often as necessary, information regarding their qualifications for office or employment under this Act and their responsibilities under applicable laws relating to standards of conduct for state officers or employees.

(y)   The commission shall prepare and maintain a written plan that describes how a person who does not speak English or who has a physical, mental, or developmental disability can be provided reasonable access to the commission's programs.

(z)   The commission may not adopt rules restricting competitive bidding or advertising by a person regulated by the commission except to prohibit false, misleading, or deceptive practices by the person. The commission may not include in its rules to prohibit false, misleading, or deceptive practices by a person regulated by the commission a rule that:

(1) restricts the use of any medium for advertising;

(2) restricts the person's personal appearance or use of the persons's voice in an advertisement;

(3) relates to the size or duration of an advertisement by the person; or

(4) restricts the person's advertisement under a trade name.

SECTION 6. (a) A person desiring to act as a real estate broker in this state shall file an application for a license with the commission on a form prescribed by the commission. A broker desiring to engage a person to participate in real estate brokerage activity shall join the person in filing an application for a salesperson license on a form prescribed by the commission. A person previously licensed as a broker may apply for inactive status. A person previously licensed as a salesperson may apply for inactive status without the participation of a broker. The person must apply for inactive status on a form prescribed by the commission not later than the first anniversary of the date of the expiration of the broker or salesperson license.

(b) To be eligible for a license, an individual must be a citizen of the United States or a lawfully admitted alien, be at least 18 years of age, and be a legal resident of Texas at the time of the filing of an application, and must satisfy the commission as to the individual's honesty, trustworthiness, integrity, and competency. However, the competency of the individual, for the purpose of

qualifying for the granting of a license, shall be judged solely on the basis of the examination referred to in Section 7 of this Act.

(c) To be eligible for or to renew a license, a corporation must designate one of its officers and a limited liability company must designate one of its managers to act for it. The designated person must be a licensed real estate broker as shown in the records of the commission. A corporation or limited liability company may not act as a real estate broker unless the designated person is a licensed real estate broker.

(d) For an individual to be eligible for a registration or a renewal of a registration under Section 9A of this Act, the individual must be a citizen of the United States or a lawfully admitted alien and be at least 18 years of age.   For a corporation, limited liability company, partnership, limited liability partnership, or any other entity to be eligible for a registration or renewal of a registration under Section 9A of this Act, it must designate one of its officers, partners, or managers to act for it. The designated person must be an individual registered under Section 9A of this Act.

SECTION 6A.   (a) If, at any time before a person applies for a license under this Act, the person requests the commission to determine whether the person's moral character complies with the commission's moral character requirements for licensing under this Act and the person pays a fee set by the commission for the moral character determination, the commission shall make its determination of the person's moral character.

(b) Not later that the 30th day after the day on which the commission makes its determination, the commission shall give the person notice of the determination.

(c) If the person later applies for a license under this Act, the commission may conduct a supplemental moral character check of the person. The supplemental check may cover only the time since the day on which the person requested the original moral character determination.

SECTION 7. (a) Competency as referred to in Section 6 of this Act shall be established by an examination prepared by or contracted for by the commission. The examination shall be given at such times and at such places within the state as the commission shall prescribe. The examination shall be of scope sufficient in the judgment of the commission to determine that a person is competent to act as a real estate broker or salesperson in a manner to protect the interest of the public. The examination for a salesperson license shall be less exacting and less stringent than the examination for a broker license. The commission shall furnish each applicant with study material and references on which the applicant examination shall be based. When an applicant for a real estate license fails a qualifying examination, the applicant may apply for reexamination by filing a request therefor together with the proper fee. The examination requirement must be satisfied not later than six months after the date on which the application for a license is filed. Courses of study required for a license may include but are not limited to the following, which shall be considered core real estate courses for all purposes of this Act:

(1) Principles of Real Estate (or equivalent) shall include but not be limited to an overview of licensing as a real estate broker and salesperson, ethics of practice, titles to and conveyancing of real estate, legal descriptions, deeds, encumbrances and liens, distinctions between personal and real property, appraisal, finance and regulations, closing procedures, real estate mathematics, and at least three classroom hours of instruction on federal, state, and local laws relating to housing discrimination, housing credit discrimination, and community reinvestment.

(2) Real Estate Appraisal (or equivalent) shall include but not be limited to the central purposes and functions of an appraisal, social and economic determinant of value, appraisal case studies, cost, market data and income approaches to value estimates, final correlations, and reporting.

(3) Real Estate Law (or equivalent) shall include but not be limited to legal concepts of real estate, land description, real property rights and estates in land, contracts, conveyances, encumbrances, foreclosures, recording procedures, and evidence of titles.

(4) Real Estate Finance (or equivalent) shall include but not be limited to monetary systems, primary and secondary money markets, sources of mortgage loans, federal government programs, loan applications, processes and procedures, closing costs, alternative financial instruments, equal credit opportunity acts, community reinvestment act, and state housing agency.

(5) Real Estate Marketing (or equivalent) shall include but not be limited to real estate professionalism and ethics, characteristics of successful salesmen, time management, psychology of marketing, listing procedures, advertising, negotiating and closing, financing, and the Deceptive Trade Practices-Consumer Protection Act, as amended, Section 17.01 et seq., Business & Commerce Code.

(6) Real Estate Mathematics (or equivalent) shall include but not be limited to basic arithmetic skills and review of mathematical logic, percentages, interest, time-valued money, depreciation, amortization, proration, and estimation of closing statements.

(7) Real Estate Brokerage (or equivalent) shall include but not be limited to law of agency, planning and organization, operational policies and procedures, recruiting, selection and training of personnel, records and control, and real estate firm analysis and expansion criteria.

(8) Property Management (or equivalent) shall include but not be limited to role of property manager, landlord policies, operational guidelines, leases, lease negotiations, tenant relations, maintenance, reports, habitability laws, and the Fair Housing Act.

(9) Real Estate Investments (or equivalent) shall include but not be limited to real estate investment characteristics, techniques of investment analysis, time-valued money, discounted and nondiscounted investment criteria, leverage, tax shelters, depreciation, and applications to property tax.

(10) Law of Agency (or equivalent) shall include but not be limited to the principal-agent and master-servant relationships, the authority of an agent, the termination of an agent's authority, the fiduciary and other duties of an agent, employment law, deceptive trade practices, listing or buying representation procedures, and the disclosure of agency.

(11) Law of Contracts (or equivalent) shall include the elements of a contract, offer and acceptance, the statute of frauds, specific performance and remedies for breach, unauthorized practice of law, commission rules relating to use of adopted forms, and owner disclosure requirements.

(b) The commission by rule may establish the title and content of additional core real estate courses.

(c) The commission shall waive the examination of an

applicant for a broker license who has, within one year previous to the filing of the application, been licensed in this state as a broker, and shall waive the examination of an applicant for a salesperson license who has, within one year previous to the filing of his application, been licensed in this state as either a broker or salesperson. The commission by rule may provide for the waiver of some or all of the requirements for a license under this Act for an applicant who was licensed under this Act within the six years preceding the date of filing the application.

(d) Each applicant for a broker license shall furnish the commission satisfactory evidence that the applicant has had not less than two years active experience in this state as a licensed real estate salesperson or broker during the 36-month period immediately preceding the filing of the application; and, in addition, shall furnish the commission satisfactory evidence of having completed successfully 60 semester hours, or equivalent classroom hours, of core real estate courses or related postsecondary education courses accepted by the commission. These qualifications for a broker license may not be required of an applicant who, at the time of making the application, is duly licensed as a real estate broker by any other state in the United States if that state's requirements for licensure are comparable to those of Texas. As a prerequisite for applying for a broker license, those persons licensed as salespersons subject to the annual education requirements provided by Subsection (e) of this section shall, as part of the hours required by this subsection, furnish the commission satisfactory evidence of having completed all the requirements of Subsection (e) of this section.

(e) Each applicant for a salesperson license shall furnish the commission satisfactory evidence of having completed 12 semester hours, or equivalent classroom hours, of postsecondary education, six hours of which must be completed in core real estate courses, of which a minimum of two hours must be completed in Principles of Real Estate as described in Subsection (a)(1) of this section, a minimum of two hours must be completed in Law of Agency as described in Subsection (a)(10) of this section, and a minimum of two hours must be completed in Law of Contracts as described in Subsection (a)(11) of this section. The remaining six hours shall be completed in core real estate courses or related courses. As a condition for the first renewal of a salesperson license, the applicant shall furnish the commission satisfactory evidence of having completed a minimum of 14 semester hours, or equivalent classroom

hours, eight hours of which must be completed in core real estate courses. As a condition for the second renewal of a salesperson license, the applicant shall furnish the commission satisfactory evidence of having completed a minimum of 16 semester hours, or equivalent classroom hours, 10 hours of which must be completed in core real estate courses. As a condition for the third renewal of a salesperson license, the applicant shall furnish the commission satisfactory evidence of having completed a minimum of 18 semester hours, or equivalent classroom hours, 12 hours of which must be completed in core real estate courses.

(f) Insofar as is necessary for the administration of this Act, the commission is authorized to inspect and accredit educational programs or courses of study in real estate and real estate inspection and to establish standards of accreditation for such programs conducted in the State of Texas, other than accredited colleges and universities. The commission shall determine the acceptability of real estate courses and real estate inspection courses offered to satisfy the requirements of this Act, and by rule may provide reasonable criteria for the approval of those courses. Schools, other than accredited colleges and universities, which are authorized to offer real estate educational courses pursuant to provisions of this section, shall be required to maintain a corporate surety bond, or other security acceptable to the commission, in the sum of $10,000, payable to the commission, for the benefit of a party who may suffer damages resulting from failure of a commission approved school or course to fulfill obligations attendant to the approval.

(g) Notwithstanding any other provision of this Act, each applicant for a broker license shall furnish the commission with satisfactory evidence:

(1) that the applicant has satisfied the requirements of Subsection (d) of this section;

(2) that the applicant is a licensed real estate broker in another state, has had not less than two years' active experience in the other state as a licensed real estate salesperson or broker during the 36-month period immediately preceding the filing of the application, and has satisfied the educational requirements for a broker license as provided by Subsection (d) of this section; or

(3) that the applicant has, within one year previous to the filing of the application, been licensed in this state as a broker.

(h) Notwithstanding any other provision of this Act, the commission shall waive the requirements of Subsection (e) of this section for an applicant for a salesperson license who has, within one year previous to the filing of the application, been licensed in this state as a broker or salesperson. However, with respect to an applicant for a salesperson license who was licensed as a salesperson within one year previous to the filing of the application but whose original license was issued under the provisions that the first, second, and third renewal of the license would be conditioned upon furnishing satisfactory evidence of successful completion of additional education, the commission shall require the applicant to furnish satisfactory evidence of successful completion of any additional education that would have been required if the license had been maintained without interruption during the previous year.

(i) Not later than the 30th day after the date on which a licensing examination is administered under this Act, the commission shall notify each examinee of the results of the examination. However, if an examination is graded or reviewed by a national testing service, the commission shall notify examinees of the results of the examination not later than the 14th day after the date on which the commission receives the results from the testing service. If the notice of examination results graded or reviewed by a national testing service will be delayed for longer than 90 days after the examination date, the commission shall notify the examinee of the reason for the delay before the 90th day. If requested in writing by a person who fails a licensing examination administered under this Act, the commission shall furnish the person with an analysis of the person's performance on the examination.

(j) All license applicants must complete at least three classroom hours of course work on federal, state, and local laws governing housing discrimination, housing credit discrimination, and community reinvestment or at least three semester hours of coursework on constitutional law.

(k) The commission may accept examinations administered by a testing service as satisfying the examination requirements imposed under this Act. The commission may negotiate agreements with those testing services relating to examination development, test scheduling, examination site arrangements, and test administration, grading, reporting, and analysis. The commission may require a testing service to correspond directly with the license applicants regarding the administration of the examinations and may require that a testing service collect fees for administering the examinations directly from the applicants. The commission also may require a testing service to administer examinations at specific locations and specified frequencies. The commission shall retain the authority to establish the scope and type of all examinations. The commission shall adopt rules and standards as necessary to implement this section. In the absence of an agreement with a testing service, the commission shall administer any required qualifying examination in accordance with this Act.

SECTION 7A. (a) To renew an active real estate broker license or an active real estate salesperson license that is not subject to the annual education requirements of this Act, the licensee must provide the commission proof of attendance at at least 15 classroom hours of continuing education courses approved by the commission during the term of the current license. The commission by rule may provide for the substitution of relevant educational experience or correspondence courses approved by the commission instead of classroom attendance. In addition, supervised video instruction may be approved by the commission as a course counting as classroom hours of mandatory continuing education. At least six hours of instruction must be devoted to the rules of the commission, fair housing laws, landlord-tenant law and other Property Code issues, agency laws, antitrust laws, the Deceptive Trade Practices-Consumer Protection Act (Subchapter E, Chapter 17, Business & Commerce Code), disclosures to buyers, landlords, tenants, and sellers, current contract and addendum forms, the unauthorized practice of law, case studies involving violations of laws and regulations, current Federal Housing Administration and Department of Veterans Affairs regulations, tax laws, property tax consulting laws and legal issues, or other legal topics approved by the commission. The remaining hours may be devoted to other real estate-related topics approved by the commission. The commission may consider equivalent courses for continuing education credit. Property tax consulting laws and legal issues include but are not limited to the Tax Code, preparation of property tax reports, the unauthorized practice of law, agency laws, tax laws, laws concerning property taxes or assessments, deceptive trade practices, contract forms and addendum, and other legal topics approved by the commission. Real estate related courses approved by the State Bar of Texas for minimum continuing legal education participatory credit and core real estate courses under

Section 7(a) of this Act shall automatically be approved as mandatory continuing education courses under this Act. The commission may not require examinations except for correspondence courses or courses offered by alternative delivery systems such as computers. Daily classroom course segments must be at least one hour long but not more than 10 hours long.

(b)   An applicant for an active real estate broker license or an active real estate salesperson license who is not subject to the education requirements of Section 7 of this Act must provide the commission with proof of attendance of the number of classroom hours of continuing education that would have been required for a timely renewal as specified in Subsection (a) of this section during the two-year period preceding the filing of the application.

(c)   As a condition of returning to active status, an inactive salesperson whose license is not subject to the annual education requirements of this Act must provide the commission with proof of attendance at at least 15 hours of continuing education as specified in Subsection (a) of this section during the two-year period preceding the filing of the application.

(d)   The commission may adopt rules and set and collect reasonable fees to implement this section, including a fee not to exceed $400 for an application for approval of a provider of continuing education and a fee not to exceed $100 for an application for a course of study to be offered for continuing education. If the commission determines that an applicant satisfies the requirements of this section and any rules adopted by the commission under this section, the commission may authorize a provider to offer continuing education for a period of two years or authorize the offering of a course of study for a period of two years. (Effective August 31, 1991.)

(e)   On or before September 25, 1991, the commission shall:

(1)   identify each real estate broker that:

(A) has been licensed under this Act for at least 10 years as of September 1, 1991, and holds a license as a real estate broker on that date; and

(B) on June 1, 1991, has the principal place of real estate brokerage business, as designated on the real estate broker's license pursuant to Subsection (a) of Section 12

of this Act, located in a county with a population of 225,000 or less, according to the 1980 federal decennial census; and

(2)   send a written notice to each real estate broker identified under Subdivision (1) of this subsection stating that the real estate broker may qualify to opt out of the mandatory continuing education requirements required by this Act in accordance with Subsection (f) of this section if the real estate broker has held a broker's license for 10 years or more and holds a broker's license on September 1, 1991.

(f)   Notwithstanding any other provision of this Act, a real estate broker identified and receiving a notice under Subsection (e) of this section who has held a broker's license for 10 years or more and holds a broker's license on September 1, 1991, is not required to comply with the mandatory continuing education requirements of this section to renew the real estate broker's license if after October 1, 1991, and on or before October 30, 1991, the real estate broker:

(1)   notifies the commission in writing that the real estate broker is opting out of those requirements; and

(2)   pays a one-time fee to the commission in the amount determined by the commission to be adequate to recover the cost to process the application not to exceed $100.

(g)   The commission may adopt rules that establish procedures under which a license may be issued, renewed, or returned to active status before the applicant completes the continuing education requirements of this section. The commission may prescribe an additional fee, not to exceed $200, for the issuance, renewal, or return to active status of a license before the applicant completes the continuing education requirements of this section and may require the applicant to complete the required continuing education not later than the 60th day after the date the license is issued, renewed, or returned to active status.

SECTION 8. (a)   The commission shall establish a real estate recovery fund which shall be set apart and maintained by the commission as provided in this section. The fund shall be used in the manner provided in this section for reimbursing aggrieved persons who suffer actual damages by reason of certain acts committed by a duly licensed real estate broker or salesperson, a duly registered person under Section 9A of this Act, or by an unlicensed employee or agent of a broker or salesperson, provided the registrant, broker, or salesperson was registered or licensed by the State of Texas at the time the act was committed and provided recovery is ordered by a court of competent jurisdiction against the registrant, broker, or salesperson. The use of the fund is limited to an act that constitutes a violation of Section 15(a)(3) or (6) of this Act if the judgment debtor was at the time of the violation a licensed real estate broker or salesperson. The use of the fund is limited to an act that constitutes a violation of Section 9A(c)(1) of this Act if the judgment debtor was at the time of the violation registered under Section 9A of this Act.

(b) On application for an original license pursuant to this Act, the applicant shall pay, in addition to the original license application fee, a fee of $10 which shall be deposited in the real estate recovery fund. On application for an original registration under Section 9A of this Act and for each renewal of such registration, the registrant shall pay, in addition to the registrant's original application fee or renewal fee, a fee of $50, which shall be deposited in the real estate recovery fund.

(c) If on December 31 of any year the balance remaining in the real estate recovery fund is less than $1 million, each real estate broker and each real estate salesperson, on the next renewal of his license, shall pay, in addition to his license renewal fee, a fee of $10, which shall be deposited in the real estate recovery fund, or a pro rata share of the amount necessary to bring the fund to $1.7 million, whichever is less. If on December 31 of any year the balance remaining in the real estate recovery fund is more than $3.5 million or more than the total amount of claims paid from the fund during the previous four fiscal years, whichever is greater, the amount of money in excess of the greater amount shall be transferred to the general revenue fund.

(d) No action for a judgment which subsequently results in an order for collection from the real estate recovery fund shall be started later than two years from the accrual of the cause of action. When an aggrieved person commences action for a judgment which may result in collection from the real estate recovery fund, the registrant, real estate broker, or real estate salesperson shall notify the commission in writing to this effect at the time of the commencement of the action.

(e) When an aggrieved person recovers a valid judgment in a court of competent jurisdiction against a registrant, real estate broker, or real estate salesperson,

on the grounds described in Subsection (a) of this section that occurred on or after May 19, 1975, the aggrieved person may, after final judgment has been entered, execution returned nulla bona, and a judgment lien perfected, file a verified claim in the court in which the judgment was entered and, on 20 days' written notice to the commission, and to the judgment debtor, may apply to the court for an order directing payment out of the real estate recovery fund of the amount unpaid on the judgment, subject to the limitations stated in Subsection (n) of this section.

(f) The court shall proceed on the application forthwith. On the hearing on the application, the aggrieved person is required to show that:

(1) the judgment is based on facts allowing recovery under Subsection (a) of this section;

(2) the person is not a spouse of the debtor, or the personal representative of the spouse; and the person is not a registrant under Section 9A of this Act or a real estate broker or salesperson, as defined by this Act, who is seeking to recover a real estate commission or any compensation in the transaction or transactions for which the application for payment is made;

(3) the person has obtained a judgment under Subsection (e) of this section that is not subject to a stay or discharge in bankruptcy, stating the amount of the judgment and the amount owing on the judgment at the date of the application;

(4) based on the best available information, the judgment debtor lacks sufficient attachable assets in this state or any other state to satisfy the judgment; and

(5) the amount that may be realized from the sale of real or personal property or other assets liable to be sold or applied in satisfaction of the judgment and the balance remaining due on the judgment after application of the amount that may be realized.

(g) A recovery on the judgment against a single defendant made before payment from the recovery fund must be applied by the creditor first to actual damages.

(h) The court shall make an order directed to the commission requiring payment from the real estate recovery fund of whatever sum it finds to be payable on the claim, pursuant to and in accordance with the limitations contained in this section, if the court is satisfied, on the hearing, of the truth of all matters required to be shown by the aggrieved person by Subsection (f) of this section and that the aggrieved person has satisfied all of the requirements of Subsections (e) and (f) of this section. The commission may relitigate any issue material and relevant in the hearing on the application that was determined in the underlying action on which the judgment in favor of the applicant was based. If the court finds that the aggregate amount of claims against a registrant, real estate broker, or salesperson exceeds the limitations contained in this section, the court shall reduce proportionately the amount it finds payable on the claim.

(i)   A license or registration granted under the provisions of this Act may be revoked by the commission on proof that the commission has made a payment from the real estate recovery fund of any amount toward satisfaction of a judgment against a registrant under Section 9A of this Act or a licensed real estate broker or salesperson.   The commission may probate an order revoking a license. No registrant, broker, or salesperson is eligible to receive a new registration or license until the broker or salesperson has repaid in full, plus interest at the current legal rate, the amount paid from the real estate recovery fund on the broker or salesperson's account.

(j)   The sums received by the real estate commission for deposit in the real estate recovery fund shall be held by the commission in trust for carrying out the purposes of the real estate recovery fund.   These funds may be invested and reinvested in the same manner as funds of the Texas State Employees Retirement System, and the interest from these investments shall be deposited to the credit of the real estate recovery fund, provided, however, that no investments shall be made which will impair the necessary liquidity required to satisfy judgment payments awarded pursuant to this section.

(k) When the real estate commission receives notice of entry of a final judgment and a hearing is scheduled under Subsection (h) of this section, the commission may notify the Attorney General of Texas of its desire to enter an appearance, file a response, appear at the court hearing, defend the action, or take whatever other action it deems appropriate.   In taking such action the real estate commission and the attorney general shall act only to protect the fund from spurious or unjust claims or to insure compliance with the requirements for recovery under this section.

(l)   When, on the order of the court, the commission has paid from the real estate recovery fund any sum to the judgment creditor, the commission shall be subrogated to all of the rights of the judgment creditor to the extent of the amount paid.   The judgment creditor shall assign all his right, title, and interest in the judgment up to the amount paid by the commission which amount shall have priority for repayment in the event of any subsequent recovery on the judgment. Any amount and interest recovered by the commission on the judgment shall be deposited to the fund.

(m) The failure of an aggrieved person to comply with the provisions of this section relating to the real estate recovery fund shall constitute a waiver of any rights under this section.

(n)   Notwithstanding any other provision, payments from the real estate recovery fund are subject to the following conditions and limitations:

(1)   payments may be made only pursuant to an order of a court of competent jurisdiction, as provided in Subsection (e) of this section, and in the manner prescribed by this section;

(2)   payments for claims, including attorneys' fees, interest, and court costs, arising out of the same transaction shall be limited in the aggregate to $50,000 regardless of the number of claimants; and

(3)   payments for claims based on judgments against any one licensed real estate broker, licensed real estate salesperson, or registrant under Section 9A of this Act may not exceed in the aggregate $100,000 until the fund has been reimbursed by the licensee or registrant for all amounts paid.

(o)   Nothing contained in this section shall limit the authority of the commission to take disciplinary action against a registrant or licensee for a violation of this Act or the rules and regulations of the commission; nor shall the repayment in full of all obligations to the real estate recovery fund by a registrant or licensee nullify or modify the effect of any other disciplinary proceeding brought pursuant to this Act.

(p)   Any person receiving payment out of the real estate recovery fund pursuant to Section 8 of this Act shall be entitled to receive reasonable attorney fees as determined by the court, subject to the limitations stated in Subsection (n) of this section.

(q) A registrant, broker, or salesperson registered or licensed under this Act shall notify consumers and service recipients of the availability of the real estate recovery fund established under this section for reimbursing certain aggrieved persons. The notice must include the name, mailing address, and telephone number of the commission and any other information required by commission rule. The notification may be provided with the notice required by Section 5(q) of this Act or:

(1) on a written contract for the services of a registrant, broker, or salesperson;

(2) on a brochure distributed by a registrant, broker, or salesperson;

(3) on a sign prominently displayed in the place of business of a registrant, salesperson, or broker; or

(4) in a bill or receipt for service provided by a registrant, broker, or salesperson.

SECTION 9. *(Amended by S.B. No. 577, effective January 1, 1998)* (a) When an applicant has satisfactorily met all requirements and conditions of this Act, a license or certificate of registration shall be issued which may remain in force and effect so long as the holder of the certificate of registration or license remains in compliance with the obligations of this Act, which include payment of the renewal fee as provided in Section 11 of this Act. Each active salesperson license issued shall be delivered or mailed to the broker with whom the salesperson is associated and shall be kept under his custody and control.

(b) An applicant is not permitted to engage in the real estate business either as a broker or salesperson until a license evidencing the applicant's authority to engage in the real estate business has been received. A person may not engage in the business of selling, buying, leasing, or transferring an easement or right-of-way for another for compensation until the person is licensed or registered under this Act.

(c) The commission by rule may adopt a system under which licenses and registrations expire on various dates during the year. Dates for payment of the renewal fee shall be adjusted accordingly. For the year in which the renewal date is changed, renewal fees payable shall be prorated on a monthly basis so each licensee or registrant shall pay only that portion of the fee which is allocable to the number of months during which the license or

registration is valid. On renewal of the license or registration on the new renewal date, the total renewal fee is payable.

(d) Any other provision of this Act notwithstanding, the commission may issue licenses and registrations valid for a period not to exceed 24 months and may charge and collect renewal fees for such period; provided, however, that such renewal fees shall not, calculated on an annual basis, exceed the amounts established in Section 11 of this Act, and further provided that the educational conditions for renewal established in Subsection (e) of Section 7 of this Act shall not be waived by the commission.

(e) The commission shall require, in any application for a broker or salesperson license or a renewal of a broker or salesperson license, the applicant to disclose whether the applicant has entered a plea of guilty or nolo contendere to, been found guilty of, or been convicted of a felony and the time for appeal has elapsed or the judgment or conviction has been affirmed on appeal, irrespective of an order granting probation following the conviction or suspending the imposition of sentence.

SECTION 9A. *(Added by S.B. No. 577, effective January 1, 1998)* (a) A person may not sell, buy, lease, or transfer an easement or right-of-way for another for compensation, or with the intention or in the expectation or on the promise of receiving or collecting compensation, for use in connection with telecommunication, utility, railroad, or pipeline service unless the person is:

(1) licensed as a real estate broker or real estate salesman under this Act;

(2) exempt from this Act for the purpose of selling, buying, leasing, or transferring an easement or right-of-way; or

(3) registered with the commission under this section.

(b) The commission shall maintain a registry of persons who are registered under this section.

(c) The commission shall investigate a signed complaint received by the commission that relates to the acts of a person registered or required to be registered under this section. The commission may revoke or suspend the registration of a registrant under this section who:

(1) engaged in dishonest dealings, fraud, deceptive acts, misrepresentations, bad faith, unlawful discrimination, or untrustworthiness;

(2) failed within a reasonable time to make good a check to the commission after the commission has mailed a request for payment to the registrant's last known address as reflected in the commission records;

(3) failed to provide to a party in a transaction a written notice promulgated by the commission that is to be given before the party is obligated to sell, buy, lease, or transfer a right-of-way or easement and that contains the name of the registrant, the certificate number of the registrant, the name of the person the registrant represents, a statement advising the party that the party may seek representation from a lawyer or real estate broker in the transaction, and a statement generally advising the party that the right-of-way or easement may affect the value of the property; or

(4) disregarded or violated a provision of this Act or a rule of the commission relating to registrants under this section.

(d) The commission may adopt rules to administer and enforce this section.

SECTION 10. (a) If the commission declines or fails to register or license an applicant, it shall immediately give written notice of the refusal to the applicant. Before the applicant may appeal to a district court as provided in Section 18 of this Act, the applicant must file within 10 days after the receipt of the notice an appeal from the ruling, requesting a time and place for a hearing before the commission. The commission shall set a time and place for the hearing within 30 days from the receipt of the appeal, giving 10 days' notice of the hearing to the applicant. The time of the hearing may be continued from time to time with the consent of the applicant. Following the hearing, the commission shall enter an order which is, in its opinion, appropriate in the matter concerned.

(b) If an applicant fails to request a hearing as provided in this section, the commission's ruling shall become final and not subject to review by the courts.

(c) The commission may issue a probationary license. The commission by rule shall adopt reasonable terms and conditions for a probationary license.

SECTION 11. (a) The commission shall charge and collect the following fees:

(1) a fee not to exceed $100 for the filing of an original application for a real estate broker license;

(2) a fee not to exceed $100 for annual renewal of a real estate broker license;

(3) a fee not to exceed $50 for the filing of an original application for a real estate salesperson license;

(4) a fee not to exceed $50 for annual renewal of a real estate salesperson license;

(5) a fee not to exceed $50 for an application for a license examination;

(6) a fee not to exceed $20 for filing a request for a license for each additional office or place of business;

(7) a fee not to exceed $20 for filing a request for a license or certificate of registration for a change of place of business, change of name, return to active status, or change of sponsoring broker;

(8) a fee not to exceed $20 for filing a request to replace a license or certificate of registration lost or destroyed;

(9) a fee not to exceed $400 for filing an application for approval of an education program under Section 7(f) of this Act;

(10) a fee not to exceed $200 a year for operation of an education program under Section 7(f) of this Act;

(11) a fee of $15 for transcript evaluation;

(12) a fee not to exceed $10 for preparing a license or registration history;

(13) a fee not to exceed $50 for the filing of an application for a moral character determination;

(14) an annual fee of $20 from each real estate broker and each registrant to be transmitted to Texas A&M University for the Texas Real Estate Research Center as provided by Section 5(m) of this Act;

(15) an annual fee of $17.50 from each real estate salesperson to be transmitted to Texas A&M University

for the Texas Real Estate Research Center as provided by Section 5(m) of this Act;

    (16) an annual fee of $80 from each registrant under Section 9A of this Act; and

    (17) any fee authorized under Section 8 of this Act for the real estate recovery fund.

SECTION 11A. Increase in Fees. *(Amended by S.B. No. 1058, effective August 30, 1993).*

    (a) Each of the following fees imposed by or under another section of this Act is increased by $200:

    (1) fee for filing an original application for an individual real estate broker license; and

    (2) fee for annual renewal of an individual real estate broker license.

    (b) Of each fee increase collected, $50 shall be deposited to the credit of the foundation school fund and $150 shall be deposited to the credit of the general revenue fund. This subsection applies to the disposition of each fee increase regardless of any other provision of law providing for a different disposition of funds.

SECTION 12.   (a)   Each resident broker shall maintain a fixed office within this state. The address of the office shall be designated on the broker's license. Within 10 days after a move from a previously designated address, the broker shall submit an application for a new license, designating the new location of the broker's office, together with the required fee, whereupon the commission shall issue a license, reflecting the new location, provided the new location complies with the terms of this section.

    (b) If a broker maintains more than one place of business within this state, the broker shall apply for, pay the required fee for, and obtain an additional license to be known as a branch office license for each additional office the broker maintains.

    (c) The license or licenses of the broker shall at all times be prominently displayed in the licensee's place or places of business.

    (d) Each broker shall also prominently display in the broker's place or in one of the broker's places of business the license of each real estate salesperson associated with the broker.

    (e) The certificate of registration of a registrant under Section 9A of this Act shall at all times be prominently displayed in the registrant's place of business. Within 10 days after a move from a previously designated address, the registrant shall notify the commission of the move and obtain a new certificate of registration reflecting the new location.

SECTION 13.   (a)   When the association of a salesperson with the salesperson's sponsoring broker is terminated, the broker shall immediately return the salesperson license to the commission. The salesperson license then becomes inactive.

    (b) The salesperson license may be activated if, before the license expires, a request, accompanied by the required fee, is filed with the commission by a licensed broker advising that the broker assumes sponsorship of the salesperson.

SECTION 13A. (a) A real estate broker who holds a license issued under this Act and who is not acting as a broker or sponsoring a salesperson may apply to the commission in writing to be placed on the inactive status list maintained by the commission. The broker must apply for inactive status before the expiration of the broker's license. The broker shall terminate the broker's association with any salesperson sponsored by the broker by giving written notice to the salesperson before the 30th day before the date the broker applies for inactive status. A person on inactive status under this section is required to pay the annual renewal fees.

    (b) A person on inactive status under this section may not perform any activities regulated under this Act.

    (c) If the person has been on inactive status, the commission shall remove the person from the list on application, payment of the required fee, and proof of attendance of at least 15 classroom hours of continuing education as specified in Subsection (a) of Section 7A of this Act during the two-year period preceding the filing of the application.

SECTION 14.   (a)   It is unlawful for a licensed broker to employ or compensate directly or indirectly a person for performing an act enumerated in the definition of real estate broker in Section 2 of this Act if the person is not a licensed broker or licensed salesperson in this state.   However, a licensed broker may pay a commission to a licensed broker of another state if the foreign broker does not conduct in this state any of the negotiations for which the fee, compensation, or commission is paid.

(b) A resident broker of another state who furnishes the evidence required under Section 7(g) of this Act may apply for a license as a broker in this state. A resident of another state who is not licensed as a broker but who was formerly licensed as a salesperson or broker in this state may apply for a license in this state not later than the first anniversary of the date of the expiration of the previous license. An application by a nonresident is subject to the requirements under this Act for the type of license applied for. A nonresident licensee need not maintain a place of business in this state. The commission may in its discretion refuse to issue a license to an applicant who is not a resident of this state for the same reasons that it may refuse to license a resident of this state. The commission shall judge the competency of a nonresident applicant solely on the basis of the examination conducted under Section 7 of this Act.

(c) Each nonresident applicant shall file an irrevocable consent that legal actions may be commenced against the applicant in the proper court of any county of this state in which a cause of action may arise, or in which the plaintiff may reside, by service of process or pleading authorized by the laws of this state, or by serving the administrator or assistant administrator of the commission. The consent shall stipulate that the service of process or pleading shall be valid and binding in all courts as if personal service had been made on the nonresident in this state. The consent shall be duly acknowledged, and if made by a corporation, shall be authenticated by its seal. A service of process or pleading served on the commission shall be by duplicate copies, one of which shall be filed in the office of the commission and the other forwarded by registered mail to the last known principal address which the commission has for the nonresident against whom the process or pleading is directed. No default in an action may be taken except on certification by the commission that a copy of the process or pleading was mailed to the defendant as provided in this section, and no default judgment may be taken in an action or proceeding until 20 days after the day of mailing of the process or pleading to the defendant. Notwithstanding any other provision of this subsection, a nonresident of this state who resides in a city whose boundaries are contiguous at any point to the boundaries of a city of this state, and who has been an actual bona fide resident of that city for

at least 60 days immediately preceding the filing of his application, is eligible to be licensed as a real estate broker or salesperson under this Act in the same manner as a resident of this state. If a person is licensed in this manner, the person shall at all times maintain a place of business either in the city in which the person resides or in the city in this state which is contiguous to the city in which the person resides, and the person may not maintain a place of business at another location in this state unless the person also complies with the requirements of Section 14(b) of this Act. The place of business must satisfy the requirements of Subsection (a) of Section 12 of this Act, but the place of business shall be deemed a definite place of business in this state within the meaning of Subsection (a) of Section 12.

SECTION 15. (a) The commission may, on its own motion, and shall, on the signed complaint in writing of a consumer or service recipient, provided the complaint, or the complaint together with evidence, documentary or otherwise, presented in connection with the complaint, provides reasonable cause, investigate the actions and records of a real estate broker or real estate salesperson. The commission may suspend or revoke a license issued under the provisions of this Act at any time when it has been determined that:

(1) the licensee has entered a plea of guilty or nolo contendere to, or been found guilty of, or been convicted of, a felony, in which fraud is an essential element, and the time for appeal has elapsed or the judgment or conviction has been affirmed on appeal, irrespective of an order granting probation following such conviction, suspending the imposition of sentence;

(2) the licensee has procured, or attempted to procure, a real estate license, for the licensee or a salesperson, by fraud, misrepresentation or deceit, or by making a material misstatement of fact in an application for a real estate license;

(3) the licensee, when selling, buying, trading, or renting real property in the licensee's own name, engaged in misrepresentation or dishonest or fraudulent action;

(4) the licensee has failed within a reasonable time to make good a check issued to the commission after the commission has mailed a request for payment by certified mail to the licensee's last known business address as reflected by the commission's records;

(5) the licensee has disregarded or violated a provision of this Act;

(6) the licensee, while performing an act constituting an act of a broker or salesperson, as defined by this Act, has been guilty of:

(A) making a material misrepresentation, or failing to disclose to a potential purchaser any latent structural defect or any other defect known to the broker or salesperson. Latent structural defects and other defects do not refer to trivial or insignificant defects but refer to those defects that would be a significant factor to a reasonable and prudent purchaser in making a decision to purchase;

(B) making a false promise of a character likely to influence, persuade, or induce any person to enter into a contract or agreement when the licensee could not or did not intend to keep such promise;

(C) pursuing a continued and flagrant course of misrepresentation or making of false promises through agents, salespersons, advertising, or otherwise;

(D) failing to make clear, to all parties to a transaction, which party the licensee is acting for, or receiving compensation from more than one party except with the full knowledge and consent of all parties;

(E) failing within a reasonable time properly to account for or remit money coming into the licensee's possession which belongs to others, or commingling money belonging to others with the licensee's own funds;

(F) paying a commission or fees to or dividing a commission or fees with anyone not licensed as a real estate broker or salesperson in this state or in any other state for compensation for services as a real estate agent;

(G) failing to specify a definite termination date that is not subject to prior notice in a contract, other than a contract to perform property management services, in which the licensee agrees to perform services for which a license is required under this Act;

(H) accepting, receiving, or charging an undisclosed commission, rebate, or direct profit on expenditures made for a principal;

(I) soliciting, selling, or offering for sale real property under a scheme or program that constitutes a lottery or deceptive practice;

(J) acting in the dual capacity of broker and undisclosed principal in a transaction;

(K) guaranteeing, authorizing, or permitting a person to guarantee that future profits will result from a resale of real property;

(L) placing a sign on real property offering it for sale, lease, or rent without the written consent of the owner or the owner's authorized agent;

(M) inducing or attempting to induce a party to a contract of sale or lease to break the contract for the purpose of substituting in lieu thereof a new contract;

(N) negotiating or attempting to negotiate the sale, exchange, lease, or rental of real property with an owner, lessor, buyer, or tenant, knowing that the owner, lessor, buyer, or tenant had a written outstanding contract, granting exclusive agency in connection with the transaction to another real estate broker;

(O) offering real property for sale or for lease without the knowledge and consent of the owner or the owner's authorized agent, or on terms other than those authorized by the owner or the owner's authorized agent;

(P) publishing, or causing to be published, an advertisement including, but not limited to, advertising by newspaper, radio, television, or display which is misleading, or which is likely to deceive the public, or which in any manner tends to create a misleading impression, or which fails to identify the person causing the advertisement to be published as a licensed real estate broker or agent;

(Q) having knowingly withheld from or inserted in a statement of account or invoice, a statement that made it inaccurate in a material particular;

(R) publishing or circulating an unjustified or unwarranted threat of legal proceedings, or other action;

(S) establishing an association, by employment or otherwise, with an unlicensed person who is expected or required to act as a real estate licensee, or aiding or abetting or conspiring with a person to circumvent the requirements of this Act;

(T) failing or refusing on demand to furnish copies of a document pertaining to a transaction dealing with real estate to a person whose signature is affixed to the document;

(U) failing to advise a purchaser in writing before the closing of a transaction that the purchaser should either have the abstract covering the real estate which is the subject of the contract examined by an attorney of the purchaser's own selection, or be furnished with or obtain a policy of title insurance;

(V) conduct which constitutes dishonest dealings, bad faith, or untrustworthiness;

(W) acting negligently or incompetently in performing an act for which a person is required to hold a real estate license;

(X) disregarding or violating a provision of this Act;

(Y) failing within a reasonable time to deposit money received as escrow agent in a real estate transaction, either in trust with a title company authorized to do business in this state, or in a custodial, trust, or escrow account maintained for that purpose in a banking institution authorized to do business in this state;

(Z) disbursing money deposited in a custodial, trust, or escrow account, as provided in Subsection (Y) before the transaction concerned has been consummated or finally otherwise terminated; or

(AA) discriminating against an owner, potential purchaser, lessor, or potential lessee on the basis of race, color, religion, sex, national origin, or ancestry, including directing prospective home buyers or lessees interested in equivalent properties to different areas according to the race, color, religion, sex, national origin, or ancestry of the potential owner or lessee;

(7) the licensee has failed or refused on demand to produce a document, book, or record in licensee's possession concerning a real estate transaction conducted by the licensee for inspection by the commission or its authorized personnel or representative;

(8) the licensee has failed within a reasonable time to provide information requested by the commission as a result of a formal or informal complaint to the commission which would indicate a violation of this Act; or

(9) the licensee has failed without just cause to

surrender to the rightful owner, on demand, a document or instrument coming into the licensee's possession.

(b) The provisions of this section do not relieve a person from civil liability or from criminal prosecution under this Act or under the laws of this state.

(c) Notwithstanding Subsection (b) of this section, a person is not subject to civil liability or criminal prosecution because the person did not inquire about, make a disclosure related to, or release information related to whether a previous or current occupant of real property had, may have had, has, or may have AIDS, HIV-related illnesses, or HIV infection as defined by the Centers for Disease Control of the U.S. Public Health Service.

(d) The commission may not investigate under this section a complaint submitted more than four years after the date of the incident involving a real estate broker or salesperson that is the subject of the complaint.

(e) The commission may request and, if necessary, compel by subpoena the attendance of witnesses for examination under oath and the production for inspection and copying of books, accounts, records, papers, correspondence, documents, and other evidence relevant to the investigation of alleged violations of this Act. If a person fails to comply with a subpoena issued under this subsection, the commission, acting through the attorney general, may file suit to enforce the subpoena in a district court in Travis County or in the county in which a hearing conducted by the commission may be held. The court, if it determines that good cause exists for the issuance of the subpoena, shall order compliance with the requirements of the subpoena. Failure to obey the order of the court may be punished by the court as contempt. *(Added by S.B. 842, effective September 1, 1993.)*

SECTION 15A. Repealed August 28, 1989.

SECTION 15B. (a) Notwithstanding any other provision of the Act, there shall be no undercover or covert investigations conducted by authority of this Act unless expressly authorized by the commission after due consideration of the circumstances and determination by the commission that such measures are necessary to carry out the purposes of this Act. No investigations of licensees or any other actions against licensees shall be initiated on the basis of anonymous complaints whether in writing or otherwise but shall be initiated only upon the commission's own motion or a signed written complaint from a person. Upon the adoption of such motion by the commission or upon receipt of such complaint, the licensee shall be notified promptly and in writing unless the commission itself, after due consideration, determines otherwise.

(b) In addition to any other authority granted by this Act, the commission may revoke or suspend a license, place on probation a person whose license has been suspended, or reprimand a licensee for a violation of this Act or a rule of the commission.

(c) The commission may, upon majority vote, rule that an order revoking, canceling, or suspending a license be probated upon reasonable terms and conditions determined by the commission. *(Added by S.B. No. 177, effective September 1, 1989.)*

(d) If a license suspension or revocation is probated, the commission may require the licensee:

(1) to report regularly to the commission on matters that are the basis of the probation;

(2) to limit practice to the area prescribed by the commission; or

(3) to continue to renew professional education until the licensee attains a degree of skill satisfactory to the commission in those areas that are the basis of the probation.

(e) The commission may authorize a commission employee to file a signed written complaint against a licensee and to conduct an investigation if:

(1) a judgment against the licensee has been paid from a recovery fund established under this Act;

(2) the licensee is convicted of a criminal offense that may constitute grounds for the suspension or revocation of the licensee's license; or

(3) the licensee fails to make good a check issued to the commission.

SECTION 15C. (Amended by S.B. No. 489, effective January 1, 1996) (a) A licensee under this Act who represents a party in a proposed real estate transaction shall disclose that representation at the time of the licensee's first contact with:

(1) another party to the transaction; or

(2) another licensee who represents another party to the transaction.

(b) The disclosure required under Subsection (a) of this section may be made orally or in writing.

(c) A licensee who represents a party in a real estate transaction acts as that party's agent.

(d) Except as provided by Subsection (e) of this section, a licensee shall furnish to a party in a real estate transaction at the time of the first face-to-face meeting with the party the following written statement:

"Before working with a real estate broker, you should know that the duties of a broker depend on whom the broker represents. If you are a prospective seller or landlord (owner) or a prospective buyer or tenant (buyer), you should know that the broker who lists the property for sale or lease is the owner's agent. A broker who acts as a subagent represents the owner in cooperation with the listing broker. A broker who acts as a buyer's agent represents the buyer. A broker may act as an intermediary between the parties if the parties consent in writing. A broker can assist you in locating a property, preparing a contract or lease, or obtaining financing without representing you. A broker is obligated by law to treat you honestly.

"IF THE BROKER REPRESENTS THE OWNER: The broker becomes the owner's agent by entering into an agreement with the owner, usually through a written listing agreement, or by agreeing to act as a subagent by accepting an offer of subagency from the listing broker. A subagent may work in a different real estate office. A listing broker or subagent can assist the buyer but does not represent the buyer and must place the interests of the owner first. The buyer should not tell the owner's agent anything the buyer would not want the owner to know because an owner's agent must disclose to the owner any material information known to the agent.

"IF THE BROKER REPRESENTS THE BUYER: The broker becomes the buyer's agent by entering into an agreement to represent the buyer, usually through a written buyer representation agreement. A buyer's agent can assist the owner but does not represent the owner and must place the interests of the buyer first. The owner should not tell a buyer's agent anything the owner would not want the buyer to know because a buyer's agent must disclose to the buyer any material information known to the agent.

"IF THE BROKER ACTS AS AN INTERMEDIARY: A broker may act as an intermediary between the parties if the broker complies with The Texas Real Estate License Act. The broker must obtain the written consent of each party to the transaction to act as an intermediary. The written consent must state who will pay the broker and, in conspicuous bold or underlined print, set forth the broker's obligations as an intermediary. The broker is required to treat each party honestly and fairly and to comply with The Texas Real Estate License Act. A broker who acts as an intermediary in a transaction:

(1) shall treat all parties honestly;

(2) may not disclose that the owner will accept a price less than the asking price unless authorized in writing to do so by the owner;

(3) may not disclose that the buyer will pay a price greater than the price submitted in a written offer unless authorized in writing to do so by the buyer; and

(4) may not disclose any confidential information or any information that a party specifically instructs the broker in writing not to disclose unless authorized in writing to disclose the information or required to do so by The Texas Real Estate License Act or a court order or if the information materially relates to the condition of the property. With the parties' consent, a broker acting as an intermediary between the parties may appoint a person who is licensed under The Texas Real Estate License Act and associated with the broker to communicate with and carry out instructions of one party and another person who is licensed under that Act and associated with the broker to communicate with and carry out instructions of the other party.

"If you choose to have a broker represent you, you should enter into a written agreement with the broker that clearly establishes the broker's obligations and your obligations. The agreement should state how and by whom the broker will be paid. You have the right to choose the type of representation, if any, you wish to receive. Your payment of a fee to a broker does not necessarily establish that the broker represents you. If you have any questions regarding the duties and responsibilities of the broker, you should resolve those questions before proceeding."

(e) A licensee is not required to provide the written information under Subsection (d) of this section if:

(1) the proposed transaction is for a residential lease for not more than one year and no sale is being considered; or

(2) the licensee meets with a party who is represented by another licensee.

(f) In the written information required to be provided under Subsection (d) of this section, the licensee may substitute the word "buyer" with "tenant" and "seller" with "landlord" as appropriate.

(g) The written information required to be provided under Subsection (d) of this section may be printed in any format that uses at least 10-point type.

(h) A real estate broker may act as an intermediary between the parties if:

(1) the real estate broker obtains written consent from each party to the transaction for the real estate broker to act as an intermediary in the transaction; and

(2) the written consent of the parties under Subdivision (1) of this subsection states the source of any expected compensation to the real estate broker.

(i) A written listing agreement to represent a seller or landlord or a written agreement to represent a buyer or tenant which also authorizes a real estate broker to act as an intermediary in a transaction is sufficient to establish written consent of the party to the transaction if the written agreement sets forth, in conspicuous bold or underlined print, the real estate broker's obligations under Subsection (j) of this section.

(j) A real estate broker who acts as an intermediary between parties in a transaction:

(1) may not disclose to the buyer or tenant that the seller or landlord will accept a price less than the asking price unless otherwise instructed in a separate writing by the seller or landlord;

(2) may not disclose to the seller or landlord that the buyer or tenant will pay a price greater than the price submitted in a written offer to the seller or landlord unless otherwise instructed in a separate writing by the buyer or tenant;

(3) may not disclose any confidential information or any information a party specifically instructs the real

estate broker in writing not to disclose unless otherwise instructed in a separate writing by the respective party or required to disclose such information by this Act or a court order or if the information materially relates to the condition of the property ;

(4) shall treat all parties to the transaction honestly; and

(5) shall comply with this Act.

(k) If a real estate broker obtains the consent of the parties to act as an intermediary in a transaction in compliance with this section, the real estate broker may appoint, by providing written notice to the parties, one or more licensees associated with the broker to communicate with and carry out instructions of one party and one or more other licensees associated with the broker to communicate with and carry out instructions of the other party or parties. A real estate broker may appoint a licensee to communicate with and carry out instructions of a party under this subsection only if the written consent of the parties under Subsection (h) or (i) of this section authorizes the broker to make the appointment. The real estate broker and the appointed licensees shall comply with Subsection (j) of this section. However, during negotiations, an appointed licensee may provide opinions and advice to the party to whom the licensee is appointed.

(l) The duties of a licensee acting as an intermediary provided by this section supersede and are in lieu of a licensee's duties under common law or any other law.

(m) In this section:

(1) "Face-to-face meeting" means a meeting at which a substantive discussion occurs with respect to specific real property. The term does not include a meeting that occurs at a property being held open for prospective purchasers or tenants or a meeting that occurs after the parties to the transaction have signed a contract to sell, buy, rent, or lease the real property concerned.

(2) "Intermediary" means a broker who is employed to negotiate a transaction between the parties subject to the obligations in Subsection (j) of this section and for that purpose may be an agent of the parties to the transaction. The intermediary shall act fairly so as not to favor one party over the other. Appointment by the intermediary of associated licensees under Subsection (k) of this section to communicate with, carry out instructions of, and provide opinions and advice to the parties to whom the licensees are appointed is a fair and

impartial act.

(3) "Licensee" means a real estate broker or real estate salesperson and includes a licensed associate of a licensee.

(4) "Party" means a prospective buyer, seller, landlord, or tenant or an authorized representative of a party, including a trustee, guardian, executor, administrator, receiver, or attorney-in-fact. The term does not include a licensee who represents a party.

(5) "Subagent" means a licensee who represents a principal through cooperation with and consent of a broker representing the principal and who is not sponsored by or associated with the principal's broker.

SECTION 15D. No licensed real estate broker, licensed real estate salesperson, or not for profit real estate board or association which provides information about real property sales prices or terms of sale for the purpose of facilitating the listing, selling, leasing, financing, or appraisal of real property shall be liable to any other person as a result of so providing such information unless the disclosure of same is otherwise specifically prohibited by statute.

SECTION 15E. Notwithstanding any other provision of this Act or any other law, a licensee shall have no duty to inquire about, make a disclosure related to, or release information related to whether a:

(1) previous or current occupant of real property had, may have had, has, or may have AIDS, HIV-related illnesses, or HIV infection as defined by the Centers for Disease Control of the U.S. Public Health Service; or

(2) death occurred on a property by natural causes, suicide, or accident unrelated to the condition of the property.

SECTION 15F. *(Added by S.B. 489, effective January 1, 1996)* (a) A party is not liable for a misrepresentation or a concealment of a material fact made by a licensee in a real estate transaction unless the party knew of the falsity of the misrepresentation or concealment and failed to disclose the party's knowledge of the falsity of the misrepresentation or concealment.

(b) A licensee is not liable for a misrepresentation or a concealment of a material fact made by a party in a real estate transaction unless the licensee knew of the falsity of the misrepresentation or concealment and failed to disclose the licensee's knowledge of the falsity of the misrepresentation or concealment.

(c) A party or a licensee is not liable for a misrepresentation or a concealment of a material fact made by a subagent in a real estate transaction unless the party or licensee knew of the falsity of the misrepresentation or concealment and failed to disclose the party's or licensee's knowledge of the falsity of the misrepresentation or concealment.

(d) The provisions of this section shall prevail over common law and any other law. This section does not diminish a real estate broker's responsibility for the acts or omissions of the broker's salespersons associated with or acting for the real estate broker, as provided by Section 1 of this Act.

(e) In this section, "licensee," "subagent," and "party" have the meaning assigned to those terms by Section 15C of this Act.

SECTION 16. (a) A license or registration granted under the provisions of this Act shall be suspended or revoked by the commission on proof that the licensee or registrant, not being licensed and authorized to practice law in this state, for a consideration, reward, pecuniary benefit, present or anticipated, direct or indirect, or in connection with or as a part of the licensee's employment, agency, or fiduciary relationship as a licensee, drew a deed, note, deed of trust, will, or other written instrument that may transfer or anywise affect the title to or an interest in land, except as provided in the subsections below, or advised or counseled a person as to the validity or legal sufficiency of an instrument or as to the validity of title to real estate.

(b) Notwithstanding the provisions of this Act or any other law, the completion of contract forms which bind the sale, exchange, option, lease, or rental of any interest in real property by a registrant under Section 9A of this Act, a real estate broker, or a real estate salesperson incident to the performance of the acts of a broker as defined by this Act does not constitute the unauthorized or illegal practice of law in this state, provided the forms have been promulgated for use by the commission for the particular kind of transaction involved, or the forms have been prepared by an attorney at law licensed by this state and approved by said attorney for the particular kind of transaction involved, or the forms have been prepared by the property owner or prepared by an attorney and required by the property owner.

(c) A Texas Real Estate Broker-Lawyer Committee is hereby created which, in addition to other powers and duties delegated to it, shall draft and revise contract forms capable of standardization for use by real estate licensees and which will expedite real estate transactions and reduce controversies to a minimum while containing safeguards adequate to protect the interests of the principals to the transaction.

(d) The Texas Real Estate Broker-Lawyer Committee shall have 12 members including six members appointed by the commission and six members of the State Bar of Texas appointed by the President of the State Bar of Texas. The members of the committee shall hold office for staggered terms of six years with the terms of two commission appointees and two State Bar appointees expiring every two years. Each member shall hold office until the member's successor is appointed. A vacancy for any cause shall be filled for the expired term by the agency making the original appointment. Appointments to the committee shall be made without regard to race, creed, sex, religion, or national origin.

(e) In the best interest of the public the commission may adopt rules and regulations requiring real estate brokers and salespersons to use contract forms which have been prepared by the Texas Real Estate Broker-Lawyer Committee and promulgated by the commission; provided, however, that the commission shall not prohibit a real estate broker or salesperson from using a contract form or forms binding the sale, exchange, option, lease, or rental of any interest in real property which have been prepared by the property owner or prepared by an attorney and required by the property owner. For the purpose of this section, contract forms prepared by the Texas Real Estate Broker-Lawyer Committee appointed by the commission and the State Bar of Texas and promulgated by the commission prior to the effective date of this Act shall be deemed to have been prepared by the Texas Real Estate Broker-Lawyer Committee. The commission may suspend or revoke a license issued under the provisions of this article when it has determined that the licensee failed to use a contract form as required by the commission pursuant to this section.

SECTION 17. (a) If the commission proposes to suspend or revoke a person's license or registration, the person is entitled to a hearing before the commission or a hearings officer appointed by the commission. The commission shall prescribe procedures by which all decisions to suspend or revoke are made by or are appealable to the commission. The commission shall prescribe the time and place of the hearing. However, the hearing shall be held, if the licensee so desires, within the county where the licensee has the licensee's principal place of business, or if the licensee is a nonresident, the hearing may be called for and held in any county within this state. The hearing is governed by the procedures for a contested case under Chapter 2001, Government Code.

(b) The commission may issue subpoenas for the attendance of witnesses and the production of records or documents. Process issued by the commission may extend to all parts of the state and may be served by any person designated by the commission.

SECTION 18. A person aggrieved by a ruling, order, or decision of the commission has the right to appeal to a district court in the county where the hearing was held, and an appeal is governed by the procedures under the Administrative Procedure and Texas Register Act (Article 6252-13a, Vernon's Texas Civil Statutes).

SECTION 18A. (a) Any listing contract form adopted by the commission relating to the contractual obligations between a seller of real estate and a real estate broker or salesperson acting as an agent for the seller shall include a section that informs the parties to the contract that real estate commissions are negotiable.

(b) When appropriate to the form, it shall include a section explaining the availability of Texas coastal natural hazards information important to coastal residents.

SECTION 18B. (a) If a person files a complaint with the commission relating to a real estate broker or salesperson, the commission shall furnish to the person an explanation of the remedies that are available to the person under this Act and information about appropriate state or local agencies or officials with which the person may file a complaint. The commission shall furnish the same explanation and information to the person against whom the complaint is filed.

(b) The commission shall keep an information file about each complaint filed with the commission that the commission has authority to resolve.

(c) If a written complaint is filed with the commission that the commission has authority to resolve, the commission, at least quarterly and until final disposition of the complaint, shall notify the parties to the complaint of the status of the complaint unless the notice would jeopardize an undercover investigation authorized under Subsection (a) of Section 15B of this Act.

SECTION 18C. Repealed September 1, 1991.

SECTION 19. *(Amended by S.B. No. 577, effective January 1, 1998)* (a) A person acting as a real estate broker or real estate salesperson without first obtaining a license or a person required to register under Section 9A of this Act who sells, purchases, leases, or transfers a right-of-way or easement without first obtaining a certificate of registration under Section 9A of this Act is guilty of a misdemeanor and on conviction shall be punishable by a fine of not less than $100 nor more than $500, or by imprisonment in the county jail for a term not to exceed one year, or both; and if a person other than an individual, shall be punishable by a fine of not less than $1,000 nor more than $2,000. A person, on conviction of a second or subsequent offense, shall be punishable by a fine of not less than $500 nor more than $1,000, or by imprisonment for a term not to exceed two years, or both; and if a person other than an individual, shall be punishable by a fine of not less than $2,000 nor more than $5,000.

(b) In case a person received money, or the equivalent thereof, as a fee, commission, compensation, or profit by or in consequence of a violation of Subsection (a) of this section, the person shall, in addition, be liable to a penalty of not less than the amount of the sum of money so received and not more than three times the sum so received, as may be determined by the court, which penalty may be recovered in a court of competent jurisdiction by an aggrieved person.

(c) When in the judgment of the commission a person has engaged, or is about to engage, in an act or practice which constitutes or will constitute a violation of a provision of this Act, the county attorney or district attorney in the county in which the violation has occurred or is about to occur, or in the county of the defendant's residence, or the attorney general may maintain an action in the name of the State of Texas in the district court of such county to abate and temporarily and permanently enjoin the acts and practices and to enforce compliance with this Act. The plaintiff in an action under this subsection is not required to give a bond, and court costs may not be adjudged against the plaintiff.

(d) Notwithstanding any other provision of this section, this Act, or any other law, if, in the judgment of the commission, a person has engaged or is about to engage in an act or practice that constitutes or will constitute a violation of this Act, the commission, acting through the attorney general, may maintain an action in the name of the state in district court in the county in which the violation has occurred or is about to occur, or in the county of the defendant's residence, to abate and temporarily or permanently enjoin those acts or practices and to enforce compliance with this Act. In an action under this subsection the commission is not required to give bond, and court costs may not be recovered against the commission. In addition to injunctive relief the commission may recover court costs, reasonable attorney's fees, and a civil penalty, payable to the state if a person received money or other consideration as a fee, commission, compensation, or profit by or in consequence of a violation of Subsection (a) of this section. The court shall set the civil penalty in an amount not less than the amount of the money so received, but not more than three times the amount so received.

SECTION 19A. (a) If a person licensed under this Act violates this Act or a rule or order adopted by the commission under this Act, the commission may assess an administrative penalty against the person as provided by this section.

(b) The penalty for each violation shall be set in an amount not to exceed $1,000.

(c) In determining the amount of the penalty, the administrator named under Subsection (i) of Section 5 of this Act shall consider:

(1) the seriousness of the violation, including the nature, circumstances, extent, and gravity of the prohibited acts;

(2) the history of previous violations;

(3) the amount necessary to deter future violations;

(4) efforts to correct the violation; and

(5) any other matter that justice may require.

(d) If, after investigation of a possible violation and the facts surrounding that possible violation, the administrator determines that a violation has occurred, the administrator may issue a violation report stating the facts on which the conclusion that a violation occurred is based, recommending that an administrative penalty under this section be imposed on the person charged, and recommending the amount of that proposed penalty. The administrator shall base the recommended amount of the proposed penalty on the seriousness of the violation determined by the consideration of the factors set forth in Subsection (c) of this section.

(e) Not later than the 14th day after the date on which the report is issued, the administrator shall give written notice of the report to the person charged. The notice shall include a brief summary of the charges, a statement of the amount of the penalty recommended, and a statement of the right of the person charged to a hearing on the occurrence of the violation or the amount of the penalty, or both the occurrence of the violation and the amount of the penalty.

(f) Not later than the 20th day after the date on which notice is received, the person charged may accept the determination of the administrator made under Subsection (d) of this section, including the recommended penalty, or make a written request for a hearing on the determination.

(g) If the person charged with the violation accepts the determination of the administrator, the commission shall issue an order approving the determination and ordering the payment of the recommended penalty.

(h) If the person charged requests a hearing or fails to timely respond to the notice, the administrator shall set a hearing and give notice of the hearing. The hearing shall be held by a hearing examiner designated by the administrator. The hearing examiner shall make findings of fact and conclusions of law and promptly issue to the commission a proposal for decision as to the occurrence of the violation, including a recommendation as to the amount of the proposed penalty if a penalty is warranted. Based on the findings of fact, conclusions of law, and recommendations of the hearing examiner, the commission by order may find a violation has occurred and may assess a penalty or may find that no violation has occurred. All proceedings under this subsection are subject to the Administrative Procedure and Texas Register Act (Article 6252-13a, Vernon's Texas Civil Statutes).

(i) The administrator shall give notice of the commission's order to the person charged. The notice shall include:

(1) the findings of fact and conclusions of law separately stated;

(2) the amount of the penalty ordered, if any;

(3) a statement of the right of the person charged to judicial review of the commission's order, if any; and

(4) other information required by law.

(j)   Within the 30-day period immediately following the date on which the order becomes final as provided by Subsection (c), Section 16, Administrative Procedure and Texas Register Act (Article 6252-13a, Vernon's Texas Civil Statutes), the person charged with the penalty shall:

(1) pay the penalty in full; or

(2) if the person files a petition for judicial review contesting either the amount of the penalty or the fact of the violation or contesting both the fact of the violation and the amount of the penalty:

(A) forward the amount to the administrator for placement in an escrow account; or

(B)   in lieu of payment into escrow, post with the administrator a supersedeas bond in a form approved by the administrator for the amount of the penalty, the bond to be effective until all judicial review of the order or decision is final.

(k)   If a person charged is financially unable either to forward the amount of the penalty for placement in an escrow account or post a supersedeas bond for the amount of the penalty, the person may satisfy the requirements of Subdivision (2) of Subsection (j) of this section by filing with the administrator an affidavit sworn by the person charged, stating that the person is financially unable either to forward the amount of the penalty or post a bond.

(l)   Failure to forward the money to or to post the bond or file the affidavit with the administrator within the time provided by Subsection (j) of this section results in a waiver of all legal rights to judicial review. Also, if the person charged fails to pay the penalty in full as provided under Subdivision (1) of Subsection (j) of this section or forward the money, post the bond, or file the affidavit as provided by Subsection (j) or (k) of this

section, the administrator may forward the matter to the attorney general for enforcement.

(m)   Judicial review of the order or decision of the commission assessing the penalty shall be under the substantial evidence rule and shall be instituted by filing a petition with a district court in Travis County, as provided by Section 19, Administrative Procedure and Texas Register Act (Article 6252-13a, Vernon's Texas Civil Statutes).

(n)   If the penalty is reduced or not assessed by the court, the administrator shall remit to the person charged the appropriate amount plus accrued interest if the penalty has been paid or shall execute a release of the bond if a supersedeas bond has been posted.   The accrued interest on amounts remitted by the administrator under this subsection shall be paid at a rate equal to the rate charged on loans to depository institutions by the New York Federal Reserve Bank and shall be paid for the period beginning on the date the penalty is paid to the administrator under Subsection (j) of this section and ending on the date the penalty is remitted.

(o)   A penalty collected under this section for a violation by a person licensed as a real estate broker or salesperson shall be deposited in the real estate recovery fund.   A penalty collected under this section for a violation by a person licensed or registered as a real estate inspector shall be deposited in the real estate inspection recovery fund.

SECTION 20.   (a)   A person may not bring or maintain an action for the collection of compensation for the performance in this state of an act set forth in Section 2 of this Act without alleging and proving that the person performing the brokerage services was a duly licensed real estate broker or salesperson at the time the alleged services were commenced, or was a duly licensed attorney at law in this state or in any other state.

(b) An action may not be brought in a court in this state for the recovery of a commission for the sale or purchase of real estate unless the promise or agreement on which the action is brought, or some memorandum thereof, is in writing and signed by the party to be charged or signed by a person lawfully authorized by the party to sign it.

(c) When an offer to purchase real estate in this state is signed, the real estate broker or salesperson shall advise the purchaser or purchasers, in writing, that the purchaser or purchasers should have the abstract covering the real estate which is the subject of the contract examined by an attorney of the purchaser's own selection, or that the purchaser or purchasers should be furnished with or obtain a policy of title insurance. Failure to advise the purchaser as provided in this subsection precludes the payment of or recovery of any commission agreed to be paid on the sale.

(d) This section does not apply to an agreement to share compensation between persons licensed under this Act. This section does not limit a cause of action between brokers for interference with business relationships.

SECTION 21.   Repealed September 1, 1991.

SECTION 22.   Repealed July 1, 1991.

SECTION 23.   REAL ESTATE INSPECTORS.

(a) DEFINITIONS. In this section:

(1) "Apprentice inspector" means a person who is in training under the direct supervision of a professional inspector or a real estate inspector to become qualified to perform real estate inspections.

(2) "Committee" means the Texas Real Estate Inspector Committee.

(3) "Core real estate inspection courses" means educational courses approved by the commission, including but not limited to structural, electrical, mechanical, plumbing, roofing, business, legal, standards of practice, report writing, appliances or ethics, all of which must relate to a real estate inspection.

(4) "Direct supervision" means the instruction and control by a professional inspector or real estate inspector licensed under this section who is:

(A) responsible for the actions of an individual performing a real estate inspection or preparing a report of a real estate inspection;

(B)   available if and when needed to consult with or assist an individual performing a real estate inspection or preparing a report of a real estate inspection; and

(C)   physically present at the time and place of the inspection.

(5) "Indirect supervision" means the instruction and control by a professional inspector licensed under this section who is:

(A) responsible for the actions of an individual performing or preparing a real estate inspection; and

(B)   available if and when needed to consult with or assist an individual performing a real estate inspection or preparing a report of a real estate inspection, but who is not required to be physically present at the time and place of the inspection.

(6) "Inspector" means a person who is licensed as an apprentice inspector, real estate inspector, or professional inspector under this section.

(7)   "License" means an apprentice license, a real estate inspector license or a professional inspector license issued under this section.

(8)   "Licensee" means a person holding an apprentice inspector license, a real estate inspector license or a professional inspector license issued under this section.

(9)   "Professional inspector" means a person who represents to the public that the person is trained and qualified to perform a real estate inspection and who accepts employment for the purpose of performing a real estate inspection for a buyer or seller of real property.

(10)   "Real estate inspection" means a written or oral opinion as to the condition of the improvements to real property, including structural items, electrical items, mechanical systems, plumbing systems, or equipment.

(11)   "Real estate inspector" means a person who represents to the public that the person is trained and qualified to perform real estate inspections under the indirect supervision of a professional inspector and who accepts employment for the purpose of performing a real estate inspection for a buyer or seller of real property.

(b) TEXAS   REAL   ESTATE   INSPECTOR COMMITTEE. (1) The Texas Real Estate Inspector Committee is created. In addition to other powers and duties delegated to it by the commission, the committee shall recommend:

(A) rules for the licensing of inspectors in this state in accordance with this section;

(B)   rules relating to the education and experience requirements for licensing as an inspector under this section;

(C)   rules relating to the qualifying examination required for licensing as an inspector under this section;

(D) rules establishing a code of professional conduct and ethics for an inspector under this section;

(E)   reasonable fees to implement this section, including an application fee for licensing, an examination fee, a renewal fee for a license, and any other fee required by law;

(F) rules relating to continuing education requirements for a licensed inspector;

(G) rules relating to the standards of practice for a real estate inspection;

(H) rules relating to granting or denying an application for the licensing of an inspector;

(I) the form and format for any applications and forms required under this section; and

(J) any other action by the commission as may provide a high degree of service and protection to the public when dealing with licensed inspectors.

(2) The committee is composed of nine members appointed by the commission. The members of the committee hold office for staggered terms of six years, with the terms of three members expiring February 1 of each odd-numbered year. Each member holds office until the member's successor is appointed. Appointments to the committee shall be made without regard to the sex, race, color, age, handicap, religion, or national origin of the appointees. In the event of a vacancy during a term, the commission shall appoint a replacement who meets the qualifications for appointment under this subdivision to fill the unexpired part of the term. A member of the committee must be a professional inspector actively engaged in the practice of real estate inspecting at the time of appointment and must have been primarily engaged in the practice of real estate inspecting for at least five years before the member's appointment. No more than three members of the committee may hold a real estate broker license. Each member of the committee is entitled to a per diem allowance and to reimbursement of travel expenses necessarily incurred in performing functions as a member of the committee, subject to any applicable limitation in the General Appropriations Act. The committee shall annually elect from its members a chairperson, a vice-chairperson, and secretary. A quorum of the committee consists of five members.

(3) The commission may remove a committee member if the member:

(A) does not have at the time of appointment the qualifications required by Subdivision (2) or this subsection;

(B) cannot discharge the member's duties for a substantial part of the term for which the member is appointed because of illness or disability; or

(C) is absent from more than half of the regularly scheduled committee meetings that the member is eligible to attend during each year, unless the absence is excused by the committee.

(4) The validity of an action of the committee is not affected by the fact that it was taken when a ground for removal of a committee member exists.

(5) If the administrator of the commission has knowledge that a potential ground for removal exists, the administrator shall notify the chairperson of the commission that a potential ground exists.

(6) The commission shall adopt procedural rules to be used by the committee in implementing its powers and duties.

(7) The committee is subject to the open meetings law, Chapter 271, Acts of the 60th Legislature, Regular Session, 1967 (Article 6252-17, Vernon's Texas Civil Statutes), the open records law, Chapter 424, Acts of the 63rd Legislature, Regular Session, 1973 (Article 6252-17a, Vernon's Texas Civil Statutes), and the Administrative Procedure and Texas Register Act (Article 6252-13a, Vernon's Texas Civil Statutes).

(8) The committee shall meet semiannually and at the call of the commission. The committee may also meet at the call of a majority of its members.

(9) The committee shall act in an advisory capacity to develop and recommend to the commission rules under this section. The committee shall review commission rules relating to this section and recommend changes in the rules to the commission. The commission shall submit all proposed rules, all proposed rule changes and all requests for proposed rules or rule changes that relate to the regulation and licensing of inspectors under this section to the committee for development or recommendation. The commission may modify the rules developed by the committee if the commission finds such modifications are in the public interest. This section does not prohibit the commission from developing and adopting rules relating to the regulation and licensing of inspectors under this section if the committee fails to develop or recommend rules under this section within a reasonable period of time

after the commission submits the proposed rules, rule changes or requests for proposed rules or rule changes to the committee. If the committee determines that a rule requested by the commission should not be developed or recommended for adoption by the commission, the committee shall submit a report on the matter to the commission. The chairperson of the commission and the chairperson of the committee shall then appoint three members each from their respective bodies to meet as an ad hoc committee to consider the report and recommend possible action by the commission. The chairperson of the commission or a member of the commission designated by the chairperson shall serve as the seventh member of the ad hoc committee. At least one member of the ad hoc committee must be a public member of the commission.

(c) LICENSE REQUIRED. (1) A person may not act as a professional inspector in this state for a buyer or seller of real property unless the person possesses a professional inspector license issued under this section.

(2) A person may not act or attempt to act as a real estate inspector in this state for a buyer or seller of real property unless the person possesses a real estate inspector license issued under this section and is under the indirect supervision of a professional inspector.

(3) A person may not act or attempt to act as an apprentice inspector in this state for a buyer or seller of real property unless the person is licensed under this section and is under the direct supervision of a real estate inspector or professional inspector.

(d) ELIGIBILITY; APPLICATION. (1) To be eligible for a license as an apprentice inspector, an applicant must be an individual, a citizen of the United States or a lawfully admitted alien, and a resident of this state at the time of the filing of the application. The applicant must be sponsored by a professional inspector licensed under this section. The applicant must be at least 18 years old. The applicant must satisfy the commission as to the applicant's honesty, trustworthiness, and integrity.

(2) To be eligible for a license as a real estate inspector, an applicant must have met the requirements and been licensed as an apprentice inspector for at least three months and have performed at least 25 real estate inspections under direct supervision before filing an application. The applicant must satisfy the commission

as to the applicant's honesty, trustworthiness, integrity, and competency. An applicant for an original real estate inspector license must submit satisfactory evidence to the commission of successful completion of not less than 90 classroom hours of core real estate inspection courses. The commission by rule may specify the length and content of the core real estate inspection courses required by this subdivision. The commission shall determine the competency of an applicant on the basis of an examination required by Subsection (i) of this section. The applicant must be sponsored by a professional inspector licensed under this section. Notwithstanding this subdivision of this subsection, an applicant is eligible for and has satisfied all requirements for a license as a real estate inspector if the applicant was previously licensed as a real estate inspector during the preceding 24-month period immediately preceding the filing of the application, the applicant is sponsored by a professional inspector, and the applicant satisfies the commission as to the applicant's honesty, trustworthiness, and integrity.

(3) To be eligible for a license as a professional inspector, an applicant must have met the requirements and have been licensed as an apprentice inspector for at least three months and licensed as a real estate inspector for at least 12 months and have performed at least 175 real estate inspections under indirect supervision before filing an application. An applicant for an original professional inspector license must submit satisfactory evidence to the commission of successful completion of not less than 30 classroom hours of core real estate inspection courses and eight classroom hours related to the study of standards of practice, legal issues, or ethics related to the profession of real estate inspections. These classroom hours are in addition to those required for an apprentice inspector license or a real estate inspector license. The commission shall determine the competency of an applicant on the basis of an examination required by Subsection (i) of this section. Notwithstanding this subsection, an applicant is eligible for and has satisfied all requirements for a license as a professional inspector if the applicant was previously licensed as a professional inspector during the preceding 24-month period immediately preceding the filing of the application and the applicant satisfies the commission as to the applicant's honesty, trustworthiness, and integrity.

(4) The commission by rule shall provide for the substitution of relevant experience or additional education in lieu of the number of real estate inspections required by this section and in lieu of the requirement

that the applicant be licensed as an apprentice inspector or a real estate inspector before issuance of a license as a real estate inspector or professional inspector. The rules adopted by the commission under this subdivision may not require an applicant to complete more than 60 additional classroom hours of core real estate inspection courses.

(5) An applicant must file an application for a license with the commission on forms prescribed by the commission.

(6) Before a licensed professional inspector may sponsor an apprentice inspector or a real estate inspector, the professional inspector must provide sufficient proof to the commission that the professional inspector has completed not less than 200 real estate inspections while licensed as a professional inspector under this Act.

(e) ISSUANCE OF LICENSE. The commission shall issue an apprentice license, a real estate inspector license, or a professional inspector license to an applicant who possesses the required qualifications, passes the appropriate examination if required, and pays the fee required by Subdivision (2) of Subsection (o) of this section.

(f) EXPIRATION OF LICENSE; RENEWAL.
(1) A license issued under this section expires one year after the date it is issued.

(2) A person may renew an unexpired license by paying to the commission before the expiration date of the license the required renewal fee.

(3) If a person's license has been expired for 90 days or less, the person may renew the license by paying to the commission the required renewal fee and a fee that is one-half of the examination fee, if any, for the registration or license.

(4) If a person's license has been expired for longer than 90 days but less than one year, the person may renew the license by paying to the commission all unpaid renewal fees and a fee that is equal to the examination fee, if any, for the license.

(5) If a person's license has been expired for one year or longer, the person may not renew the license. The person may obtain a new license by submitting to reexamination, if required, and complying with the requirements and procedures for obtaining an original

license. However, the commission may renew without reexamination an expired license of a person who was licensed in this state, moved to another state, and is currently licensed and has been in practice in the other state for the one year preceding application. The person must pay to the commission a fee that is equal to the examination fee for the license.

(6) At least 30 days before the expiration of a person's license, the commission shall send written notice of the impending license expiration to the person at the person's last known address according to the records of the commission.

(g) CHANGE OF ADDRESS. A licensee under this section shall notify the commission and pay the required fee within 30 days after the date a change of place of business occurs.

(h) FEES. (1) The commission shall charge and collect reasonable and necessary fees to recover the cost of administering this section as follows:

(A) a fee not to exceed $75 for the filing of an original application for a license as an apprentice inspector;

(B) a fee not to exceed $125 for the filing of an original application for a license as a real estate inspector;

(C) a fee not to exceed $150 for the filing of an original application for a license as a professional inspector;

(D) a fee not to exceed $125 for the annual license renewal of an apprentice inspector;

(E) a fee not to exceed $175 for the annual license renewal of a real estate inspector;

(F) a fee not to exceed $200 for the annual license renewal of a professional inspector;

(G) a fee not to exceed $100 for taking a license examination; and

(H) a fee not to exceed $20 for a request for a change of place of business or to replace a lost or destroyed license.

(2) All fees may be paid by cash, check, cashier's

check, or money order.

(3)   The fees shall be reviewed annually and reduced to the extent that the costs of administering this section are funded by the real estate inspector regulation account established under Subdivision (4) of Subsection (o) of this section.

(i) EXAMINATION.   (1)   The commission shall prescribe the licensing examinations, which shall be prepared by or contracted for by the commission. A licensing examination shall evaluate competency in the subject matter of all required core real estate inspection courses. The licensing examination shall be offered not less often than once every two months in Austin. If a license applicant fails the examination, the applicant may apply for reexamination by filing a request with the commission and paying the examination fee. Each license applicant must satisfy the examination requirement not later than six months after the date on which the license application is filed. A license applicant who fails to satisfy the examination requirement within six months after the date on which the license application is filed must submit a new license application with the commission and pay the examination fee to be eligible for examination.   If a license applicant fails the examination three consecutive times in connection with the same application, the applicant may not apply for reexamination or submit a new license application with the commission for six months from the date he failed the last examination.

(2) Not later than the 30th day after the date on which a licensing examination is administered under this section, the commission shall notify each examinee of the results of the examination. However, if an examination is graded or reviewed by a national testing service, the commission shall notify examinees of the results of the examination not later than the 14th day after the date on which the commission receives the results from the testing service. If the notice of examination results graded or reviewed by a national testing service will be delayed for longer than 90 days after the examination date, the commission shall notify the examinee of the reason for the delay before the 90th day.

(3) If requested in writing by a person who fails a licensing examination administered under this section, the commission shall furnish the person with an analysis of the person's performance on the examination.

(j)   WAIVER FOR OUT-OF-STATE APPLICANTS.

The commission may waive any license requirement for an applicant with a valid license from another state having license requirements substantially equivalent to those of this state.

(k) CONTINUING EDUCATION PROGRAMS. The commission shall recognize, prepare, or administer continuing education programs for inspectors. Participation in the programs is mandatory. A real estate inspector must submit satisfactory evidence to the commission of successful completion of at least four classroom hours of core real estate inspection courses annually before a license renewal is issued.   A professional inspector must submit satisfactory evidence to the commission of successful completion of at least eight classroom hours of core related real estate inspection courses annually before a license renewal is issued.

(l)   Prohibited acts.   A professional inspector, real estate inspector or an apprentice inspector licensed under this section may not:

(1)   accept an assignment for real estate inspection if the employment or fee is contingent on the reporting of a specific, predetermined condition of the improvements to real property or is contingent on the reporting of specific findings other than those known by the inspector to be facts at the time of accepting the assignment;

(2)   act in a manner or engage in a practice that is dishonest or fraudulent or that involves deceit or misrepresentation;

(3)   perform a real estate inspection in a negligent or incompetent manner;

(4)   act in the dual capacity of inspector and undisclosed principal in a transaction;

(5)   act in the dual capacity of inspector and real estate broker or salesperson in a transaction;

(6)   perform or agree to perform any repairs or maintenance in connection with a real estate inspection pursuant to the provisions of any earnest money contract, lease agreement, or exchange of real estate; or

(7)   violate the rules adopted by the commission or any provisions of this section.

(m)   OFFENSES.   (1)   A person commits an offense

if the person knowingly or intentionally engages in the business of real estate inspecting without a license under this section or performs an inspection during a period in which the inspector's license is revoked or suspended.

(2) An offense under this subsection is a Class B misdemeanor.

(3) The commission may authorize the committee to conduct administrative hearings or recommend the entry of final orders, or both, in contested cases regarding a licensed inspector. The commission may authorize specific employees to conduct hearings and render final decisions in contested cases regarding a licensed inspector.

(4) The commission may investigate the actions of a licensed inspector and may, after notice and hearing in accordance with the provisions of Section 17 of this Act, reprimand, place on probation, suspend or revoke a license for a violation of this Act or a rule of the commission. If the commission revokes a license of a person, the person may not apply to the commission for one year after the revocation.

(n) EXEMPTIONS. This section does not apply to any electrician, plumber, carpenter, any person engaged in the business of structural pest control in compliance with the Texas Structural Pest Control Act (Article 135b-6, Vernon's Texas Civil Statutes), or any other person who repairs, maintains, or inspects improvements to real property and who does not represent to the public through personal solicitation or public advertising that the person is in the business of inspecting such improvements. The provisions of this section shall not be construed so as to prevent any person from performing any and all acts which the person is authorized to perform pursuant to a license or registration issued by this state or any governmental subdivision of this state.

(o) REAL ESTATE INSPECTION RECOVERY FUND. (1) The commission shall establish a real estate inspection recovery fund, which shall be set apart and maintained by the commission as provided by this subsection. The fund shall be used in the manner provided by this subsection for reimbursing aggrieved persons who suffer actual damages by reason of certain acts committed by a duly licensed inspector, provided the inspector was licensed by the State of Texas at the time the act was committed and provided recovery is ordered by a court of competent jurisdiction against the inspector. The use of the fund is limited to an act that is a violation of Subsection (1) of this section.

(2) When a person receives notice that he has successfully completed the licensing examination provided by Subsection (i) of this section, the person shall pay, in addition to any other fees required by this section, a fee not to exceed $200, which shall be deposited in the real estate inspection recovery fund prior to the commission's issuing the person an inspector license.

(3) If on December 31 of any year the balance remaining in the real estate inspection recovery fund is less than $300,000, each inspector, on the next renewal of the person's license, shall pay, in addition to the license renewal fee, a fee of $75, or a pro rata share of the amount necessary to bring the fund to $450,000, whichever is less, which shall be deposited in the real estate inspection recovery fund.

(4) If on December 31 of any year the balance remaining in the real estate inspection recovery fund is greater than $600,000, the amount in excess of $600,000 shall be transferred to a separate account in the general revenue fund to be known as the real estate inspector regulation account. The money in the real estate inspector regulation account may be used only for the payment of costs incurred by the commission in the regulation of inspectors.

(5) No action for a judgment that results in an order for collection from the real estate inspection recovery fund shall be started later than two years from the accrual of the cause of action. When an aggrieved person commences action for a judgment that may result in collection from the real estate inspection recovery fund, the inspector shall notify the commission in writing to this effect at the time of the commencement of the action.

(6) When an aggrieved person recovers a valid judgment in a court of competent jurisdiction against an inspector on the grounds described in Subdivision (1) of this subsection, the aggrieved person may, after final judgment has been entered, execution returned nulla bona, and a judgment lien perfected, file a verified claim in the court in which the judgment was entered and, on 20 days written notice to the commission and to the judgment debtor, may apply to the court where the judgment was rendered for an order directing payment out of the real estate inspection recovery fund of the

amount unpaid on the judgment, subject to the limitations stated in Subdivision (15) of this subsection.

(7) The court shall proceed on the application forthwith. On the hearing on the application, the aggrieved person is required to show:

(A) that the judgment is based on facts allowing recovery under Subdivision (1) of this subsection;

(B) that the person is not a spouse of the debtor, or the personal representative of the spouse and the person is not an inspector, as defined by this section;

(C) that the person has obtained a judgment under Subdivision (6) of this subsection that is not subject to a stay or discharge in bankruptcy, stating the amount of the judgment and the amount owing on the judgment at the date of the application;

(D) that based on the best information available, the judgment debtor lacks sufficient attachable assets in this state or any other state to satisfy the judgment; and

(E) the amount that may be realized from the sale of real or personal property or other assets liable to be sold or applied in satisfaction of the judgment and the balance remaining due on the judgment after application of the amount that may be realized.

(8) The court shall make an order directed to the commission requiring payment out of the real estate inspection recovery fund of whatever sum it finds to be payable on the claim, pursuant to and in accordance with the limitations contained in this subdivision, if the court is satisfied, on the hearing, of the truth of all matters required to be shown by the aggrieved person by Subdivision (7) of this subsection and that the aggrieved person has satisfied all of the requirements of Subdivisions (6) and (7) of this subsection. The commission may relitigate any issue material and relevant in the hearing on the application that was determined in the underlying action on which the judgment in favor of the applicant was based. If the court finds that the aggregate of claims against an inspector exceeds the limitations contained in this section, the court shall reduce proportionately the amount it finds payable on the claim.

(9) A recovery on the judgment against a single defendant made before payment from the real estate inspection recovery fund must be applied by the creditor first to actual damages.

(10) A license granted under the provisions of this section may be revoked by the commission on proof that the commission has made a payment from the real estate inspection recovery fund of any amount toward satisfaction of a judgment against a licensed inspector. The commission may probate an order revoking a license. No inspector is eligible to receive a new license until the person has repaid in full, plus interest at the current legal rate, the amount paid from the real estate inspection recovery fund on the person's account.

(11) The sums received by the commission for deposit in the real estate inspection recovery fund shall be held by the commission in trust for carrying out the purpose of the real estate inspection recovery fund. These funds may be invested and reinvested in the same manner as funds of the Employees Retirement System of Texas, and the interest from these investments shall be deposited to the credit of the real estate inspection recovery fund. However, investments may not be made that will impair the necessary liquidity required to satisfy judgment payments awarded pursuant to this subsection.

(12) When the commission receives notice of entry of a final judgment and a hearing is conducted under Subdivision (8) of this subsection, the commission may notify the Attorney General of Texas of the commission's desire to enter an appearance, file a response, appear at the court hearing, defend the action, or take whatever other action it deems appropriate. In taking such action the commission and the attorney general shall act only to protect the fund from spurious or unjust claims or to ensure compliance with the requirements for recovery under this subsection.

(13) When, on the order of the court, the commission has paid from the real estate inspection recovery fund any sum to the judgment creditor, the commission shall be subrogated to all of the rights of the judgment creditor to the extent of the amount paid. The judgment creditor shall assign all his right, title, and interest in the judgment up to the amount paid by the commission. The amount paid by the commission shall have priority for repayment in the event of any subsequent recovery on the judgment. Any amount in interest recovered by the commission on the judgment shall be deposited to the fund.

(14) The failure of an aggrieved person to comply

with the provisions of this subsection relating to the real estate inspection recovery fund shall constitute a waiver of any rights under this subsection.

(15) Notwithstanding any other provision, payments from the real estate inspection recovery fund are subject to the following conditions and limitations:

(A) payments may be made only pursuant to an order of a court of competent jurisdiction, as provided by Subdivision (6) of this subsection, and in the manner prescribed by this subsection;

(B) payments for claims, including attorney fees, interest, and court costs, arising out of the same transaction shall be limited in the aggregate to $7,500 regardless of the number of claimants; and

(C) payments for claims based on judgments against a licensed inspector may not exceed in the aggregate $15,000 until the fund has been reimbursed by the licensee for all amounts paid.

(16) Nothing contained in this subsection shall limit the authority of the commission to take disciplinary action against a person licensed under this section for a violation of this section or the rules of the commission, nor shall the repayment in full of all obligations to the real estate inspection recovery fund by a person nullify or modify the effect of any other disciplinary proceeding brought pursuant to this section.

(17) A person receiving payment out of the real estate inspection recovery fund under Subdivision (15) of this subsection shall be entitled to receive reasonable attorney fees as determined by the court, subject to the limitations stated in that subdivision.

(18) An inspector licensed under this section shall notify consumers and service recipients of the availability of the real estate inspection recovery fund established under this section for reimbursing certain aggrieved persons. The notice must include the name, mailing address, and telephone number of the commission and any other information required by commission rule. The notification may be provided:

(A) on a written contract for the services of an inspector;

(B) on a brochure distributed by an inspector;

(C) on a sign prominently displayed in the place of business of an inspector; or

(D) in a bill or receipt for service provided by an inspector.

(p) INACTIVE LICENSES. The commission by rule may adopt terms and conditions by which an inspector may apply for, renew, or place a license on inactive status and rules by which an inactive inspector may return to active status.

(q) The commission shall consider the recommendations of the Texas Real Estate Inspector Committee relating to the qualifications and licensure of inspectors to assure the public of a quality professional inspection system in real estate transactions in Texas.

(r) The commission by rule shall prescribe standard forms and adopt rules that require inspectors to use the forms to reduce discrepancies and create consistency in preparing reports of real estate inspections.

SECTION 24. RESIDENTIAL RENTAL LOCATORS. *(Added by S.B. No. 1334, effective January 1, 1996)* (a) In this section, "residential rental locator" means a person, other than the owner of the property or a person exempted by Section 3 of this Act, who offers, for consideration, to locate a unit in an apartment complex for lease to a prospective tenant.

(b) A person may not engage in business as a residential rental locator in this state unless the person holds a license issued under this Act to operate as a real estate broker or real estate salesperson and complies with the continuing education requirements under Section 7A of this Act.

(c) The commission by rule shall adopt regulations and establish standards relating to permissible forms of advertising by a person licensed under this section.

(d) Each residential rental locator shall post in a conspicuous place accessible to clients and prospective clients the locator's license, a statement that the locator is licensed by the commission, and the name, mailing address, and telephone number of the commission as provided by Section 5(q) of this Act.

(e) A violation of this section by a residential rental locator constitutes grounds under this Act for the suspension or revocation of the person's license and for the assessment of an administrative penalty under Section 19A of this Act.

(f) A person commits an offense if the person engages in business as a residential rental locator in this state without a license issued under this Act. An offense under this subsection is a Class B misdemeanor.

(g) Repealed September 1, 1997.

Appendix B

CANONS/TEXAS REAL ESTATE COMMISSION

Canons of Professional Ethics and Conduct for Brokers and Salesmen

Article 1:

Fidelity

A real estate broker or salesman, while acting as an agent for another, is a fiduciary. Special obligations are imposed when such fiduciary relationships are created. They demand:

(a) That the primary duty of the real estate agent is to represent the interests of his client, and his position, in this respect, should be clear to all parties concerned in a real estate transaction; that, however, the agent, in performing his duties to his client, shall treat other parties to a transaction fairly;

(b) that the real estate agent be faithful and observant to trust placed in him, and be scrupulous and meticulous in performing his functions;

(c) that the real estate agent place no personal interest above that of his client.

Article 2:

Integrity

A real estate broker or salesman has a special obligation to exercise integrity in the discharge of his responsibilities, including employment of prudence and caution so as to avoid misrepresentation, in any wise, by acts of commission or omission.

Article 3:

Competency

It is the obligation of a real estate agent to be knowledgeable as a real estate brokerage practitioner. He should

(a) be informed on market conditions affecting the real estate business and pledged to continuing education in the intricacies involved in marketing real estate for others;

(b) be informed on national, state and local issues and developments in the real estate industry;

(c) exercise judgment and skill in the performance of his work.

Appendix C

REAL ESTATE MATH REVIEW
PERCENT

Percent (%) means part per hundred. For example, 25% means 25 parts per hundred; 10% means 10 parts per hundred. Percentages are related to common and decimal fractions as follows:

$$5\% \quad = \quad 0.05 \quad = \quad {}^{1}/_{20}$$
$$10\% \quad = \quad 0.10 \quad = \quad {}^{1}/_{10}$$
$$25\% \quad = \quad 0.25 \quad = \quad {}^{1}/_{4}$$
$$75\% \quad = \quad 0.75 \quad = \quad {}^{3}/_{4}$$
$$99\% \quad = \quad 0.99 \quad = \quad {}^{99}/_{100}$$

A percentage greater than 100% is greater than 1. For example:

$$110\% \quad = \quad 1.10 \quad = \quad 1{}^{1}/_{10}$$
$$150\% \quad = \quad 1.50 \quad = \quad 1{}^{1}/_{2}$$
$$200\% \quad = \quad 2.00 \quad = \quad 2$$
$$1{,}100\% \quad = \quad 11.00 \quad = 11$$

To change a decimal fraction to a percentage, move the decimal point two places to the right and add the % sign. For example:

$$0.001 \quad = \quad 0.1\%$$
$$0.01 \quad = \quad 1\%$$
$$0.06 \quad = \quad 6\%$$
$$0.35 \quad = \quad 35\%$$
$$0.356 \quad = \quad 35.6\%$$

A percentage can be changed to a common fraction by writing it as hundredths and then reducing it to its lowest common denominator. For example:

$$20\% \quad = \quad 20/100 \quad = \quad {}^{1}/_{5}$$
$$90\% \quad = \quad 90/100 \quad = \quad {}^{9}/_{10}$$
$$225\% \quad = \quad 225/100 \quad = \quad 2{}^{1}/_{4}$$

ADDING AND SUBTRACTING DECIMALS

To add decimals, place the decimal points directly over one another. Then place the decimal point for the solutions in the same column and add. For example:

```
 6.25
 1.10
10.277
17.627
```

If you are working with percentages, there is no need to convert to decimal fractions; just line up the decimal points and add. For example:

```
 68.8%
  6.0%
 25.2%
100.0%
```

When subtracting, the same methods apply. For example:

$$
\begin{array}{rr}
1.00 & 100\% \\
-0.80 & -80\% \\
\hline
0.20 & 20\%
\end{array}
$$

When there is a mixture of decimal fractions and percentages, first convert them all either to percentage or to decimal fractions.

MULTIPLYING AND DIVIDING DECIMALS

Multiplying decimals is like multiplying whole numbers except that the decimal point must be correctly placed. This is done by counting the total number of places to the right of the decimal point in the numbers to be multiplied. Then count off the same number of places in the answer. The following examples illustrate this:

$$
\begin{array}{cccccc}
0.6 & 0.2 & 1.01 & 6 & 6 & 0.03 \\
\times\,0.3 & \times\,0.2 & \times\,2 & \times\,0.1 & \times\,0.11 & \times\,0.02 \\
\hline
0.18 & 0.04 & 2.02 & 0.6 & 0.66 & 0.0006
\end{array}
$$

When dividing, the process starts with properly placing the decimal point. A normal division then follows. When a decimal number is divided by a whole number, place the decimal point in the answer directly above the decimal point in the problem. For example:

$$
3\sqrt{\,3.09\,} = 1.03 \qquad 3\sqrt{\,0.099\,} = 0.033
$$

To divide by a decimal number, you must first change the divisor to a whole number. Then you must make a corresponding change in the dividend. This is done by simply moving both decimal points the same number of places to the right. For example, to divide 0.06 by 0.02, move the decimal point of each to the right two places.

$$
\begin{array}{ll}
0.02\sqrt{\,0.06\,} & \text{becomes } 2\sqrt{\,6\,} \\
0.5\sqrt{\,3\,} & \text{becomes } 5\sqrt{\,30\,} \\
0.05\sqrt{\,30\,} & \text{becomes } 5\sqrt{\,3,000\,}
\end{array}
$$

When multiplying or dividing with percentages, first convert them to decimal form. Thus 6% of 200 is

$$
\begin{array}{r}
200 \\
\times\,0.06 \\
\hline
12.00
\end{array}
$$

PROBLEMS INVOLVING RATES

The basic equation for solving rate problems is: **Percent** times **Base amount** equals **Result**

$$
P \times B = R
$$

If you know the result and the percent and you want the base amount, then divide both sides of the equation by P to get:

$$
B = \frac{R}{P}
$$

If you know the result and the base amount and you want to know the percentage, divide both sides of the equation by B to get:

$$P = \frac{R}{B}$$

An equation will remain an equation as long as you make the same change on both sides of the equal sign. If you add the same number to both sides, it is still an equation. If you subtract the same amount from each side, it is still equal. If you multiply both sides by the same number, it remains equal. If you divide both sides by the same number, it remains equal.

One way to remember the basic equation for solving rate problems is to think of a campaign button that looks like this:

$$R = P \times B \qquad P = \frac{R}{B} \qquad B = \frac{R}{P}$$

A simple way to solve rate problems is to think of

the word **is** as = (an equal sign).
the word **of** as × (a multiplication sign).
the word per as ÷ (a division sign).

for example:

"7% of $50,000 is $3,500"

translates:

"7% × $50,000 = $3,500"

Problem 1

Beverly Broker sells a house for $60,000. Her share of the commission is to be 2.5% of the sales price. How much does she earn?

Her commission is 2.5% of $60,000
Her commission = 0.025 × $60,000
Her commission = $1,500

This is an example of Result = Percent × Base.

Problem 2

Sam Salesman works in an office which will pay him 70% of the commission on each home he lists and sells. With a 6% commission, how much would he earn on a $50,000 sale?

His commission is 70% of 6% of $50,000
His commission = 0.70 × 0.06 × $50,000
His commission = $2,100

This is an example of Result = Percent × Base.

Problem 3

Newt Newcomer wants to earn $21,000 during his first 12 months as a salesman. He feels he can average 3% on each sale. How much property must he sell?

3% of sales is $21,000
0.03 × sales = $21,000
sales = $21,000 ÷ 0.03
sales = $700,000

This is an example of Base = Result ÷ Percent.

Problem 4

An apartment building nets the owners $12,000 per year on their investment of $100,000. What percent return are they receiving on their investment?

$12,000 is ____% of $100,000

$12,000 = ____% × $100,000

$\frac{\$\ 12,000}{\$100,000}$ ÷ $100,000 = 12%

This is an example of Percent = Result ÷ Base.

Problem 5

Smith wants to sell his property and have $47,000 after paying a 6% brokerage commission on the sales price. What price must Smith get?

$47,000 is 94% of selling price

$47,000 = 0.94 × selling price

$\frac{\$47,000}{0.94}$ = selling price

$50,000 = selling price

Problem 6

Miller sold his home for $75,000, paid off an existing loan of $35,000, and paid closing costs of $500. The brokerage commission was 6% of the sales price. How much money did Miller receive? The amount he received is 94% of $75,000 less $35,500.

amount = 0.94 × $75,000 – $35,500

amount = $70,500 – $35,500

amount = $35,000

Problem 7

The assessed valuation of the Kelly home is $10,000. If the property tax rate is $12.50 per $100 of assessed valuation, what is the tax?

The tax is $\frac{\$12.50}{\$100}$ of $10,000

tax = $\frac{\$12.50}{\$100}$ × $10,000

tax = $1,250

Problem 8

Property in Clark County is assessed at 75% of market value. What should the assessed valuation of a $40,000 property be?

Assessed valuation is 75% of market value

Assessed valuation = 0.75 × $40,000

Assessed valuation = $30,000

Problem 9

An insurance company charges $0.24 per $100 of coverage for a one-year fire insurance policy. How much would a $40,000 policy cost?

Cost is $\dfrac{\$0.24}{\$100}$ of \$40,000

Cost = $\dfrac{\$0.24}{\$100} \times \$40,000$

Cost = \$96

AREA MEASUREMENT

The measurement of the distance from one point to another is called *linear* measurement. Usually this is along a straight line, but it can also be along a curved line. Distance is measured in inches, feet, yards, and miles. Less commonly used are chains (66 feet) and rods ($16\frac{1}{2}$). Surface areas are measured in square feet, square yards, acres (43,560 square feet), and square miles. In the metric system, the standard unit of linear measurement is the meter (39.37 inches). Land area is measured in square meters and hectares. A hectare contains 10,000 square meters or 2.471 acres.

To determine the area of a square or rectangle, multiply its length times its width. The formula is:

Area = Length × Width
A = L × W

Problem 10

A parcel of land measures 660 feet by 330 feet. How many square feet is this?

Area = 660 feet × 330 feet
Area = 217,800 square feet

How many acres does this parcel contain?

Acres = 217,800 ÷ 43,560
Acres = 5

If a buyer offers \$42,500 for this parcel, how much is the offering per acre?

\$42,500 ÷ 5 = \$8,500

To determine the area of a right triangle, multiply one-half of the base times the height:

A = $\frac{1}{2}$ × B × H   A = $\frac{1}{2}$ × B × H
A = $1\frac{1}{2}$ × 25 × 50   A = $\frac{1}{2}$ × 40 × 20
A = 625 square feet   A = 400 square feet

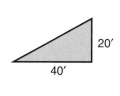

To determine the area of a circle, multiply 3.14 (π) times the square of the radius:

A = $\pi \times r^2$
A = 3.14×40^2
A = $3.14 \times 1,600$
A = 5,024 sq ft

Note: Where the diameter of a circle is given, divide by two to get the radius.
To determine the area of composite figures, separate them into their various components. Thus:

20' × 60' = 1,200 sq ft
10' × 50' = 500 sq ft
1,700 sq ft
20' × 70' = 1,400 sq ft
10' × 30' = 300 sq ft
1,700 sq ft

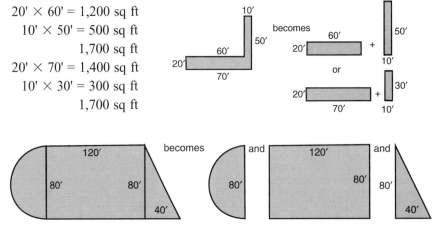

$(3.14 × 40'^2 × \frac{1}{2}) + (80' × 120') + (\frac{1}{2} × 40' × 80') = 13,712$ sq ft

VOLUME MEASUREMENT

Volume is measured in cubic units. The formula is:

Volume = Length × Width × Height
V = L × W × H

For example, what is the volume of a room that is 10 ft by 15 ft with an 8 ft ceiling?

V = 10' × 15' × 8'
V = 1,200 cu ft

Caution: When solving area and volume problems, make certain that all the units are the same. For example, if a parcel of land is one-half mile long and 200 ft wide, convert one measurement so that both are expressed in the same unit; thus the answer will be either in square feet or in square miles. There is no such area measurement as a mile-foot. If a building is 100 yards long by 100 feet wide by 16' 6" high, convert to 300 ft by 100 ft by 16.5 before multiplying.

RATIOS AND PROPORTIONS

If the label on a five-gallon can of paint says it will cover 2,000 square feet, how many gallons are necessary to cover 3,600 sq ft?

A problem like this can be solved two ways:
One way is to find out what area one gallon will cover. In this case 2,000 sq ft ÷ 5 gallons = 400 sq ft per gallon. Then divide 400 sq ft/gal into 3,600 sq ft and the result is 9 gallons.
The other method is to set up a proportion:

$$\frac{5 \text{ gal}}{2,000 \text{ sq ft}} = \frac{Y \text{ gal}}{3,600 \text{ sq ft}}$$

This reads, "5 gallons is to 2,000 sq ft as 'Y' gallons is to 3,600 sq ft." To solve for "Y," multiply both sides of the proportion by 3,600 sq ft. Thus:

$$\frac{5 \text{ gal} × 3,600 \text{ sq ft}}{2,000 \text{ sq ft}} = Y \text{ gal}$$

Divide 2,000 sq ft into 3,600 sq ft and multiply the result by 5 gallons to get the answer.

FRONT-FOOT CALCULATIONS

When land is sold on a front-foot basis, the price is the number of feet fronting on the street times the price per front foot.

Price = front footage × rate per front foot

Thus a 50 ft × 150 ft lot priced at $1,000 per front foot would sell for $50,000. Note that in giving the dimensions of a lot, the first dimension given is the street frontage. The second dimension is the depth of the lot.

Appendix D

PRACTICE EXAM 1

1. The requirement that real estate contracts be in writing is called:
   A. Statute of Frauds
   B. Law of Agency
   C. Regulation Z
   D. Specific Performance

2. The use of land that produces the greatest current value is called:
   A. market value
   B. highest and best use
   C. income approach
   D. projected gross income

3. If a salesperson lists and sells a property for $90,000 and receives 60% of the 7% commission paid to her employing broker, how much does the salesperson receive?
   A. $2,520
   B. $3,780
   C. $5,400
   D. $6,300

4. Sara Seller is satisfied with all of the terms of an offer to purchase her property from Bill Buyer except the date of possession, which she changes from April 9 to April 10. Which of the following is correct?
   A. Sara's acceptance creates a valid contract
   B. Sara cannot make a counteroffer
   C. Sara can always accept Bill Buyer's original offer if the April 10th date is not accepted
   D. Sara has rejected Bill Buyer's offer

5. The best method to appraise a residential property is the:
   A. cost approach
   B. income approach
   C. market approach
   D. highest and best use

6. At the time of listing a property, the owner specifies that he wishes to net $65,000 after satisfying a mortgage of $25,000 and paying a 7% brokerage fee. For what price should the property be listed?
   A. $90,000
   B. $94,550
   C. $96,300
   D. $96,774

7. When an option is exercised, it becomes which of the following?
   A. lease
   B. offer
   C. multiple listing
   D. contract of sale

8. The person borrowing money to purchase real estate is the:
   A. mortgage
   B. mortgagor
   C. mortgagee
   D. grantor

9. A real estate broker sells a tract of land (described in the figure below) for $1,600 per acre and earns a 9% commission. How much does the broker receive? (answers rounded)
   A. $661
   B. $952
   C. $992
   D. $1,983

10. Charging a rate of interest higher than permitted by law is called:
    A. usury
    B. Fannie Mae
    C. alienation
    D. adjustable rate

11. The real estate secondary market for mortgages includes all of the following EXCEPT:
    A. FNMA
    B. GNMA
    C. FHLMC
    D. mortgage brokers

12. Texas Home Equity mortgages are limited to_____ of market value.
    A. 70 percent
    B. 50 percent
    C. 80 percent
    D. 125 percent

13. The practice of not lending money in a specific area is called:
    A. disintermediation
    B. redlining
    C. intermediation
    D. channeling

14. The party who assigns a contract interest to another is the:
    A. grantor
    B. assignee
    C. assignor
    D. grantee

15. From the standpoint of both the agent and the seller, the best type of listing contract is:
    A. open
    B. exclusive agency
    C. net
    D. exclusive right to sell

16. The Texas Real Estate Commission members are appointed by the:
    A. Texas legislature
    B. Texas Association of REALTORS®
    C. Governor of Texas
    D. Texas attorney general

17. If the monthly payment on a $60,000 fully amortizing mortgage loan at 12% APR for a 20-year term is $660.65, how much is the principal reduced by the first monthly payment?
    A. $60.65
    B. $72.00
    C. $600.00
    D. $612.20

18. Hypothecate most nearly means:
    A. selling real estate
    B. pledging real estate as collateral for a loan
    C. leasing real estate
    D. giving an easement

19. Texas real estate brokers must notify consumers and service recipients of the procedures for directing complaints to the commission:
    A. with a TRELA posting
    B. on a sign prominently displayed in place of business
    C. no notice is required
    D. on a salesperson's business card

20. Which of the following most accurately describes the major purpose of a mortgage or a deed of trust?
    A. to secure the payment of a note
    B. to convey a title to the trustee
    C. to provide for equity of redemption
    D. to prevent assumption

21. The acceleration clause provides for which of the following?
    A. equity of redemption
    B. prepayment penalty
    C. right of lender to require immediate payment of principal balance when borrower is in default
    D. alienation by borrower

22. Which of the following liens takes priority over mortgage foreclosure sale proceeds?
    A. mortgage lien
    B. second lien
    C. property tax lien
    D. mechanic's lien

23. The TREC may assess an administrative penalty against a licensee for each violation of the TRELA for an amount not to exceed:
    A. $100
    B. $500
    C. $1000
    D. $5000

24. A lending institution's sharing in the appreciation in value of property and sharing in the equity of property is called:
    A. shared appreciation mortgage
    B. amortization
    C. liquidation
    D. hypothecation

25. All of the following may be required prepaid items by the mortgagee EXCEPT:
    A. real property taxes
    B. hazard insurance
    C. property owner's assessment
    D. broker's commission

26. FHA requires which of the following documents to be signed by borrowers purchasing a home built before 1978?
    A. commission disclosure form
    B. lead-based paint test results disclosure
    C. lead-based paint information disclosure
    D. Fair Housing Disclosure form

27. Within what period from notice must an applicant request an appeal if the commission declines to license an applicant?
    A. 30 days
    B. 60 days
    C. 90 days
    D. 10 days

28. The financing arrangement in which the borrower and lender hold equitable title to the real estate and a disinterested third party holds legal title is:
    A. deed of trust
    B. note
    C. junior mortgage
    D. contract for deed

29. To be eligible for a license under the TRELA an individual must be:
    A. a resident for 60 days
    B. a resident for 6 months
    C. 21 years of age
    D. a legal resident at time of filing application

30. Minor changes to a signed accepted offer to purchase require each amendment or change to be initialed by:
    A. all parties
    B. buyer only
    C. broker and seller
    D. seller only

31. A blanket mortgage usually contains which of the following?
    A. closed-end clause
    B. release clauses
    C. good faith estimate
    D. due-on-sale clause

32. A listing broker is permitted by law to do which of the following?
    A. make a secret profit in addition to the commission
    B. agree to reduce the asking price without the seller's approval
    C. present an offer from the broker's sister with full disclosure of the relationship
    D. accept a bonus from the buyer without the seller's approval

33. Which of the following regulates the advertisement of credit terms available for a house offered for sale?
    A. RESPA
    B. Fannie Mae
    C. Equal Credit Opportunity Act
    D. Regulation Z

34. The TREC may not suspend or revoke a license when it has been determined that:
    A. licensee has entered a plea of guilty of a felony
    B. licensee has engaged in misrepresentation
    C. licensee failed to make clear to all parties which party licensee is acting for
    D. licensee states the owner will accept the list price

35. If a lease specifies the rent to be 2% of the gross sales per annum, with a minimum annual rent of $8,000, what is the annual rent if gross sales are $1,200,000?
    A. $8,000
    B. $12,000
    C. $24,000
    D. $28,000

36. Which of the following provides the grantee with the greatest assurance of title?
    A. special warranty deed
    B. deed of gift
    C. general warranty deed
    D. grant deed

37. Which of the following is a benefit of recording a deed?
    A. it prevents any liens from being filed against the property
    B. it protects the grantee against the grantee's creditors
    C. it protects the grantee against future conveyances by the grantor
    D. it makes a mortgage lien subordinate

38. Under TRELA a party is not liable for a misrepresentation or a concealment of a material fact by a licensee in a real estate transaction unless:
    A. party is a subagent
    B. the party knew of the falsity
    C. no exception
    D. party chooses to be liable

39. An action between two brokers may not be brought in a court in this state for recovery of a commission for the sale or purchase of real estate unless the promise or agreement is:
    A. written
    B. oral
    C. either written or oral
    D. part of purchase agreement

40. All of the following are rights of a life tenant EXCEPT:
    A. encumber
    B. use
    C. alienate
    D. waste

41. Which of the following statements is correct?
    A. an easement provides right of possession
    B. an easement in gross has no servient tenement
    C. an easement is a fixture to real estate
    D. an appurtenant easement can be obtained by necessity

42. The requirement to disclose representation at the time of the licensee's first contact with another party can be:
    A. oral
    B. written
    C. either oral or written
    D. no disclosure required

43. A meeting at which a substantive discussion occurs with respect to specific real property is called by the TRELA a(n):
    A. intermediary meeting
    B. face to face meeting
    C. settlement party
    D. subagency

44. A claim, lien, charge, or liability attached to and binding upon real property is a(n):
    A. encumbrance
    B. community property
    C. license
    D. syndication

45. An owner of a condominium office:
    A. has a proprietary lease
    B. is assessed by the property owners association for maintenance to his office unit
    C. may pledge his property as security for a mortgage loan
    D. owns a share of stock in the corporation that owns the real estate

46. Timesharing is commonly associated with which of the following?
    A. cooperatives
    B. profits
    C. joint ventures
    D. condominiums

47. Which of the following clauses in an accepted offer to purchase protects the buyer from losing her earnest money in the event financing is not obtained?
    A. habendum
    B. contingency
    C. defeasance
    D. subordination

48. The Fair Housing Act of 1968 prohibits discrimination in the rental of all of the following EXCEPT:
    A. offices
    B. apartments
    C. houses
    D. residential lots

49. The Fair Housing Act of 1968 prohibits all of the following EXCEPT:
    A. discriminatory advertising
    B. use of brokerage services
    C. steering
    D. redlining

50. Inducing an owner to list property by telling the owner that people of a certain national origin are moving into the neighborhood is called:
    A. steering
    B. redlining
    C. blockbusting
    D. profiteering

51. Representing that goods are new if they are reconditioned is a violation of the:
    A. Agency Law
    B. Deceptive Trade Practices Act
    C. Statute of Frauds
    D. Parole Evidence Rule

52. A property manager's fee usually consists of a base fee plus:
    A. a percentage of the rental income received
    B. a percentage of the gross potential income
    C. a percentage of the net income
    D. a percentage of the stabilized budget

53. When a lessee installs trade fixtures, these are:
    A. a permanent part of the real estate
    B. owned by the lessor
    C. the personal property of the lessee
    D. real property

54. A person living on the managed premises as a salaried employee engaged to manage and lease apartments is called a(n):
    A. property manager
    B. rental agent
    C. employee manager
    D. resident manager

55. An alienation clause makes a mortgage:
    A. defeasible
    B. unassumable
    C. incontestable
    D. adjustable

56. A real estate salesperson, while acting as an agent for another, is a(n):
    A. intermediary
    B. broker
    C. facilitator
    D. fiduciary

57. A buyer assumes a seller's existing 11%, $80,000 first deed of trust on the settlement date of June 12. The seller makes the monthly payment on June 1 with interest in advance. Which of the following is a correct settlement statement entry for the interest?
    A. $293.28 buyer's credit
    B. $439.92 seller's credit
    C. $293.28 seller's debit
    D. $439.92 seller's debit

58. Which of the following types of listing contracts gives the broker commission entitlement if anyone sells the listed property during the listing term?
    A. net
    B. open
    C. exclusive agency
    D. exclusive right to sell

59. A real estate salesperson advises a prospective buyer that the property the buyer is considering is scheduled for annexation into the city limits. This disclosure constitutes which of the following?
    A. disloyalty to principal
    B. misrepresentation
    C. required disclosure to buyer
    D. violation of disclosure of information by salesperson

60. A real estate agent owes what level of obligation to his principal?
    A. no obligation
    B. very lowest obligation
    C. very highest fiduciary obligation
    D. no fiduciary obligation

61. A salesperson receives two offers for a listed property within a 10-minute period. One offer is 2% less than the listed price, and the other is 6% less than the listed price. The salesperson should present to the seller:
    A. neither offer
    B. both offers
    C. the highest offer
    D. the first offer

62. Closing on a commercial property is April 18. The property taxes for the previous year were $5,760.Which of the following is the correct closing statement entry for taxes?
    A. $1,728 buyer's credit
    B. $4,032 buyer's credit
    C. $1,728 seller's credit
    D. $4,032 seller's credit

63. The amount of a purchase money mortgage appears in the closing statement as:
    A. seller's credit only
    B. buyer's debit only
    C. seller's debit; buyer's credit
    D. seller's credit; buyer's debit

64. A seller paid an annual hazard insurance premium of $540 for a policy effective February 12. At settlement on April 16 of the same year, the buyer purchased the policy from the seller. This transaction is correctly entered on the settlement statements as:
    A. $96 buyer's credit
    B. $444 buyer's credit
    C. $96 seller's credit
    D. $444 seller's credit

65. The amount of earnest money appears on closing statements as a:
    A. credit to buyer
    B. debit to seller
    C. credit to seller
    D. debit to buyer

66. When listing real property for sale, a real estate broker:
    A. does a competitive market analysis
    B. makes an appraisal to estimate market value
    C. estimates residual income
    D. correlates reproduction cost

67. An apartment building produces an annual net income of $10,800 after deducting $72 per month for expenses. What price for the property would provide a buyer with a net return of 12%?
    A. $90,000
    B. $97,200
    C. $116,641
    D. $129,600

68. An apartment building contains 30 units. Each unit rents for $200 per month. The vacancy rate is 4%. Annual expenses are $3,000 for maintenance, $1,100 insurance, $1,600 taxes, $1,200 utilities, and 15% of the gross effective income for management fee. What is the investor's net rate of return for the first year if he paid $260,000 for the property?
    A. 6.69%
    B. 11.64%
    C. 14.94%
    D. 19.94%

69. A subagent would have to disclose to the listing broker all of the following facts about the buyer except that the buyer:
    A. has a daughter who is a real estate attorney
    B. has an option on two adjoining parcels
    C. has a known poor credit rating
    D. has defaulted on three previous transactions through the subagent

70. Which of the following methods is used to estimate the value of the land only, on which an apartment building is to be located the next year?
    A. cost approach
    B. income approach
    C. market data approach
    D. replacement cost

71. Gross rent multipliers are used in connection with which of the following?
    A. condominiums
    B. schools
    C. vacant land
    D. income property

72. Adherence to which of the following has the effect of maximizing land value?
    A. principle of contribution
    B. principle of change
    C. principle of anticipation
    D. principle of highest and best use

73. Texas law presumes that all property acquired after marriage is:
    A. separate
    B. community
    C. unity of person
    D. right of survivorship

74. An urban homestead can consist of a lot or lots amounting to no more than:
    A. one acre of land
    B. 100 acres of land
    C. 200 acres of land
    D. one section of land

75. When land is torn away by the violent action of a river it is called:
    A. erosion
    B. avulsion
    C. reliction
    D. alluvion

76. The characteristic of land that has the greatest effect on land value is:
    A. nonhomogeneity
    B. location
    C. indestructibility
    D. immobility

77. All of the following are examples of public land use controls EXCEPT:
    A. deed restrictions
    B. building codes
    C. zoning
    D. environmental control laws

78. An estate created for the life of a person other than the life tenant is called a life estate:
    A. in remainder
    B. pur autre vie
    C. by dower
    D. in reversion

79. The person making the will is known as the:
    A. devisee
    B. bequestor
    C. legatee
    D. testator

80. A formal declaration by a person signing a deed that he or she, in fact, did sign the document is called:
    A. a commissioning
    B. a conveyance
    C. a recorded plat
    D. an acknowledgment

81. A trespass on the land of another as a result of an intrusion by some structure or other object is an:
    A. encroachment
    B. easement
    C. estate
    D. emblement

82. As a result of a salesperson's negligence in filling in the provisions in a contract of sale, the seller incurs a financial loss. Liability for this loss may be imposed on:
    A. both the salesperson and the employing broker
    B. the salesperson's employing broker only
    C. the salesperson only
    D. neither party

83. A gift of real property at death is a(n):
    A. devise
    B. bequest
    C. escheat
    D. demise

84. Of the following types of deeds, which provides the grantee with the LEAST assurance of title?
    A. bargain and sale
    B. quitclaim
    C. grant
    D. special warranty

85. Recording protects which of the following parties?
    A. grantor
    B. seller
    C. vendor
    D. grantee

86. All of the following are rights of a mortgagor EXCEPT:
    A. defeasance
    B. foreclosure
    C. equity of redemption
    D. possession

87. Which of the following gives the mortgagee the right to declare the entire principal balance immediately due and payable if the mortgagor is in default?
    A. acceleration clause
    B. alienation clause
    C. statutory foreclosure clause
    D. assignment clause

88. On June 16, a seller closes on the sale of her home. Annual taxes of $861 for the current year were paid in full by the seller prior to the sale. If these payments are prorated, which amount will be returned to the seller?
    A. $357
    B. $397
    C. $430
    D. $464

89. If the GIM is 7.5 and the annual gross income is $250,000, what is the estimated property value?
    A. $1,875,000
    B. $2,500,000
    C. $3,000,000
    D. $3,333,000

90. A salesperson licensee may receive commissions from which of the following?
    A. cooperating broker
    B. buyer
    C. seller
    D. sponsoring broker

Appendix E

PRACTICE EXAM 2

1. To foreclose on a home equity loan in Texas requires:
   A. judicial foreclosure
   B. non-judicial foreclosure
   C. subordination
   D. fiat money

2. While a broker was inspecting a property for listing, the property owner told the broker that the house contains 2,400 square feet of heated living area. Without verifying this information, the broker listed the property and represented it to prospective buyers as containing 2,400 square feet. After purchasing the property, the buyer accurately determined that the house has only 1,850 square feet and sued for damages for the difference in value between 2,400 square feet and 1,850 square feet. Which of the following is correct?
   A. the broker is not liable because he relied on the seller's positive statement as to the square footage
   B. the seller is not liable because the broker, not the seller, represented the property to the buyer as containing 2,400 square feet
   C. the theory of caveat emptor applies; thus, neither the seller nor the broker is liable to the buyer
   D. both the broker and the seller are liable to the buyer

3. The sales associates of Executive Realty, Ltd., obtained several excellent listings in Exclusive Estates by advising homeowners that a number of Chinese families were moving into Exclusive Estates and therefore their property values would be substantially depressed. This activity is most accurately described as:
   A. steering
   B. blockbusting
   C. soliciting
   D. redlining

4. A real estate salesperson earned $48,000 in commissions in one year. If she received 60% of the 6% her broker received, what was her average monthly sales volume?
   A. $66,666
   B. $80,000
   C. $111,111
   D. $133,333

5. The type of listing contract that is most beneficial to the broker and the seller is:
   A. exclusive right to sell
   B. net
   C. open
   D. exclusive agency

6. A real estate broker is responsible for all of the following EXCEPT:
   A. acts of sales associates while engaged in brokerage activities
   B. appropriate handling of funds in trust, or escrow, accounts
   C. adhering to commission schedule recommended by the local real estate organization
   D. representing property honestly, fairly, and accurately to prospective buyers

7. A triangular tract of land is 8,000 feet long and has highway frontage of 4,000 yards. If Ajax Realty Company lists this property at 9% commission and sells it for $1,600 per acre, what amount of commission does Ajax receive?
   A. $105,785
   B. $158,678
   C. $218,160
   D. $317,355

8. When listing a home for sale, the broker advises the seller that because he owns only one house, the listing is exempt from prohibitions of the Fair Housing Act of 1968. Which of the following statements about the broker's advice is true?
   A. the broker is acting correctly in advising the seller about the exemption
   B. the broker always should give good legal advice to sellers and buyers
   C. the broker is in error because the exemption is from the Civil Rights Act of 1866
   D. the broker is acting incorrectly in that the property is not exempt because the seller is using a broker

9. A construction loan can also be called a(n):
   A. reverse mortgage
   B. blended-rate loan
   C. blanket mortgage
   D. Interim loan

10. A salesperson associated with Metro Realty, Inc., obtained an offer for a property listed by Preferred Real Estate Company, which she gave to Sam Slicker, the listing agent with Preferred, for presentation to the property owner. Realizing that the amount of the offer was such that it probably would not be accepted, Sam increased the amount by $3,000 prior to presentation. Which of the following statements correctly characterizes Sam's action?

    A. to make the change a proper and appropriate act, Sam should have obtained the approval of Metro Realty before changing the offer

    B. Sam's action was in violation of his fiduciary obligations and was completely improper

    C. Sam's action would have been appropriate with the seller's consent

    D. Metro Realty, Inc., will be entitled to the entire commission because of Sam's actions

11. In the process of preparing an offer for commercial property, a broker was asked by two potential purchasers to recommend the most beneficial way for them to take title to the property. Which of the following should the broker recommend?

    A. tenants in common

    B. in severalty

    C. ask an attorney

    D. ask the listing broker

12. Upon the broker's recommendation, a seller accepted an offer that was 8% below the listed price. The broker did not disclose to the seller that the buyer was the broker's brother-in-law. Which of the following is correct?

    A. the broker violated his obligations as agent of the seller

    B. the fact that the buyer is related to the broker is not required to be divulged to the seller

    C. the broker has done nothing wrong as long as he doesn't take any commission

    D. the broker has done nothing wrong if the appraised value of the home matches the offered price

13. A VHAP loan is available to:

    A. all Texans

    b.. women only

    C. men only

    D. Texas veterans

14. Combining the interest rate with other costs of a loan is known as the:

    A. trigger rate

    B. annual percentage rate

    C. finance charge

    D. amount financed

15. If the closing date is November 10 and the seller had paid the real property taxes of $2,880 for the current tax year of January 1 through December 31, which of the following is the correct closing statement entry for taxes?

    A. seller's credit of $400

    B. seller's debit of $2,480

    C. buyer's credit of $400

    D. buyer's debit of $2,480

16. RESPA requires lending institutions to provide borrowers with which of the following at the time of or within three days after application for a mortgage loan for housing?

    A. good faith estimate

    B. HUD Form No. 1

    C. disclosure statement

    D. nonrecourse note

17. The buyer assumes a 9% loan with a balance of $74,000 mortgage at closing on July 12. The seller has already made the July 1 payment; the next payment of $638.69, including principal and interest for July, will be due on August 1. Which of the following is the correct closing statement entry for interest?

    A. buyer's debit of $222.00

    B. buyer's credit of $638.69

    C. seller's debit of $222.00

    D. seller's credit of $638.69

18. No covenants or warranties are found in a:

    A. General Warranty deed

    B. Special Warranty deed

    C. Quitclaim deed

    D. Sheriff's deed

19. Under the right of eminent domain the government can take ownership of privately held land for all of the following EXCEPT:

    A. streets

    B. an elementary school

    C. a single family residence

    D. public housing

20. A single taxpayer sells her residence for $122,000. The original cost was $86,000. The taxpayer has lived in the home for $3^1/_2$ years and is in the 28% tax bracket. What is the amount of income tax due?
    A. $36,000
    B. $10,080
    C. $7,200
    D. $0

21. A property manager's responsibilities include all of the following EXCEPT:
    A. maintenance
    B. collecting rents
    C. commingling
    D. negotiating leases

22. Which of the following is one of the basic responsibilities of a property manager?
    A. appraising the property annually
    B. evicting all minority tenants to provide for a more stable complex
    C. producing the best possible net operating income for the owner
    D. preparing the annual tax returns and attending audits with the IRS

23. What net annual operating income must a property manager produce from a property to provide an 8% return to the owner, who paid $763,000 for the property?
    A. $9,538
    B. $61,040
    C. $95,375
    D. $104,849

24. Which of the following most accurately describes a property manager?
    A. fiduciary
    B. trustee
    C. escrow agent
    D. resident manager

25. When all parties agree to the terms and conditions of a real estate contract, there is said to be:
    A. mutual satisfaction
    B. *sui juris*
    C. meeting of the minds
    D. equitable consent

26. A roofline extending without permission onto an adjoining property is an example of:
    A. easement appurtenant
    B. encroachment
    C. license
    D. easement in gross

27. John owns an apartment building in a large city. After discussing the matter with his legal advisers, he decides to alter the type of occupancy in the building from rental to condominium status. This procedure is known as:
    A. conversion
    B. partition
    C. deportment
    D. amendment

28. The members of the Texas Real Estate Commission serve for a term of:
    A. 6 months
    B. 18 months
    C. 3 years
    D. 6 years

29. An owner's office building is producing a net annual operating income of $140,000. If the owner paid $1,166,666 for the property, what rate of return is she receiving on her investment?
    A. 8.3%
    B. 12%
    C. 14%
    D. 16.3%

30. All of the following statements about options are correct EXCEPT:
    A. they must be in writing to be enforceable
    B. they are binding upon optionor and optionee
    C. when exercised, they become contracts of sale
    D. optionor and optionee must be competent

31. Which of the following is both a contract of sale and a financing instrument?
    A. installment land contract
    B. sale and leaseback
    C. lease with option to purchase
    D. executed contract

32. A lease providing for rental changes based on changes in the Consumer Price Index is which of the following?
    A. escalated
    B. graduated
    C. percentage
    D. index

33. If the commission proposes to suspend or revoke a person's license, the person is entitled to a hearing before the commission:
    A. at a place the commission selects
    B. within the county of licensee's business
    C. both a and b
    D. in Austin only

34. Public land use controls in the form of zoning ordinances are an exercise of:
    A. power of eminent domain
    B. general plan for development
    C. police power of the government
    D. Interstate Land Sales Full Disclosure Act

35. A property owner in a recently zoned area is permitted to continue to use his property in a manner that does not comply with the zoning requirements. This use is described as:
    A. exclusive-use zoning
    B. deviation
    C. nonconforming use
    D. private control of land use

36. A real estate broker, acting as an agent for another in a transaction, has a primary duty to:
    A. get the transaction closed successfully
    B. help the parties reach a mutually beneficial agreement
    C. treat all parties impartially
    D. represent the interests of his client

37. Which of the following actions of the broker is most likely to result in the creation of an agency with the buyer?
    A. show buyer an available property
    B. transmit buyer's offer to seller
    C. discuss the financing alternatives
    D. negotiate on buyer's behalf

38. A deed is made eligible for recording on the public record by which of the following?
    A. abstract
    B. avoidance
    C. alienation
    D. acknowledgment

39. The listing broker should follow all of the seller's instructions EXCEPT:
    A. show the property on Fridays
    B. extend the closing if necessary
    C. conceal the cracked foundation
    D. lease the property prior to closing

40. Which of the following provides the exclusive right of possession and control of real property?
    A. easement
    B. leasehold
    C. license
    D. encumbrance

41. A co-owner of real property automatically received a deceased co-owner's share of ownership. This is called:
    A. intestate succession
    B. inheritance by devise
    C. right of survivorship
    D. inheritance by descent

42. Four brothers received title to a large tract of land from their grandfather, who gave each brother a one-fourth undivided interest with equal rights to possession of the land. All four received their title on their grandfather's seventieth birthday. The brothers most likely hold title in which of the following ways?
    A. in severalty
    B. as tenants in common
    C. as tenants by the entirety
    D. as remaindermen

43. John and his wife, Mary, live in a community property state. Mary inherits a large shopping mall in the city where they live. Which of the following statements about Mary's ownership of the mall is correct?
    A. Mary and John hold the property as tenants by the entirety
    B. Mary may encumber or convey the title only with John's participation in a mortgage or deed
    C. Mary holds title as separate property
    D. the property is considered community property because of the marriage status at the time of inheritance

44. Which of the following statements about the creation of a condominium is FALSE?
    A. a Declaration, Articles of Association, and Association Bylaws must be recorded in the public record in the county where the property is located
    B. a parking garage with rental spaces can be converted to condominium ownership
    C. an apartment complex can be converted to condominiums only with a majority vote of the tenants
    D. a shopping center can be converted to condominium ownership

45. A real estate agent can do which of the following?
    A. complete TREC-approved forms
    B. prepare a deed
    C. draw a real estate note
    D. prepare a deed of trust

46. The state took a part of an owner's property for construction of a building. Which of the following statements about this event is correct?
    A. the property owner must be compensated for the difference in market value of the property before and after the partial condemnation
    B. the building to be constructed may be used for the sole use and benefit of a private corporation
    C. the property owner has no recourse to challenge taking his property
    D. the value established is the average of the owner's desired value, the state's desired purchase price, and an independent appraisal

47. It is unlawful for a licensed broker to compensate which of the following for a real estate sale?
    A. another broker
    B. a friend who made referral
    C. a broker licensed in another state
    D. the broker's salesperson

48. A property with a market value of $80,000 is entitled to a homestead exemption of $20,000. What is the tax rate per $100 if the tax bill is $900?
    A. $1.125
    B. $1.50
    C. $11.25
    D. $15.00

49. An encroachment is which of the following?
    A. lien
    B. party wall
    C. trespass
    D. fixture

50. In estimating the value of an office building containing 22,400 square feet, an appraiser established the annual rental income to be $400,000. The appraiser also learned that monthly expenses averaged $16,700. If the average investor in this type of property was realizing a net return of 13.5%, what would be the appraiser's estimate of the value of the property?
    A. $1,478,518
    B. $1,484,444
    C. $2,962,962
    D. $2,964,600

51. A competitive market analysis is performed when:
    A. assessing property
    B. pricing property
    C. appraising property
    D. condemning property

52. For which of the following types of property would the market data approach be the most relevant appraisal method?
    A. vacant industrial land
    B. library
    C. condominium office
    D. farm land with a large hog operation

53. The principle providing that the highest value of a property has a tendency to be established by the cost of purchasing or constructing a building of equal utility and desirability is the principle of:
    A. highest and best use
    B. competition
    C. supply and demand
    D. substitution

54. When an offer to purchase real estate is signed, the real estate broker or salesperson must give written notice that title insurance or an abstract should be obtained by the:
    A. seller
    B. title company
    C. buyer
    D. seller and buyer

55. The broker, when acting as an intermediary, must obtain written consent from:
    A. seller
    B. buyer
    C. TREC
    D. all parties to transaction

56. A real estate broker who is acting as an intermediary must:
    A. disclose to buyer that seller will accept less
    B. disclose to seller that buyer will pay more
    C. disclose confidential information
    D. treat all parties honestly

57. A building now 21 years old has a total economic life of 40 years. If the replacement cost of the building is $1,200,000, what is the value?
    A. $228,571
    B. $252,631
    C. $570,000
    D. $630,000

58. Which of the following is the most likely result of the homogeneous development of a residential subdivision?
    A. overinflated values
    B. maximized values
    C. stabilized values
    D. depressed values

59. Which of the following approaches to value is the most appropriate for estimating the value of a condominium apartment?
    A. cost approach
    B. income approach
    C. comparable approach
    D. gross rent multiplier

60. Which of the following statements by the listing broker to the buyer might lead a court to infer an agency relationship with the buyer?
    A. "This is a good buy."
    B. "Let's test the seller with a low offer and then go up if we have to."
    C. "Now is the time to submit an offer."
    D. "Let me tell you about the type of loans available at the bank today."

61. A rural homestead for a single person can consist of not more than:
    A. 200 acres
    B. 640 acres
    C. 120 acres
    D. 100 acres

62. The monthly payment necessary to fully amortize a 15-year mortgage loan of $100,000 at 8.5% APR is $984.74. How much interest will the mortgagor pay over the 15-year term?
    A. $77,253.20
    B. $127,500.00
    C. $176,892.41
    D. $276,892.41

63. A person who dies leaving a valid will is said to have died:
    A. intestate
    B. testate
    C. in succession
    D. in descent

64. A lender charges a 2% loan origination fee and three discount points to make a 95% conventional insured mortgage loan in the amount of $47,500. What is the cost of these charges to the borrower?
    A. $922
    B. $1,188
    C. $1,425
    D. $2,375

65. Which of the following could be considered separate property?
    A. dividends from husband's inherited stocks
    B. one spouse's salary
    C. rents from real estate inherited by the wife
    D. real estate inherited by the husband

66. A security device on a home rental must be re-keyed by landlord within what time period after tenant turnover?
    A. 3 days
    B. 7 days
    C. 10 days
    D. 30 days

67. All of the following are ways in which a seller may finance the sale of her property for a buyer EXCEPT:
    A. wraparound purchase money mortgage
    B. contract for deed
    C. FHA-insured mortgage
    D. purchase money first mortgage

68. Bill and Betty Brown execute and deliver a $50,000 mortgage to Ajax Financial Associates at 10:30 a.m. on April 1. At 11:30 a.m. on the same day, they give a $10,000 mortgage pledging the same property to Fidelity Finance, Inc. Fidelity's mortgage is recorded at 1:10 p.m. that day, and the mortgage to Ajax is recorded at 1:42 p.m. on April 1. Which of the following statements about these mortgages is correct?
    A. because the mortgage to Ajax was executed and delivered first, Ajax holds the first mortgage
    B. Fidelity has the second mortgage because it was executed and delivered after the mortgage given to Ajax
    C. Ajax and Fidelity will be co-first mortgage holders because both mortgages were signed on the same day
    D. because the mortgage to Fidelity was recorded first, Fidelity holds the first mortgage

69. When a buyer signs a purchase contract and the seller accepts, the buyer acquires an immediate interest in the property known as:
    A. legal title
    B. statutory title
    C. equitable title
    D. defeasible title

70. Regulation Z specifies that the only specific credit term that may appear in an advertisement of a house for sale without the requirement of a full disclosure is which of the following?
    A. SAM
    B. APR
    C. ECOA
    D. RESPA

71. In the sale of their home, Van and Vera Vendor were required to satisfy their existing first mortgage of $40,000 so the buyers could obtain a first mortgage to finance their purchase. The Vendors' closing statement contained a debit in the amount of $800 because the Vendors paid off their loan prior to the full term. From this information, it can be determined that the Vendors' mortgage contained a(n):
    A. acceleration clause
    B. alienation clause
    C. prepayment clause
    D. defeasance clause

72. A developer gave the seller a $385,000 purchase money first mortgage to secure payment of part of the purchase price for a tract of land. The developer was able to convey unencumbered titles to the first six lot purchasers by paying only $8,000 on the purchase money mortgage because the mortgage contained:
    A. release clauses
    B. due-on-sale clauses
    C. prepayment clauses
    D. mortgaging clauses

73. In the purchase of an office building, the buyer gave the seller a mortgage for $200,000 more than the seller's first mortgage and took title to the property subject to the first mortgage. The purchase money mortgage required payments of interest only for the first five years, at which time the principal has to be paid and a new purchase money mortgage created. All of the following statements about these financial arrangements are correct EXCEPT:
    A. the purchase money mortgage is a wraparound term mortgage
    B. for this arrangement to work satisfactorily, the seller's first mortgage must not contain an alienation clause
    C. this arrangement must be approved by Fannie Mae
    D. the purchase money mortgage has a balloon payment

74. The Texas provision that provides for the transfer of real estate belonging to any person who dies without a will and has no heirs is:
    A. eminent domain
    B. escheat
    C. right of redemption
    D. ad valorem

75. Which of the following actions of the broker is most likely to result in the creation of an agency with the buyer?
    A. show buyer an available property
    B. transmit buyer's offer to seller
    C. discuss the financing alternatives available
    D. negotiate on buyer's behalf

76. A property description reading "$1/4$ of the northeast $1/4$ of section 22" describes how many acres?
    A. 20
    B. 40
    C. 160
    D. 240

77. The private ownership of land is known as:
    A. feudal ownership
    B. government ownership
    C. allodial ownership
    D. eminent domain

78. All of the following are powers of government EXCEPT:
    A. police power
    B. escheat
    C. taxation
    D. deed restrictions

79. An owner whose property is condemned is entitled to be compensated for:
    A. book value
    B. assessed value
    C. market value
    D. mortgage value

80. A listing contract creates an agency relationship in which:
    A. the broker is a general agent
    B. the seller is the principal
    C. the seller is a general agent
    D. the broker is the principal

81. When a real estate broker or seller conceals a known defect, this is an example of:
    A. mutual mistake
    B. unintentional misrepresentation
    C. fraud
    D. mistake of law

82. Upon application for an original license, pursuant to TRELA, the applicant shall pay a fee to the real estate recovery fund of:
    A. $10
    B. $100
    C. $500
    D. $1,000

83. A lease is all of the following EXCEPT:
    A. contract
    B. nonfreehold estate
    C. freehold estate
    D. binding obligation on the parties

84. During a licensee's period of inactive status the person may:
    A. practice real estate
    B. refer buyers for a fee
    C. list homes for sale
    D. pay annual license renewal fees

85. A licensed real estate practitioner may not:
    A. sell or exchange real estate
    B. negotiate listings
    C. advise sellers on legal matters
    D. aid in locating rental real estate

86. Which of the following enables the mortgagee to sell the mortgage in the secondary mortgage market?
    A. assignment clause
    B. due-on-sale clause
    C. mortgaging clause
    D. power-of-sale clause

87. When a buyer purchases a home using a VA-guaranteed loan, he is allowed to:
    A. pay a loan origination fee
    B. pay discount points
    C. purchase the property to be used as a rental
    D. both a and b

88. Redlining applies to which of the following?
    A. brokers
    B. developers
    C. lenders
    D. landlords

89. A lease is a contract that is:
    A. bilateral
    B. unilateral
    C. collateral
    D. trilateral

90. Which of the following is a deductible expense for homeowners?
    A. real property taxes
    B. maintenance
    C. mortgage principal payments
    D. energy usage

Appendix F

ANSWER KEY

Chapter 2

1. B
2. E
3. E
4. A
5. B
6. B
7. A
8. D
9. B
10. C
11. C
12. D
13. E
14. A
15. A
16. B
17. D

Chapter 3

1. B
2. E
3. B
4. D
5. C
6. D
7. C
8. A
9. C
10. C
11. B
12. D
13. C
14. E
15. D
16. D
17. C
18. E
19. A
20. A

Chapter 4

1. B
2. C
3. A
4. B
5. D
6. C
7. B
8. A
9. C
10. D

11. A
12. E
13. A
14. D
15. C

Chapter 5

1. D
2. C
3. D
4. C
5. B
6. C
7. C
8. B
9. A
10. C
11. A
12. C
13. C
14. D
15. A
16. D
17. B
18. C
19. C
20. C

Chapter 6

1. D
2. C
3. A
4. D
5. D
6. C
7. C
8. A
9. B
10. B
11. C
12. B
13. D
14. B
15. D
16. B
17. D
18. B
19. C

Chapter 7

1. E
2. D

3. D
4. A
5. C
6. C
7. D
8. B
9. C
10. D
11. D
12. D
13. D
14. C
15. A
16. A
17. D
18. B
19. B
20. B

Chapter 8

1. D
2. E
3. A
4. C
5. C
6. C
7. D
8. B
9. B
10. D
11. C
12. C
13. E
14. D
15. B
16. C
17. A
18. A
19. A

Chapter 9

1. C
2. D
3. B
4. B
5. B
6. C
7. A
8. D
9. B
10. C
11. D

12. C
13. A
14. B
15. C
16. C
17. A
18. C
19. C
20. C

Chapter 10

1. D
2. B
3. A
4. E
5. C
6. B
7. D
8. C
9. A
10. A

Chapter 11

1. D
2. D
3. B
4. C
5. C
6. D
7. D
8. B
9. A
10. B

Chapter 12

1. A
2. D
£. B
4. D
5. C
6. C
7. C
8. C
9. C
10. C

Chapter 13

1. A
2. C
3. C
4. C
5. B

6. D
7. C
8. C
9. D
10. B
11. B

Chapter 14

1. A
2. C
3. A
4. A
5. D
6. D
7. A
8. C
9. D
10. A
11. C
12. B
13. C
14. A
15. B
16. D
17. A
18. C
19. D
20. A

Chapter 15

1. E
2. D
3. B
4. E
5. C
6. C
7. C
8. D
9. D
10. C
11. C
12. C
13. A
14. D
15. C
16. B
17. D
18. B
19. A
20. A

Chapter 16

1. A
2. B
3. C
4. B
5. B
6. D
7. C
8. D

9. C
10. C
11. C
12. B
13. A
14. D
15. E
16. B
17. B
18. A
19. B
20. C

Chapter 17

1. C
2. B
3. A
4. A
5. D
6. C
7. D
8. D
9. A
10. C
11. A
12. C
13. C
14. C
15. C
16. C
17. D
18. A
19. A
20. C

Chapter 18

1. C
2. D
3. D
4. C
5. E
6. B
7. C
8. A
9. A
10. B
11. C
12. D
13. A
14. D
15. B
16. D
17. C
18. C
19. B
20. B

Chapter 19

1. A
2. A

3. C
4. C
5. D
6. E
7. B
8. A
9. C
10. B
11. C
12. B
13. D
14. C
15. C
16. C
17. B
18. E
19. D
20. C

Chapter 20

1. A
2. C
3. B
4. D
5. C
6. C
7. A
8. C
9. B
10. A
11. D
12. B
13. C
14. B
15. B
16. C
17. C
18. C
19. D
20. B
21. C
22. C
23. B
24. A

Chapter 21

1. C
2. A
3. B
4. C
5. A
6. D
7. A
8. A
9. B
10. C
11. A
12. D
13. A
14. B

15. C

Chapter 22

1. D
2. C
3. A
4. B
5. C
6. C
7. A
8. D
9. A
10. B
11. C
12. A
13. A
14. D
15. C
16. D
17. D
18. C

Chapter 23

1. C
2. D
3. D
4. C
5. D
6. A
7. D
8. C
9. B
10. A
11. B
12. A
13. B
14. D
15. C
16. D
17. B
18. C

Chapter 24

1. D
2. D
3. C
4. A
5. C
6. A
7. C
8. A
9. D
10. A
11. C
12. A
13. D
14. B
15. A

ANSWER KEY TO
PRACTICE EXAM 1 (APPENDIX D)

1. A	24. A	47. B	70. C
2. B	25. D	48. A	71. D
3. B	26. C	49. B	72. D
4. D	27. D	50. C	73. B
5. C	28. A	51. B	74. A
6. D	29. D	52. A	75. B
7. D	30. A	53. C	76. B
8. B	31. B	54. D	77. A
9. C	32. C	55. B	78. B
10. A	33. D	56. D	79. D
11. D	34. D	57. B	80. D
12. C	35. C	58. D	81. A
13. B	36. C	59. C	82. A
14. C	37. C	60. C	83. A
15. D	38. B	61. B	84. B
16. C	39. C	62. C	85. D
17. A	40. D	63. C	86. B
18. B	41. D	64. D	87. A
19. B	42. C	65. A	88. D
20. A	43. B	66. A	89. A
21. C	44. A	67. A	90. D
22. C	45. C	68. D	
23. C	46. D	69. A	

ANSWER KEY TO
PRACTICE EXAM 2 (APPENDIX E)

1. A	24. A	47. B	70. B
2. D	25. C	48. B	71. C
3. B	26. B	49. C	72. A
4. C	27. A	50. A	73. C
5. A	28. D	51. B	74. B
6. C	29. B	52. A	75. D
7. B	30. B	53. D	76. B
8. D	31. A	54. C	77. C
9. D	32. D	55. D	78. D
10. B	33. C	56. D	79. C
11. C	34. C	57. C	80. B
12. A	35. C	58. B	81. C
13. D	36. D	59. C	82. A
14. B	37. D	60. B	83. C
15. A	38. D	61. D	84. D
16. A	39. C	62. A	85. C
17. C	40. B	63. B	86. A
18. C	41. C	64. D	87. D
19. C	42. B	65. D	88. C
20. D	43. C	66. B	89. A
21. C	44. C	67. C	90. A
22. C	45. A	68. D	
23. B	46. A	69. C	

170–171; *illustrated,* 169; loan size, 170; monthly payments, 169–170; partially amortized, 171–172; repayment methods, 168

Amount financed: amount of credit provided to the borrower, 186

Amount realized: selling price less selling expenses, 242

Analysis,   299

Annexation,   15, 82

Annual percentage rate (APR):   a uniform measure of the cost of credit that includes interest, discount points, and loan fees, 186

Anticipation, principle of: what a person will pay for a property depends on the expected benefits from the property in the future, 301

Antitrust laws,   368

Apartment buildings: as investments, 421–422

Apartment locators: firms that specialize in finding rental units for tenants, 7

Apparent authority,   354

Appraisal: an estimate of value, 279–303; appraisal report, 297–299; appraiser's best estimate, 295–296; buyer's and seller's markets, 303; as career, 8; characteristics of value, 300–301; cost approach, 288–291; developing, 296–297; income approach, 291–295; market approach, *see* **Market approach;** market value defined, 280; multiple meanings of value, 302–303; professional appraisal societies, 296–297

Appraisal district,   236

Appraisal Foundation,   296

Appraisal letter: a valuation report in the form of a business letter, 298

Appraisal reports,   298–299

Appraisal Review Board,   238

Appraisal societies,   296

Appraise.   *See* **Appraisal**

Appreciation: an increase in property value, 415

Appropriation process: the enactment of a taxing body's budget and sources of money into law, 235

Appurtenance: right or privilege or improvement that belongs to and passes with land but is not necessarily a part of the land, 16

"As is" clause,   359–360

Assemblage: the process of combining two or more parcels into one, 303

Assessed value: a value placed on a property for the purpose of taxation, 302–303

Assessment district.   *See* **Improvement district**

Assessment roll: a list or book, open for public inspection, that shows assessed values for all lands and buildings in a taxing district, 238

Assessments,   239–241, 326

Assessor parcel number,   25–26

Asset integrated mortgage,   227

Assets,   257, 264

Assign: to transfer to another one's rights under a contract, 274–275

Assignee: one to whom a right or property is transferred (also called an assign), 274

Assignment: the transfer of one's rights under a contract to another, 274

Assignor,   274

Association: a not-for-profit organization that can own property and transact business in its own name, 66; prorating payment to, 257

Association dues: fees paid by a condominium or PUD unit owner to the owner's association for upkeep of the common elements, 393

Assumed name certificate,   315

Assume the loan: the buyer obligates himself to repay an existing loan as a condition of the sale, 154, 176–177

At-risk: the amount of money an investor stands to lose, 418

Attorney-in-fact: one who is authorized by another to act in his (her) place, 104

Avulsion: the removal of land by the action of water, 82

Balloon loan: a loan in which the final payment is larger than the preceding payments, 171

Balloon payment: the name given to the final payment of a balloon loan, 171

Banks: as mortgage lenders, 203

Bargain and sale deed: a deed that contains no covenants, but does imply that the grantor owns the property being conveyed by the deed, 75

Base line: an east-west or geographer's line selected as a basic reference in the rectangular survey system, 21

Basis: the price paid for property; used in calculating income taxes, 242

Bench mark: a reference point of known location and elevation, 20, 26–27

Beneficial interest: a unit of ownership in a real estate investment trust, 66

Beneficiary: one for whose benefit a trust is created; the lender in a deed of trust arrangement, 66, 197–198

Bequest: personal property received under a will, 78

Bilateral contract: results when a promise is exchanged for a promise, 102

Bill of sale: a written agreement by which one person transfers his personal property to another, 14

Deed of trust: a document that conveys title to a neutral third party trustee as security for a debt, 143, 147–153; advantages, 163; compared to a mortgage, 143; *illustrated document,* 148–152; lending practices, *see* **Lending practices;** parties to, 147–148; to secure assumption, 154–158

Deed restrictions (deed covenants): provisions placed in deeds to control how future landowners may or may not use the property, 40, 409; violation of, 40

Default: failure to perform a legal duty, such as failure to carry out the terms of a contract, 132, 133

Defeasance clause: a mortgage clause that states the mortgage is defeated if the accompanying note is repaid on time, 142

Deficiency judgment: a judgment against a borrower if the sale of pledged property at foreclosure does not bring in enough to pay the balance owed, 161

Delayed exchange: a nonsimultaneous tax-deferred trade, 137–138

Delinquent loan: a loan wherein the borrower is behind in his payments, 160

Delivery and acceptance of deed, 72

Demand: a need or desire coupled with the purchasing power to fill it, 301

Department of Housing and Urban Development (HUD). *See* **HUD**

Department of Veteran Affairs, 178–181; certificate of eligibility, 179; certificate of reasonable value, 179

Depository Institution's Deregulation and Monetary Control Act, 203

Depreciation: loss in value due to deterioration and obsolescence, 290–291, 294–295, 416; economic obsolescence, 291; fictional depreciation, 295; functional obsolescence, 291; physical deterioration, 290–291; tax calculations, 416

Deregulation Acts (1980 and 1982), 203

Dereliction: the process whereby dry land is permanently exposed by a gradually receding waterline, 110

Descent, title by, 78

Description, 94

Development, land, 8

Devise: a transfer of real property by means of a will, 78

Devisee: one who receives real property under a will, 78

Diminishing marginal returns, principle of: we should invest dollars whenever they will return to us more than $1 of value and should stop when each dollar invested returns less than $1 in value, 302

Disaffirms: revokes, 107

Disclosure, 358, 366, 429; of ARM features, 222; broker, 358; Regulation Z amendment, 300; seller, 360, 362–363

Disclosures in contract, 128–129

Disclosure forms, 362–363

Discount broker: a full-service broker who charges less than the prevailing commission rates in his community, 349

Discount points: charges made by lenders to adjust the effective rate of interest on a loan, 174–175

Discrimination. *See* **Fair housing laws**

Disintermediation: the movement of money out of savings accounts into corporate and government debt instruments, 202

Divorce, effect on ownership, as community property, 44

Dollars per hundred: property tax rate, 236

Dollars per thousand: property tax rate, 236

Dominant estate: the parcel of land which benefits from an easement, 39

Dower: the legal right of a widow to a portion of her deceased husband's real property, 43–44

Downside risk: the possibility that an investor will lose his money in an investment, 428

Downzoning: rezoning of land from a higher-density use to a lower-density use, 407

Drilling rights, 48

Dual agency (divided agency): representation of two or more principals in a transaction by the same agent, 364

Due-on-sale: a clause in a note or mortgage that gives the lender the right to call the entire loan balance due if the property is sold or otherwise conveyed, 153, 215–216

Durable power of attorney: power of attorney that does not lapse because of the passage of time unless a time limitation is specifically stated in the instrument creating it, 104

Duress: the application of force to obtain an agreement, 107

Early payoff of a loan, 232, 234

Earnest money contract. *See* **Purchase contract.**

Earnest money deposit: money that accompanies an offer to purchase as evidence of good faith, 155

Earth's center, 14

Easement: the right or privilege one party has to use land belonging to another for a special purpose not inconsistent with the owner's use of the land, 38; appurtenant, 38–39; dominant estate, 39; in gross, 39; by implication, 38; party wall, 39; by prescription, 38, 81–82; servient estate, 39; termination, 39

Loyalty to principal: a requirement that an agent place his principal's interest above his own, 355–356

Maggie Mae: a real estate industry nickname for the MGIC Investment Corporation, 213

Maintenance fees: fees paid by a condominium or PUD unit owner to the owners' association for upkeep of the common elements, 393

Majority: the minimum age required for legal competency (in most states 18 years), 103

Maker: the person who signs a promissory note, 144

Map books, 25

Mapping a curve, 20

Margin: the amount added to the index rate that reflects the lender's cost of doing business, 220–221

Market approach: a method of valuing property based on recent sales of similar properties, 280–288; competitive market analysis, 285–286; condominium, townhouse, and cooperative, 285; gross rent multipliers, 287–288; single-family residence, 280–284; vacant land, 285

Market exposure, 345

Market value: the cash price that a willing buyer and a willing seller would freely agree upon, given reasonable exposure of the property to the marketplace, full information as to the potential uses of the property, and no undue compulsion to act, 280

Marketable title acts: state laws aimed at cutting off rights and interests in land that have been inactive for long periods; not used in Texas

Married persons: community property, 43–44, 60–61; as joint tenants, 58; as tenants by the entirety, 60

Master deed: a document that converts a parcel of land into a condominium subdivision, 392

Master limited partnership: limited partnership that can be traded on a stock exchange, 429

Maturity: the end of the life of a loan, 167, 170–171

Mechanic's lien: a lien placed against real property by any unpaid workman or supplier who has done work or furnished building materials, 41, 94

Meeting of the minds. *See* **Mutual agreement**

Menace: threat of violence to obtain a contract, 107

Meridian: a north-south line running from the starting point as the correlated base line used as references in mapping land, 21

Metes and bounds: a detailed method of land description that identifies a parcel by specifying its shape and boundaries, 18–20; bench marks, 20; *illustrations,* 19, 20; monuments, 19

MGIC: Mortgage Guarantee Insurance Corporation, 213

Middleman: a person who brings two or more parties together but does not represent either party, 366

Mill rate: property tax rate that is expressed in tenths of a cent per dollar of assessed valuation, 236

Mineral rights, 47–48

Minor, Infant: a person under the age of legal competence; in most states, under 18 years, 103

Minorities, 384–385

Misrepresentation. *See* **Innocent misrepresentation.**

Mistake: refers to ambiguity in contract negotiations and mistake of material fact, 107

MLS Plus, 345

Modification: the influence on land use and value resulting from improvements made by man to surrounding parcels, 29

Money damages: compensation paid in lieu of contract performance, 111

Monthly income, 196

Monument: an iron pipe, stone, tree, or other fixed point used in making a survey, 19

Mortgage: a pledge of property to secure the repayment of a debt, 141–165; alienation clause, 153; amortized mortgage, 168–171; assumption of the loan, 154; availability and price of money for, 214–215; chattel mortgage, 92, 160; compared with a deed of trust, 143, 147–148; covenants, 148; debt priorities, 159–160; deed as security, 143; early mortgages, 141–142; equitable mortgages, 142–143; financing methods, *see* **Financing methods;** first lien mortgage, 159; foreclosure, 160–163; hypothecation, 141–142; interest rates, *see* **Interest rates;** intermediate theory, 142; junior mortgages, 159; lending practices, *see* **Lending practices;** lien theory, 142; mortgage loan analysis, 195–198; novation, 154, 159; pledge methods, 142–143; points, 174–175; primary market, 201–208; promissory note, 143–146; reduction, 415; regular mortgage, 142; secondary market, *see* **Secondary mortgage market;** second lien mortgage, 159; "subject to" clause, 153–154; subordination, 159; title theory, 142

Mortgage banker: a person or firm that makes mortgage loans and then sells them to investors, 204

Mortgage broker: a person who brings borrowers and lenders together, a loan broker, 204

Mortgage company: a firm that makes mortgage loans and then sells them to investors. 203–204

Mortgage financing, career in, 10

Mortgage insurance: insures lenders against nonrepayment of loans, 177, 181–182

Mortgage lien: a pledge of property by its owner to secure the repayment of a debt, 41

Mortgage pool: a common fund of mortgage loans in which one can invest, 210

Opinion of title: an attorney's opinion as to the status of title, 94

Option: a right, for a given period of time, to buy, sell or lease property at specified price and terms, 230, 274; fee, 135; lease-option, 134

Optionee: the party receiving the option, 135

Optioner: the party giving the option, 135

Oral contracts, 109, 118

Oral earnest money contract, 118

Oral will, 105

Origination fee: a charge for making a loan, 174

Ostensible authority: results when a principal gives a third party reason to believe that another person is his agent even though that person is unaware of the appointment, 354

Outside of escrow. *See* **Outside of the closing**

Outside of the closing: means that a party to the closing has paid someone directly and not through the closing, 262

Overall rate: a mortgage-equity factor used to appraise income-producing property, 294

Overencumbered property: a property where market value of that property is exceeded by the loans against it, 230

Owner, protecting, 341–342, 356

Owner-broker relationship, 353–360; agent's authority, 354; antitrust laws, 368; bargain brokers, 349; broker compensation, 346–347; broker's obligations to his principal, 354–358; broker's obligations to third parties, 358–360; listing agreement, 339–344; procuring cause, 347–348; property disclosure statements, 360–363; terminating employment contract, 348–349

Owner's policy: a title insurance policy designed to protect the fee owner, 96–97

Ownership, 55–68; associations, 66; concurrent ownership by states *table,* 59; corporations, 65–66; inter vivos and testamentary trust, 66–67; joint tenancy, 57–60; joint venture, 63; land trusts, 67; partnership, 61–63; real estate investment trusts (REITS), 66; severalty, 55; sole, 55; syndication, 65; tenancy by the entirety, 60; tenants in common, 55–57; trusts, 66–67; of waterways, 17

Ownership rights, 36–49; transfer, *see* **Title transfer**

Package mortgage: a mortgage secured by a combination of real and personal property, 223

Parcel map, 25

Parcel number. *See* **Appraisal district's parcel number**

Parol evidence rule: permits oral evidence to augment a written contract in certain cases, 109

Partial performance of a contract, 110–111

Partial reciprocity, 315

Partial release: a release of a portion of a property from a mortgage, 153

Partially amortized loan: a loan that begins with amortized payments but ends with a balloon payment, 171; *table* 172

Participation certificate: a secondary mortgage market instrument whereby an investor can purchase an undivided interest in a pool of mortgages, 212

Participation loan: one that requires interest plus a percentage of the profits, 203

Partition: to divide jointly held property into distinct portions so that each co-owner may hold his or her proportionate share in severalty, 57

Partnership: a form of co-ownership for business purposes, 61–63, 426; limited partnership, 62–63

Party (parties): a legal term that refers to a person or a group involved in a legal proceeding, 101

Party wall: a fence or wall erected along a property line for the mutual benefit of both owners, 39

Passive investor, 417

Patent, 82

Payment cap: a limit on how much a borrower's payments can increase, 221

Pension funds as lenders, 205

Percentage basis: rent is based on the tenant's sales, 274

Percolating water: underground water not confined to a defined underground waterway, 16

Performance: principal is expected to do whatever he reasonably can to accomplish the purpose of the agency, such as referring inquiries by prospective buyers to the broker, 368; of contracts, 109, 111

Periodic estate: a tenancy that provides for continuing automatic renewal until canceled, such as a month-to-month rental, 47, 269

Permanent reference mark, 19

Personal property: a right or interest in things of a temporary or movable nature; anything not classed as real property, 14, 48

Personalty: things of a temporary or movable nature as distinguished from realty, 14, 48

Physical characteristics of land, 27–28

Physical deterioration: deterioration from wear and tear and the action of nature, 290–291

Pipeline disclosure, 128

PITI payment: a loan that combines principal, interest, taxes, and insurance, 171

Planned unit development (PUD): individually owned houses with community ownership of common areas, 391, 397–398

Seller's affidavit of title: a document provided by the seller at the settlement meeting stating that he has done nothing to encumber title since the title search was made, 251

Seller's market: one with few sellers and many buyers, 303

Senior mortgage: the mortgage against a property that holds first priority in the event of foreclosure, 159

Separate property: spouse-owned property that is exempt from community property status, 60–61

Service the loan, 203

Servient estate: the land on which an easement exists in favor of a dominant estate, 39

Set-up rental, 274

Settlement: the process of consummating a real estate transaction, 250–265

Settlement funds, 188, 195

Settlement meeting: a meeting at which the seller delivers his deed to the buyer, the buyer pays for the property, and all other matters pertaining to the sale are concluded, 250–265

Settlement statement: an accounting statement at settlement that shows each item charged or credited, to whom, and for how much, 261–262, 265

Severalty ownership: owned by one person, sole ownership, 55

Severance damages: compensation paid for the loss in market value that results from splitting up a property in a condemnation proceeding, 35

Shelley* v. *Kraemer, 374

Sheriff's deed: a deed issued as a result of a court-ordered foreclosure sale, 78, 161

Sherman Antitrust Act, 368

Short-form acknowledgment, 91

Signature: acknowledgment, 96, 119–20; deeds, 94, 96; promissory note, 144; witnesses, 89–90

Simple assumption, 176

Situs: refers to the preference by people for a given location, 30

Sole ownership: owned by one person, 55

Special agency: an agency relationship created for the performance of specific acts only, 353

Special assessments: charges levied to provide publicly built improvements that will benefit a limited geographical area, 239–241

Special warranty deed: contains only one covenant–the covenant against encumbrances, 75

Specific lien: a lien on a specific property, 42

Specific performance: contract performance according to the precise terms agreed upon, 149

Specific property offering: property purchase method whereby the organizers buy properties first and then seek partners, 427

Spot zoning: the rezoning of a small area of land in an existing neighborhood, 407

Square-foot method: an appraisal technique that uses square-foot construction costs of similar structures as an estimating basis, 289

Standard mortgage: a pledge of property to secure the repayment of a debt, 142

Standard parallel: a survey line used to correct for the earth's curvature, 21

Statute of Frauds: a law requiring that certain types of contracts be written in order to be enforceable in a court of law, 71, 108–109, 270

Statute of limitations: a legal limit on the amount of time one has to seek the aid of a court in obtaining justice, 112

Statutory dedication, 82

Statutory estates: estates created by law and including dower, curtesy, community property, and homestead rights, 43–44

Steering: the practice of directing home seekers to particular neighborhoods based on race, color, religion, sex, national origin, nonhandicapped, or adult only housing, 377

Step-up rental: a lease that provides for agreed-upon rent increases, 232, 274

Straight-line depreciation: depreciation in equal amounts each year over the life of the asset, 417

Street numbers, as a means of describing property, 18

Subchapter S Corporation, 65–66

Subdivision regulations, 409

Subject property: the property that is being appraised, 280

Subject to the existing loan: the buyer of an already mortgaged property makes the payments but does not take personal responsibility for the loan, 154

Sublease: a lease that is given by a lessee, 47, 275

Sublessee: a lessee who rents from another lessee, 47, 275

Sublessor: a lessee who rents to another lessee, 47, 275

Subordination: voluntary acceptance of a lower property priority than one would otherwise be entitled to, 160; as a financing tool, 229

Subprime loans, 198

Substitution, principle of: maximum value of a property in the marketplace tends to be set by the cost of purchasing an equally desirable substitute property provided no costly delay is encountered making the substitution, 301